C0-AWU-691

HETERICK MEMORIAL LIBRARY
OHIO NORTHERN UNIVERSITY
ADA, OHIO 45810

Painting the Cannon's Roar

For James King

Painting the Cannon's Roar

Music, the Visual Arts and the Rise of an Attentive
Public in the Age of Haydn, *c*.1750 to *c*.1810

THOMAS TOLLEY

Ashgate

Aldershot • Burlington USA • Singapore • Sydney

© Thomas Tolley, 2001

All rights reserved. No part of this publication may be reproduced, stored in a retrieval system, or transmitted in any form or by any means, electronic, mechanical, photocopying, recording or otherwise without the prior permission of the publisher.

Thomas Tolley has asserted his moral right under the Copyright, Designs and Patents Act, 1988, to be identified as the author of this work.

Published by
Ashgate Publishing Limited
Gower House
Croft Road
Aldershot
Hants GU11 3HR
England

Ashgate Publishing Company
131 Main Street
Burlington
Vermont, 05401–5600
USA

Ashgate website: http://www.ashgate.com

British Library Cataloguing in Publication Data

Tolley, Thomas
    Painting the Cannon's Roar: Music, the Visual Arts and the Rise of an Attentive
    Public in the Age of Haydn
    1. Hadyn, Joseph, 1732–1809—Criticism and interpretation. 2. Art and music—
    History—18th century. 3. Performing arts—Audiences. I. Title.
    700.9'033

US Library of Congress Cataloging in Publication Data

Tolley, Thomas
    Painting the Cannon's Roar: Music, the Visual Arts and the Rise of an Attentive
    Public in the Age of Haydn / Thomas Tolley.
        p.   cm. – (Modern Economic and Social History Series)
    Includes bibliographical references.
    1. Art and music—History—18th century. 2. Performing arts—Audiences.
    3. Haydn, Joseph, 1732–1809—Criticism and interpretation I. Title.
    ML3849.T65 2001
    700'.9'033–dc21   00–054303

ISBN 0 7546 0393 8

This book is printed on acid free paper.

Typeset by Express Typesetters Ltd, Farnham, Surrey.

Printed and bound in Great Britain by MPG Books Ltd, Bodmin, Cornwall.

700.9033
T651p

Contents

List of Illustrations

(between pp. 236 and 237)

Preface

Everything is authentic in my painting.
I get the drums to go
Boom, boom, boom . . .
You can hear the muskets:
Bang, bang, bang . . .
I've even painted the cannon's roar.
Louis Hurtaut Dancourt, *La Rencontre imprévue* (1763)[1]

Painting the Cannon's Roar is an account of a cultural development of the eighteenth century that has hitherto received little critical attention. The book describes the emergence of a kind of meeting of aural and visual perceptions in the public sphere, well recognized at the time, which, though largely running its course by the early nineteenth century, left a substantial legacy to the subsequent development of Western culture. This meeting of perceptions may reasonably be considered as one outcome of the aesthetic debates of the age of the Enlightenment, though we still live with its consequences today.

The book is founded upon the seemingly implausible premise that, across much of Europe during the period *c.*1750 to *c.*1810, the paths of the history of music and of the history of painting crossed, with interesting and lasting consequences. More precisely, it is argued that changes in aesthetic response and public behaviour in both the practice of listening (to music) and also the practice of viewing (of the visual arts) during this period reveal similar concerns at the same time, to the extent that they may be considered part of the same movement. This may be studied and understood at many levels. My intention has been to show that these activities, musical and artistic, though previously occupying quite distinct spheres of human accomplishment and endeavour, came during the eighteenth century to share a close affinity within the public sphere, resulting in a kind of parity in popular estimation.

By this I do not mean to imply that the distinct qualities of music and the various visual arts became confused, at least not for the broad mass of audiences for music and the visual arts. After all, most people, then as now, would agree that just as ears serve one purpose and eyes another, so music is one thing and painting is something quite different. What is here suggested, however, is that the autonomy of music and of each of the visual arts did not constrain possibilities for developing new kinds of experience through the creative combining of visual and aural sensations. Attempts had often been made since the sixteenth century to safeguard the independence of each of the arts in the West through academies established to cultivate and promote them in the public domain. But this did not prevent continuous assaults on what were perceived as the boundaries of possibility for music and the visual arts.

The sense that the arts could not be circumscribed left some people with the notion that there might be areas of overlap worth pursuing. Some of these areas of overlap involved both music and the visual arts in following parallel courses stemming from their literary connections. Poetry had long been considered the dominant partner in its relative associations with both music and painting, so it is not surprising that literary themes continued to impress themselves on the other arts. One example is the development of the 'conversational' mode in the writing of string quartets, which closely parallels the development of the 'conversation piece' in painting. The cultivation of polite and intelligent conversation may be considered an important literary manifestation of the eighteenth century, already well refined by the time that the first developments in music and painting just mentioned began.

But, as I argue in Chapter 1, the strong bonds previously connecting both music and painting with the literary arts were generally somewhat eroded in the eighteenth century, to be replaced in large measure with new associations, especially linking music and the visual arts, which is the theme of this book. Issues connecting music and painting which had been raised in vague terms from time to time in the seventeenth century and earlier started to be considered more seriously and widely by the middle years of the eighteenth century. Can music depict objects, in the manner of a painting? Can a work of art be heard as well as seen? Are sounds colourful? The fact that many who interested themselves in such questions felt that they could answer them affirmatively is a token of the increasing proximity of music and the visual arts for many listeners and viewers by the third quarter of the eighteenth century. The title of this book provides one concrete example of this. Derived from an opera first heard in 1764, in which the theory of a direct relationship between aural experience and painting is demonstrated (through images and music) and discussed, the title is intended to suggest how this works at its most popular. Although the concept of analogy between music and the visual arts is satirized in the opera, as a prominent feature of a entertainment designed to be seen by large audiences its precepts were clearly well understood in the public domain at the time.

Although it would be a gross exaggeration to suggest that historians of music and historians of visual culture take little notice of each other's activities, the number of studies genuinely considering these two realms of human activity together as cultural history is negligible. Only in the sphere of musical iconography has there been any extensive common interest, and even then usually with separate and often rather conventional agendas in mind. Music historians tend to look, for example, to the visual arts for evidence of performance practice, the form of musical instruments and the notation of compositions (sometimes otherwise unrecorded). Art historians, who often give wildly inaccurate descriptions of musical phenomena in the visual culture they study, more often have their sights set on giving interpretations or explanations of musical iconography, perhaps in terms of allegories or genres, sometimes as indications of social trends.

In some respects this reluctance on the part of different kinds of cultural historian to investigate the broader affinities for their chosen field of study is understandable. It is relatively more straightforward to plot the development of a single concept – the rise of 'the symphony', the development of 'landscape painting', the œuvre of a composer or an artist – than a rather nebulous one involving more than one human faculty. Tracing the fortunes of a single concept is of course certainly a very valid approach to studying cultural history; few would choose to challenge the assumption that clearly defined products of human creativity – such as symphonies, landscape paintings and individual œuvres – have their own autonomous histories.

However, our reluctance today to transgress boundaries between different fields of historical inquiry may arguably result in a rather limited, perhaps even distorted view of the past and its cultural achievements. The wide range of mankind's intellectual and emotional attainments sometimes defies ready categorization. Men and women have always had both ears and eyes, and it may reasonably be assumed that they have ever used both faculties simultaneously. If this is so, then it may be suggested that there came a point in the development of Western culture (and probably other cultures) when creative forces tried to appeal to both senses together, not just separately. We of course today think little of this notion when, for example, we turn on our television sets then sit back to watch *and* to listen. Few programmes escape the introduction of music at some point, which we have all come to expect. But why? And when did this kind of expectation begin?

The unwillingness of cultural historians to address questions of this kind partly stems from the ways Western educational systems function. Disciplines are studied separately, and students are rarely encouraged to make use of categories of knowledge and information drawn from a variety of spheres in relation to what is learnt in a principal subject area. Academics tend to be 'specialists' in single, distinct 'fields'. Perhaps the most extreme example of the categorization of knowledge is the division between disciplines based on 'science' and those based on the 'arts'. The former are supposedly founded on the notion of a quest for absolute knowledge, tested through experimentation, and 'proved' through mathematical certainty; whereas the latter are often perceived to be less objective in their methods, depending more on *interpretation* of texts, documents and other material survivals than on incontestable facts. This gross simplification of what really happens in the sciences and arts is, of course, a caricature of the situation put forward here to indicate how many such preconceived notions of the distinctions between sciences and arts do not stand up to close scrutiny. These notions are not only unhelpful when applied to historical contexts, but also arguably in present-day contexts. Just as it can be shown that the issues and objectives of scientific inquiry between the thirteenth and the nineteenth centuries were clearly aligned with the development of the visual arts during the same period (as indicated, for example, in Martin Kemp's *The Science of Art*), so too, many issues engaging contemporary scientists might, were there the will and imagination, be seen to have implications for contemporary historians of all kinds. The Darwinian theory of evolution, for example, underpins much science pursued today; but it would be hard to pinpoint many cultural historians finding it necessary to grapple with this concept, except where 'evolution' is used (mistakenly) to signal 'development'. Because evolution is perceived somehow only to be relevant to prehistory, and the changes it produces are thought to take place imperceptibly over prolonged periods, it is presumed that the notion of evolution can have no relevance to cultural historians concerned with the Classical world and later.

This conclusion is reinforced by the general tendency of historians to chart cultural change chiefly through the material products of societies rather than through the perceptions and opinions of the people comprising these societies. Histories of art, for example, still generally tend to place emphasis in the first instance either on 'works of art' and how they came into being, or on the creators of such objects and their supposed intentions. An understanding of the context of a 'work of art' might (for instance) look to available documentation to discover the requirements of its patron(s), its original setting and its function(s) as a means of building up a picture of its 'significance'. Histories of music might look to similar issues, with special emphasis on study of manuscript and published sources. This is, of course, not to imply that there is anything wrong with direct study of artists/composers and their œuvres; on the contrary, this is clearly essential primary work. What, however, emerges as problematic is the pretence that the totality of such study comprises a history of human cultural achievement. It may lead to a 'history of paintings', or a 'history of musical compositions'; but this is not the same thing as trying to understand how cultural objects or compositions have attained significance, which stems from how individuals and audiences have viewed or heard such works. In other words, meaning cannot be found in the work itself, or in the intentions of its creator in bringing it into being, but in those who perceive it, which may change from person to person, from age to age, and even from day to day.

As research is increasingly showing, clear signs of human evolution may in fact be detected taking place in all periods, including the most recent, and at rates so rapid that it might be easy to overlook them. Evidence is increasingly coming to light that during the past three or four hundred years several significant changes have taken place concerning both the form and functioning of the human body and its faculties, especially in the West. Some examples may help to make this point more tangible: thus the average voice of Westerners is probably pitched a semitone or more lower than it was little over two centuries ago; the average Westerner is today significantly taller than his counterpart in the later Middle Ages; in only a couple of generations puberty is taking place for the majority of Westerners at a discernibly younger age; the capacity for humans to memorize at length appears to be diminishing as this function of the brain gives up its role to artificial ways of storing information; the body's interior clock, once determined chiefly by hours of sunlight, and therefore formerly showing change throughout the year, is now increasingly dependent on artificial light, resulting in a more uniform inner functioning throughout all seasons because of the more regularized hours for daily activities. If these examples are not misleading, then it may be argued that such major and quick changes in the human condition may also have a bearing on other facets of the human development, with implications for the writing of all kinds of history concerned with charting cultural change.

It is a major premise of this book that the ways Westerners have used their visual and aural faculties reflects comparable kinds of change, conditioned by environmental and social factors and shaped by aesthetic expectations. These ways have as yet only made a limited impact on the scholarship of cultural history. One key exception of which I am aware is the notion of 'the period eye' elucidated by Michael Baxandall in a study of visual culture in fifteenth-century Italy and developed by Svetlana Alpers in her account of Dutch visual culture in the seventeenth century. The aural equivalent, what might be called 'the period ear', has been the subject of a study by James Johnson tracing the development of listening habits in Paris in the eighteenth and nineteenth centuries. Recently the idea of a 'history of listening', reasonably conceived as complementing the history of music, has aroused wider interest, as indicated, for example, by the articles in a special issue of *The Musical Quarterly*, subtitled *Music as Heard* (82/3–4, 1998). In all these studies the authors aim to build up a sense of the experiences, prejudices, education and tastes of looking or listening audiences in various societies at different periods in order to understand broad changes in human behaviour in relation to visual or aural culture. In so doing readers engage with the cultural survivals of various societies in order to sense what were the dominant issues framing the ways they understood what was seen or heard in former periods.

From the foregoing it will be clear that I see much scope for pursuing the notion of a history of visual culture which places its emphasis on Man's *visual* faculties and how these have developed in relation to the environment mankind has created around itself. For the sake of clarity I use the term 'pictorialism' to describe this. Pictorialism implies the whole range of visual culture, not just 'art', and how this range was used and perceived in its historical context. It may be helpful to use the designation 'history of pictorialism' to distinguish this field of inquiry from the traditional objectives of 'Art History'. The former would be concerned with sight and how mankind has *evolved* culturally using his eyes, and would seek to explore the dominant visual characteristics of whole societies and their development; the latter tends traditionally to be concerned with objects ('Art') and contexts for understanding how these came into being, often stressing individual artists, patrons, styles and iconography. Whilst Art History seeks to be objective about reconstructing and analysing the circumstances in which 'works of art' came into being and the contexts for displaying the works themselves, and is therefore allied in its objectives with – though distinct from – the discipline of History, 'pictorialism' might begin by asking questions about the nature of visual culture *today* – like the one I posed about why television programmes are always accompanied by music – and might then proceed to answer them by tracing comparable phenomena in earlier periods. In this respect 'pictorialism' might aspire to study visual culture in ways analogous to the approach of the discipline of Linguistics in an understanding of the development of oral/verbal culture. To put it another way, 'pictorialism' might be a way of articulating the view that Man's faculty of sight (in its intellectual sense), as it has evolved and as it has been conditioned until now, may be understood as a cumulative reflection of all the major stages in the development of visual culture.

Painting the Cannon's Roar has therefore been conceived as a study in the history of pictorialism, taking what it is here argued was one of the major developments, if not *the* major development in the history of vision in the West in the later eighteenth century as its subject – its association with music. My method has been to look for evidence from a wide range of sources touching on the relationship between the visual arts and music in order to compile as rounded a view as possible of the episode itself. Many readers may find that the interpretation of the evidence under consideration, whilst pertinent, is often pushed too far – beyond the limits generally considered acceptable in an academic study. In defining a subject previously underexplored it is, however, not at first always clear what the precise (or desirable) limits of possibility for interpretation may be. Further reflection is always needed to refine new ideas, but in relation to the content of this book this will have to wait. Some readers may also object that the content of this book too frequently fails to acknowledge music and each of the visual arts as autonomous arts. But as I hope to have already indicated, it is not my intention to denigrate the individual identities of the various arts in question, which would be nonsensical, their autonomy being here taken for granted. A principal objective of the book, however, is to stress how in the public sphere, for a period, it was the *connections* between the arts which counted for something and enabled them to take on new meanings. Since this is a study which cuts across disciplines and tries to establish a new way of thinking about visual history, conventional stylistic labels have not always been especially helpful. Although such terms are not applicable to modes of looking or listening, being only descriptive of works of human creativity, I have not thought it necessary to dispense with them, though I have tried to use them only where there is a historical basis for their application. Few would wish, for instance, to challenge the notion that Canova was a 'neoclassical' sculptor, though applying the term 'classic' to eighteenth-century music is much more problematic in a historical context and it was therefore easy to dispense with it. I have also not found it necessary to engage with prevailing musicological or art historical debates on scholarly practice relating to the period studied since the work presented here negotiates its way across traditional divisions with the aim of discovering something new. This does not mean that I have not made use of the theoretical positions of previous scholars interested in this period, but I have not necessarily followed them all the way along the same path. I particularly have in mind the theory of topoi set out by Leonard Ratner in defining the 'Classic' style in music – echoes of ordinary features of popular music, used by distinguished composers as elements in their formal and expressive discourse. Several of Ratner's 'topics' have direct relevance to the subject of this book, their visual implications being included in this study. But I have couched these examples in terms relevant to my own argument so that I am not obliged to deal with all the ramifications of a theory which, though wholly persuasive, does not coincide precisely with the views I wish to advance here.

Ratner's notion of topoi (though not the ones he discusses) have also been helpful to me in forming my own reading of works by popular artists discussed in this book, such as prints after caricatures by Bunbury and Gillray. What seems to me to be crucial to Ratner's argument and also to the thesis of this book is the sense of an increasing and ever more receptive audience for music (and equally for the visual arts) in the later eighteenth century which potentially included all social strata in most Western countries, and which made for an ever increasing range of 'topics', associations and other referents. What may be shown to have been popular with these audiences therefore assumes special significance in establishing general patterns of behaviour in relation to the public's proclivities in looking and listening. Popularity is an important measure of the kind of change which pictorialism seeks to chart. The corollary of this is that compositions and works of art came to be considered as commodities in the public domain, with institutions (such as public exhibitions and public concerts) and genres (like the printing of popular songs and popular prints) receiving development to cater for very broad kinds of public demand. If readers think they might find it objectionable for musical compositions and works of art to be discussed chiefly as the products of commercialism, at the expense of any consideration of the artistic integrity of their creators, then they should perhaps put this book down now. But the fact is that those composers and artists in the later eighteenth century who best adapted themselves to the market place were those who were most successful in their own lifetimes.

Since the book is concerned with the popular in culture, it is closely structured around the career and visual interests of the most popular cultural figure to live during the period in question, the composer Joseph Haydn. As I seek to show in Chapter 2, Haydn's contemporary reputation – in terms of its extent and persistence, across continents as well as in the main centres of influence in Europe – far exceeded that of any other musician, painter, sculptor, or even writer during the period of his mature working career. A case may therefore be made that he was the first truly international cultural celebrity in the modern sense, famed not just as a performer but as a creator. Although long before Haydn's lifetime, musical performers, especially opera singers, gained significant international reputations at the height of their careers, it can hardly be claimed that this kind of celebrity matched Haydn's since it was felt by only a fraction of the population and was much more transitory in character. Only the widespread reputation of Canova can be said to have approached that of Haydn, but only then at a slightly later date and with a much more limited audience.

Contemporary references to many of Haydn's compositions show that they held significance not only in musical circles, but in artistic debates as well. Although it may strike many readers as odd that a study which aims principally to make a contribution to an understanding of the history of visual culture should have at its heart an assessment of a composer, they will only be able to judge whether I have been successful in this aim after having read it. The argument builds on the premise that Haydn consciously set about ensuring that he was in tune with many aspects of popular visual culture as a means of assessing what engaged broad audiences and in order to further his own reputation. His own collection of prints is perhaps the best indicator of Haydn's own fascination with the visual (discussed in Chapter 7). His responsiveness to popular imagery has implications not only for ways in which his own music was understood when first heard, but also for how the artists he himself most admired were viewed. The picture which emerges from this presents a very different kind of 'Haydn' from the one generally projected in the public sphere since the nineteenth century. Little trace remains of the naive, poorly educated composer, out of tune or out of sympathy with the intellectual and aesthetic issues of his times, still often reflected in popular accounts of the composer's life available today. Although it would be totally misleading to suggest that Haydn was motivated primarily by ambition, carrying the implication that his own artistic integrity was of secondary importance to him (an impression I may unintentionally suggest to some readers as the argument develops), this does not mean that the commercial and business factors in the world in which he operated were not crucial to how he built on his own success to become the best-known cultural figure of his time. At one level Haydn was determined, often uncompromising, and even unscrupulous in his dealings with publishers and entrepreneurs, to the point where some of his business practices brought him to the brink of legal challenges. It is at this intensely commercial level of his creativity that it is here submitted that Haydn's visual interests came into play, at least in the period after his compositions started to be published with his own authority. By emphasizing Haydn above all other creative figures in this study, I have not intended to give the impression that he was alone in his time in pursuing the popular. Many, perhaps most, contemporary composers and artists sought exactly such a relationship with their public. By the end of the eighteenth century democratization had become a noble ideal infecting many countries, with major repercussions for how composers and artists presented themselves to their audiences. But in the pursuit of popularity, Haydn's success was unprecedented and unmatched in his lifetime. This book is intended to go some way towards explaining this.

Many colleagues in the University of Edinburgh have helped me with aspects of this book. I have particularly benefited from discussion of individual points with Professor Andrew Barker, Professor Kerr Borthwick, Michael Bury, Professor Harry Dickinson, David Howarth, Professor David Kimball, Professor Duncan Macmillan and Roger Tarr. The resources of the Reid Music Library have been of inestimable value to me in completing the work. I am grateful to the staff of the library for their help. To Imre Kovács I owe a particular debt of gratitude for translating a number of texts from Hungarian into English relating to the content of Chapter 3. My special thanks go to Professor Richard Thomson for his constant encouragement and support in this project. Finally, I am very grateful to Rachel Lynch and to Bonnie Blackburn for seeing this project through to publication.

Note

1. The text comes from a speech made by Vertigo, a painter. Translation from the booklet accompanying the recording of Gluck's *Les Pèlerins de la Mecque ou La Rencontre imprévue* by John Eliot Gardiner and the Opera de Lyon (Radio France/Erato Disques, 1991), 149.

Abbreviations

AMZ	*Allgemeine musikalische Zeitung* (Leipzig, 1798–)
BMC	*Catalogue of Prints and Drawings in the British Museum: Division I. Political and Personal Satires.* The chief volumes used in this book are those by Dorothy Mary George: vol. V [1771–83], vol. VI [1784–92], vol. VII [1793–1800] (repr. London, 1978)
CCLN	*The Collected Correspondence and London Notebooks of Joseph Haydn*, ed. and trans. H.C. Robbins Landon (London, 1959)
CCP	*The Collected Correspondence and Papers of Christoph Willibald Gluck*, ed. Hedwig and E.H. Mueller von Asow, trans. Stewart Thomson (London, 1962)
Dies	Albert Christoph Dies, *Biographische Nachrichten von Joseph Haydn nach mündlichen Erzählungen desselben entworfen und herausgegeben von Albert Christoph Dies, Landschaftmaler* [Vienna, 1810], ed. Horst Seeger (Kassel, n.d. [1959])
Carpani	Giuseppe Carpani, *Le Haydine: lettere sulla vita e le opere del celebre maestro Giuseppe Haydn* (Milan, 1812)
Griesinger	Georg August Griesinger, *Biographische Notizen über Joseph Haydn* [Leipzig, 1810], with notes by Peter Krause (Leipzig, 1983)
Haydn, *Briefe*	*Joseph Haydn: Gesammelte Briefe und Aufzeichnungen*, ed. Dénes Bartha (Kassel, 1965)
Hob.	Anthony van Hoboken, *Joseph Haydn, Thematische-bibliographisches Werkverzeichnis*, 3 vols (Mainz, 1957–78)
Hörwarthner	Maria Hörwarthner, 'Joseph Haydns Bibliothek – Versuch einer literarischen Rekonstruktion', in *Joseph Haydn und die Literatur seiner Zeit*, ed. Herbert Zeman (Eisenstadt, 1976), 157–207; translated as 'Joseph Haydn's Library: An Attempt at a Literary-Historical Reconstruction', trans. Katherine Talbot, in *Haydn and His World*, ed. Elaine Sisman (Princeton, 1997), 395–461
New Grove	*The New Grove Dictionary of Music and Musicians*, ed. Stanley Sadie (London, 1980)
Novello	Vincent and Mary Novello, *A Mozart Pilgrimage, Being the Travel Diaries of Vincent & Mary Novello in the Year 1829*, transcribed by Nerina Medici di Marignano, ed. Rosemary Hughes (London, 1955)

Révolution   [Abbé Gaspard Michel Le Blond], *Mémoires pour servir à l'histoire de la révolution operée dans la musique par M. le chevalier Gluck* [or *Révolution de la musique*] (Naples, 1781; repr. Amsterdam, 1967)

CHAPTER ONE

Introduction: Painting and Music at the Crossroads

In contemporary Western culture viewing images at the same time as listening to music is such an everyday occurrence that the combined experience is usually taken for granted. Whether it is a film, a television programme, a video, or a commercial, we are quite comfortable about using our ears as well as our eyes in order to sense fully the visual medium, music inevitably playing an expected part in the pleasure of the experience.

Even at the beginning of the cinematic age, before coordinated sound became a reality for motion pictures, it took little time before pianists, and later organists, were employed to improvise to what the audience saw; not only was music thought to enhance the visual experience, it also had the very real effect of drawing in the crowds in ever greater numbers. At the very beginning of the twentieth century, therefore, there was an expectation that this form of popular visual culture was incomplete without a musical element. During the course of the century, this combination may be experienced in various spheres. In recent decades, for example, directors of art museums in major Western cities have discovered that their galleries often make very suitable spaces for musical performances. Chamber concerts, in which the aural experience reflects something of the period of the art objects surrounding performers and audience, have proved one way of attracting viewers to rooms otherwise ignored by the public. At the other end of the cultural spectrum, the most successful rock concerts cannot do without coordinated lighting and other sophisticated visual effects, which could hardly have been imagined fifty years ago. The music video is perhaps the latest development in the need to satisfy both senses simultaneously.

These are small symptoms of what may be considered a vital cultural phenomenon of recent times, which has a bearing on almost everyone in Western society. It takes as its starting point the notion that the way we *see* may be affected by what we *hear*, or vice versa. In other words, when music and the visual arts are designed to attract mass audiences they occupy similar social and cultural territory, subject to comparable influences and considerations. But this has hardly always been the case.

1. The Middle Ages and Renaissance

Although Aristotle had considered the possibility that sensations stimulated by sound might be related to, or have a direct bearing on, feelings aroused by vision, the implications of this were largely ignored throughout Classical Antiquity and the Middle Ages.[1] When arguments were adduced comparing the senses, ranking them in order of importance, it was sight that was generally considered the superior sense, a view first formulated by Aristotle and Plato.[2] Some conception that a practical analogy between sight and sound might be feasible, however, was certainly known and understood. There is a report, for example, that the ancient Greek painter Theon painted a picture of a soldier 'rushing to the aid of his country', which on being first unveiled was provided with the accompaniment of a trumpet, apparently not only to attract the attention of viewers, but also to heighten the illusion.[3] Although the report of this unusual exhibition indicates that it was highly successful in intensifying viewers' experience of the picture, there is little to suggest that the experiment itself was thought worth repeating. In general, Antiquity seems to have bequeathed to later periods in the West a clear division in how the visual and aural senses were thought to operate.

Thus throughout the development of Western medieval thought many formative figures (like St Augustine) found themselves drawn to considerations of music, its effect on the mind treated as either spiritual (and consequently beneficial), or sensual (and therefore generally damning). The same authorities rarely thought it necessary to mention the visual arts. This was perhaps in part because since at least the time of St Gregory the Great (d. 604) there had been a sense that artistic images might lead to the dangers of idolatry (breaking the Second Commandment; Exod. 20: 4), and could accordingly only be justified on the grounds of teaching the illiterate religious narratives.[4] This association meant that painting and sculpture were usually held in low esteem by scholars and other writers, exciting little extended discussion of a positive nature. St Thomas Aquinas may be considered typical of such attitutdes. He has much to say about music, emphasizing how its spiritual qualities might be used to promote faith and devotion.[5] Painting and sculpture, however, are never discussed in this way, nor even mentioned.[6] But the fact that Aquinas considered that only the senses of seeing and hearing led to a recognition of both good and evil, and that these same two senses alone are capable of distinguishing beauty, shows how in the Middle Ages there existed the potential for the pictorial arts and music being treated comparably.

This is apparent, for example, in the way the liturgy was complemented by both music (plainchant and later polyphony) and images (such as altarpieces and illuminated liturgical manuscripts), which for those large numbers attending church services would have been experienced simultaneously;[7] or the way, in the later Middle Ages, some writers imagined memory-working, sight and hearing, represented by eye and ear, acting as doors of *equal* importance to the inner workings of the mind.[8] Occasionally during this period, evidence suggests that the impetus for music intended to be heard in ecclesiastical settings may have come from artistic sources, and that consideration was given during the course of composition to satisfying the two senses together.[9] There are even examples of celebrated composers being brought up in the households of distinguished painters.[10]

In social practice, however, music and pictures generally occupied very different spheres in the Middle Ages. Music was one of the respectable liberal arts, with its origins in the study of mathematics. As such, music was rational and could be understood as a means to approaching the divine. Music was allied with astronomy, so notions of the music of the spheres helped the educated to comprehend the sacred. On the other hand, the visual arts were, at best, placed among the so-called mechanical arts, occupying in social terms a very different realm.[11] While music was seen to have distinct intellectual qualities, the visual arts were discussed in terms of materials and labour. Medieval society, inheriting Christ's view, as related in his dealings with Mary and Martha, that contemplation should be set above action, was able to pigeon-hole musical and artistic activities quite separately, with music occupying the elevated ground. Vision may have been deemed the higher sense, but only at a common level of human endeavour. Hearing was more important for the intellect because it related to the acquisition of knowledge, a notion which again stemmed from Aristotle.

Attitudes during the period of the Renaissance changed much of this. The visual arts gradually took on many of the liberal characteristics previously associated with music. The application of mathematics, a liberal art, to painting and sculpture occasionally led artists and theorists to explore the relationship of music to visual art. Perhaps the most notable example of this is in the literary remains of Leonardo da Vinci.[12] Those interested in architecture often found musical proportions, intervals and modes irresistible.[13] Music itself during the Renaissance period, however, often suffered in common esteem from new associations with the vulgar or the lustful in society, bringing it firmly down to earth. Whereas music had often been associated with divine love in the Middle Ages, by the sixteenth century it was as likely to be allied with earthly love.[14] That music might be intrinsically sinful was a notion always simmering beneath the surface. St Augustine, a powerful force in shaping Western opinion, confessed to having grievously sinned when he found himself moved more by singing than by the words being sung. The conclusion he drew from this was that music was good for those with weak minds since it might arouse in them feelings of devotion.[15] Indeed some of the sinful associations reduced music to still lower depths. The hellish goings-on involving a range of stringed and blown musical instruments in paintings by Bosch, for example, leave little room to doubt that the pleasure music affords the human ear is not only corrupting, but leads ultimately to damnation, a view expressed less violently in countless later allegories of music.[16]

With music, though hanging on to its sacred roots, moving into less exalted social territory, and painting and sculpture on the ascent, there arguably comes a point, sometime in the early sixteenth century, when it is possible to detect a kind of crossing of paths of the arts associated with looking and with listening, at least at the popular level, in terms of the majority of those who looked and listened. A symptom of this is the way celebrated composers and artists were occasionally paired to aid understanding of their importance: Ockeghem and Donatello (both cited as founding figures) is one example; Josquin des Prez and Michelangelo (both bringing their art to states of perfection) is another.[17] This common ground explains attitudes to looking at visual works of art in the High Renaissance. Paintings created in the Rome of Pope Leo X, such as Raphael's *Stanze*, may be shown to have been designed to be heard, metaphorically, as well as seen.[18] The same attitude is evident at precisely the same period in northern Europe. The *Angel Concert* in Grünewald's Isenheim Altarpiece, created for use in a hospital, not only acts as a divine serenade for the infant Christ within the scene, as so often in earlier medieval iconography, but more interestingly functions as a kind of therapy for the sick who would have viewed the work, the artist and the hospital authorities finding biblical sanction for the idea that music heals.[19] For Grünewald, looking and listening clearly went together, as indeed they also seem to have for the extraordinary scribe known by the pseudonym Alamire. In the first decades of the sixteenth century Alamire worked for most of the leading courts of Western Europe, his versatility demonstrated by the role he assumed as a secret agent, as well as acting in several cultural capacities. Alamire was responsible for some of the most magnificent musical codices of the period, containing the finest polyphonic compositions of his age, sumptuously decorated by the leading illuminators available.[20] But he also acted as a dealer, both in musical instruments and in paintings. The evident duality of his interests presumably to some extent reflected those of the men and women who employed him. These included such notable patrons of the visual arts and music as Margaret of Austria and Henry VIII. Perhaps attitudes favourable to perceiving the musical and visual arts as being of comparable importance, especially at court, were stimulated by the convention of the *Paragone* – the comparison between the various arts – which became popular at this time.[21] In the development of this tradition, the visual arts (especially painting) were generally held in higher esteem than music, a position largely arrived at by taking up earlier conceptions of the primacy of vision over hearing. But this was not always so, especially in the early years of the sixteenth century, when the debate concerning the relative importance of the arts was at its most intense, and when the relative merits of the arts were finely balanced.[22]

An attempt to articulate a practical relationship between painting and music was made later in the sixteenth century by Giuseppe Arcimboldo, a Milanese painter who worked for the imperial court in Prague. According to one account, Arcimboldo made correspondences between different colours and the twelve semitones of the octave involving Pythagorean proportions and various gradations of tone from black to white.[23] Exactly how this was managed is hard to gauge from the account. Although the painter's colour harmony was sufficiently intelligible to receive satisfactory musical performance, on a harpsichord adapted for the purpose, it seems not to have engaged his contemporaries with any desire to follow through its implications.

Tracing any appreciable kind of continuous interplay between musical sound and vision beyond this moment in the sixteenth century would at best be disjointed. Having crossed, the paths of music and the visual arts proceeded largely in separate directions. Although musicians, singers, musical instruments and musicality proved a rich source of imagery for artists throughout the sixteenth and seventeenth centuries (and later), constantly exploited in portraits, allegories, concert pieces, still lifes and in all manner of religious and secular iconography, this hardly indicates that the realms of music and the visual arts occupied the same sphere of interest in popular estimation.[24] When artists during these centuries depicted the attributes of music, or even musicianship, in their paintings, they were not for the most part implying an affinity between their activities and those of musicians, but tapping into a rich vein of associations for music which allowed them to say something about the world in which they operated, without having to spell it out.

In several paintings by Caravaggio, for example, music-making is clearly important. But these paintings are not *about* music; the imagery of music is an attribute to express other ideas, sometimes sacred, more often profane, reflecting the world in which Caravaggio operated.[25] In seventeenth-century Rome (where Caravaggio worked at the height of his career) there were many patrons, who indulged both musical and artistic interests; but in general terms these patrons – the most prominent were connected with the papal court – had no reason to foster any sense that an integration of the visual and musical arts might be helpful. When evidence survives of cases where parity is extended to painting and music, there is generally a literary point of connection, not a direct one.[26]

In a very different context, though in the same century, many paintings by Vermeer and his Dutch contemporaries suggest how the private music-making of women from prosperous backgrounds was an important pastime, sometimes appreciated by men of the same social class, who probably supplied the pictures shown hanging on the walls.[27] Looking and listening may well go together in this closely knit environment. But Vermeer structures the world he creates so that it is reasonably clear the real agenda is about something quite different: human feelings, desire, anticipation, longing. Performing music is important to this artist and his contemporaries because it provided a means for commenting on heightened sensations, which were otherwise difficult to convey in paint.

From a different perspective, Nicholas Lanier, Master of the King's Music at the Stuart court in London, was a musician with distinct visual interests, charged with purchasing paintings in Mantua for his patrons in London and occasionally himself using paint and brush.[28] The friend of distinguished painters like Van Dyck and Guido Reni, Lanier rather unusually for his age balanced visual and musical pursuits, and perhaps encouraged his artist friends to take music seriously; but there is little to suggest the two sides of his interests had much bearing on each other. However, the fact that Lanier gained a reputation for activities in both spheres and that distinguished painters of this period often interested themselves in music – some, like Domenichino and Vermeer, even being noted for their musical ability – points to a growing receptivity to the notion that the practice of music was good for painting, and the business of image-making was beneficial for music.

A key outcome of this process of coming together were some ideas suggested by the great Jesuit polymath, Athanasius Kircher. In a remarkable compendium of ideas about light, astronomy, cosmology and optics, published in Rome in 1646, Kircher made a general analogy between light and sound, claiming that the characteristics of human voices resemble different colours.[29] In another compendium, on music, published four years later, a more refined idea was advanced: that 'sound is the ape of light', a concept which drew on notions of reflection in the laws of optics.[30] In a later treatise, the *Phonurgia nova*, which received wide circulation in a translation into German, this correspondence was taken further.[31] It is difficult to gauge how influential Kircher's ideas were. But an indication that his compendium on music of 1650 was widely appreciated comes from the Austrian composer Heinrich Biber, who 'borrowed' Kircher's notations for birdsong for one his own compositions.[32] Another Austrian composer, Joseph Haydn, later owned a copy of the *Phonurgia nova*, and may have found its parallel between light and sound of relevance to his own compositions.[33] Kircher's illustration of 'The Harmony of the World's Creation', relating the days of creation as described in Genesis to the six registers of an organ, may also have had a bearing on Haydn's musical treatment of the same material in his oratorio *The Creation*.[34]

Despite Biber's borrowings, Kircher cannot be said to have made any coherent impact on the relationship between music and the visual arts in the seventeenth century. During this post-Renaissance period, though both music and painting occupied important positions in the run of social activities, they were quite distinct in the way they operated: there remained no real coming together. Perhaps the only meaningful point of social contact was the analogous relationship both music and the visual arts developed in relation to the literary arts. The notion that pictures were the illiterate person's substitute for words, which pervaded Western medieval visual culture following its first clear articulation by St Gregory, may have lost its impact by the Renaissance, but it still underpinned many views of the *Ut pictura poesis* idea which came to replace it.[35] A painting might be like a poem, but a commonly expressed view was that it was neither as important nor as useful as a poem because it could rarely stand by itself, without a literary idea or a narrative underlying its foundation. Numerous arguments were put forward dismissing this continuing denigration of the visual arts, though it was never effectively eliminated from popular thinking. A similar prejudice existed before the nineteenth century concerning music, which though accepted as one of the Arts, was none the less frequently considered an inferior one because it relied on poetry or texts.[36] Before the wider recognition of instrumental music in the eighteenth century, true music was held to concern the human voice, and that implied not just singing, but singing words. So music was often held to be merely a kind of decoration for the lofty literary element.

The similarity of the relationships between the visual arts and literature and music and literature by the later seventeenth century, shows that the potential for a closer cultural interaction between eye and ear existed by this time. It is certainly possible to point to musical spectaculars executed for members of the court of Louis XIV, treating the Arts of Painting and Music on equal terms, though never on their own terms since they are always matched by other Arts (like Agriculture or Navigation), or dominated by Poetry.[37] It is not until well into the eighteenth century that evidence starts to come to light showing painting and music treated with parity, and without any kind of literary intermediary. The frontispiece to the collected edition of Watteau's engravings, published after the artist's death by his friend the collector Jean de Jullienne, apparently depicts the two men together, one in the act of painting, the other playing music.[38] Admittedly, this is essentially a representation of friendship. But behind this, the iconography suggests an unmistakable pairing, or perhaps even alliance, of musical and artistic pursuits unhindered by other activities, which the public was presumably ready to accept.

2. Newton's *Opticks*

What effectively provided a genuine pretext for music and the visual arts moving closer together, undermining the position of literature in keeping them apart and subservient (at least in popular esteem), was a thesis advanced by one of the heroes of the eighteenth-century Enlightenment, Sir Isaac Newton. In the *Opticks* (1704), Newton implied, though without stating it unequivocally, that there exists a scientific relationship between sight, represented by the movement of light rays, which are perceived as colour, and sound, represented by the vibrations of a sounding body, such as a string on a musical instrument.[39] A musical tone could be shown to be equivalent to a particular colour, their connection determined – in theory, if not demonstrably – through their frequencies and proportions: thus Newton considered the seven colours of the spectrum (of a prism or rainbow) to be visual counterparts of the seven principal intervals of the musical scale.[40] Colours which (he considered) are harmonious when seen together related to the perfect proportions of concordant intervals. The respectability of Newton, and the apparently indisputable nature of his supposed discovery – founded (or so he claimed) on mathematics, one of the bases of reason – led educated men and women until early into the nineteenth century to reassess the ways they looked and listened. Newton's notions about light and sound may have gone unnoticed by artists and composers immediately after publication, and were opposed in several details by several leading authorities; but beginning with men of letters, his theory began to change popular preconceptions about the relationship between music and painting, exposing them together to greater public scrutiny, and raising their standing closer to that long enjoyed by the literary arts.

Among those who helped to make Newton's ideas widely known were Count Francesco Algarotti, who also wrote popular essays on painting and opera, and Voltaire, whose *Éléments de la philosophie de Newton* (1738) includes a chapter on the relationship of proportions in sound and light.[41] But it was left to the Jesuit L.B. Castel, who took seriously the notion that the vibrations which cause sounds have exact equivalents in the light waves generating colours, to devise a practical demonstration of this concept. His *Clavecin oculaire* was created with the intention of matching coloured lights (or cards in its earliest incarnation) with the sounds of a keyboard instrument.[42] Castel admitted taking the basic premise from Kircher.[43] Contrary to Newton, who matched the colours of the prismatic spectrum to the notes of the diatonic scale, Castel based his instrument on mixtures of the primary colours (the 'normal colours of painters'), allowing a twelve-colour scheme equivalent to the twelve notes of the chromatic scale, refined with a twelve-point system for shading from light to dark. Castel's faith in the parallelism he advocated went so far as to imagine whole operas represented as tapestries, and even extended to cover other senses, conceiving instruments for performance on perfumes and tastes.[44]

Although Castel's instrument was generally deemed a failure, its several incarnations meant that its premise became well known. As a concept it was found intriguing, provoking continuing discussion into the nineteenth century. Diderot considered it sufficiently important to merit an article in the *Encyclopédie*.[45] Distinguished composers like Rameau and Telemann came temporarily under the spell of Castel's thinking.[46] By the mid-eighteenth century his premise had become so pervasive in educated circles that it started to play a part in the way those with cultural pretensions borrowed concepts related to one art when discussing another. Louis de Cahusac (one of Rameau's librettists), for example, discussing *opéra-ballet* and *tragédie*, found the difference between the two was most easily conveyed by comparing a pretty painting by Watteau, with its grace, precision and brilliant range of colours, to a picture showing a vast composition, like those by Raphael or Michelangelo.[47]

3. Harmony for Ear and Eye

Although Newton's 'discovery' and its aftermath was found to have limited practical application from the point of view of most writers on the visual arts and music in the eighteenth century, its impact may be felt in the way theorists became increasingly concerned to discuss painting and music as though they were precisely comparable and, more importantly, on an equal footing with poetry.[48] When Dubos re-examined the old *Ut pictura poesis* principle in 1719, part of his agenda was to show that music (by which he meant opera) affects the ear in much the same way that painting affects the eye.[49] Batteux's influential book on the fine arts reduced to the same principle ('imitation' of nature), published in 1746, and the *Discours préliminaire* (1751) of the prestigious *Encyclopédie* (by d'Alembert) impressed on readers how closely, despite important distinctions, the leading art-forms operate in conveying their message.[50]

One consequence of this process was that during the eighteenth century any earlier published hints about the musical interests of Old Master painters were seized on as a means of understanding their work and imitating their strengths. In 1674, for example, the Venetian commentator Boschini discussed Veronese's celebrated *Marriage Feast at Cana* (Fig. 1), identifying the musicians in the foreground of the painting as portraits of the leading painters in Venice at the time it was executed.[51] When Napoleon had it moved to Paris in 1799, this aspect of the picture remained one of the main points of interest in viewing the work.[52] Following this example, pictures showing concerts of music were scrutinized for further portrayals of musical painters, their choice of instruments supposedly providing insights into their artistic temperaments. An edition of *The Tatler* in 1710 discussed such a picture (and the principle), a sufficiently memorable essay for it to be recalled in Charles Avison's 'On the Analogies between Music and Painting', published in 1753.[53] The *Concert* in question was at this time attributed to Domenichino, a painter known to have been musical and to have associated with others in the artistic fraternity in seventeenth-century Rome who toyed with notions of harmony linking music with colour.[54] One of Domenichino's close contemporaries was Poussin. On the strength of a famous letter in which Poussin tried to explain one of his pictures in terms of musical modes, it was generally assumed in the following century that he had used the range of modes to 'compose' his pictures.[55] How this worked nobody was quite willing to commit to words; but that it was considered crucial is evident from those who celebrated Poussin, like Félibien.[56] Antoine Coypel, Director of the French Academy, writing in 1721, advocated to his students generalized advice stemming from this tradition (reinforced by Newton's propositions), which by this date amounted to a doctrine:

> Each picture must have a mode which characterizes it. Its harmony will be now sharp and now sweet, now sad and now cheerful, according to the different nature of the subject one wants to represent. In this one can follow the enchanting art of music ... What should move the heart by passing through the ears should also move it by passing through the eyes.[57]

Possibly the most extreme case of 'musicalization' of a celebrated seventeenth-century painter was Salvator Rosa, who on slender evidence was actually treated as a composer in the eighteenth century.[58]

But the painter who experienced the greatest transformation in public esteem as a result of principles of music being applied to looking at his pictures was Rubens. Roger de Piles, Rubens's greatest champion in the late seventeenth and early eighteenth centuries, developed a sustained use of musical analogies to draw attention to what he considered the most moving kind of painting, which resulted primarily from the arrangement of colours (in which it was generally believed Rubens had excelled), producing 'a music for the eye'.[59] By placing emphasis on painting appealing to the senses and passions, as much as to reason, de Piles invited anyone to respond to Rubens, without need of intellectual qualification. This probably explains why a string of musicians and writers on music in the eighteenth century show considerable interest in Rubens. Thus in 1738, an account of a rehearsal of Handel's funeral anthem for Queen Caroline, held in the Banqueting-House (Whitehall), compared Handel's music with 'the Beauties form'd by magic Dyes [colours]' of Rubens's famous ceiling:

> Such Charms the two contending Arts dispense;
> So sweetly captivate each ravish'd sense,
> We ne'er can fix; but must by Turns admire
> The mimic Pencil, and the speaking Lyre.[60]

Another example of Rubens being used to praise a musical composition appeared in a eulogy on the composer Mondonville by Alexandre Tanevot (1756). 'What sublime drawing!', wrote Tanevot about the music, 'What rich pictures! ... The brush of Rubens guides *your harmony.*'[61]

The tendency towards 'musicalizing' Rubens was enduring. It may be felt in the career of the composer Abbé Vogler, who was much celebrated across Europe in the last decades of the century for his improvised keyboard recitals. For a time in the 1780s he was court composer to the Elector Palatine, whose famous picture gallery at Düsseldorf provided the setting for some of Vogler's documented concerts.[62] Vogler arranged for a fortepiano to be placed in turn in front of key paintings in the collection and then improvised music suited to their individual style and content. Rubens seems to have been selected more than any other painter represented in the collection.[63] Vogler was particularly drawn to a painting known as *Castor and Pollux*, representing the story of the abduction of the daughters of Leucippus (Fig. 2).[64] Its subject had only been recognized a short time before Vogler's recitals, so the painting itself was likely to have been topical at the time.[65] It subsequently inspired him to write an opera on the subject, with a libretto loosely drawn from Rameau's popular *Castor et Pollux*, first performed in 1737.[66] Rubens's famous *La Kermesse* also provided Vogler with inspiration for another opera, given the same title.[67]

The implications of Newton's *Opticks* were also felt in other spheres. Close scrutiny of the career of Handel shows the great composer frequently providing music with a visual aspect, perhaps to satisfy a kind of expectation on the part of his audiences. The clearest indication of this is Handel's refined use of tone-painting, in which the music consciously acts to evoke images in the listener's mind.[68] In his early oratorio, *La resurrezione*, for example, the libretto provided him with several opportunities to suggest visual phenomena – stormy sea, sunrise, birds, calm after tempest – which he carefully integrated into his musical setting.[69] The oratorio, performed in Rome in 1708, also emphasized the general theme of the conflict between Lucifer and Christ, by musical ideas conveying the notion of darkness giving way to light. Unambiguous evidence that the audience was encouraged to experience the oratorio visually comes from documentation showing that the patron caused an elaborate 'set' to be erected in the performing venue, showing a range of images and lighting effects, including a large canvas painting depicting the Resurrection and demons plunging into the abyss.[70]

The sets of the operas on which Handel worked after moving to London may, in some cases, also have been calculated to coordinate musical and visual effects.[71] One such designer was Marco Ricci, who had previously painted scenery for a production of Alessandro Scarlatti's *Pirro and Demetrio* in London. Ricci's experience of this encouraged him to paint a series of scenes showing opera rehearsals, featuring portraits of the performers (*c*.1709).[72] What is noteworthy about these pictures in the present context is that the rooms in which the rehearsals take place are hung with paintings, some of which seem to comment on the actions of the opera performers.[73] This use of pictorial material conspicuously displayed in relation to the main content of images was taken up by Hogarth. Several of his most admired works mercilessly satirize the practice and conventions of music, especially Italian opera.[74]

Ricci's paintings, which survive in several versions, and Hogarth's popular prints provide one measure of how London audiences in the decades after the publication of the *Opticks* became responsive to the idea of thinking about music in relation to visual culture. Handel's choice of themes for operas sometimes also reflects this interest, works of art (statues, monuments, portraits, etc.) often playing a part in the plot-line. In one of Handel's most enduring operas, *Admeto* (1727), for example, an important subplot is built around a series of portraits.[75] This preoccupation perhaps helps explain why one of the earliest biographical accounts of Handel, written within a year of his death, concluded by drawing an analogy between the most commanding features of the composer's style and two of the most celebrated works of ancient art, both much admired in the eighteenth century: the 'force' and 'energy' of Handel's harmony is compared with the Farnese *Hercules* (Naples, Museo Nazionale), 'which seems to be nothing but muscles and sinews'; and the composer's melody is likened to the *Venus de' Medici* (Florence, Uffizi), 'which is all grace and delicacy'.[76]

Handel himself was certainly sensitive to artistic matters. He seems to have gone out of his way to acquire paintings believed to be by distinguished artists, such as Rembrandt.[77] He also amassed an impressive collection of prints, including, predictably, a number after paintings by Poussin, Rosa and Rubens.[78] The engraver of these particular items, Joseph Goupy, was another of Handel's designers, providing, for instance, sets for *Admeto*. The two men seem to have fallen out in the 1730s, after which Goupy worked for Frederick, Prince of Wales, one of Handel's greatest opponents. Goupy subsequently produced a caricature in which Handel appears as 'the Harmonious Boar', ridiculed for having written such noisy music: an ass brays, cannon fire and clouds of smoke fill the room.[79] It seems that Goupy here had in mind Handel's *Fireworks Musick*, written in 1749 as part of the public celebrations for the Peace of Aix-la-Chapelle.[80] This music was almost certainly originally conceived to coordinate with the most lavish of eighteenth-century displays of fireworks, commissioned by the government, and realized by another of Handel's former stage designers, Servandoni. Although fireworks displays had previously been ordered for public celebrations of treaties, the idea of matching the spectacle – which also included paintings, statues and transparencies – to music appears to have been a novelty, probably conceived to acknowledge a general feeling that on such occasions both eye and ear needed to be satisfied. In the event the music was probably performed before the fireworks, but even at the rehearsal it attracted the largest single audience of the composer's lifetime (12,000 listeners). Nobody could have doubted that this was music composed to accompany fireworks, especially when the firing of cannon was a memorable feature of both the rehearsal and the performance proper.

The public rehearsal for the *Fireworks Musick* took place at Vauxhall Gardens. At this time Vauxhall was fast becoming the most popular venue for entertainment in London. The attraction was that it combined pleasures for all the senses, chiefly the visual and aural. More paintings were commissioned for the various supper boxes than might be seen at any other public location in Britain.[81] An account of the Gardens written in 1739 explains how music was performed, though with intervals to enable visitors to enjoy the promenades or to view the paintings.[82] Much of the music was by Handel, who was commemorated in a prominent statue, erected in 1738, which is known to have pulled in the crowds.[83] After Vauxhall was first developed as a kind of pleasure park in the 1730s, its principal clientele seems to have been aristocratic. Frederick, Prince of Wales, the ground landlord, was a regular visitor. His well-known enthusiasm for the visual arts and music soon acted as an incentive for those from more diverse backgrounds to visit the Gardens and experience for themselves visual and musical culture together.[84] By the 1740s many of the songs performed at Vauxhall were published for sale, with illustrations often relating to the visual delights available to visitors.[85] A selection of the paintings were also engraved, as were views of the Gardens (1752), advertised as on sale at the venue itself. These developments point to not only to a broadening of the social range drawn to Vauxhall, but also to the very popularity of experiencing music and the visual arts together.

One feature of this development is that the parity being established between music and the visual arts gradually enabled them to be perceived as independent of literary culture, at least in the public sphere; occasionally the previous dominance of literature hardly seems relevant. In 1719 Jonathan Richardson, in his discourse on connoisseurship, could not think of making a comparison between 'the Noblest Works' of Raphael and 'the most Ravishing Musick' of Handel without also introducing a literary correlation: 'the most Masterly Strokes' of Milton.[86] Six years later, when expounding his theory of painting, Richardson's view had changed. After explaining the advantages of painting over words, he points out that the pleasure afforded by painting is precisely comparable to music: 'its beautiful Forms, Colours and Harmony, are to the Eye what Sounds, and the Harmony of that kind are to the Ear'.[87] This trend continued. When the castrato Farinelli, a great international celebrity, had his portrait painted with a group of friends about 1750, he chose to include a singer, a poet and a painter, representing a balance between the leading arts.[88] Twenty years later he was visited by the music historian Charles Burney, who saw the picture in the singer's collection.[89] Burney's account, however, leaves no doubt that by this stage in his life Farinelli's interests were exclusively artistic and musical. Indeed he interestingly combined the two by labelling the various keyboard instruments he had acquired with the names of Old Master painters, the character of the sound of the instrument reflecting the choice of painter. Farinelli's favourite instrument was a pianoforte, made in Florence in 1730, which he labelled his 'Raphael'.[90]

4. The Crossroads

The diaries and correspondence of a leading cultural figure like Sir Horace Walpole show how carefully visual interests, generally pursued during the day

– visiting collections, exhibitions and print shops – and musical diversions, usually undertaken in the evening – like attending the opera – were balanced in the decades after 1750. Both pursuits provided topics for conversation in the literary salons Walpole frequented. The men of the French Enlightenment, the *philosophes* who were Walpole's friends, though principally literary figures, increasingly paid attention to what was going on in both music and the visual arts, reflecting and advancing the exhibitions at the Salon, as well as the rise of public concerts and other public musical activities.

These cultural developments were quickly taken up by young aristocrats on the Grand Tour. Many found themselves matching visits to the antiquities and collections of Italy, the original object of their journey, with trips to the opera and, later, even visits to professional musicians for lessons. Analysis of portraits commissioned in Italy lends an insight into how this came about. In 1758, for example, one of the painters most favoured by Britons in Rome, Mengs, was commissioned to paint a portrait of John, Lord Brudenell, then aged 23.[91] With its bust of Cicero, its pile of books and papers, and not least the affectionate dog, the portrait suggests a typical attempt to characterize a British aristocrat as an erudite and dutiful representative of his class. Only Brudenell's fur-lined coat seems rather out of place for a man in his position, especially since the view behind shows the season to be summer. The coat betrays the influence of Brudenell's hero, the great writer on antiquities, Winckelmann. A similar garment was sometimes worn by Winckelmann, as Mengs (a close acquaintance) would certainly have known.

In the same year, Batoni, Mengs's rival, was also commissioned to paint Brudenell's portrait. In this painting the sitter appears more relaxed, holding a mandoline, and leafing through the pages of a musical manuscript on which the name of the composer Corelli is visible at the end of the composition.[92] The painter actually copied out a long section from the end of the sixth sonata from Corelli's Opus 5. For a viewer to gain a full appreciation of this portrait, a recognition of Corelli, and this piece in particular, was helpful to building up a sense of what Brudenell was like. The sonata was certainly a favourite of Brudenell's since, in the portrait, it appears in the middle of what is evidently a manuscript, presumably intended to suggest Brudenell's own personal compilation of musical favourites. This is a portrait which was designed to be seen by Brudenell's closest friends, for whom such tastes would have been meaningful. On the other hand, the more imposing portrait by Mengs, which makes no reference to the sitter's musical abilities (a dubious asset for a British aristocrat at this date since instrumental performance at this level of society was more readily associated with women), was probably intended to satisfy the interests of Brudenell's family. It therefore emphasizes stability, traditional scholarship, even domesticity. Although Brudenell's two portraits were designed to function in separate social spheres, what is interesting about them in the present context is that they were conceived at the same moment and therefore suggest the coming together of visual and musical enthusiasms in his persona. Brudenell was for someone in his situation not only a pioneer in advertising his musicality, which would have had distinctly negative connotations for many at home (notwithstanding portraits of the cello-playing Prince of Wales), he was also a pioneer among British aristocrats in taking an interest in Italy's Greek antiquities, under the inspiration of Winkelmann, for which he would probably have been applauded in Britain. In 1758 the duality of these interests was unusual; by the end of the eighteenth century in Britain and France they were taken for granted.

It was really with the education of women that popular attitudes allowing musical and visual pursuits to be combined first achieved momentum, beginning at court and filtering through to the gentry. Madame de Pompadour is well known as a major patron of the visual arts in the middle of the eighteenth century.[93] She also took singing and harpsichord lessons from the best teachers available, something unexceptional for a woman in her position. More unusual, though far from unprecedented, were the drawing lessons she took. Distinctly remarkable for a woman in her position, however, were her attempts to learn etching and engraving (a number of examples of her work survive).[94] Madame de Pompadour's efforts to interest herself and those around her in what may be termed the mechanics of musical performance and artistic production, not just their promotion, made a lasting impact. Indeed she was pleased to display the fruits of her labours, as is evident from some of the portraits of her, by Boucher and Delatour, suggesting her musical abilities – she was often shown leafing through a musical manuscript – and featuring what have been interpreted as examples of her own graphic work.[95] In the next generation, Marie-Antoinette took up the mantle of Madame de Pompadour and made a conscious effort to bring together musical and visual interests so that they acted simultaneously in the same sphere. The painting by J.-B.-A. Gautier-Dagoty, featuring the Queen playing the harp surrounded by her admirers, the scene itself being recorded by a painter, is one visual testimony of this among many.[96] Like other female members of the imperial family educated in Vienna, Marie-Antoinette (like other princesses in the eighteenth century) was taught both musical performance and some techniques of drawing. But Gautier-Dagoty's painting shows how in her adult life Marie-Antoinette considered it entirely appropriate in a courtly environment to enjoy musical and visual diversions together.

In Britain a similar development occurred. Mrs Delany, a significant figure at court, came from a literary background. She left her mark not only by performing with some celebrity at the harpsichord, but also through her botanical pictures, executed in a kind of paper collage technique of her own devising.[97] While family connections made her naturally comfortable in the company of literati, like Swift, the enthusiasms she herself developed brought her close friendship with Handel, and made visits to the houses of painters like

Benjamin West a routine occurrence. After she died, Horace Walpole paid tribute to her combined interests by designing a new frame for the portrait of her painted by Opie, featuring attributes of painting and music equally balanced.[98] By the end of the eighteenth century, of course, it was commonplace for young women not only to learn to draw and to play a musical instrument, both activities treated on a par with each other, but also to appreciate the best examples of the two arts. Late eighteenth- and early nineteenth-century novels, such as those by Jane Austen, offer clear insights into the parity of the visual and musical arts in the social sphere at the time, and also how even those with literary inclinations could afford to ignore neither.[99]

During the second half of the eighteenth century public interest in linking the visual arts and music naturally extended to the professional practitioners themselves. Many composers, for instance, showed their concern with the visual arts by forming collections of images. The best known (since an itemized list was published) and perhaps the most extensive was the one formed by C.P.E. Bach.[100] Part of it appears in a drawing by the artist A. Stöttrup, which revealingly also features the artist himself portraying the composer.[101] On account of his exposure to this collection, Bach's son managed to resist becoming a musician (like almost everyone in his extended family) and trained as a painter, notwithstanding his father's resentment of the costs of tuition in Rome.[102]

Bach's exact contemporary, the painter Gainsborough (they both died in 1788), is well known for having preferred the correspondence and company of musicians to painters.[103] The friend of J.C. Bach, he once claimed that he could not wait to give up portrait-painting in order to devote himself to playing his beloved viola da gamba, a sentiment of a kind echoed by a number of British painters at this time.[104] One influential musician with whom Gainsborough had dealings was Thomas Linley, who became music director at the Drury Lane Theatre. Linley's precocious son Tom (who like the rest of the family sat for Gainsborough) was a friend of the young Wolfgang Amadeus Mozart when they were together in Florence in 1768. It is interesting that Leopold Mozart, as he toured his son around Europe, paid almost as much attention to viewing works of art as attending musical events; this, at least, is the impression gained from his correspondence. Tom Linley's father was probably much the same. When the Mozarts arrived in Louvain in 1763, for example, Leopold claimed to have stood transfixed in front of an altarpiece by the fifteenth-century painter Dirk Bouts, rather an unusual artist to get excited about at this date, and testimony that Leopold took picture-viewing seriously.[105] During his extended itineraries designed to expose his prodigy son to the ears and eyes of cultured European society, Leopold made a point of seeing as many paintings by Rubens as circumstances permitted. His highest praise was reserved, in accord with many commentators of the period, for the

Descent from the Cross in Antwerp.[106] Rubens was, as previously indicated, a much more conventional artist to admire in the eighteenth century than Bouts; but Leopold's persistence in seeking out paintings by Rubens for his son to absorb suggests that he believed viewing such works would actually help to cultivate his infant son's musicality. Presumably Leopold was under the impression that there was something for the composer to learn from studying the colour, form and immediacy of Rubens's paintings, a view probably stemming ultimately from the writings of de Piles. The value Leopold set on paintings is also evident in the portraits he commissioned of his young children in 1763, attributable to Lorenzoni. These are not just records of the appearance of Wolfgang and Nannerl, of value to Leopold in encouraging public interest in his gifted children; they also record splendid clothes given to the children by members of the imperial family, a very useful visual association worth exploiting.[107] Leopold evidently recognized that pictures might be very helpful to aspiring musicians.

What practical effect the viewing of paintings by Rubens and others could have had on the formation of the younger Mozart as a composer is difficult to say. It can hardly have taught him how to draw, though he delighted in the occasional pictorial scribble in letters to his family.[108] Writing in 1800, Mozart's sister recalled that her 10-year-old brother had shown 'a natural affection for all artists. Every composer, *painter*, *engraver*, and the like, whose acquaintance he made on journeys, had to give him some memento of his skill and these he would carefully preserve.'[109] Constanze, Mozart's widow, went further than this, recalling that her husband had been 'fond' of painting and sculpture, 'and could draw himself'.[110] Vincent Novello, the British publisher, who reported this after a visit to Constanze in 1829, noted that one of her rooms was hung with 'a very numerous Collection of Portraits of the greatest painters – among whom I particularly noticed Vandyk and Rembrandt'.[111] Some of these prints were probably acquired by Mozart himself. He certainly also enjoyed the company of painters as an adult. In 1781 he proudly reported to his father that one of his compositions had been performed in the house of the court painter Joseph Hickel.[112] His brother-in-law was the painter/actor Joseph Lange, whose portrait of Mozart was considered by his family the best likeness of him.[113]

Leopold's encouragement to his son to view pictures therefore seems to have had some bearing on Mozart's subsequent interests and associations. Indeed there is a good visual record of how Leopold seems to have introduced his son to the company of those whose principal concerns were the visual arts in a painting by Pietro Fabris, reflecting an occasion of music-making when the Mozarts were in Naples in 1770 (Fig. 3). Leopold and his son are both identifiable playing keyboard instruments, along with three further instrumental players, including Sir William Hamilton, the distinguished collector, antiquarian and British envoy in Naples. On the walls hang various antiquities and paintings copying those found at Pompeii and Herculaneum. In the foreground is the painter himself with his easel. Fabris surveys the scene, holding his painting in one hand and his brush in the other. Here, the practice of painting and that of music clearly go together.[114]

Mozart, however, did not always appreciate such social situations. When he was in Paris in 1778, he grew furious when, having been invited to perform in the house of a duchess, who along with her guests completely ignored him – or so it seemed to him – they passed the time in silence sketching each other.[115] On his threatening to leave, however, they implored him earnestly to continue. They had, it transpires, been listening to him *very attentively*, but they could indulge their artistic interests at the same time without losing their aural concentration. This is another clear example of the practice advanced by Marie-Antoinette of pursuing musical and artistic activities at social gatherings at the same time, in equal measure.

Later, it seems, Mozart did find a use for the visual education his father had insisted on, though it takes an unexpected form. In a small number of compositions, Mozart's manuscript notation makes use of five colours.[116] Conventional notation needs no colour at all, so the trouble Mozart went to in purchasing various coloured inks to write the music reflects, at the very least, some visual concerns. These colours have sometimes been dismissed as a kind of joke; but a further possibility is that Mozart was experimenting with using colours to convey expressive qualities in the interpretation of the music, which standard notion could not otherwise indicate.[117]

Another infant prodigy, contemporary with Mozart, was the painter Angelica Kauffman, one of the most popular artists of the period, her reputation extending across Western Europe. Kauffman's earliest biographer relates how as a child she was undecided whether to pursue a career in painting or one in music.[118] She claimed to have shown considerable talent in both, an assertion reasonably supported by a self-portrait, painted at the age of 13, showing her with a sheet of difficult vocal music which she had learned to sing.[119] Advice led her to give up music and devote herself to painting. The practice of self-portraiture, however, stayed with her. In 1782 Kauffman painted herself in the character of Painting inspired by Poetry, a representation of that old idea of painting depending on literature for its existence.[120] Twelve years later, Kauffman executed a further self-portrait, this time showing her choosing between following one of two female figures personifying Painting and Music, whose paths have met, but now go off in separate directions (Fig. 4).[121] This painting is iconographically rather subtle. On the one hand, it subverts the ancient iconography of the *Choice of Hercules* which, especially in Britain (where Kauffman enjoyed her greatest success), had become a kind of emblem for a moral crusade since the time it was discussed by the Earl of Shaftesbury, the philosopher, in the early eighteenth century.[122] On the other hand, the painting suggests how music would have been the easy route to have taken, associated as in the past with pleasure, whilst painting was difficult, associated with virtue. But leaving these considerations aside, the picture is especially interesting for the point in the development of Western culture when it was conceived. Although it refers to a decision taken in Kauffman's childhood, 35 years before it was executed, such a painting could not have been imagined at that time, when literature then still generally underpinned both painting and music, as still implied in the portrait of 1782.

But by the 1790s, painting and music could be understood in the public sphere as a real choice, both occupying similar social ground, almost, though not quite, eclipsing literature in the realm of human endeavour.[123] As one near-contemporary London newspaper report put it, 'picture mania rages as strongly as the musical mania', a statement which might also have been made in Paris, Vienna, Berlin, or almost any other major Western city.[124] It became almost second nature for many educated during this period to think of one art in terms of the other. When, for example, William Crotch expressed in 1831 the notion that J.S. Bach was 'the Michael Angelo of our art, and Handel was our Raffaelle', he was trying to convey something about music history which was most conveniently disclosed with reference to widely understood notions of the key characteristics of celebrated artists.[125] Crotch probably first encountered this way of thinking as a young man in the early 1790s, at a time when he heard Haydn perform his symphonies in London, and when he started to read the *Discourses* of Sir Joshua Reynolds, a work originally intended for students of visual culture, but the principles of which Crotch himself later applied to music. Although Crotch was a professional musician, like several other composers of the early nineteenth century – Mendelssohn is perhaps the best-known example – he spent much of his time developing his skills as an artist.

It may reasonably be suggested, therefore, that Kauffman's image of Painting and Music at the crossroads precisely reflects, not just the actual weight of common opinion concerning the respective merits of visual and musical culture, but also the point in the history of the two arts when their paths crossed, as they had done briefly in the sixteenth century. On this occasion, however, the outcome of this crossing of paths in the public sphere was longer-lasting and more deeply felt. Arguably, some of its consequences have remained features of Western culture, despite the fact that the actual proximity of visual and musical culture as suggested in Kauffman's painting of 1794 extended only briefly into the nineteenth century, partly because new cultural issues came to the fore, and partly because of the turmoil in which Europe found itself as a result of the rise of Napoleon. It is the aim of the remainder of this book to discuss how this rapport between music and the visual arts came into being and to provide an account of some of its most momentous features.

CHAPTER TWO

Popularity, Music and the Visual Arts

1. An International Language

The period when the visual arts and music came to be treated with parity in the public sphere during the later eighteenth century coincides with the emergence of a new kind of cultural reputation. Distinguishable from earlier brands of celebrity by reaching out and affecting many more people from the outset for a prolonged period, this new kind of reputation had the potential for becoming a worldwide phenomenon. The development of Western commercial interests in the eighteenth century, increasingly inter-continental in outlook, encouraged many involved in the arts to address themselves to what might appeal to the greatest possible audience, not necessarily restricted to a particular class or nationality, but which might aspire to a universal popularity.

Although by the 1780s the names of leading cultural figures – like Michelangelo, Shakespeare and Handel – were recognized and found meaningful throughout Europe and many other regions of the world, it was only during the later eighteenth century that it became possible for a *contemporary* figure to gain what amounts to a global reputation.[1] The fact that such a development took place at this time testifies to the possibility of a kind of international culture, which for some had desirable aspects, in terms both of its commercial advantages and also its benefits to mankind in general, as a means of uniting humanity.

The figure who first achieved this standing was neither a writer, nor an artist, but a composer of music. By the time of his death in 1809 the name and music of Franz Joseph Haydn were known and admired throughout the known world, a reputation which had then been evident for the best part of three decades. The situation was accurately summed up, for example, by Haydn's own patron, Prince Miklós II Esterházy, who in paying tribute to the composer in 1802 acknowledged 'the well-known reputation of your famous, universally esteemed works'.[2] In the words of Giuseppe Carpani, one of Haydn's first biographers (writing within three years after the composer's death) and a friend during his last years, the Austrian's compositions were heard 'from Mexico to Calcutta, just as from Naples to London, [and] from Pera [a suburb of Constantinople] to Paris'.[3]

Carpani did not exaggerate. During the last two decades of Haydn's life institutions representing most European countries paid official tribute to the composer, reflecting widespread popular enthusiasm for his work. Gifts bestowed on him by most crowned heads further acknowledged general admiration for Haydn throughout Europe.[4] Carpani's desire to emphasize

Haydn as more than merely a European phenomenon, stretching from the Americas to Asia, was also not overstated. Mentions of Haydn and his work in the *Diario de México*, the principle chronicle of cultural events in Mexico in the early nineteenth century, indicate the high regard for him in educated circles in central America. The same journal published a long obituary of Haydn in 1810 which attempted to account for this success:

> All of the natural gifts that can possibly distinguish an artist are united in Haydn: fluency of invention, immense facility, boldness to expand the limits of his art, variety of resources which lend freshness to his compositions, and above all the most delicate taste that prevents him from passing those limits beyond which genius degenerates into extravagance.[5]

In fact Haydn's reputation had probably already reached Latin America by the early 1780s since the Venezuelan revolutionary General Francisco de Miranda made a point of visiting 'the famous Haydn' in Hungary during a European tour in 1785.[6]

By this date Haydn was equally well known in the homes of the well-to-do in North America, especially through pieces or arrangements for voice and keyboard.[7] In 1783 Thomas Jefferson, a future president of the United States, drew up a catalogue of his library at Monticello, with mention of five keyboard sonatas and two concertos by Haydn which he intended to acquire. Whether or not these were purchased when he was in Europe in the mid-1780s is not known; but the musical education his young daughter Martha received during their time in Paris, when Jefferson acted as American Minister to France, undoubtedly put Haydn to the fore. Among the works acquired for her were keyboard arrangements of Symphonies Nos 53, 73 and 75 in editions published in London, where Haydn compositions had been advertised for sale since the mid-1760s. Jefferson and his family regularly attended concerts featuring Haydn symphonies when they were in Paris, and also after their return to the United States, as is evident from his personal account books. The numerous entries concerning payment for concerts, pianoforte lessons and keyboard tuning are interspersed with those covering the range of Jefferson's other interests, including many artistic matters, such as the acquisition of prints and paintings, and their framing.[8] Several entries during the Parisian period relate to negotiations with the sculptor Houdon for various items, in particular a statue of George Washington commissioned by the Assembly of the State of Virginia, for which Jefferson was entrusted with the arrangements.[9] Jefferson told Washington that Houdon possessed 'the reputation of being the *finest statuary of the world*', and that his 'bust' of *Voltaire* 'is said to be the *finest in the world*'.[10] In seeking out and befriending Houdon, Jefferson was acting to ensure that the interests of the fledgling American republic were served by the most talented and widely recognized artist then available. Similarly, in paying special attention to Haydn, Jefferson reveals his concern for promoting, within his own sphere and more widely throughout his country, the figure who in recent years had most successfully captured the imagination of the musical public in Europe.

Early American interest in Haydn was not restricted to city-dwellers and landowners. Perhaps the first Americans to be especially attentive to Haydn were those in the Moravian communities of Pennsylvania and North Carolina, where a copy of at least one early Haydn symphony had arrived by 1770.[11] Such was the level of interest in the United States that a Haydn Society had been founded in New York by 1798, and another followed in Philadelphia in the year of his death.[12] Knowledge of these perhaps prompted Carpani to compare Haydn with Christopher Columbus, both opening up 'ways to the New World'.[13]

Carpani had also not been misinformed about performances of Haydn's compositions in India, where the British even encouraged natives to attend concerts of Western music as part of the process of establishing European cultural values within their settlements.[14] Haydn was represented in India both by chamber music, intended for private consumption at home, and also by symphonies, performed in subscription concert series during the 1780s. For example, one of Martha Jefferson's favourites, Symphony No. 73 (composed about 1781 and published in London about 1783), was billed in concert programmes for the 1789 season in Calcutta, where it was particularly identified as 'the celebrated one of "La Chasse"'.[15] Indeed Haydn may himself have proudly told Carpani about the reception of his music in India, the composer having learnt of it from members of the British community who returned to London during his visits to the English capital in the early 1790s. One Haydn enthusiast from India whom the composer seems to have met at this time was John Shore, later Lord Teignmouth.[16] Shore was a friend of the leading orientalist resident in India during this period, Sir William Jones, whose book on the music of the Hindus (in translation) formed part of Haydn's library, having been dedicated to him by its German translator in 1802. Jones was also keen on Haydn. Writing to Shore from Calcutta in 1787, his prescription for good health was: 'Take a concerto of Corelli, An air of Leo, or Pergolesi, – a trio of Haydn, &c. Mixtura fiat.'[17] Such a mix of composers indicates that for many enthusiasts (Jefferson may also be included) Haydn's music, at least by this period, presented no threat to more established tastes, something which could not be said for the music of many other contemporary Continental composers. In fact Jones implies that Haydn's music was a force for good in the world, a view shared, for example, by the architect George Dance, who knew Haydn well. Dance wrote concerning the performance of works by Haydn and others like them that their 'beneficial influence upon the taste and judgment of the rising generation cannot be doubted'.[18]

In 1790, when Haydn began a journey to London, his first major trip outside the Habsburg empire, the notion that the work of a *living* individual might have an appeal throughout the world, crossing cultural boundaries, was a novel concept. It had not happened for writers because the problems of translation into many languages precluded such a possibility at this date. Nor had it occurred for artists, the difficulties of effective reproduction of contemporary works of art prohibiting any significant *global* appreciation of them. Music, however, was somewhat different, as Haydn himself had come to realize by the time of this first visit to London. Shortly before setting out, his friend Mozart had tried to dissuade him from undertaking such a journey at his age (he was then 58 years old), explaining to him that 'you have had no training for the great world, and you speak too few languages'. Haydn's reply to this was simple: '*my language* is understood all over the world'.[19]

The idea that music could be conceived as a kind of international language, with the power for mass communication, was not exactly a novelty, having already been suggested in the first volume of the famous *Encyclopédie* published in 1751.[20] It was developed further by Rousseau in an essay on the origins of language (published in 1781, but written *c*.1760) which argued that music was originally a natural part of spoken language.[21] Rousseau's leading advocate in England, Dr Burney, the historian of music and a friend of Haydn's, took up the idea to the extent that by 1795 he could quite naturally list together Dr Johnson (a writer), Metastasio (a librettist) and Haydn (a composer), and treat each one as an example of 'a favourite *author*', purposely not bothering to distinguish between literary authors and a composer of music.[22] Arguably, this kind of tendency resulted in most newly composed music published during the late eighteenth century (not just Haydn's) showing considerable stylistic homogeneity, distilling elements from various national traditions in ways which could hardly have been imagined in the first half of the century.[23] But his generalized drive towards a musical *linga franca* can only partly account for Haydn's success. It has been recognized that the dominant element in this musical unity was Italian opera. Haydn certainly fully absorbed this; but Italian opera was only one of a considerable number of factors which governed the development of his instrumental music, on which his reputation was chiefly built. A distinction may therefore be made between the large number of composers who sought to appeal to broad audiences by striving for a musical common denominator, the chief idiom of which was Italian opera, and Haydn, whose instincts led him to develop a notion of the possibility of music as a kind of shared universal language, understood by everyone. This more focused and compelling concept seems to have been recognized by Haydn himself as a factor in his own resounding success by the time of his final meeting with Mozart in 1790. As the report concerning Haydn's departure for England suggests, Haydn had evidently had a sustained and serious interest in considering his own music in terms of a language with the power to 'speak' in a distinct voice capable of being understood by a international audience, a much more ambitious and powerful point of motivation than the desire of many serious contemporary composers simply to reach larger audiences by refining popular musical traditions into a stylistic unity. Like Burney, Haydn perhaps first encountered this notion through the writings of Rousseau.

Although by 1770 Haydn would have been well aware of the extent of his reputation throughout the southern German-speaking world, his music being widely requested and performed in the aristocratic households and monasteries of Austria and neighbouring regions, it was probably a little later that he fully recognized how extensively his music was being pirated and published in many cities across most of Europe, with neither his permission and nor prospect of financial gain for himself. By the 1770s Haydn's name alone was sufficient to guarantee a measure of success for compositions, among undiscriminating as well as discriminating listeners. Publishers, anxious to issue works by Haydn when none was available, had few qualms about printing other composers' compositions under his name. As a result of this, by the 1780s, Haydn determined to take control of his own interests very carefully. This entailed not only dealing directly with publishers in major European cities himself, so that something of the commercial fruits of his labours would return to him; but also deliberately exploiting what made his work widely popular, in order to ensure that his reputation was constantly being cultivated still further. Several sources testify to Haydn studying the musical preferences of different nations in order to be sure of pleasing each of them, an approach which arguably led by the 1790s to a kind of composition intended to please as large an audience as possible, a notion which would have been inconceivable and unnecessary in the systems of musical patronage existing in Haydn's youth. This quality of universality in Haydn's mature work was what many contemporaries thought distinguished him from other composers. One critic writing in 1801 expressed it by suggesting that 'If ... one wanted to describe the character of Haydn's compositions in just two words, they would be – it seems to me – *artful popularity* [*kunstvolle Popularität*] or *popular* (easily comprehensible, effective) *artfulness* [*populäre Kunstfülle*].'[24]

Haydn's experience of actively striving to communicate with a universal audience – one consequence of thinking about music as though it were an international language – is hard to find reflected in the fortunes of contemporary composers, who were generally writing with specific audiences in mind and only occasionally found it necessary to adapt themselves to meeting the needs of other kinds of audience. For example, some composers of Italian opera, like Paisiello and Cimarosa, were certainly enormously successful in the leading opera houses across *all* of Europe in the later eighteenth century. But their success, by comparison with Haydn's, was restricted because it rested chiefly on just one privileged section of the musically interested public. Arrangements of popular arias or keyboard variations of favourite themes from operas by these composers might reach a slightly larger public, but not considerably so since such publications were largely aimed at cashing in on interest generated in the opera house itself. The audience for opera also tended to have little sense of extended loyalty to a composer, fashions changing rapidly as new operas featuring fresh novelties were staged for the public's delectation. This is probably one reason why Haydn himself was reluctant to compose operas for stages other than the princely opera house run by his own patron at Eszterháza in Hungary.

In many centres opera was a very competitive business, as Mozart discovered in trying to establish himself in Vienna. Although Mozart's mature operas were not unsuccessful in Vienna and Prague during his lifetime, their success was quite limited by comparison with those by other popular opera composers of the day, such as Paisiello and Salieri, whose works were performed much more widely.[25] It was only after his death (1791) that Mozart began to receive the kind of broad and sustained acclamation that has come to be associated with him today. Despite the fact that he was well travelled within Europe in his formative years, that his talents were widely recognized as those of a genius from the very outset of his career, and that examples of his music were performed in many leading centres of Western Europe by the 1780s, compositions by Mozart were often not especially well received within his lifetime outside the circles in which his name was meaningful, at least consistently and by comparison with those by Haydn. This was notwithstanding Haydn himself having been among Mozart's staunchest advocates.[26] Both in London and Vienna in the early 1790s, Haydn attempted to promote appreciation of Mozart's music, though he himself certainly felt that far too few heeded him. Obviously, Mozart had many close and loyal supporters, who were willing to pay more than the going rate to acquire or hear his compositions. But the typical music-lover in his lifetime was much more likely to be attracted to Haydn's music than Mozart's. This is reflected also in the variety of offers of engagements or employment Haydn received during the time he knew Mozart, which contrast with the difficulties Mozart himself encountered in securing a suitable position. Although Mozart's personality may – or may not – account for his lack of success in gaining any prestigious post, the history of patronage tends to suggest that most enlightened patrons were prepared to put up with almost any personal characteristics in employees in order to obtain the services of the man (or woman) who could provide the desired product. Specific criticisms of Mozart's compositions, such as the Emperor Joseph II's judgement of *Die Entführung aus dem Serail* (1782) that it was '*too* beautiful for our ears' and had 'an *enormous* number of notes' at a time when economy of composition was often sought in music – found in works by composers like Haydn and Paisiello – only partly explains the reception first given to much of Mozart's mature music on the international stage.[27]

Perhaps a more substantial reason for the comparative lack of lustre attached to Mozart's name on the broader European front during his adulthood may be detected in a certain reluctance on his part to compromise his style. This is not to imply that Mozart was unwilling to please any particular category of listener. Many instances of him writing to satisfy specific individuals or groups with varied tastes might be mentioned. But these are more about Mozart directing himself to meet the requirements of a commission, or an occasion, than about him modifying his compositional procedures or aims to suit the ways different kinds of people listened. While Haydn's mature music travelled well and was (it is here submitted) calculated to do so, Mozart seems to have been on the whole less concerned with satisfying varied tastes or preferences, so his music often failed to make a substantial impact on early listeners outside the environments either in which he himself worked and had direct experience, or in which the music was originally intended to be heard. A comparison of the sets of quartets dedicated to the cello-playing king of Prussia, Friedrich Wilhelm II, by Haydn (Op. 50) and Mozart (K. 575, 589, 590) may serve to highlight the contrast between the two composers and their attitudes. Mozart incontestably wrote his quartets, with their prominent cello parts, to please the king. But it did not follow from this that these parts, much more demanding than usual for the cello in a quartet, would necessarily be appreciated elsewhere. On the other hand, there is no real evidence to suggest that Haydn took any significant note of the king's performing abilities in conceiving his music, as a comparison with both earlier and later quartet series by him suggests.[28] Although Op. 50 has different characteristics from Haydn's previous published set of quartets (Op. 33), unlike the distinguishing feature of Mozart's Prussian quartets these differences do not betoken a particular kind of audience for the music, but, it may be argued, build on general appreciation of his music that had previously been generated.

As the anecdote concerning the attempt to dissuade Haydn from visiting London implies, Mozart in 1790 seems not to have been fully prepared to conceive music in terms of a language which might speak to everyone, from different nationalities and backgrounds, at the same time, within the same composition. This is certainly not to suggest that Mozart was uninterested in his music reaching the widest possible audiences, or that he did not share the Enlightenment ideals of his time which found in music a force for improving the human condition. But with Mozart other issues seem often to have intervened to hamper any attempt to satisfy any notion of a universal audience of the time. Sometimes these seem to have stemmed from his own prejudices, which he frankly admitted. Many such prejudices, for example, become evident in correspondence with his father during 1778, when the younger man was travelling to Paris in search of employment. Just when Leopold reminded his son that his purpose in going to the French capital was to 'build up your own name and reputation *in the world*' by taking on whatever was available (and would pay), Wolfgang saw fit to inform his father that 'I become quite powerless whenever I am obliged to write for *an instrument which I cannot bear* [the flute].'[29] This was the kind of statement which exasperated Leopold, who instantly recognized that such attitudes provided no basis on which to build success, let alone a world reputation. Although Mozart wrote (most of) the required pieces, his lack of enthusiasm perhaps betrayed itself to the patron, a situation which Haydn always worked hard to avoid, even when called on to write for the most unusual instruments.

Not long afterwards, Mozart received a commission in Paris for some choruses for inclusion in a composition by another composer, but in writing them he confessed to his father that he found this to be 'hack-work' and beneath him (though he readily took on such work many times in the future).[30] Again, this betrays an attitude that Haydn himself took care never to hint at even remotely in connection with his own work, though during the course of his career he was often required to rewrite parts of compositions of others to render them suitable for local performance. In composing for publication in Paris, Leopold urged his son to 'make it easy, suitable for amateurs and *rather popular*', a lesson instinctively heeded by Haydn, but which Mozart seems to have found more difficult to follow.[31] The prospect of writing an opera for Paris led Leopold to offer his son advice that 'before you write for the French stage ... listen to their operas and find out what pleases them ... endeavour, I hope, to acquire *the correct accent*'.[32] It was advice of this sort that Haydn certainly put to practical effect when he himself subsequently composed for audiences in Paris and London; but Mozart *fils*, despite on occasions following his father's instincts (as, for example, in the 'Paris' symphony), never managed to pick up 'the correct accent'. Mozart insisted that the opera in question had to be 'a grand opera or none at all', an attitude which at the end of the day left him with no commission and very little to show for his time in Paris.[33] His lack of success resulted in him referring repeatedly in his letters to 'these stupid Frenchmen', and forming a hostility to many things French which remained with him for the rest of his life. For example, he found the French language itself 'so detestable for music. It really is hopeless; even German is divine by comparison.'[34] Mozart's ambition in Vienna to be able to write operas in German is well documented later in his career; and though this may be interpreted as a desire to be understood by everyone within the society in which he worked, it also betrays more than a hint of antagonism to other national cultures. Had this been widely sensed (which seems quite likely), it could hardly have been conducive to any claims that a universal audience might interest itself in Mozart and his music. Haydn was careful to avoid suggesting that he held any prejudices along these lines – indeed, there is little evidence that he did during his working career – and even in his two late oratorios he went to the trouble of ensuring that they were published with translations into all the major European languages. Whilst the course of Mozart's career after his final trip to Paris obliged him (by choice or necessity) to become increasingly reliant on the German-speaking world for his prospects, which at times were frequently exceptionally good, the course of Haydn's career during this period brought about a loosening of national boundaries in relation to the diffusion and understanding of his music, and a continual enlargement of his reputation. This was a situation during the 1780s and later that he worked hard to maintain, despite the fact that for long periods he worked in comparative isolation at his patron's palace in rural Hungary.

It is understandable therefore why Mozart, in contrast to Haydn, found it unnecessary to develop skills which would have enabled him to deal effectively with widely differing kinds of patron and publisher, and their varied needs. On the other hand, ever conscious of how to follow and how to lead the tastes of his audience simultaneously, Haydn seized every opportunity to send his music overseas and to accept commissions from abroad, even in the most unusual circumstances, or for the oddest combinations of instruments, knowing that in so doing, this could only serve, not hinder, the extent of his reputation. Music for unusual combinations could always be rearranged for more conventional groupings, as in the case of the Concertos and Notturni for lire organizzate (commissioned from Naples), some of which were performed in London with oboe and flute (or two flutes). Mozart of course also made many arrangements of his own music and music by other composers; but in these cases the motivation seems to have been in the first instance to satisfy his own interests or the interests of those he respected, rather than what a broad listening public might want from him.

It was only after Mozart's death that pan-European audiences came to listen to his music more appreciatively; but even then it is possible to detect prejudices against it, including on the part of the most enlightened of thinkers. For example, one of Haydn's English friends, the playwright Thomas Holcroft – a man who embraced many of the notions of an international brotherhood of mankind stemming from the French Revolution – noted in his diary early in 1798 that an acquaintance had 'adopted the cant which from Germany has spread to England, of affirming Mozart to be a greater man than Haydn. In Germany, his theatrical pieces have given Mozart his great popularity; he was undoubtedly a man of uncommon genius, but *not* a Haydn.'[35] Holcroft was certainly among Haydn's most enthusiastic supporters, to the extent that in 1794 he wrote a poem in tribute to the composer and half filled his music library with Haydn's compositions.[36] His coolness towards Mozart may partly be explained by a feeling that if he admitted Mozart to be as great a composer as Haydn, his idol would somehow be diminished. Later in 1798, Holcroft attended a private musical occasion at which music by both Haydn and Mozart was performed. Afterwards he noted:

> ... both men of uncommon genius, but the latter [Mozart] impatient after novelty and superior excellence, often forgets the flow of passion in laboriously hunting after new thoughts which, when thus introduced, have the same effect in music, as the *concetti* of the Italians in poetry; and for these Mozart is frequently extolled as superior to Haydn.[37]

Holcroft tried to listen to both Haydn and Mozart objectively, but he persuaded himself, as many others at this date seem to have, that he could detect in Haydn's music a quality inspiring in the listener a sense of universal association, which he found wanting in Mozart, whose appeal, though considerable, was conditioned by characteristics which struck him as betraying a national disposition, excluding some listeners from a full appreciation of the music.

Haydn's notion of music as a kind of world language also indicates how he thought of his achievement in terms of culture as a whole, not within the sphere of music alone. As a man who held firm Christian views, Haydn wanted his achievement to reflect itself in the promotion of good within the world, that it should benefit the unfortunate in society, as well as himself. He was hardly alone in holding such views, which were held by many advocates of the ideals of the Enlightenment. He was, however, in rarer company in actually putting these notions into practice. There is no doubt that Haydn believed that any prosperity which accrued to an individual as a result of commercial success placed obligations on that individual to repay the community responsible for the success. One practical means Haydn found to do this was to involve himself in charitable works. His oratorio *Il ritorno di Tobia*, for example, was first performed in Vienna in 1775 for the Tonkünstler-Societät, an organization of musicians which gave biannual concerts to raise funds in support of the widows and orphans of members. The oratorio, performed as far away as Rome, Berlin, Lisbon and Leipzig long before Haydn dreamt of leaving his homeland, was an immediate success. In the words of a contemporary report, '*the whole very numerous public* was delighted and Haydn was the great artist once again, whose works are loved in the whole of Europe and in which foreigners find the original genius of a master'.[38] Haydn's involvement with the Tonkünstler-Societät lasted most of the remainder of his life. His later oratorios were repeatedly put on, often with his own involvement, to help support its activities financially.

But as Haydn grew older, the range of his charitable interests broadened. Performances of his oratorios supported military as well as musical charities. A performance of *The Creation* given on 16 January 1801, for example, raised substantial sums for wounded soldiers. Haydn's early biographer, G.A. Griesinger, reporting on this occasion, sensed that Haydn himself intended that the work should function in this way: 'This music seems to have been made to help collect money for good works, and this time it in no way failed its purpose.'[39] The community in general also benefited from Haydn's generosity to the extent that the authorities in Vienna conferred on him the privilege of becoming a freeman of the city in 1804. In the letter to the composer announcing their decision, they wrote that Haydn had

> helped the poor men and women ... of St. Marx by giving public performances of Cantatas [oratorios?] the proceeds of which were given to these people. Not only did he show considerable generosity ... but he also demonstrated himself always prepared to lend his services voluntarily and without payment. ... By this notable ... act of generosity, the people in the hospital, made infirm through age, poverty and poor health, enjoyed for prolonged periods of time consolation and ease ... In addition, through his extraordinary talent he has done a great deal to elevate the aesthetic judgement of a large part of the community ...[40]

Another facet of Haydn's expanding charitable concerns was his support for organizations responsible for artistic activities. His first public engagement after returning to Vienna from his first visit to England was at the masked ball of the Society of Visual Artists[41] held on 25 November 1792, the first such event to be held by this body, attended by many leading figures in Viennese society. For this occasion Haydn composed twelve Deutsche Tänze and twelve Minuets, which he himself conducted, offering the music and his services without remuneration.[42] He may also have arranged an earlier dramatic work especially for the occasion.[43] The ball, for which 2,181 tickets were sold, was in aid of the widows and orphans of painters, sculptors and other artists. Documentation concerning the event refers to Haydn 'als Kunstverwandler', that is, he was a friend of visual art, and provides the information that the dances were arranged by the composer for keyboard soon after the event 'at the request of the Empress', to whom they were presented in gratitude for her support.[44] The speed with which the keyboard version of the dances was issued by Haydn's publisher, Artaria, less than a month after their first performance, and the Empress's admiration for the pieces suggest that they struck the listener at the time as entirely novel. This impression may have been given because the Deutsche Tänze were danced in a new manner, possibly in a style which in due course was to develop into the waltz.[45]

Haydn evidently went to considerable trouble to demonstrate his support for the artistic community in Vienna, though he had only just returned from England. For this, the very first ball in support of the society, it would have been easier to call on a resident composer, as was the case in subsequent years. When Beethoven provided music for the dances at the same ball in 1795, it was reported that he composed them 'as a token of his desire for solidarity between the various branches of the Arts'.[46] Haydn was probably among the first to promote this attitude in Vienna, impressing it on Beethoven, who became the older composer's pupil shortly before the ball of 1792. Haydn himself, though like Mozart always enthusiastic about fraternity between different kinds of creative individual, may have been particularly encouraged in this by the experience of England, where he would have observed in operation a more developed system of charitable patronage, and where it was not unusual for artists of one kind to mix with creative figures of another. For example, Haydn's friend Thomas Holcroft, essentially a literary figure, spent a considerable portion of his time fraternizing with both musicians and painters. Having begun learning the violin at the age of 5, and acquiring a reputation for complete mastery in vocal music as a teenager, Holcroft had a sufficiently distinguished voice to sing tenor in the famous Handel celebrations in Westminster Abbey of 1784.[47] He later belonged to a musical club, whose members included the composers Shield and Clementi, and the violinist and impresario Salomon, all of whom became well known to Haydn. Holcroft was also on good terms with well-known painters like Opie, Beechey and Barry, and regularly visited auction rooms in search of paintings. Indeed he put together quite an impressive collection which he was pleased to show visitors; he was particularly proud of two landscapes by Richard Wilson, an unusual taste for a political radical.[48] Such was the kind of fellowship which Haydn certainly encountered in London, and which he may have hoped to sponsor in Vienna by supporting the Society of Artists.

Haydn's substantial collection of engraved prints, including reproductions of Old Master paintings and works by contemporary artists, is clear testimony of his considerable interest in the visual arts, also demonstrable through his friendly relations with many leading artists of his time, especially in London, where evidence suggests he enjoyed the company of painters and printmakers as much as, if not more than, that of the musical fraternity.[49] In later life his favourable attitude to artists is evident in his dealings with another of his earliest biographers, the landscape painter A.C. Dies, whose interviews with Haydn during the last years of the composer's life – no fewer than thirty between 1805 and 1808 – provided the basis of the *Biographische Nachrichten von Joseph Haydn* (1810), the author's designation as 'Landscape painter' (*Landschaftmahler*) conspicuously featuring on the title-page.[50]

Since 1797 Dies had been employed teaching landscape painting at the Vienna Akademie. He was appointed professor in 1806. Before this he had spent 20 years in Italy, employed initially in the workshop of Piranesi, then earning a living giving drawing lessons. Goethe met him in 1788 and engaged him in an exercise in colouring a landscape which was intended to help the German 'learn more and more about colour and harmony'.[51] In 1792 Dies became involved in an important project to publish 72 views of Italy, the *Mahlerisch-radirte Prospecte von Italien*, to which he had contributed 24 plates by 1795. After settling in Vienna, he landed a curatorial job in the picture gallery of Prince Esterházy. An interest in art theory is also clear from a commentary Dies wrote on Lessing's famous essay *Laocoön, or The Limits of Painting and Poetry* (1766), published in 1802.[52] Although hardly distinguished, Dies's experience in various fields of the visual arts was certainly considerable. In his own judgement, and that of Haydn, it evidently provided adequate qualification to write a serious musical biography. Since no one disputed this, it may be understood as an indication that a career in painting was considered as appropriate to writing about composers as one in music.

Dies's idea to write Haydn's biography stemmed from a conversation with his friend the sculptor Anton Grassi, who had been on good terms with Haydn for several years.[53] Grassi told Dies that Haydn had neither written any account of his life himself, nor had he been willing for anyone to do it. According to Grassi, however, Haydn was full of stories and comical experiences which would make the basis of an excellent account. This needed to be done before it was too late, so that posterity could be left an accurate picture of such a unique figure, who had grasped the secrets of harmony better than anyone.[54] Dies asked Grassi to use his influence with the composer to exhort him to agree to be interviewed for a biography. Despite Grassi's powers of persuasion, Haydn absolutely refused, protesting that 'his life could interest nobody'.[55] It was only when Haydn was told that Dies was *an artist*, who claimed to have attempted a few musical compositions himself, that the composer seemed impressed, finally consenting to the plan.

Dies was aware that his scheme was flawed as an accurate piece of biographical writing since by this date Haydn's memory was often far from perfect. He therefore determined to produce 'so true a *representation* that every contemporary of Haydn's might find again in the portrait the characteristics of the original, as if looking in a mirror'.[56] But the portrait was to be neither an 'idealized picture', nor one which concentrates on details alone: 'I ... scrupulously checked myself from immortalizing, like Denner's *paintbrush*, the wrinkles in place of the face.'[57] As a painter Dies understandably drew on his artistic experience in his writing, as when he introduces Balthasar Denner, 'the pore-painter', famed for the excessive naturalism of his portraits, in order to explain the kind of impression of the composer he was hoping to present.[58] Dies was also ever conscious of stressing the visual as a means of stimulating Haydn's memory. He talks about 'The pictures [*Die Bilder*] I raised in Haydn's imagination', a ruse to shift Haydn's attention away from the impediments of old age and to focus his recollections on the triumphs of the past.[59]

The experience of Dies, a painter, in being permitted to record Haydn's life is not an isolated instance of Haydn, the most famous composer of his age, attracting the professional interest of an individual as much concerned with the visual arts as with music. For Giuseppe Carpani, the third of Haydn's early biographers, Haydn's achievement acted as a kind of catalyst for developing a new style of writing. This attempted to convey a sense of the character of Haydn's music, and its effect on listeners, by comparing it with the visual arts, with which Carpani assumed his readers had some familiarity.

2. Musical Biography: Carpani Exploding the Cannon

One measure of Haydn's continuing popularity at the end of his life is the number of publications about him which appeared at the end of his life and shortly afterwards. Few composers had previously been considered sufficiently worthy candidates for monographic treatment. By and large, before the early years of the nineteenth century there appears to have been no sustained interest on the part of the public in details of composers' lives and affairs. Short notices of major composers were published from time to time in the eighteenth century, such as the anonymous 'Account of Joseph Haydn, a celebrated composer of music', which appeared in London in 1784.[60] But such notices, consisting of brief collections of essential items of biographical information, rarely betray any sustained attempt to analyse their subjects in depth. For most readers at this date the notion that the life of a musician might be a matter worthy of public attention could hardly be taken seriously. While it was certainly becoming increasingly fashionable for the educated classes to concern themselves with *knowledge* of music, there was as yet no clear view about what kind of writing might best inform a popular audience. Treatises for professional musicians were clearly quite inappropriate for a general readership. The musical entries in the *Encyclopédie* (1751–72) and the publications on music that this spawned, like Rousseau's *Dictionnaire de musique* (1768), went some way to meet a growing need; but these were principally aimed at those of an elevated frame of mind, often drawn from the leisured classes. They did not cater for the average reader who might interest him/herself in the activities of a composer. Later musical dictionaries, such as E.L. Gerber's *Historisch-biographisches Lexicon der Tonkünstler* (1790–92), did provide information on composers, which certainly contributed to their reputations. Gerber's treatment , for example, of Haydn, whom he calls 'one of our greatest men' and 'the glory of our age', gives a indication of how fervently Haydn was admired in Germany at the time of his first visit to London. But such dictionaries were intended for use by specialists rather than by the general public. By their nature, they were obviously limited in the kind of information they contained.

The English writer on music Charles Burney recognized the problem of satisfying a broad readership for music in preparing his *General History of Music*, one of the earliest attempts to provide a comprehensive overview of the development of Western music, published between 1776 and 1789. The *General History* was intended to show that music was capable of sustaining a continuous and logical history in the same way that had long been accepted for the visual arts and literature. Giorgio Vasari's *Le vite de' più eccellenti architetti, pittori, e scultori italiani* (first published in 1550), in which might be found assembled many details of the lives of celebrated Italian artists, had been a cornerstone of the libraries of educated men with cultural interests since it first appeared. Indeed Burney himself had two editions of Vasari (1648 and 1759) in his own library, and certainly referred to them in preparing his own *History*. The connection in his mind between his project to write a music history and examples of history-writing already published concerning other arts, especially painting, is clear from a letter sent at the time he first contemplated the project:

> I find it [the writing of a history of music] connected with Religion, Philosophy, History, Poetry, Painting, Sculpture, public Exhibitions & private life. ... It is somewhat extraordinary that nothing of this kind has been attempted in our language, which abounds with histories of every other art, as well as of its Professors. Yet I see no reason why the life of an eminent musician should not afford as much entertainment to the Public *as that of a Painter*. The Former is more frequently thrown into the highest society, his life is more chequered, & he obtains more easy access to the Great than the Latter.[61]

Burney proceeds to give as an example of a musician with a comparable colourful life, the celebrated castrato Farinelli, whose singing had created a sensation across Europe earlier in the eighteenth century. After commenting on Farinelli's career, Burney continues: 'Now amongst all the Painters whose lives had been written by Vasari, there is no one except Leonardo da Vinci, who furnishes such great & interesting events.'[62]

During the course of researching his *History* Burney made two extended trips to the Continent, one to France and Italy, and the other to the Netherlands, Germany and Austria. Partly as a means of financing his main project, Burney had the idea of publishing (in an edited form) his journals and notes from the trips. Although these were primarily aimed at conveying to a general readership a flavour of contemporary musical activity across Europe, their content throughout points to Burney's concern to show that music did not exist in a cultural vacuum, but was part of a respectable canon of creative accomplishments, including painting, sculpture and architecture, a position which many at the time of publication thought unconvincing. Burney's success may be measured both by those who read his musical tours, and where they placed Burney's volumes within their library. Jefferson, for example, owned all of Burney's musical tours and, in cataloguing his own library, arranged them close to essential volumes for the eighteenth-century connoisseur of the visual arts, including Richardson's *Theory of Painting and Essay on a Connoisseur* and Félibien's *Lives of Painters and Architects* (an imitation of Vasari).[63] Everywhere he went, Burney made a point of viewing the major works of art, galleries, churches, collections of paintings, buildings and monuments, as well as describing and often giving his opinion on them, something which his audience would have perceived as an indication of his status as an educated gentleman and also of his competency to write about cultural matters. His travelogues therefore gave the ordinary reader a way into an understanding of music, its institutions and public manifestations, through the visual arts, about which Burney takes for granted the notion that every self-respecting reader would have some interest and knowledge. He thereby prepared the public for the appearance of his main work, the *General History*, and made its subject-matter more approachable to the ordinary reader. As a consequence of this approach, Burney frequently found himself drawing pictorial-musical analogies, generally by informing music through the language of painting. For example, when discussing the development of dynamics in the Mannheim school he compares the treatment of *piano* and *forte* to 'the use of red and blue in painting', and in weighing up the abilities of the composer Hasse, he draws a parallel with a painter who understands how to cast the light onto the principal figure in a painting.

A significant aspect of Burney's historical method in the *General History*, as he anticipated at the outset, was to provide biographical information on the leading musicians whose work comprised the story he was telling. When in the fourth volume (1789) he came to give an account of Haydn, he prepared his readers for what he considered was an exceptional episode in the history of recent music by injecting a personal element into his prefatory comments:

> I am now happily arrived at that part of my narrative where it is necessary to speak of HAYDN! The admirable and matchless HAYDN! From whose productions I have received more pleasure late in my life, when tired of most other Music, than I ever received in the most ignorant and rapturous part of my youth, when every thing was new, and the disposition to be pleased undiminished by criticism or satiety.[64]

Most of the biographical information about Haydn which follows was received, upon request, from the British envoy in Vienna. But Burney was not satisfied with presenting this and a discussion of Haydn's chief compositions. Consideration of Haydn lead him to a reflection on the nature of originality: 'his compositions are in general so new to the player and hearer, that they are equally unable, at first, to keep pace with his inspiration. But it may be laid down as an axiom in Music, that whatever is *easy* is *old*, and what the hand, eye, and ear are accustomed to; and, on the contrary, what is *new* is of course *difficult*, and not only scholars but professors have it to learn.'[65] Here, reflections on Haydn gave Burney a pretext for introducing a philosophical element into his *History*. At an earlier stage in the work, the section treating Corelli, Burney found himself instinctively drawn to thoughts about Haydn in reflecting on Corelli's reputation and its unprecedented durability:

> [Corelli's] productions have contributed longer to charm the lovers of Music by the mere powers of the bow, without the assistance of the human voice, than those of any composer that has yet existed. Haydn, indeed, with more varied abilities, and a much more creative genius ... has captivated the musical world in, perhaps a still higher degree; but whether the duration of his favour will be equal to that of Corelli, who reigned

supreme in all concerts, and excited undiminished rapture full half a century, must be left to the determination of time, and the encreased [*sic*] rage of depraved appetites for novelty.[66]

By the time Burney actually met Haydn in London in 1791, when he presented him with a copy of his *General History*, he could have been in no doubt that Haydn's reputation was indeed of a kind which would last, and which the world had not previously seen.

The *General History*, though intended for a serious readership, was an important step in the direction of popular musical biography. It was, however, the phenomenon of Mozart, whose unprecedented rise and fall, ending with his early death in 1791, which perhaps did most in the eighteenth century to lead the general public into sensing that the lives of composers might provide the subject matter of worthwhile reading. The subject of Mozart's life embraced several themes which were irresistible to later eighteenth-century sensibilities and were quickly mythologized: infant prodigy, genius recognized but unrewarded, premature death, and most absorbing of all, his pauper's burial in an unmarked grave.[67] Within a decade of Mozart's demise, several accounts of his life had appeared to satisfy curiosity.[68] The most conscientious of these early biographies is the one by F.X. Niemetschek (1798).[69] But even this could not escape depicting Mozart's demise as though it were an episode from an eighteenth-century novel, with scenes of the composer's premonition of death vividly portrayed on the flimsiest of factual evidence. Niemetschek also suggested another approach to popularizing Mozart's life when he referred to the subject of his biography as 'our Raphael in music'. The parallel with this particular sixteenth-century painter, one of the most admired artists in the eighteenth century, was a way of conveying to Niemetschek's readership notions of pure classical form, ideal beauty, noble simplicity, and perfection which he wanted to imply Mozart's music might impart, and which were traditionally associated with Raphael.

The correlation between composer of the Enlightenment and painter of the Renaissance was elaborately and systematically taken up in an article published in 1800 by Friedrich Rochlitz, one of Mozart's most eloquent early champions.[70] Much of the cultural baggage of Raphael's reputation that the art-loving public of the late eighteenth century had grown up with was now grafted onto Mozart, substantiating the slender view of him hitherto available in print. Beginning with straightforward comparisons of the relationship of father to son, noting that in both cases the son adopted the same profession as the parent, Rochlitz proceeds to compare aspects of Mozart's operas with the most famous works by Raphael, well known to many readers through popular prints. Thus the frescoes depicting stories from the fable of Psyche in the loggia of the Villa Farnesina in Rome are compared with *The Magic Flute* and *La clemenza di Tito*; the *School of Athens*, Raphael's most famous fresco in the Vatican, is discussed as though it were a companion to both the finale of Act I of *Don Giovanni* and the same opera's celebrated 'hell scene' in Act II, notwithstanding the difference in media. The analogy with Raphael proved a potent one for conceptions of Mozart throughout the nineteenth century.[71]

The idea for such musical-pictorial parallels was invented by neither Niemeschek nor Rochlitz. Both may have been familiar with the comparisons made by Burney in his north European travelogue (1773). Burney wrote that while Hasse (a popular composer of opera) 'may be regarded as the Raphael ... of living composers', Gluck 'gives such energy and colouring to passion, as to become at once poet, painter, and musician. He seems to be the Michael Angelo [*sic*] of living music, and is as happy in painting difficult attitudes, and situations of the mind, as that painter was of the body.'[72] Burney also found it useful to compare J.S. Bach with Michelangelo in the *General History*. The Bach/Michelangelo analogy was one which struck a chord with later writers in Germany; but by the time Niemetschek and Rochlitz were comparing music and the visual arts, Hasse's star no longer seemed as bright as that of Raphael, who was now the perfect match for projecting Mozart in the public sphere. By 1800 such analogies had gained a certain resonance. In that year, for example, one critic could quite confidently liken a living composer, Cherubini, to a long-deceased painter, Veronese.[73] In Rome, where Mozart's star was slow coming into ascendancy, a Canova bust of Cimarosa was set up in proximity to the tomb of Raphael, as a means of commenting on the character and eminence of the music of an *Italian* composer.[74]

Following Niemetschek's *Mozart*, musical biography developed one stage further with the appreciation of the life and work of J.S. Bach by J.N. Forkel, director of music at Göttingen.[75] Although Bach's music was unknown to most of the musical public at the beginning of the nineteenth century, Forkel gave his pioneering biography a populist slant by implying that Bach should be a source of pride and national sentiment for the German people: 'no other nation has anything to be compared'. Forkel dedicated his biography to another early Bach enthusiast, Baron Gottfried van Swieten, the imperial librarian in Vienna and arranger/author of the word-books for Haydn's late oratorios.[76] In 1799 it was announced that Haydn would be an editor in a new history of music devised by Forkel in a series of *Denkmäler* (memorials), featuring engraved portraits of leading composers, another indication that by the turn of the century there was thought to be a market for biographical writing about composers. Haydn's personal attitude to the series, which was never fully realized, was actually less than enthusiastic. Perhaps he had reservations about Forkel's overtly nationalistic approach. But it is equally likely that at this date Haydn simply found the idea of writing about composers' lives somewhat tedious, though he enjoyed collecting portrait prints of great musicians. He himself, as indicated above, refused cooperation with any serious attempt at a biography of him until 1805. He may have changed his mind and come round to the view that his own life was worthy of literary commemoration on reading Forkel's *Bach*, a copy of which was acquired for his own library.[77]

Once Haydn had accepted the idea that composers were worthy of biographical treatment, it was not long before a stream of authors set about packaging his life and work in various forms suitable for easy public consumption. One example is an account by G.S. Mayr amounting to a monograph on *The Creation*, among Haydn's best-loved works.[78] Most of these popular accounts, however, were published in France.[79] A German equivalent was *Joseph Haydn, seine kurze Biographie und äesthetische Darsellung seiner Werke*, one of a series of eight composer biographies written by I.T.F.C. Arnold, for the benefit of the young. These volumes were designed to follow up the success of a similar publication devoted to Mozart, written anonymously by Arnold, which appeared in 1803.[80] The set seems to have appealed sufficiently to the public for the same publishers to reissue all the biographies later the same year in a two-volume set, with one important change.[81] In place of the biography of Haydn, Arnold introduced a new section consisting of a comparison between the works of Haydn and Mozart.[82] Arnold may have felt that it was necessary to keep abreast of developments concerning biographical writing about Haydn by attempting something new. He was clearly not in a position to compete with biographers who had enjoyed personal contact with the composer, such as Dies. A comparison between two such popular composers was perhaps intended to sustain public interest at a time when so many lightweight accounts of Haydn had been available to the public in recent years.

Some of these short biographical works are valuable sources for aspects of Haydn's career. Framery (1810), for example, is particularly informative about Haydn's French connections. None of them, however, is as complete as Dies, nor as thorough and conscientious as the most accurate of Haydn's first biographers, Griesinger, who knew Haydn during the last decade of his life. Griesinger was in correspondence with G.C. Härtel, of the Leipzig music-publishing firm of Breitkopf & Härtel, which at the time of his first interview with Haydn (1799) was planning to issue a set of volumes of the composer's works. He acted as an intermediary with Haydn for the publishing house, and in the course of their meetings collected material for a biography of the composer, though he apparently concealed this fact from Haydn, judging the old man might object. The first evidence of Griesinger's efforts appeared in a short article entitled 'Haydns Lebensabriss' (1805).[83] Griesinger expanded this into a full biography, first published immediately *after* Haydn's death in 1809 in a series of articles in the leading musical journal of the period, the *Allgemeine musikalische Zeitung*, published by Breitkopf & Härtel, to which Haydn himself had subscribed and once been asked to contribute. In 1810 these notes, with additions, were republished as a book because, in Griesinger's words, 'the man whom they [the notes] relate to is *of interest to many persons* who perhaps do not read the above musical journal'.[84] Griesinger's biography is an honest, unpretentious account of Haydn's life. Its interest derives not from any special treatment or view of the composer, but in its attempt at a reliable portrayal of the man, mostly related in a basic narrative style. As Griesinger says at the beginning of his volume, 'Since I was lucky enough to be continuously associated with Joseph Haydn during the last ten years of his life and to be honoured with his trust, my story may claim both truth and accuracy, and I consider it my duty here and there to introduce Haydn's very own words, just as I noted them on returning from seeing him.'[85]

Griesinger did an accomplished job in presenting the essence of Haydn's life and character. However, he made little attempt to explain why Haydn was such a towering figure. At this date serious music criticism was still in its infancy, having only become established as a feature of the musical world with the founding of publications like the *Allgemeine musikalische Zeitung*. The language of music criticism had yet to develop to a point where it might help the general public to appreciate distinctions between composers without actually having to hear performances or study scores. As musical biographies began to become more plentiful, it became evident that there was a need to find a way of describing music. Griesinger ignored the issue entirely. His emphasis on factual information leaves a dry impression, which in the long term hardly served the interests of Haydn's reputation. Dies's biography, written in the form of descriptions of his thirty visits to the composer, has a much greater sense of Haydn's presence about it. However, like Griesinger, Dies did not really have a satisfactory method of explaining to readers why Haydn's music was noteworthy, though he was mindful that in writing about a musician this was an issue. Conscious that his meetings with Haydn had left the field of aesthetics unexplored (perhaps because Haydn himself, sensitive to criticism of his work in later years, was unwilling to discuss such issues), Dies attempted to rectify the omission objectively by including at the end of his book one rather critical review of Haydn's music which had originally appeared in the *Allgemeine musikalische Zeitung* in 1801. This solution was clearly unsatisfactory. Indeed in some respects it made the problem all the more conspicuous. A small number of other early biographers of Haydn, such as Framery and Arnold, were not insensitive to the difficulty of expressing the aesthetic characteristics of music, though their solution was little better. Arnold relied on the use of analogies, not between musicians and artists as Burney and Rochlitz had suggested, but between musicians and writers.[86] Evidently the youthful audience Arnold had in mind for his biographies were considered more likely to have literary than artistic leanings. But this probably represents more a prejudice on Arnold's part than any true reflection of the position music was generally held to occupy in the wider cultural discourse of the period.

It was left to Carpani, the last of Haydn's first major biographers, to forge a more informative approach to the character of Haydn's music, an approach which was soon to have wider application.[87] Carpani, whose book *Le Haydine* first appeared in 1812, was in many respects ideally suited to this task.[88] Unlike Haydn's other early biographers, Carpani was not only a literary man, but one who also had a genuine interest in writing which might absorb, entertain and even provoke readers, as well as extending Haydn's reputation and the appeal of his music. By comparison with the biographies by Griesinger and Dies, which Carpani knew, *Le Haydine* places the emphasis not on providing posterity with factual information about Haydn which, though not ignored, was often unapologetically inaccurate, but on trying to convey what he saw as the essence of Haydn's musical achievement in terms that might be understood by specialists and educated amateurs alike.

Trained in Pavia as a lawyer, Carpani discovered at an early point that his true vocation lay in writing, first poems and plays, later libretti, criticism and biographies. Napoleon's Italian campaigns forced him to leave his native country and settle in Vienna, where his abilities and long-standing loyalty to the house of Habsburg secured him a nomination as court poet. His interest in music eventually brought him into contact with almost every composer in the imperial capital, most of whom had occasion to set his words. He even composed a little himself. But his most successful advancement of music's cause was in writing about composers and their work, his subjects including Salieri, Weber and, late in life, Rossini.

He first met Haydn at about the same time as Dies, and soon found himself championing the composer's music by providing Italian translations of van Swieten's texts for *The Creation* and *The Seasons*, which helped an appreciation of Haydn among his compatriots. *Le Haydine*, dedicated to the music conservatory in Milan, was similarly designed to further Haydn's popularity in Carpani's native country, where Haydn's late compositions, which departed radically from canons of taste generally accepted in Italy, were regarded with suspicion. Before Napoleon's invasion in 1796, much of northern Italy had been subjected to Austrian rule, and Italians naturally felt antipathy to examples of Austrian influence. Carpani's book also marked a new venture in writing about music in Italy, where (notwithstanding Mayr) musical biographies remained largely unknown.

Written as a sequence of seventeen letters addressed to a friend, the format enabled Carpani to use his particular talents to advantage.[89] For though the letters are loosely tied together by the story of Haydn's life, their main appeal derives more from a series of digressions on aesthetic issues, personal musings, and reflections on the history of music, all of which stem from aspects of the study of Haydn. Collections of letters were a well-established literary formula for books intended for general consumption in this period, first popularized in England.[90] Carpani, however, makes the device his own by bringing the considerable range of his cultural knowledge to bear on the composer. This was something new. Carpani's subject springs to life in the reader's imagination by drawing not one single parallel with great literary figures, as Arnold had, but with several, including Homer, Pindar, Virgil, Petrarch, Racine and Collin. Statements like 'Haydn is the Ariosto of music' are numerous.[91] But he takes the idea further by implying connections with the worlds of science and philosophy. Whilst Haydn's character, he claims, has something in common with Newton's, his compositions suggest that he was music's answer to Kant.[92]

But the principal strength of Carpani's study is its elaborate series of comparisons between music, generally that of Haydn, and the visual arts, which were designed to convey the composer's major strengths to a culturally alert readership.[93] Carpani was well qualified to attempt such an approach. According to a catalogue of writings compiled after his death he was responsible for several guides to works of art and collections, including accounts of paintings in Santa Maria presso San Celso in Milan and by Elisabeth Vigée-Lebrun.[94]

Although Carpani's theoretical opinions on the visual arts were hardly original, he played an important part in popularizing the views he espoused.[95] His advocacy of neoclassicism, for example, is evident in a guide written in 1806 to the cenotaph of the Archduchess Christine in the Augustinerkirche in Vienna, recently completed by the leading neoclassical sculptor Antonio Canova (Fig. 5).[96] This was recognized as one of the most prestigious and outstanding monuments of the early nineteenth century, by a sculptor at the height of his powers, who was then the most celebrated of all living artists.[97]

The Christine monument was commissioned when Canova was visiting Vienna in August 1798 by her recently bereaved husband, Duke Albert of Sachsen-Teschen.[98] Canova, who personally supervised the erection of the cenotaph in 1805, developed the design from one he had evolved in the early 1790s as a monument to the painter Titian, intended for the church of the Frari in Venice, though abandoned in 1795. The design for the Vienna monument was finalized by 12 July 1800, after Canova had made several alterations in response to Duke Albert's impressions of it received during the previous year. Unlike Canova's earlier schemes for funerary monuments, which were essentially neoclassical reworkings of Baroque designs, the completed Christine monument was entirely original in concept. The main structure, bearing an identifying inscription and a portrait-medallion of the Archduchess, is in the form of a pyramid, a feature which on account of its use for ancient tombs had become topical in the later eighteenth century, especially during that phase of the Egyptian revival associated with Napoleon's campaign in Egypt (1798).[99] In front of an entrance to the pyramid Canova created a group of free-standing statues, all in attitudes of mourning, each one shown as though moving in procession towards the entrance to the pyramid. These statues (representing two young girls, two women, an elderly man and a young child) were clearly intended to suggest a range of ages and characteristics, from graceful youth to the infirmities of old age. The interpretation of the figures is (deliberately) ambiguous, and might suggest either an allegory of virtues, a depiction of a funeral cortège (one of the figures carries a funerary urn), or a representation of humanity (as the three ages of man) paying tribute to the deceased.[100] Carpani, who knew Canova, presumably saw his task to elucidate the monument's meaning, though he was not the only one to attempt this at the time.[101] What makes the monument particularly striking is the sense of sorrow implied by the figures as they move towards the pyramid's darkened entrance, conveying the notion of mankind's inescapable journey towards death. Although themes of death or dying had naturally featured on earlier tombs, humankind's inevitable progress towards death was a new concept for an artist to portray in this context.

As Carpani would have been well aware, the idea of humanity moving inexorably towards its earthly end had some topicality in Vienna at exactly the moment that Duke Albert sent his final views to Canova on the form of the monument. A series of *bozzetti* show the sculptor developing the idea of a complete procession of grieving figures only at a late stage in its conception, the impoverished elderly figure at the end not occurring in the *bozzetti*.[102] It seems possible that this may have been a response to one of the themes of Haydn's last oratorio, *The Seasons*, on which he and his librettist, van Swieten, were then working. At one level, *The Seasons* works as an allegory of man's life on earth. This is especially evident in the fourth part, *Winter*, in which in a moving aria (No. 38) the elderly labourer Simon pictures to himself his life's progress (*erblicke deines Lebens Bild*), equating the ages of man with each of the seasons in turn, ending with winter, which points towards the open grave (*zeiget dir das offne Grab*). According to his pupil Neukomm, Haydn, now at the end of his composing career, identified with this part of the oratorio in particular.[103]

The notion of the ever-changing seasons as a metaphor for life's progress was clarified for the public by the engravings decorating the title-page of the first editions of both the vocal score and the full score of *The Seasons*, both published by Breitkopf & Härtel in 1802. In the design used for the full score, each of the seasons, as in several illustrations to James Thomson's *The Seasons*, on which the oratorio was based, is represented as a personification.[104] All four are arranged together in a ring (to suggest continuity) and are associated with a band of stars (to indicate that the seasons change in tandem with the path of the sun through the zodiac during the course of the year).[105] Unlike earlier *Seasons* illustrations, however, the design clearly differentiates between each personification, with Spring at the top, shown as a young woman holding flowers, and Winter (the only male personification) below, shown as an old man. Haydn was particularly pleased with this engraving, which he called a 'gar e lieber Narr'.[106] The frontispiece for the vocal score also shows the seasons as personifications, again three women of various ages and a man (Fig. 6). Summer and Autumn are shown decorating a double-headed herm (presumably representing the year) with swags of flowers. Behind them, Winter appears as an old, hunched man, leaning on a staff, his right arm linked with the left arm of Spring, who guides him along and carries another swag of flowers.

The iconography of these personifications has much in common with the figures from Canova's memorial to Archduchess Christine. Indeed the arrangement of Winter and Spring is so close to the rear figures in Canova's procession that a direct connection cannot be ignored. Since these were the last figures to be included and finalized in Canova's design, it seems likely that their conception owed much to the Viennese context of the monument. The concept of including a moving cortège on the memorial (representing humanity's progress towards death) was perhaps suggested to Canova by Duke Albert, who certainly wished to approve final designs for the tomb. He told Canova, for example, to modify one design he was sent so that the old man carried not a lance (a motif which originated with Canova, and may have been a misunderstanding of his patron's wishes), but a staff. Canova's design was realized in full-scale models, placed on exhibition in Rome, in the latter half of 1800. But work on *The Seasons* had probably commenced at the time Canova was in Vienna in mid-1798 to secure his pension from the Emperor, when he received the commission. It was exactly then that Haydn and his librettist, Gottfried van Swieten, were basking in the glory of the first performances of *The Creation* and planning their further collaboration.

Van Swieten's work on arranging the text-book for *The Seasons* closely coincided with Duke Albert's commission for his wife's memorial. Indeed it seems possible that the two projects came into contact with each other. When van Swieten wrote 'Der Erde Bild ist nun ein Grab, wo Kraft und Reiz erstorben liegt' (The picture of earth is now a tomb, where power and charm lie buried) in describing the winter landscape, he may have formulated the words with the memorial to the Archduchess in mind. As the imperial librarian, van Swieten's apartment and workplace, part of the Hofburg Palace, actually adjoined the Augustinerkirche, where the Archduchess's memorial was erected. Van Swieten would undoubtedly have taken an interest in it. He had long known Duke Albert, the Emperor's uncle by marriage, whose outstanding collection of prints and drawings was housed nearby. It seems conceivable that the Duke asked van Swieten to advise on the form of his wife's monument, which would explain the later changes in the iconographic conception of Canova's design, and their connections with concepts and images in *The Seasons* and the frontispieces of its first publication. In particular, the theme of the ages of man in the monument might well have originated with the oratorio; and the motif of an old, blind man being led by a younger woman seems also to have been first devised to illustrate the music.

In the title-page of the vocal score, the artist made much of the floral swags, a feature incorporated into the Christine monument in its final form, but which does not appear in the drawings confirming the design sent to Duke Albert. The implication here is that this and other motifs were imposed on the sculptor as the monument was realized by those responsible for the commission in Vienna.

The special significance of *The Seasons* for the imperial family is indicated by the fact that 'at the request of the imperial court', its second performance was given for them. In later performances the Empress – a fanatical supporter of Haydn's late vocal music – herself sang the part of Hanne, Simon's daughter. There is every likelihood, therefore, that knowledge of Haydn's new oratorio, which would have been a topic of considerable general interest in many circles (taking into account the huge success of his previous oratorio *The Creation*), may have influenced Duke Albert's dealings with Canova concerning the form of his wife's memorial, especially considering that the most relevant aspect of the oratorio, 'Winter', was also the part which held the greatest significance for Haydn personally.

Moreover, the initial impact of *The Seasons* on its first audiences may have counted for something in Carpani's decision to write about Canova's monument for Archduchess Christine. From the outset, the oratorio was intended to reach not only the highest echelons, but every rank of society. At its very first performance (24 April 1801), a privately arranged concert in the palace of Prince Schwarzenberg, 'every honest man was permitted to attend', a clear reflection of Haydn's desire to be of benefit to men of all back-grounds.[107] According to a contemporary report of this event, 'The public was very numerous and *mixed*. The Archduke and the [ordinary] citizen, the Prince with his star and the modest scholar, were all together here. The performance was worthy of Viennese artists, the applause *undivided* and noisy.'[108] Carpani, who was present on this very occasion, also mentions the great acclaim given to *The Seasons*, though he reports Haydn himself as feeling that it did not match that paid to *The Creation* because in this the characters had been 'angels', whereas in *The Seasons* they were only 'peasants'.[109] Between his attendance at this Haydn première and work on his biography of Haydn, Carpani found himself drawn to writing about Canova, so the connection between composer and sculptor stemming from their dealings with van Swieten and Duke Albert is likely to have been appreciated by him, and may have influenced the broader musical/pictorial analogies he sought to draw in *Le Haydine*.[110]

Though a man of limited ability, Carpani recognized at the time he knew Haydn that there was scope in writing about the arts to cater for the interests of a new kind of audience, reaching from 'the Prince with his star' to 'the modest scholar'. Carpani had in mind a populist readership; he wanted to bring about a greater understanding of cultural developments – the phenomenon of

Haydn, a key monument by Canova – within the wider public domain. He recognized that the parity with which the visual arts and music had come to be treated in the public sphere demanded a new approach to writing on cultural issues. By drawing on the critical vocabulary established since the time of Vasari for discussing the visual arts, Carpani foresaw a means of informing a non-specialized readership about music. Carpani's experience as the official censor for theatres in Venice, an appointment held before settling in Vienna, may have helped him to understand the nature of popular appeal in certain kinds of visual culture – especially opera and Venetian painting. Furthermore he could assume readers to have a basic grasp of the characteristics of Old Master painters, particularly of the Italian schools, from the recent success of Luigi Lanzi's *Storia pittorica della Italia*, a comprehensive history of Italian painting, systematically covering all regions of Italy. As the first (incomplete) edition clarified in its title, the *Storia pittorica* was intended for *dilettanti*. Subsequent editions explained that part of its purpose was 'to facilitate knowledge of styles of painting'.[111] Lanzi worked under the patronage of the Grand Dukes of Tuscany, who also made an extensive collection of Haydn's church music, a combination of interests which could only have encouraged Carpani to consider Haydn in visual terms.[112]

Carpani's method of comparing Haydn with aspects of the visual arts in *Le Haydine* works at several levels. At its simplest, he suggests direct parallels with well-known artists whose stylistic characteristics, as defined by the well-established canon of writing on the visual arts (Vasari, Bellori, Félibien, Roger de Piles, etc.), would have been well understood by many readers. He argues, for example, that Haydn is the 'Tintoretto of music'.[113] Carpani may have been deliberately provocative in this choice of comparison, Tintoretto having been a painter much disparaged in the seventeenth and eighteenth centuries, the negative appraisal of him starting with Vasari, who thought the Venetian 'eccentric, fanciful, quick and resolute', working haphazardly and without *disegno* (design), and continuing into Carpani's own time with painters like Fuseli who valued the power of drawing of central Italian artists, especially Michelangelo, over the *colorito* of the Venetians.[114] However, Vasari's statement that Tintoretto 'loved all the arts, *especially* music' provided Carpani with the basis of a rather different conception of the Venetian's significance. Some seventeenth-century writers on Tintoretto and his Venetian contemporaries made much of their supposed musicality, to the extent that it was believed that Veronese had painted portraits of Tintoretto and other distinguished painters as the musicians in his famous *Marriage Feast at Cana* (Fig. 1).[115] Seventeenth-century authorities (especially Ridolfi and Boschini) had also been more inclined to see in the work of Tintoretto a much more acceptable balance than Vasari had allowed between, on the one hand, an enthusiasm for colour associated with the Venetian school of painting (typified by Titian) and, on the other hand, a strength in drawing characteristic of the Florentine school (the greatest exponent being Michelangelo). Roger de Piles helped promulgate the positive interpretation of Tintoretto's achievement when in his famous 'balance of painters' he awarded Tintoretto 16 (out of 20) for colour, no less than 14 for drawing, and 15 for composition (though only 4 for expression).[116]

With this in mind, Carpani could claim Tintoretto as the obvious artistic counterpart to the Austrian composer. Haydn's work, he suggests, unites the Venetian feeling for colour with Michelangelesque qualities of vigour and invention in drawing. Throughout *Le Haydine* there is a basic assumption that drawing is the equivalent of melody in music, and colour equates with musical instrumentation (or orchestral colour). According to Carpani, however, Haydn was a more profound artist than Tintoretto because he had a greater understanding of the potential of drawing (shades of the Vasarian view underlying his perspective). Something of the sheer scale and force of Michelangelo's imagination may be heard in Haydn. In the final analysis, however, Haydn falls short of Michelangelo because the latter excelled in history painting, the pictorial equivalent of opera, in which (in Carpani's view) Haydn failed to make his mark.[117]

Haydn made his name with symphonies, which for Carpani is the musical counterpart of landscape-painting. In this genre the composer comes closest to the greatest of all colourists, Titian, whose knowledge of 'how to arrange his colours on a canvas' provides the closest approximation of the various effects of orchestration experienced by the listener during a performance of a Haydn symphony.[118] According to Carpani, therefore, time is to music as space is to painting. Haydn is also like Titian in that he developed a grand style in church compositions just as the Venetian painter perfected the design of large altarpieces, for which the Venetian school was to become best known. Haydn's 'musical brush' was every bit as rich and varied as Titian's.[119] In Haydn, the colouring of Titian matches the drawing of Raphael and the grace of Correggio.[120]

Carpani followed up his Haydn/Tintoretto analogy with a list of thirty-two celebrated composers, mostly Italians, all of whom are paired with famous painters, thereby implying a common critical language for describing both composer and painter. Most of the painters are Old Masters of the fifteenth to seventeenth centuries, though the composers all belong to the eighteenth century. Carpani's intention was clearly to use the names of painters, all of whom had well-established critical reputations, to suggest characteristics in the music of the composers. Examples include Pergolesi paired with Raphael, Handel with Michelangelo, Porpora (one of Haydn's teachers) with Perugino (Raphael's teacher), Gluck with Caravaggio, and Mozart with Giulio Romano.

Some of Carpani's other musical/pictorial parallels have a deeper purpose to them. To help explain Haydn's practice of keeping a notebook for jotting down musical themes as they occurred to him, Carpani makes a comparison with what was then believed to be Leonardo da Vinci's habit of collecting in notebooks drawings of 'strange or characteristic physiognomies' when he encountered them.[121] Apart from *The Last Supper* in Milan, knowledge of which was widely disseminated through engravings and copies, Leonardo was best known to eighteenth-century audiences through the so-called 'grotesque' heads, several series of which had been engraved in the seventeenth and early eighteenth centuries.[122] Mariette, who published one series in 1730, implied that Leonardo had become 'a great physiologist' partly as a result of his interest in fidelity to nature, and partly because he informed this through an understanding of the expression of the Passions and their classification, an interest which was otherwise in the eighteenth century particularly associated with the French painter Charles Le Brun.[123] Carpani, citing Leonardo and Le Brun, took these notions and applied them to Haydn, giving them a moral dimension in the process. According to Carpani, Haydn's instrumental music often suggests an exemplary story, the characters in which were portrayed with a variety of passions and idiosyncrasies, corresponding to the figures of Leonardo and Le Brun.[124] Haydn's sketchbooks are like arsenals of characters which may be drawn on when needed in the supposed manner of Leonardo. The implications of this comparison would have had further resonance for Carpani's readers since the period leading up to the time when *Le Haydine* was written saw considerable progress in popular understanding of Leonardo's life and activities. Engravings of a much wider selection of drawings from his notebooks led to a greater awareness of the extent of Leonardo's interests, and research into his life emphasized the view of him as a universal man, whose work had extended far beyond the realm of the visual arts as it was generally understood in the eighteenth century.[125] Carpani's comparison between the working methods of Haydn and Leonardo would therefore have implied for Haydn a kind of universality and range of intellectual achievement not usually expected of contemporary composers.

In another example of musical/pictorial analogy, Carpani sought to assess Haydn's achievement by viewing him as a landscape painter of the standing of Claude Lorraine, a painter of the countryside of the standing of Nicolaes Berchem, a battle painter of the standing of Jacques Courtois (Il Borgognone) and a flower painter of the standing of Jan van Huysum.[126] These painters were often upheld as the leading practitioners of their chosen genre. Mention of earlier Dutch painters like Berchem and Van Huysum – Rembrandt is also cited – may possibly reflect interest in Dutch painting stimulated by the publication in the 1790s of the three-volume *Galerie* by the prominent art dealer J.-B.-P. Lebrun (husband of the famous painter Elisabeth Vigée-Lebrun, who inspired one of Carpani's 'guides'), whose house on the rue de Cléry in Paris was celebrated not only for exhibitions of paintings, but also for concerts. After the Revolution these seem to have been made available to the public.[127] Lebrun placed special emphasis on Dutch genre over other previously more favoured categories and schools of painting, like Flemish history painting, and particularly stressed what he saw as the democratic character of such art, a view in keeping with the times in which he was writing. Carpani may have felt that this taste in painting, iconographically and stylistically, struck a chord with the character of Haydn's oratorio *The Seasons*, which portrays aspects of peasant life in both landscape and interior settings. However, in his references to Claude Lorraine and other admired landscape painters, such as Salvator Rosa and Joseph Vernet, Carpani seems to have had in mind analogies with symphonic music as much as oratorios.[128] The distinctive quality of light associated with each well-known landscape artist may be felt in Haydn's instrumental music, which may often be experienced in terms of a stroll through a landscape. Elsewhere Carpani explains Haydn's supreme understanding of the balance of forceful and tranquil passages in a piece of music in terms of the distribution of light and shade (chiaroscuro) in a successful painting by Caravaggio or Rembrandt.[129]

Carpani reserved his most elaborate discussion of musical/pictorial analogies for his accounts of Haydn's two late oratorios.[130] Both works are treated as though they were collections of paintings. The scenes in *The Creation* are discussed as 'beautiful pictures of the harmonic gallery', while in describing *The Seasons*, he says: 'You have to imagine a gallery full of paintings, all different in style, subject and colouring.'[131] Carpani attributes the initial impetus for this kind of overt pictorialism in music to Haydn's collaborator, van Swieten,

> ... a man learned in music and himself a composer not without merit. The Baron had noticed that, although music did *not* constitute a language, it could nevertheless express the passions, and thus might also colour and portray pictures, by imitating analogous effects. I remember one such [picture] where music was called 'an invisible painting'. The Baron had also observed that though traces of this imitation might be heard in the works of the great masters, the field in general still remained completely open for exploration, and he pointed this out to Haydn; the undertaking to be attempted was an oratorio of a completely descriptive kind. Haydn accepted the invitation ... [132]

In analysing the aesthetic aims underpinning these late oratorios, Carpani argues that music may imitate visible things in one of two ways: 'the physical and the sentimental: one is direct, the other indirect'.[133] 'Physical' imitation often starts with a sound (or sometimes an object) in nature, which when conveyed musically may call an image to mind. Carpani gives several examples of this from works by earlier composers, including an aria from Gluck's *Les Pèlerins de la Mecque*, suggesting the murmuring of a brook, and Handel's vivid portrayals of natural and supernatural effects in *Israel in Egypt*.[134] Van Swieten was perhaps aware that Handel's original patrons when listening to works like *Israel in Egypt* seem to have been unappreciative of the composer's efforts in musical painting, but that by *c*.1800 audiences were much better prepared for hearing such 'painting' and taking pleasure from it. The second form of pictorial/musical imitation Carpani identifies, which he terms 'Sentimental', depends on recreating musically the sensations that may be provoked when perceiving something in nature. This form of 'painting' replies chiefly on expression. To help explain it Carpani defers to the influential musical theorist Lacépède, whose *La Poétique de la musique*, published in 1785, was an early attempt to relate eighteenth-century aesthetics to practical musical composition.[135] In describing the measures that a composer should take in order to depict feelings, Lacépède constantly turns to the visual arts for appropriate language to convey his purpose. He maintains, for example, that 'In order to *paint* the feelings the musician will also make use of accompaniments against which to set his melodies', and 'The mode that the musician selects, too, will surely contribute to the fidelity of the *picture*.'[136] At times Lacépède's pictorial analogies are more precise, as when he considers the importance of proportion for the composer, which he relates not just to painting but to architecture, as indeed does Carpani:

> The simplicity or grandeur of the subject and the size of the building in which the music is to be performed will determine a preference for phrases of sixteen, eight or two bars – and so on. Pleasant, small-scale subjects that are to be studied closely require detailed work and *delicate brush strokes*, whilst *large canvases* that are to be viewed from a distance call for *bold brush strokes* and grand gestures. Similarly, musical compositions that are only to be performed in small rooms, compositions that are *miniature paintings* and which are only intended to charm the ears of those who perform them, such pieces call for short phrases – those, that is, of two and eight measures.[137]

Apart from Lacépède, Carpani brings to his subject several key eighteenth-century figures who helped form opinion on the cross-fertilization of the visual arts and music: Dubos, Batteux, Castel and Sulzer. Although Carpani himself brings to bear his knowledge of the visual arts in his appreciation of Haydn, like many contemporary writers on music with a grounding in theory, he was not entirely convinced by Haydn's own pictorialism, though any lack of taste or judgement in this he attributes to van Swieten. It is known from several sources that Haydn himself, especially after hearing early criticism of *The Seasons*, was unhappy about the extent to which van Swieten had pushed him into the kind of word-painting depending on the imitation of sounds in nature. Both Griesinger and Dies comment on Haydn's reluctance to set van Swieten's croaking of frogs to music, but the Baron coerced him into doing it by showing him an example of how it had been managed in French music.[138] A letter stemming from Haydn was even published indicating that the composer himself regretted writing 'this French trash' which had been forced on him.[139] However, the croaking of frogs had already featured in a symphony representing the 'Transformation of the Lycian Peasants into Frogs' (from Ovid's *Metamorphoses*) by Haydn's friend Karl Ditters von Dittersdorf, performed in Vienna in 1786, which was certainly known to van Swieten and probably to Haydn also, and also in a composition by Werner (1748), Haydn's predecessor as Esterházy Kapellmeister.[140] Haydn's objections to setting frogs croaking probably had less to do with any actual or imagined antipathy towards musical painting on his part than resentment about portraying a creature which struck him as too lowly to include in an oratorio planned on a grand scale. In other words, for Haydn, setting frogs to music was just too tasteless, just as 'the peasants' of the same oratorio seemed to the composer hardly of the same order as 'the angels' of *The Creation*; so when *The Seasons* faced criticism for being overly concerned with painting, the composer allowed it to be widely known that his own instincts had been against this particular example, for which he understandably incurred van Swieten's displeasure.[141]

At the outset of their collaboration Haydn and van Swieten would almost certainly have seen eye to eye on the desirability of developing 'painting' as a key feature of the work they produced together. Both composer and librettist intended that the fruits of their collaboration should reach the largest possible audience, that the oratorios should be genuinely popular and have a mass appeal, objectives in which they largely succeeded. However, it was hardly van Swieten alone who recognized that musical pictorialism might become a factor in guaranteeing this. By the time that Haydn entered into partnership with the Baron, his own experience of what was then proving to be popular in music would have led him to the conclusion that this was an avenue worth pursuing. He had already by that point been engaged in a consideration how to develop his composition to reach ever expanding audiences for over a decade and a half.

3. Vox populi

In 1776 Haydn was asked to contribute an autobiographical sketch for publication in a national journal; his celebrity was starting to catch up with him.[142] He recorded succinctly and accurately the main features of his life until 1761, when he entered the employment of the Esterházys, the family he was to serve for the remainder of his life. But in detailing the course of his life, Haydn stresses certain aspects over others: his humble origins in a country town; how his father, a wheelwright, raised him as well as he could; how music came to him and his family 'by nature' without having to be taught or understanding its notation; how at the age of 7 his talent was recognized by a visiting Kapellmeister, a leading musician from Vienna, who took him to the city; and how hard work enabled him to overcome poverty until his ability was recognized by prominent patrons. In presenting this outline, the life story Haydn constructed for himself bears a striking correspondence with the well-known story as told by Vasari and others of the rise to fame of the painter Giotto, whose career in the eighteenth century was commonly held to mark the starting point from which all later European painting developed. Vasari's Giotto also grew up in modest circumstances in a country town. His father, 'a simple field labourer', brought him up 'well for his position in life'. Giotto learnt to draw, but 'never had any master but Nature'. At the age of 10 his talent was recognized by the leading painter from Florence, who took him to the city, where study and his natural ability combined to make him the most sought-after painter of his time. It is tempting to consider that Haydn, in need of a model to help construct his life's story in a form acceptable to the public, found inspiration in Vasari. But if this is so, it is difficult to see Haydn having taken this initiative himself.

In the same letter in which he wrote this sketch, Haydn also notes that he had been 'lucky enough to please *all nations* except the Berliners. ... Despite this, they go to great lengths to procure all my works, as I was informed last winter by Herr Baron v. Sviten [van Swieten], the Imperial and Royal Ambassador at Berlin.'[143] It is clear that even at this comparatively early date in Haydn's career, van Swieten took an interest in Haydn's popularity. He personally informed the composer that even in northern Germany, the one place in Europe that his compositions had seemingly not gone down well – Burney commented on the same hostility[144] – all was not what it was reported to have been. Six years later, in correspondence with Artaria, the Viennese publishing company with which he had recently entered into a business arrangement, Haydn specifically cites the Baron for encouraging him to make greater use of his popularity: 'Herr Baron v. Svieten led me assuredly to understand that henceforth I should dedicate my compositions directly to the public [*dem Publico meine Compositionen widmen solle*].'[145] Although this probably refers primarily to the need for Haydn to ensure that publication of his works was achieved under his own control, and that he therefore did not lose out financially on publishing deals (as he had done in the past), the Baron may also have had in mind the desirability for Haydn of ensuring that the character of his compositions should address popular taste. Whatever the case, there is no doubt that van Swieten took a sustained interest in Haydn and the development of his popularity. He therefore makes a good candidate for having advised the composer on the form of his autobiographical outline, which was the first opportunity Haydn received to present himself to his expanding public through words.[146]

Before working directly with Haydn, van Swieten had been President of the Court Commission on Education in Austria, a position which ensured that he kept abreast of issues which were of interest across the entire spectrum of Austrian society. As a leading personality committed to the ideals of the Enlightenment and to implementing Joseph II's policies on liberalization, van Swieten recognized that music potentially had a role to play in maintaining a unified society. Although inevitably he did not question the prerogative of princes and aristocrats as the foremost patrons of music, there was no reason in his view why the music itself should not reach and affect the *entire* nation. In realizing such ideals the figure of Haydn himself was important, not only because he wrote music which captivated a wide listening audience, but because his own story, from modest origins to successful figure of national significance, provided a good model for the youth of the country. Early relations between van Swieten and Haydn may have encouraged the latter to think of himself in these terms.

The idea that the cultivation of popularity might be a virtue, or rather a force for good in society, became increasingly part of Haydn's own thinking as his career progressed. Griesinger reports Haydn being especially flattered by the award he received from the city of Vienna, 'for it made me think of this: *vox populi: vox Dei* [the voice of the people is the voice of God]'.[147] Haydn was especially fond of peppering his discourse with Latin quotations, so Griesinger's account rings true.[148] The composer presumably quoted this particular Latin tag to indicate his view, widely shared at the time, that the collective judgement of the people enjoyed divine sanction, a notion which survived to haunt subsequent generations. When Beethoven very late in life, for example, was informed of 'the exclusive interest in Italian opera' which then prevailed in Vienna, he gave utterance to the 'memorable' words: 'It is said *vox populi, vox Dei*. I never believed it.'[149] Beethoven perhaps heard Haydn utter this same Latin adage when taking lessons with him in the early 1790s. Their contrasting attitudes to it, symptomatic of a failure to see eye to eye on most matters, suggests how for Haydn the idea of public approbation had a compelling attraction, whereas for Beethoven it never meant much, signifying still less with the passing of time. At any rate, this is what early writers on Beethoven led their readership to believe.

The motto *vox populi, vox Dei* may have become familiar to Haydn when he was in England, where its use may be traced back to the Middle Ages.[150] Another German-speaking anglophile, Georg Christoph Lichtenberg, was certainly very struck with the phrase and incorporated it into one of his famous aphorisms written in the early 1770s: 'In the words *Vox populi vox Dei* there is more truth than we usually manage to get into four words nowadays.'[151] An indication of how familiar it was in eighteenth-century England comes from a poet known to have been read by Haydn, Pope, who played on and subverted its meaning: 'The People's voice is odd, / It is, and it is not, the voice of God.'[152] By the 1780s the motto had acquired an even sharper satirical edge, as is evident from its appearance in political caricatures the spirit of which, given Haydn's undoubted interest in the art of caricature during the time he was in England, may well have been known to him.[153] It was particularly associated with the leading Whig politician Charles James Fox, who tried to identify himself with the voice of the people in order to distinguish himself and his supporters from the Tories, the party of king and country, which from 1783 to 1801 formed the government under the premiership of William Pitt. The play on words between Fox and *vox* made the connection irresistible to caricaturists, many of whom were in the pocket of Pitt's followers. *Vox populi, vox Dei*, for example, is the title of an anonymous print the publication of which coincided with the Westminster election of 1784, an important test of public opinion followed nationwide and with phenomenal popular enthusiasm in the capital.[154] Fox, the winning candidate, is represented in the print holding the staff and cap of Liberty, establishing his supposed credentials as defender of the people and their freedom. Characteristically depicted as overweight and unshaven, Fox stands triumphant, a laurel wreath placed on his head by a cherub trumpeting 'victory'. Behind him his defeated opponent leaves the scene weighed down by the burdens of 'Deceit', 'Ingratitude' and 'Perjury'. Supporting Fox is the Duchess of Devonshire, who canvassed during the election, not hesitating to use her celebrated charms to elicit votes on his behalf. She holds the 'shield of virtue' to repel arrows labelled 'malice', 'envy' and 'woman hater'. Although women had no vote, important Whig politicians did not shrink from using their wives to stir the electorate, often to the horror of conservatives, who viewed this in terms amounting to an attack on the constitution.

During Haydn's visits to England, Fox and Pitt still dominated the political scene and many of the issues they had previously debated continued to fill the newspapers, now only further polarized as a result of their contrasting reactions to the French Revolution. The composer took great interest in the political scene in England, not so much from a partisan point of view or to understand the issues, but to observe how public opinion was formed and manipulated in a democratic country, something which of course he could not have experienced in Austria. In notebooks kept during his first visit to London (1791–92) Haydn reminded himself of two amusing anecdotes about Fox, the first of which relates directly to his electioneering and also to his relationship to the Duchess:

> When Mr Fox, in looking to be elected to Parliament, addressed the voters, one man said he would rather give him a rope than a vote. Fox answered that he could not deprive him of a family treasure.
> Duchess of Devonchire [*sic*], his protectress. Anecdote about the foot under her skirt.[155]

Judging from such detailed knowledge of Fox, Haydn could hardly have missed the popular association of *vox populi* with the politician. Indeed it seems very likely that Haydn met Fox since they had many acquaintances in common. For example, the composer was a regular performer and guest at soirées given by the Prince of Wales, one of Fox's closest associates. Only two years before Haydn's first visit to London Fox had been instrumental in introducing the Regency Bill in support of the Prince of Wales during the constitutional crisis resulting from George III's temporary mental incapacity, a measure which Pitt successfully resisted.

Haydn also cultivated the friendship of those at the radical end of the political spectrum in England, men like Thomas Holcroft, who during the period of Haydn's second visit to England stood trial for high treason, and was considered by the authorities too dangerous to be allowed to air his views unchallenged at a time when Britain was at war with France. Through Holcroft Haydn is likely to have come into contact with other leading radicals who wished to perpetuate the movement towards reform precipitated by the French Revolution, such as William Godwin, author of the *Enquiry concerning Political Justice* (1793), who stood trial with Holcroft in 1795, and Godwin's future wife Mary Wollstonecraft, author of *A Vindication of the Rights of Woman* (1792). Holcroft's interest in Haydn's music, in which he seems to have found a spirit sympathetic to his own ideals, has already been noted. But in turn Haydn seems to have been more than curious about Holcroft's work; his library contained the first three volumes of Holcroft's *The Adventures of Hugh Trevor* (1794), a novel which, while denouncing the Establishment and its institutions, nevertheless presents an optimistic and moral view of the world, with goodness promoted and truth triumphant.[156]

But Haydn was not only interested in radicals; it was the entire political spectrum which fascinated him. Although he seems to have successfully avoided revealing his own political views when in England, it seems reasonably clear that Haydn's instincts made him a natural supporter of Pitt, especially after the outbreak of war with France (1793), when Britain became Austria's ally. Haydn was particularly friendly with Pitt's foreign secretary, the Duke of Leeds.[157] Already in November 1791, when he attended the Lord Mayor's banquet, Haydn particularly noted seeing the Duke and the Prime Minister in person and that 'No toast was more applauded than that of Mr Pitt.'[158] Haydn's admiration was sufficient for him to purchase a portrait-print of Pitt, which he kept until he died.[159] The admiration was possibly swelled by Pitt's attendance at concerts.[160] Fox, on the other hand, was known to have been tone-deaf; and though his supporter, the Duchess of Devonshire, liked (and even composed) music, her family patronized the composer and violinist Felice Giardini, whose contemptible behaviour towards Haydn during his stay in London can hardly have endeared him to their party.[161]

Haydn's respect for Pitt may have owed something to an important political painting executed between 1793 and 1795 by his fellow-countryman, K.A. Hickel, who in London styled himself 'Painter to the Emperor of Germany'. Hickel's brother Joseph was court painter in Vienna and, as previously indicated, was on friendly terms with Mozart.[162] Hickel's enormous picture (Fig. 7), which Haydn would certainly have known when it was first exhibited in London, portrays Pitt speaking in the House of Commons and includes portraits of 96 Members of Parliament, many taken from sittings during

1794.[163] The painting was inspired by debates in Parliament in February 1793 following the execution of Louis XVI, marking the beginning of hostilities with France. These sessions were naturally widely reported and aroused public interest. Hickel originally had in mind a second painting which was to have shown the Leader of the Opposition replying to Pitt, though this never advanced further than initial sketches. Fox had at first opposed Pitt's motion condemning Louis XVI's death, though he subsequently supported the war. Hickel's completed painting, which he doubtless calculated would strike a chord with the public during the initial stages of the war, when patriotism and respect for national institutions were at their height, was put on show in May 1795 only a stone's throw from the venue where the concerts of Haydn's last London season took place. It was announced in *The Times*, together with an invitation to subscribe to a print of the picture.[164] Pitt himself was one subscriber to the print, causing *The Times* to comment that 'this, no doubt, will make the subscriptions fill even with more rapidity than ever'.[165] Earlier the same newspaper had reported that the picture provoked 'not only general admiration but a numerous attendance of the most fashionable Nobility'. The reputation of the picture was such that it was subsequently acquired by the Austrian Emperor Francis I. His interest in it, presumably stemming from its function as a commemoration of the Austro-British alliance, would also have been especially meaningful to Haydn.

Haydn's cultivation of friendships across the political board was not only important for him in terms of trying to attract audiences for his music drawn from all tiers of society, but also in helping him to appreciate how difficult it was to escape the politicization of cultural activity in a 'free' society, a position at its most acute in time of war. Whether it was a novel like *Hugh Trevor*, or a painting such as Hickel's *House of Commons*, literature and the visual arts might consciously be used to galvanize public opinion in the interests of a particular cause. Music need be no exception to this, and in many of the works Haydn produced for his second visit to England and in major compositions thereafter it is possible to ascertain evidence of this thinking in operation. This is not so much connected with propaganda, though Haydn sometimes allowed himself to be drawn into overtly propagandistic projects – the proposal to set Selden's fiercely patriotic lines *Mare Clausum* as an oratorio was eventually abandoned – but a matter of using the arts as a means of benefiting the greatest number of people, a process of moral popularization, in order to act as a force for the common good: *vox populi, vox Dei*. Needless to say, Haydn was of course never interested in pandering to the lowest common taste to achieve this purpose; but in developing his style and in selecting compositional formats, he became increasingly concerned to attract the attention of as many listeners as possible, from all classes and all backgrounds.

In Britain the notion that the arts might be used to address a general public was first articulated early in the eighteenth century, especially in relation to painting (though not without regard for music), by Shaftesbury, who imagined a republic of the fine arts structured in such a way that painting might endeavour to promote virtue in the public sphere. Taking his cue from classical sources which had ranked the genres of painting, Shaftesbury saw in the highest of these, history-painting, the greatest potential for benefiting mankind. His identification of the good with the beautiful, derived from the popular tradition of Christian aesthetics, gave his view a further dimension, reinforcing arguments of subject matter with those of style.[166] Such ideas took on a particular resonance with the founding in 1768 of the Royal Academy in London, an institution with responsibility for promoting the appreciation of the visual arts in society. Sir Joshua Reynolds, the first President of the Academy, believed that painting, ideally though not exclusively of the type recommended by Shaftesbury, might help to build a better, more virtuous society, in all nations.[167]

During his visits to England Haydn certainly digested many notions stemming from Shaftesbury. He owned a copy of the *Characteristicks* (an edition of 1790), the principal treatise in which Shaftesbury set out his views on the relationship of morals and aesthetics, and met many members of the Royal Academy, including (if Carpani is to be believed) Reynolds at the end of his life.[168] Moreover the idea that the Fine Arts constituted a republic, that is, they belonged to all the people, was especially influential. Though working for a Grand Duke who became an Emperor, Lanzi compared the structure of the Fine Arts to a Roman-style Republic in which artists ventured to become like other enfranchised citizens. The notion was also applied to literature (the 'republic of letters'), and sometimes to music: Couperin, for example, refers to the sharing of Italian and French elements in the 'Republic of Music' in France in the preface to *Les Goûts réünis* (1724). At the beginning of *Le Haydine*, Carpani gives a telling slant to this construction by conceiving of music *before* the time of Haydn as a monarchy in which the human voice was sovereign; with the rise of instrumental music in the eighteenth century, the chief 'light' of which was Haydn, this realm gave way to a republic.[169]

The process of democratization of music, in which Haydn was understood from an early stage to play the leading role, borrowed much of its impetus and language from the visual arts. It also advanced through Haydn's determination to succeed with his music across the political and social board. Haydn told his first biographers that though he was pleased to have associated with men and women of the highest status in society, he in fact felt most comfortable with people from modest backgrounds, similar to his own. None the less, Haydn took special pleasure in the challenge of persuading those initially prejudiced *against* his music in the most elevated of positions to change their opinion. The best example of this is George III, whose reluctance to listen to anything other than Handel was well known. By the time of Haydn's visits to England,

Handel had become such a national institution that one of Haydn's admirers, Sir William Jones, who Burney called 'a decided republican', felt himself obliged to ignore Handel in his musical recommendations, probably because the latter had come to be so much associated with the Establishment that for Jones he smacked too much of insular nationalism.[170] Griesinger relates an occasion when Haydn had very much wanted to have something of his own played at an annual concert patronized by the King, though only Handel was requested.[171] Apparently there was a rule that only music more than 30 years old could be performed. During his second stay in England, however, Haydn got his way. An acquaintance of Haydn's who performed in this concert, the oboist William Parke, continues the story:

> At the end of the first part of the concert Haydn had the distinguished honour of being formally introduced to His Majesty George III, by His Royal Highness the Prince of Wales. My station at the time was so near to the King, that I could not avoid hearing the whole of the conversation. Among other observations, His Majesty said (in English) 'Doctor Haydn, you have written a great deal.' To which Haydn modestly replied, 'Yes, Sire, a great deal more than is good.' To which the King neatly rejoined, 'Oh no, the world contradicts that.' ... The gracious reception Haydn experienced from the King was not only gratifying to *his* feelings, but flattering to the science he professed; and while it displayed the condescension and liberality of a great and good monarch, it could not fail proving a powerful stimulus to rising *genius*.[172]

Haydn himself proudly noted the occasion in his notebook: 'There was nothing played except my own compositions; I sat at the pianoforte; in the end I had to sing too. The King, who previously could or would only hear music of the Handel sort, was rapt; he conversed with me, and introduced me to the Queen, who said many compliments to me.'[173] Griesinger expands on this, presumably reporting what Haydn told him:

> The King and Queen wanted him to remain in England. 'I will give you an apartment in Windsor for the summer,' said the Queen, and then she added slyly, squinting at the King, 'and then sometimes we'll together make music *tête à tête*. 'Oh! I'm not jealous of Haydn,' said the King, 'he's a good upright German man.'[174]

Whilst his character and nationality may have contributed to Haydn winning over the King, it seems likely that eventual acceptance of his music played a part in the process, which naturally gratified the composer. In his dealings with leading figures at the height of his career Haydn never allowed his music to be perceived as though it belonged to any particular grouping, or stemmed from any political persuasion, which of course it did not. He thus freed himself, in so far as it was possible, from much prejudice based on political opinion.

His attitude and the benefits accruing from it are particularly evident when compared with attitudes of other leading cultural figures of the time, whose political convictions became so firmly associated with their works that when governments toppled, the political change adversely affected their careers and appreciation of their work. The painter J.L. David, for example, embraced the ideals of the French Revolution so eagerly that he took on the design of huge propaganda processions extolling republican virtues. As an elected *député*, he voted for the execution of Louis XVI. With the fall of Robespierre David was thrown into prison, only to become an equally passionate Bonapartist after meeting Napoleon in 1798. After Waterloo (1815) David fled, spending the remainder of his life in exile in Brussels. The fate of the composer Cimarosa was even more dramatic. Having been successful in producing operas for the courts of St Petersburg and Vienna, he returned to his native Naples where a Bonapartist-inspired revolution overthrew the Bourbon monarchy in 1799. Cimarosa quickly espoused the revolutionary cause, composing a patriotic anthem which was sung during the burning of the royal banner. When soon afterwards the revolution failed, the returned king, Ferdinand IV, instituted an investigation into the composer. Despite trying to ingratiate himself by writing a cantata in honour of the Bourbons, Cimarosa was thrown into prison and only narrowly avoided a sentence of death. He died not long after being released in Venice, rumoured to have been poisoned on the instructions of Queen Carolina.

The impartiality shown by Haydn in his relations with political figures extended to a tolerance of religious practice. Although a practicing Catholic throughout his life, 'Haydn left every man to his own persuasion and recognized all as brothers.'[175] Visiting a Protestant country, where established forms of discrimination against those who practised his own religion still existed,[176] seems to have presented no problem for him. Just over a decade before he came to England the anti-Catholic Gordon riots had left many Catholics in England devastated. For example, the portrait painter George Romney was terrified into searching his home for any item which might bear a Roman Catholic interpretation lest his house be burnt down.[177] In the aftermath of this, when the first plans were drawn up to bring Haydn to England, attempts were made to use his faith to discredit him, but all trace of this seems to have died away when he actually arrived. In fact the composer seems to have been particularly fascinated by Christians of other denominations who paid attention to his music, presumably because this was clear evidence that his appeal knew no religious impediment. This is evident, for example, in his contribution (of six items composed in 1794) to the *Improved Psalmody*, new settings of the Psalms suitable for parish worship in the Anglican communion by the Rev. William D. Tattersall and others. Haydn received a piece of plate to commemorate his cooperation in this project, which marked the start of a period when melodies by Haydn were often adapted for use in public worship in Protestant churches.[178] A clear instance of Haydn's interest in how his music affected Protestants is his account in his notebook of a concert held in March 1792. An English clergyman was present who, Haydn records, fell 'into the deepest melancholy' on hearing the slow movement from Symphony No. 75 because he had dreamt the previous night 'that this piece was a presentiment of his death'. A month later the composer added: 'Today ... I heard ... that this Evangelical [Protestant] clergyman had died.'[179] Reflecting on the incident with Dies in 1806 Haydn still found this coincidence 'an amazing occurrence', a hint perhaps that he derived a certain pleasure from his own implication that his music could have exerted such a powerful force in suggesting a premonition of death. Dies, however, was sceptical.[180]

Contemporaries seem often to have found Haydn's Adagio movements (like the one from Symphony No. 75) so moving that those of a devout disposition connected the feelings aroused in them with religious revelation. Haydn himself had prepared the ground for such experience in the sequence of slow movements comprising *The Seven Last Words*, musical meditations on incidents described in the Bible concerning the Crucifixion and death of Christ, first published in its original version for orchestra in 1787, and subsequently popularized throughout Europe in various arrangements of the material, including one for string quartet. Haydn himself wrote that he intended this music to arouse 'the very deepest impression on even the most uncultivated listener'.[181] Something of the experience felt by listeners to such movements was recorded by the composer Samuel Wesley, who saw Haydn perform in London, and whose perspective was coloured by an interesting religious background, his uncle being the founder of Methodism, and he an Anglican with strong leanings to Roman Catholicism: Haydn's 'Adagios are so pathetic and tender that although performed by inarticulate Instruments, their effect is irresistibly pathetic and affecting.'[182]

Haydn also took special interest in leaders of nonconformist denominations, such as the Moravian minister C.I. Latrobe (a friend of Burney), who later, recalling his friendship with Haydn, wrote: 'I never perceived in Haydn any symptoms of that envy & jealousy, which is, alas, so much the besetting sin of musicians. He appeared to me to be a religious character, & not only attentive to the forms & usages *of his own Church*, but under the *influence of a devotional spirit*. This is felt by those, who understand the *language of Music* ...'.[183] As this passage indicates, Moravians (a Protestant sect advocating a strict life and daily prayers) placed special emphasis on the part music might play in developing spiritual awareness, a facet of their religion which Haydn himself was concerned to exploit. Haydn was probably also aware that Moravians had been seminal in introducing his music to America. Like Methodists (who made the final break with the Anglican church at the end of Haydn's period in England), the Moravians later established a tradition for performing large-scale vocal works, especially oratorios by Handel and Haydn.[184] *The Creation*, though a religious oratorio in the sense that it is partly based on the Creation story as told in the Bible, conspicuously avoids any possibility of inter-denominational dispute by ending the narrative before the Fall, thereby neatly sidestepping the issue of sin which had divided Christians since the Reformation.

John Wesley, the founder of Methodism and one of the great social reformers of his age, had for a time been under the spell of the Moravian Church in London. His concern to attend to the spiritual needs of the lowest strata of society – especially those engaged in low-paid, industrial activities (like coal mining), largely ignored by the established Church – and his emphasis on the certain conviction of salvation would have appealed to Haydn. The composer's own family background would have helped him to identify with the values of Methodism: simple virtues, study of the Bible, honest toil, thrift and charity. Haydn's late oratorios, *The Creation* and *The Seasons*, may be seen to have been calculated in their subject matter to provide for the needs of that section of society which also concerned Wesley, and for whom musical provision had not previously been a priority. The figure of Adam in *The Creation* offered a special message of hope, the making of man in God's image representing not only the triumph of Creation, but also an allegory of the common man, suggesting a purpose for all men in the divine plan. This was an ecumenical message; but it was also relevant to other faiths. It is symptomatic of Haydn's customary attitude towards his fellow men that there is no record that he ever voiced anything which might be construed as anti-semitic, though animosity to Jews was commonplace in the society in which he grew up and was even given expression by otherwise the most enlightened of composers, including Beethoven. *The Creation* was aimed at all men and generally succeeded in commanding the attention of people from all backgrounds. In the words of Samuel Wesley, 'Haydn's oratorio ... is acknowledged *universally* to be a masterly and imperishable Work, in Contrivance, Expression, and Variety.'[185]

The trouble Haydn took to please his public is evident from many sources connected directly with him. He would perform, or take on menial commissions from figures with all manner of backgrounds and occupations, especially if he knew they were likely to propagate his reputation still further. The British officer who came to Haydn (probably in 1794) requesting the composition of two marches by the end of a fortnight, when he was to sail for America (or India according to another source), was obliged by him, as was the young woman from Coburg who (about 1780) requested the composition of a song to her own words telling the tale of a faithful poodle, with which she hoped to elicit an offer of marriage from her sweetheart, the poodle's owner.[186] Haydn also worked for connoisseurs and amateurs, the young and the old, soldiers and sailors, bankers and merchants, religious communities, charitable institutions, as well of course as the publishers and aristocratic patrons who might be expected to support an established composer of the time. Whilst the

English sources provide a detailed picture of Haydn's willingness and desire to satisfy musically as varied a cross-section of the public as possible, sources from France enable a corresponding picture of Haydn's listening public to be drawn which, since the composer never visited the country, acts as a useful barometer of attitudes towards him, unprejudiced by direct contact with the man himself.

As in London, works by Haydn were published in Paris by the mid-1760s. By 1770 he was already popular, judging from the way publishers fell over themselves to obtain his works; and during the 1780s he became the most frequently performed composer in concerts held in the city.[187] His *Stabat Mater* (composed in 1768) and several symphonies originally composed for Haydn's patron Prince Esterházy were especially well received at performances given in the fashionable concert series, the *Concert spirituel*, and often published.[188] The six 'Paris' Symphonies (Nos 82–87) were commissioned for the Parisian *Concert de la Loge Olympique* and composed in 1785–86, and a further three symphonies ordered by the same organization (Nos 90–92) followed in 1788–89.[189] This concert series was initiated in 1781 to provide Parisians with a high standard of orchestral playing and replaced the earlier *Concert des Amateurs*. The musicians performed wearing eye-catching blue coats with swords at their sides in a room resembling a theatre, with boxes for spectators in tiers. It was one of the series's founders, C.-F.-M. Rigoley, Comte d'Ogny, who took the initiative to approach Haydn directly for symphonies, paying him exorbitant amounts, more than five times what Mozart had received in 1778 for his 'Paris' symphony for each one. D'Ogny, who in 1785 inherited the post of *Intendant Général des Postes*, belonged to an old noble family and assembled one of the most extensive music libraries of the eighteenth century, adding to it Haydn's autographs of the 'Paris' Symphonies presumably in about 1787.

As Haydn would have been well aware, the symphonies were primarily for the ears of an aristocratic audience, representing French taste of the 1780s at its most sophisticated. Haydn included in the music many features evidently calculated to appeal to listeners drawn primarily from the French nobility. Two of the symphonies (Nos 82 and 83), for example, include thematic material suggestive of animals – a clucking chicken and a dancing bear – resulting in popular nicknames being given to them, *L'Ours* and *La Poule*, very much in the spirit of the titles of many pieces of eighteenth-century French music. Although Haydn may not have intended these precise associations, there can be little doubt that the character and diversity of the music was conceived to encourage such impressions in the listener's imagination. Later, when he was assured how most listeners would react to such associations, he was able to develop this kind of 'painting' with confidence and exactitude in the late oratorios.

In Symphony No. 85 the first movement includes bold 'quotations' from the opening of an earlier Haydn symphony, No. 45 (1772), popularly known from the dwindling character of its last movement as 'The Farewell' (*Les adieux*). Many Parisian listeners to Symphony No. 85 are likely to have recognized 'The Farewell' references. This earlier symphony was the subject of a long review in the *Mercure de France* in 1784 and was performed, most appropriately and presumably with the audience's understanding of the choice, at the final concert of the *Concert spirituel* in its venue in the Tuileries before moving to a new one.[190] The theme of farewell was one which struck a special chord in Paris during the last decades of the *Ancien régime*, when it played an important part in the cult of *sensibilité*. For example, in the celebrated *Le Monument du Costume*, two series of engravings after designs by the artist Moreau le jeune documenting 'the manners and dress of the French in the 18th century', the first series (published in 1776) records the rise of a young married woman in aristocratic society and includes a scene of flirtation at the Opéra entitled *Les Adieux*. The second movement of Symphony No. 85, a set of variations, is based on an old French 'folk-song' known as 'La gentille et jeune Lisette', which Haydn knew would further delight Parisian audiences. This symphony was first published in Paris in 1788 with the title *La Reine de France*, an indication that it was Marie-Antoinette's favourite. Four years later when the Queen's family was placed under guard in the Temple in Paris, one visitor reported that the royal prisoners were permitted a harpsichord and some music, including *La Reine de France*. When seen by the Queen, it prompted her to remark 'Times have changed', at which the assembled company could not restrain their tears.[191]

Since Haydn's music was so closely associated with the *Ancien régime* in the 1780s it might have been expected that his reputation would have plummeted at the Revolution. Many composers who had thrived under the old order, such as Grétry, never quite recovered their former prestige after the change, and the same applies to leading painters, like Fragonard and Hubert Robert (who spent a period in prison). Some artists, like Vigée-Lebrun, one of Marie-Antoinette's favourite painters, decided to leave France altogether, disgusted by the course of events and realizing the precarious situation they found themselves in. But although times changed, Haydn and his music kept firmly abreast of them. In fact the Revolution and its ideals only served to further Haydn's reputation, as his music now started to reach new audiences drawn from less privileged or new social groupings.

Like many contemporary artists, Haydn promptly embraced the principles of the early Revolution, not only mindful which way the wind was blowing, but anxious to preserve his reputation. After hearing the news of the fall of the Bastille and the creation of the new National Assembly in France, he wrote to Sieber, one of the Parisian publishing firms with which he had dealings, indicating that he wanted one of the symphonies they expected to publish 'to be entitled the "National" Symphony'.[192] Nothing came of this project, presumably because of deteriorating relations with France as the Revolution developed; but that nobody doubted Haydn's music could only broaden its appeal in the new spirit of democratization, and that Haydn himself was favourable to this is unmistakable. Earlier associations for music written for France may have assumed positive new values during the period of the National Assembly (1789–91). A hen protecting her eggs (cf. Symphony No. 83, *La Poule*), for example, became a symbol used in popular prints in 1790 for the protection of the new French nation.[193]

It was only when the course of the Revolution resorted to extreme violence and the lives of the royal family were at stake that Haydn's attitude hardened. Marie-Antoinette was an Austrian princess and any threat to her was an affront to all Austrians. Haydn's feeling on this matter is evident from his acquisition of a portrait engraving of the Queen (after a painting by Dies) which he kept in his collection until death, a reminder of his former success at the French court.[194] However, although the political confrontation in Europe which followed the execution of Louis XVI in January 1793 placed Haydn and the French on opposite sides, resulting in a hiatus in communication and dissemination of new works, the appreciation of his works in France once again quickened during the later 1790s, building its prestige throughout the first two decades of the nineteenth century.[195] Partly as a result of regular new concert series being promoted, such as the *Concert de la Rue Cléry*, a stone's throw from where the art dealer Lebrun had his gallery, Haydn symphonies became the most performed of all music, few concerts failing to include a work by him, with often two symphonies appearing on one programme. Newspaper notices supported the often vociferous enthusiasm of concert-goers, emphasizing that Haydn's was the kind of music which appealed to everyone, possessing 'the rare privilege of always captivating spectators', and appealing to 'the least experienced listeners as well as the most demanding experts'.[196]

It is not surprising therefore that when *The Creation* was given in Paris for the first time, on Christmas Eve 1800, it was considered an event of such public significance that Napoleon, then First Consul, felt he had to make an appearance at the theatre, despite under normal circumstances having little time for most music other than Paisiello's. The occasion became famous because of an attempt on Napoleon's life on his way to the performance. The bomb intended for him destroyed another carriage, killing 22 persons, wounding 57 and damaging 42 houses; but notwithstanding this, Napoleon still felt it crucial to be seen at the theatre. The subsequent success of the oratorio in Paris was overwhelming, even for a city which had become used to grand spectacular occasions, many designed by J.-L. David. When reports started reaching Haydn, he could hardly control his excitement.[197] The last music he was ever to hear, the aria from *The Creation* describing the creation of man and woman (No. 24), was sung by a French captain in May 1809 a few days before his death, Napoleon having retaken Vienna earlier the same month. The French Emperor, mindful of the enormous prestige enjoyed by Haydn in his own country, took the trouble to ensure that the composer's house was guarded during his last days to protect him, in so far as it was possible, from the bombardment then taking place. As in 1805, when Napoleon had previously been in Vienna, he completely ignored Haydn's music, in contrast to most of his fellow-countrymen and the Viennese.[198]

The Creation owed part of its success to its portrayal of mankind. The figure of Adam, who embodies the notion of humanity, has significance for all men. Not only may he be understood in the context of the traditional Judeo-Christian explanation for the beginning of the human predicament – Man created in God's image – but he is also seen in Enlightenment terms. Indeed light itself, betokening the dissemination of good in the world – an Enlightenment as well as a biblical metaphor – is a key feature of the work's aesthetic, Haydn's gift for expressing musically the effects of light overwhelming many early listeners. Furthermore the oratorio stresses man as the summit of the natural world, with intellect, virtue and beauty to match. Man commands authority over Nature, but his respect for it gives him moral credentials. Adam is therefore presented as the ideal model for the ordinary man, encouraging self-improvement through his love for his companion (Eve) and his regard for the world around him. There is neither wrong-doing nor sin in *The Creation*, so the view of Adam it propounds, in contrast to that often advocated in the eighteenth century in which he was held partly responsible for the suffering of mankind (on account of his part in instigating Original Sin), emphasizes strength rather than weakness, and virtue rather than sin. In *The Seasons* these characteristics are even more marked. The honest, simple virtues of the protagonists, their working with nature, their persistence in the face of adversity, and above all their contented lives present them as ideal exemplars for human behaviour. This may be the world of ordinary labourers, working on the land, but theirs is a message for all men, a point emphasized in early performances when the venues were the homes of the aristocracy and the singers included members of the imperial family.

The Seasons, however, should not be confused with the kind of peasant performance practised by Marie-Antoinette at Versailles in the spirit of a return to nature advocated by Rousseau. The characters devised by van Swieten and Haydn suffer the hardships and fears of real peasants. Like Adam and Eve in *The Creation*, they were certainly intended to appeal to a post-Revolutionary audience which had absorbed the *Declaration of the Rights of Man and of Citizens by the National Assembly of France*, its rhetoric and ideals, much of which is reflected, though not promoted, in both oratorios. This is not to say that either work is a product of the French Revolution, only that both oratorios were conceived in part as responses to it, projecting the concerns of a more enlightened society and also, more importantly, of a fairer one, in which the common man might assume the centre stage. This point could hardly have been missed in France in the early years of the nineteenth century. But the characters in *The Seasons* are satisfied with their lot in life and place their trust absolutely in God. These are peasants who are certainly not going to undermine the foundations of society.

One measure of the intention of van Swieten and Haydn to reflect the issues of a post-Revolutionary world, rather than aim at mere conventionality, is their treatment of women in *The Creation* and *The Seasons*. Both men knew that, ever since Haydn's music had begun to command attention in the public sphere, women had been as important as, if not more important than, men in comprising the composer's extended audience. It was helpful therefore that his representation of women should seem progressive. Taking some account of influential feminist thinking, such as the ideas expressed in Mary Wollstonecraft's *A Vindication of the Rights of Woman*, was one way of achieving this. Wollstonecraft argued that women's oppression was chiefly a reflection of their inadequate education, which fostered that 'weak elegance of mind, exquisite sensibility, and sweet docility of manners supposed to be the sexual characteristic of the weaker vessel'. In *The Creation* though Eve, in line with traditional exegesis, submits herself to her husband – 'Thy will is my law' (No. 29) – and Haydn's music contrasts the strength of Adam with the sweetness of Eve (especially in No. 24), the expression of her subjugation was evidently contrived to be less repressive than that formulated by Milton in *Paradise Lost*, one of the principle sources for the oratorio's text.[199] Moreover, since sin is not an issue in the oratorio, Eve's customary role as temptress and inciter of Man's Fall is never mentioned; she is her husband's companion, both presented as equals in aspiration and achievement. In *The Seasons*, whilst woman's place as her husband's supporter is generally affirmed (a position which passed unchallenged by Wollstonecraft), one section of the oratorio, *Winter*, specifically demonstrates womankind's capacity for intellect and honour. In the *Spinning Song* (No. 34), traditional female virtues of industry and purity are stressed as those required to gain a husband. This is mischievously followed up in the song with chorus which comes next (No. 36), in which Hanne tells the story of a wealthy lord who tries to seduce a young woman working on the land, the chorus (that is the country-people assembled listening to the story) interjecting with questions, expressions of disapproval and laughter. After he steals a kiss and offers her gifts and anything she desires, the woman coyly pretends to respond to his advances, but urges caution since her brother is working nearby. When the aristocrat goes to take a look at the brother, the woman swiftly mounts his horse and rides off proclaiming her revenge for his improper proposal, while the lord is left gaping and ashamed. The chorus expresses its approval at this just outcome. This story does not occur in the textual source on which the oratorio was based, Thomson's popular poem *The Seasons*, but was borrowed from one written in 1762, part of a musical play called *Annette et Lubin* by Madame Favart, in order to lighten the mood of an otherwise serious section of the oratorio.[200] However, as the audience for the story in 1801 might have anticipated, the ending of such tales more often than not had a different outcome, with the woman submitting to the man, and having to pay for the moment of weakness.

Haydn had followed this path just twenty years earlier in his choice of texts for the twelve German songs which comprised one of the earliest collections of his works published with his approval. The fourth of these, 'An all too Common Story', opens in a very similar vein to the song from *Winter*, with the same notes and rhythm, and in the same key.[201] In the earlier song the man tries to gain entrance to the woman's house as night falls, but is refused. As he is about to leave, the key turns and she admits him, though 'only for a moment'. The neighbours burn with curiosity, but end up laughing when he is discovered leaving the next morning. In the next song in the cycle, 'The Abandoned Woman', the woman of the title complains that all members of her sex, who are characterized as meek and pleasing, share weak hearts, falling into the traps of men, only too willing to be deceived.[202] By the time that *The Seasons* was conceived such characterization of the female sex was no longer acceptable in a work aimed at a universal audience. This point may have been impressed on Haydn by a key figure in Wollstonecraft's circle, Holcroft, who translated 'An all too Common Story' into English. So whilst the mood of this song was what Haydn wanted to recreate in the oratorio, its message was completely changed to keep abreast of the times.

Haydn's instinct for keeping in tune with developments in popular culture is also evident from his arrangements of traditional Scottish songs. Whilst the late oratorios were intended to appeal to a very wide audience, the Scottish songs (and later arrangements of Welsh and Irish melodies also) show Haydn trying to lend his reputation a grass-roots quality, using material which supposedly stemmed directly from the ordinary man, generally admitted to be beautiful though with rough edges, and presenting it in a form suitable for private performance in drawing-rooms the length and breadth of Europe. There seems to have been little financial incentive to take on such work (at least initially), but since he undertook so many his commitment to this genre is undoubted, suggesting that he both truly enjoyed it and found value in it both for himself and in terms of furthering the popularity of the songs.[203]

He made his first arrangements, technically undemanding and straightforward, for the London-based Scottish publisher William Napier when he was in England: 100 arrangements in 1791–92 in a volume dedicated to the Duchess of York, and a further 50 in 1794–95, this time dedicated to Queen Charlotte.[204] The venture seems to have been sufficiently successful to rescue Napier from bankruptcy. Haydn may have been encouraged to participate in this project, knowing how widespread the taste for things Scottish was becoming. For some intellectuals this taste connected with a view that study of traditional culture provided a tool for understanding the origins of music and the arts. Burney, for example, in devising the *General History*, considered that 'authentic' singing from Naples was 'a very singular species of music, ... as different from that of all the rest of Europe *as the Scots*, and is, perhaps, as ancient, being amongst the common people merely traditional'.[205] This was the period when study of local customs and dress was starting to be reflected in the visual arts. Thus the Scottish painter David Allan, whose patrons, the Cathcart family, later took a special interest in Haydn, depicted scenes observing the habits of local people in both Naples and Scotland.[206] The sense of spectacle and movement in his *Highland Wedding* (1780) gives some sense of what was soon to catch the imagination of people outside Scotland, like the musical spectacular Haydn saw at the Little Haymarket Theatre in London in July 1794:

> They performed a National opera, N.B. a piece in Scottish dress. The men wore flesh-coloured breeches, with white and red bands wrapped round their stockings, a short brightly-coloured striped masons' apron [i.e. kilt], brown coat and waistcoat, over the coat a large, broad officer's sash in the same design as the apron, and black hat shaped like a shoe and decorated with ribbons. The women all in white muslin, brightly-coloured bands in their hair, very broad girdles in the same design round their bodies, as well as for their hats.[207]

Haydn would also perhaps have heard some of the Scottish songs, first popularized by the castrato Giusto Tenducci in arrangements by Johann Christian Bach, which were often introduced into English operas in the later eighteenth century.[208] These provide a musical parallel to the exceptional and widespread interest in the 'primitive' poetry of Ossian, presented to the public as though it formed part of the ancient literary heritage of Scotland 'in translation', and thus selected for illustration by several leading artists, but in fact a fabrication by James Macpherson.

In taking on the Scottish songs Haydn was therefore contributing to a wider movement which, as conceived by some of its promoters, aimed to project Scottish music to a more prominent position within the firmament of European culture. Arguably the fascination with things Scottish – its landscapes, customs, history and cultural traditions – which spread throughout Europe in the first decades of the nineteenth century helped to stimulate a broader fascination with traditional or native music across the continent. Perhaps Haydn, in associating himself so prominently with Scottish 'folk' music, felt himself to be making a personal contribution both to the project to extend appreciation of indigenous Scottish music, and also, more importantly, to the idea that all traditional forms of music, when appropriately presented, have claims to be heard by even the most discriminating of listeners. Stendhal perhaps reflected something of this mood in describing a visit to Scotland, during the course of which he was put in mind of Haydn:

> This race ... must be musical. ... as I rode round the crofts, I heard music welling up from all sides. Admittedly, it was not *Italian* music – no, it was something far better; for this was Scotland, and the music was native to the soil from which it had sprung. If Scotland, instead of being poor and barren, were a land of wealth and prosperity ... I do not doubt for an instant that the subterranean springs of natural music ... would have been carefully caught, preserved, purified and distilled into a quintessence of *ideal beauty*, and that, in due course *Scottish music* would have sounded as familiar in our ears as ... *German music* does today [1824]. The land which has given us Ossian, ... the land which finds its pride in Robert Burns, might unquestionably be expected to give Europe a new Haydn or another Mozart.[209]

Stendhal went on to make a comparison between Haydn and Burns, which was very apt since many of Haydn's arrangements were to songs with words by Burns, though as far as it has been possible to tell Haydn was never actually sent the words, only the melodies.[210] Burns provided encouragement and lyrics for the most ambitious and thoughtful of the publishers of Scottish songs in Haydn's time, George Thomson, whose firm was based in Edinburgh, and with whom Haydn was in correspondence between 1799 and 1805.[211] Although Thomson has been criticized for lack of respect for 'authenticity' in achieving his arrangements, and for bowdlerizing Burns's lyrics, this ignores his ambition of bringing Scottish musical achievement before a universal audience and of ensuring that the form in which it was transmitted was appropriate for performance anywhere in the civilized world and did not give offence. He was conscious of the danger of over-refining his material for the genteel palate – being very critical of other publishers whom he found guilty of this – and tried to follow Burns's advice that

> Whatever Mr Pleyel [Thomson's first arranger] does, let him not alter one iota of the original Scots Air; I mean in the song department. ... But, let our National Music preserve its native features. – They are, I own, frequently wild, & unreduceable to the more modern rules; but on that very eccentricity, perhaps, depends a great part of their effect.[212]

Haydn was almost certainly Thomson's first choice as arranger for his collection, being in his view 'the unsurpassed and unrivalled genius of the realms of music'.[213] But because Haydn was already committed to Napier in the early 1790s, Thomson approached Pleyel, a former pupil of Haydn's, who was in London at the same time as Haydn; and when Pleyel dried up, he turned to Kozeluch, the Imperial Court Composer in Vienna. Between them they managed two volumes of 50 songs each. Dissatisfied with the quality of arrangement he was receiving for an endeavour he intended should 'ever remain the standard of Scottish Music', he managed to engage Haydn for the third and fourth volumes and for new arrangements of songs already set by

Pleyel and Kozeluch. Haydn's sensitivity and variety of treatment were infinitely preferable to the approach of his predecessors and much appreciated by Thomson. He was less happy when he learnt, probably in 1803, that Haydn was also undertaking arrangements of Scottish songs for another Edinburgh publisher, William Whyte, and with so much work he was farming out some of the arrangements. Haydn's pupil Neukomm later claimed to have provided 70 of these. Even if true – others were probably also involved – this in no sense diminishes Haydn's commitment to the indigenous song of Scotland. Haydn arranged or oversaw almost 400 such songs (including those from other regions of the British Isles), and only increasing infirmity prevented him from continuing.[214]

Haydn's seriousness of purpose in devoting so much of his late activity to Scottish music is reflected not only in his acquisition of several publications relating directly to 'Scottish' music, but also in his purchase of a German translation of the *History of Scotland* by William Robertson, principal of the University of Edinburgh, one of the most celebrated historians of his age.[215] He also possessed an edition of the same author's *History of America*.[216] Presumably both works were read, at least partly, with a mind to discover aspects of those nations which might be relevant to satisfying them musically. Since Haydn claimed that he had to change many things in his musical style to suit the taste of the English, it seems possible that he had in mind the need for equivalent modifications in relation to other countries, though, having never visited them, he was reliant on other sources of evidence regarding stylistic characteristics supposedly favoured by their peoples.[217] The work in his library which most conclusively suggests Haydn's interest in the world beyond the one with which he was familiar is an edition (in English) of Captain Cook's *Complete Collection of Voyages round the World*.[218] For many Europeans James Cook's 'voyages of discovery' represented both a sense of the exotic and a growing realization of the commercial possibilities in establishing links with distant parts of the globe. Since Cook had permitted artists to accompany him on some of his trips, something of the wonder of what was to be seen in the far corners of the earth, in terms of its flora and fauna, and the customs and appearance of its peoples, was made available in Europe. Lichtenberg records seeing drawings (now lost) relating to Cook's second voyage (1772–75) at the end of 1775 when he visited one of the artists who had been on the voyage, William Hodges;[219] it seems likely that Haydn may have seen associated material in London in the 1790s. He might also have viewed the ethnographical collections relating to Cook's third voyage in 1781 which were acquired by Sir Ashton Lever to form the basis of a natural history museum called the *Holophusikon*.[220] Lever was obliged to give the collection up in 1786, but it was still open to visitors during the period Haydn was in London. The excitement caused by reports of Cook's expeditions also gave rise to a number of popular theatrical entertainments based on them, abroad as well as in Britain. One which Haydn may have known (by reputation) was *Il Capitano Cook agli Ottaiti*, a ballet first performed in Florence and given to the new Emperor Leopold II in Vienna in 1791.

Haydn himself met several people directly connected with Cook's voyages when he was in London. Captain James Burney, Dr Burney's son, took part in the last voyage (1776–81), during which Cook was killed, and was later to write a *History of Discoveries in the South Seas*. The artefacts he brought back from Polynesia and Hawaii inspired fashions which were reported in the press in early 1781.[221] Of greater significance to Haydn in the long term was his contact with Sir Joseph Banks, the celebrated botanist, who had participated in Cook's first voyage to the South Pacific (1768–71), returning with considerable collections of scientific and artistic interest which resulted in him being feted in society: no fewer than 30,000 plants and 1,000 animals, including many unknown species; art and artefacts from various islands, and over 1,200 drawings and paintings.[222] A portrait of Banks by Benjamin West taken on his return depicts him wearing a Maori cloak and surrounded by objects he had collected in New Zealand and Polynesia.[223] Banks's regard for Haydn is well documented by the survival of handbills indicating his attendance at concerts of Haydn's music during the composer's first year in London.[224] One of these handbills, for Haydn's benefit concert on 16 May 1791, was kept with a ticket signed by Haydn, an indication that Banks was acquainted with the composer by that date.[225] What is interesting about Banks's devotion to Haydn's music is how it appealed to a man of science who had circumnavigated the globe. It seems possible that Banks perceived a quality in Haydn's music which transcended the aesthetic limitations of traditional Western music and suggested a more universal appeal. It is known that Banks was keen on music on board ship and himself learnt to play various instruments, including the flute and guitar. Haydn, like Burney, may have been hopeful to learn from Banks about musical provision in the primitive societies he visited in regions of the world remote from Europe.

Haydn perhaps first found out about Cook and his voyages from the engraver Johann Jacobe, professor of mezzotint in the Vienna Academy from 1782 until his death in 1793.[226] Between 1777 and 1780 Jacobe had been in London on a state scholarship, perfecting his knowledge of mezzotint. Most of the plates he engraved in London were after paintings by Reynolds, including one dated 1777 of Omai, the South Sea Islander who travelled to England in 1774 as a result of Captain Cook's second voyage.[227] Although his garb is entirely inauthentic, Reynolds's portrait of Omai, shown at the Royal Academy in 1776, conveys something of the elegance in deportment and good manners which struck many Westerners on meeting him. Omai spent much of his time in England with Banks and was taught English by James Burney. He created such an impression with the public that he and his relations with

Westerners later formed the basis of a famous pantomime called *Omai, or A Trip round the World*, first performed in 1785 with music by William Shield and spectacular stage designs by Philippe de Loutherbourg, some of which were based on drawings by artists like Hodges and John Webber who had actually accompanied Cook on his voyages.[228] The pantomime ended with the descent of 'a grand painting' by Loutherbourg entitled *The Apotheosis of Captain Cook Being crowned by Brittania and Fame*, which inspired several derivatives and was published as a print shortly before the beginning of the composer's second London visit. The depiction of Cook devised by Loutherbourg presented him as a great agent for civilizing the world, an image intended to consolidate his popular reputation in Britain.[229]

Loutherbourg later designed an equivalent print to demonstrate the power of music as a civilizing force in the world, choosing Haydn and Mozart to represent the summit of human musicality, showing them, as he had shown Cook, approaching the light of divinity. Haydn in fact met both Shield and Loutherbourg in England. The composer's interest in the South Pacific, and in the peoples of Polynesia, Australia and New Zealand with whom Cook and his colleagues came into contact, might therefore have been stimulated by a large number of English acquaintances.

It seems very likely that Haydn was concerned that his music should appeal to all men and women, regardless of their origins or religious views. Although he would have had little sense of non-European musical traditions, he probably hoped that his compositions had the potential to enchant people from all parts of the globe. The presence in Britain of Omai, who seems to have experienced little difficulty in adjusting to life in the West (though he never lost the desire to return home), played an important part in changing attitudes towards people from parts of the world viewed by Westerners as uncivilized. Many educated Europeans who had grown up in the first half of the eighteenth century, taking for granted the notion that Africans and natives of other 'savage' regions of the world were suitable for exploitation as slaves, came to change their opinion on contact with Omai and others like him, who integrated themselves in the West and were sufficiently articulate to tell their stories. Joshua Reynolds is a good example of such a person, in later years becoming a convinced abolitionist. Omai may not have been a Christian (no one seems to have attempted to convert him), but for many he represented living proof of Rousseau's notion of the 'noble savage', that man, unfettered by Western values and raised in a state of nature, led a more content and morally superior existence. Another popular play with music by Shield, *Inkle and Yariko*, first performed in 1787 and loosely based on a true story, presented the abolitionist case even more succinctly.[230] Its principle character, a beautiful Indian woman tricked into slavery, was sung by Mrs Billington, from whom Haydn probably learnt the plot and understood the significance of the piece in national politics. One of Haydn's favourite artists, George Morland, made a further contribution to changing attitudes with two paintings, contrasting native hospitality to shipwrecked British sailors with the treatment of blacks by English slave traders, published as prints in 1791.[231] Slavery thus became a matter of national debate during Haydn's time in England; in 1792 William Wilberforce achieved his first major success on the road to full abolition when a measure he proposed advocating education for black slaves in preparation for their eventual emancipation received Parliamentary approval. The debate had relevance for Haydn because, as indicated below, many of those who lent their voice to the argument for change were among his champions. This is an extension of the view expressed by Jones, Dance and others that Haydn's music was a force for good in the world. For one significant part of Haydn's audience in London, therefore, there are grounds for considering that his music had associations with the idea of establishing a world free from prejudice based not only on religion, but also on race. This very much fits with Griesinger's assertion that Haydn was not only happy to leave everyone to their own (religious) convictions, but also considered *all* men to be his brothers.[232] Griesinger wrote this long after notions of the brotherhood of mankind had been firmly integrated into Western thinking as a result of the ideals of the French Revolution. But there is still every reason to assume that this was a fundamental aspect of Haydn's thinking, intrinsic to his composition, long before the Revolution, indeed probably throughout most of the time he spent in princely service.

Although Haydn probably encountered few men or women of non-European origin before coming to Britain, one he certainly knew was George Bridgetower, a black, who like Haydn himself had been in service to Prince Miklós I Esterházy. After leaving Eszterháza in unknown circumstances, Bridgetower came to England in 1789. Mrs Papendiek, a friend of Haydn's, takes up his story:

> About this time ... Bridgetower ... came to Windsor, with a view of introducing his son, a most prepossessing lad of ten or twelve years old, and a fine violin player. He was commanded by their Majesties to perform at the Lodge, when he played a concerto of Viotti's and a quartet of Haydn's, whose pupil he called himself. Both father and son pleased greatly. The one for his talent and modest bearing, the other for his fascinating manner, elegance, expertness in all languages, beauty of person, and taste in dress. He seemed to win the good opinion of every one, and was courted by all and entreated to join society.[233]

Sources indicate that both Bridgetowers were in contact with Haydn in England in 1791.[234] The designation of the younger as 'pupil' of Haydn received no objection from the composer and was presumably therefore more than a mere marketing point. Haydn, or at any rate his name, helped to ensure a favourable reception in Paris as well as London for the young violinist (and composer), who later became the original dedicatee of one of Beethoven's violin sonatas.

Another black Haydn probably knew in Austria (at least by reputation) was Angelo Soliman. Taken into slavery at the age of 7, an unusual chain of events ended with Soliman serving in several princely Viennese households, commanding great esteem throughout society for his noble bearing and education.[235] However, he incurred the wrath of one patron by marrying a European, the widow of a Dutch general, for which he was dismissed. Although temporarily ostracized, Soliman made his way back to become tutor to the son of Prince Liechtenstein and a member of the same Masonic lodge as Mozart, whom he knew. Haydn himself is very likely to have identified with the situations of Bridgetower and Soliman. His own skin was apparently darker than most Europeans, which in his early career apparently resulted in him suffering some discrimination. Carpani describes how his first Esterházy patron decided to employ Haydn after hearing his music, but did so without seeing him in person.[236] When Haydn was eventually presented to his new employer, his appearance was not what was expected and the Prince called him 'Blackamoor', a name which stuck with his new colleagues. Even if the story has no factual basis, it presents clear of evidence of how people judged by appearances and of disrespectful attitudes to blacks.

Haydn would therefore have been alert to the prejudice suffered by blacks in Britain. He could hardly have failed to learn about such distinguished blacks as Ignatius Sancho and Oloudah Equiano, both of whom had accounts of their lives published during the 1780s.[237] Sancho was brought as a slave to England at the age of about 2. During an unhappy placement in a London household he attracted the interest of members of the family of the Dukes of Montagu, a lifelong connection which enabled him to develop a taste for the arts. In later life Sancho gained a reputation as a man of letters, for publishing criticism on painting, and for musical composition.[238] Although he died before Haydn visited England, several of the composer's English friends had been on close terms with Sancho and are likely to have drawn Haydn's attention to his life and published compositions.[239] Equiano was also captured by slave-traders as a boy, and after working on a plantation in Virginia and in the Royal Navy, succeeded in buying his freedom.[240] In England he toured the country in support of the abolitionist cause, using the life he wrote of himself, *The Interesting Narrative*, to publicize the plight of many blacks. Subscribers to the first edition included such personalities as the composer Thomas Attwood (a pupil of Mozart), the painters Richard Cosway and William Hodges (one of the artists who accompanied Cook), the writer Hannah More and the famous entrepreneur/potter Josiah Wedgewood. Among Equiano's other subscribers several were closely involved with Haydn, including the Prince of Wales, the Duke of York, C.I. Latrobe and Lord Cathcart. It seems possible that their social objectives impinged to some extent on their musical enthusiasms, and that for some, as in sentiments expressed by Dance and Jones, Haydn's music was indeed perceived as a force for extending good.

The available documentation does more than hint at Haydn's concern for the predicament of non-Europeans subject to European domination and his disapproval of slavery. Abolitionism was a social ideal to which the evidence indicates he undoubtedly subscribed. However, in common with many in Britain, Haydn probably connected the moral argument against slavery with the benefits to be gained from increasing trade across the globe. Successful commerce is dependent on freedom to trade, and freedom itself is antithetical to slavery. The moral justification for expanding commercialism, extending prosperity throughout the world, also had ramifications for the world of music. All men of non-European origin might be seen as potential new audiences for Western music, which for popular published composers like Haydn might present new challenges and new rewards. This is perhaps in part why Haydn let it be known that he took an interest in non-European musical tastes and practices. The translation of Sir William Jones's work on Hindu music, presented to the composer about 1802, is evidence for this, as is Haydn's own recording in his notebook of a number of details about China and its Emperor which he probably heard directly from Lord Macartney, who headed a delegation to Peking to promote British trading interests in the Far East in 1793.[241] Macartney is known to have been interested in music in general and in Haydn's music in particular.[242] He was friendly with Burney, through whom he was probably introduced to Haydn. His delegation to China included no fewer than five German musicians, whose abilities must have been wide-ranging, since they took with them 11 Western instruments (two violins, viola, cello, oboe, bassoon, two basset-horns, clarinet, flute and fife), all procured for Macartney by Burney with a view to introducing Western music to the Chinese.[243] In Peking the musicians gave a concert every evening, attracting an audience which included 'the chief mandarin of the Emperor's orchestra, who attended constantly and listened to the performance with the airs of a virtuoso'.[244] Unfortunately, exactly what music was played at these concerts is unknown, though given the musical tastes of Burney and Macartney it seems inconceivable that Haydn would not have been included. Macartney's own musical interests were such that he seems to have taken seriously a list of enquiries about the nature of Chinese music drawn up by Burney. In his journal, for example, Macartney described in detail the music-making accompanying the Emperor's birthday celebrations.[245]

The embassy to China did not achieve the hoped-for trading agreement. The Chinese were generally indifferent to the West: the Emperor's official edict, issued on the departure of the British, stated that they had 'never valued ingenious articles', nor did they have 'the slightest need for your country's manufactures'.[246] Only portraits by Reynolds of George III and Queen Charlotte in state robes attracted any great attention, along with the concerts given in Peking.[247] It was perhaps hearing this from Macartney after the latter's return to Britain that prompted Haydn to note details of the mission in his own journal.

Macartney's delegation to China was about furthering British commercial interests. It is of course a token of the status enjoyed by painting and music in the public sphere in Britain that the organizers of the embassy considered it worth including them in the package of Western goods on offer to the Chinese. Part of Haydn's own interest in visiting Britain was probably to learn how the marketing of music operated in a country in which commercialism had developed further than in his homeland. Despite several offers to compose for and perform in concert series in London during the 1780s, it was only after English publishers started to press him hard about coming to London, and one in particular, John Bland (with whom Haydn stayed on first arriving in the English capital), took the trouble twice during the later 1780s to present himself in person to the composer as an indication of just how significant a figure Haydn was to publishers of music in London, that the composer seems to have seriously started to entertain the idea of making the journey. Salomon's coup in actually persuading Haydn to accompany him to England following the death of Miklós I was probably managed so easily not simply because Salomon (Haydn's future impresario in London) happened to be in an opportune place at the right time, but because the composer was already mentally prepared for the journey through his recent dealings with London publishers. Long before setting foot in England Haydn would have been attracted by the commercial opportunities for music in London, including not only regular series of public concerts and musical performances in theatres, but also, and just as importantly, a comparatively advanced level of publishing and selling of music. When the Prince of Wales was asked his opinion of a project devised by Haydn's friend, the singer and composer Michael Kelly, to open a shop for the sale of his own music, the Prince replied that 'in a *commercial country* like ours, nothing can be more creditable than for a man to sell the produce of his own abilities, or, indeed, of any other person's'.[248] Haydn is likely to have been encouraged when he heard views of this kind.

In Austria in the 1780s the composer had already taken measures to control the commercial exploitation of his music, by making or sanctioning arrangements of large-scale compositions so that they might be performed at home with very limited forces. He was probably, however, unprepared for the extent of such arranging in Britain, where music devised for one kind of audience was soon modified to reach another. For example, Salomon made published arrangements of all twelve London Symphonies for both keyboard trio and for quintet.[249] Many of Haydn's earlier symphonies were known to English audiences through keyboard arrangements, some appearing in more than one version. Burney himself adapted several symphonies.[250] Instrumental music by Haydn dating from before 1790 probably reached its largest audiences in the form of (mostly anonymous) arrangements for voice and keyboard.[251] Four collections appeared between 1786 and 1788, each with twelve numbers.[252] The words, usually strongly sentimental in tone, were drawn from a large variety of sources, including Ovid, Petrarch and modern poets, such as Thomas Gray.[253] The character of the music was often rigorously adapted to fit the words, with frequent changes of tempo and key. Thus the second movement of Symphony No. 73 was made to fit Dr Johnson's *An Evening Ode*, and the same author's *The Winter's Walk* was set to the last movement of a keyboard sonata (Hob. XVI: 24), one of several which Burney also published with his own addition of a violin accompaniment (in 1784). Such 'adaptions', however, could apparently be performed quite readily by those who knew the original works by Haydn. One of the most popular of these arrangements, adapting part of the first movement of the keyboard sonata in C major (Hob. XVI: 35) to words concerning a woman awaiting the return of her beloved, entitled 'William', formed part of a collection of music probably played by Jane Austen, who also seems to have owned a manuscript copy of the sonata itself.[254]

Stage composers in London also regularly incorporated borrowings from Haydn's symphonic output into their own productions. One which Haydn himself saw in 1794 was Samuel Arnold's *Auld Robin Grey*, which featured a shipwreck scene set to the earthquake music from *The Seven Last Words*.[255] The original *Auld Robin Grey* – telling the story of Jenny's love for Jemmy, who she believes drowned, and her marriage to Auld Robin, who can provide for her elderly parents – came from a ballad written (anonymously) by Lady Anne Lindsay, who in 1772 set the words to a well-known tune. Its popularity may be measured by the number of prints which were published illustrating key moments in the narrative.[256] Parts of the ballad were subsequently 'adapted' in the early 1780s to favourite movements from Haydn symphonies performed at the Bach–Abel concerts.[257] Haydn almost certainly knew both the words and the musical theme when he arranged the same song for Thomson in 1800.[258] Long before Haydn worked in England, therefore, the composer's audiences would have been quite used to the notion that his music might suggest a range of extra-musical associations, perhaps literary and certainly visual, which the composer himself further exploited in compositions of the London period and later.[259]

The pictorialism of the late oratorios was thus already deeply rooted in the average listener's expectations of Haydn's creativity. It was also a major factor in the intense commercialization of Haydn's music. Although Haydn could not stop the exploitation of his music once it had become a form of public property following publication, he did succeed in later years in controlling the initial dissemination of his work to his own satisfaction. Haydn's own publication of *The Creation*, almost two years after the first performances, is a good example of this. As he stated in announcements for this first edition: 'The work is to appear in full score, so that on the one hand the public may have the work in its entirety, and so that the connoisseur may see it *in toto* ... while on the other, it will be easier to prepare the parts, should one wish to perform it anywhere.'[260] Haydn's publication was intended for audiences in both German- and English-speaking countries (translations for other countries followed later), so it featured parallel texts in the two languages, and included a long list of subscribers, drawn chiefly from Austria and Britain. Among those included were Lord and Lady Macartney, Lady Banks, Charles Wesley (Samuel's brother), Mrs Papendiek, Dr Burney, and several members of the royal and imperial families, including George III, Queen Charlotte and the Empress Marie-Therese. By the time of Haydn's death, *The Creation* had appeared in a considerable number of published arrangements and reductions, most of which had nothing to do with him directly and from which he derived no profit.[261] These testify to the continuing popularity of Haydn; but since all of them could only derive from the score he himself published, no other sources being publicly available (in contrast to earlier works), they tend to confirm the value of his strategy in preserving the integrity of his composition.

One consequence of the success of *The Creation* was that it led to Haydn's election in 1802 as a foreign member of the newly formed, though already prestigious, Institut National des Sciences et des Arts (soon to become known as the Institut National de France) in the class of 'Literature and Fine Arts'. 1802 saw a temporary cessation of hostilities in Europe following the Treaty of Amiens, a peace which helped to turn such internal affairs for the French into matters of international significance, viewed with interest in Britain and Austria. Haydn received the honour of election to the Institut at the same time that it was awarded to two of his most distinguished admirers: Jefferson, now President of the United States; and Banks, President of the Royal Society. Banks, who was elected in the class of 'Sciences, Physics and Mathematics', was pleased to inform a correspondent that he had been honoured concurrently with Haydn.[262] Banks's reaction to Haydn's election, however, was somewhat at variance with the view generally held in England, where the honour bestowed on Haydn by the French was met with howls of protest.[263] This disapproval, well documented in press reports, has been given as one reasons why Haydn's last oratorio, *The Seasons*, was never performed in England during the composer's lifetime.[264] It stemmed principally from the fact that another candidate for membership of the Institut had been proposed, the playwright Richard Brinsley Sheridan, who naturally received support from the British public. Only one foreigner at a time could be elected a member of the Institut in each class, and since Sheridan seems to have been the only other serious candidate in the 'Literature and the Fine Arts' class, the (unfounded) suspicion arose in England that Haydn had deliberately set out to rival Sheridan and to campaign for his own election. There was a strong feeling that Haydn should not have been eligible for election because he lacked literary ability and was, at best, 'only a very eminent *composer* of Musick'.[265] In the words of one of the literary attacks on Haydn,

> ... music is still only an accompaniment to the art of poetry and acts merely to dignify the latter. To elevate a musician to the leadership of the Fine Arts is much the same as awarding to the weaver who made the canvas, or to the joiner who made the frame for a painting, the prize that rightfully belongs to the great painter.[266]

Sheridan, Whig politician and friend of Fox, was merciless in attacking Haydn, to the extent of devising appalling English verse – published satirically under Haydn's name – to mock the composer and his fitness for such an honour. Even though Sheridan married into a musical family (his father-in-law was Thomas Linley) and had worked with musicians all his life, he and his friends could not accept how a composer might represent a category labelled 'Literature and the Fine Arts'. This view, of course, demonstrates the tenacity of earlier prejudices against music in relation to the other arts, particularly poetry and painting.

The venom of Sheridan's attack on Haydn effectively marked the beginning of a steady decline in Haydn's standing in England. Although Haydn's reputation in other countries, especially France, continued to grow for several years, when the decline eventually set in, it coincided, as in England, with a shift in the relationship of the arts. The situation which had developed in many countries by the 1790s, allowing music a kind of parity with literature and the visual arts, was dissipated in the early nineteenth century as literature again reasserted its superiority in the mind of the public. This was not a return to the comparative standing of the arts of the first half of the eighteenth century, since music had firmly established itself in the canon of respectable accomplishments. But during the Napoleonic era the particular bond which had developed by the end of the eighteenth century between music and the visual arts, especially with painting, evaporated as literature again assumed the high ground in the public's perception. One symptom of this is that the tail-end of the union between music and the visual arts provided inspiration and material not so much for serious composers and painters, who increasingly came to despise the nature of the bond because of its roots in 'popular' culture, but for major *literary* figures like Stendhal, Wackenrode, and even Goethe, who found the connection irresistible.

CHAPTER THREE

Steps to Parnassus

1. 'How eye and ear are entranced': Haydn and Esterházy Patronage

On 1 May 1761 Haydn signed a contract appointing him Vice-Kapellmeister to Prince Pál Antal Esterházy, head of the most influential of the Hungarian noble families owing their allegiance to the Austrian monarchy. Although he only succeeded to the post of full Kapellmeister in 1766, after the death of G.J. Werner, his predecessor, Haydn had responsibility for directing most of the musical activities expected of a Kapellmeister from the outset of his appointment.[1] The terms of Haydn's post stipulated that all his compositions were to be for the exclusive use of the Prince and might not be copied for performance outside Eisenstadt without permission. After Pál Antal died, however, the conditions of this agreement were gradually relaxed and Haydn's music was heard elsewhere.[2]

Miklós I, whom Haydn served faithfully from 1762 until the Prince's death in 1790, was the most perceptive of Haydn's Esterházy patrons, his support for the composer and his personal enthusiasms playing a major part in shaping Haydn's career.[3] The lack of interest in music shown by Miklós I's successor enabled Haydn to travel to London in the early 1790s, though nominally remaining an Esterházy employee. But when Miklós I's grandson succeeded as Miklós II in 1795, Haydn returned to service as composer of an annual mass in honour of the Princess's name-day, the last of which was first performed in 1802. In contrast to Miklós I, Miklós II was a man of meagre musical understanding, though he was undoubtedly enthusiastic about musical performance. His passion for collecting works of art, however, may have played a part in stimulating aspects of Haydn's late compositional style.

Before entering Esterházy's service, Haydn had been employed by several aristocrats: notably Baron Fürnberg, for whom he wrote several divertimenti; and Count Morzin, whose musical establishment Haydn headed in the later 1750s. It was for Morzin that Haydn probably wrote his earliest symphonies (as many as 18). As patrons, however, the Esterházys were in a different league, their status and broad cultural aspirations establishing them as one of Eastern Europe's leading families.[4] Miklós II was even offered the crown of Hungary by Napoleon in 1809, though he chose to remain loyal to the Habsburgs.

Under Pál Esterházy (d. 1713), the first Prince, the extensive Esterházy estates were consolidated and governed from their seat at Eisenstadt (originally Hungarian Kismarton, about 30 miles south-east of Vienna), where remains of the medieval castle were transformed into a Baroque country house by the imperial architect C.M. Carlone. The most spectacular aspect of the castle's decoration remains the ceiling fresco of the main hall (1665–71), painted by Tencala. Three principal scenes show episodes from the story of Eros and Psyche, conceived as an allegory of the pleasure resulting from the Esterházy marriages. Smaller scenes depict incidents from the story of the golden apples of the Hesperides, interspersed with various female figures personifying the regions of greater Hungary.[5] It was in this setting celebrating Esterházy power that many of Haydn's earliest compositions for the family were first performed. Prince Pál's interests are also reflected in the considerable collection of (now unidentifiable) paintings he amassed at Eisenstadt (where he also kept an orchestra), and in the publication of *Harmonia caelestis* (1711), a book of vocal music composed by the Prince himself.

This combination of artistic and musical enthusiasms was followed by Pál's grandsons, Haydn's first two Esterházy patrons. Exactly what paintings the Esterházys acquired in the eighteenth century cannot be clearly determined since the collection was only first catalogued in 1812. By this date it had been substantially enhanced by Miklós II, one of the most outstanding collectors of Old Master paintings, drawings and prints of his time.[6] Italian paintings were Miklós II's particular passion. In one year, 1794, he returned from his annual visit to Italy with no fewer than 50 paintings. The catalogue, compiled by the engraver and landscape painter Jószef Fischer, an authority on Dutch and Flemish painting, included 528 paintings, only just over a half of all the paintings known to have been in the collection at this time.[7]

Under Miklós I, the Esterházy collection was already recognized for its quality and diversity. Although it is unclear whether he or his grandson acquired the most famous Esterházy painting, a *Madonna* by Raphael,[8] there is no doubt that the principal patron of Haydn's maturity had a thorough knowledge of the major painters of the post-Renaissance Western tradition, an appreciation inherited by his grandson. Whilst aspects of the Esterházys' artistic tastes were entirely conventional, favouring works attributable to Old Masters of the Renaissance and later periods – painters whose reputations had been substantiated by Vasari and other leading authorities – or internationally recognized painters of the later eighteenth century (like Mengs and Kauffman), some acquisitions reveal the Esterházys as pioneers in artistic taste. For example, a *Parnassus*, purchased in Germany in 1807, was in 1812 attributed to the then reasonably well-known (though unfashionable) seventeenth-century painter Eustache Le Sueur; it was subsequently reattributed to Simon Vouet, a name much less familiar in the early nineteenth century.[9] Indeed Haydn's patrons showed a consistent interest in seventeenth-century French painting, collecting works by artists such as Philippe de Champaigne, Laurent de la Hyre, Jacques Stella and Le Brun at a time when they were not in general terms highly regarded elsewhere. The Esterházys' later interest in Spanish painting, from the sixteenth century until Goya, may also be considered rather idiosyncratic for the period.

Even less conventional was the acquisition of a number of works by little-known Italian painters of the period before the time of Raphael. One example is a *Madonna* by Carlo Crivelli.[10] As an artist who had spent his mature career in an artistic backwater (the Italian Marches), Crivelli was almost completely forgotten after his death. A brief section on him in Lanzi's *Storia pittorica* brought him to the attention of a wider audience. But it was Napoleon's Italian campaigns which led to the painter's works reaching the international markets known to Miklós II.[11] None the less, the acquisition of a painting by Crivelli would still have represented early nineteenth-century taste at its most exceptional.[12]

This enlightened aspect of his collecting habits was not matched, however, by the Prince's connoisseurship, which, like his understanding of music, reveals more obsession than discrimination. His determination to acquire a Correggio, for example, led him in 1795 to purchase a picture in Rome passed off as one by the dealer, but generally known to be a student work by Ignaz Unterberger.[13] Only when Unterberger himself informed the Prince of his authorship was the painting returned to Rome from Vienna.[14] Miklós II evidently lacked judgement; but this episode also illustrates an enthusiasm for pictures which counts as a family trait.

The first compositions Haydn executed for Prince Pál Antal in 1761 indicate how, even at the outset of his appointment, he recognized his patron's appreciation of *visual* culture. The set of three symphonies Haydn entitled respectively *Matin, Midi* and *Soir* feature two unmistakable visual allusions, and the possibility cannot be excluded that the entire cycle was written to an illustrative programme, now unidentifiable.[15] Pictorial elements were not uncommon in mid-eighteenth-century instrumental music. At the start of his career Haydn had even been required to improvise to visual gestures.[16] But it had apparently not previously occurred to him (or to his earlier patrons) to include such elements in symphonies.

Composing 'pictorially' was probably therefore a concession to Eszterházy taste. The *Musikalischer Instrumental-Kalendar* (1748), a set of twelve suites by Werner (still nominally Kapellmeister to the Esterházys at the time Haydn entered their service), contains several pictorial movements illustrating their titles, including 'The Earthquake', 'The Storm' and 'The Hunt'.[17] Even the sign of Cancer (*Sonne in Krebs*) connected with the month of June was given a pictorial association in the form of a 'crab' canon, in the second movement of the suite for this month. In another Esterházy favourite, Vivaldi's *Four Seasons*, the vivid pictorial programme was spelt out in the descriptive sonnets accompanying the music.[18] Haydn probably had long known these concertos, their original publication bearing a dedication to a member of the Morzin family, Haydn's employers before he entered Esterházy service. But perhaps the main impetus for Haydn choosing to compose with a visual aspect came from Telemann. Evoking images in music had been explored by the Hamburg composer since the 1730s when he had come under the spell of Castel and his *clavecin oculaire*.[19] Telemann's cantata depicting times of the day, *Die Tageszeiten* (1759), is therefore a possible source for Haydn taking up the same theme in 1761.[20] But the longer and more substantial tradition of illustrating the times of the day in the visual arts was perhaps also taken into account in shaping the material.[21]

Having satisfied his new audience through conventional aspects of musical pictorialism at the beginning of his tenure, a visual dimension in Haydn's music seems to have been restricted for most of the 1760s to the field of word-painting.[22] Here again he was contributing to a well-established tradition. What probably reawakened interest in exploring further the possibilities of visual stimuli as shaping forces in music was Prince Miklós's creation of a new palace at Süttör, renamed 'Eszterháza' in 1765. The opportunities presented by this project, in terms of working alongside artists and in terms of the Prince's conception for the palace and its setting, offered Haydn new challenges, some of which could be met with reference to appealing to the eyes as well as the ears of his listeners.

Eszterháza was one of the grandest princely residences set within specially designed grounds in Eastern Europe.[23] The idea of building on a magnificent scale on such a remote site must have daunted the numerous architects and artists employed on the project, with whom Haydn cooperated during the later 1760s. The palace was habitable by 1766. But the opera house, marionette theatre and quarters for musicians were only ready for use in 1769. The extensive grounds, featuring sculptures, fountains and various pavilions, were completed over succeeding years. Work on the park was still in progress in 1784, when a grand waterfall with allegorical sculptures was constructed. Inspiration throughout stemmed from the Prince's taste for things French, especially rococo ornament and formal gardens. Even before Eszterháza was finished it was nicknamed 'the little Versailles of Hungary', a description which accurately reflects the Prince's aspirations.[24]

What distinguished Eszterháza from other aristocratic residences, and even from the Versailles of Louis XIV, was the extensive provision for music-making which formed an *integral* part of the original plans.[25] Eszterháza was a place designed for viewing an array of spectacular visual delights – from the picture gallery to the fountains and statues, from the porcelain collections to the Chinese pleasure house. But all early accounts of the palace and its grounds stress how visitors were intrigued not only by what appealed to the eye, but also by what satisfied the ear, an aspect of the Eszterházy experience always associated with Haydn. 'It is indescribable how eye and ear are entranced' was how one guide (1784) expressed the combination of sensations available.[26]

Major orchestral concerts probably took place in the main *salle*, at the core of the palace, on the first floor, reached from the courtyard by a pair of staircases. Unlike rooms designated for music in other stately residences of this period, the 'concert room' at Eszterháza was at the very heart of the complex, effectively the focal point of the three grand *allées* stretching across the park.[27] The ceiling of the *salle* was decorated with a huge fresco depicting Apollo, the sun god, driving his chariot across the sky bringing light to the world, designed by the Prince's chief painter J.B. Grundemann (1766–67). At the corners of the room are statues of the Four Seasons, by J.J. Rössler. The iconographic programme, elaborating a solar theme, reflects the influence of Versailles.[28] The association of Louis XIV with the sun had inspired aspects of Habsburg propaganda by the end of the seventeenth century. But Prince Miklós's adaptation of this motif was a reminder that Apollo was the god of music as well as the sun god.[29] At Eszterháza light and music are conceived together.

A possible stimulus for this conception was the publication in 1763 of a collection of seventeenth-century texts, treating both painting and music.[30] The original author of this compilation was G.B. Doni, whose interest in ancient music had led him to invent a double lyre, partly based on evidence drawn from antique sources associated with Apollo.[31] The instrument illustrated in Doni's treatise, conceived for realizing 'the music of the ancients', bears a clear resemblance to the form of the baryton, the curious instrument played by Prince Miklós himself. Haydn wrote a considerable quantity of baryton music for the Prince between about 1764 and 1775.[32] It is conceivable that the Prince's enthusiasm for this instrument stemmed from a belief that it represented the closest modern equivalent to Apollo's lyre. Just as Louis XIV was famously projected at Versailles through association with the sun god, Prince Miklós probably saw himself at Eszterháza in the same role. The designation of pavilions as 'Temples' to the Sun and to Diana (the moon goddess, Apollo's sister) bears out this suggestion, as does the choice of themes for festivities. During the visit of Maria Theresa in 1773, for example, a sequence of classical gods, including Apollo and Diana, appeared in the marionette operas by Haydn performed for her entertainment. The performance, a panegyric on the house of Habsburg, established a connection between the Empress and her court and Jupiter and the gods on Olympia.[33] The notion that Eszterháza was a place of light was emphasized in these festivities by vast displays of pyrotechnics and other illuminations. On the occasion of the Empress's visit the fireworks were combined with painted images to further glorify the monarchy. This spectacle was followed by a viewing of a purpose-built pavilion, which revealed at one level a series of paintings of allegorical figures skilfully illuminated, and below, a set of transparencies, lit from behind, reproducing well-known paintings by Van Dyck.

One implication of this emphasis on parallels with ancient gods and on various displays of light was that Eszterháza presented an analogy to Parnassus, the realm where Apollo, accompanied by the Muses, promoted all forms of artistic creativity. Parnassus was a popular theme for courtly entertainments.[34] Since the sixteenth century it had a further connotation as a symbol of the Republic of Letters and, later, of Music.[35] In due course, this association led to Parnassus being used in the titles of scholarly works aimed at teaching the rudiments of a discipline, the scholar progressing towards the summit of the mount as the techniques are mastered.[36] From this, it was a short step to Parnassus being adopted by highborn society as a symbol of its aspiration to be at the forefront of Enlightenment culture. In music, the greatest Parnassus treatise was Fux's *Gradus ad Parnassum* (1725), which Haydn studied closely throughout his career.[37] He must have taken the notion of mounting the summit of Parnassus quite seriously since, in 1781, he referred derisively to Kapellmeister Hofmann's attempts to scale 'the heights of Mount Parnassus'.[38] Perhaps this image stuck with him as a result of the engraving of Parnassus, featuring Apollo and the Muses, decorating the frontispiece of Fux's treatise, which reproduced a design by the imperial painter Jan van Schuppen, distantly derived from Raphael's *Parnassus* in the Vatican.[39]

In terms of the development of Haydn's compositional technique, the relevance of perceiving Eszterháza as a modern Parnassus is that it provides a context for understanding several changes in Haydn's approach to composition during the early 1770s. After 1769, Haydn was required to provide concert music intended for audiences at Eszterháza who were there as much for visual entertainments as musical ones. There is at least one documented concert at which there was an implicit expectation that the audience would *look* as well as *listen*; it was held in the picture gallery, occupying the large west wing of the palace.[40] On this occasion the principal guests were the Archduchess Christine and her husband, Albert of Sachsen-Teschen, whose later connection with Haydn has been discussed in the previous chapter. The imperial couple were regular visitors to Eszterháza during the 1770s, often arriving unexpectedly.[41] Their enthusiasm for music is known from many sources. They both followed, for example, the career of Mozart, from his first appearance in Vienna until the works of his last year.[42] The couple's devotion to music was matched only by their passion for the visual arts. Like the other daughters of Maria Theresa, Christine was taught to draw as a child, and her efforts show her to have been the most conscientious and talented of all her siblings.[43] One early portrait of her actually depicts her in the act of drawing, her musical interests acknowledged in the same work by the inclusion of a selection of sheets of music shown behind her.[44] Albert was one of the foremost collectors of prints and drawings of his time, the imperial couple regularly making trips to enhance their collections.[45] The notion that Christine and Albert might have been expected to look *as well as* to listen simultaneously during a concert held at Eszterháza would therefore not have struck them as anything unusual.

The original idea and much of the subsequent impetus for Albert's collection was not his own, but came from Count Giacomo Durazzo, one of the most prominent figures in Viennese cultural life from the 1750s until the 1790s. Durazzo was an important collector himself. But he was equally acclaimed for his part in developing the musical life of Vienna, particularly in expanding the possibilities of Viennese musical theatre.[46] Durazzo's achievements benefited from the close interest of the Austrian Chancellor, Prince Kaunitz, another key figure in promoting the musical and artistic life of Vienna in equal measure. Kaunitz himself played the cello and personally knew many artists and composers. He believed that the country's economic well-being could be improved by promoting all the arts. This is evident in his special interest in restructuring the art academies in Vienna. In 1766 he founded an academy for the teaching of engraving, causing large numbers of prints to be sent from Paris and London for the benefit of students, some of whom (like Jacobe) were given scholarships to study abroad. In subsequent years Kaunitz worked towards the foundation of a new Akademie in Vienna, for the study of all the visual arts, opened in 1772. He aimed to create the right kind of conditions to encourage innovation. To avoid sterility, he insisted that artists had to be taught not only techniques, but also art history, aesthetics and other humanities. His proposals included teaching the principles of colour and its optical properties, as well as the more traditional method of learning through copying.

Haydn was in contact with all these figures who in various ways advanced visual and musical culture jointly in Austria.[47] There is evidence that around the time he reached the age of 40, in the early 1770s, he embarked on a complete re-evaluation of his techniques of composition, 'to strengthen himself in his art and to learn its secrets better'.[48] The evidence for this comes from Anton Reicha, who knew Haydn towards the end of his life. Reicha's account even implies that some principles involved in this study may have been derived from the visual arts. Writing c.1815, he reports Haydn to have told him repeatedly that no day should pass without devoting time to one's art. He added, parenthetically: 'Principe d'Apelle et de Raphael: *Nullus dies sine linea.*'[49] The story of Apelles, one of the greatest painters of Antiquity, and the line was told by Pliny. He recounts how in contest with a rival, Apelles was able to paint unaided the straightest and narrowest of lines, 'more esteemed than any masterpiece'. Pliny goes on to say that Apelles never let a day pass without engaging in some artistic activity, even if it were only drawing a line.[50] He implies that the dictum 'No day without a line' was proverbial in his own time on account of Apelles's habit. As a consequence of this, the story was in the post-Renaissance period a kind of summons to self-discipline, especially attached to another famous painter, Raphael, who was considered to have achieved so much in a short lifetime. Since there were many other ways Reicha might have expressed the notion of Haydn's daily devotion to work and study, his decision to emphasize the point by referring not only to the motto, but also to two of the most admired artists of all time, may have been intended to say something about the nature of Haydn's study during the period he was relating, that is, as the composer approached the age of 40. Perhaps Haydn indicated to him that visual stimuli had been part of his course, though if this is a correct interpretation it could have only been a very small part of the overall programme. Whatever the case, much instrumental music written during this period shows evidence of Haydn finding inspiration in devices which may be shown to have a visual point of departure.

This visual aspect is perhaps at its most evident in Symphony No. 45, first performed in the autumn of 1772. Early sources indicate that Haydn's intention in the symphony was to help the musicians at Eszterháza return to their families at Eisenstadt, by implying to Prince Miklós that the time had come to leave.[51] He managed this by ending the symphony, contrary to custom, with a slow movement; the instruments cease playing in turn, until by the end only two violins remain. To aid the sense of departure, Haydn instructed the musicians to blow out their candles at the conclusion of their parts and then to leave.[52] Apparently the Prince understood the message and gave orders to leave the following day.

The fact that the orchestra was playing by candlelight suggests that this symphony, soon known as 'The Farewell', was performed at night. In view of the significance attached to light during the eighteenth century, the age of Enlightenment, the idea of deliberately extinguishing the performers' lights would have been particularly telling, all the more so in view of the Prince's apparent interest in associating himself with Apollo, the god of light. This suggests that Haydn consciously conceived this music to be heard in carefully controlled visual conditions, the relevance of which would have been readily appreciated by his patron. The notion that visual aspects of the listening environment were important to perceptions of Haydn's music had perhaps already been brought into play at the time of '*Matin*', '*Midi*' and '*Soir*', and it undoubtedly remained an issue.[53]

Gradually snuffing out lights in order to bolster the concept of 'farewell' in the music was an idea perhaps suggested to Haydn by the traditional extinguishing of candles during *Tenebrae* ('darkness'), the combined Offices of Matins and Lauds at the end of Holy Week.[54] Part of these Offices included plainsong settings of the Lamentations of Jeremiah, the *Incipit* from which Haydn quoted in the Trio of the symphony's third movement.[55] Through this combination of visual and musical stimuli Haydn was evidently successful in suggesting to his patron the lamentable, and increasingly bleak feelings of the musicians. He skilfully prepared his audience for the visual aspects of the composition through the character of the symphony's opening movement, composed in the unusual key of F sharp minor, a tonality which in the eighteenth century had associations of gloom, distress or depression, and melancholy.[56] This choice of key is as far from the most commonly used key in the eighteenth century, C major, as it is possible to travel. By contrast with F sharp minor, C major was associated with rejoicing, purity and splendour.[57] It also was credited with visual characteristics. In 1779 Vogler claimed that it was 'Perhaps the key most fit for a painting, for pure water arias, for pure subjects.'[58] Given its associations with purity and brilliance, it is entirely understandable why C major for Haydn came to be thought of as the sonic equivalent of bright light.[59] It has reasonably been suggested, therefore, that Haydn composed his 'Farewell' symphony in the key of F sharp minor, a tonality opposed to the radiance of C major, to suggest the remoteness of Eszterháza or, more particularly, the sense of longing on the part of the musicians for their families.[60] F sharp minor, understood in these terms, is as dark as it is possible to imagine. These associations may have determined Handel's choice of this key for two especially poignant operatic duets; in both of these, pairs of lovers are obliged to bid each other 'adieu'.[61] On another occasion Handel chose this key to help depict the darkness of night.[62] Haydn is unlikely to have known these examples, though he was evidently familiar with the kinds of context in which earlier composers had chosen to use this key. Familiarity with Werner's *Musikalischer Instrumental-Kalendar*, in which the form of the minuets corresponds to the number of hours of light during the day, would have provided Prince Miklós with the means to understand Haydn's use of light (and darkness).

The connection between light and sound in the 'Farewell' Symphony provided a mechanism for Haydn conveying his message. But this does not account for his very daring idea of representing the very notion of farewell in symphonic music, undoubtedly an innovation.[63] This theme received much publicity a few years earlier with the publication of Chodowiecki's first international success, an etching after his own painting, *Les adieux de Calas à sa famille*.[64] Calas was a French Protestant executed in 1762 for the murder of his son, a Catholic convert. As a result of a campaign organized by Voltaire, the son's suicide was discovered and the father was rehabilitated. The case had reverberations across Europe. Chodowiecki's picture showed Calas, in chains, bidding his final grief-stricken farewells to his family, a representation which succeeded in recreating the torment of the situation for a wide audience.[65] The artist built on the success of the image by producing a second print depicting four men viewing and discussing the painting. This was subsequently used as an illustration in Lavater's celebrated book on physiognomy.[66] Given the popularity of Chodowiecki's prints and their topicality, it seems not unlikely that they may have acted as a stimulus in Prince Miklós's understanding of Haydn's message, even if Haydn himself did not consciously refer to the prints in formulating it. The Prince would certainly have known the relevant prints and understood their sub-text exposing injustice and intolerance.

One other symphony of this period may be connected with a near-contemporary print. Early sources for Symphony No. 64 are inscribed *'Tempora mutantur'*, which seems likely to reflect a reading of the music which derived from the composer himself. The symphony features several examples of delayed resolutions and other devices implying time being out of joint.[67] The title has been related to a popular epigram by the Welshman John Owen.[68] Composing a symphony around the theme of changing times, however, suggests a response to topical issues. The Partition of Poland, in which Austria participated in 1772–73, seems one clear possibility.[69] *Tempora mutantur* was also the title of an English caricature attacking the administration of Lord Bute, who at the conclusion of the Seven Years' War (1763) reversed the policy of his predecessor and made an unpopular peace with France.[70] Bute was soon obliged to resign. Although this print refers to an earlier conflict, it might well have acted as a visual stimulus during the period of the Poland crisis.[71] One feature of *Tempora mutantur* is that George III is depicted blindfolded. The King is entertained by a rattle labelled 'Peace', apparently oblivious to the damage being caused to Britain's defences. Such a portrayal of monarchy would have been inconceivable in Austria. For this reason the caricature would have been especially memorable, particularly since its iconography incorporated details from Apelles's *Calumny*, one of the most famous pictures known from Antiquity, descriptions of which were fundamental to the visual education of the well-to-do in the sixteenth century and later.[72] Whether or not Haydn himself knew this print cannot now, of course, be determined with certainty, though he would undoubtedly have had opportunity to see it at the time of the crisis. The important point here, however, is that the print is very likely to have been known to early audiences for the symphony, whose sense of what the music conveyed might have been conditioned by the content of this eye-catching work.

In view of his patron's artistic interests, it would have been a reasonable procedure for Haydn to select an image, especially a popular one, as a starting point for a composition. This is not to suggest that he sought to translate into music the form of an image, only that images may have provided initial inspiration.[73] Haydn may have been aware of precedents for such an approach, especially by composers active in Austria. Biber's set of sonatas for violin and keyboard on the mysteries of the Rosary (*c*.1676), for example, are each identified in the surviving manuscript with engravings depicting fifteen biblical events associated with the Rosary (there are no titles).[74] In some cases the character of the music may clearly be associated with the equivalent picture. For example, in the sixth sonata, the engraving for which depicts Christ's Agony in the Garden, the first movement, entitled 'Lamento', suggests a gradual increase in intensity as the agony builds up, leading to a

climax in the second movement Presto. The following *recitativo*, with its
sequence of ascending motifs, seemingly portrays Christ's petition 'My
Father, if it be possible, let this chalice pass from me. Nevertheless not as I
will but as Thou wilt'; and the final quiet movement suggests Christ resigning
Himself to his earthly end. A work appended to the series, a Passacaglia for
solo violin, is prefixed by an image of a child with its guardian angel. The
capacity of audiences to perceive such images in listening to these pieces
(presumably having already been stimulated by some knowledge of the
'programme') is evident in the way such music was subsequently discussed.
In the preface to the set of 'Bible' sonatas by Kuhnau (1700), which have
themselves a clear pictorial programme, the composer refers to earlier pictorial
programmes in music, including works by Froberger, the court organist in
Vienna in the mid-seventeenth century. Haydn would have certainly been
aware of such compositional procedures from reading about them in
Mattheson's *Der vollkommene Kapellmeister*, a copy of which was in his
music library.[75] Mattheson, for instance, noted that 'Froberger could depict
whole histories on the clavier, giving a representation of the persons present
and taking part in it, with all their natural characteristics.'[76] A lost suite by
Froberger is also mentioned by Mattheson 'in which the passage across the
Rhine of the Count von Thurn, and the danger he was exposed to from the
river, is most clearly *set before our eyes* in twenty-six little pieces.'
Froberger's documented association with Athanasius Kircher perhaps underpinned such experimentation with the possibilities of visual representation in
musical composition.

If Haydn did start to reconsider the possibilities for music having pictorial
qualities, perhaps as a result of the programme of study he apparently set
himself (mentioned by Reicha), then Mattheson's treatise is a plausible
starting point for such a re-evaluation. Devotional imagery in particular,
similar to that used by Biber, may have motivated him during this period. In
later life Haydn indicated to all three of his early biographers that in one
symphony – he could not remember which – his intention had been to
represent a dialogue between an unrepentant sinner and God, who pleads with
the reprobate to reform.[77] Haydn's description suggests a visual stimulus in
popular devotional material. One broadsheet of the period, for instance,
headed *Cantique spirituel*, features a conversation between God and 'the
sinner', ending with a prayer to Christ.[78] The words were apparently designed
to be sung to favourite airs. But the most striking aspect of the sheet is the
large central image depicting Christ, looked on by four repentant sinners.[79]
Just as purchasers would have kept this in view in using the sheet devotion-
ally, Haydn may have had such an image in mind when composing the
symphony.

Griesinger provides further evidence for Haydn's responsiveness to images
when he says that Haydn told him that his symphonies often portrayed 'moral

characters' (*moralische Charaktere*), giving the aforementioned case of God and the sinner as an example.[80] Carpani, citing the same story, which he claims symbolized the parable of the Prodigal Son, goes on to say that the nicknames by which several of Haydn's symphonies came to be known were derived from similar tales.[81] Although this is manifestly untrue in several of the cases he cites, and others cannot now be identified, at least one example lends support to his general assertion. 'La Roxolane' takes its name from the main character in C.S. Favart's *Les Trois Sultanes*, a play for which Haydn wrote incidental music. It was from this that Haydn formed the symphony (No. 63). Although Carpani does not mention it, the same pattern applies to 'Il distratto' (No. 60), the composition of which stemmed from Haydn's incidental music for J.F. Regnard's play, *Le Distrait*, performed at Eszterháza in 1774.[82] In these symphonies the music derives from characters in plays. But in a symphony Carpani calls 'The Schoolmaster in Love', there seems to be no source in any theatrical character.[83] Identifying this symphony is problematic;[84] but the point is that by the time Carpani was writing, it was assumed that one of Haydn's compositional procedures might involve describing musically traits in human character. If Haydn could write a symphony depicting the actions of a confused man in 1774 (No. 60), then it seems possible that compositions written in the years preceding this might have also been inspired by human characteristics, though because they did not derive from theatrical productions, Haydn's precise notions went unrecorded. Haydn's words 'Thus one friend flees from the other', added to the end of the final fugue in the C major quartet from Op. 20 (1772), suggests a further example.[85]

Carpani certainly believed that Haydn illustrated 'the diverse characters of men' in instrumental music, within the framework of moral stories, and connected this with Le Brun's theory of expression of the Passions.[86] Generations of art students had to study Le Brun's ideas, copying his illustrations of facial expressions from the various engravings of them published from 1696 onwards. It was believed that this training equipped artists to portray those moments of moral significance selected from the stories of heroes which formed the most noble genre of art, history painting. The method was conceived as a comprehensive system of human visual expression, covering the full range of emotion – from admiration to ecstasy, from hope to jealously, and from laughter to rage.[87]

Evidence that composers found Le Brun's scheme relevant to music comes from the *Mémoires* (1789) of Grétry, a self-proclaimed Haydn enthusiast. Grétry was concerned with the relationship between painting and music in general terms.[88] But his main conviction was that the best kind of orchestral writing was concerned with 'painting the Passions', or expressing a range of emotional or mental conditions. This, he claimed, does not entail direct imitation of their sounds – laughter, for example, mimicked by a series of outbursts in the music – but may be achieved by 'indirect imitation', expressing the sensations associated with each of the Passions.[89] According to Grétry, almost any human emotion may be expressed musically by a talented composer. Heavy, melancholic music, featuring the darkest registers, and long, sudden pauses, for example, might suggest a hypochondriac.[90] Unrestrained elements in music produce the image of a rake.[91] For Grétry, the possibilities were endless.[92] Opera composers had hitherto only treated a narrow range of characters because of the nature of the stories they set.[93] The composer of orchestral music with a grasp of the Passions now had all manner of new possibilities before him.

Grétry's descriptions of a hypochondriac and a rake provide parallels to Haydn's confused man and his schoolmaster in love. But Grétry's discussion suggests other aspects of the doctrine of the Passions which may have a bearing on Haydn's musical thinking during the period when the implications of moving to Eszterháza may have resulted in new compositional procedures being developed. As Grétry indicates, Le Brun's formula suggests not only possibilities for unlimited variety in music, but also encouragement to pursue *extremes* of emotion. Conscious variety and extremes of form and expression are undoubted characteristics of Haydn's music during the early 1770s. These are further evident in terms of Haydn's choice of key, tempo, dynamic markings and use of instruments. By *c.*1772 even the most unexpected contrasts of mood become features of a movement. In Symphony No. 52/II, for example, the gentle, playful opening is soon interrupted by what seems a temporary fit of uncontrollable temper and grumbling.[94] Structures which are regular and symmetrical, suggesting perhaps positive characteristics, based on feelings of contentment, are juxtaposed with those which are irregular or unbalanced, implying unsettled or disturbed qualities. The symmetry reaches its apogee in the *Menuet al Roverso* from Symphony No. 47 (1772), in which the second parts of both the Minuet and the Trio are the first parts exactly reversed.[95] Although this kind of writing was not new (having been employed in earlier learned styles of music), in terms of Haydn's development, like other mathematically related devices used in his composition, it hints at a reflective aspect in the creation of the music. It might be compared with a painter holding up a mirror to paint a self-portrait, satisfied with, though not unquestioning of, his choice of subject matter.[96]

Since Le Brun's method was a fundamental of study at the French Académie – a *Prix d'expression* was instituted in 1759 to encourage detailed study of heads in expressions of emotion – it was almost certainly reinforced in Vienna during Kaunitz's reforms of the Akademie. Haydn might have learned about this from knowledge of one of the Akademie's most notorious teachers, the sculptor F.X. Messerschmidt. In about 1770 Messerschmidt began what was to become an extensive series of male busts covering a considerable emotional range in extreme forms. He was still working on them when he died in 1783. Sixty-nine pieces were found in his studio after his

death, the majority of which were exhibited in Vienna in 1793 as
Characterköpfe, each one given a title. All the heads show strongly
characterized expressions, the features of the faces contorted to such an extent
that later observers felt uneasy, even with those where the mood depicted is
ostensibly contented rather than distressed (cf. Fig. 8). The range extends from
'An Old Cheerful Smiler' to 'The Troubled One', from 'The Melancholic
One' to 'The Vexed One'.[97]

As a protégé of Van Meytens, court painter and director of the Akademie,
Messerschmidt established a considerable reputation during the 1760s. At this
time he made full-length statues of Maria Theresa and her husband, busts of
the same couple, as well as of other members of the imperial family, including
Albert of Sachsen-Teschen, and also of Gerhard van Swieten, the father of
Haydn's later collaborator. These works show Messerschmidt working in the
late Baroque vein so much admired in imperial Vienna during the reign of
Maria Theresa. The supposed grandeur and magnificence of the figures
portrayed is conveyed through the use of devices like grotesquely inflated
draperies and extensive arrangements of hair. There could hardly be a greater
contrast with the style of the *Characterköpfe*, in which all emphasis is placed
on individual facial expression, suggesting an intensity of inner mood. No
clothing is depicted and hair is either missing or kept to a minimum. Several
of these heads evidently portray the same person; it seems likely that these are
self-portraits, showing the sculptor in various dispositions he himself
experienced. The stylistic change apparent in Messerschmidt's work
beginning about 1770 is not dissimilar to the change in Haydn's instrumental
style of the same period. Both men appear to move away from conceiving their
individual pieces as projections of courtly taste and values, towards a
conscious emphasis on variety of expression, often so intensely conveyed that
they suggest reflections of the artist's own individuality of temperament and
experience.

By 1769 Messerschmidt was acting as assistant professor of sculpture at the
Akademie and was expected to succeed to the post of full professor. When this
became vacant in 1774, however, he was not proposed for the job because, it
appears, he had for three years suffered from some kind of mental illness
which alienated him from colleagues. This is known from a letter to Maria
Theresa from Kaunitz, commenting on Messerschmidt's suitability for the
post. Despite being offered a pension, Messerschmidt left Vienna, convinced
that he was being persecuted. He later settled in Pressburg (Bratislava),
devoting himself to his grimacing heads. There he attracted several important
visitors, including the occasional writer on music, Friedrich Nicolai. Nicolai's
sympathetic account of Messerschmidt's activities in 1781 shows the sculptor
as articulate and cheerful, though 'a man of fiery passions', who held several
unconventional views.[98] One of these included a theory of the relationship
between feeling in parts of the body and facial expression. To test it, Nicolai

reports the artist pinching himself all over and pulling various faces which were studied in a mirror.

A regular visitor to Pressburg, Haydn may have known of Messerschmidt's activities there. Among Messerschmidt's more developed heads are some showing the figure sticking out its tongue in an insulting or joking manner, a gesture which in musical terms may be closely paralleled with a feature of one of Haydn's Op. 33 quartets (1781).[99] The composer himself promoted this set of quartets by claiming that they had been composed 'in a new and special way', a means perhaps of drawing attention to their witty aspects, including movements labelled *Scherzo* (Joke) in place of the conventional minuet. There is no doubt that this kind of humour, a musical counterpart it is here suggested of the face-pulling preoccupations of Messerschmidt, was understood by early listeners to the quartets. Early accounts of them emphasizing their wit and the nickname ('The Joke'), which came to be applied to the second quartet in particular on account of its teasing ending, provide clear evidence for this. The likelihood of Haydn taking an interest in facial characteristics in devising these quartets is suggested by the fact that one of the people he tried to enlist in promoting the series was the Swiss authority on physiognomy J.C. Lavater, as though the composer anticipated that those in Lavater's circle might have a special interest in the range of varied facial expressions which the quartets might prompt in listeners because of the 'new and special' manner of their composition.

It seems likely that the composer would have first come across Messerschmidt (whose celebrity was evident) in Vienna, where the *Charakterköpfe* series was begun, probably inspired by Le Brun's system. Although the sculptor's obsession with these heads subsequently turned the series into something else – he may have suffered from a psychotic illness – the initial project, which for an artist working in conservative Vienna has a quality not just of novelty but almost of revelation about it, might well have provided inspiration for Haydn's own 'moralische Charaktere'. The often dark, intense and troubled characters Messerschmidt felt compelled to depict from 1770 onwards provide a persuasive parallel to the musical language Haydn developed in instrumental music in the early 1770s. Interestingly, in neither case was pursuit of serious and concentrated expression to the exclusion of the comic or the light-hearted, as indicated above. Indeed, by the time of Maria Theresa's visit to Eszterháza (1773), there is a distinct lightening in Haydn's overall output. If Messerschmidt's projected series of *Charakterköpfe* had provided a point of focus for Haydn's aesthetic interests in the early 1770s, then it seems possible that some knowledge of Messerschmidt's emerging mental disorders, which may be connected with his compulsive attitude to the heads series (to the exclusion of all else), may have alerted Haydn to the desirability of pursuing other courses. Haydn, or his employers, may have been sensitive to the published view of some critics who suspected (without foundation) the composer himself of insanity on the basis of study of his music.[100] Whatever the case, there is no doubt that Haydn subsequently understood the value of different facial expressions in a musical context. One critic, describing an early performance of *The Creation* conducted by Haydn, was fascinated by the range of the composer's grimacing: it 'could hardly have been more exaggerated if he had tried', conveying his precise intentions in each passage, 'and how he must have felt in composing them'.[101] Of course, the writer of this passage might well have been alerted to the significance of Haydn's facial gestures through knowledge of Messerschmidt's heads, which had gone on exhibition in Vienna some years earlier. But Haydn might himself have benefited from studying the same set of heads long before, closer to the time when they were created, though they may have continued to have varying repercussions for him throughout his career.

Activities at the Vienna Akademie may have provided further incentives to explore a fuller range of emotion and colour in music of the early 1770s. Kaunitz's emphasis on colour probably stimulated the *Essay on a System of Colours* (1771) by the Viennese entomologist Ignaz Schiffermüller.[102] Although his starting point was an attempt to define colours for use in identifying insects, Schiffermüller's achievement was to suggest a theory of colour harmony, providing advice on the acceptability of colour combinations, using Castel's colour circle (which had originally been devised with musical equivalencies in mind) as the basis for discussing his findings.[103] Schiffermüller also made original observations from experimenting with colour mixtures, noting differences in results when combining pigments on a spinning-disk and on a palette.[104] He illustrated his essay with a diagram showing the colour circle in the sky, with the sun in its midst, demonstrating how sunlight, divided into constituent parts, was a compound of all colours. Haydn, contracted to work for a patron who took seriously the significance of light, may have been drawn to Schiffermüller's essay because it represented a mode of thinking about light which encouraged variety, an investigation of the effects of contrasts and mixtures, and the value of experimentation.

Although there is no decisive evidence that Haydn knew Schiffermüller's work, one early publisher of Haydn's compositions arguably recognized that qualities in his music written in 1772 might be understood as musical expressions of issues concerning sunlight and its effects. Hummel's publication of the Op. 20 quartets in 1779 used the image of the sun to decorate the title-pages of the parts, from which the pieces derive their name – 'Sun Quartets'.[105] Like Schiffermüller, Hummel gave his sun a human face, the image thereby suggesting both enlightenment, and also the range of creative possibilities implied though Schiffermüller's work. By the mid-1770s the wider appreciation of Newtonian views on light evidently led to a certain receptivity on the part of the musical public to the notion of considering music as a medium for expressing visual concepts. Haydn was certainly aware of the value of introducing himself to the public in this context. The first major work he designed specifically to appeal to a broad Viennese public, the oratorio *Il ritorno di Tobia* (1775), was built around the theme of restoring sight. The story of Tobias's journey to reverse his father's blindness had long been popular in the visual arts, but had not previously been treated musically.[106] The oratorio contains some highly developed examples of word-painting;[107] but its most insistent theme, a major preoccupation of Enlightenment culture, was light and the ability to perceive it.[108] A report on the first performance picked up on this, noting that, 'His choruses, above all, were *lit by a fire* otherwise only to be found in Handel.'[109] The writer perhaps had in mind the final number in Part One, which treats different aspects of light within a prayer for the recovery of Tobit's vision.[110] After this, the association of Haydn with light was to prove a potent combination, both in terms of his own creativity and in assessments of his achievement.[111] Carpani later referred to Haydn as the 'sun' and 'light' of instrumental music, its dawn represented by composers like Sammartini and Jomelli.[112]

2. Artaria & Compagnie: Dealers in Prints and Music

On 1 January 1779, Haydn entered into a new contract with Prince Miklós, one which formally permitted the sale of his compositions. This provided for Haydn to explore the commercial aspects of his music, the first step being to establish contacts with publishers. The Viennese firm of Artaria Co. (founded in 1771), which published many of Haydn's works in the 1780s, was not however exclusively concerned with music. Like its rivals, Torricella, which also published compositions by Haydn, the main business of Artaria was dealing in prints, relatively inexpensive works of art intended for a broad public.[113] Many of the prints sold by Artaria were imported, especially from England.[114] But with Kaunitz's promotion of engraving in Vienna, works by local artists were encouraged. Many were views of the city of Vienna itself. Artaria's *Collection de 50 vues de la ville de Vienne*, featuring prints after works by Carl Schütz and others, first appeared in 1779, but was reissued several times, usually in new states to ensure the contemporaneity of topography.[115] Some prints received dedications, often to personages associated with Haydn, like Albert of Teschen-Sachsen and van Swieten.[116] The print representing the Kohlmarkt, where Artaria had its main premises, features a group of bystanders viewing an array of prints exhibited on the shop's façade, an important indicator of the rise of print culture in Vienna at about the time Haydn entered into dealings with the company.

Artaria therefore catered for clients with both musical and artistic tastes. Many customers are likely to have been anxious to develop both interests.

Kaunitz and Joseph II took a lead in encouraging public appreciation of the visual arts by arranging for the imperial painting collection to be reorganized, catalogued and, in 1781, opened to the public. Chrétien de Mêchel, the Basel-based print dealer brought in to achieve this in 1778, divided up the paintings specifically with a view to present 'the history of art in visual terms'. Paintings were hung according to notions of chronology and the history of style. Mêchel intended the collection, which was moved to the larger Belvedere palace, to be viewed more as a means 'of instruction than for casual enjoyment'. He described the new gallery as being like 'a well-stocked library, in which anyone who wants to learn will find works of every kind and every period'. It was hoped that access to the finest examples of painting would help to stimulate higher standards of taste and connoisseurship.

These attempts to improve public understanding of visual culture were matched by developments in musical culture. The emergence of subscription concerts and the greater availability of printed editions of recent music not only helped to satisfy the need for simple leisure activities, but also created an appetite for collecting printed music in order to develop the ear and intellect. Newspaper announcements made by both Torricella and Artaria in 1785, advertising rival sets of quartets by Mozart (for sale in their respective art shops, both in the Kohlmarkt), provide clear indications of how such productions were aimed at those who thought of themselves as 'connoisseurs', who were not necessarily going to perform the works.[117] In the 1780s musical connoisseurs and art connoisseurs would often have been identical, visiting the same venue to make their purchases. This explains why music publishers took great trouble to produce title-pages with a strong visual appeal.

Haydn's *Six Divertissements à 8 Parties Concertantes*, published by Artaria in 1781, for example, features several references designed to attract the eye of the aspiring connoisseur.[118] At the top of the page is a medallion showing the three Graces. The Classical origins of this group alone recommended the image as a mark of distinction. In post-Renaissance iconography the Graces sometimes personify painting, poetry and music. Their traditional significance, based on ancient sources, was as an allegory of generosity or friendship.[119] According to one popular iconographic manual, the figures embrace because one kindness begets another, and friends should always be mutually grateful; one is seen from behind while the others face to suggest that a favour given is twice returned; and they are nude because a favour should always be given without interest.[120] Above all, however, the Graces implied beauty, especially that aspect of beauty which satisfies the intellect.[121] Winckelmann's famous writings, in which this view is advocated, perhaps also encouraged the designer to include Classical fragments in the lower part of the title-page. The prominent vase would have excited the interest of those familiar with illustrations of such objects in publications by d'Hancarville and Piranesi, probably available from Artaria's shop.[122]

The introduction of music printing to Vienna, which gradually diminished the role of the music copyist, through whom dissemination of new music had previously relied, served to protect the commercial interests of composers like Haydn, and eventually to make their music known to a wider public. But these new publishing ventures had another important consequence. By bringing the commercial aspects of music and the visual arts together, the new publishing houses implied a kind of parity between musical and artistic culture within the public sphere. The point was not lost on Haydn, who increasingly took advantage of Artaria's non-musical activities to further his own interests. Prints provided a good indication of popular taste, abroad as well as at home. Keeping an eye on what grasped the public's imagination visually was a useful measure of what might appeal musically, of particular value to a composer fascinated by the scope of his own reputation.

3. Haydn and Goya

The impression that Haydn's music had made on sections of Madrid society by the end of the 1770s is evident from *La música*, a lengthy work in verse by the distinguished fabulist and composer Tomás de Yriarte, published in 1779.[123] Twenty lines in the poem's final canto concern Haydn, emphasizing the power of his compositions to inspire and delight. Wherever his works are performed, says Yriarte, they bring distinction and fame to their composer. Above all, Haydn possesses that rare quality of boundless originality:

> To your divinity alone, prodigious Haydn,
> Do the Muses concede this grace,
> *Always to be new* . . .[124]

In a note appended to this passage in a subsequent edition, Yriarte wrote that

If [this] eulogium of Haydn were to be measured by the esteem in which his works are held at this moment in Madrid, it would appear exaggerated ... in the extreme. The author of this poem, without entering into any odious comparisons, or wishing his readers to be as partial to Haydn as he is himself, has contented himself with pointing out some prominent excellencies in the compositions of that great composer, which no one can dispute ... This eulogium, however, will be found inferior to his deserts by those who have heard his numerous symphonies ... his quintets, quartets, trios and sonatas; his oratorio, *Il ritorno di Tobia* ... his *Stabat mater*, etc.[125]

For most Spaniards, therefore, the taste for Haydn was a rarefied matter when Yriarte was writing. Who exactly was listening attentively to Haydn in Madrid, however, may be determined from correspondence and from evidence of early collections of his music in Spain. These indicate that he was first taken seriously by leading figures at the Spanish court, and by those with the most liberal and enlightened leanings in particular. Since these grandees applied directly to Haydn for his music, they must be considered among his first major patrons outside the Habsburg sphere of influence. That these same men and women were also among the earliest consistent patrons of Francisco Goya, the most impressive Spanish painter of the period, raises important issues concerning how two great creative forces, one a composer, the other a painter, were perceived in relation to each other by their contemporaries, first in Spain and later abroad. It also raises questions about what, if anything, these two figures knew of each other's work, one being resident exclusively at this time in Spain, the other spending much of his time in distant Hungary.

La música stresses the importance of music to social well-being. This favourite theme of the Enlightenment is even reinforced through the engravings which illustrate the poem, an indication that Yriarte had artistic as well as musical interests. In one of these plates, for example, a group of infants playing musical instruments is contrasted with a series of lone labourers working in the countryside, the significance of which is clarified by the caption: 'Art is no less agreeable and necessary to the man in society than to the recluse.'[126] Haydn might have seen this for himself since he possessed an illustrated edition of La música.[127]

The poem, however, was not Yriarte's first tribute to Haydn. In a verse-letter dated 20 May 1776, addressed to 'a Lady who inquired of the author what friends he had', Yriarte referred to the composer as one of three 'friends'. The others were the Roman poet Horace and the painter Mengs, who at the time of writing was primer pintor de camára (first painter) to Carlos III of Spain.[128] Haydn, Horace and Mengs were chosen as favourite representatives of each of the principal arts: music, poetry and painting. They may also have been selected because of their reputations for defining one art in relation to another. Horace was especially celebrated, for example, for his famous simile ut pictura poesis.[129] And according to Mengs's friend and patron Cavaliere d'Azara (who organized the publication of Mengs's writings after his death in 1779), the painter executed his last work in the style of a sonata by the composer Corelli.[130] Yriarte is likely to have been familiar with Mengs's pictorial theories developed during his last years in Spain. Characterizing painting in terms of music contributed to Azara's considering his friend a 'painter-philosopher'. Indeed the title pintor filósofo was used to describe both Mengs and Goya partly to draw attention to the range of extra-pictorial interests they brought to their work. It is not surprising therefore that in his 1776 letter featuring praise for the music of Haydn, a 'rare' composer, he distinguished it for being like 'painting without colouring'.[131]

Tomás de Yriarte's interests were chiefly literary and musical. His elder brother Bernardo, however, was a leading figure in promoting the visual arts in Madrid and a key politician advocating enlightened reform. A member of the Academy of San Fernando (the principal institution for the visual arts in

Spain), the elder Yriarte was appointed its Vice Protector in 1792. He was probably instrumental in organizing the opening of the galleries of the Academy to the public for ten days every year to exhibit works by teachers and students. Bernardo became friendly with Goya, who in 1794 asked him for advice about exhibiting a series of paintings at the Academy. Three years later Goya painted Bernardo's portrait. Tomás was therefore in an excellent position to view the musical and visual arts from an equal perspective.[132]

Although Carlos III is known to have despised most forms of musical activity,[133] he ensured that his children received musical instruction of the highest standards, resulting in tastes covering an international spectrum. Thus his son Ferdinand, who reigned as King of the Two Sicilies, took pleasure in performing on a modified version of a Neapolitan street instrument, the lira organizzata, for which Haydn was commissioned to write several compositions in the 1780s. More importantly, another son, the Prince of Asturias (the future Carlos IV), was taught to play the violin by the Italian Felipe Sabbatini.[134] Although Carlos III also secured a keyboard teacher for the Prince, it was the violin that Prince Carlos really enjoyed. When he was old enough to pursue his own interests, the court composer Gaetano Brunetti was employed to perfect the Prince's violin technique. In 1785, at the death of his disgraced uncle, Luis Antonio, Prince Carlos continued to pay the wages of the members of his uncle's large musical staff, including (briefly) the composer Luigi Boccherini. Luis Antonio had the distinction of being the first member of the royal family to value Goya, not merely as one of a large number of tapestry designers in royal service, but as a distinguished portraitist, Goya emerging as the artist with the talent and ability to fill the void left by the death of Mengs. Prince Carlos now also came to appreciate Goya, though as the painter himself noted after one of his visits to his royal patron, Carlos seemed more concerned with continuing his performance on the violin than in entering into dialogue with his painter.[135]

Until his appointment as court painter on the accession of Carlos IV in 1789, Goya's principal royal commissions had been for tapestry cartoons. Of the 63 designs he made before 1792, 20 were for tapestries to decorate the private rooms of Prince Carlos and his wife in the palace of El Pardo. In line with the wishes of Carlos III, the subjects of most of these cartoons reflect themes and preoccupations specifically Spanish in character. Many involve music-making and sometimes dancing, contributing to a trend which by 1787 had obliged Madrid to abandon Italian opera seria in favour of recognizable Spanish music, heard especially in comedies. In the same year William Beckford noted the craze at court for women singing 'gypsy' songs, which some artists are known to have taken the trouble to learn to lend authenticity to their pictures. Haydn's music was therefore one of the few cultural imports of this period which withstood the general vogue for asserting Spanish identity at every opportunity at the expense of things foreign.

By 1781 relations between Haydn and the Spanish court were so close that a Viennese newspaper reported the King of Spain to have unexpectedly rewarded Haydn, 'long celebrated through his original compositions', for music which the composer had sent to Madrid:

> [Haydn's] reward was a golden, jewel-studded tabatière and also what must far outweigh gold and jewels in the eye of a great artist, namely the flattering way it was presented. The Secretary of the Legation of the Spanish Court ... had, upon the explicit order of the monarch, to bring the present personally to Eszterháza and, apart from presenting the gift in person, he was to report to Madrid upon the box's delivery and also to assure [Haydn] of the ever well disposed wishes of his Catholic Majesty.[136]

Considering Carlos III's disdain for foreign music, it seems unlikely that he was personally responsible for such an elaborate tribute. It would have been Prince Carlos who masterminded this display of esteem. He was certainly the recipient of Haydn compositions sent to him by the composer. A complete score of Haydn's 1779 opera *L'isola disabitata*, bearing a flattering dedication addressed to the Prince by Haydn himself, survives as the clearest testimony of this.[137] But surviving sources indicate that Haydn sent copies of other compositions directly to the Prince, including Symphonies Nos 62 and 74 (both written *c*.1780) and probably a series of baryton trios (originally composed for Prince Miklós I) with the baryton part designated for violin. Pasticcios (re)arranged or derived from other compositions may also have been sent during the later 1770s or at the beginning of the 1780s. The Spanish court, presumably on instructions from Prince Carlos, also acquired from Vienna a score of *Il ritorno di Tobia*, understandably in view of the fact that its libretto was written by Luigi Boccherini's brother. Other sources show that the Prince expanded his collection of Haydn scores and performance material to include no fewer than 55 orchestral works (mostly symphonies) by the time he ascended the throne in 1789; and with a new team of copyists he seems to have continued the collection thereafter, with many of Haydn's late symphonies featuring by the later 1790s.

Prince Carlos evidently had a sustained and deep interest in Haydn. The composer's decision to send his *L'isola disabitata* to Spain in response to requests for his music was certainly a shrewd move. Even were Haydn unaware of the disdain for Italian opera in court circles in Madrid (which seems unlikely), *L'isola disabitata* (though in Italian) was largely free of those features which caused critics like Carlos III to hold opera in contempt. Alone among Haydn's operas, *L'isola disabitata* is composed with continuous orchestral accompaniment to the action, rather than the alternation of *secco* recitatives and arias usually associated with Italian opera. The opera was based on a libretto by Metastasio, the friend of the castrato Farinelli, who (still in living memory) had been responsible for much of the musical entertainment at the Spanish court in the years before the accession of Carlos III, one of whose first actions as King had been to dismiss him. However, in contrast to most Metastasio libretti, *L'isola disabitata* is a comparatively short, small-scale work, with a simple, unaffected story line involving just four characters. Free from complicated subplots, the action is set not in the elegant palaces and cities usually expected of Italian opera, but in the wild. The natural emotions displayed by each character in turn, their sincerity and naive charm, would doubtless have struck a chord with a Spanish audience looking for values deemed true-to-life, down-to-earth, and free from affectation and over-refinement. Haydn's use of *concertante* elements, the sonorities of different instruments skilfully employed to help distinguish the various temperaments of the characters, would evidently have enhanced the effect. Although the work is predominantly serious in tone, comic touches stemming from misapprehensions about the opposite sex would certainly have been appreciated in Madrid. When the 14-year-old Silvia, who has never before seen a man (and has been taught by her elder sister that all men are faithless beasts), first sees Enrico she assumes he cannot be a man because of his handsome appearance; in fact he seems so very handsome that she cannot help herself being attracted to him in a way she has never previously experienced.

L'isola disabitata, and perhaps other works by Haydn sent to the Prince, may have been understood as having aesthetic objectives common to Goya's tapestry designs of the same period, also undertaken for the Prince. Both the opera and the tapestries feature few characters, engaged in straightforward activities, taking place in natural settings, with much incident and amusing details. Soon after the Prince became Carlos IV, he specifically requested of Goya that his tapestry designs should be *jocoso* (humorous or facetious). Indeed the tastes in music cultivated by the Prince, and what these tastes were supposed to convey about him, provide a good parallel to his attitudes towards the visual arts. The Prince evidently wished to indicate that he understood the popular trends of the day based on traditional Spanish culture, though he aspired to rise above them, embracing notions which suggested that he was a man of the Enlightenment, with broader European roots. To demonstrate his liberal credentials he, like other leading members of Spanish society, needed to develop critical skills to be able to judge the arts and predilections for the latest international cultural trends. It was also helpful to present himself as receptive to what was provocative or out of the ordinary.

Such aims, of course, bordered on the pretentious, and their expression might appear on occasions ridiculous. A letter written by Goya in early 1783 describes the reception given a painting by Francisco Bayeu, Goya's brother-in-law, when presented at the Palace.[138] After the King had seen the picture, and '*as usual*' commented on it "Good, good, good", Prince Carlos and his wife 'came to see it':

They have never had a good word for Bayeu, but they criticize him constantly – everyone knows they are impossible to please. Don Juan de Villanueva, the architect, arrived and the Prince asked him what he thought of the picture. 'Very good, Your Highness', he replied. 'You're a fool,' said the Prince, 'this painting has *no chiaroscuro, no effect* of any sort, and *very little*, if any, *merit*. Go and tell Bayeu he's a complete idiot.' ... Some say that the Prince was speaking as if he knew something about art, but he doesn't understand very much.

For Bayeu such an experience was obviously humiliating and illustrates a negative side to court patronage. But since several Academicians witnessed the event, it may in part be interpreted as the Prince making a show of exercising his own critical judgement and displaying his 'knowledge' in contrast to the King's apparent lack of discrimination. Although the attempt may not have impressed Goya, in the long term Goya himself was the clear beneficiary of the Prince's determination to rely on his own assessments of artistic matters.

Carlos's distinct enthusiasm for Haydn may be seen in the same light, distinguishing the Prince as a patron abreast of the most refined tastes on offer and receptive to what would have been automatically rejected by most of the society of which he was a part. The kind of distinction he rather bluntly drew between Bayeu ('the complete idiot') and Goya (in a position to pay visits to the Prince) is reflected in a similar story about the composer Boccherini. Apparently the Prince, probably around 1780, asked to perform as a violinist in one of this composer's quintets.[139] Carlos was given a rather monotonous part to play, and unable to appreciate the parts of the other players around him, quickly grew frustrated: 'This is abominable! Any beginner could write stuff like this.' The composer urged the Prince to persevere, only to find the music soon referred to as the work of 'a bad beginner'. Boccherini was now bold enough to suggest that before pronouncing judgement an adequate 'understanding' of music was appropriate. This was too much for the Prince, who refused Boccherini admittance to his household again. Although Boccherini (like Bayeu) may have been treated shabbily by Carlos, one inference which may be drawn from this episode is that, from the Prince's point of view, other composers (notably Haydn), provided him with superior music. Haydn's position was in the Prince's scheme of things equivalent to Goya's. Just as Haydn kept his popularity with a small number of enthusiasts in later eighteenth-century Madrid, so Goya retained his own popularity among an almost equally small number of enthusiasts in the same city, most of whom were in common. Both composer and painter enjoyed the same limited though loyal public, which was affluent, powerful and apparently appreciative of even the most unconventional aspects of their creativity.

Another patron who went to considerable lengths to support both Haydn and Goya was the Countess of Benavente, the future Duchess of Osuna, one of the most wealthy and cultured women of her age, who ran a prominent musical establishment in Madrid.[140] A contract was drawn up on 20 October 1783 between Haydn and a Spanish representative in Vienna, Carlos Alejandro de Lelis, who in his dealings with the composer negotiated with Tomás de Yriarte acting on the Duchess's behalf.[141] The contract was amended in February 1785, the terms of which obliged Haydn to give *all* his compositions to Lelis, except work undertaken in fulfilment of private commissions. At least twelve orchestral or instrumental compositions had to be included annually, eight of which were to be symphonies. This arrangement seems to have been effective until at least 1789. It probably worked for Haydn since he could draw on a considerable number of compositions originally written much earlier for Eszterháza, unlikely to have been known in Spain. However, in leading the Spanish to think he was providing them with new works, Haydn was almost caught out since the Duchess requested chamber works for unusual combinations of instruments, which could not easily be satisfied by rearranging pre-existing material. According to a letter by Lelis of 24 March 1785, the Duchess had asked for quartets for oboe, 'trompa' (probably horn), violin and cello, a rare combination, though one which seems to have found favour in Paris.[142] Haydn actually sent the Duchess two quartets without wind instruments, claiming by way of apology that he could not write well for wind, the most disingenuous of excuses, as the sharp-witted Duchess would certainly have recognized.

An assessment of the Duchess of Osuna written in 1803 by Lady Holland gives a good insight into her distinctive qualities:

> [The Duchess] is the most distinguished woman in Madrid from her talents, worth and taste. She has acquired a relish for French luxuries, without diminishing her national magnificence and hospitality. She is very lively, and her natural wit covers her total want of refinement and acquirement. Her figure is very light and airy. She was formerly the great rival of the celebrated D[uche]ss of Alba in profligacy and profusion. ... Her revenues are greater even than the D[uke] of Osuna's, who is a very tolerable sensible man and of considerable knowledge.[143]

Lady Holland also described El Capricho at La Alameda, the Osunas' private country retreat, for which Goya provided a series of paintings in 1786–87 and others later:

> The distance from Madrid is about a league and a quarter on the road to Alcalá de Henares. It is a creation of her own, as she found 24 years ago the same sterility and nakedness which characterizes the environs of Madrid; it is now cheerful and woody. The garden is rather crowded with a profusion of diff[eren]t ornaments, some in the German sentimental taste, others in a tawdry, citizenlike style. Gardens contrived for coolness, innumerable grottoes, temples, *chaumières*, hermitages, excavations, canal, ports, pleasure boats, islands, mounts, &c., &c., *La Casa della vieja* is very pretty. The mansion is excellent and well fitted up.[144]

Judging from the grounds created by the Duchess, she wished to include almost every sophistication in garden design derived from fashions belonging to several European nations in the later eighteenth century. The Duchess's musical preferences were apparently based on similar principles. For example, the set of 24 minuets and 24 'other dances' which Haydn sent her before 22 April 1789 were clearly dances of northern European origin by a German-speaking composer.[145] Such cosmopolitanism also extended to her attire. Whereas many of Goya's sitters expected to be depicted wearing Spanish costume, his first portrait of the future Duchess, completed in 1785, shows her dressed in the latest French style.[146] The group portrait of the Osunas with their four children, painted by Goya in 1788 to commemorate their succession to the title, extends this sense of fashion still further, not only through the sitters' dress and the heightened feeling for light and atmosphere Goya brought to a complicated composition, but also in terms of the very conception of the portrait, which seems to owe something to a knowledge of Gainsborough.[147] The English portraitist's works would have been known in Spain by this date through prints, which may have been drawn to Goya's attention by the Duchess herself. The inclusion of toys and pets in this family portrait perhaps reflects the couple's desire to bring up their children according to the most enlightened principles of the day, which some contemporaries would have found excessively liberal, not to be advertised in a portrait.

Apart from portraits of the Osunas, Goya also executed for them several other sets of paintings, beginning with seven decorative *asuntos de campo* (country scenes) for La Alameda, originally set into the walls of one of the principal saloons. The subject-matter in these scenes clearly derives from themes favoured in the designs for the royal tapestries; but since the La Alameda series was always intended to be seen in the medium of paint, Goya was able to express himself with greater immediacy, the paintings having more bite to them, often with a hint of menace or social comment, doubtless encouraged in Goya by the Duchess. The set shows a great range of invention. At one extreme is a rather joyful, undemanding picture of a woman swinging, of the type painted by Fragonard in the 1770s, and at the other extreme is a rather morbid scene set on a building site, where an accident has taken place, which Goya himself described in submitting his account for the painting: '... a pair of oxen carry a stone and a poor man who has hurt himself is carried on a ladder by three carters who look as if they are sorry for him'.[148] This darker side of Goya's creativity also found expression in some of the designs he worked on at the same time for tapestries originally destined for Prince Carlos's dining-room at El Pardo, the sketches for which (like others originally presented to the King) were acquired by the Osunas and displayed in the Duchess's study.[149] The subject matter of these cartoons stemmed from the tradition of depicting the four Seasons, a theme Haydn was later to take up.

The design for *Winter* shows the full force of a snow storm, the wintry blast taking its toll on a group of travellers on foot.

Even more sinister in tone is one of two large paintings commissioned by the future Duchess of Osuna for a chapel in Valencia Cathedral, for which she had responsibility, completed in 1788.[150] The painting shows an episode in the life of St Francis Borgia, an ancestor of the Duchess. The saint stands at the end of the bed of an impenitent man dying in convulsed agony. Beside the expiring man appears a group of terrifying monstrous apparitions, glaring or grinning at him, including one featuring the head of a goat and another with the wings of a bat, its claws resting on the bed. The tiny figure of Christ on the crucifix held aloft by the astonished saint is miraculously shown as having come to life, pointing towards the impenitent and sending streams of blood over him, spattering the bed clothes. This is far from being a conventional religious image of the eighteenth century. Goya's nightmarish vision is known to have impressed local artists; the power of its message for believers, and potentially also for unbelievers, was unmistakable.

Goya's disturbing use of the supernatural in the *Impenitent* was clearly to the taste of the Osunas; in 1798 they acquired for La Alameda a cycle of six paintings by Goya on fantastic subjects connected with witchcraft or the supernatural, featuring flying witches, a black sabbath with an infernal goat, an exorcism and other demonic occurrences.[151] One of the subjects was *Don Juan and the Stone Guest*, drawn from the famous play by Tirso de Molina (published in 1630), or from the later reworking of the legend by Antonio de Zamora, which formed the basis of several eighteenth-century operas, including the *Don Giovanni* of Mozart and Lorenzo Da Ponte (1788). In 1781 Haydn directed an operatic version of the story, the one composed in 1776 by Vincenzo Righini, which was partly reworked for performance at Eszterháza.[152] The popularity of this Spanish subject elsewhere in Europe may therefore have been partly responsible for the painted version delivered to the Osunas in 1798. Indeed since Haydn was preparing to perform it at the very time he was visited by a delegation from the Spanish court in 1781, this may have counted for something with patrons in Madrid interested in both Haydn and Goya. Whatever the case, it seems clear that the Duchess of Osuna played a forceful role in encouraging Goya to develop imaginative and very individualist subject matter, just as she tried, though apparently unsuccessfully, to persuade Haydn to compose for out-of-the-ordinary combinations of instruments, which she seems to have thought would develop his musical frame of reference.

One further patron of Goya at this time did, however, succeed in commissioning from Haydn original compositions of his choosing as well as in building up an enormous collection of the composer's music. This was the Duke of Alba, whose beautiful wife Cayetana became the social rival of the Duchess of Osuna and belonged to one of the leading families in Spain, traditionally associated with musical activities.[153] The Duke's own interest in music in general, and Haydn in particular, is evident from the portrait of him by Goya datable to 1795.[154] Portraits associating their sitters with music, though common elsewhere in Europe, were unusual in Spain at this date, so in this work Alba was evidently making a statement about the importance of music in his life, distinguishing himself personally from the bulk of Spanish society, and connecting his world with the mainstream of European culture. Goya was clearly happy to oblige him in these prerequisites and has portrayed him leaning against a keyboard instrument on which rests a violin. The Duke is shown holding open some sheets of music, the cover of which bears an inscription in Spanish: 'Cuatro canc.s / con Acomp.t de Forzp.o / del Sr Haydn' (Four songs with Fortepiano accompaniment by Sr Haydn).

It is possible that this collection of songs may be identical with four lost (German) songs which are only known through incipits written by Haydn, the date of which cannot now be determined (Hob. XXVIa: 48a–d). However, it is equally likely that these pieces were a selection from the two well-known sets of songs by Haydn to German texts published by Artaria in 1781 and 1784, which sources indicate may have been available in groups of four songs only (Hob. XXVIa: 1–24).[155] What the Duke holds is clearly *not* a published edition, printed music being rare in Spain, but a manuscript. Since Goya had recently become deaf at the time that Alba sat for him, it must be assumed that the decision to refer to these Haydn songs in the portrait was the Duke's rather than the artist's; the manuscript and the care taken over the inscription therefore point to it representing some favourite pieces of music, which perhaps he himself was fond of singing. The choice may conceivably have been aimed at his wife, who sat for Goya at the same time in a pendant portrait (dated 1795) and subsequently was the recipient of several personal works painted by him. Her open rejection of the refined values associated with foreign culture, and her adoption of the fashion and customs of ordinary Spaniards made a deep impact on elevated Madrid society in the later eighteenth century. Moreover, her amorous affairs were well known. Many of the Haydn songs (including the four now lost) were about love. One example is *Cupido* (Hob. XXVIa: 2), which describes how Cupid shoots his arrows, bringing lovesickness to a young woman: 'and nothing can relieve the pain, except a man'. There is evidence that after the Duke's death, Cayetana became on intimate terms with Goya.[156] Some special affection between the artist and his sitter is already evident in Goya's 1795 portrait of the Duchess. She is shown as though pointing down to an inscription drawn in the ground, Goya's signature, written in the form of a dedication to her with the date. This inscribed tribute to the Duchess may be seen to juxtapose with the inscription on the matching portrait of the Duke, referring to Haydn, which appears on an object held up by the sitter, the inference being that the respective interests of the two sitters are being sharply contrasted in order to characterize their personalities and the differences between them. A comparison between looking (the pointing Duchess) and listening (the musical Duke) also seems to have been intended by the artist, who had lost his own hearing.

Goya painted the cover of the manuscript with such detail that it seems likely to have been based on something owned by the Duke. However, the fact that it is written in Spanish rather than in Italian, the language which was generally used in connection with music in most grand aristocratic establishments in Spain at this time, seems to exclude the possibility that this reproduces accurately an actual manuscript in the Duke's possession. The title here given to Haydn ('Sr', rather than the 'Dr' by which he was generally known after 1791) and especially the form of decoration on the cover are features consistent with manuscripts written by copyists actually used by the composer himself in the mid-1780s. It seems possible therefore that the manuscript Goya painted was derived from something originating in Vienna, modified for the purposes of the commission. If this is so then Goya's portrait of Alba provides evidence of compositions sent to the Duke directly from Austria at that time.

Unfortunately this hypothesis may not be easily checked since the Duke's musical legacy has been lost, destroyed in two disastrous fires, one in the very year that Goya painted the Duke's portrait.[157] None the less, the surviving correspondence of Lelis shows that Alba commissioned directly from Haydn some 'quartets' at some point in the first half of the 1780s, for which he was still waiting two years after the order had been accepted. It seems very probable that these works are those referred to by Haydn himself in a letter to Artaria dated 5 April 1784: 'those quartets which I am presently at work on, of which half are now ready, are very brief and consist of three movements [*Stuck*] only; they are [intended] for Spain'.[158] Elsewhere in the same letter the composer mentions quartets (definitely string quartets) which he says he is working on and which he expects Artaria to publish. These are probably the set of six quartets published as Op. 50 in 1787. But Haydn distinguishes between these and those 'intended for Spain', which are not for publication, at least not by Artaria. It has often been suggested that the single short string quartet in D minor, now known as Op. 42, is one of the quartets written for Spain and therefore destined for the Duke of Alba. The autograph of this quartet, distinguished by comparison with the quartets of Op. 50 by its brevity, concise style and technical ease (features which might well have been stipulated by the Duke), is dated 1785. So if Haydn was truthful to Artaria in April 1784 in saying that he was at that very moment working on *quartets* for Spain, which took priority over the quartets the Viennese firm hoped to publish, it seems that there is at least one *lost* quartet written for Alba.

Op. 42 was published by Hoffmeister, Artaria's rival in Vienna, in 1786. Why this particular quartet, apparently destined for Spain, should have been singled out for publication is unclear, as is the survival of its autograph – those of its companions have evidently perished, assuming they ever existed. Perhaps Haydn in his haste to fulfil obligations to Spain, at a very busy stage in his career, sent the autographs of the lost quartets in 1784 without keeping copies of them, contrary to his usual practice. Later, when he wrote Op. 42, he ensured that he did not make the same mistake again, and under pressure to publish works of this type in Vienna, he gave it to Hoffmeister. Whatever the case, there is no doubt that the Duke of Alba relished Haydn quartets. Part of the collection of Haydn music copied for Prince Carlos includes a set of parts of the Op. 17 quartets, each headed 'Bibla. Villafranca'.[159] Villafranca was the Duke's family name, so these parts were probably taken from his library and never returned.

When Goya worked for the Duke and Duchess of Alba in 1795 he had probably long been familiar with the name (and music) of Haydn. Apart from members of the court who commissioned paintings from him and also enthused about Haydn, there were others far from Madrid, in Cádiz, who valued the painter and his work, and who also admired Haydn.

Cádiz had a reputation as a liberal city. An English visitor in the 1780s claimed to find there 'a more liberal way of thinking, a character even of luxury and vice from the rest of the nation; more cheerful manners, more confidence, credit, sociability ...'.[160] Goya was in Cádiz during two prolonged periods in 1792–93 and in 1796–97 (following a stay at the Andalucian estate of the Duchess of Alba, where she went after the death of her husband). On both occasions he was recuperating from serious illness, the first of which left him with temporary paralysis in the hands and rendered him permanently deaf. During his first visit he stayed at the home of Sebastián Martínez, one of the most prolific and individual collectors of works of art and literature related to art in eighteenth-century Spain (he owned 743 paintings, including works attributed to Murillo, Velázquez, Rubens, Batoni and Mengs); and on the second occasion Goya seems to have lodged with the writer Leandro Fernández de Moratín, who had recently returned from an extended visit to England and other northern European countries. The experience of Goya's visits to Cádiz has been recognized as playing a crucial role in his subsequent artistic development, chiefly through the stimulation offered him by his mutual friends, Martínez and Moratín.

Goya's portrait of Martínez indicates the painter's undoubted regard for his sitter since it is inscribed (on the verso of an engraving held in the sitter's hand) 'D.n Sebastian / Martinez / Por su Amigo / Goya / 1792'.[161] The portrait was presumably painted at the beginning of the painter's first visit to Cádiz. With his wig, cravat and fine silk French-style dress-coat, Martínez as seen by Goya suggests a person of great refinement and mature tastes: his business interests were based on trading in wine and fabrics (including silk). But in terms of fashion, he appears slightly behind the times, perhaps intentionally, to convey a hint of caution in his personality, rather like Haydn at much the same date. The informality of the pose (Martínez is casually seated) and the sincerity of his gaze (he looks straight at the viewer), however, reveal a confident trustfulness, which he no doubt expressed in the artist himself. Probably after recovering from illness Goya painted a series of three overdoors for Martínez's house in Cádiz, each showing a reclining female figure provocatively attired, sleeping or dozing. The two which have been clearly identified today are painted very softly, suggesting a dream-like quality. After his recuperation sleep seems to have been associated by Goya with reason and artistic imagination, two of the driving forces of the Enlightenment. In one print from the set called the *Caprichos* (published in 1799), a seated sleeping painter, with sinister creatures flying up behind him, is captioned 'The sleep of reason produces monsters' (No. 43). In an early commentary on the plate, possibly written by Goya himself, the image is given an even more lucid explanation: 'Imagination abandoned by reason produces impossible monsters: united with her, she is the mother of the arts and the source of wonders.'[162] The sleeping women Goya painted for Martínez suggest therefore that the artist's notion of the value of dreaming to the artistic temperament first inspired him creatively during the time he spent in Cádiz. Martínez's magnificent collection of prints, to which Goya would have had access, may have been a catalyst for the artist, not only leading him to see the medium of print-making as a possibility for greater self-expression in his work, but also providing him with examples of fantastic imagery which he later developed further himself.[163]

Martínez's collection featured a considerable range of prints by all the leading engravers, as well as prints after major Old Master paintings. It also contained a significant number of prints after paintings by contemporary artists, particularly from England. An item in Martínez's inventory, for example, for 'Saul consulting the Witch [of Endor]' is probably the engraving published by Boydell in the late 1780s after the picture of this subject by a painter who Haydn himself later sought out when he was in London, Benjamin West.[164] Goya's slightly later series of paintings on supernatural and witchcraft themes for the Duchess of Osuna might well have been precipitated by a work of this kind, which combines terrifying imagery with the power of the unknown. West's electrifying evocation of the Prophet Samuel brought back from the grave in order that the King might consult him causes Saul to collapse on the ground with his arms outstretched. The figure of the risen Prophet is particularly frightening because his face is unseen (as also is Saul's), covered by the shroud draped over his head, so his expression has to be left to the imagination of the viewer. West probably derived this device from Pliny's famous description of Timanthes's painting of the *Sacrifice of Iphigenia*, in which the artist showed Agamemnon hiding his face in his cloak unable to witness the death of his daughter, the idea being that the terrible inner turmoil experienced by the father (who had unwittingly brought about the sacrifice) could not adequately be portrayed in art.[165] What may be a reflection of West's borrowing of this device is the principal figure in the third of Goya's *Caprichos,* called 'el coco' (the bogey-man), who is completely shrouded, as is West's Samuel, and terrifies a little girl who extends her arms in the manner of West's Saul. The sense of fear potentially conveyed to an audience by depicting figures whose facial expression is hidden made such an impact on Goya that he periodically exploited the device throughout his remaining career.

In Cádiz Goya was probably introduced to another kind of print developed in England which made a great impression on the course of his art, caricature.[166] His friend Moratín was certainly fascinated by them, as is revealed in his diary (which also includes several references to Goya):

> The English caricatures are very amusing: there are stalls in London that may be called shops, so great is their number. Everything is a fit subject for these plates: literature, morality, and politics especially, provide material of all kinds for those who manufacture those grotesque squibs, and are thus able to bring out new inventions every day. ... A caricature often supplements or even exceeds criticism or the bitterest satire. I have seen the manners of every country, its customs and even its virtues ridiculed in these sheets: the gravity of the English magistrates, the affectation of the young women, the vigour of elderly women, the vanity of noblemen, the baseness of men of fashion and courtesans, in short all the vices of man in society are exposed to laughter and public scorn. Debates in Parliament, Ministers' projects, Government resolutions, political affairs, national or foreign, all are depicted, sometimes by the use of allegory, sometimes by narrative compositions. They show the King of England shitting into a chamber-pot while holding a privy council with his Ministers portrayed as wolves, weasels, foxes and birds of prey. ... In others, the Prince of Wales is seen springing from a runaway phaeton and is depicted falling upon his mistress Lady Fitz-Herbert, who is already on the ground, stomach in the air and legs splayed ready to receive him. In others Lord Macartney, the English Ambassador, kisses the behind of the Emperor of China with great devotion.[167]

As will become evident at a later stage in this book, Haydn was also fascinated by caricatures of exactly the same kind, and at much the same date, as those described by Moratín. Their mixture of satirical vulgarity, comic ridicule, and social or political commentary evidently intrigued him, and arguably played a part in determining the character of some of his late large-scale instrumental compositions intended for public consumption. Coming from a country where there were no visual traditions, at least in published form, for satirizing the Establishment, works by Gillray (Fig. 20) and others in the same tradition came as a revelation.

The same is true of Goya, whose considerable experience of the precepts of English caricature, as described by Moratín, is evident in many of the *Caprichos.*[168] But unlike the caricaturists based in London, who never feared poking fun at the most personal level, Goya generalizes the satire, thereby perhaps hoping to escape censure by the Spanish authorities. As the first advertisement of the series in a Madrid newspaper indicates: 'In none of the compositions which form part of the collection has the author proposed to ridicule the particular defects of any one individual ...'.[169] A second advertisement makes the position even plainer: 'The Author, convinced that the censure of human errors and vices can be as much the subject of painting as it is of eloquence and poetry, has chosen for his work themes from the multitude of follies and wrong-doings which are common to society ...'.[170] Issues such as the abuse of power, indifference to injustice, the neglect of education, the arrogance of the nobility and social evils (such as prostitution) were taken up by the artist and set starkly before the eyes of his audience to provoke outrage, to entertain and to urge humanity to do better. But again, unlike the London caricaturists, Goya's ridicule places the emphasis on moral indignation rather than on humour. The cumulative effect of the eighty plates also leads one to suppose that there remains very little hope for mankind; the message becomes ever darker as the visual imagination strives to give expression to ever bleaker thoughts.

This dark strand in Goya's creativity may be (and often has been) related to his illnesses and the state of mind in which these left him. But one other experience connected with Cadíz may also have been a contributory factor. A short distance from Martínez's house in Cadíz is the elliptical Oratory of the Santa Cueva, constructed between 1793 and 1796 by the neoclassical architect Torcuato José Benjumeda. Goya would have witnessed the building work in progress during his recovery. About 1795 he received a commission from the oratory (perhaps instigated by Martínez) for three lunette-shaped paintings, probably completed by the time of its consecration in March 1796.[171] Evidence that Goya conceived the compositions for his own paintings in conjunction with Martínez comes from a visual source unambiguously used by Goya in designing the central painting of the series, a *Last Supper* intended for a position high above the entrance to the chapel, overlooking the altar. The composition is based on Poussin's representation of the same subject in *Eucharist* (Fig. 9), one of a series of paintings representing the Seven Sacraments (1647). The original Santa Cueva was the meeting-place of a religious confraternity for devotion to the Sacrament of Eucharist. Since the iconographic series to which Goya's painting belongs complements the Eucharistic theme, Poussin's famous painting would have been an obvious source.[172] Goya could not have known the painting itself, but was presumably familiar with its composition through an engraving of it in Martínez's collection.[173] As a painter admired in the eighteenth century for 'the moral and intellectual seriousness' of his subjects,[174] Poussin might well have been suggested to Goya as a model for the Cádiz commission by Martínez.

Before construction work on the oratory began Goya would also have known the *original* Santa Cueva (Holy Cave), built in 1756, above which the oratory was erected. It was for this grotto that Haydn composed what in his lifetime was to become one of his most popular works, *The Seven Last Words of Our Saviour on the Cross*, intended as part of the commemorations for Good Friday, probably first performed in Cádiz in 1787, and in all likelihood in subsequent years as well.[175] Like Goya's paintings for the same foundation, *The Seven Last Words* seems to have been the idea of a local priest, Don José Sáenz de Santa María, Marqués de Valdeíñigo, who may have conceived both music and paintings as part of a distinctive programme of meditations and devotions intended for the Confraternity.

Unfortunately, the original documentation and performing material of this music has been lost, but an account of how it came into being was dictated by Haydn to Griesinger in 1801 to act as a preface to the publication of *The Seven Last Words* in its vocal arrangement:

> It is about fifteen years since I was asked by a clergyman in Cádiz to provide instrumental music for the Seven Words of Jesus on the Cross. It was then the custom, every year at Easter, to perform an oratorio in the Cathedral of Cádiz, and the following arrangements must have contributed in no small measure to the effectiveness of the performance. The walls, windows and columns of the Cathedral were draped in black cloth, and only one large lamp, hanging in the centre, lighted the religious darkness. At noon all the doors were closed; then the music began. After a suitable prelude the Bishop ascended the pulpit, pronounced one of the seven Words, and followed it with his comments. When he had finished, he descended from the pulpit and fell on his knees before the altar. This pause was filled by music. The Bishop ascended and descended a second time, a third, and so on, and each time the orchestra resumed at the conclusion of his discourse. My composition must be judged in the light of these circumstances, The task of producing a succession of seven Adagios, each of which was to last about ten minutes, without wearying the listener, was no easy one; and I soon found that I could not keep to the prescribed duration. The music was originally without text, and in that form it has been printed [1787] ... The partiality with which this work has been received by discerning connoisseurs leads me to hope that it will not fail to make an impression on the public at large.[176]

By the time this was written Haydn's memory was either failing or (more likely) he deliberately distorted the original venue to make the occasion seem more imposing, as he already had done when the piece was performed in England in 1791.[177] It is hard to imagine the windows of a whole cathedral blacked out in order to produce the 'religious darkness' required for the occasion, though such an effect would have been easily achieved in the grotto. Clearly for Haydn the experience of listening to this music was enhanced by controlling in visual terms the environment in which it was performed. Darkness intensified the beauty and power of the music. Even if performance in these conditions was not feasible, then *imagining* them was advantageous for favourable listening, hence the trouble Haydn went to in describing them in the 1801 foreword. Taking into account the lighting effects of venues for music-making was something which undoubtedly interested Haydn, as the circumstances of the original performance of the 'Farewell' symphony demonstrates. The composer was evidently receptive to the notion that what one sees conditions the way one hears. Indeed it seems possible that the authorities in Cádiz may have been aware of the story of the 'Farewell' symphony, and this acted as an inducement to approach Haydn for this particular and very unusual commission, in which an audience (congregation) were prevailed on to respond both visually and musically to the theme of Christ's last earthly utterances and death. As a commentator on the piece wrote after hearing a performance in Bonn at Easter 1787: 'The idea of expressing these thoughts [Christ's seven last words] by purely instrumental music is *curious* and *daring* and only a genius like Haydn would take such a risk.'[178]

According to Dies, Haydn was taken to task in some quarters for (apparently) attempting the meaning of the words through music in *The Seven Last Words*. Dies jumps to Haydn's defence, explaining that 'The objective was to excite the listener's feelings. The spoken words acted only to *guide* those feelings in the right way.'[179] As an artist, Dies was particularly anxious to convey the visual aspects of Haydn's composition, recognizing that in its conception '*several arts were brought together on friendly terms*', which 'secretly help to enhance the effect'.[180] After describing the setting for the original performance (coinciding exactly with Haydn's 1801 description), Dies says:

> Consequently, the music might effortlessly move hearts already worked upon into a state of extreme sensibility and keep them there. The dark, barely lit church offered *the eye* no object to distract its attention. [An image of] *Christ on the cross* was the only *visible* object on which it must fix itself. The overt pomp that otherwise always accompanies services of the Catholic Church is completely absent. The listener will be taken unawares by a really disarming simplicity, and his feeling for the religious will be totally engaged.[181]

If the original circumstances of the performance are not recreated, Dies suggests that the music will be 'robbed of a significant aspect of its existence', and it will no longer have 'the powerful effect that it has on listeners in Cádiz'.[182]

Since some aspects of Haydn's 1801 account of the first Cádiz performance of his *Seven Last Words* – decking the walls, *windows*, and columns of the church with black cloth – cannot be accurate in terms of what in fact took place, it needs to be asked what inspired this description. The idea of a darkened space (reiterated by Dies), with columns, windows blocked to prevent daylight shining through, draped black cloths and '*only one large lamp, hanging in the centre*' corresponds closely to Poussin's *Eucharist*, which inspired Goya in his central image for the Santa Cueva. If this observation is tenable, then it seems likely that the commission given to Haydn from Cádiz included some description or perhaps even a copy of this painting which stayed in his mind at the time of composition and long afterwards. This strengthens the suggestion that Goya's friend Martínez, who owned the engraving after Poussin which influenced his painter-friend, was not only crucial to Goya's participation in the decoration of the oratory, but also played a part in drawing up the commission for Haydn, and possibly the choice of composer.

Martínez was clearly the kind of intellectual figure, rather aloof from most of Spanish elevated society, who would have revered Haydn, like the Duchess of Osuna and the Duke of Alba. Although his collections show that his principal interests were in the visual arts, some items point to a concern for music. For example, Martínez possessed a French edition of James Beattie's *An Essay on Poetry and Music as they Affect the Mind*, first published in Edinburgh in 1776.[183] This is a revealing item for Martínez to have owned since the author was concerned not only with the relationship between poetry and music, but also the relationship between music and painting, which he alludes to throughout his discussion of music.[184] Beattie disagrees with earlier authorities, such as Dubos and Batteux, that music is imitative in the same sense as found in painting. He suggests – Handel's *Water Music* and Corelli's Christmas Concerto (often claimed at the time to be based on a Nativity scene) are given as examples – that musical images derive from association, not from anything intrinsic in the music. Vocal music is in his view superior to instrumental music because, being united with poetry, it conveys absolute ideas, not just general sentiments. It was perhaps just such a view that Haydn and his patrons in Cádiz were trying to challenge in *The Seven Last Words*, originally a purely instrumental piece which makes use of devices (of association) to convey images and feelings stemming from Christ's death on the Cross.[185] However, Beattie also argued that 'the end of *all* genuine music is to introduce into the human mind certain affections or susceptibilities of affection', a notion which Haydn and his listeners would certainly have applauded. Beattie's notion that the production of music should act towards the betterment of humanity, helping to create a more just and tolerant society, would also have struck a chord in the thinking of Martínez and those in his circle, including Goya, who after his stay in Cádiz took up these principles in his own art, especially evident in the *Caprichos*.

Evidence therefore supports the view that Martínez may have played a part in drawing up the commission from Cádiz for Haydn's *Seven Last Words*.[186] This makes it all the more likely that when Goya was first in the city (before losing his hearing) he experienced the composition in some form, perhaps attending a Good Friday performance in the Santa Cueva, in the kind of darkened surroundings described by the composer and conceived by Sáenz de Santa María, perhaps with the help of Martínez. It is known that the piece was given annually in Cádiz for many years after it was written, always in the circumstances in which it was first intended.[187] Given that it is known to have caused a stir among those who first heard it elsewhere in Europe, even in customary performing conditions, on someone like Goya a performance of the piece as originally envisaged would probably have made a considerable impact. The generally slow, sustained music meditating on Christ's suffering would have been compelling enough; but followed by the violent force of the music describing the earthquake and the darkness at Christ's death in the final movement, it is possible to see that for someone of Goya's disposition, the effect might have been considerable. It arguably may also have been a contributory factor in the darker outlook he brought to his art thereafter.

Goya might have become curious about Haydn at this point in his career, not only on account of the composer looming large in the interests of his leading patrons (Carlos IV, the Osunas, the Albas and perhaps Martínez), but because the earliest attention paid to the artist outside of his native country came from Austria. When Goya made his first venture into print-making in 1778, etching eight of Velázquez's paintings, it was the Viennese representative in Madrid, P.P. Giusti, who seems to have taken most notice.[188] In a letter to Kaunitz, Giusti spoke of 'An event which is not without significance for the development of the Fine Arts in this country', meaning Goya's etchings, a set of which accompanied his letter. Giusti continued: 'If the author [Goya], who is a painter and not an engraver, and the first to try this particular manner of engraving in Spain, continues to improve and has the courage to persevere, the set will make an important contribution to the world of the arts. It will also prove instructive to other artists ...'.[189]

Kaunitz was of course at this time trying to build up print-making at the Vienna Akademie. It seems very likely, since Goya did indeed 'improve' and found 'the courage to persevere', that Kaunitz and others in Vienna would have sought to obtain other works from the artist, perhaps through Giusti, who became a corresponding member of the Royal Academy of History in Madrid in 1781.[190] Evidence that the Kaunitz family maintained an interest in Goya at a time when he was still otherwise largely unknown outside Spain comes from the acquisition by Prince Alois Wenzel Kaunitz (the Chancellor's nephew) of two paintings by the artist datable c.1810.[191] Interestingly, when these two works were sold in Vienna in 1820 they were bought on behalf of Haydn's last patron, Miklós II Esterházy. Although Miklós II was a voracious collector, the purchase of paintings by a *contemporary* Spanish artist, representing ordinary working people (probably allegories on national themes), may be considered unusual, there being no acknowledged tradition for collecting such works outside the Iberian peninsula at this time.[192] It seems probable that Goya's name continued to be known in very restricted aristocratic circles in Austria since the time of Giusti's correspondence. Aristocratic connections may have counted for something. The young aunt of the Duchess of Alba, Mariana, second wife of the Marquis of Santa Cruz, was a daughter of the Austrian family of Waldstein. Goya was close to her around 1799 and painted her portrait. Furthermore, in the 1780s a taste for things Spanish may be identified in Vienna, reflected in the content of several favourite operas.[193] In one of these, *Don Giovanni*, its librettist (Lorenzo Da Ponte) claimed that the Spanish style of the costumes became infectious, all ladies wishing to be seen in this manner. This fad may have led to a more sustained curiosity about contemporary Spanish visual culture.[194] By the later 1790s such associations, as well as a connection with Haydn, may have made prints by Goya desirable in elevated circles in Austria and it is not inconceivable that Haydn himself knew something of the artist.

There is a basis for considering therefore that by the last years of the eighteenth century the refined audience for Goya's works in Spain, which had also formed an appreciation of Haydn, was matched in Austria by an equally exclusive group of aristocrats who knew something of Goya and listened to Haydn's most polished compositions, those intended for the ears of 'connoisseurs'. Indeed it may be instructive to make a comparison between works by the two men both published in 1799, though in both cases worked on at least two years earlier: Goya's *Caprichos* and Haydn's six quartets, Op. 76. There is clearly no direct connection nor mutual influence between these works. What is here suggested is that the cognoscenti who first appreciated them were conditioned in comparable ways and discerned similar qualities in these works, reflecting equivalent stages reached by both artist and composer in their respective creative aims.

Both sets represent the height of sophistication and the most refined taste in the eighteenth century, and were intended by their creators to be perceived in this way. These are works which not everyone will respond to favourably. The tone is serious and intimate, often sombre, reflective and absorbing, though humour and jokes are never far away. However, in both cases there is a gulf between the kind of jollity and wit which were associated with both Haydn and Goya in the 1770s and 1780s and the works in question. What was formerly intended or perceived as witty, amusing or even eccentric has now what may now be described as exhibiting a sustained mocking quality. Humour acts not simply to induce a grin or delight in itself, but as a means of commenting on notions of social consequence suggested to the audience. This is repeatedly evident in Goya's plates, in which a long series of figures unwittingly expose their pretension by placing themselves in ridiculous situations, seemingly unaware of the derision they cause around them.

To attempt the expression of this mocking quality is extraordinary in instrumental music, but none the less Haydn employed several devices to achieve it. The first three movements of No. 1 are predominantly light in mood, with the character of the writing sounding at times almost tongue-in-cheek, especially at the very opening of the quartet, where three massive chords immediately give way to a gentle, almost trivial theme begun by the solo cello and finished by the solo viola. During the course of the movement its simple contours and rhythms are explored and developed to suggest a series of adventures, leading the listener from a state of innocence to full maturity. The last movement, however, takes an unexpected, and (in instrumental music) unprecedented turn by beginning in the relative minor and maintaining almost throughout an unyielding and uncompromising character. Unlike the finales of most earlier Haydn quartets, and others in the set, this one is substantial and very taxing for the listener (though of course most of Haydn's finales, despite their light character, are compositionally and technically challenging for the players). But almost at the end of the movement (bar 180), before the final close, Haydn introduces an entirely new and very commonplace theme played by the first violin, irritatingly based on repetitions of a opening motif of the main theme of the movement, but inverted. With pizzicato accompaniment and the simplest of harmonies, this artlessness seems to deride the sense of purpose and high seriousness of what has gone before, suggesting that Haydn intended leaving his listeners with a kind of sting in the tail. Examples of parody may certainly be found in earlier quartet series by Haydn; one senses, however, in these earlier works that the element of mimicry stemmed from Haydn parodying himself.[195] In the Op. 76 set, devices like the one just described seem to go beyond simple parody to suggest what is here interpreted as mockery, with the capacity to imply a kind of social commentary.

What may be taken for mockery is also heard in the last movement of the D minor quartet (No. 2), based on a characteristic Hungarian-style violin melody in the minor. The first movement of this quartet is characterized throughout by the motif of a falling fifth, starkly repeated in almost every imaginable guise to the point where Haydn impresses on even the most inexperienced listener that this particular interval is significant and memorable. The mood is serious and intense throughout. In the finale, the opening section also features a fifth, but this time the interval *rises*. Haydn draws conspicuous attention to this by marking pauses to be played over both notes, as though to relish a moment ridiculing previously heard material. But Haydn is far from finished. At the recapitulation, the main theme returns without the rising fifth, and played in the major. For the first time in the movement he marks the passage *pianissimo*, thereby leaving his audience uncertain what to expect and having to listen hard to find out; a new joke now trumps the old one. The trouble Haydn took to impress on listeners the sound of a falling fifth at the outset of the quartet, a kind of perfect and rational motif, is again used to effect towards the end of the exposition of the last movement by writing a sequence of giant descending intervals (beginning at bars 66–67) suddenly reduced, as the music continues, to a series of repetitions of the smallest of all intervals (a diminished second), wild musical exaggerations which suggest the music being almost pulled apart and mocking the perfect fifth on which the opening part of the quartet was structured. The 'hee-haw' effect of these falling leaps led by the nineteenth century to the quartet sometimes being referred to by the nickname 'the Donkey', and the device was sufficiently memorable for Mendelssohn to borrow from it for the music suggesting Bottom (transformed into an ass) in *A Midsummer Night's Dream*. When in the recapitulation the same passage reappears, it is varied by inverting the first of the giant leaps so that they ascend rather than descend, a final twist suggesting that Haydn tried to capture musically the idea that those who mock live to see themselves mocked in turn.

That such music could put some listeners in mind of an ass is pertinent to establishing a connection in audience perceptions between Haydn's listeners and the viewers expected for Goya's the *Caprichos*: several of the prints feature this beast of burden (Fig. 10), a pervasive symbol of folly or corruption in European culture since the Middle Ages, and a particular favourite with political polemicists.[196]

The third movement of the same quartet, the main part of which consists of a strict canon in two parts, its relentless *forte* dynamic and seemingly crude character sustained throughout, also gave rise to a nickname: 'Witches' Minuet' (*Hexenmenuett*). The grotesque character of this music is matched by the frequent appearance of witches and other hags in Goya's *Caprichos*, their extreme crudity possessing, as in Haydn's 'minuet', its own particular kind of charm and compulsion.[197] Other 'minuets' in the Op. 76 series were written to be played so fast – *Presto* in the case of nos 1 and 6 – that they lose all connection with the original character of the dance which Haydn had previously led listeners to believe was a mainstay of his quartets (and those by every other composer of this genre before Beethoven). Such wild transformation is another feature of the *Caprichos*, in which human figures sprout wings or their bodies take on the form of animals.[198] Haydn also employed unexpected changes in tempo to lend a mocking quality to what has gone before. In the first movements of Nos 5 and 6, the gentle *Allegretto* of their main sections gives way to more vigorous, though brief, endings marked *Allegro*, based on the same thematic material. This lends the music a sense of excitement and energy which parallels the potency of some of Goya's scenes in which action is featured as part of their message. In two movements in the set (Nos 3/i and 4/iv) Haydn required the players to quicken the tempo towards the end, not only intensifying the music, but giving the impression of one's feet leaving the ground. Again, this most unusual effect (unprecedented in instrumental music), may be seen to correspond with the various figures which take off, defying gravity in the *Caprichos*.[199] In one movement, No. 2/ii, Haydn employs the opposite notion, slowing the music down, and allowing it to lose volume, which might suggest the increasing infirmities of old age, another of Goya's concerns.

In several movements in the Op. 76 quartets Haydn very conspicuously inverts motifs heard in principal themes. As a compositional device this was nothing new; but the attention he draws to it indicates that for these compositions it had taken on a particular significance in communicating with his audience. For example, in the fourth quartet the beautiful, gliding opening theme of the first movement is based on a rising motif played on the first violin (giving the quartet its nickname, 'The Sunrise'). Played on the cello in an inverted form, descending rather than ascending, the same material forms the basis of the movement's second subject. Haydn thereby expresses musically the notion of topsy-turviness. This inversion of what might be expected, an upside-down quality, is also a favourite aspect of Goya's visual language, girls carrying chairs on their heads upside down (no. 26) or donkeys riding men (no. 42), for example, being unambiguous expressions of this idea.[200]

In the middle section of the minuet from the last quartet, Haydn takes this concept to its most ludicrous degree. With its label '*alternativo*', rather than the traditional 'trio', and through composed, Haydn signals that there is something to be noted about this section. Whilst the main section of the movement is characterized by a theme with a sequence of *increasing* intervals (major third, fifth, octave and major tenth), the *alternativo* turns the tables on this by having no changes of interval in its main subject. This consists melodically of a mere descending scale, initially played *piano*, which in a series of twenty-four variations comprises the entire section. Here Haydn delights in using the most basic of material – it is not possible to become more mundane – and turns it into something literally uplifting. In the process of developing his scale, Haydn inevitably inverted it for some of the variations so that aurally the section becomes a kind of conflict between the scale in its descending and ascending versions. In the end it is the ascending form, now played *forte*, that triumphs, leaving the listener unambiguously on an optimistic note, unpromising and prosaic material having been transformed into something inspirational.

The repeated rising and falling aspect of this section is in many respects reminiscent of the great wheel of Fortune, constantly turning, elevating individuals to the height of their power and then bringing them back down again. This was a persistent image in medieval culture, sometimes surviving in various forms into the eighteenth century.[201] One example is featured in Handel's *Giustino* (1737), in which the goddess Fortuna appears to the peasant hero in a dream and eventually leads him to become emperor.[202] One of Goya's *Caprichos* (no. 56) presents a variant of this. Labeled *Subir y basar* ('To rise and to fall'), the print depicts rising and falling figures and was originally given the explanation: 'Fortune maltreats those who court her. Efforts to rise she rewards with hot air and those who have risen she punishes by downfall.'

This image and its message are presented as a kind of warning about social climbing, proffered as a means of improvement for the viewer and thus ultimately optimistic in tone. The same may be said of the *alternativo* in Op. 76/6, clearly conveyed through Haydn's ending of the section with the theme played in its transformed *rising* mode, rather than the *descending* form with which it began. As so often in his quartet, the view of the world that Haydn seems to convey here and throughout the Op. 76 series is essentially cheerful and hopeful for the future, though the process involved in arriving at this view might be turbulent. This was, of course, a view shared by most creative artists (including Goya) and composers working in the late eighteenth century, though Haydn must be counted among the most successful in communicating this, to the extent that listeners in the later nineteenth century assumed that naive optimism was the dominant trait of the composer himself, not just his music. This was a conclusion which was never reached in relation to major contemporaries, like Mozart, for whom darker forces were often perceived to be at work.

In Goya's art of the later 1790s there has never been any doubt that the use of imagery which suggested the world turned upside down was part of a social commentary, drawing attention to injustices, persecutions and follies of his age. Although some early observers of the *Caprichos* may have seen in places references to prominent figures in Spanish society and considered that they were the object of the artist's satire – and indeed Goya himself may have had these figures in mind in designing the prints – it is clear that in their final published version of 1799 he took the trouble to ensure that his moralizing was aimed at society in general, not at individuals.[203] Goya much later claimed that it was because the prints led to him being denounced by the Inquisition that he surrendered the plates and 240 copies of the set to the King (who deposited them in the Real Calcografía) in 1803.[204] Even if the real motivation for this act was because the prints did not sell well (only 27 sets are known to have been purchased between 1799 and 1803) and the King was trying to help Goya (by giving him a pension for his son) in return for what remained, it is evident that the King valued Goya's work and did not feel threatened by it. This suggests that the set was perceived, and probably intended, as a product of the Enlightenment, an exercise in trying to persuade, through art, those in positions of authority to examine their society and help create a better one.

It seems likely that a similar objective was held by Haydn in Op. 76, and perhaps in some of the earlier quartet series. The nature of instrumental musical, unlike figurative art, may mean that it is an unsuitable vehicle for drawing attention to social issues (as James Beattie hinted); but an experienced, inventive and conscientious composer like Haydn may have thought differently. Taking into account Haydn's own charitable interests at this date and the musically perceptive audience who first listened to the quartets (enlightened Viennese aristocrats), it does not seem implausible that the mocking and topsy-turvy devices he employed in these works were created to help inspire more advanced attitudes towards society at large.

As with Goya, there is of course no explicit criticism of any individual; Haydn after all was a figure of the Establishment by this time. What it may be argued he set out to do was encourage his listeners to face up to issues confronting a post-Revolutionary age. If those in power never strive towards creating an improving society, then chaos, of the kind seen in Revolutionary France, will ensue. Haydn himself provides an unambiguous social context for perceiving the set by introducing the theme of his recently composed 'Emperor's Hymn' – intended as an Austrian equivalent to 'God save the King' at a time when Napoleon had recently been threatening the well-being of the nation – into No. 3/ii. Haydn personally arranged this movement (as written for the quartet) for keyboard, indicating not only his well-known love for the theme, but also his particular concern with its presentation in the quartet.[205] The tune, evidently representing imperial power, the bedrock of Austrian society, is the basis for a set of variations. In each of these the theme itself is heard intact (with no changes), on each instrument in turn, suggesting all elements in society acknowledging the Emperor as the foundation of secular authority. With all kinds of differing accompaniment taking place above and below the theme, it is therefore presented as a kind of beacon which shines out clearly and constantly no matter what else takes place.

The political sympathies that this scheme underpinned, however, may be construed as having been put in question by two other slow movements in the set, those of Nos 4 and 6. A discriminating listener would have recognized that these two movements are closely related, arguably deliberately so, indicating that there is an integrity about the Op. 76 set as a whole. Not only are both movements marked *Adagio* and have the same time signature, but the main thematic material (the opening five notes) on which both movements is constructed is the same in both cases (though in different keys). Given that Haydn had a reputation for never repeating himself, this affinity would undoubtedly have drawn attention to itself among his aficionados: on a previous occasion, in publishing a set of six sonatas written at different times (though not originally conceived as a set), he had even felt it necessary to ask his publisher to print a kind of excuse on the reverse of the title-page, 'in order to forestall the criticisms of any witlings', when he realized that he had unwittingly repeated himself between two sonatas.[206] In Op. 76/4 this five-note theme is used ingeniously, but in a structure which Haydn often employed, based on sonata form.

In No. 6, however, neither the structure nor its annotation may be considered in the least conventional, a perception which Haydn forces on the listener since No. 4/ii provides a standard by which to judge this. Labelled 'Fantasia', the main tonality of the movement in question in No. 6 is in B major, already quite remote from the E flat major of the other movements (and clearly less conventional that the relationship of keys between the corresponding movements in No. 4). But Haydn actually dispenses with any key signature (before the recapitulation), largely because he takes the music relatively rapidly through no fewer than thirteen modulations, many of them in successively unrelated keys. The impression this gives the listener is quite disconcerting and involves much dissonance. It is unclear where the composer is taking his audience, which suggests a sense of aimless wandering and uncertainty. This is all resolved in the recapitulation, when the B major tonality comfortingly re-establishes itself without contention; but for a while Haydn deliberately allows the listener to become lost, an aesthetic goal which is all the more telling since it comes in the last quartet in the series. The effect is somewhat similar to the unusual key relationships Haydn devised at much the same time to express Chaos in *The Creation*. In the oratorio the composer set himself the task of depicting theological Chaos; in the quartet he may have aimed at suggesting the equivalent notion of social chaos, what might happen when the accepted order of things starts to disintegrate, a possibility which certainly exercised the minds of leading intellectuals in Vienna after the French Revolution. Ultimately Haydn's view, as always (and as with most discriminating composers of the period of the Enlightenment) is optimistic, though his princely audience would surely have wondered about this at times in listening to the series, just as Goya's audience would have in turning the sheets of the *Caprichos*. The Enlightenment principle that the arts contributed to the well-being of society, curing it of its ills, would have been uppermost in the minds of both Haydn and Goya as they worked on both these projects.

When in February 1799 Goya announced the publication of the *Caprichos* in the *Gazeta de Madrid*, the advertisement tellingly appeared on the same page with others for books on *music*, including works by Haydn. This may be seen as a clear indication that the market Goya intended for his series of prints coincided with that for Haydn's music, which had been developing in Madrid since the 1770s. It may also be understood as a small indication that the stunning new visual language the artist developed in the *Caprichos* owed something to music, arguably Haydn's music in particular, in the sense that the series tried to communicate something about the state of the world from a personal point of view in such a way that its message was experienced without being clearly defined. Such ambiguity had previously been the preserve of music. But with Haydn's mature quartets, enthusiastically studied by men of the standing of the Duke of Alba, it may be argued that the composer attempted to use instrumental music as a means to communicate a range of extra-musical notions in ways not hitherto imagined, thus bringing the possibilities for music closer to the realm occupied by the visual arts. The aesthetic goals of both Haydn and Goya in the later 1790s may therefore be understood as having much in common, in large measure a result of common interests and aspirations in their audiences.

A good example of a member of their combined audience is Count Jacob Gustaf de la Gardie, a prominent aristocrat, diplomat and writer. In Vienna in 1800 the Count produced the first Swedish translation of the text of Haydn's *Creation*. In Spain sometime afterwards he became one of the earliest foreign purchasers of the *Caprichos*.[207] No doubt in Vienna he also heard performances of Haydn's quartets.

CHAPTER FOUR

Talking Pictures and Moving Images: The Discourse on the Visual Arts in Eighteenth-Century Opera

For nearly a quarter of a century – from 1766, the date of Haydn's succession to the title *Kapellmeister*, until 1790, when Miklós I died – the focus of Haydn's musical activities was opera.[1] Not only did he compose no fewer than seventeen operas during this period, he also had responsibility for all musical decisions in the running of the princely opera house. His duties included selecting operas by other composers suitable for staging at Eszterháza, reworking them, hiring and rehearsing the singers, and directing the performances. During the 1780s alone, Haydn produced no fewer than 96 operas. In this decade over a hundred operatic performances were given each season.[2] In 1786, the busiest year, seventeen new operas were produced. Many of these operas were very recent, suggesting that Haydn considered it his duty to keep abreast of the latest developments. The Prince's personal investment in opera is indicated by the fact that after the original opera house at Eszterháza burnt to the ground late in 1779, the replacement building, ready in October 1780, did not meet his approval. The new façade had to be pulled down and rebuilt, delaying the production of the opera Haydn had composed especially for the occasion, *La fedeltà premiata*.

Although preference at Eszterháza was for *opera buffa*, presumably reflecting princely taste (which to some extent mirrored the main enthusiasms in the Vienna of Joseph II), taken as a whole the repertoire was quite diverse and a reasonable reflection of prevailing trends in opera.[3] Some notable composers, like Gluck, are conspicuous by their absence.[4] While all leading opera houses during the eighteenth century naturally reflected local conditions and tastes, in general terms what was novel in one major centre was likely to be followed elsewhere shortly afterwards.[5] Opera and its performance throughout the eighteenth century always had an international dimension; but as the century advanced the extent of this internationalism increased. Eszterháza, despite its isolation, was not out of line with this.

Opera also came to be experienced by an increasing proportion of the population, not only by aristocrats, who had been its principal supporters earlier in the century. Again, local conditions show considerable variations in this: Italian opera houses had often made provision for those whose incomes automatically excluded them from audiences in northern Europe. But with the growth in prosperity of the middle classes and, later, democratizing attitudes stemming from the French Revolution, the possibilities for experiencing opera for anyone who wished to do so, assuming the venue to lie within convenient range, greatly increased. Publication of popular items from operas in arrangements suitable for performance at home, permitting favourite moments to be experienced repeatedly, and the development of sets of keyboard variations, based on well-loved themes from successful operas (a genre which both Mozart and Beethoven exploited), extended further the appeal of the operatic experience. Eszterháza also played its part in opening up opera to a wider public. The Prince made performances available free of charge to anyone who wished to attend, though the very remoteness of his opera house meant that few could take advantage of the opportunity. In order to attract a decent audience he apparently encouraged servants to attend, even permitting them to appear 'uncombed, drunk and dishevelled', a concession not available on other occasions.[6]

1. Sacrificing Iphigenia: Algarotti, Tiepolo and Vanloo

It is of course in the nature of opera that, from the audience's point of view, the experience is a combination of visual and auditory sensations. It had always been appreciated that the dramatic and musical effects of opera were enhanced if the spectacle on stage impressed, or was seen to complement qualities otherwise heard. Theatre directors who recognized this, and had the means at their disposal, often went to the trouble of persuading leading artists to execute scenery for them. When, for example, Lord Manchester, an opera enthusiast, succeeded in 1709 in persuading two prominent Venetian painters to come to England, Pellegrini and Marco Ricci, the *first* task they were given was to paint scenery for Scarlatti's opera *Il Pirro e Demetrio*, before they went on to decorate aristocratic residences, work to which they were more accustomed.[7]

In general terms, however, emphasis on the visual aspects of opera was unusual in the first half of the eighteenth century. What counted for most opera-lovers was neither the painted sets, nor even the music, but the words. There was general agreement that the role of the musician was subservient to that of the poet: music was an art of a lower order. What an opera looked like on stage, its visual aspect, was rarely worth mentioning. Opera texts by famous librettists like Metastasio were treated as sacrosanct, revered by audiences and composers alike. Surviving correspondence shows that Metastasio was in the habit of instructing those involved in creating opera on the most detailed matters relating to the musical setting and performance of his texts, indicating that it was taken for granted that a librettist's concept for an opera had to be respected in all particulars.[8] The same libretti were often set many times by different composers, but the librettist's intentions had to be respected.

By the 1780s, however, ways were being found of challenging these earlier conventions, allowing music to take priority over the words to the point of depriving a libretto of any autonomous distinction. Mozart's working practice for *Die Entführung aus dem Serail* (1782) shows an approach to opera which considered the music and its dramatic potential before any concern with the words, as is evident from the composer's correspondence with his father.[9] A few years later, this stance had become so topical that it could even be turned into the idea for a satirical opera: *Prima la musica e poi le parole* ('First the music, then the words'), by Salieri, a composer Mozart considered to have intrigued against him.[10]

This shift in the relationship between composer and librettist, undermining the latter's commanding position in the production of opera, had repercussions for the relationship of the visual arts to opera. There was a feeling in some quarters that painters could have much to contribute to opera beyond the mechanics of scenography. In his *Réflexions d'un peintre sur l'opéra* of 1743, the painter Mont d'Orges argued that since painters are students of Nature, they were in the best position to give advice to singers on the language of gesture. This line of thinking must have been taken seriously since it was repeated by J.G. Noverre, perhaps the most influential and international of eighteenth-century choreographers, who was known to Haydn through his occasional activities at Eszterháza.[11] Noverre suggested that the study of paintings by great masters would be helpful to those aspiring to devise ballets, especially in matters concerning perspective, lighting and colouring.[12]

Another facet of the shifting relationship between the component parts of opera in the middle of the century was the way the activities of several leading painters began to hinge on an appreciation of opera and its workings. A key figure in this development was Francesco Algarotti, a significant friend of painters, who commissioned works for his own modest collection, and also for two of the greatest collections put together in his lifetime: those of Frederick the Great at Sans Souci, and Augustus, King of Poland and Elector of Saxony, at Dresden.[13] Apart from a large range of international contacts (including Voltaire), Algarotti left his mark on the development of eighteenth-century culture and taste though an extensive body of writings, including original essays on opera and painting.

His first work, *Il Newtonianismo per le dame* (Newtonianism for Ladies; 1737), is a useful starting point for considering Algarotti's thinking for, as its title suggests, it aimed at making accessible to a wide audience (there were English and French translations) Newton's theories on the relationship of colour to sound, or more precisely to musical pitch.[14] Newton's authority as a physicist gave this concept – defining clear relationships between phenomena affecting eye and ear – a new scientific respectability, previously wanting in speculations on the relationship, which appealed to Algarotti. Newton's suggestion that the movement of light rays, which are perceived as colour, was analogous to the vibrations of a sounding body, such as a bell, and that mathematics was the key to understanding the relationship, provided the basis for a general canon of aesthetics, which Algarotti recognized might underpin much of human creativity.[15] A musical tone could be shown to be equivalent to a particular colour, their connection determined – in theory, if not demonstrably – through their frequencies and proportions: thus Newton considered the seven colours of the spectrum (of a prism) to be visual counterparts of the seven principal intervals of a musical scale.[16] In Algarotti's *Newtonianismo* therefore the achievements of great artists and musicians are treated as though they were interchangable. He did not attempt, however, to turn his interpretation of Newton into practical advice for artist or composer, satisfying himself that promoting Newtonian ideas was sufficient to encourage a broader appreciation of the arts and better artistic practice.[17]

Algarotti's enthusiasm for Newton led him to keep in mind music when treating artistic matters, and painting when considering opera.[18] This is nowhere more evident than in his dealings with his friend Tiepolo, whom he first met in Venice in 1743 when commissioning paintings for Dresden. The subject Algarotti gave Tiepolo was 'Timotheus, or the Effects of Music'. For this Algarotti drew up an elaborate programme, including Alexander having to be depicted in raptures at the music of Timotheus, his eyes 'trembling and lascivious'.[19] Details such as these may have been too much for Tiepolo at this point in his career since the picture was never painted. Algarotti, however, tried again, giving him instructions for a 'Caesar presented with the Head of Pompey', a more appropriate subject for a patron called Augustus. Unfortunately, neither Algarotti's programme nor Tiepolo's painting (completed by 1746) survives. It seems probable that Algarotti's choice and programme were inspired by an opera commissioned by Frederick the Great to inaugurate his opera house in Berlin in 1742, C.H. Graun's *Cleopatra e Cesare*, which features an episode in which the head of Pompey is presented to Caesar by Ptolemy.[20] Frederick himself had given the subject of this opera to the librettist, and achieving its performance had been one of his main aims on succeeding to the throne in 1740. Subsequently Algarotti often helped Frederick translate libretti for his opera house. Indeed the King himself wrote libretti for Graun to set, the most celebrated being *Montezuma*, which Algarotti in his *Essay on Musical Opera* cited as a model opera.

Algarotti's first choice of subject for Tiepolo, the Timotheus painting, might also have been inspired by a recent musical production. His interest in this theme may have been prompted by knowledge of Dryden's poem *Alexander's Feast or The Power of Music*, which also describes the emotional impact of music on the Emperor.[21] This poem, with additions from *The Power of Music* by Newburgh Hamilton, was used as the basis of Handel's oratorio *Alexander's Feast*, first performed in London in February 1736.[22] Algarotti was in London at this time, making an impact on English society.[23] It seems entirely plausible that he would have been caught up in the general enthusiasm for Handel's work, 'the grandeur of his music, the majestic choruses, reflective of all the pomp and richness of the story, [and] the beautiful words of Dryden'.[24]

Commissions Tiepolo subsequently received from Algarotti show an increasing interest in musical themes or imagery. *Maecenas presenting the Arts to Augustus*, one of a pair of small canvases destined for the chief minister of the Elector Augustus, was sent to Dresden in 1744.[25] In this painting, the arts comprise three female personifications (representing painting, sculpture and architecture) and a blind old man (Homer) representing poetry, who is led by a youth holding a trumpet, presumably representing music. Although Algarotti makes it clear in the *Saggio sopra l'opera* (1755) that he upheld the traditional view of the poet as 'chief engineer' of an opera, whose duty, he suggested, was 'to give directions to the dancers, the machinists, the painters; ... even to those who are entrusted with the care of the wardrobe and dressing the performers',[26] his instructions (now lost) for the *Maecenas* seem to have implied a role for music, if not exactly anticipating Mozart's views on the relationship of music to text, then at least as one which should provide the librettist with a sense of direction.

In the same year, Tiepolo also completed a *Banquet of Cleopatra and Anthony* (Fig. 11) for Augustus of Saxony under Algarotti's direction.[27] Although this painting was apparently begun for another client, its significance to Algarotti is clear from his acquisition of what he described as Tiepolo's *modello* for the painting, and from its subject matter, combining an element from the first programme for a painting he suggested to Tiepolo (a feast) and one from his second suggestion (Cleopatra). Among the many differences between the *modello* and the painting Augustus received, differences which may have resulted from Algarotti's intervention, is that the painter introduced more prominent musicians in the version sent to Dresden. Tiepolo returned to the same subject on several subsequent occasions, most notably in his decorations for the Palazzo Labia in Venice, completed by 1746–47. In this *Banquet of Cleopatra* the number and variety of musicians was again significantly increased, and their position, much closer to the banqueteers, ensured that they were viewed as a more vital element in the composition. Apart from the instrumentalists, Tiepolo also included figures who may be interpreted as singers, holding sheets of music. These musicians, together with the dramatic qualities of this fresco and of its companion piece (the *Meeting of Cleopatra and Anthony*), the staging of the main figures in both scenes, and the elaborate costumes, even more theatrical than in his earlier works – all these aspects of the Palazzo Labia paintings – betray more than a casual interest in the world of opera, a source of inspiration for Tiepolo very much connected with Algarotti's own interests.

Tiepolo's debt to opera, which has been identified in a number of works from this period and later in his career, is perhaps at its most manifest in his decorations painted in 1757 for the Villa Valmarana (Vicenza), which feature subjects frequently treated in opera, including the love of Angelica and Medoro (from Ariosto's *Orlando furioso*) and the story of Armida and Rinaldo (from Tasso's *Gerusalemme liberata*), both of which he depicted on several other occasions.[28] Perhaps beginning with Tiepolo, the treatment of these subjects in opera and painting draws attention to their frivolous character. Many situations described by Ariosto and Tasso were recognized for their potential for comedy, rather than the seriousness of purpose which had previously been emphasized. Reynolds seems to have sensed this when he wrote that 'The Venetians like the wild imaginations of Tasso or Ariosto, the same mixture of serious and ludicrous.'[29] And other contemporary writers, including Voltaire and Goethe, were much quicker to find the humorous and the fanciful in Ariosto than the serious.[30]

One reason why a lighter approach to Tasso and Ariosto caught the public imagination was that modern editions of these works made them very widely known, and in the process of becoming popular entertainment, the cheerful, not the sombre had to be stressed. When Benjamin West first made a name for himself in London in the 1760s, after a period of study in Italy, *Angelica and Medoro* and *Rinaldo and Armida* were among the subjects through which he chose to introduce himself to the public; and although these were early attempts to attach himself to the revered tradition of history painting, the results show that the desire to please through light-hearted sentiment far outweighed the need to emulate the grand manner.[31] The same may be said of the Ariosto and Tasso subjects painted by West's friend Angelica Kauffman, which were chiefly intended to be engraved and thus reach a very considerable audience.[32] Projects to illustrate editions of Ariosto by Mortimer in England in the early 1770s, and, more extensively, by Fragonard in France at about the same date show the same tendencies.[33] The tone was particularly well set by Fragonard in the drawing he probably intended as the design for the frontispiece of the publication (which never appeared), showing Ariosto being inspired by two putti representing Love and Folly. Fragonard became interested in Ariosto and Tasso during a youthful spell in Italy, where his approach may have been influenced by visits to see Tiepolo frescoes.

In Germany the extent of the popularity of this material may also be shown from its use in calendar illustrations by Chodowiecki published in Germany in the 1780s.[34] This partly explains why Haydn's opera on the Angelica and Medoro theme, *Orlando paladino* (1782), was the most successful of his operas in his lifetime.[35] This *dramma eroicomico*, with a libretto by Nunziato Porta, broke new ground by consciously balancing serious elements (Angelica and Medoro's love for each other) with comic ones (the bungling attempts by Pasquale, Orlando's squire, to woo the shepherdess Eurilla), which anticipate a similar mixture of elements in another pioneering opera, Mozart's *Don Giovanni* of 1787. Porta's treatment of the Orlando story suggests a striving to interest broader kinds of audience by giving a new twist to familiar material.[36] The status of Orlando's madness in this mixture of the serious and comic is rather ambiguous; at the outset Orlando is cast as the villainous pursuer of Angelica, only to be transformed into a ridiculous victim of his insanity when, in the manner of Don Quixote (whose character was also being re-explored in the visual arts and opera at this time), he is unable to distinguish one character from another, mistaking Pasquale for Angelica.[37] In early eighteenth-century Orlando operas, such as those by Handel and Vivaldi, Orlando's state of mind was generally given serious expression (though not devoid of comic aspects); but in a work which was a major source for Haydn's librettist, *Le pazzie d'Orlando* by Guglielmi (first performed in London in 1771), with a libretto by one of Haydn's later collaborators, Badini, Orlando's insane obsession with Angelica is comically matched by most of the other characters falling in love with the wrong partners. In Haydn's opera the transformation of Orlando from villain to buffoon before he is finally cured is a clever piece of character development. Like other aspects of the opera, this is only partly derived from earlier portrayals of Ariosto's story in opera, owing as much to recent pictorial developments of the subject matter, beginning with Tiepolo, to which the public seem to have responded well. However, the experimental balance struck in Haydn's Orlando opera, despite its success with the public, does not seem to have wholly satisfied him since he returned to the traditional *opera seria* format for his next opera, *Armida*, based on Tasso, first performed in 1783.

The subject depicted by Tiepolo in the Villa Valmarana which would have had the most resonance with contemporary audiences in relation to opera was the sacrifice of Iphigenia.[38] In order to fulfil a vow to the goddess Diana, whom he had offended, Agamemnon, King of Mycenae, is obliged to sacrifice his own daughter Iphigenia in order to gain favourable winds to sail against Troy. From an eighteenth-century perspective this was one of the most famous episodes of the Trojan War. Though it was not mentioned by Homer, it assumed a kind of Homeric status. Tiepolo's treatment of this subject, painted in the entry hall to the villa, is particularly striking since the walls are turned into a kind of three-dimensional stage on which the noble action takes place, an illusion intensified for the viewer by the appearance of the goddess Diana on the ceiling, who gesticulates to the scene, saving Iphigenia from death by replacing her with a hind at the moment that the knife of the priest was to have been plunged into her breast. This is the pictorial equivalent of the *dea ex machina* effect towards the end of many operas treating this subject. The situation, combining tragic consequences of duty with sensations of relief at the unexpected outcome, was one of the most emotional episodes considered appropriate for the stage.

It was Racine who initiated an interest in sacrifice dramas with his *Iphigénie en Aulide* (1674), the starting point for several libretti of eighteenth-century operas on the subject. In his preface, Racine actually stated that the classical tradition for Diana's intervention was too absurd for modern audiences. He therefore invented a rival for Iphigenia, Ériphyle, an intriguer who at the moment of sacrifice stabs herself at the altar, removing the need for Iphigenia to die as well. But despite Racine's objection, Diana's miraculous appearance proved popular on stage. Algarotti, for example, wrote his own libretto in French on the *Iphigénie en Aulide* story, with which he concluded his essay on opera (1755). Though owing much to Racine, Algarotti ended his libretto with Diana descending from the clouds to rescue Iphigenia, leaving in her place a hind, as in Tiepolo's fresco. One of Algarotti's aims in appending this libretto to his essay was to use it as a method of demonstrating his view that restraint and simplicity in the construction of opera plots and in their visual trappings were preferable to the complicated workings of subplots, with their gratuitous reliance on intrigue and confidants (like Ériphyle). Algarotti also considered that features like the choruses and ballets, often introduced merely to pander to the expectation that opera should contain spectacle, should only be used where they could be naturally integrated into the action. He was also scornful of many other conventions of opera developed by Metastasio. His views may have been shaped by knowledge of Graun's *Ifigenia in Aulide*, first performed for Frederick the Great in 1748, with a libretto by Villati (to whom the King had given a copy of Racine's play). This featured several innovative elements which would have appealed to Algarotti and later opera reformers: a large proportion of the recitative accompanied by the orchestra, rather than just the cembalo; arias without the traditional da capo repetitions, and a plaintive march accompanying Iphigenia's processional entrance before her sacrifice. Graun's *Ifigenia* made such an impression that a local critic, C.G. Krause, in his essay on poetry for music (1752), dedicated to Graun, advocated it as *the* model for librettists and composers to follow.[39]

Apart from its possible repercussions for Tiepolo, by way of Algarotti, Graun's *Ifigenia* had further pictorial consequences. It stimulated Frederick the Great in 1755 into commissioning a painting on the subject of the sacrifice of Iphigenia from Carle Vanloo, a favourite at the French court.[40] Mme de Pompadour, for example, had promoted Vanloo by involving him in several decorative schemes in which music and the visual arts were paired.[41] In fact the painter's musical interests were directly relevant to his success. Not only was his wife a celebrated Italian opera singer, who played a part in introducing Italian music into France, but Vanloo launched his career in Paris by exhibiting at the *Salon* of 1737 a pair of *portraits déguisés* representing respectively the arts of painting and music, and featuring the quasi-Turkish costume then coming into vogue at the French court: *The Pasha Having his Mistress's Portrait Painted* includes a self-portrait; and *The Pasha Giving a Concert to his Mistress* shows Christine Vanloo performing an aria from Handel's *Admeto*.[42]

Vanloo's picture for Frederick the Great, which conceivably reflects operatic practice, proved to be one of the most fiercely discussed paintings of the eighteenth century, provoking a stream of correspondence and pamphlets by distinguished critics when exhibited at the *Salon* of 1757.[43] Much of the comment centred on Vanloo's failure to follow the classical custom of depicting Agamemnon with some item of clothing acting as a veil, shielding from the gaze of viewers his grief, caused by what he imagines is the death of the daughter he is obliged to sacrifice. The veil was known to have been a much admired feature of a picture by the ancient Greek painter Timanthes, who had been inspired by Euripides' play on the same subject. According to ancient sources, Timanthes portrayed a number of degrees of grief in this painting, the most extreme of which was that of Menelaos, to whom he gave 'a look of sorrow that was the ultimate effect of this sort his art could achieve'. Quintilian, who gives this account, ended it by explaining that Timanthes, 'after thus exhausting his capacity to convey such emotion and being at a loss as to how to express the face of the father in an adequate way, covered his [Agamemnon's] head with a veil and left it to the imagination of the viewer to judge the extent of the pain'.[44]

Following the discovery of a painting at Pompeii apparently related to Timanthes' lost version, the later eighteenth century saw a revival of interest in the subject of Iphigenia's sacrifice. This raised the issue of the appropriate mode of portraying Agamemnon's grief. Tiepolo, perhaps prompted by Algarotti into considering operatic treatments of the subject, had followed the tradition, showing the father holding up his cloak to his face to obscure the terrible deed from view.[45] This motif exactly reflects Euripides, as the French sculptor Falconet pointed out in a comment on his own translation of the section on Timanthes' painting in Pliny's *Natural History*. The passage was sufficiently well known for Reynolds to draw attention to it in his *Discourse* of 1778. Vanloo, however, solved the same problem by showing Agamemnon too distressed to bring himself to witness the rescue of his daughter, contrasting his unawareness of the event with the surprise of those who do see. This solution – not in fact as original as some at the time imagined – was praised by Voltaire and the French theorist the Comte de Caylus. But it was attacked by Diderot's friend Melchior Grimm, who defended the approach first devised by Timanthes, by drawing attention to two concepts: firstly, propriety, which dictated that extreme grief should be *hidden* from view, since the visual arts were incapable of representing it adequately; and secondly, the incapacity, of even great artists, to distinguish in paint the extremity of grief suffered by Agamemnon from the anguish, pain or remorse of others witnessing Iphigenia's sacrifice.

2. Gluck and the Visual Arts

The controversy generated by Vanloo's picture was also relevant to the approach to the Iphigenia story in later opera, where conflicts arose concerning the appropriate mode of musical setting. Both Algarotti and Diderot had reached the conclusion in 1757 that the sacrifice of Iphigenia was the ideal subject for operatic treatment. When Gluck therefore decided the time was ripe to introduce his music to Parisian audiences he used the same story as a vehicle for this. He was particularly well placed to express musically Timanthes' view of Agamemnon since he had already treated in opera a character in turmoil on account of not being able to look at the object of his love, in this case because of a prohibition placed on him by the gods. This character was Orpheus in his opera *Orfeo ed Euridice* (1762). Gluck's *Iphigénie en Aulide*, first performed in 1774 (the same year that his Orpheus opera was reworked for a Parisian audience) with a libretto by Du Roullet adapted from Racine, was described by his former pupil, Marie-Antoinette, as 'a great triumph'. Nevertheless, as the Queen's account of the opera makes clear, it provoked a heated debate:

> On the 19th [April] we had the first performance of *Iphigénie*: I was carried away by it, and people can no longer talk of anything else. All heads are fermenting as a result of this event, as much as could be imagined – it is incredible, there are dissensions and quarrels, as though it were a matter of some religious dispute; at court, although I publicly expressed myself in favour of this inspired work, there are partisanships and debates of a particular liveliness; and in town it seems to be still worse ...[46]

For Parisians, Gluck's *Iphigénie* opera represented a new kind of musical experience, placing the emphasis on conveying a sequence of extreme emotions musically, something which partisans of the old conventions of French opera found disarming, used as they were to the notion that music was merely an embellishment to telling a story by means of words (i.e. the libretto). As one early reviewer put it: 'We haven't said anything about the lyrics of *Iphigénie* because no one talks about them. The music absorbs all the attention of the spectators; none remains for the poem.'[47] This conveying of emotion to an audience was not simply a matter of the expression in the parts written for the singers and their performance of them, but more importantly a matter for the entire musical score, such that the orchestra throughout acts as much to create the mood of the drama as to accompany the singers, the task with which it was traditionally associated.[48] On occasions, whilst the words of a singer may betray the particular state of mind of an individual character, the tone and direction of the drama will be set by the orchestra, which may suggest a conflicting notion to that given by the singer. Audiences were being expected to listen carefully not just to the singers, or to the words, but to the entire musical context in order to grasp exactly what was taking place. Starting with Gluck, a libretto had to be written with a particular composer in mind, and the days when a libretto, such as one by Mestastasio, could be set repeatedly, were numbered.

In Gluck's *Iphigénie* (1774), the drama hinges on Agamemnon's agonizing over fulfilling his vow to kill his daughter. This maintains a sense of tension for the audience since, for much of the opera, his oath is unknown to the other characters and to the people (the chorus). Whilst Tiepolo and Vanloo had to express the conflicting claims of love and duty which constitute Agamemnon's remorse in a single image, Gluck was of course able to explore the discord within him in a sequence of episodes in which his troubled character is fully developed. In Act I, for example, after the arrival of his wife Clytemnestra and Iphigenia in preparation for her marriage to Achilles, the chorus congratulates Agamemnon on his restored domestic well-being, to which he is only able to respond by uttering bitter asides. In Act II, a ceremonial quartet and chorus anticipating the marriage leads to the revelation that Agamemnon waits at the altar to sacrifice his daughter, not to witness her marriage to Achilles. When Agamemnon is later left alone with his conscience, Gluck composed a kind of lament for the solo oboe, which represents the devastation in Agamemnon's heart. Here the orchestra says what cannot be expressed in words, the musical equivalent of Timanthes' veil concealing what cannot be rendered in paint. The pressure is kept up until the very moment that the sacrifice is due, with Agamemnon in conflict with Achilles, Thessalians ready to attack the Greeks, and Clytemnestra's frenetic, almost violent outburst presaging the grim events of the future. For the actual rescue of Iphigenia, Du Roullet followed Racine in rejecting the intervention of Diana in person, leaving the task to Calchas, the high priest and Diana's agent. On hearing that the gods have been appeased, and that fair weather has been granted so that Agamemnon and his men may prepare to sail, the four principals are so stunned that they can only manage to utter each other's names before singing a quartet expressing their delirious happiness: all are then reconciled and reunited. But as the final preparations are made for the marriage of Iphigenia and Achilles, the music – in D minor and in bare octaves, marked with loud beats of the drum – betrays a future rather different from the one the celebrations are intended for, of impending tragedy rather than contentment.

Gluck seems to have considered the episode of Calchas proclaiming Diana's change of mind to have had insufficient weight for the dénouement of the opera; and for its revival in 1775, he altered the scene, introducing Diana as *dea ex machina*. Presumably, despite Racine's objections, so strongly was the audience's anticipation of Diana's appearance that her failure to emanate was deemed an anticlimax. Part of such expectation was of course a result of familiarity with paintings like those by Tiepolo and Vanloo. Gluck may perhaps originally have had in mind a scene closer to Batoni's *Sacrifice of Iphigenia*, in which Diana does not appear, but is represented by a statue behind the altar, on which Agamemnon mournfully fixes his gaze whilst holding his swooning daughter's hand, thus solving the difficult problem of the father's expression in facing up to Iphigenia's end; Clytemnestra has fainted at her daughter's feet; and Achilles turns away from the scene also unable to look.[49] It is conceivable that Gluck may have known a version of Batoni's picture.[50]

Whatever the precise visual inspiration behind the *Iphigénie* of 1774, it is clear that Gluck, at least in part, conceived his mature operas in visual terms, not as a stage designer might, but like a painter depicting episodes in the subjects he set. The evidence for this comes from his own words. In the preface to the first edition of *Alceste* (Vienna, 1769), Gluck wrote a kind of manifesto of his aims in composing serious opera, repudiating the practice and conventions associated with Metastasio, and taking one stage further the criticisms of Algarotti. In order to articulate his points – the most important of which were: firstly, that music should be integral to the drama, not just decoration for a libretto; and secondly, that simplicity counted for more than virtuoso display – Gluck borrowed from the popular vocabulary for debating the visual arts, no equivalent language having then developed for enthusiasts to discuss aspects of opera. Gluck begins the preface in defensive mood,[51] but proceeds to explain his own aims, suggesting that they were really those of a painter:

> I have endeavoured to restrict music to its true purpose of serving poetry through expression and through the telling of the episodes of the story, ... and I thought that [music] should do this in the same way that lively colours affect an accurate and well-executed drawing, and that a careful contrast of light and shade helps to bring the figures to life without changing their form. ... Furthermore, I believed that my most important task should be to concentrate on seeking to beautify simplicity, and I have avoided making a spectacle out of complications at the expense of clarity.[52]

In the letter of dedication of his next opera, *Paride ed Elena* (1770), Gluck made further use of musical–visual analogies in defending *Alceste*, which he claimed had been misunderstood on account of bad performances (rehearsals) in inappropriate venues:

> ... it was imagined what the effect would be like in a theatre from what took place in a room, and with the same deception that was once used in a city in Greece to judge statues, designed to be seen very high up on columns, but from only a few feet away. ... The more truth and perfection are aimed for, the more crucial it is to be precise and exact. The qualities

which distinguish Raphael from a mass of other painters are imperceptible, and, even the smallest change of form, which might make little difference in caricature, would completely ruin the portrait of a beautiful woman. ... the text of *Paride* ... did not present the composer's imagination with those strong passions, those great portraits, and those tragic situations, which move the audience in *Alceste*, and which present so much scope for artistic effect; one should not therefore expect the same force and energy in the music; just as in paintings set in full light one does not expect the same effects of chiaroscuro, or the same strong contrasts that the painter might use in a subject which requires him to show a low level of lighting. ... I was obliged to look for some variety of colour ...[53]

In composing *Armide* (1777), the opera he wrote after *Iphigénie en Aulide*, Gluck even went as far as to claim that he had 'endeavoured to be ... *more painter* and poet than musician'.[54] In fact Gluck became well known in Paris for statements of this kind. A letter published in the *Journal de Paris* in 1777 reported a conversation at the Opéra about *Iphigénie en Aulide*, in which the parties agreed that the opera could not be considered music: 'Just as in looking at pictures by Correggio, Titian and Van Dyck, true connoisseurs have always said: "that's not painting".' The correspondent who overheard this, whilst disgusted by the ignorance of such a supposedly clever remark, nevertheless found something important behind it:

[Gluck] has more than once said that in composing an opera, he makes only one vow, to forget that he is a musician. This assertion, full of sense and profundity, and which the fools [overheard at the Opéra] ought to have understood (though they took it for a bit of stupidity), reminds me of something similar of M. Chardin's ... Someone asked the famous painter for a picture and particularly wanted the colours to be clear and bright. [Diderot had praised Chardin for the veracity and harmony of his colouring.] 'Ah! Who told you', wrote the artist with enthusiasm, 'that pictures are made with colours?' Woe betide every imitator who in his works betrays too much of the means by which he enabled his imitation to be made.[55]

It has sometimes been claimed that key texts signed by Gluck setting out the objectives of his operatic reforms were in fact written by his librettist for the relevant operas, Ranieri de' Calzibigi, who had previously compiled an edition of Metastasio's works and written an essay on them.[56] It is true that Calzibigi also refers to the visual in opera, as when, in explaining Gluck's comparative lack of success in Italy, he employed the same visual comparison as the composer used in his letter of dedication, only in greater detail, implying that he, not Gluck, was the force behind them:

They are pieces for the theatre and not for the chamber, rather like the *Athena* of Phidias [the celebrated sculptor], which at first sight in the studio looked raw, rude and carelessly hewn out; but afterwards, seen on the noble site for which it was predestined, had an effect of the most surprising beauty. ... The Italian public has as yet little idea of these theatrical optics.[57]

But Gluck's clear interest in the visual arts, which may be established from other sources, tends to militate against Calzabigi being the principal instigator of their reforms. Gluck's wife, for example, practised as a miniature painter.[58] In Paris the composer shared a house and much time with a painter, J.C. von Mannlich.[59] He counted as a particular friend the engraver J.-M. Moreau, whose drawings were sent from Paris to the composer in Vienna.[60] It was Moreau who designed the sets for Gluck's most accomplished serious opera, *Iphigénie en Tauride*, the success of which when performed in Vienna in 1781 the composer himself generously attributed in part to Moreau's visual contribution.[61] Moreau was best known in France as a book illustrator, his first major work also proving a fruitful partnership with a composer, the *Choix de chansons* (1773), with music by J.B. de La Borde, whom Gluck also knew during his visits to Paris.[62] Moreau also provided drawings for illustrations to Caylus's *Recueil d'antiquités* and the famous *Encyclopédie* of Diderot and d'Alembert.[63] Furthermore, he collaborated with another French book illustrator with whom Gluck had dealings, Charles Monnet, who designed the frontispiece to the Paris publication (1764) of his Orpheus opera, usually considered the first of Gluck's operas to put into practice the principles stemming from Algarotti's 1755 essay, and the first of his collaborations with Calzibigi.[64]

Among his other artistic interests, Gluck was especially proud of the portrait of him exhibited at the *Salon* of 1775 by J.-S. Duplessis, an official painter to Louis XVI. The portrait, which was in the composer's possession, shows Gluck at the keyboard in a kind of romantic rapture that seems to have particularly struck those who saw it. It was, for example, admired in Gluck's house in 1783 by J.F. Reichardt, former Kapellmeister to Frederick the Great and noted writer on music, who mentions it in an account of the visit: 'Hanging in the room was the beautiful, life-size oil painting by Duplessis of Paris, which shows the artist brimful of vitality, heaven in his eyes and love and goodness on his lips. ... [I] had no sooner expressed a wish to possess a good and faithful copy of the beautiful painting than Gluck readily promised [me] one. Several months later it arrived in Berlin, most welcome and with an obliging letter from the great artist.'[65] This account was published in 1813. The composer obliged at least one other admirer of his portrait with a copy of it.[66] Since the family to whom it was sent were significant collectors of pictures, it may be assumed that the copy was requested as much for its artistic merit as for its claim to be an accurate record of Gluck's appearance. The family in question, called de la Ferté, were great patrons of the visual arts according to papers left by the painter Joseph Vernet.[67]

Gluck's undoubted interest in the visual arts lends support to his sole authorship of those texts bearing his name explaining his aims in writing operas from the time of *Orfeo* and after. It has to be admitted, however, that both he and Calzabigi owed much in the shaping of their aesthetic ideals to one of the most influential figures in the development of later eighteenth-century culture, Winckelmann. Taking as his starting point the reforming ideals of Algarotti, in whose footsteps he for a time followed, Winckelmann went far beyond such concepts in the direction of what he saw as the pure values of Greek antiquity: not for him the showy, inauthentic visualizations of the classical past of Tiepolo.[68] In his widely read essay entitled 'Thoughts on the Imitation of Greek Works in Painting and Sculpture' (1755), written in Dresden before having gained any experience of studying Greek art through direct observation, Winckelmann attacked the decorative qualities of the rococo style in vogue at the German courts with which he was familiar, just as Gluck, over a decade later, attacked the excesses of contemporary opera.[69] For both men, true beauty and expression stemmed from simplicity, which in its noblest form, together with a certain quiet grandeur, had been bequeathed to Western culture by the ancient Greeks. Alongside their seriousness in recreating the Classical past such that it touched the emotions of contemporaries, both Winckelmann and Gluck advanced their cases by implying that the cause of simplicity had a moral dimension: in opposing the extravagances of the artists and conventions they abhorred, they believed their position to be closer to God.

Gluck first encountered Winckelmann in Rome in 1756 (when he received a papal knighthood) at the residence of the latter's future patron, Cardinal Albani, who offered to help the composer in a feud with some local musicians. Winckelmann was at the time starting his study of the visual remains of Classical Rome – he was soon to be engaged in looking after the cardinal's unique collection of antiquities – and befriending Mengs, who was then working on his two theoretical writings, the 'Thoughts on Beauty' and the 'Reflections on the Three Great Painters Raphael, Correggio and Titian'.[70] Gluck's next contact with Winckelmann would have been on the occasion that the latter accepted an invitation in 1768 to Vienna from Prince Kaunitz. It was on his return trip to Rome the following year that Winckelmann was murdered in Trieste, an event which shocked the Western world. Kaunitz had hoped to persuade Winckelmann to take up a position at the Vienna Akademie, which the Prince had been active in reconstructing, just as he had been energetic in developing and securing the production of opera in the Austrian capital. Kaunitz was one of Gluck's greatest supporters. He was also proactive in putting into practice his theory that the 'support of the Fine Arts in a state is an important part of the concern of a wise ruler', the value of music and the visual arts being not simply aesthetic but economic.[71]

During the period between Gluck's visit to Rome and Winckelmann's visit to Vienna, the latter completed his most famous work, the 'History of the Art of Antiquity' (1764) which, in a posthumous reprint reflecting the author's wishes, was dedicated to Kaunitz.[72] Winckelmann's 'History' appeared as a revelation. Through observation and through his considerable knowledge of ancient literary sources concerning the visual arts, Winckelmann was able to give in a structured form a convincing account of the development of the style of ancient Greek art (in four stages), presented in terms of a kind of organic evolution which passed for progress and then decline, and also to place into systematic order the visual remains of antiquity, such that the perceptive reader was given a clear and seemingly comprehensive insight into the visual aspects of classical culture.[73] Furthermore, his scheme was given modern relevance by making a parallel for each of its four phases with the development of Italian painting from the precursors of Raphael until the death of Carlo Maratta (1713), who was often considered the last of the great Old Master painters. Before Winckelmann, attempts to present ancient visual material to the public had been arbitrary and fragmented, and chiefly based on information in ancient sources. His achievement therefore made an enormous impact on men of learning, the 'History' often considered as *the* history of ancient art by the end of the century. Winckelmann's presence in Vienna at the behest of Gluck's chief supporter is likely to have had its effect on the composer himself, shaping his preface to *Alceste* (which appeared the following year), and encouraging him to practise and strengthen still further his aesthetic goals, in operas like *Iphigénie en Aulide*.

The part played by the visual arts in Gluck's account of his reforming aims in opera was not unique in writings on music at this time. The debate which Gluck's reforms provoked shows that his supporters in particular frequently resorted to drawing on analogies taken from study of painting and sculpture in framing their arguments. There was, of course, nothing unusual in a writer reviewing a work of art on one occasion, and a piece of music on the next. Diderot and Grimm had since the 1750s been writing criticism of both the visual arts and aspects of opera. What the Gluck controversy generated, however, was a more ambitious development, writing on music in which arguments could be drawn from the sphere of painting and sculpture. The writings of the main protagonist, Gluck himself, had instigated this. But part of the inspiration is likely to have stemmed from Jean-Jacques Rousseau, who in 1748 had been commissioned to write the articles on music for Diderot's great *Encyclopédie*, which following revisions formed part of his musical dictionary of 1767. In a discussion of melody which first appeared in the same year as Winckelmann's 'History' (1764), for example, Rousseau explains its function in music by drawing a closely argued analogy with the role of drawing in painting.[74]

Although Rousseau, in another section of the same essay, denied the kind of colour and sound analogies stemming from Newton which had intrigued Algarotti, his paralleling of painting and music nevertheless provided a kind of forum for Gluck's supporters to challenge the criticisms levelled at the composer's work. One main line of criticism of Gluck's reform operas was that in emphasizing expression at the expense of beauty, his settings were too forceful in their representation of suffering, portraying nature without refining it into a true work of art. This meant that they were considered by some as lacking the melodic inspiration of Italian opera, concentrating instead on harmony and instrumentation. In Rousseau's terminology, there was too much colour, insufficiently defined by drawing. Rousseau had been active in supporting the cause of Italian opera in France, partly because of his view that the French language was unsingable. Gluck therefore went to great lengths to forestall opposition from Rousseau and his followers to his *Iphigénie en Aulide*, by writing a letter to a French journal in which he diplomatically referred to Rousseau, saying that he hoped to collaborate with him in order to seek 'a noble, inspiring and natural melody with a declamation in line with the prosody of each language and the character of each people'.[75] Thus, with this goal in mind, he would produce 'a kind of music suited to all nations' and eliminate 'the ridiculous distinctions between national types of music'.[76]

It was important for Gluck to neutralize criticism from this quarter because Rousseau had argued that the music of ancient Greece was entirely melodic, its legendary power a result of union with words. Since Gluck's operas attempted to recreate on stage the power of ancient Greek legend, claiming to revive Greek notions of music-drama, he could not afford to be censured by those suggesting that his means were inappropriate to his subject matter. Rousseau in fact came to be not unenthusiastic about Gluck's music. But others raised objections to his work, mostly connected with his emphasis on 'colour' at the expense of 'drawing'. Gluck's supporters therefore found it appropriate to face this challenge by again, where appropriate, resorting to the language of the visual arts to analyse the issues.

The debate was at its most intense in 1777. Following an attack on Gluck by J.F. de Laharpe, published in a French journal in October of that year, Gluck called on one of his champions, J.B.A. Suard, a member of the Academy, to defend him.[77] Suard wrote a long letter treating in detail all the points raised by Laharpe and demonstrating his error of judgement. He begins by discrediting Laharpe's competence to discuss the matters at issue. Like other literary types, Laharpe, he claims, goes to the opera as he goes to see the pictures at the Louvre, only so that he can talk about them over dinner.[78] Suard then moves to deal with Laharpe's view that Gluck is good in instrumental music but weak in melody, melody being the rarest quality in music.[79] Advising Laharpe to consult a musician or to read Rousseau's dictionary, Suard finds that Laharpe's terminology is often misleading, words like 'aria' (*air*), 'recitative' (*récitatif*) and 'melody' (*mélodie*) being used at random and contradictorily.[80] Suard further undermines Laharpe's position by examining his most recent article on painting, in which the terminology is again found wanting. Laharpe knows only one artistic expression, 'reflection' (*reflet*), but his use of it is completely unintelligible. The trouble, according to Suard, is that Laharpe's facility with words is not matched by his understanding of art.

Whereas in the Renaissance the greatest painters benefited from contact with the leading poets, and vice versa, modern painting suffers from lack of constructive engagement by men of letters:

> Several factors force painters ultimately to sacrifice great artistic ideas to the expediency of their profession. Small, painstaking, over-stylish, highly refined pictures, cold reproductions of still life, portraits and miniatures have replaced those works of genius in which the great minds of antiquity, the great traditions of history and all human passions were represented on canvas. Our connoisseurs are trained in the school of the picture-dealers and adopt its ridiculous jargon. When you speak to an artist about inspiration, character and expression, he talks of *relish*, *silvery tones* and *sweet touches*. The same trend seems to be coming into music. It is not enough for you, Monsieur [Gluck], to be moving, powerful and sublime; people want sweeping outlines, soft colours and elegant forms; one finds only applause for country songs ... they want to put tragedy into ariettas, just as the Marquis de Mascarille [otherwise unknown] proposed to write the history of Rome in madrigals.[81]

Later, Suard seeks to show that what Laharpe desires from opera is neither possible nor really conceivable. Every artist has his own merits, and no individual artist embraces all the qualities admired in other artists. It would be ridiculous to try to attempt such an idea. The point is made forcefully by again drawing on the visual arts. The range of Old Master painters and classical works of art suggests that Gluck's knowledge of the visual arts went far beyond the superficial:

> If I said to a painter, 'I would like you to fuse force with grace, perfection in draughtsmanship with the magic of colour', he would doubtless reply that he would like to be able to do it. But if I said to him, 'I'm hoping to find in a picture the haughty, bold, expert touches of Michelangelo together with the pure, graceful, soft strokes of Correggio, the true and profound expressions of Domenichino, the lissome, enticing heads of Parmigianino, the effects of light, the brilliant, glowing colours and the soft, harmonious passages that captivate me in the paintings of Titian, those huge bodies and strong contrasts of light and shade that lend such movement and grandeur to the compositions of Annibale Carracci', then my painter would probably say to me, as Apelles said to Megabises: 'Don't speak too loud in case the one who is mixing my colours should laugh at you.' There are certain kinds of beauty which, by their very nature, are beyond the province of art. It would be absurd, wouldn't it, in looking at the figure of Laocoön as he utters his cries, his features convulsed, his muscles swollen with pain, to look for the grace and nobility, the elegance of form, and the imposing calm shining out from the figure of the *Apollo Belvedere*?[82]

Gluck next came under fire from the famous writer J.-F. Marmontel, an ardent supporter of Italian opera, and in particular of Piccinni, the Italian composer brought to Paris and set up as a rival to Gluck. In his 'Essay on the Progress of Music in France' (1777),[83] Marmontel reacted against the prevailing enthusiasm for Gluck in Paris by introducing a kind of test of the worth of music, that it should not only excite the passions, it should also be pleasing, a quality which in Gluck's music is found wanting:

> We know that the set rule of the ancients was never to allow grief to deform the appearance of beauty. The dying *Gladiator, Niobe,* and *Laocoön* [three sculptures from antiquity, each portraying extreme expressions] are examples of this. Not that a convulsed expression on the face would not have been much more frightening; rather, the pain this would have inflicted would not have been mixed with pleasure. The Greeks took the same care in tragedy to give the most violent passions, either in action, or in language, all the charm of expression: even strength had its own elegance.[84]

In this passage Marmontel brings the world of opera into contact with a subject of recent discussion by Europe's literati, focusing attention on one of the most celebrated of ancient sculptures. This is the group showing the Trojan priest Laocoön and his two young sons, their bodies crushed by giant snakes after Laocoön had warned his countrymen about accepting the wooden horse as a gift from the Greeks.[85] The sculpture was described by Pliny as among the most famous in imperial Rome, and the one he himself considered superior to all others. In the eighteenth century, it sparked a consideration of the acceptable limits of expression in the visual arts. For Winckelmann, who in 1755 compared it with Virgil's description of Laocoön's death in the *Aeneid*, the sculpture perfectly balanced the needs of beauty with those of expression; thus, for example, he claimed that the partly open mouth of the figure of Laocoön appropriately suggested the groans of the dying priest, which he contrasted with the violence of the cries of Virgil's Laocoön: 'His shrieks were horrible and filled the sky, like a bull's bellow when an axe has struck awry ...'.[86] In the sculpture, Winckelmann thought, its artists ensured that the subject was treated with a dignity, restraint and taste commensurate with the ideals of simple, quiet grandeur of classical Greek statuary, unlike the explicit description of Virgil, with its vivid and gruesome details, which leaves a very different kind of impression on the mind.

Lessing's influential essay *Laocoön* (1766) takes as its starting point Winckelmann's assertion (in discussing the Laocoön group) that 'noble simplicity and sedate grandeur in Gesture and Expression' were characteristic of Greek sculpture. Lessing challenged the notion which had prevailed since the Renaissance that painting – and by extension sculpture – was merely a mute form of poetry, realizing for the eyes the images and descriptions of literature.[87] Lessing wished to distinguish clearly the visual from the literary arts. According to his analysis, the visual arts are in essence figurative arts, which make their effect in space; poetry, however, is concerned with continuing action, which makes its impact in time. Beauty in the visual arts derives from the depiction of the human body and its proportions. For Lessing, this explains why the sculptors of the *Laocoön* represented the figures naked, the human body in its most beautiful and purest form; this was not, and could not be, relevant to Virgil, who indicates that his Laocoön was clothed. In their striving for beauty, the sculptors had to ensure that the suffering of the figures was not represented such that it destroyed their corporeal beauty and the harmony of the composition.

Although neither Winckelmann nor Lessing was concerned directly with music, their arguments were so well known that they made an impact on the writers of the Gluck controversy. Marmontel, in the passage quoted above, distorts them to underline his case that the representation of extreme emotion in any of the arts only achieves merit if it is done with beauty, leaving an impression of pleasure. According to Marmontel, Gluck fails this test. Unlike Lessing, Marmontel does not distinguish between the visual and literary arts. His main analogy is between poetry and music; but he uses the visual arts (his knowledge of which seems to have been limited) to bolster his position, perhaps because of their topicality. The confusion between literary and pictorial values, which Lessing had attempted to disentangle, is really in Marmontel's line of thought further confounded because he treats music as though it were a branch of poetry, and the kind of beauty which leads to pleasure in painting is also found in poetry. Suard, however, seems to accept Lessing's view that the visual arts obey the laws of beauty, not those of the literary arts. This allows him to perceive a new kind of alliance between the visual arts and music, in which beauty, embracing a range of notions, is a common factor. For Suard, the *Laocoön* was certainly a beautiful sculpture, but its beauty is only one of a range of different kinds of beauty. What he considered the extreme emotion of the *Laocoön* may stand at the opposite end of the spectrum from the quiet grandeur of the *Apollo Belvedere*, but, just as Gluck's heightened expressivity seemed far removed from the soothing and melodious strains of Piccinni, both in fact are excellent examples of beauty.

Marmontel seems to have been ill at ease in coming to terms with the use of notions drawn from criticism of the visual arts in contributions to the Gluck debate by his opponents. Later in the 'Essay on the Progress of Music in France', for example, he twice quotes from a letter published by an anonymous Gluck enthusiast who, like Suard, had found it useful to draw on pictorial analogies. Marmontel cites such passages verbatim, perhaps in an attempt to ridicule them.[88] A year later, he published a still more forceful attack on Gluck, which is known to have incensed the composer. Part of this piece concerns the competence of individuals to judge artistic matters; according to Marmontel the identity of the writer should be taken into account in weighing up the worth of criticism, otherwise

> Anyone who believed he had been endowed by nature with the gift of judging everything without having learned anything would be allowed to congratulate himself on possessing this rare gift from heaven; but if in his

enthusiasm, he denied soul and intelligence to anyone who had the misfortune not to admire what he admires or to like what he does not like; if with one hand he sought to knock down the statues of the most famous artists and with the other to erect a great monument to the glory of someone whom he had chosen to idolise; his name would reveal if this fanaticism was sincere or feigned.[89]

Here the 'anyone' refers to Gluck's supporters, some of whom wrote anonymously, as in the case of the article Marmontel quoted in his 'Essay'. By adding a phrase in which Marmontel adopts the language of the Gluckian party, he was pointedly hitting back at them, making out that they were the destroyers of an illustrious past (knocking down 'the statues of the most famous artists'), sacrificing this for something which had yet to be adequately tested (building 'a great monument to the glory of someone', the 'someone' evidently being Gluck). Suard could not let such an assault go unanswered. Replying in October 1778, he turned the tables again by suggesting the logic of Marmontel's position was that a public would forget the great artists of the past if it were deluged by the products of new ones, whatever their merit: 'It follows from [Marmontel's] theory that ... when Italy had more great painters than she has great musicians today, the new pictures must, of necessity, make them forget those of Michelangelo and Raphael.'[90] This was of course nonsense. But by choosing examples from Italy, the land of Marmontel's favourite composers, Suard met Marmontel's challenge head on. In reminding his readers that the Italian Renaissance produced many more painters than the eighteenth century had produced Italian composers, though this had done nothing to damage the subsequent reputations of artists like Michelangelo and Raphael, Suard was showing not only that support for Gluck was no threat to the standing of any artist, past or present, but also that advocates of Gluck who called on the visual arts to support their cause had made a more stimulating contribution to the discourse on the development of modern opera than the Italianists, like Marmontel, who relied on familiar literary conventions.

Suard was not the only writer on music to follow Gluck in making use of the visual arts in projecting a case to the public. A year before his appointment as Kapellmeister to Frederick the Great in 1775, Reichardt (whose subsequent enthusiasm for Gluck has already been discussed) published his 'Letters of an Attentive Traveller', in which he related some recent musical experiences.[91] In the first letter, for example, concerning the Berlin of his future employer, Reichardt demonstrates a comparison of the operas of Graun with those of Hasse; both are beautiful, but Hasse knows how to create an effect from the point of view of the audience, in which Graun fails:

In this connection, the story of the two Greek sculptors is in point. Each is asked to make a goddess to be set up in a temple at a considerable height. This being done, the two figures are exhibited to the crowd. Scarcely have they been unveiled when everyone runs to the one figure, shouting : 'This is beauty! This is art! With what industry and paints all this is worked out! As to that other one – fie on its distorted face! What a broad high forehead it has! What a nose, and what a big space between it and the mouth! Who ever saw such a face on a goddess?' The shrewder artist is silent and asks only that the two figures be placed in position. His is the first to be elevated. As it rises further and further from the floor it seems to undergo a transformation; astonishment overcomes the crowd and confused mutterings are heard. At length it stands in position, and the crowd grows still, standing as though rooted to the spot, blinded by its beauty. Then the other figure is elevated in its turn. It too is transformed, for no one can any longer recognise it. ... The one artist recognises his mistake and disappears, while the other, surrounded by the crowd, is crowned with the triumph, honour, and praise that accompany him for the remainder of his life.[92]

Reichardt's point in this passage and perhaps the story itself were probably derived from the examples of Gluck (the letter of dedication to *Paride ed Elena* of 1770) and Calzibigi. Gluck is also likely to have been the source of Reichardt's view that 'Both *forte* and *piano* are in Adagio very different from what they are in Allegro; the painter, similarly, uses very different degrees of light and shade in depicting a sad or gentle situation and in a merry banquet scene or furious battle piece.'[93] In fact Reichardt frequently resorts to such parallels, suggesting that his readership in Berlin were well prepared for such notions, perhaps as a result of Algarotti's presence in the city at mid-century.[94] Indeed Reichardt continued to develop such parallels throughout his career. In his *Musikalischer Almanach* published in Berlin in 1796, for example, he distinguished the compositions of the sons of Johann Sebastian Bach by claiming that Friedemann worked in black, Emanuel in grey and Christian in colours taken from nature.

By the time that Reichardt was experimenting in Berlin with Gluckian notions of comprehending music through knowledge of the visual arts, new associations between opera and the visual arts were developing in Paris as a result of Gluck's growing reputation. Gluck's popularity in Paris was recognized through the exhibition of a marble bust of him at the Salon of 1775 by the rising sculptor Jean-Antoine Houdon (1741–1828), whose informal portrayal of the composer – his open shirt, his lively, but unkempt appearance, his pockmarked face, and the tilt of his head – suggests an attempt to convey the spontaneous and unorthodox appeal of his music.[95]

In the same year the celebrated singer Sophie Arnould, whose reputation was established the previous year in the title role of Gluck's *Iphigénie en Aulide*, made an agreement with the same sculptor for an equally unconventional marble bust, showing her in the character of Iphigénie.[96] Houdon shows her wearing a sash decorated with crescent moon and stars, indicating her dedication to Diana, whose mercy she implores, expressed through her face and her over-large eyes looking upwards. This pose and other features of the bust – its chaste eroticism, the contrived state of disarray, with one breast exposed and hair dishevelled, and the mixture of grace and abandon

– presumably reflect Mlle Arnould's appearance on stage on the point of Iphigénie's sacrifice, the moment that Agamemnon could not bear to behold.

Although portraits of well-known personages, including actors, shown with the attributes of theatrical characters had long been popular, basing the portrait of a singer on her performance in a celebrated *operatic* role, which itself had a string of cultural associations, was a rarity. Like the bust of Gluck, it was exhibited at the Salon of 1775; but as an image, Houdon's bust of Arnould must have achieved very widespread popular circulation since the document of commission stipulated that the sculptor was personally to 'finish' no fewer than thirty plaster copies, and more if subsequently required; these were doubtless intended to satisfy the interest of the growing number of Gluck's supporters, whose newly discovered musical enthusiasms had very likely been encouraged by Arnould's performance.

A further token of esteem for Gluck from an artist working in Paris at this time comes from Fragonard's drawing known today as *Homage to Gluck*, showing three busts representing the composer in the august company of Homer and Virgil; beneath Gluck (represented in the middle) is a plaque inscribed 'AMANTI DEGLI ARTI'; and in front of them an admiring artist, palette and brushes at the foot of his chair.[97] This was probably executed to celebrate one of Gluck's operatic triumphs in Paris in the 1770s. Fragonard was certainly influenced by opera. It has been shown that his two paintings from the story of Armida and Rinaldo took their inspiration not directly from Tasso, but either from Lully's 1686 *Armide*, revived in 1761 and 1764, or from Gluck's 1777 *Armide*, based on the same libretto.[98]

Gluck's last opera for Paris, *Iphigénie en Tauride*, which tells how Iphigenia was reunited with her brother Orestes 15 years after she had been rescued from sacrifice, also attracted the attention of at least one leading artist at its première in 1779. Gabriel de Saint-Aubin is best remembered for his unique views of Salon exhibitions and his helpful sketches of paintings in his copies of Salon *livrets* and in contemporary sale catalogues.[99] He recorded, for example, the appearance of one of Fragonard's Armida paintings when it was sold in 1778, thus confirming the identification of the subject matter of the painting. Saint-Aubin's depiction of the appearance of Diana towards the end of Gluck's highly successful opera – another *dea ex machina* – helps to clarify a number of points about the relationship of opera to images in the public sphere by the end of the 1770s. From the artist's point of view, it indicates that the business of making a visual record of an episode in an opera which caught the public imagination was only a step away from recording those paintings which, for whatever reason, the public found remarkable at the same period. In other words, what was seen on stage at the Opéra came to be perceived at this time as part of the same realm – affecting the same perceptive processes – as what was seen at the Salon or at an auction of paintings. It was therefore subject to the same standards and language of critical appreciation.

The culmination of this process may be shown in relation to one of the most celebrated paintings of the time, J.-L. David's *Oath of the Horatii*, first exhibited in France at the Salon of 1785. David's picture put into paint a subject, and to some extent a sentiment, already well known in Paris through Corneille's play *Horace* (1639), the dénouement of which corresponds in some details with the painting, and through Noverre's 1777 ballet, *Les Horaces*, with music by Josef Starzer. This has been shown to anticipate many aspects of David's conception, most notably the use of the three swords.[100] Noverre, who also collaborated on the ballets in Gluck's operas, may have come to David's attention through one of his close literary mentors, M.-J. Sedaine, whose accomplishments included writing opera libretti.

The huge impact of David's painting on the public inspired in turn the production in Paris of an opera the following year, *Les Horaces*, with music by Salieri, Gluck's closest musical follower, and words by Guillard, who had also supplied the libretto for Gluck's *Iphigénie en Tauride*. Although *Les Horaces* was not a success, this did not dissuade David turning to a musical source again two years later in *Paris and Helen*. The subject and character of this have been shown to relate closely to Gluck's *Paride ed Elena*, a relationship unlikely to have been lost on many who saw the painting when first exhibited in 1788.[101] It is no coincidence that the word which came to be used for the catalogues of the *Salon* exhibitions sold to members of the public in the eighteenth century was the same word used in French for an opera libretto: *livret*.

Another factor which brought closer the spheres the *Salon* exhibitions and the *Opéra* in the public domain was the growth of popular criticism. By the 1780s, the kind of parody which had developed in the *vaudevilles* associated with the *Opéra comique* had found a new target in the *Salon* exhibitions, which anyone might visit free of charge. Farcical characters, generally representing the underprivileged, but whose cultural presence was felt by all ranks of society, were used as protagonists in musical critiques, disseminated to visitors in the form of pamphlets.[102] At the 1785 Salon exhibition, for example, one of these protagonists was Figaro, the servant hero of Beaumarchais's celebrated plays, made even more famous in operas by Paisiello and Mozart.[103] Beaumarchais characterized Figaro by his good humour and love of song. An engraving in the pamphlet shows Figaro at the exhibition: 'Today I am a critic', he says, 'To inspire my studies I'll mix them with some songs.'[104] Behind him appear several paintings, including David's *Horatii*. This mixing of musical and pictorial elements at the popular level probably coloured the way Haydn's music was perceived in Paris. Haydn's 'Paris' symphonies made the same overwhelming impact on Parisian audiences as David's *Horatii* a year or so earlier.[105] It seems likely that the new range of emotions conveyed to viewers of the painting were closely connected with those experienced by audiences for the music.[106]

Saint-Aubin's drawing from the first production of Gluck's *Iphigénie en Tauride*, representing the dénouement of the opera, suggests that by the late 1770s there were artists who consciously looked out for the most pictorial and memorable scenes in opera as the basis of their own work, probably because they knew that in a sense the public had already been prepared for the concept, and thus interest had already been aroused. Such was the rapport that the same kind of relationship could work in the other direction, an opera taking its cue from a painting. Saint-Aubin's selection of the scene of the appearance of Diana in *Iphigénie en Tauride* shows how Gluck's instinct to include an equivalent scene in the revised version of his earlier *Iphigénie* opera for Paris had been in tune with public taste. Audiences in Paris were treated to a very similar experience shortly afterwards when the same libretto was given to Gluck's rival, Piccinni, whose setting was staged in 1781.[107] Popular fascination with such scenes at this time is further attested by Diana's appearance in similar circumstances at the conclusion of Haydn's *La fedeltà premiata* (1780), a kind of comic parody of the sacrifice operas associated with Gluck, the libretto for which was originally set by Cimarosa.

An important factor in the pictorial appeal of these scenes is that the Diana character alludes to images connected with her cult: in Gluck's opera she orders the Scythians to restore to the Greeks statues of her taken from her temples in Greece; and in Haydn's opera – the sacrifice demanded being a pair of lovers – the image which has to be restored is of the goddess's heart.[108] Such details derive, of course, from the ancient legends concerning Iphigenia and from Euripides' play. According to Classical sources Iphigenia alone on Tauris had the right to handle the sacred image of Diana (Artemis); and Orestes travelled there (unaware of his sister's presence there) to reclaim it in the belief that this would save him from the torments he experienced as a consequence of having murdered Clytemnestra, their mother, an act which avenged Clytemnestra's murder of their father, Agamemnon.

In earlier operatic versions of the story, images of Diana play an even more fundamental role in the plot. As a result of the success of a play on this subject staged in Paris in 1757, praised by Diderot and other critics, the Iphigenia on Tauris story was taken up by a number of opera composers not long afterwards, notably Tommaso Traetta.[109] Although in Traetta's *Ifigenia in Tauride* (Vienna, 1763) Diana herself does not appear, the plot resolving itself through human means, the chief premise of this version of the story is Orestes' quest to reclaim the image of Diana from her temple in Tauris and return it to Greece. A statue of Diana would therefore have been a prerequisite for performance of this opera, which proved to be enormously successful, early productions taking place in cities as far apart as Milan, St Petersburg and Copenhagen. Indeed Traetta's *Ifigenia* may be considered an important precursor of the 'reform' operas by Gluck, who is known to have conducted it in Florence in 1767.[110] Before working in Vienna, Traetta had been in Parma, where his Bourbon employers encouraged him to set translations of libretti originally written for Rameau, such as *Castor et Pollux*, which in Traetta's version became *I Tintaridi* (1760). The chief minister in Parma, Guillaume du Tillot, who was responsible for much of the French cultural influence at this time, was on close terms not only with Algarotti, but also with Durazzo in Vienna. Together they helped to shape Traetta's view of music drama by advocating the introduction of French elements into traditional Italian opera, including choruses, ballets and an appreciation of ancient Greek drama.[111] One measure of the respect in which Traetta's *Ifigenia* opera was held is that it was produced as late as 1786 at Eszterháza, a fairly rare intrusion into the prevailing taste for comic operas: Haydn inserted at the beginning of the opera a newly composed recitative and aria for Orestes, explaining to his companion Pylades how he felt himself ever pursued by the grim, pitiless apparition of his murdered mother surrounded by the Furies, a torment which the quest to retrieve Diana's statue was intended to expiate.[112]

Another token of the popularity of the Iphigenia in Tauris story by the 1760s, and possibly of Traetta's opera in particular, is that one of Benjamin West's first paintings exhibited in London after having studied in Italy was based on this theme.[113] It shows the friends Orestes and Pylades brought before Iphigenia the high priestess, with a view of the statue of Diana depicted as a huntress in the background. Although West probably derived the essential elements of his scene from Euripides, the group of disputing soldiers to the right of Orestes and Pylades do not correspond to anything in the play and may have a basis in some knowledge of Traetta's opera.[114] West's painting became widely appreciated on the Continent, partly on account of a print of it published by Boydell in 1771, and partly because the heads of its chief characters were engraved as illustrations in one of the most popular books of the age, J.C. Lavater's *Physiognomische Fragmente*, in the first edition of 1775. The *Fragmente* enthusiastically advanced the theory that the face is the mirror of the inner being. West was one of only two living artists (the other was Chodowiecki) used for his illustrations by Lavater, who described West's painting as 'one of the most beautiful pieces I know', praising it as a demonstration of the harmony between physical and moral beauty. West responded to this by giving Lavater one of his paintings which was also used as an illustration to an additional volume of the *Fragmente* published in 1778.[115] Lavater's grand opus captured the public imagination. Haydn certainly came under its spell;[116] and it seems not unlikely that Gluck studied the sections concerning West's picture and Lavater's theory that human appearance betrays inner moral character when preparing his *Iphigénie en Tauride*.

Not everyone agreed, however, that West's contribution was beneficial to the work. The painter Henry Fuseli, who counted Lavater a friend since their youth, objected to the use made of a painting by his rival in the *Fragmente*, and probably for this reason the relevant illustrations were dropped in later editions. Fuseli, however, also found himself drawn to the Iphigenia in Tauris story, though to rather different elements from those which inspired West. What appealed to Fuseli was the torment suffered by Orestes through his vision of the Furies accompanying the ghost of his mother. Such visions, or terrifying dreams involving spectres and other supernatural creatures, were a preoccupation of Fuseli throughout his career. They have often been seen as one aspect of his expression of the Burkean sublime. Although it is possible to point to disturbing dream images by artists working before the mid-eighteenth century, examples are rare and do not suggest a source for Fuseli's fascination.[117] It has usually been assumed that Fuseli's inspiration was primarily literary and that, for example, passages in Shakespeare's tragedies involving ghosts caught his imagination at a time when the illustration of Shakespeare was becoming an issue for artists working in London. But his earliest depiction of a dream of this type, a drawing of Orestes witnessing a vision of his mother accompanied by the Furies (c.1763), may be connected with Traetta's opera, not only on account of the proximity of the dates of their execution, but also because the opera was unusual for its time in depicting on stage both the sleeping Orestes in torment, and also the cause of his torment, the Furies and the ghost of Clytemnestra.[118] This was such a distinctive and successful scene that it was later imitated in Gluck's opera on the same subject. Before Fuseli's drawing of Orestes, post-Renaissance artists had been reluctant to show both vision as well as dreamer within the same image in depicting subjects of this type. Their preference was to show the dreamer alone, experiencing a vision otherwise invisible, implying the workings of a deluded mind.[119] Traetta's opera of 1763 may have been the catalyst for this change since it also marks an important development in the portrayal of the workings of the mind in music drama, setting to music both the physical state of the dreamer as well as the vision itself.[120]

3. Painting the Cannon's Roar

In January 1764, only months after the first performances of Traetta's *Ifigenia*, audiences in Vienna were exposed to another new opera which acted as a forum for commenting on the visual arts. This was one outcome of the dual interests of Kaunitz and his theatre intendant, Durazzo.

The opera which excited so much attention at the beginning of 1764 was an *opéra-comique* in French by Gluck called *La Rencontre imprévue*. The libretto was adapted from *Les Pélerins de la Mecque*, a successful musical play first performed in Paris in 1726.[121] Set in Ottoman Cairo, the plot centres on the attempt by a prince to rescue his beloved from the harem of the Sultan, who at the end of the opera reunites the lovers and pardons all misdemeanours. In the original text, a minor episode concerned a French painter called Vertigo, his name hinting at his deranged state of mind, the pretext for some comic diversion.[122] Although Vertigo plays no part in the plot proper, in Gluck's opera his role was greatly expanded, the comedy he generates playing on the public's knowledge of, and preconceptions about, artists and artistic practice.

Although Gluck's Vertigo was not an entirely original creation, the part was given topicality because a well-known artist trained in Paris, who had subsequently spent part of his career in Constantinople, had been in Vienna only months earlier making drawings of, among others, Kaunitz and the numerous imperial children. This artist was Liotard, whose admirers included Mme de Pompadour, Horace Walpole and Mrs Delany. His reputation had been guaranteed by the notoriety he lent himself by adopting Turkish habits and wearing Turkish dress when in Western society.[123] His enormous beard made a particular impact. Liotard was also responsible for giving the West some of its best images of what Turkish life might be like. His drawings were probably used in designs for Gluck's opera. His theory that the best judge of a work of art was the ignorant man on the street, rather than the educated critic or the academy painter, also endeared him to certain sections of the public. Liotard was, therefore, a meaningful figure in Vienna when Gluck's opera was premièred. The audience would have had little trouble relating Liotard's extravagant persona to the stage presence of the equally eccentric Monsieur Vertigo, who is described as 'famous', but who now prefers to adopt the habit of a Muslim, like Liotard.

During Vertigo's first brief appearance in the opera his eccentricity is established when he refers to himself as 'a supernatural being', a reference to a favourite eighteenth-century notion about great artists, that they belonged to a select group of eternal geniuses, a status to which ordinary mortals could not aspire.[124] Vertigo likens himself to a string of Old Master painters, whose names derive from the famous catalogue of artists by de Piles, only he prefaces the list with the names of Cato and Socrates, and ends it with a number of fabulous beasts. In the aria which ends his first appearance on stage, Vertigo compares his 'divine paintbrush' to the work of Prometheus, who in Greek mythology fashioned the first man from clay and stole fire from the gods to give to mankind. The aria ends with Vertigo proclaiming that he was about to abandon the earth to his rivals and fly into the skies in order to paint the effect of *thunder*.

Such nonsense was probably intended to satirize some of the latest artistic theories emanating out of Paris. Socrates and Prometheus were among the heroes of the Enlightenment, inspiring both artists and composers. The vogue among the *philosophes* for comparing themselves with Socrates in particular was followed by artists, such as the sculptor Falconet, who reminded his readers that the ancient Greek had been a sculptor *before* becoming a philosopher.[125] A picture depicting thunder was claimed by Pliny to have been painted by Apelles, the most famous painter of antiquity, so Vertigo is attempting something which the most famous of painters had already achieved. The idea that a painter could depict something which one primarily *hears* rather than *sees*, of course, fascinated Enlightenment thinkers, especially following the renewed interest in Pliny generated by Falconet's translation of, and commentary on, the sections on painting and sculpture in the *Natural History*.[126]

Vertigo's other appearance in *La Rencontre imprévue* occurs in an extended scene in which two of the main characters are obliged to wait for an audience with the Sultan. Together they are kept amused by inspecting a series of paintings by Vertigo which were shown on stage. Since designs for the opera have not survived, the only evidence for the form of these pictures comes from the libretto; this is sufficient to indicate that Vertigo was an artist abreast of the times.

Vertigo's first painting portrayed a splendid banquet with 20 people enjoying themselves. The table showed a superb display of food, with the guests entertained by a group of musicians. The most celebrated of banqueting paintings featuring musicians was, of course, Veronese's *Marriage at Cana* (Fig. 1), then still in San Giorgio Maggiore in Venice, but widely known through prints and imitations by later artists. Fragonard drew it in 1761.[127] It probably inspired some of the banqueting scenes by French artists which became popular for the decoration of aristocratic dining rooms in the 1730s.[128] Perhaps Vertigo's banqueting scene was a late example of this genre; but its inspiration might equally lie with the series of paintings by Tiepolo illustrating Cleopatra's banquet (Fig. 11), suggested by Algarotti, whose writings would certainly have been read by part of Vertigo's audience.

Vertigo himself says that he painted the musicians in his banquet scene with such skill that it is easy to see that they are playing *Italian* music. To his fury, however, the characters to whom he shows his pictures repeatedly fail to identify correctly the kind of music Vertigo intended his performers to be playing. Their first guess is that it is an Adagio, when it actually transpires that it is a 'presto prestissimo'. This is a clear parody of the idea, evidently well understood, that a picture is capable of conveying musical sounds to the sensitive viewer, which discussion of Newton's theory had helped to foster in the public sphere. Finally appreciating the intensity of sound Vertigo put in his picture, one of the characters is obliged to respond, for want of anything better to say, by commenting on the incredible number of brush-strokes needed to paint so much noise.

Vertigo's second painting is a landscape, which we are informed was painted in 'his true style', provoking comments of 'What *nobility*!' and 'What *majesty*!' The scene itself, it appears, showed a herd of young white cows frolicking with a group of young black bulls, and some admirable perspectival effects, including rustic shacks forming colonnades of 'sublime taste'. The painting left its viewers speechless: 'The only thing one can say is ... well, didn't you paint another picture?'

Vertigo's landscape might at first seem to belong in essence to that genre of Dutch seventeenth-century landscape paintings featuring groups of cattle, quietly reposing, rediscovered in eighteenth-century France, where they became prized by collectors.[129] However, the subject matter of Vertigo's painting is, of course, complete nonsense: groups of bulls do not frolic with herds of cows, and rustic shacks never form colonnades. It seems likely that what it was expected Viennese audiences 1764 would understand by this painting was a kind of caricature of the latest painting fad from Paris. Among the most discussed painters at the 1763 Salon was the young Loutherbourg, exhibiting a group of landscapes for the first time. These paintings caught the eye of Diderot, who established Loutherbourg's reputation by praising him above many better-known painters exhibiting the same year. As a result of this Loutherbourg soon achieved widespread fame as a painter of pastoral scenes, often featuring cattle and rustic sheds.[130]

Diderot's Salon criticisms were intended principally to give readers abroad a sense of developments in visual culture in Paris. Nowhere were they read more avidly than in Vienna, where Kaunitz's French alliance heightened public sensitivity to anything new from Paris, the European capital of fashion. A sense of how men like Durazzo were anxious to hear what was culturally newsworthy from Paris comes from the way he maintained a correspondence with the Parisian entrepreneur, Favart, who supplied him with the original libretto of *Les Pèlerins*. For example, towards the end of 1761, Favart reported to Durazzo how Greuze's most recent success at the Salon of the same year, *L'accordée de village*, was within months turned into a *tableau vivant* by a Parisian theatre, apparently set to music. Greuze was one of the painters most praised by Diderot, a position soon to be challenged by Loutherbourg.

According to Diderot writing in 1763, Loutherbourg was a 'rare phenomenon': 'He's great, he's already mature; is there anything he isn't?'[131] In his Salon criticisms of that year, Diderot described in detail one painting by Loutherbourg which particularly impressed him.[132] In this canvas he urged his readers to note 'the bulls ... don't they come to life? Can't you see them chewing the cud? Can't you see their their true colour, their true character, the real skin of those animals? What intelligence and what vigour! That child [Loutherbourg] was born with his thumb clasping a palette.'[133] Later in his discussion, Diderot could not help touching on the aural aspects of the picture: 'the conversation of that herdsman and that peasant woman will amuse us; our ears will not be offended by the rustic sounds of the drover, who charms the silence of that lonely place and banishes the boredom of his condition by playing the flute.'[134]

It has to be remembered that most of Diderot's readers would not actually have had the opportunity of seeing the works he comments on, hence the colourful language he adopts was intended to help to bring the pictures to life. But for his aristocratic readers in Vienna, used to Old Master paintings and the late Baroque tradition, the points Diderot was trying to make about Loutherbourg probably seemed hopelessly ridiculous. Vertigo's landscape, with its frisky cows and bulls parodying the pastoral lovers depicted by Loutherbourg and others, deliberately mocks not only the tone of Diderot's enthusiasm, but also the notion that any landscape merited such weighty attention.

Vertigo's third picture was a battle-piece, a pendant to the banquet scene. 'I painted the horror', proclaims Vertigo, 'I inspire terror.' On one side appeared the cavalry with clashing sabres; on the other was the infantry, amidst the noise of gunfire, drums and trumpets. Vertigo's picture would be impossible to copy, because only he could capture in paint the *sound* of the batteries and the muskets, and all the other *noise* of the battlefield. As Vertigo himself points out, he even painted the cannon's *roar*.

Leaving aside the continuing emphasis on depicting sound in painting, which gave Gluck some splendid opportunities for musical word-painting, it is tempting to view this work as a conventional battle-piece of the type made popular by seventeenth-century artists like Wouwermans and Salvator Rosa; however, the actual form of Vertigo's painting again shows evidence of recent influences from Paris. Apart from seeing the launch of Loutherbourg's career, 1763 also marked the beginning of the same painter's reputation as an expert on battles, which he had already been painting as a student in the studio of another painter well known in this genre, Casanova. Loutherbourg subsequently painted several contemporary battles, adding authenticity by visiting the battlefields and taking copious drawings of the associated paraphernalia. Concerning Loutherbourg's battle-piece exhibited in 1763, Diderot wrote: 'among his pictures, he showed a small one with his name, Loutherbourg, written on the frame in large letters; its subject is a battle. It is exactly as though he were telling the whole world: "Gentlemen, remember those pieces by Casanova which so surprised you two years ago; look closely here and judge to whom belongs the merit of those others."[135] In other words, contemporaries recognized that this painting marked the end of Loutherbourg's work for Casanova, who had hitherto taken credit for Loutherbourg's contribution. The younger artist now announced himself to the world as an independent artist. The painting spoke volumes.

Vertigo's fourth painting may also be connected with Loutherbourg. An uncontrollable torrent, rushing down the side of a mountain, lays waste the countryside, destroying all in its path. Everywhere is devastation and horror. A human element is included in the form of a labourer transfixed with fear and terror. The content of this painting – with the enormity of its mountains, the overwhelming force of the workings of nature, the terror this provokes, and man's inability to withstand it – is an early response to Burke's theory of the sublime, first published in 1757, which made an immediate impact on writers like Diderot. Loutherbourg, among many artists, became obsessed with the representation of the theme of the supreme force of nature overpowering mankind, painting a series of avalanche pictures, showing snow or water cascading down the side of a mountain about to strike a small group of helpless humans, the best known of which was painted towards the end of his career.[136] Such paintings were, of course, not based on actual observation of natural phenomena, but artificially arranged to maximize the effect of terror.

The impact of the sublime in Vertigo's painting, however, was completely undermined because he included *in the same picture* 'a clear little stream', slowly winding its way across a plain, its banks covered with brightly coloured flowers, its gentle murmuring inviting beholders to sleep. As Vertigo himself says, 'the sighs of love could not be sweeter'. In a painting which portrays total devastation, the inclusion of such an idyllic, peaceful scene could not be more inappropriate. Such an element is again total nonsense, deliberately intended to make fun of the concept of the sublime. Presumably the librettist had in mind a pastoral scene of the type in which Boucher specialized, about as far from the sublime as it was possible to paint in 1763. Commenting on just such a painting by Boucher, exhibited the same year, Diderot wrote:

> ... a bit of landscape, and Heaven knows how many more details, all piled on top of one another; then paint the whole in the most brilliant colours, and you'll have the *Shepherd Scene* by Boucher. ... Must a painter paint everything? Can't he leave anything at all to my imagination? ... This man is the ruin of our young painters. As soon as they are able to hold brush and palette, they begin to sweat over garlanded putti, ... to indulge in all sorts of extravagances which are not saved by the warmth, originality, prettiness or magic of their model, but have all its faults.[137]

Gluck's music, of course, helps to emphasize the point. The 'sweet murmurings', which 'can be *heard* through one's *eyes*', can also be heard through one's ears in the form of some of Gluck's most delicate music, making a splendid contrast with the dramatic and energetic musical tone-painting accompanying the account of the devastation caused by the torrent.[138]

The colourful pastoral scene with the stream leads, in Gluck's opera, to a pretext for discussing Vertigo's handling of colour. This was certainly a very topical subject, widely discussed at the Paris Salons exhibitions. There is plenty of evidence that many of the more adventurous artists in mid-eighteenth-century Paris were disgusted by the level of much art criticism which was more concerned with quibbling about the appropriateness of an artist's choice of colour than the true artistic concept behind a painting. On being praised for what he can achieve with a limited range of colours on his palette, Vertigo admits to being an expert in 'the art of mixing colours'. Agreeing with him, one of his guests chooses an unfortunate turn of phrase in an attempt to complement him: 'you really have to know how to *marry* colours together'. The word 'marry' instantly sends Vertigo into a state of apoplexy. He suddenly sees a vision of a monster, who turns out to be Hymen, the god of marriage. For Vertigo, Hymen appears with wizened features and as a coward, characteristics which start to intrigue the painter as he considers their artistic possibilities. Vertigo therefore makes his final exit chasing after this apparition, protesting that he wants to paint Hymen 'in his true colours'.

Hymen was certainly iconographically significant in painting of the middle years of the eighteenth century, as his appearance in works by, for example, Reynolds and Zoffany testifies.[139] By turning him into an apparition, Gluck and his collaborators were, of course, parodying the use of apparitions in recent operas, like Traetta's *Ifigenia*, which in turn depended on the contemporary interest in the visionary in painting.

At Vertigo's first appearance in Gluck's opera it is clearly established that one of his main character traits is that he hated his wife, whom he abandoned; any talk of marriage sends him into a frenzy. When his painting of a banquet is mistaken for a *wedding* feast, all attempts to bring his mind back to sanity fail until the painting is eventually re-identified as a celebration of divorce.[140] Although many eighteenth-century painters really did leave their wives in order to pursue artistic careers, the source of the notion of artistic and matrimonial incompatibility as portrayed in Gluck's opera is almost certainly the Pygmalion legend, as told by Ovid, in which the sculptor Pygmalion resolves to lead a celibate life, horrified at the dissolute ways of the women around him, only to fall in love with his own creation, a beautiful statue of a woman, who following an invocation to Venus, the goddess of love, comes to life.

Some members of the audience at early performances of Gluck's *Rencontre imprévue* may have made the connection between Vertigo and Pygmalion through Falconet's version of the subject, exhibited at the Salon of 1763, or rather through Diderot's comments on it.[141] But in any case, the eighteenth century was the great age of the Pygmalion legend, starting in 1700 with La Barre's opera *Le triomphe des arts*, in which the art of sculpture was represented by an enactment of this very tale.[142] Countless operas, ballets, paintings and engravings indicate how this tale of a work of art coming to life was found to be enormously appealing throughout the century. In almost all the pictorial representations of the story, like the engraving by de Ghendt (in fact an illustration of Rousseau's opera on the subject), the moment chosen for portrayal is that of the first stirrings of animation in the statue. The story was so familiar that by 1800 Thomas Rowlandson could confidently parody the whole idea of the animated statue by leaving little to the imagination concerning what was on Pygmalion's mind in willing the statue into life. Jean Raoux's *Pygmalion amoureux de sa statue* (1717) even includes the torch-bearing figure of the god Hymen, clarifying still further the origins of the characterization of Vertigo in the Pygmalion legend.[143] It is not surprising therefore that a drawing illustrating a Pygmalion ballet of 1758 is evidently related to this painting, and significantly found its way into the collection of Durazzo, who commissioned Gluck's opera.[144]

Another landmark opera which depended on the Pygmalion legend and also presented the practice of the visual arts on stage, set to music, was Duni's *opéra-comique Le peintre amoureux de son modèle* of 1757, in which an aged painter and his young apprentice both fall in love with the same young woman who models for them.[145] The opera was so popular that a parody of it appeared the following year entitled *Gilles, garçon peintre*, connecting Pygmalion with the world of popular theatre, particularly the character best known from the depictions of him by Watteau.[146] The popular theatre of Paris also made use of another story about a statue coming to life, the Don Juan/Don Giovanni story which, after Molière had popularized it, was repeatedly treated both musically and pictorially. However, long before Italian opera took up the story of the dead Commendatore taking revenge on his assassin by the statue on his monument coming to life, it had appeared in Paris in *commedia dell'arte* versions, several of which contained musical elements. In one version, the Don's amorous exploits were illustrated in a large picture shown to the audience and explained by his servant, useful evidence for how the story came to appeal to the visual imagination.[147] What all musical versions of the story concentrated on, and most pictorial versions illustrated, was, as in the Pygmalion story, the episode of the statue first coming to life. In some operatic versions, libretti provide very detailed instructions on the form the Commendatore's monument, which (in the context of the story) is only just approaching completion. This explains why in several operas on the subject the Don and his servant find themselves in the middle of the night in the mausoleum, satisfying themselves on the form of the monument before it has been unveiled to the public. A version of 1734, for example, explicitly states that there should be represented on stage a 'grand temple in the gothic style with magnificent monuments adorned with marble figures in the midst of which is the equestrian statue of the deceased Commendatore'.[148] Most of the images created in connection with Mozart's *Don Giovanni* chose this moment in the opera for illustration, suggesting that the animation of a monumental statue really did succeed in capturing the public's imagination.[149]

Another stage work which managed the same idea and made a comparable impact on audiences at this date was Shakespeare's *Winter's Tale*. Towards the end of the play the character of Hermione, who is believed to have died long before, is revealed convincingly to other characters in the play as a standing statue, which after its lifelike qualities are observed, really does come to life, drawing the play to a happy conclusion. To emphasize the wonder of this moment, Shakespeare himself demanded that this scene should be played to music.[150] When Garrick adapted the play in the 1750s, he had the whole episode set to music especially composed by William Boyce.[151] The statue scene was the moment in eighteenth-century productions of the play that was particularly chosen for illustration; many of these images were engraved, becoming popular prints of the period, testifying to the public's fascination with the notion of a work of art coming to life.[152]

The Winter's Tale may quite properly be included in a discussion of opera because another situation treated in its plot, the suspicion of Hermione's husband that she had been unfaithful with his best friend, provided the basis of an *opéra-comique* first performed in Paris in 1769 called *Le tableau parlant* (The Talking Picture), with a libretto by Anseaume (who was also responsible for *Le peintre amoureux de son modèle*) and music by the popular French composer Grétry.[153] In this comic version, with characters drawn from the *commedia dell'arte*, the action takes place around a near-completed portrait of Cassandre. In order to spy on a pair of lovers, Cassandre cuts out the face of his image, putting himself in its place. Much amusement is derived from one of the lovers rehearsing a confession to the portrait which, to general astonishment, eventually replies.[154] Indeed one eighteenth-century source actually claims that the idea for this talking portrait was adapted from a real story concerning the portrait-painter Ranc. According to this, Ranc placed one of his models behind a hole in a canvas showing the model's portrait in order to deceive some friends who had criticized his ability at capturing a likeness.[155] Apparently it had the desired effect. The story may have a whiff of Apelles' grapes deceiving the birds about it, but the evidence of his brand of portraiture suggests that it may have been true.[156]

Certainly, the whole concept of deceiving pictures, shown to an audience in a musical context, commanded undoubted attention. In another version of *Le peintre amoureux de son modèle*, the painter actually on stage begins to draw a picture of his ideal model with a series of carefully choreographed pen-strokes, the instructions and diagrams for which have survived, drawing particular attention to her ample breasts. When his wife enters unexpectedly, he quickly turns the picture upside-down, indicating the beginnings of an innocuous, though mountainous landscape.[157]

In 1771 Grétry completed another iconic *opéra-comique*, *Zémire et Azor*, a reworking of the 'Beauty and the Beast' story in an oriental setting, with a libretto by Marmontel.[158] What became the most memorable episode in the opera is a scene in which the beast reveals to the heroine a magic picture showing her father and sisters, who not only come to life, but may also be heard lamenting the loss of their loved one.[159] Several prints, drawings and paintings of this picture scene based on early performances are testimony to its particular appeal (Fig. 12). These show that the 'picture' took the form of what appears as an elaborately framed canvas painting of life size, but which was of course a small stage with its own proscenium and lighting.[160] As befits dedications to Mme du Barry of the opera proper, and to Marie-Antoinette of a print illustrating this *Tableau magique*, there was certainly no dubious taste involved in either the visual or the musical aspects of the work, unlike the version of *Le peintre amoureux* just mentioned. Dr Burney, who noted Grétry's special friendship with Liotard, saw *Zémire* in 1772 in Brussels, and described the opera as written 'with great art, taste, and genius', its music 'full of new ideas and imagery', its scenes 'rich, ingenious, and elegant'.[161] Grétry's music for the picture scene was clearly intended to enhance the enchantment of the imagery, played as it was by an offstage windband and making use of a mesmerizing repeated motif, apparently originally suggested by Diderot. In a sense it is not unreasonable to understand this musical-visual episode as a sophisticated response by Marmontel and Grétry to Vertigo's pictures in Gluck's *Rencontre imprévue*, bearing in mind that Gluck was one of their chief rivals. Although it is often difficult in the world of eighteenth-century opera to distinguish today between parody and the supposedly serious, in the case of *Zémire*, despite the context being a fairy tale, there is every reason to assume that the notion of the moving/talking picture was designed to be understood as plausible and realistic within the make-believe sphere of the opera's subject matter.[162] In his *Mémoires*, Grétry included a section discussing the relationship of sound to colour, or music to vision. This provides evidence that attempts to entertain an audience with an experience simultaneously pictorial and musical was a clear aesthetic objective.

Zémire and Grétry's earlier opera proved enormously popular, especially in London, where reworkings of the material appeared on stage within a year of the original Paris performances.[163] The London version of *Le tableau parlant* was called *The Portrait* to distinguish it from *The Picture*, an earlier opera by Thomas Arne, which itself had been based on a short play by Molière, *Le Sicilien, ou l'amour peintre* (The Sicilian, or Love makes the Painter), first performed in 1666 with music by Lully.[164] The main feature of these works is a character who impersonates a portrait-painter in order to observe his beloved. Much comic play is made of artistic conventions, especially the correct posing of the young woman who is the object of affection, in order to create the most flattering image: ensuring, for example, that her eyes are properly fixed on the painter, who may thereby pursue his seduction without being suspected.

The story was given another musical treatment in London in 1775, marking the beginning of an intensive period when portraits, talking and otherwise, and other works of art played a role in the plots of many operas. For instance, Cimarosa's *Il pittor parigino* (The Parisian Painter) of 1781, a very popular opera, especially in London, reprises many of the themes already discussed. In 1790 Parisians were treated to one opera called *Le portrait* and another entitled *Les portraits*.[165] Three years later in London, Mozart's friend the composer Stephen Storace successfully reworked *Le tableau parlant*, in a version entitled *My Grandmother*, after the figure portrayed in the portrait of this opera.[166] Isaac Cruikshank used the opera as the basis of a caricature satirizing the relationship between the Prince of Wales, who appears in a portrait, and his latest rather elderly mistress, portrayed in the caricature as the 'grandmother' of the opera's title.[167] Even Mozart's mature operas, though hardly known for such pictorial elements today, introduce portraits, galleries and other artistic details which seemingly reflect the public's appetite for seeing such images at the opera.[168]

Unfortunately, evidence for how audiences responded to the iconic element in musical theatre is scarce. In view of the public's evident enthusiasm for the interaction between music and image, it seems likely that the interaction itself came to have an effect on the ways people in Western society learned to look and to listen, and their expectations. The example of the 17-year-old Prince of Wales attending a performance of *The Winter's Tale* – as already indicated, an important stimulus to the development of moving images and talking pictures in opera – provides an insight into the consequences of this development. The Prince became infatuated with an actress in the performance, Mrs Robinson, one of the most frequently painted women of her time, who briefly became his mistress.[169] He wrote to her signing himself Florizel, the name of her beloved in the play, showing how closely he identified with the character on stage. He even imitated the behaviour of leading personalities in these operas, by sending her a miniature portrait of himself, in the manner of Ferrando or Guglielmo in Mozart's *Così fan tutte*. Before giving up the stage for him, the last role in which Mrs Robinson appeared was *The Miniature Picture*, a play with music by Lady Craven, whose wide circle of admirers included Walpole and Kaunitz.[170] Another of the same author's musical plays, *The Statue Feast*, a reworking of the Don Juan story, suggests the extent of interest in introducing unmistakable references to visual culture into musical theatre.[171]

From this panoply of evidence for the interaction between visual culture and opera in the eighteenth century a straightforward conclusion may be drawn – that the public developed a taste for musical entertainments in the theatre, the most memorable parts of which drew inspiration from the visual arts. Operas came to feature not only references to paintings, sculptures and well-known artists, but they also highlighted issues such as the public's perception of what the theory and practice of painting and sculpture might be about, how the ordinary man or woman should respond to works of art, and what the conduct and temperament of a typical artist might be like. In a variety of ways the content of a considerable number of operas composed between the 1750s and the 1790s draw on material of this kind. Often music and image were tied together in such a way that they appealed because they were experienced together. Although this was at its most dynamic during the period Haydn was directing opera at Eszterháza, the tradition never died.[172]

Haydn himself may not have been at the forefront of these developments; but he was keenly aware of their implications and contributed to them. He introduced key operas to Eszterháza, including Cimarosa's *Il pittor parigino* and Grétry's *Zémire*. His own version of *La Rencontre imprévue* (*L'incontro improvviso*) may have dispensed with the character of Vertigo, who would have seemed a bit dated by 1775 (when the opera was produced), but the picture scene was retained: the opera's hero, disguising himself as a painter in an unsuccessful attempt to escape the Sultan, claims the skill to depict all the features of Vertigo's paintings.[173] In Haydn's opera, however, these elements are not simply comic; they become so implausible that detection of the bogus painter is inevitable. Haydn's *La vera costanza* (1778) also features a picture. In Act I the Baroness gives her nephew a portrait of the woman she intends him to marry; straightaway, he seems besotted, apparently rejecting the woman he has secretly married. The use of a portrait as a mechanism for falling in love had become an operatic convention by this time, later featured in two operas by Mozart.[174] The convention was so well understood that in Haydn's opera it was easily subverted, the nephew remaining true to his wife.

Haydn's operatic experience of the 1770s and 1780s allowed him an appreciation of the discourse on musical–artistic interaction in one of its most popular incarnations. By the time of his visits to London in the 1790s, he was in an excellent position to extend the public's taste for such interaction. Nowhere had the interplay of music and image on stage been more successful than in London.

CHAPTER FIVE

Musical Icons and the Cult of Haydn

On 29 July 1794 Haydn attended the Little Haymarket Theatre in London and noted the inscription over the proscenium arch: *SPECTAS ET TU SPECTABERE*.[1] 'See and you will be seen' was a lesson he took to heart. Issues concerning appearance, image and public perception, which the composer closely observed at work in the fortunes of leading theatrical and musical personalities in London, showed him just how crucial to the management of an individual's reputation the business of portraiture was becoming.[2] As a leading personality in London in the early 1790s, the implications of this for Haydn could not be ignored. In recognizing the extent to which portraiture was treated as a growing commercial venture in late eighteenth-century London, Haydn came to appreciate how portraiture was starting to play a part in promoting music, particularly in maximizing the possibilities of earnings to be gained from music, both in the concert hall and in terms of musical publication, issues which were soon to become as meaningful in the Vienna to which he returned in 1795.

1. A Public Image

Haydn had already started to sense the connection between the reception of his music in the public sphere and his own image in the early 1780s, when he first mused over the idea of travelling to London and the commercial rewards such a trip might bring. On 18 June 1781 his publishers in Vienna, Artaria, announced that they were issuing a print of Haydn's portrait, continuing a series of engravings of well-known personalities which they were making available to the public (Fig. 13).[3] The publishers probably hoped that this would stimulate sales of the composer's music, which Artaria had begun issuing the previous year.[4] The print itself was the work of J.E. Mansfeld, who was responsible for many engravings issued by Artaria. Though it proved useful in publicizing Haydn's music, later portraits of the composer by more distinguished artists suggest that it was an image aimed more at showing the composer's features in the best possible light – replete with suitable classical allusions – than in providing the public with a reliable likeness.[5]

What is unclear about Mansfeld's engraving is the source actually used for the portrait, since subsequent correspondence shows that the composer never actually sat for him. Haydn first mentions the engraving as an afterthought in his letter to Artaria of 27 May 1781: 'P.S. Very many people are pleased with my portrait. Return the [original] painting to me in the same case.'[6]

Presumably Artaria sent Haydn proofs on which they may have asked him to comment, probably with regard to whether he considered it a suitable likeness. Haydn was certainly happy with it, though this may have stemmed more from the way Mansfeld had flattered him than from any physiognomic accuracy. The composer evidently provided Artaria with a painted portrait to act as a model, though it is not known what this was. If it had been one of the early portraits of the composer still known today, such as the one showing him in Esterházy livery which Prince Miklós supposedly commissioned c.1768 from his painter Grundmann,[7] or the one probably painted by Ludwig Guttenbrunn when he was employed at Eszterháza between 1770 and 1772,[8] then it is clear that Mansfeld played down Haydn's less attractive features and aimed to present to the public an altogether more good-looking Haydn.

Several anecdotes given by Haydn's early biographers shed light on the composer's attitude to his own features. Dies, for example, says: 'Haydn believed himself to be ugly, and he told me of a prince and his wife who could not stand his face, "because", said he, "I was too ugly for them". This presumed ugliness, however, was not in the least fundamental, but merely a matter of heavily pock-marked skin and brown complexion.'[9] Carpani, for whom 'Haydn was certainly not the colour of lilies', has a story about the composer's first encounter with his Esterházy patron, who referred to him as 'a Blackamoor'.[10] His colouring, however, was not his only difficulty in relations with patrons; his nose also presented a problem: 'His hawk's nose (he suffered considerably from a nasal polyp, which undoubtedly enlarged this member) and other features also were deeply pock-marked; the nose even seemed so that each nostril appeared to have a different shape.'[11]

The composer resumed his comments on the Mansfeld engraving on 23 June 1781, opening his next letter to Artaria not with business matters, but with the engraving itself, the effect that it had provoked moving it from the bottom to the top of his business agenda:

> The portrait-painting, together with the 12 impressions you enclosed of the most beautifully engraved portrait-print, I received with the greatest pleasure. Even more thrilled was my gracious Prince, for as soon as his attention was drawn to it, he immediately asked me to give him one. Since these 12 examples are not enough, I would ask you, my dear Sir, to send me a further 6 at my expense.[12]

On 20 July he returned to the subject: 'Once again I am in your debt for the portraits you sent; but do they sell? I'm interested. Whatever the case the frame-makers and gilders have prospered from those you sent me.'[13]

The engraving does indeed seem to have sold and undoubtedly helped to further Haydn's reputation outside his native country. At least one impression, for example, was sold to the composer Wenceslaus Pichl, as is evident from his letter to the great Bolognese historian of ancient music Padre Martini dated 20 May 1784. In the letter, Pichl thanked the Italian for the honour of being requested to send to his correspondent his (Pichl's) portrait, which he enclosed for Martini, together with another of Cherubini, already recognized as a young composer of great ability, and also a printed portrait of Pichl's friend Haydn, whom he calls a man of great talent.[14] Since at this date only one *printed* portrait of Haydn existed, it was clearly a Mansfeld 'Haydn' which Pichl sent to Martini. The Italian, in fact, had a collection of musical portraits and was anxious to extend it, as his correspondence often reveals.

Another famous collector of musical portraits was the composer C.P.E. Bach, who acquired the Mansfeld engraving of Haydn sometime between 1781 and his death in 1788.[15] When Burney visited Bach in Hamburg in 1772, the portrait collection was already considerable; the English musician was shown into 'a large and elegant music room, furnished with pictures, drawings and prints of more than a hundred and fifty musicians: among whom, there are many Englishmen, and original portraits, in oil of his father [J.S. Bach] and grandfather'.[16] When a catalogue of Bach's estate was published by his widow in 1790, the number of portraits stood at nearly 400; so either Burney was not shown the full extent of the collection, or it had grown substantially in the last sixteen years of the Hamburg composer's life, which, in view of the rise in popularity of engraved portraits of musicians during these years, is not unlikely. The original *idea* for this particular collection, however, seems to have been due to J.S. Bach (d.1750), whose own acquisitions may have included engravings of Handel (a mezzotint of 1748 by John Faber, after a painting by Thomas Hudson) and Antonio Vivaldi (engraved by François Morellon La Cave in 1725).[17] These and many of the more important celebrities in C.P.E. Bach's collection, including Mansfeld's 'Haydn', were shown under glass in attractive black frames; though as space on his walls became limited, some of the collection probably had to be kept in portfolios. But the intention of publishers was certainly to display such prints in places where they could be easily seen.[18]

Haydn himself collected a respectable number of printed portraits, some of which were framed and displayed, and others kept in a portfolio.[19] One item in the inventory of his collection of engravings, for example, specifies '6. portraits of composers', though there is no indication who these might be.[20] A few portraits are even mentioned in correspondence. In a letter to Artaria of 2 August 1787, he requested a portrait of the soprano Anna Morichelli, who later sang at some of the concerts he gave in London, and another of his friend the composer Antonio Salieri; both portraits had been engraved by Mansfeld and published by Artaria.[21] Another letter of 29 November 1789 shows Haydn requesting a portrait of one of his most enthusiastic German princely patrons from the prince's agent in Vienna: '... but only as a silhouette, since I am an amateur collector of the leading figures [represented in this format]'.[22]

Most of the catalogued portraits from Haydn's collection, however, were of celebrities connected with his London period.[23] It seems possible that, like many other casual collectors of such images, Haydn was stimulated to acquire these prints by the first volume of Gerber's *Tonkünstler-Lexikon* (1790), an early example of a music dictionary to include musical biographies (including Haydn's) as well as definitions of musical terms.[24] In a series of appendices, Gerber's dictionary featured information on musicians' portraits, medallions, busts etc., much of which was derived from the C.P.E. Bach catalogue of the same year. Such guides to musical iconography, intended for interested amateurs as well as professional musicians, meant that by the 1790s that section of the public which was taking the business of music increasingly seriously was now not only able to develop its musical tastes and collecting habits, they were also in a position to expect that their tastes and collecting habits could be satisfied by the production of a steady flow of new portrait engravings representing in image the musical enthusiasms of the moment.[25]

By the time Haydn had arrived in England, therefore, he would have realized that he could hardly postpone indefinitely having to sit properly for his portrait if he were to retain and expand the interest in him on the part of the English public: his publishers and supporters in London would certainly have demanded it. The need for some kind of action would have become apparent to him through contact with one of his most ardent admirers in London, Latrobe, who was introduced to Haydn by Burney not long after the composer's arrival in London. Apart from translating Burney's 'Verses on the Arrival of Haydn in England' into German for the benefit of the composer – his command of English being then non-existent – Latrobe left his own account of Haydn.[26] The composer decided to pay Latrobe a visit:

> When [Haydn] entered the room, he found my wife alone, & as she could not speak German, & he had scarcely picked up a few English words, both were at a loss what to say. He bowed with foreign formality, & the following short Explanation took place.
> H. 'Dis, Mr Latrobe house?' The answer was in the affirmative.
> 'Be you his woman?' (meaning his wife).
> 'I am Mrs. Latrobe' was the reply.
> After some pause, he looked around the room, & saw his picture, to which he immediately pointed, & and exclaimed, 'Dat is me. I am Haydn!' My wife instantly, knowing what a most welcome guest I was honoured with, sent for me to a house not far off, & treated him with all possible civility.[27]

When exactly this exchange took place is not known; but circumstances suggest that it occurred in the spring of 1791.[28] If this is correct, then the portrait Haydn saw on Latrobe's wall can only have been the Mansfeld engraving, since no further portrait was issued until April 1791. The Mansfeld image had been known in England since at least 1784, when it was used as the basis of the portrait that illustrated the biographical account of Hadyn published in that year.[29] That Mrs Latrobe did not immediately recognize

Haydn is therefore understandable: not only had the engraving been made a decade earlier (and even then probably based on a still earlier portrait), but it smoothed over Haydn's most noticeable features. This episode would probably have suggested to Haydn that the time had come to update the image of himself available in the public sphere, even if having to sit for a portrait was an experience which, as it would remain for the remainder of his life, left him feeling more than a little uncomfortable.

2. Updating the Image

At least six portraits of Haydn were taken in London during his two visits. Five of these date from his first visit (1791–92), of which three were engraved within a short period of their creation (two others followed in the early 1800s).

The first portrait to be engraved was by A.M. Ott, the print of which was made by Bartolozzi and published on 4 April 1791, only a few months after Haydn had arrived, and within weeks of the start of his first concert season.[30] Ott's portrait is a miniature, executed in pastel on ivory, so it would not have taken as long to execute as a life-size oil painting. Since both Ott and his technique were French, there exists the possibility that the portrait may initially have been taken as much with a French market in mind, as a British one. Notwithstanding his French aristocratic patrons of the 1780s, Haydn's music remained popular in France throughout the Revolutionary period and later, so it is likely that there would have been a demand for his image across the Channel. Ott's presence within the swelling ranks of the émigré community in London in the spring of 1791 is an indication of how artists and composers at the time were working not only for an English audience, but for a newly arrived French one.[31]

Ott's patron, the anglophile Duke of Orléans, who embraced the Revolution during its early stages, and (styling himself 'Philippe Egalité') was to make his own bid for the throne before becoming one of its victims during the Terror, was much revered in England for supporting practical reform in France. Opinion turned against him, however, when he became a signatory to the execution of Louis XVI in January 1793.[32] Reynolds's portrait of him, painted for the Prince of Wales in 1785, had been highly praised as an excellent likeness at a dinner he attended at the Royal Academy.[33] The portrait was prominently displayed at Carlton House (the London residence of the Prince of Wales) until, as the painter Farington relates, 'the detestable conduct of the Duke in what related to the late King of France, caused the Prince to have it taken down'.[34] Haydn himself may have seen the portrait at the numerous soirées hosted by the Prince at which the composer was the star attraction. This perhaps encouraged him to approve Ott's designation as 'Painter to the Duke of Orleans', which appears on the engraving of Ott's portrait of Haydn. During the months immediately after it was published this would have been a tremendous boost to its sale, not only because of the favourable view of the Duke in England at the time, but more importantly because the Duke's collection of paintings – the most prestigious collection in France with the exception of that of the King – became a topic of public interest when it was presented at auction in London in order to help finance the Duke's bid for the throne.[35]

By 1793 the association of any public image with the disgraced Duke would have been bad publicity. This probably explains, in part, why Haydn himself disliked the Ott portrait, though it was engraved by the leading engraver of the time, Bartolozzi, who knew the composer well and had years of experience in portraits. By comparison with Mansfeld's engraving, Bartolozzi's presents a less flattering image, the nose noticeably hooked and the countenance severe. The accuracy of the likeness (difficult to assess today) may therefore also have played a part in the composer's unfavourable view of the engraving. Griesinger reported Haydn's opinion of it in 1799: '... Haydn is not satisfied with the portraits which are being sold to the public; he was engraved three times in England, and one of them was corrected by Bartolozzi himself, but it is *not* a good likeness.'[36] Whatever the merits (or demerits) of this portrait, the image of Haydn it introduced into the public domain was not the way the composer himself wished to the seen.

Soon after this 1799 exchange, Haydn's correspondence reveals that his preferred portrait of himself at this stage in his career was one published by Artaria in 1800, by which date it may be assumed that the market for the (by then) rather dated Mansfeld image had been exhausted. The portrait in question, painted by Johann Zitterer after 1791 (it features the celebrated theme from the second movement of the 'Surprise' Symphony, which dates from this year), was engraved by Johann Neidl, an artist who may have commanded Haydn's particular respect since the composer acquired for his own collection a copy of this engraver's portrait of Nelson. The composer's preference for Neidl's 'Haydn', which Carpani later used to illustrate his biography, may stem partly from the fact that Neidl worked in stipple, an engraving technique developed in England in the 1760s, which Haydn particularly appreciated,[37] and partly from the way the image reflects Guttenbrunn's more youthful portrait, for which Haydn probably sat in early 1770s. Nelson was actually in Vienna at the very moment Haydn wrote to Artaria concerning a request he had received from Pleyel, one of his former pupils. Pleyel, who had founded a publishing house in Paris and was planning a 'complete' edition of Haydn's quartets, had apparently asked the composer for an appropriate portrait of Haydn that could be reproduced on the title-page. Pleyel himself would almost certainly have possessed (or could have easily acquired) an older portrait of Haydn, so he was presumably hoping for something more recent. However, Haydn himself seems to have felt that he had nothing to offer Pleyel, so he pursued the matter with Artaria, with the Zitterer–Neidl engraving in mind:

> But I want to help him [Pleyel] with my portrait, and so I would be obliged to you, my dear Sirs, if you would send to Dresden [where Pleyel was then visiting], in my name, an impression of the *very good portrait* which I saw in your premises last time, and which has presumably been issued by now. He will have it copied and publish a reduction of it with the Quartets. I will reimburse you at the first opportunity.[38]

Haydn's concern that Pleyel should use the most recent Artaria portrait for such an important publication is evident in Haydn's letter to him of May 1801, in which, after enquiring when the edition of the quartets would appear, he asked pointedly whether the portrait had been received from Artaria.[39] Perhaps by then Haydn had sensed that Artaria had either been slow in responding to his request, or had deliberately ignored it, a real possibility by the end of 1800 because Artaria may not have wished to help a firm which had recently entered into an agreement with a rival publishing house (Breitkopf & Härtel) for the distribution rights of the quartets in Germany.[40]

Since nothing was received from Artaria, Pleyel was obliged to find another solution to the problem of a Haydn portrait for his *Collection Complette des Quatuors*. Pleyel's engraver, Louis Darcis, worked from a (lost) drawing by P.-N. Guérin, which was probably worked up from two sources: firstly, an engraving created for the first volume of the *Oeuvres Complettes* of Haydn, published in 1800 by Breitkopf & Härtel, based on a drawing the publishers had commissioned in 1799, itself dependent in part on Guttenbrunn's portrait;[41] and secondly, on Bartolozzi's engraving after Ott's portrait. Since the latter may have been intended from the outset for a French market, it is not surprising that Pleyel would have made use of it. Pleyel had been in London in 1792, engaged by a rival group of concert promoters to the Salomon–Haydn series, and would have had the opportunity to acquire the engraving then, assuming he did not purchase it in Paris. In December 1802, Haydn thanked Pleyel for his 'exceptionally fine edition of the Quartets', praising 'their beautiful printing, the paper – and their having been so well corrected'; indeed, for their general appearance, he 'will be remembered forever'.[42] It is very telling of Haydn that the only thing he failed to mention on seeing the actual publication was the portrait, despite his previous obsession with it.

The second portrait of Haydn to be engraved when he was in London was executed by Thomas Hardy, who was also responsible for the print after it was published on 13 February 1792. Both oil painting and engraving were probably commissioned by John Bland, one of Haydn's London publishers.[43] Bland had been sufficiently keen to publish works by Haydn not known to other publishers that he travelled to Eszterháza, where he met Haydn early in November 1789.[44] Haydn used the visit to bargain with Artaria; though not long afterwards, at Bland's insistence, he sent the London publisher the three 'sonatas' for keyboard with the accompaniment of flute or violin, and cello.[45] These were issued with a special note drawing attention to the circumstances in which they had been obtained, thus leading the English public to believe that they enjoyed a particular relationship with the composer: 'This & the Two following Trios were wrote at the particular request of the Publisher when he was with Mr. Haydn in Novr. last ... J. Bland thinks this sufficient notice to other Publishers not to pirate the same.'[46] In the absence of adequate copyright laws, a personal connection with the composer seems to have gone some way to protecting a publisher who had actually contracted with a composer for compositions. Bland's commission for the Hardy portrait, of course, served to confirm this connection at the expense of rivals.

Haydn, however, liked the outcome no more than the portrait by Ott, as Griesinger's comments quoted above suggest. Hardy's portrait does not show the composer with a hooked nose, and indeed suggests a quietly confident, amiable, even rather jolly sitter. But the engraved version alters the composer's appearance slightly, and in so doing presents a more sombre Haydn, less jovial, less at ease. Notwithstanding this, Hardy's engraving was the model for several prints of Haydn mostly engraved on the Continent, which, with one exception, Haydn does not seem to have approved, if indeed he was aware of them.[47] The exception, inscribed 'A Chaponnier del. Laurens sculp 1803', was sent to Haydn early in 1804 by Zelter. The composer replied (only the draft survives): 'I am very grateful to you for the portraits you sent me [Zelter enclosed several copies of the same print], but there is a small error: 1733 should read 1732 [the date of Haydn's birth] ... It is *very much* [Haydn originally wrote *quite*] like me.'[48] Haydn's apparent change of attitude towards the portrait type deriving from Hardy presumably stems either from a wish not to offend Zelter for his kindness, or, more likely, from a recognition that, now his composing career had ended, there was no point in objecting to a portrait on the basis that it did not represent him the way he wished to appear to his public; but there certainly still remained a point in promoting a portrait which served to further his reputation abroad and satisfied a still curious public with a reasonable likeness.

3. The Reluctant Sitter

The third portrait of Haydn to be published in London was painted by Guttenbrunn and engraved by Ludwig Schiovanetti, who had worked with Bartolozzi ; it was issued in 1792.[49] Guttenbrunn had worked on decorations at Eszterháza and executed a portrait of Prince Miklós in 1770. He probably painted Haydn for the first time shortly afterwards. In 1772 the Prince sent him to Italy, which the painter decided suited him better than Hungary. He consequently never returned to Eszterháza. In Italy Guttenbrunn built something of a reputation for himself: in 1782 he became a member of the Academy in Florence and, like other celebrated artists of this period, he was invited to contribute to the Grand Duke of Tuscany's famous collection of artistic self-portraits.[50]

From 1789 to about 1795 Guttenbrunn was in London, where he evidently renewed his acquaintance with Haydn. The composer must have respected Guttenbrunn's talents at this time since he acquired for his collection a portrait engraving by him after an English sitter and an *Apollo and the Muses* published in 1794.[51] Haydn also recorded him as a painter working in London in his first London notebook along with 'Mr Ott', which suggests that the composer had come into contact with him within a few months of his arrival, Ott's 'Haydn' having been published in early April 1791.[52] In the second London notebook Haydn records Guttenbrunn's name a second time in a list of all the artists responsible for having made portraits of him during his first visit to England.[53] The composer does not say, however, that he had actually sat for Guttenbrunn during this period, only that he had been painted by him. This is an important distinction because the portrait used as the model for the engraving by Schiovanetti was simply another version of the portrait he is believed to have painted 20 years earlier in Eszterháza. Although, in the absence of further documentary evidence, it could be suggested that both of Guttenbrunn's Haydn portraits were painted in London, this is most unlikely since in both portraits Haydn has the appearance of a man no older than 40, his age when Guttenbrunn left Eszterháza. It seems therefore that in London Guttenbrunn painted a portrait of Haydn which was intended to be a revised version of a much earlier work. Whose idea this was, and why it was managed, are not entirely clear.

Unfortunately, the early history of neither of Guttenbrunn's portraits is known. Something, however, is known about one of them during the period after Haydn's return to Vienna since it is mentioned in Griesinger's correspondence with Breitkopf and Härtel, who were then looking for a portrait to engrave in their projected complete edition of Haydn's works.[54] On 12 June 1799 Griesinger noted that 'The painting by Guttenbrunn, which he [Haydn] gave for drawing to one of his acquaintances, is said to be better [than Bartolozzi's engraving].'[55] Early in July matters seem to have been arranged since Griesinger reports: 'Haydn will deliver to me Guttenbrunn's portrait in three days; he is afraid that it would make a bad impression as a copper engraving, because he is painted in a pose as if studying one of his compositions. It seems to me that Messrs. Kininger [the artist commissioned to redraw the portrait] and Kohl [the engraver] should decide about this.'[56]

Later in July Griesinger returned to the portrait: 'Haydn has gone to ... Eisenstadt ... and his wife ... put me off for some time before she allowed one of her acquaintances to fetch Guttenbrunn's portrait and deliver it to me. It seems to be a good likeness, Haydn's wife holds it to be *the best*, and Mr. Kininger, to whom I gave it at once, is also satisfied with it.'[57] By November Griesinger had asked Haydn why his wife had been so reluctant to hand over the portrait. The reply was such a revelation: 'Guttenbrunn ... had once been her lover, and so she parted with the portrait as seldom as possible.'[58]

Since Haydn's wife had been unwilling to hand over the portrait, and told Griesinger it was the best likeness of her husband (which she surely knew was disputable), there is no reason to doubt what Haydn told Griesinger: the portrait acted as a memento of an affair she had had more than a quarter of a century earlier. This suggests that the portrait that was in her possession in 1799 was one dating from the time of her affair, and which she had held on to, with her husband's knowledge, since the time Guttenbrunn had departed for Italy in 1772. When Haydn came across Guttenbrunn in London almost 20 years later, at a time when he was considering how he could convey into the public sphere the most advantageous image of himself, he might well have remembered Guttenbrunn's portrait from the 1770s still in his wife's possession. This image had the advantage of representing a much younger, more elegant Haydn than any artist in London, no matter how competent, was able to depict. Although there is no conclusive proof, it seems likely that what happened was that Haydn, or Guttenbrunn, or both, prevailed upon Frau Haydn (who remained in Austria during her husband's trips to England) to send the portrait to London in order to have a copy made. Since it is very small this would have presented no problem.

There would have been advantages for both Guttenbrunn and Haydn in such an action. Guttenbrunn had become a fashionable artistic entrepreneur in London, the newspapers often carrying advertisements for his exhibitions. The *Morning Herald* of 24 April 1794, for example, contains a list of items featured in Guttenbrunn's 'Exhibition of Ancient and Modern Pictures, No. 4 Little Maddx-street four doors down from New Bond-street', which opened its doors to the public daily.[59] One of the exhibits was a portrait of the 'late Queen of France [Marie-Antoinette] *taken from life* in the year 1789'. Guttenbrunn was therefore very much in the business of displaying portraits of famous personalities as part of a commercial enterprise. Exhibiting a portrait of Haydn, one of the leading personalities in London during the early 1790s, would certainly have been profitable, especially if he himself could accurately make the claim that it had been *taken from life*, though without the trouble of having to undertake fresh sittings. Guttenbrunn might well have been prevailed upon to copy his Eszterháza portrait of Haydn if there were financial gain to be had, both from the copied portrait (the original would presumably have been returned to Haydn's wife) and from Schiovanetti's engraving. From Haydn's point of view such an arrangement would have been admirable since it presented him to the public in the way he wanted to be remembered: youthful and handsome.

Another of the portraits of Haydn painted whilst he was in London at this time provides further evidence of his sensitivity about portraiture and how he was only prepared to be painted if it suited his own view of himself. The portrait in question is the one by Hoppner for which Haydn sat at the end of 1791 (Fig. 14).[60] Hoppner's portrait was different to those by Ott, Hardy and Guttenbrunn (the London version) in that it was not originally intended as the basis of an engraving. Since it was commissioned by the heir to the throne, it nevertheless posed a dilemma of image for the composer, who by this date would have been well aware how portraits by the most fashionable painters in London – and Hoppner was among *the* most fashionable – were often closely scrutinized and compared with their sitters. Discussion generated by works like Reynolds's *Duc d'Orléans*, still at this date occupying pride of place at Carlton House, would probably have revealed to Haydn the critical position of portraiture within cultured British society. Indeed, early the next century, a groundless story had arisen that Haydn had sat for Reynolds, and this was the starting point of a piece which appeared in the *Quarterly Review* in 1817:

> Sir Joshua Reynolds had been nearly three years in his grave at this period; and the person to whom Haydn sat for his portrait was the late Mr. Hoppner, who if he [Haydn] had languished for a conversation 'in his native tongue,' was very capable of gratifying him [Hoppner's mother was German]. We [the author of the article: probably William Gifford, editor of the *Quarterly Review*, and a friend of Hoppner] knew Haydn, and well remember the circumstance of his sitting for his picture. He was a coarse and hard-featured man, who, among other amiable weaknesses, cherished that of conceiting himself to be somewhat of an Adonis. He would sit with exemplary patience to be painted; but no birthday beauty was ever more solicitous to choose the favourable moment. Many a time, when an hour had been fixed for his attendance, he would get up from his chair, gaze steadfastly and wistfully in the glass, and say, 'I don't tink I look well to-day; I will not see Mr. Hoppner'; and Salomon was accordingly despatched with his excuses. The picture was not quite finished when Haydn left England; it was, however, so striking a likeness of this extraordinary man, that the Prince of Wales, for whom it was painted, would not permit Hoppner to touch it after his departure, and the portrait is now in His Royal Highness's possession.[61]

Although some aspects of this account are obviously wrong, such as the implied date (1795, instead of 1791) and the reason the portrait was left unfinished (Haydn did not leave England for several months after he is recorded to have sat for Hoppner, and he subsequently returned to London when further sittings might have been possible had they been deemed necessary), and the author has clearly embellished his recollection with fanciful detail, there is no reason to suspect its gist. It has, however, to be understood in the context of an account of the painting of the same portrait, which the article in the *Quarterly Review* was intended to refute, originally published by Carpani, who would have heard it from the composer himself.

Carpani mistakenly thought that the painter Haydn referred to was Reynolds. The reason for this is that in the same part of his book Carpani gives an anecdote in which Haydn was asked for his opinion of a portrait by Reynolds of the singer Mrs Billington, which he probably also heard from the composer.[62] Stendhal repeated this error in his plagarism of Carpani, an inaccuracy which would have been read in London through the popular English translation (*The Life of Haydn, in a series of Letters written in Vienna*) first published by John Murray in 1817, the very year in which the misinformation was corrected in the *Quarterly Review*. But apart from this error, and some understandable embellishment, Carpani's version of the story of the Prince of Wales's portrait of Haydn contains several details that can be verified from other sources:

> The Prince of Wales, keen to have a portrait of Haydn, commissioned one from Reynolds. Sensitive to such an honour, our maestro presented himself at the studio of the painter and work was begun. Everyone knows how tedious it is to stay as still as a statue when sitting for a portrait painter. Such tedium shows itself commonly in portraits, even the best executed. Reynolds, who wanted to paint, to the best of his ability, the inner man and not just the features of the celebrated maestro, set about finding a suitable pose for him which he felt should neither be at the keyboard, nor as the leader of the orchestra; he therefore began to consider how best to enliven Haydn, how to produce an alert likeness, how to make him think of things to ensure Haydn looked contented. Haydn had never been either an actor or a courtier in his life, and thus did not know *alienum sumere vultum* [to take on another face]. He was bored and was unable to express anything other than what his feelings told him. Reynolds was obliged to give up work for the day. On the next day, there was another sitting and the same boredom set in. The experiment was repeated a third time, and yet again with the same outcome. In the end Reynolds went to see the Prince, explaining the impossibility of painting such a portrait, and begged H.R.H. to let him give up the task since he did not wish to falsify such a distinguished man by turning him into a sprightly *fantasia* or the *aria* of a mummy. The Prince laughed at the story, and thought up a strategy which worked a miracle. He invited for a fourth time the good maestro to sit for the stupified painter. Haydn presented himself displaying his usual gloomy countenance; as he sat down the painter took up his brush; and at this point, a canvas, which had acted like a screen, was drawn back in front of the maestro revealing a pretty smiling young woman, dressed in white and crowned with roses, who took the maestro's hand, and spoke to him in his own language:
> 'How it pleases me, kind sir, to see and be with you!'
> Haydn, astonished and full of immense joy, patriotically embraced this woman from his homeland; the dark expression disappeared from his face, and Reynolds, hurrying with his brushstrokes, created a handsome Haydn, joyous and exultant, such that *the portrait really spoke the composer's music*. The enchantress, who worked this beautiful transformation, was a chambermaid of the Queen, a Saxon by birth. She was spirited and attractive, and this marvellous deed was not for her a difficult undertaking.[63]

The German lady-in-waiting to the Queen may be identified as Mrs Papendiek, actually the Queen's Assistant Keeper of the Wardrobe. Hoppner, whose mother had been in royal service, was apparently on good terms with Mrs Papendiek. She mentions Hoppner and his wife in her memoirs written many years later. As the wife of a flautist, who taught music to the royal family, her memoirs also describe aspects of concert life in London, including accounts of Salomon's playing and even the first concert of his first season with Haydn. Mrs Papendiek even mentions Haydn himself, not quite as in the context described by Carpani, but sufficient to indicate that she had been privy to information about the way the composer conceived his compositions, which could well have come from the composer's own lips during sittings for Hoppner.[64] In 1799, when Haydn was looking for English subscribers for *The Creation*, he wrote to Mrs Papendiek's husband, hoping that he would be able to persuade members of the royal family to lend their names to the venture.[65] At the end of the letter, Haydn, perhaps recalling his conversations with Mrs Papendiek, remembered her to her husband: 'P:S: my respectful compliments to your dear wife.'[66]

Apart from Carpani's story gaining credibility from the identification of the woman brought in to entertain Haydn during his sittings with Hoppner, it also agrees with what is known about late eighteenth-century practice regarding how sittings were managed. It was understood by painters that sitters could not be expected to keep still for any useful length of time without some kind of diversion. This usually took the form of relatives or friends being encouraged to attend and amuse the sitter in the painter's studio. Farington's diary entry for 15 March 1794, for example, records a visit to his friend the architect and artist George Dance: 'Lady Susan Bathhurst was sitting for a profile – Lady Triphina Bathhurst and Lady Beaumont Lysons were also there.' Five days later Haydn himself sat for Dance, and since Dance's drawing turned out to be Haydn's favourite portrait of his London years, it may be imagined that on that occasion he was as well occupied as Susan Bathhurst.

In Carpani's account of Hoppner's ('Reynolds's') portrait of Haydn, it is the painter who recognizes the difficulty that Haydn's bored expression presented in order to create a work which was worthy of the status of the sitter and also of the artist. Perhaps this is how Haydn related it to Carpani. But it might just as well have been Haydn himself, already sensitive to his appearance on any given day, as the account in the *Quarterly Review* suggests, who recognized the necessity for looking right on each of the appointed days since this was how posterity was going to see him. Considering the difficulties with the sitter, Hoppner's portrait is really very successful, and doubtless the Prince of Wales was right (if Gifford's account is accurate) that there was no need for Hoppner to finish the painting in the way he would have done for most commissioned portraits. This after all was a private commission, intended to be seen chiefly by the Prince himself.[67] The portrait itself shows

Haydn in relaxed, confident mood, and conveys something of his quiet sense of humour. Since the pose of a sitter adopted for a portrait was often in English portrait practice a matter of negotiation and agreement between painter and sitter, it may be suggested that Haydn himself contributed some aspects of the composition.[68] In one hand he holds a quill pen, a motif also used for the portraits engraved by Bartolozzi and Schiovanetti. This feature first occurs in Guttenbrunn's early portrait; it seems to have appealed to Haydn, who perhaps requested it of both Ott and Hoppner.[69]

However, the sense given in the accounts of both Carpani, and especially Gifford, that Haydn was not really happy with Hoppner's portrait and its progress, which offers an alternative explanation of why the picture was never fully completed, finds support in another account of a session in which Haydn sat for his portrait, one which actually took place several years after his return to Austria. The story again comes from Carpani, but this time the source is unlikely to be the composer but the painter:

> Other portraits of Haydn which may be had from printsellers, engraved at different times, all have a defect stemming from a little weakness of Haydn himself. He – rather like a former famous Austrian minister of the last century [Kaunitz] – could not bear to be portrayed as being old, and he forced a painter who was taking his portrait in the year 1800, that is when the composer was in his seventieth year, to do the work again. Rather losing his self-control, he called the painter a traitor for choosing from the life of the gentleman who he wanted to portray the period exactly when he was visually least presentable. Flying into a rage, he added:
>> 'If I was Haydn when I was forty years old, why do you want to leave to posterity a Haydn who is seventy? Neither I nor you have anything to gain from this decision.'
> The painter had no option but to submit to the composer's wishes. One may see on the title-page of Haydn's Opus 73 [76] as printed by Artaria an example of the comic result of the composer's rebukes. This particular image, at the top of the page, showing him aged between thirty-five and forty, at a time when the original was esteemed more than the copy, was truly ridiculed by those who saw it.[70]

Carpani as usual did not take care with precise dates of events and the age of his subject when the events were supposed to take place, so it is not clear which portrait of Haydn the story refers to. The painter in question may have been Johann Rösler, whose portrait of Haydn is dated 1799.[71] Rösler is known to have travelled to Eisenstadt in mid-September 1799, when it seems likely sittings with Haydn could have taken place.[72] The story could have been told to Carpani when he was in Vienna in 1800, or after 1805, the year he settled in the city permanently. That the picture, which was often copied and engraved, was considered a good likeness is attested by its first documented owner, Rochlitz, who attached a note to the back of the picture indicating that it had been 'painted in Vienna *from life* and after formal sittings of the master by Rösler in 1799, shortly after Haydn's second stay in London, and *so much like him* that I who had shortly before talked to him [Haydn] when he passed through Leipzig [on Haydn's return from London to Vienna] *recognized him at first glance* before I had any idea whom the picture was supposed to present.'[73]

4. Age and Youth

There can be little doubt that Haydn's main objections to portraits of him were based not on considerations of accuracy of likeness – he seems to have been quite content to settle for a bad likeness so long as it made him appear presentable – but on matters to do with what the public might perceive about him (and presumably his music) from contemplating his image. This was more of an issue if he was aware that the portrait was to be engraved; and as he became older the issue became more acute.

The extent to which this was beginning to weigh on his mind during the London years, when he reached his seventh decade, may be shown from his acquisition of an engraving entitled *Age and Infancy*, after a painting by Opie, the subject matter of which evidently struck a chord with him.[74] The contrast of youth and age, beauty and ugliness, was of course a popular theme in the 1780s and 1790s for English caricaturists, like Rowlandson and Gillray, always anxious to appreciate the latest fad to capture the public's imagination.[75]

At least one correspondent later sensed that for Haydn the visual aspect of growing older proved difficult for him, perhaps more so than with other men of his background. Writing to the composer in 1804, Zelter reassured him that 'There is no work by you in which your *great age* is to be noticed. Your *Seasons* is a work *youthful* in strength and *old* in mastery.'[76] The theme was still very much on Haydn's mind when Cherubini visited him in Vienna in 1806. When the younger man addressed the older as 'Father', as younger composers who revered Haydn were encouraged to do in his presence, Haydn responded with 'Yes, as far as *age* is concerned, but not as far as the *music* goes.'[77]

It was about this time that Haydn had a calling card printed with the opening words and music of one of the part-songs he had composed in the late 1790s: 'Gone is all my strength, old and weak am I.'[78] Soon after this he gave a copy to Dies, who movingly describes the emotions he experienced pondering Haydn's recognition of his own enfeebled state, as expressed through the music on the visiting card, which includes the very slow tempo indication *Molto Adagio*. Haydn would have had in mind the final line of the original *Lied*, 'An harmonious song was my life', which Dies probably knew and recognized the composer was now applying to himself. Although Dies emphasized the sadness the card made him feel, he ended the account of the visit on an upbeat note, recognizing that the card was as much a joke on Haydn's part, as a morose statement about his increasing infirmity. Dies noted in particular how at this advanced stage in his life, Haydn seemed 'to find pleasure in depicting his state of health' worse than it really was, commenting that 'On these occasions I usually point out that his appearance betrays no hint of indisposition. The brightness which then covers his face confirms that one has guessed the truth, although he pictured the opposite.'[79] Dies's astute observation provides a good indication that Haydn was in the habit of manipulating the way people saw him, such that, even in very old age, he would seek to engineer a visitor's perceptions of his appearance in order to receive a compliment.

In fact the discrepancy between the way Haydn wanted to appear from the time of his visits to London and later (youthful and vigorous) and the way he actually looked (old and increasingly less agile, and eventually feeble) was of such consequence to him that he deliberately set out to tamper with what the public could learn of his appearance. As publishers started to plan quite grand editions of his music by the end of the eighteenth century, they required new portraits for their title-pages. Naturally they approached him about this, but they probably were unaware what trouble they were causing themselves. In the case of Breitkopf & Härtel, Haydn dismissed all the engravings made in England, but encouraged a portrait derived from Dance's drawing (which had not been engraved at this date), a copy of which was duly requested and sent from London to Vienna. But when this either did not arrive, or more likely did not satisfy, the trail led back to Guttenbrunn's portrait made almost three decades earlier. Kininger, the artist commissioned to copy Guttenbrunn's painting, had to attempt the task of bringing an old portrait up to date no fewer than three times. The last version was messily pasted onto a previously prepared setting.[80] When in the same year (1799) Artaria published Haydn's last complete set of quartets (today known as Opus 76, but originally published as Opus 75), the title-page of the first volume included a copy of Mansfeld's old engraving, notwithstanding the fact that other portraits were certainly available by then in Vienna. Although the page was designed by Mansfeld's son, even he must have wondered at the request to use an image originating the best part of two decades earlier.[81]

Haydn's paranoia about age and public perceptions of it stem, of course, from the notion that music was often understood by audiences as a portrayal of the composer who wrote it. The attitude, which is particularly found in French writing on music in the eighteenth century, is neatly summarized in relation to Haydn in a letter from 142 French musicians to the composer congratulating him on *The Creation*: 'When in this work he imitates the fires of light, Haydn seems to have portrayed himself [*se peindre lui même*], and thus proves to us all that *his name* will shine fully as long as the star whose rays he seems to have borrowed.'[82] Haydn himself evidently shared this notion: in commenting on his last composition (the unfinished quartet published as Opus 103) in later life he told Griesinger that 'It is my last last child, but it still *looks like me.*'[83]

One consequence of connecting the appearance of a composer with the character of his music was that audiences with knowledge of a composer's appearance might judge his music as much on the basis of the image, and its character traits, as from a hearing of the music itself. Perhaps all composers whose music is well performed have had to put up with this human instinct, but Haydn seems to have suffered from it more than most. In London, Salomon's rivals had used this very idea to try to discredit him. According to Dies, a newspaper article appeared: 'Haydn only recollected that he was pictured in it as *old*, *weak*, and *incapable* of creating anything new. He had long since exhausted himself and was obliged by ailing faculties to repeat himself.'[84] The tactic, of course, did not succeed; but over a decade later, when Haydn was discussing his visits to London with Dies, it still left him uneasy. Even after he was forced to give up original composition because of failing health, Haydn found consolation by taking up the revision of his most youthful works.[85]

During the last years of his life, Haydn also remembered several occasions when admirers of his music, on meeting him in person, had been quite unable to believe that he, unattractive and peasant-like in appearance, could possibly have been responsible for the refined compositions associated with his name, to which they attached notions of beauty and genius: the image of the composer they had formed in their mind's eye on the basis of listening to the music simply did not fit the reality of seeing the composer himself.

Haydn recounted a number of these stories to Dies. One, which he claimed took place in the mid-1770s, concerns a visit he made to Vienna, where, driving down the street, he happened to hear the beginning of one of his symphonies being played in the residence of a count. When he eventually gained access to the venue – servants tried to debar him – and was recognized as the composer by some, others could not believe it:

> 'That's not Haydn – it can't possibly be! Haydn must be a *big, handsome, well-proportioned* man and not the *insignificant little* man you've got in the middle over there.'
> Everyone laughed.
> They all raised their eyes, and Haydn, more astonished than anybody, looked around to see who was contesting his very existence. In the company was an Italian priest who had been in Vienna only a short time, had heard a lot about Haydn and adored his music. ... The *picture* of Haydn that he had previously *imagined* now failed to live up to the *reality*, and stubbornness and prejudice led him sooner to charge Nature with having made a mistake than to acknowledge that the deception was his.[86]

Haydn had a similar experience on his second journey to London. He made himself known to some Prussian officers, who were enjoying the *Andante* of Symphony No. 94 played on the pianoforte. They refused to believe that he was really Haydn: "'Impossible! Impossible! You Haydn? – Already such an *old man*! – That doesn't rhyme with the *fire in your music*! – No! We shall never believe it!" In this vein the men persisted in *doubting* so long that Haydn found a letter he had received from their King which he had luckily brought with him.'[87]

With experiences like these, confronted with complete incredulity at his appearance, it is no wonder Haydn sought to protect the reputation of his music by seeking to control the image of himself which was fast becoming a kind of commodity in the public domain. Although in person he could demonstrate, despite his age and appearance, that he had the 'fire', spirit and energy to produce his much admired works, when it came to winning over sceptics like the Italian priest and the officers in the stories given to Dies, a portrait which presented him as he really appeared was unlikely to work; but one which presented him in a certain light might stand a chance. It was therefore necessary to try to ensure that the right kind of portraits went into circulation.[88]

5. The Cult of Haydn

Haydn's strategy regarding the images of him published by *c*.1800, and their limitations, had one consequence that he himself may have found hard to predict and over which he had no control: they formed the basis of what may be described as a cult of the composer, with quasi-religious overtones in its practices and manifestations. This was particularly fervent in Paris, where interestingly, though images of Haydn were known, like the one published by Pleyel, their relationship to Haydn's appearance was dubious. Dies, presumably repeating a description given him by the composer himself, records the kind of treatment a public image of Haydn could inspire in the French capital shortly after the turn of the century: 'When Prince Esterházy was in Paris in 1803, he was very agreeably surprised one evening at the *Concert des amateurs.* They had made Haydn's laurel-crowned portrait *an object of veneration* and exhibited it, fully illuminated, in a prominent position in the room.'[89] Artaria's publication of the Opus 76 quartets in 1799, reusing the old Mansfeld portrait, may have partly inspired such homage, the title-page suggesting a kind of divine status for Haydn: his image appears in clouds, a cherub playing a lyre to his side, and the Muse of music placing a wreath over his head. Since Haydn himself was probably behind the reuse of an earlier portrait in this publication, he may also have suggested other aspects of its presentation, based on works he had seen in London. One model might have been Cipriani's *The Nymph of Immortality Crowning the Bust of Shakespeare*, which Haydn acquired for his own collection.[90]

The adulation witnessed by Prince Esterházy also emulated the kind of displays of homage which had been paid to Voltaire in Paris two decades earlier. A print by C.E. Gaucher after a drawing by Moreau the Younger dated 1782, for example, shows a bust of Voltaire on the stage of the Théâtre-Française, surrounded by actors who hold laurel coronets in their hands which they raise towards the bust, recording an event which took place in March 1778.[91] Other pictorial representations of the coronation of Voltaire, including a parody of the bust-crowning scene, show that this method of paying tribute to a celebrated figure was well understood in late eighteenth-century Paris. In applying it to Haydn, however, later French audiences were paying the composer a very particular compliment; not only were they honouring a foreigner, but also a musician rather than a writer.[92]

Such veneration for Haydn in Paris, however, was by no means unusual. Gerber, in his article on Haydn in the revised version of his *Lexikon*, says that the *Concert de la rue de Clery*

> set up a bust of [Haydn] in the midst of the orchestra at its last concert and after the performance of his newest symphony crowned it to the jubilation and applause of those present. In the absence of a real bust of Haydn, they had, to be sure, to make do in this ceremony with a bust of Cato, on a pedestal of which sparkled in great gold letters the words 'To the immortal Haydn'. But since nobody in the audience was personally acquainted with Haydn, nobody was the worse for this innocent deception.[93]

The fact that nobody knew what Haydn really looked like is consistent not only with what had happened in England, but also with other evidence for Haydn iconography in Paris. The 142 French musicians, whose letter to the composer congratulating him on *The Creation* was quoted above, also presented him with a large gold medal by N.-M. Gatteaux, featuring on one side a profile representation of Haydn, and on the other side an allegory commemorating their performance of the oratorio.[94] Haydn treasured the medal for the rest of his life. He thought nothing of the fact that Gatteaux had little idea what he really looked like and had had to invent the profile using Pleyel's engraving and 'a portrait *resembling* Haydn, which was ordered from Germany', perhaps a copy of the engraving ordered by Breitkopf & Härtel.[95]

Haydn of course appreciated the Gatteaux medal – Gatteaux later designed a second one also presented to Haydn – because it was an offering representing 'Hommage à Haydn' and commemorated the successful reception of his most cherished work abroad. The idea of a commemorative medal, a token which hitherto had generally only been cast or struck in honour of rulers or heroes, was especially flattering. Since the medal was designed to preserve memory of Haydn and the sense of wonder his music had created, Haydn was unusually inspired to thank the donors of the medal by revealing his own concern for his reputation after his death, and by drawing attention to his advancing years, even though Gatteaux had been careful to portray him as mature, rather than old: 'I have often doubted whether my name would survive me; but your goodness raises my confidence, and the token of esteem with which you have honoured me strengthens my hope that perhaps *I shall not completely die* [these words emphasized]. Yes, gentlemen, you have crowned my grey hairs, and strewn flowers by the edge of my grave.'[96]

Haydn would have also liked the classical allusions suggested by a portrait reproduced in profile. In London a medallion with his portrait in profile had been made by the Scottish artist James Tassie, who developed a wax-based paste from which portraits could be cheaply modelled to give them the appearance of antique cameos and gems, which were much studied, collected and admired in the eighteenth century.[97] Many celebrities, such as Haydn's friend John Hunter, were portrayed in this way and Tassie himself enjoyed a huge reputation across Europe.[98]

The notion of authority attached to profile portraits provides one reason why Haydn's favourite London portrait of himself was the one by Dance, who drew many celebrities in this fashion during the last years of the eighteenth century.[99] Dance was clearly a very skilful draughtsman, his portraits making few concessions to vanity. On the other hand, in their simple truthfulness, they maximize the possibilities for reading into their sitters' features late eighteenth-century notions of nobility and virtue. For Haydn, Dance's profile drawing of him may also have signified friendship. A number of entries in the diary of Dance's friend Farington indicate that the two men, composer and architect, were on very close terms, in a way that does not seem to have been achieved in the case of other artists for whom Haydn sat, for reasons which should be clear.

Haydn was probably introduced to Dance through Burney, whose daughter Susan left an account of a visit by Dance to a Burney musical evening at which the architect played first cello, and later second violin.[100] Farington reports meeting Dance in June 1795 on his way to see Haydn, whom the architect intended inviting to dinner.[101] Apparently Dance also invited several English enthusiasts for music, presumably Haydn's. Haydn's account of his own earlier life recounted at this and other meetings gave Dance and others plenty of scope for recollections of the composer in later years. Although Haydn sat for Dance in 1794, it seems very likely that they knew each other from early in Haydn's first visit.[102] Dance certainly admired Haydn and all that the composer had achieved in England, as he indicated in a commentary accompanying the publication of engravings of many of the most celebrated of his portrait heads, including Haydn's, in 1814.[103] An indication of Haydn's opinion of Dance is given in a letter by Griesinger to Breitkopf and Härtel:

'The best profile is said to be by an Englishman called Danz (at least Haydn said so). A *very good* head, which he expects from England any day and which he wishes to give you for engraving.'[104]

Just as the profile representations of Haydn carried with them classical allusions, so too did the sculpted busts of the composer, all the surviving examples of which were executed during the last decade of his life, and several examples of which were catalogued among his artistic effects at his death.[105] An insight into Haydn's thinking is revealed in an item from his second will made in February 1809, in which he bequeathed to Count Harrach 'the little gold medal from Paris [Gatteaux's second medal], with the accompanying letter from the *Amateurs* of music; also the large bust in the antique style [*en Antike*]'.[106] Dies, in publishing Haydn's will in his biography of the composer, considered that the bust Haydn intended for Harrach was one by his friend Grassi, who had introduced him to Haydn. A lost life-size bust by Grassi is known to have shown Haydn in antique costume and was presumably the work Dies had in mind.[107]

From 1778 Grassi, to whom the composer became very attached, was the leading modeller for the Viennese porcelain factory, working chiefly in a neoclassical style.[108] He was best known for mass-reproduced busts of classical heroes and also for one of Joseph II, a copy of which was acquired by Prince Miklós for Eszterháza, where Haydn presumably knew it. Grassi's two surviving busts of the composer, both showing him in contemporary costume, are in unglazed white porcelain (*biscuit*), a substance which because of its marble-like texture became popular for reductions and imitations of antique sculpture in the late eighteenth century, particularly in Vienna.

Presumably Haydn himself approved such classical allusions in portrait busts of him. They suggested that he was a representative of an esteemed tradition of portraying great personages, which in the recent past had more often than not been used for those of royal or noble birth, sometimes for military heroes, occasionally for writers and artists, but rarely for composers in their lifetimes. Haydn was evidently proud of Grassi's busts of him, and in 1803 indicated to Thomson that he would try to send him one of the smaller busts intended for mass reproduction, which the composer claimed was 'very like me'.[109]

Whatever Haydn's intentions, the portrait Count Harrach actually received from the composer's estate was not the lost (large) one by Grassi, but an unsigned life-size bust in lead attributable to Franz Thaller (perhaps based on Grassi's *en Antike* portrait), which has remained in the Harrach family's possession.[110] Haydn probably made a point of bequeathing a bust and a medal to Harrach because the Count had played an important role in commemorating the composer during Haydn's lifetime. In 1793 he commissioned a monument to Haydn in the grounds of his country seat at Rohrau, Haydn's birthplace. In its original form this consisted of a large pedestal with inscriptions praising

Haydn on its two most visible sides, and topped by a sculpted lyre and other musical instruments.

The Count explained his decision to build this structure in a letter to Dies, which the latter quoted in his biography of the composer:

> I considered it appropriate and befitting, as well as a tribute for my park, to erect in the castle grounds in the vicinity of his birthplace a stone monument to the praiseworthy and famous J. Haydn. Haydn himself was then in England, was only barely known to me, and was unaware of my scheme; furthermore, it was only fortuitously that he learned only two or three years later that this monument had been erected at Rohrau, and he came to see it without my knowing.[111]

Haydn was evidently touched by this apparent act of homage and subsequently tried to ensure in his will that the monument was properly maintained in perpetuity, something which was contested by the Count, who considered that this *privilege* was the right of his own family. The Count's original motives in creating the monument, however, were not solely to do with commemorating Haydn, as he himself confessed to Dies: 'The reason that I placed a stone monument to Haydn in my garden was largely that, after coming of age, I desired to fashion the formal and kitchen gardens, the orchards and the pheasant enclosure around my castle ... I hardly dare say into an English park, but still into a neat promenade, not without some effort to economize.'[112] The Haydn monument was therefore part of a scheme to transform the grounds at Rohrau away from a formal French garden to a park of the kind created by Capability Brown, which was easier to maintain and was therefore gaining popularity throughout Europe.[113] The monument was erected on a newly created island at a picturesque bend in the River Leitha, and was set off with carefully arranged plantings of trees introduced from abroad. Haydn would certainly have appreciated the effect that the Count was trying to create since a similar change of taste is reflected in the landscaping schemes of Miklós II, who turned his back on the formal gardens constructed by Miklós I at Eszterháza, and created a new park in the English style at Eisenstadt in the 1790s.

Haydn would likewise have understood that the business of commemorating creative individuals in the form of free-standing monuments, especially during their lifetimes, was another aspect of English taste. He himself recorded seeing the statue of Handel, portrayed as Apollo, at Vauxhall Gardens which he visited in 1792.[114] This statue, the first important commission given to L.F. Roubiliac in England, was set up in 1738 when Handel was at the height of his powers. It has claims to be the first European statue erected to a creative figure in his own lifetime, preceding Pigalle's *Voltaire* by more than three decades.[115] The enormous success of the Vauxhall *Handel* led to Roubiliac being commissioned to portray the same composer in other contexts, most notably on his tomb in Westminster Abbey, for which

Handel himself made provision in his will.[116] Haydn, who attended several commemorative concerts devoted to Handel's music in Westminster Abbey during his time in London, would certainly have been familiar with this monument and many other memorials in the same church devoted not only to British royalty, nobility, politicians and military heroes, but also to literary figures and also a handful of musicians extending back before Handel. These British memorials were well known in German-speaking countries, but at the time Haydn was in England no real attempt had been made to imitate them.

One reason that Germans had not gone in for such commemoration is recorded in several aphorisms by G.C. Lichtenberg, who had studied Westminster Abbey during his visits to England in the 1770s. Despite being a celebrated Anglophile, Lichtenberg considered that Westminster Abbey 'will one day be called *the Golgotha of sculpture*'.[117] Writing at about the time Harrach commissioned his monument to Haydn, when a movement began in Germany to honour cultural figures with proper memorials, Lichtenberg recorded his views in a passage headed '*The German Pantheon*'. Recalling his unfavourable impression of the monuments at Westminster, he felt that

> these memorials stood there ... to bestow honour on the place where they stood. ... If such an institution is to be of any use at all men must be installed there whose deeds were great without glory, who acquired merit simply through acts for their country and their fellow men – no writers as such. A writer who needs a statue to immortalize him is not worthy of one.[118]

What Lichtenberg felt about memorials to writers applied in Germany equally to composers, though during the 1790s such notions were being challenged more frequently. For example, the *Allgemeine musikalische Zeitung* carried an article in 1800 about monuments to German composers. This mentions the memorials in Westminster Abbey, the one to Handel in particular, and others in the Panthéon in Paris, implying that it was outrageous that there was no equivalent in Germany; indeed the only memorials which could be cited were two plaques to C.P.E. Bach, a recent monument to Mozart in Weimar, and Harrach's monument to Haydn, which was illustrated in the article.[119]

This publicity for the Rohrau monument may have encouraged Haydn to see it for himself; indeed his interest in it was such that he managed to acquire some kind of *modello* of the memorial. Both Dies and Griesinger remembered seeing it in his house and it was recorded among Haydn's effects after his death.[120] The article in the *Allgemeine musikalische Zeitung* seems to have prompted other visits to Rohrau, such as the one made by Count Zinzendorf, who described the memorial to Haydn in his diary in September 1800.[121] The monument at Rohrau, though meagre in appearance, therefore came to hold a special place in the history of German memorials. As early as 1784 readers of the *Magazin der Musik* had learned that Haydn was to receive a monument, not in Germany, but in England, in fact in Westminster Abbey![122] The report, which specifically mentions that the monument was to be unveiled on the arrival of the composer in London (expected at any moment), was of course entirely without foundation. It evidently stemmed from some confusion (perhaps deliberate) with the monument to Handel, which had first been shown to the public in 1762 to general approval, and which again came to the fore during the famous Handel Commemoration in Westminster Abbey of 1784.[123] Given Count Harrach's interest in aspects of English taste, it seems likely that his own memorial to Haydn represented an attempt both to emulate English taste and practice, and also to instigate a German tradition for large-scale musical memorials, which could act as focal points for people enthusiastic about the persons commemorated.

The notion, however, was slow to catch on. When Novello was in Vienna in 1829, seeking information on Mozart and Haydn, he was dismayed to learn that there was no monument to Mozart, noting that this was 'a sore subject' with Viennese composers and 'every other person of good taste and feeling'.[124] By contrast, the Haydn monument at Rohrau did receive attention, if only because of the various restorations it underwent in the first half of the nineteenth century. After the lyre crowning the monument succumbed to the weather, it was replaced by a bust of Haydn copied from the one Harrach inherited from the composer; in view of Haydn's bequest, it seems that this may have been Haydn's intention all along.[125]

The ritualistic respect paid to Haydn in Paris and to a lesser extent in Vienna by about 1800 were anticipated by developments in England. By the time of Haydn's first concert in London there is evidence that the Haydn phenomenon had already reached what may be described as 'cult' status, something that reveals itself in the choice of language used in connection with him. The morning after his first concert, for example, the *Morning Chronicle* told its readers that

> never, perhaps was there a richer musical treat. It is not wonderful that to *souls* capable of being touched by music, HAYDN should be an *object* of *homage*, and even of *idolatry*; for like our own SHAKSPEARE, he moves and governs the passions at will. His new Grand Overture [possibly Symphony No. 92] was pronounced by every scientific ear to be a most wonderful composition ... we cannot suppress our anxious hopes, that the first musical genius of the age may be induced, by our *liberal* welcome, to take up his residence in England.[126]

That Haydn's very person could be considered an object of 'idolatry' perhaps stemmed from knowledge of the composer's Catholic faith, something that had become an issue for the largely Protestant readership in England since at least the mid-1780s, when newspapers suggested that Haydn's failure to take up invitations to come to England was a result of his religion and the detrimental and illiberal effects this had on him and his compatriots. In

January 1785 the *Gazetteer & New Daily Advertiser* carried a report explaining the composer's failure to show in London. According to this, Haydn was '*doomed* to reside in the court of a miserable German Prince', where he devoted his life 'to the rites and ceremonies of the Roman Catholic Church', which he carried 'even to *superstition*'. 'Would it not be 'equal to a *pilgrimage*', asks the writer, 'for some aspiring youths' to 'transplant him to Great Britain, the country for which his music seems to be made?''[127] In September 1785, the *Morning Herald* carried a fresh report of Haydn's intention of visiting England, but qualified it, saying,

> Those ... who know him best, are of the opinion, that he will never honor this land of *heresy* with his practice. This great genius is so a great a bigot to the *ceremonies of religion*, that all his leisure moments are engaged in the celebration of masses, and in the contemplation of *purgatory* ... he is glad to seek *consolation in the bosom of the Church*.[128]

When Haydn actually appeared in London in 1791, and these commentators were confounded, the choice of words revealing traditional Anglo-Saxon contempt for Catholicism was subverted and turned to Haydn's advantage. Not only did he become an object of 'idolatry', but his very person was supposedly responsible for a miracle, resulting from sight of the man himself. Dies tells the story thus:

> Haydn's muse was already *venerated* long before he set foot in London in person, but once he was actually present, the *veneration* increased as each day passed. Everybody wanted to *see* and to hear and, to satisfy his curiosity, crowded into the concert hall ... When Haydn appeared in the orchestra and sat down at the pianoforte to direct a symphony himself, all members of the inquisitive audience in the stalls left their seats and gathered around the orchestra the better to *see* the famous Haydn at close range. The seats in the middle of the floor were therefore empty, and hardly had they been unoccupied when the great chandelier crashed to the ground and broke into pieces, throwing the well-attended gathering into the greatest disarray. As soon as the initial fear was over ... several persons vocalized the state of their feelings with loud cries of 'Miracle! Miracle!' Haydn himself was deeply moved and thanked the *merciful Providence* [der gütigen Vorstehung] that had sanctioned him, in a kind of way, to be the cause ... of *saving* the lives of at least thirty people.[129]

The precise origins of the miracle story are unclear. It is even a matter of debate to which symphony the story alludes. But there can be no doubt, as Dies noted, that several versions of it had been widely circulated by the time he interviewed Haydn.[130] The composer's denial of knowledge of it to Dies was therefore certainly disingenuous, though entirely understandable. Sensing that his popularity had developed to the stage where he himself was the subject of a cult may have left him ambivalent about what was happening. On occasions he tried to make light of the whole notion, as when Dies referred to Haydn's pianoforte:

[Haydn] found the notion comical that I should have called it a 'priceless treasure' ... 'But haven't they', I said, 'offered the surgeon who owns the bullet that killed Nelson 100 guineas for that despicable little bit of lead? Surely your creative clavier is worth as much as that deadly bullet?' – 'In London,' said Haydn, 'they love that stuff! I actually saw Handel's clavier in the residence of the Queen, who bought it from his family and kept it as a *relic*.'[131]

Haydn might have dismissed the notion that his own clavier might become a relic, but Dies's anecdote betrays Haydn's awareness that exactly this was likely to be the case.

Mention of Nelson would surely also have reminded Haydn of the occasion in 1800 of his meeting with the admiral, who had asked the composer for the pen which he used for composing as a keepsake; in return Haydn received Nelson's watch.[132] This, of course, signified much more than a simple exchanging of gifts between two renowned men, and more even than the acquisition on Nelson's part of an innocent memento of his meeting with Haydn. Haydn's 'worn-out' pen symbolized the essence of his creativity, the very point at which his genius became tangible to mankind. In giving it away in such circumstances, Haydn must have been aware that within the act lay the potential for a very particular kind of reverence. Soon after this example, it seemed that everyone wanted something by which they could remember Haydn the man. An example of this is given by Griesinger, who must himself have been present at the sale of Haydn's effects after his death, and reports the commotion this caused as the Viennese outdid each other in attempting to obtain some vestige of the composer himself: 'The Vienna public showed how highly it deemed Haydn at the auction of his estate. ... Everybody wanted to buy a memento. Even people of unassuming standing outbid one another and clambered for the possessions *as though they were a saint's relics* [wie um die Reliquien eines Heiligen].'[133]

Despite the indifference he showed to the idea of becoming the focus of a quasi-religious cult, Haydn was certainly aware of what was happening and indeed to some extent may be considered, unwittingly, to have promoted it. Pohl, Haydn's nineteenth-century biographer, reports the case of a portrait-miniature of the composer executed in the later 1780s, which Haydn himself gave to a female admirer with a lock of his own hair attached, and at least one further portrait-miniature of the composer exists with a lock of his hair fastened to the reverse.[134] Although the use of locks of hair as both relics and lovers' keepsakes has a long history, Haydn's use seems to anticipate that made by Napoleon at a slightly later date, the giving of locks of hair symbolizing both a binding of a subject to his hero and a kind of sharing of his power, the association of hair with strength stemming from the biblical story of Samson and Delilah.[135] Since hair is one part of the human body which may be removed without injury to one's health and which also escapes the decay affecting other bodily remains following death, it was socially acceptable to keep locks of hair as mementos of the famous during their lifetimes and more meaningfully after their demise.

The acquisition of locks of hair was both a kind of demonstration of attachment to respected persons, in life and even more so in death, and also a trigger to recollecting their appearance. By the early nineteenth century, the fad had developed to the extent that some individuals made a habit of collecting bits of hair and displaying them. For example, one of Haydn's greatest English admirers of this period, the poet Leigh Hunt, formed an extensive collection of locks, including several of English poets, and also of Washington and Napoleon.[136] Hunt's friend, Novello, recounts how he eventually persuaded Constanze Mozart to part with a lock of her husband's hair and would undoubtedly have acquired some of Haydn's had the opportunity arisen.[137] After being shown in Vienna a framed lock of Beethoven's hair, Novello noted that Beethoven had originally refused permission for such locks to be cut, but was later reported to have said 'cut off a *bushel* if you like'.[138]

Although the collecting of such memorabilia was widely practised at this period, in some circles the practice was associated with religious conviction. Thus Charles Lamb, a Protestant, was not averse to chiding his friend Novello, a Catholic, about the latter's esteeming of personal momentos connected with the body. After having inspected Novello's album of his trip to Vienna, Lamb returned it, feigning concern about its safety: 'I am anxious, not so much for the autographs, as for that bit of the hairbrush [used by Mozart, and presented to Novello by Constanze]. I enclose a cinder which belonged to *Shield* [the English composer], when he was poor, and lit his own fires. Any memorial of a great Musical Genius, I know, is acceptable.'[139]

The quest for relics of Haydn later passed to other items which might directly be associated with the composer. By the period of Nelson's visit to Vienna there is a sense that the composer's letters and manuscripts could be considered not only potential collector's items on account of their content, but also objects of reverence in themselves because of their contact with Haydn's person. A letter from Haydn to Holcroft, written during his second London visit, for example, had added under the composer's signature the inscription 'The immortal "The Shakespeare of Music" J.H. 1805', accompanied by an asterisk and an explanation that this addition had been written by Holcroft; among other (probably early nineteenth-century) additions is one confirming the letter's authenticity: 'the handwriting of HAYDN'.[140] Another autograph letter of this period received the inscription, probably not by the original recipient, 'The celebrated Musician, Dr. Haydn'.[141] In March 1804 Zelter wrote to Haydn, replying to a letter he had received from the composer: 'I have not words, revered master, to express the pleasure I felt on receiving your affectionate letter of 25 February, which I shall bequeath as a *relic* [Reliquie] ... to my eleven children.'[142] Somewhat later, though in similar vein, the inscription 'holy relic' was added to two leaves of Haydn's sketches for one of the choruses from *The Creation*.[143]

Indeed at the very last performance of *The Creation* attended by the composer in person (27 March 1808), Haydn lived up to the cult status that had developed around him by making two quasi-religious gestures which were clearly visible to the assembled masses; these were sufficiently memorable in themselves that they became the subject of a poem by Collin.[144] According to Griesinger, at the point where Haydn depicted 'And there was light',

> the audience as always broke into the loudest applause. Haydn *made a gesture of his hands heavenward* [machte eine Bewegung mit den Händen gen Himmel] and said, 'It comes from there!' Fearing that a turmoil of emotions left too long unchecked might risk an old man's health, he allowed himself to be carried away in his chair at the end of the first part [of the Oratorio]. He took leave with streaming eyes, and *stretched out his hand in blessing* [streckte die Hand segnend] to the orchestra.[145]

Haydn's gestures were presumably spontaneous; but in the stretching of his arms at an emotional performance of *The Creation*, his most admired composition, some members of the audience might well have been reminded of the gestures of the figure of God, especially the celebrated scene of the *Creation of Adam*, in the most famous representation of the Creation, Michelangelo's ceiling in the Sistine Chapel. It was perhaps some recollection of Michelangelo's powerful iconographic motif which made the occasion so memorable. Although Haydn was obliged to leave before the moment in the oratorio actually depicting the creation of Adam, the extending of his hand towards the assembled company might not only (in retrospect) have been understood to presage the aria concerning Man's creation, but might also have acted as a reminder of the notion that Man was made in God's image, which the aria illustrates.[146] At his last appearance in public therefore, Haydn, though frail and cold – several attentive women overwhelmed him with offers of their shawls – may have been understood by some to have assumed the role of creator attending his own creation. The occasion made such an impact that Princess Esterházy had the scene painted and presented to Haydn.[147]

The composer's conduct on this occasion and probably others, and his liking for being addressed as 'papa' by younger colleagues (to whom he referred as 'his children'), reinforced a view of Haydn as a figure of cult status.[148] It is entirely understandable therefore why, by the time of his death, Haydn was referred to as the father of music.[149] Haydn's dramatic raising of his arm, echoing Michelangelo's vision of the creation of Man, was perhaps recalled on the deathbed of Beethoven, one of the 'children' who witnessed Haydn's last public appearance and the most revered composer of the decades after Haydn's death. A great flash of lightening and awful crash of thunder startled those attending the dying composer, at which Beethoven momentarily came to life and 'stretched out his own right arm majestically – "like a general giving orders to an army", and then instantly died'.[150] Although this episode was embellished on being retold,[151] there is no doubt that, as in the case of Haydn's last public gesture, those who observed it, and later those who read descriptions of it, sensed that the episode had a kind of *divine*, almost Christological significance. It represented the point at which human creativity at its most powerful was understood to come to terms with divinity, and in this special relationship lay the possibility of commemoration of a type which rivalled the saints of the medieval Church. The epithet 'divine' had been repeatedly used in relation to Michelangelo following his death to express the sense (believed of many) that the artist had enjoyed a privileged association with divinity.[152] Perhaps observers of Haydn's last public gestures recalled something of this association as they conceived how Haydn would be remembered. It was also not long after the time of Haydn's last public appearance that Beethoven (subsequently himself often compared with Michelangelo) began referring to the divine as an attribute of music, especially his own.[153] It seems probable that this line of thinking was at least in part prompted by his own observations of Haydn and reactions to him in 1808.

One popular manifestation of the cult of Haydn was reverence attached to his very name, a development which perhaps drew inspiration from devotion to the Name of Jesus which, having developed locally during the later Middle Ages, was finally given a feast day observed by the entire Roman Catholic Church in 1721.[154] Haydn was certainly very conscious of the value of a name from a commercial point of view by the early 1780s: in negotiating for publication of the keyboard arrangement of the symphony (No. 69) he had dedicated to the great field-marshal von Laudon, he noted that the name '"Laudon" will contribute more to the sale than ten finales'.[155] The point was not lost on him in later years when he played a part in associating the name of another celebrated military figure with the mass he originally entitled *Missa in angustiis*, but which within a few years of its composition in 1798 became known as 'the Nelson' throughout Austria and southern Germany. Although Haydn must have realized by the 1780s that his own name was a significant factor in affecting sales, it was not until he visited England that he was confronted with the degree of piety some of his admirers invested in it. Haydn himself records experiencing an example of such devotion, which his later discussions of it with both Griesinger and Dies show left him very moved:

> On 14 Sept [1791] I dined for the first time at Mr Shaw's. ... As I was bowing round the company, I suddenly became aware of the fact that not only the lady of the house, but also her daughters and other women each wore on their headdress *a parte* over the front a most enchanting curved pearl-coloured band of 3 fingers' breadth, with the name Haydn in gold woven into it; and Mr Shaw wore this name on his coat, worked into the edges of both his lapels in the best steel beads. ... [He] wanted a memento from me, and I gave him a tobacco-box which I had just bought ... Some

days later I went to him, and saw that he had had a silver case put over my box, on the cover of which was very beautifully engraved Apollo's harp and the following words: *Ex dono celeberrimi Josephi Haydn* [A gift from the famous Joseph Haydn].[156]

Affection for the name 'Haydn' quickly spread to the composer's homeland. Dies explains how after Haydn's first return to Vienna from London, his fame increased to such an extent that 'every cultivated [gebildete] man uttered the *name* Haydn with a tone that conveyed a sense of *national pride*'.[157]

Such reverence certainly continued. In Zelter's letter to Haydn of 16 March 1804, in which he hoped to commission a sacred work from the composer, he tried to offer encouragement, writing 'So I beg you ... to shoulder this work so that *your great name* also resonates to the *glory of God* and of Art in our circle [in Berlin], which has as its sole aim to reawaken and preserve Church or sacred music.'[158] Zelter's praise for Haydn sometimes took on what almost amounts to a Christological dimension. Later in the same letter, perhaps with prophecies of the Messiah's entry into Jerusalem in mind, he wrote: 'O come to us, come! You will be received like a god among men.' In a review of a performance of *The Creation* held in 1801, Zelter went so far as to invoke the Second Coming in order to convey to the growing readership of the journal in which his review appeared his enthusiasm for the music and his hope that Haydn would write more of the same: 'And thus, God be praised! Marvellous spirit! Appear again in new clarity, and renew the offering of your spirit, for you are a law unto yourself and your works are as you. Amen!'[159]

Rhetoric of this kind, which had the effect of projecting Haydn as a kind of saviour of music, was probably designed to counter one limited, but cogent view of Haydn's late oratorios, objecting to the pictorial aspects of the music, which were seen as retrospective (an issue which is discussed later in this book). The language of salvation applied to Haydn, however, contributed to a shifting of the focus of popular articulated admiration away from the music itself and onto its composer. During the last years of Haydn's life organizations almost fell over themselves in showering honours on Haydn, conscious perhaps that for such a gesture to be really meaningful it would need to be made before the great man died. The rate at which these honours appeared prompted Dies to write the year before the composer's death: 'The cultured whole world in Europe is in time-honoured rivalry to offer our Haydn demonstrations of its great reverence. The *name* of Haydn sparkles like a star – a great triumph for Art.'[160]

When Haydn finally died his funeral was a small-scale affair, on account of the difficult situation caused by the very recent occupation of Vienna by Napoleon's troops. His passing was properly marked a fortnight later (15 June 1809) with a grand memorial service, attended by all the French dignitaries and 'the whole art world of Vienna, most of them in mourning'.[161] Griesinger describes how on this occasion all the composer's medals, all bearing his name, as well as the ivory plaque also bearing his name (given him as a special honour, to allow attendance at concerts in London free of charge), were displayed to the public on a black satin cushion, placed at the end of the catafalque and protected by members of the French army and the local civic guard in turn: Haydn's memorial service, it seems, amounted to a kind of state occasion, which Vienna did not again witness until the death of Beethoven eighteen years later.[162] At his end, therefore, Haydn was treated in a manner usually reserved for royalty, nobility or military heroes, and this included decking out the whole church with 'black hangings ... decorated with the interwoven initials of the *name* Haydn'.[163] The medals, traditionally attributes of military heroes, were engraved and published in Carpani's biography of the composer, presumably to suggest that Haydn represented a new kind of cultural hero, appropriate for a new age.

To preserve Haydn's likeness for posterity, a death mask of the composer's face was made by his servant, Elssler, acting on instructions from Dies.[164] Although this may not be the earliest death mask of a famous composer to have been made – there was apparently one of Handel, for example[165] – earlier images of this kind had chiefly been reserved for personages of royal or noble status, though in Germany and France literary figures had begun to be honoured in this way during the second half of the eighteenth century.[166] After Haydn, death masks of many famous composers were commonly taken, most notably of Beethoven, whose features were also recorded in a life mask (1812).[167] Apart from the death mask, Elssler's devotion to Haydn's image, not just his person, may also be demonstrated from an anecdote told by Dies: '[Elssler,] when he had to fumigate Haydn's room and believed himself to be alone, used to stand with the censer before Haydn's portrait and cense him to express his veneration. He was seen doing it.'[168]

But the most extraordinary episode in the cult of Haydn was the somewhat macabre fate of his bodily remains after death. One of the gravediggers was bribed by an acquaintance of Haydn's, the former Esterházy employee Carl Rosenbaum, and by his friend J.N. Peter, a prison administrator in Lower Austria, to steal Haydn's head in order, they maintained, to 'protect it from desecration'.[169] According to Rosenbaum's diary, the two men drove to the burial ground; Rosenbaum then

> got out and received Joseph Haydn's *invaluable relic* from Jakob Demuth [the gravedigger]. It smelled terrible. Once I had the package in the coach, I had to throw up. The stench was too much for me. ... The head was already rather green but still easily recognisable. The impression this sight made on me will stay with me for ever. The dissection lasted one hour; the brain, which was of large proportions, stank the most terrible of all. I endured it to the end.[170]

The head was then macerated and bleached, and a black box with glass panels, modelled on a Roman sarcophagus, was made for it and decorated with a golden lyre, in which the skull was placed on a silk cushion. Rosenbaum built a mausoleum for displaying the box in his garden, where privileged visitors were allowed to view it.

The theft of the head was discovered in 1820 when Haydn's last patron, Prince Miklós II, was embarrassed into making good his promise to have a tomb for Haydn made at Eisenstadt, a promise known to the public since it had been mentioned in Dies's biography (1810). The Prince had been prompted into this by a visiting member of the British royal family who congratulated him on being in possession of the 'mortal remains' of the great composer. When Haydn's body was moved from Vienna to Eisenstadt the robbery was discovered and the guilty pair were identified following a police inquiry. They avoided returning the correct skull, however, by substituting another. Even when Haydn's tomb was opened up in 1909, the deception was not identified and it was only in 1954 that Haydn's actual skull was reunited with his body.[171] An account of what became of the real skull after Peter's death is given by Botstiber, who completed the last volume of Pohl's biography of Haydn in 1927:

> [Peter's] widow turned over Haydn's skull as well as that of the actress Roose [who had died shortly before Haydn, and whose head had also been stolen] ... to Dr Karl Haller, who gave both skulls to the renowned anatomist Rokitansky [a distinguished professor of pathology in the University of Vienna from 1834 to 1875]. His sons finally turned over Haydn's skull to the Society of Friends of Music, where it is kept in the museum as a *costly relic*.[172]

The authenticity of this skull was proved by experts in 1909.[173] However, even after the supposed reuniting of head and body in 1820, there must have been some in Vienna who were aware of what had really happened. Novello heard the story of the skull having been stolen (as discovered in 1820) from the Viennese composer Eybler, who informed him that 'the general opinion was that it had been taken to Paris for *phrenological* studies'.[174] Whether this supposition was correct or not, it must have been sufficiently well known to cause concern at the time of Beethoven's death in 1827. Novello was told two years later that when Beethoven 'was first buried a guard was placed every night for some time lest his body should be stolen away'.[175] Some contemporaries may have seen in this episode, as with the guards officiating at Haydn's memorial service, a messianic touch. But the truth, as reported in a letter written shortly afterwards, was more mundane: 'I must still report to you that the gravedigger of Währing, where [Beethoven] lies buried, visited us yesterday and told us that someone, in a note that he showed us, had offered him 1,000 florins C.M. if he would deposit the head of Beethoven at a specified location. The police are already engaged in an investigation.'[176] It seems that some unscrupulous persons in the mould of Rosenbaum were prepared to go to considerable lengths to procure the head of a famous composer. But the motivation for this, as in the case of Haydn's skull, was as much about studying appearance as acquiring a 'costly relic'.

6. Physiognomy, Phrenology and Frankenstein

The intense interest in Haydn's appearance during the last 20 or so years of his life and the composer's attempts to manipulate the kinds of image of himself which entered the public domain may be seen as symptoms of a preoccupation of the time with the interpretation of likenesses: the notion that facial features, formations of the body, and even characteristics of handwriting were visual manifestations of an individual's inner character. One of the most influential books of the period which helped to formulate public opinion on such concepts was the *Physiognomische Fragmente* by the Zürich-based theologian J.K. Lavater, which appeared in four volumes between 1775 and 1784.[177] In this the theory of correspondences between the visual appearance of individuals and their creative personalities was expounded at length, and an attempt was made to give it scientific justification through the observation of nature.

Haydn was certainly aware of Lavater's work by the 1780s since the Swiss writer was one of the well-known figures to whom he chose to write in 1781 in the hope of securing subscribers for the publication of the Opus 33 quartets. The composer opened his letter by saying 'I love and am pleased to read your works. As it is written, heard and reported, I also have a certain ability myself, since *my name*, it is said, is known with great credit in every country...'.[178] Haydn's telling choice of wording here, emphasizing that it was his 'name' rather than his music or he himself that was known 'in every country', was perhaps intended as a gesture to thwart any notion that he might himself become the subject of an attempt at practical application of Lavater's theories. Haydn was perhaps aware that Lavater was particularly interested in composers because the character of their music was a further element to take into consideration in equating outward features with inner characteristics.[179]

Lavater, whose collection of portrait silhouettes (some of which he apparently executed himself) certainly included one of Haydn, characterized each personality in his collection with a verse.[180] Under Haydn's he wrote: 'Something more than the commonplace I discern in the eye and the nose; / The forehead also is good; in the mouth something philistine.'[181] Lavater perhaps based this interpretation on the silhouette of Haydn by Hieronymous Löschenkohl, published in the *Österreichischer Nationalkalender* for 1786, depicting the composer with a pronounced lower lip.[182] Had Haydn been given the opportunity to hear Lavater's reading of his features, which seems likely in view of Griesinger's knowledge of it, he doubtless would have understood the spurious basis on which such theories were founded: philistinism was not a trait which fitted Haydn, as his long-standing support for many charitable works, as well as for dozens of musicians, amply indicates. But from Haydn's standpoint the real issue, taking into consideration the wide dissemination of Löschenkohl's silhouette and the popularity of Lavater's writings, was the effect such interpretations might have on how the public received his music. During the later part of his career, Haydn seems to have consciously tried to offset any damage from this source to the reception of his major compositions, like the late oratorios, by ensuring that they were presented to the public in the context of charity.

Haydn himself probably reflected on Lavater's theories and their popular appeal in some detail during his visits to London, when he came into contact with at least two men very much concerned with the Swiss physiognomist and his ideas. One was Lavater's friend and fellow-countryman, Fuseli, who translated into English another of Lavater's important works. The other was Holcroft, who was responsible for a very successful translation into English of the *Physiognomische Fragmente* published in 1789. Haydn's knowledge of Lavater and his understanding of the effect Lavater's ideas had had on public opinion undoubtedly contributed to the care and sensitivity, in matters concerning portraiture, he himself showed on numerous occasions. By the time of his second return to Vienna, it had become quite natural for him to request to see a portrait of a colleague who could not be seen in person, presumably so that he could make his own assessment of the absent man's character, though not necessarily along the lines proposed by Lavater. Dies describes an episode in Dresden when Haydn visited the composer Naumann. Not finding him at home, Haydn 'asked whether a picture of Naumann were at hand, and when the reply was in the affirmative, he asked to be shown it so that he might at least be *acquainted* with Naumann's picture'.[183]

The musical public in the Vienna to which Haydn returned was as keen on the value of physiognomical interpretation as in the London he had left, especially in the circles in which he found himself becoming increasingly active. There is a report, for example, that during the performance of an oratorio organized by van Swieten in 1789, an engraved portrait of the oratorio's composer was passed around the audience, perhaps in an attempt to lend interest to the occasion by enabling the audience, which included members of the nobility, to equate characteristics of the music with features of the composer's image.[184] This particular oratorio was by C.P.E. Bach, and the occasion took place in the residence of Prince Johann Esterházy; but it seems more than likely that this was standard practice at performances of oratorios arranged by van Swieten, and would therefore certainly have been known to Haydn, who is likely to have been the subject of such treatment on occasions when he himself was not present. The practice perhaps derived from van Swieten's knowledge of one of the first portrait prints of Handel, which was advertised for sale to subscribers of his oratorio *Alexander's Feast* in 1738.[185]

Beneath the portrait is a design by Gravelot representing the opening scene of the work. The notion that a listener would find it useful to contemplate a composer's portrait whilst listening to his music persisted long into the nineteenth century.[186]

Lavater's theories did not convince everyone. It would probably have come as a relief to Haydn that the Swiss pastor's doctrines had been undermined in some spheres through the spirited attacks on them by Lichtenberg, whose views on the monuments in Westminster Abbey have already been discussed. Lichtenberg largely dismissed Lavater's claim that physiognomy could be considered an adequate basis for the scientific analysis of character, and in its place put forward the view that expression was the true reflection of inner being. As a hunchback, Lichtenberg understandably found no basis in the study of physical traits for comprehending personality, but developed a view that facial and bodily expression not only reveal character, but might also be used to make judgements on patterns of human behaviour. The pictorial tradition of suggesting moral instruction through the representation of opposing aspects of character, the most successful exponent of which was Hogarth (who had developed the genre and the visual mechanisms for exploring such ideas in several series of satirical prints), helped to shape Lichtenberg's views and inspire his own visual schemes, which were published in popular formats in Germany from as early as 1778. Haydn, studying himself in the mirror in later life (pock marks, hooked nose, polyp and all), would therefore have drawn comfort from the great debunker of Lavater's theories. The story of 'Beauty and the Beast', which Haydn knew through Grétry's *Zémire et Azor* (presented at Eszterháza in Italian in 1782), would also have reminded him that appearances, no matter how ugly, are no guide to personality.

There is evidence by the early 1800s, when Haydn was around the age of 70 and his composing days were numbered, that his attitude to his own portraiture changed. It was now too late to be concerned about manipulating the way the public perceived him in the present; his mind was turned increasingly to the hereafter, how the public would perceive him in the future. In this sense Haydn was able to come to terms with both his age and his appearance. He recognized that from the point of view of posterity what he really looked like might be a matter of serious interest; the record would have to be put straight before it was too late. This was not an issue for a contemporary public; it was a private matter which he himself had to take care of. The change of attitude is most evident in the portraits which were in his possession at the time of his death, most of which were sculpted busts. Thus the lead bust which passed to Count Harrach shows very clearly Haydn's face covered in deep pock marks, which hardly appear at all in the earlier painted portraits. The same observation applies to the naturalistically painted wax bust said to be by Thaller in the inventory of his belongings drawn up after Haydn's death. Haydn kept this under a glass dome.[187] Novello, who saw this bust in 1829 when it belonged to the Viennese publisher Tobias Haslinger, described it as 'strikingly like, clothed in a part of the clothes which [Haydn] himself wore, and the imitation of his wig is made of his own hair'.[188]

In using his own clothes and hair to lend realism to this bust, Haydn evidently went to considerable lengths to have his appearance in later life recorded as faithfully as possible. In this he may have been influenced by the tradition of wax effigies at Westminster Abbey which were a visitor attraction when he was in London.[189] He is likely to have seen, for example, the figure of Pitt the Elder modelled by Patience Wright, Hoppner's mother-in-law, finished in 1775. When this figure was set up in the Abbey, it was said that the robes in which it was shown were those he wore when delivering his last great speech in the House of Lords. Haydn might also have heard about the wax effigy of Nelson, also displayed in the Abbey soon after his death in 1805. Nelson is known to have sat for the artist during his lifetime, and examples of his actual clothing were used for the display of the effigy, described at the time as 'a very striking resemblance ... considered by [those who knew him] to be a strong and exact representation of our departed hero'.[190] Such representations were clearly created to be seen by admirers of the figures portrayed after decease. This is probably what Haydn himself had in mind with the Thaller bust.

Thaller himself was certainly involved with one of the most distressing examples of human bodily remains being used in a visual commemoration of a dead person, which also relates to Haydn's thinking. Angelo Soliman, brought to Vienna as a slave from Africa, became a respected servant in several princely households. When Soliman died, the Emperor Francis II ordered, against the wishes of the dead man's family and the ecclesiastical authorities, that his body should be skinned and stuffed by Thaller in order to be displayed in the imperial museum as a human specimen.[191] The appalling fate of Soliman's body is perhaps the most extreme case of an attempt to preserve a well-known person's living appearance for posterity. It may be considered part of a tradition of exceptional memorial likenesses intended for public display, in which Haydn seems to have wished to include himself, though in a less gruesome form. The tradition may be considered to have reached its culmination in the 'auto-icon' of the philosopher Jeremy Bentham.[192] In his will, Bentham directed that his physical remains should be preserved and displayed in a glass case, his skeleton stuffed with straw and set in his favourite chair, dressed in his own clothes, and with his head mummified. Bentham thought that mummification might be adopted in Europe. The resulting 'auto-icons' of figures who had contributed to the well-being of mankind could act as a source of inspiration to later generations. His own preserved head was deemed by his executors to be unsuitable for public display and was replaced by a wax effigy.

That Haydn's motivation for having his portrait created in wax was not dissimilar to Bentham's in his 'auto-icon' is suggested by the composer's connections with some of the prominent medical personalities of late eighteenth-century Vienna. The surgeon who attempted to remove Haydn's nasal polyp, J.A. von Brambilla, was also the mastermind behind the foundation in 1785 of the imperial medical-surgical military academy, the Josephinum, which quickly became famed for its anatomical-pathological museum, consisting of over 1,000 wax models commissioned by the Emperor from modellers in Italy, which Haydn certainly knew.

Another physician who commanded attention at the imperial court in Vienna at the end of the century was F.J. Gall, the originator of the phrenological theory of brain structure, who arrived in Vienna in the same year as the foundation of the Josephinum. Gall developed a theory which sought to show that the brain was not only the organ of the mind, but consisted of several mental faculties, which could be physically located within the brain, their relative size being an indicator of each faculty's power of manifestation. Of greatest interest to the public at large was Gall's notion that, since the human skull ossifies over the brain during infant development, external examination of the cranium may be used as a guide to interpreting an individual's mental faculties. According to Gall there are 37 faculties of the brain, which may be catalogued under such headings as 'Benevolence', 'Spirituality' and 'Self-Esteem', the development of which affects the size and contour of the skull; a well-developed region of the head therefore testifies to a correspondingly well-developed faculty for that region. It followed from this that character analysis of a subject would be possible on the basis of study of the head. In many respects Gall's theory proceeded from Lavater's physiognomy, which had already argued that 'the exterior form of the brain, which imprints itself perfectly on the internal surface of the skull, is, at the same time, the model of the contours of the exterior surface'.[193] Gall's theory, however, was more compelling intellectually since it went beyond the simple linking of physical appearance with character by connecting the visible form of the head with the functions of the brain. Gall was able to devise a craniological chart which, as he himself said, was 'seized upon so avidly by the public; even artists took it over and distributed a large number among the public in the form of masks of all kinds'.[194] For five years Gall lectured on these subjects in Vienna; but in 1802 the Austrian authorities forbade him to disseminate his views further on the grounds that they were subversive.[195] He eventually settled successfully in Paris, declining a subsequent invitation by the Emperor to return to Vienna.

The first general knowledge of Gall's theories by the public in Vienna closely coincides with Haydn's apparent change of mind concerning his own portraiture. The lifelike busts he encouraged during his last years spent in Vienna may be understood as responding to those ideas of Gall's then capturing the public imagination. There can be no doubt that subsequently these ideas provided the principal motivation for the theft of Haydn's skull, the phrenological interests of Rosenbaum and Peter being well documented.[196] Peter's considerable collection of skulls with which he attempted to verify Gall's theory was well known; in examining Haydn's skull he was proud to find proof of 'the seat of hearing, just as it is given in the preface to Gall's book'.[197] Peter was here alluding to one of Gall's 37 faculties, called 'Tune', which phrenologists claimed is located in the external corners of the brow, of particular relevance to musicians. Subsequent handbooks on phrenology, in discussing this 'organ', claimed that it could be shown to be particularly enlarged in certain famous composers, notably Handel and Haydn.[198] Eybler's comment to Novello that 'the general opinion was that [Haydn's skull] had been taken to Paris for phrenological studies', whether true or not, certainly indicates that 20 years after Haydn's death there was a widespread view that his mortal remains had helped to advance the boundaries of scientific inquiry.

Indeed, the fate of Haydn's skull and its contribution to the fad for phrenology may be understood in the context of the renewed interest in Western society at this time in the bodily remains of the deceased, which fed into aspects of popular culture. In 1816, for example, Mary Shelley began *Frankenstein*, in which a being – 'the Creature' – is fabricated from the remains of bodies collected from the grave and dissecting room, and brought to life through the clandestine labours of its creator, thus putting into effect for the first time 'what had been the study and desire of the wisest men since the creation of the world'.[199] Shelley's friends in Scotland, where she lived from 1812 to 1814, may have inspired her with the latest developments in phrenology, which provoked particular and lasting attention in Edinburgh. As early as 1803 the *Edinburgh Review* was able to state, 'Of Dr Gall and his skulls who has not heard?' and in 1815 a debunking of the entire theory in the same journal led to Gall's collaborator, Dr Spurzheim, visiting the Scottish capital to illustrate their 'findings' with a demonstration centred on the dissection of a brain.[200]

The element in Shelley's story in which Frankenstein's Creature actually comes to life derives, of course, from another source acknowledged in the novel's subtitle, *The Modern Prometheus*, alluding to the ancient myth of the rebellious Titan who stole fire from Olympus to save mankind. Ovid refashioned the legend to make Prometheus into the creator of men; thereafter Prometheus was often seen as a kind of champion of human creativity, the fire he stole from heaven representing the inspirational spark for the cultural achievement of mankind which distinguishes man from lesser creatures. Aeschylus' play *Prometheus Bound*, which treats the punishment inflicted on Prometheus for rivalling the gods, was especially influential after it became widely available in English translation on writers in Mary Shelley's circle (including Percy Shelley and Byron), for whom the Titan embodied the struggle of man against tyranny and an expression of post-Revolutionary freedom.

The origin of early nineteenth-century popular interest in the creative aspects of the Promethean legend, however, may be traced back to the reception given to Haydn's oratorio *The Creation* in Paris in 1801.[201] The oratorio, which concerns the creation of a man, Adam, appealed to French society at the time because it suggested the formation of a new social order, portraying the newly created man free from the shackles of Original Sin – the oratorio conspicuously omits the story of the Fall – and emphasizing instead the perfection of Man's existence in Paradise. The 142 French musicians who wrote to Haydn congratulating him on *The Creation* did so in Promethean terms:

> No year goes by in which a new production by this composer does not enchant the artists, enlighten their minds, contribute to the progress of art, extend the vast ways of harmony, and prove that its expanses are *boundless* [elles n'ont point de bornes] if one follows *the luminous trails* [les traces lumineuses] with which Haydn has brilliantly illuminated the present and enriches the future. But the imposing conception of the oratorio even surpasses ... everything which this wise composer has until now offered to an astonished Europe. When in this work he imitates the *fires of light* [feux de la lumière], Haydn seems to have portrayed himself, and thus proves to us all that his name will shine fully as long as the star whose rays he seems to have borrowed.[202]

The commemorative medal which accompanied the musicians' letter reinforced these allusions visually: a flaming torch in the midst of a circle of stars appearing above a lyre, at the base of which is shown a reclining nude male figure, presumably representing the newly formed man. By implication Haydn is understood by his French admirers as the Prometheus/Creator figure, a notion of which he and others in Vienna certainly became very conscious.

One indication of this comes from 1801 when, following the success of *The Creation* in Vienna, Haydn's former pupil Beethoven was commissioned to write a ballet, *The Creatures of Prometheus*, a subject which was probably chosen to rival *The Creation*.[203] According to a near-contemporary source, Haydn soon afterwards (about the time he heard from the Parisian musicians) met Beethoven unexpectedly and congratulated him on the ballet. There followed a brief exchange between the two men punning on the word 'Creation': 'Beethoven replied: "O, dear Papa, you are very kind; but it is far from being a *Creation*!" Haydn, surprised at the answer and almost offended, said after a short pause: "That is true; it is not yet a *Creation* and I can scarcely believe that it will ever become one."'[204]

Haydn was right about Beethoven's Prometheus ballet, which was not popular in Vienna. However, the choreographer who commissioned it, Salvatore Viganò, used the same subject matter for his *Prometeo*, a grand ballet first produced in Milan in 1813, in which the figure of Prometheus acted as a mark of respect for Napoleon. Viganò retained some of Beethoven's music, but added pieces by other composers. According to Stendhal, the section which made the greatest impact on its audiences used the music depicting Chaos from the prelude to Haydn's *The Creation*, which was danced by three ballerinas to express 'the first faint stirring in the soul of an awakening to beauty'.[205] It was probably this kind of interpretation of Haydn's oratorio that had caused Parisian audiences at the beginning of the century to see the composer in Promethean terms, the music suggesting not only the Creation story as told in Genesis, but also the emergence of human creativity itself, lit by a spark of divine light captured by the composer.

Viganò's ballet was so successful and well known in Italy that his achievement was commemorated with a medal, depicting the bound Prometheus. It has plausibly been suggested that this medal and some knowledge of the production it marked is likely to have become known to Mary and Percy Shelley, who attended the ballet when they visited Milan in 1818; *Prometeo* and its element derived from Haydn's *Creation* may thus have played a part in developing the English Romantic interest in the Prometheus legend.[206] Indeed, so firmly was the Promethean legend linked with Haydn in the first years of the nineteenth century that Griesinger referred to the composer as 'this musical Prometheus',[207] and Dies chose to end his Haydn biography with a commemorative poem spelling out the connection.[208]

Although Mary Shelley is unlikely to have read the verse quoted by Dies, she might well have known the French Promethean view of *The Creation* from those radical friends of her father's who had travelled to Paris in 1802 during the peace of Amiens to observe for themselves the outcome of the Revolution in shaping French society: one such person, for example, was Haydn's friend Thomas Holcroft. Encouraged by Novello, *The Creation* certainly captured Mary Shelley's imagination and she shared this enthusiasm with another English Romantic, Leigh Hunt.[209] She was probably aware that her own novel had a further important connection with Haydn: one of her own sources for *Frankenstein*, Milton's *Paradise Lost*, was also the acknowledged textual source for *The Creation*.

7. Hero

The early nineteenth-century Promethean view of Haydn brings him into the orbit of one important strand of early Romantic thinking and image-making; but it also helps to explain why his own person was of such interest, particularly to followers of Lavater and Gall, creating a demand for images of him which allowed his features to be analysed free from the hindrance of his wig.[210] In a sense Haydn himself helped to foster such interest at the time he composed *The Creation*. In treating the creation of Adam, the first man, he set words which not only idealize Man as the 'king of nature', but also describe his 'broad and lofty forehead' which, in terms reminiscent of Lavater or Gall, betokens 'the power of intellect': 'and from the clear, bright glance the spirit shines forth, the breath and image of his Creator'.[211]

Although the creator referred to here was of course the God of the Old Testament, it is easy to see how he might be misunderstood as Haydn himself, whose image, it might be construed, was reflected in the portrayal of Adam as clad with 'dignity and honour', and endowed with 'beauty, strength and courage'.[212] In fact, poems written in praise of *The Creation* quite naturally referred to Haydn as the 'Creator', albeit the 'Creator of Harmony'.[213] Haydn was a genius in the eighteenth-century sense (as defined by Rousseau); but he was also a genius in the sense that his creativity was understood at the threshold of the nineteenth century to take humanity a stage further than this by, as Dies expressed it, rivalling the gods themselves.

Haydn himself, of course, would have seen his own creativity more in devotional terms, the fire of his inspiration certainly deriving from heaven, but with the emphasis more on prayer than on any distinctive relationship with divinity. None the less, the idea that Haydn, while working on *The Creation*, enjoyed some privileged connection with the Almighty was reflected and developed by Griesinger, who notes that because of this relationship, Haydn was 'bound to have greater success in this composition [*The Creation*] than a hundred other masters', and quotes the composer himself as saying: 'I was never so devout as during the period when I was working on *The Creation*. Every day I dropped to my knees and prayed God to grant me strength for a successful outcome to this work.'[214] Griesinger goes on to suggest that Haydn's notion that his talent was 'a gracious gift from Heaven', rather than a mark of his own genius, was in fact characteristic of great German artists, citing Albrecht Dürer, the celebrated painter and printmaker, as an example. Perhaps one reason why Dürer was chosen for comparison was that he had lived in an age when it was thought that everyone unquestioningly gave thanks to God for their achievements, which Griesinger accepted was no longer the case following the Age of Reason. Dürer was also a key figure for those German thinkers *c*.1800 who sought to connect the study of aesthetics and religion.[215] One prominent activist in this movement, Friedrich von Schlegel, even referred to Dürer in 1803 as 'the Shakespeare of painting', an interesting parallel with the often repeated notion that Haydn was 'the Shakespeare of music'.[216]

Partly on account of the special relationship he was thought to enjoy with the Almighty, Haydn plays a part in the emergence of the new concept of the hero on the eve of the Napoleonic era. Before Haydn wrote *The Creation* (1797), the Western idea of a hero, deriving from Greek antiquity, was largely restricted to the (generally) young, powerful athlete, successful in combat. But from the time of the first public performances of *The Creation* the notion of 'the art-hero' established itself. In 1799 Rochlitz could refer to Haydn, as well as Mozart, Goethe and Schiller as 'heroes and leaders'.[217] Dürer, as Griesinger was aware, came to be seen as a kind of founding father of the visual arts in Germany, and therefore a national hero.[218] The equivalent position in music was awarded to J.S. Bach, whose life was the subject of the first extended musical biography, by Forkel, which emphasized the idea of Bach as specifically a 'German' composer, his works 'a priceless national patrimony'.[219]

Rochlitz, writing in the very first volume of the *Allgemeine musikalische Zeitung* in 1798, presented a similar picture of Bach, 'the patriarch of German music ... the Albrecht Dürer of German music', comparing him also with three of the other cultural figures most admired at the time: Rubens, Newton and Michelangelo.[220] In 1801 the same journal published a series of articles by J.K. Triest which again emphasized the pre-eminent role of J.S. Bach in the development of German music, a position which Triest compared with the one Michelangelo occupied in the arts of architecture, sculpture and painting.[221] Although the Bach/Michelangelo analogy was not exactly new, having already been suggested by Burney (who perhaps was also the first to refer to Haydn as a 'hero'), the context of this and other analogies fashioned by Rochlitz and his contemporaries, pride in Germany's cultural heritage, was new.[222] Haydn was certainly very much aware of these developments in championing great cultural figures from Germany's past and probably wished to be associated with them. Dies tells the story of Haydn's approval for a cartoon aimed at showing the superiority of German compared with Italian music: J.S. Bach was depicted in the middle of the sun, surrounded by Handel, Haydn and other German composers; below, an Italian owl was shown abhorring the light of the sun, and a German hen was shown ready to fight an Italian capon.[223]

Haydn certainly shared much of the enthusiasm for J.S. Bach generated by Rochlitz. He may in extreme old age have even approved its nationalistic purpose. Haydn's music library featured works by Bach, including the B minor Mass and at least one set of 24 Preludes and Fugues. He also owned Forkel's biography of Bach. It is doubtful, however, that Haydn admired Bach more than Handel, many of whose works were also in Haydn's library, and who is known to have been specifically praised by Haydn ('He is the master of us all') during his visits to London. Handel, unlike Bach, however, was disqualified from consideration as a truly German hero, having spent most of his creative life in England, where performances of his music amounted to an English national institution.[224] It was therefore Bach with whom Haydn was linked in the last painted portrait of the Austrian composer to be executed in his lifetime, the one by Isidor Neugass dated 1805.[225] Haydn is depicted in reflective mood looking through some leaves of musical manuscripts in front of a statue of Apollo, the god of music, with whom he was often connected towards the end of his life – he even kept such a statuette in his house at Gumpendorf.[226] Behind Haydn, however, is a clearly recognizable bust of J.S. Bach, placed to imply that Haydn was inspired by the earlier composer. Neugass's portrait therefore presents Haydn not only as a composer working in the tradition of Bach, but more importantly as a new addition to the illustrious line of German art-heroes.

The use of a portrait bust to suggest a source of inspiration in a painted portrait was not unusual by the early nineteenth century, especially in England.[227] Gainsborough had shown the famous actor Garrick with a bust of Shakespeare, which became well known through the engraving by Valentine Green (1769); and in turn Thomas Stothard depicted the actress Mrs Yates reciting Sheridan's 'Verses to the Memory of Garrick' in front of a bust of the actor (engraved by J. Heath in 1783).[228] Having become established in England for literary figures, the device was appropriated for painters, as may be seen, for example, in Reynolds's *Self-portrait with a bust of Michelangelo*, presented to the Royal Academy (engraved by Green in 1780).[229] Haydn may have noted such works when he was in London. But by 1805 painters in Vienna are likely to have known them through engravings, which may have been used as models. Lichtenberg had long since advocated the use of Reynolds's portraits as models for German-speaking portrait painters, and in adapting the type to honour German 'art-heroes', it was inevitable that a composer like Haydn would be treated in this way.[230] Neugass's use of a bust of Bach in his portrait of Haydn is particularly interesting since Bach's appearance had been recorded in very few paintings dating from his lifetime and the popular tradition for his iconography had then only recently been established.[231] The engraving of Bach published in the first volume of the *Allgemeine musikalische Zeitung* probably did much to enable the public to recognize the composer and may have been used as a model by Neugass for the bust depicted in his portrait of Haydn. Neugass's use of the bust therefore indicates not only how important popular busts were becoming in conveying to the public a sense of musical identity and continuity, but also how composers had by then become accepted and desirable subjects for such busts. By the time the Novellos visited Vienna in 1829, it was to be expected that a renowned music publisher would display a series of busts of the most famous composers (including Haydn); though, in an age when it was yet to become conventional to decorate concert venues and opera houses with busts of composers, this was still enough of a novelty to receive comment.[232]

When Neugass painted his portrait of Haydn, therefore, the idea that a composer might be considered a hero had been clearly established. Haydn (and Bach) thus rubbed shoulders with other figures portrayed in busts produced for a popular market in the early nineteenth century, such as Nelson, a representative of the more traditional category of hero, and Raphael and Shakespeare, representatives of arts which the public had been willing to admit might accommodate notions of the hero before this was possible for composers.[233] Whilst at an earlier point in his career Haydn often personally attempted to manipulate the image of himself which entered the public sphere, at the end of his life it was really the public which manipulated the image of Haydn it wished to see, placing him on a pedestal and ranking him with the 'greatest' of past and contemporary figures.

What, it may be suggested, marred this standing, leading in the decades after his death to Haydn being considered merely one of a number of composers whose features were worthy of public gaze, rather than *the* representative of the musical arts, was not simply the emergence of other leading composers whose image entered the public domain following the success of Haydn (notably Beethoven), but the acknowledgement of Napoleon as the single most influential personality to capture the imagination of Western society in the early nineteenth century, even among his adversaries. The image of Beethoven presented to the public by the end of the second decade of the century tended to make a virtue of his less attractive features, gruff personality and dishevelled appearance by implying that here was a man who was prepared to confront conventionality and challenge the gods themselves. The Promethean characteristics first associated with Haydn were applied to Beethoven more appropriately; this was an image which had a lasting grip on the public's imagination.

But the same also applied to the image of Napoleon. Within only a few years of Haydn's death there would have been few people across Europe who did not have some sense of Napoleon's appearance, so extensively had his image been reproduced in printed formats; in the process of establishing (and debunking) the cult of Napoleon, every device which had been used to project Haydn in the public sphere was also used for Napoleon, but more so, with enthusiasm, and to far greater effect.[234] Even Haydn's favourite ruse of encouraging the younger generation to view him as a father-figure, implying a paternal and even a priestly dimension to the composer's public persona, which found visual expression in the quiet, unassuming portraits Haydn himself favoured late in life, was appropriated for Napoleon: a popular print, for example, by one of the greatest artists to devote himself to propagating the Emperor's achievements, J.-L.-H. Bellangé, shows a peasant pointing to an inexpensive image of Napoleon in military uniform, and saying to his parish priest, 'For me, he will always be *Our Father.*'

For almost two decades before Napoleon was declared Emperor of the French, Haydn had been one of the most 'seen' figures in Western society, his image widely known, even if in person he went unrecognized. No contemporary cultural figure knew the value and the problems of having his/her own image in the public sphere more than Haydn. He certainly sought to control the way he was portrayed with a view to influencing public perceptions of him, his music and his reputation. After his death, of course,

Haydn's image lost status in relation to other 'heroes', particularly Beethoven (a 'cultural' hero), and Napoleon (a traditional 'military' hero). To some extent his image also came to be subverted early in the nineteenth century to support a new sense of German cultural identity, far removed from the universal respect it received in the 1790s. But the process which led to Haydn's image becoming such a significant piece of cultural public property by the early nineteenth century meant that Western man never looked quite the same way again.

CHAPTER SIX

Developing Tastes: The Culture of Looking in England in the Early 1790s

1. A Visual Education: Haydn as Collector

Possibly the clearest evidence for Haydn's interest in the visual arts comes from his own collection of works of art, which may be partially reconstructed from a catalogue drawn up after his death (Appendix), and from a few items mentioned in his will.[1] The most prominent aspect of the works he acquired was a collection of over 200 prints, mostly kept in a portfolio, with a small number mounted behind glass, framed and hung on the walls of his house in the Viennese suburb of Gumpendorf.

The precise number of prints Haydn owned cannot be established since the cataloguer did not always distinguish clearly between prints and odd drawings which were kept with them. Several prints were sometimes also included under a single item and accounted for rather vaguely, as in item 609, which simply indicates 26 separate engraved theatrical scenes, with no further information. But for many items, the cataloguer provided sufficient details (often titles, and names of designers and engravers) to identify the prints. Although little care was taken in transcribing words (e.g., 'Bunbury' consistently appears as 'Bunburg', 'Barker' was turned into 'Parker'), the catalogue permits a clear picture of Haydn's taste in prints to be established. The bulk of the collection consisted of English pieces, the majority of which (judging from their dates of publication) are likely to have been acquired when Haydn was in England. The collection therefore presents unambiguous evidence for Haydn immersing himself in English visual culture of this period. As with any kind of collector, one of the main reasons for this had clearly to do with his own personal interests, tastes and curiosity at this particular time. But an examination of the specific choices he made suggests that many of the prints may have been acquired as a method of informing the composer of prevalent canons of taste within the public sphere in England during the period of his visits. A cursory investigation of the character of the collection shows that, although it was diverse (including prints after Old Master paintings, caricatures, literary prints, portraits, and various 'fancy' prints), his selections within each genre suggest that he wished to keep abreast of what made the greatest impact on the public at the time. Haydn's collection featured some of the most popular prints of the early 1790s, choices which it would be hard to account for merely in terms of Haydn's personal preferences, but which hint at a concerted effort to keep in tune with public taste. There was a pronounced emphasis on prints produced by the stipple process, which allowed a delicacy of effect and permitted colour. This technique dominated English printmaking from the later 1770s. Since it was quicker and cheaper to produce than line engraving, it was hugely successful with the public, though many lamented the consequent decline of the latter technique, thought by some to be a much nobler art.[2] The collecting of prints was therefore one way for Haydn of gauging aesthetic features to which the English at large were particularly responsive. This, it may be argued, has a bearing on the form and character of the music he composed for London audiences. This is not to suggest in any way that Haydn compromised his own artistic creativity; only that the fact of his being in England and observing English tastes presented new stimuli, which (as the composer himself acknowledged) had to be taken into account in working for an English public.

In later life, Haydn claimed, somewhat disingenuously, that he had been too impoverished throughout his career to purchase expensive works of art. In discussing works by Haydn kept unpublished in his lifetime, Griesinger claimed that 'The most interesting of these [unpublished pieces] are 46 canons, mostly to German lyrics, that hung framed in Haydn's bedroom. "I was not rich enough", [Haydn] said, "to buy myself beautiful paintings; I accordingly made myself a wallpaper that not everyone can have."'[3] These canons also appear in the inventory of Haydn's possessions drawn up after his death, where they are said to have hung in his study 'like pictures' (*als Bilder*), divided up into a set of six.[4] This arrangement and most of the compositions in question were certainly made after Haydn returned from England for the second time. Whilst it evidently indicates a pride in his own compositional ability, which could only be admitted privately, the trouble Haydn went to in framing and displaying these manuscripts implies a recognition in this type of composition that a certain aesthetic pleasure might be derived from *looking* at the scores, as well as from *listening* to their music. One of the canons featured in this arrangement – Haydn was especially proud of it – was a setting of the words 'Thy voice O Harmony is divine', submitted for his doctoral degree from the University of Oxford in July 1791. He reused this same composition for the first of his settings of the Ten Commandments in German ('You should believe in one God'). The work was designed to be read backwards and upside down, as well as conventionally; the composer most appropriately associated the form of this ingenious canon with divinity. One autograph of this work shows Haydn writing it out in circular form and using different coloured inks to indicate how it should be read. This is probably the form in which it hung at Gumpendorf.[5] Although the use of a circle in the notation of the canon was a device to aid legibility – examples survive from the Middle Ages and the Renaissance[6] – Haydn evidently also associated the shape with God, a perfect form without beginning or end. The association of divinity with the circle also cleverly refers to and overcomes the prohibition in the second Commandment: 'You should not make any graven image, nor any likeness of any thing that is in heaven above ...'. The manuscript therefore has a clear pictorial aspect beyond its musical value. The use of an abstract form to express the infinite nature of God at the same time as giving visual pleasure, though apparently intended for the composer's delectation alone, shows Haydn indulging in a form of artistic creativity and perception, almost certainly prompted by aesthetic experiences in England. For his friends in Vienna it was easier to account for his canon pictures by implying that they were in place of 'real' pictures, which he claimed were beyond his means, than explain the true motivation behind them.

Although in his youth Haydn may not have been in a position to commit large sums for purchasing artefacts, as financial success became more assured, there is no doubt that, when time permitted, his attention often turned to what visual items he might collect for his own amusement. When old age made composition impossible for him, he seems to have enjoyed looking at what he had amassed and sharing it with others. After seeing Haydn on 9 June 1806, Dies wrote:

> Haydn showed me a portfolio of copper engravings, some of which he purchased in London, others received as gifts. Many of them are portraits of celebrated musicians whom Haydn knows personally. While we were turning through the engravings, Prince Paul, son of the reigning Prince Esterházy, was announced as a visitor to Haydn [here inspection of the portfolio had to be abandoned].[7]

Unfortunately, Dies says nothing further about Haydn's prints. It seems likely, however, that the inspiration for Haydn to collect came from the extensive print collections assembled in Vienna in the second half of the eighteenth century, including those of his patron, Prince Esterházy, of the local lord where he grew up, Count Harrach, as well as those of Count Durazzo and Albert of Sachsen-Teschen.[8] By the time that Haydn was sufficiently secure financially to devote funds to the odd print, such collecting had been recognized as a valuable pastime for a German-speaking citizen with appropriate resources. In his popular and influential encyclopedia, the *Allgemeine Theorie der schönen Künste* (first published 1771–74, with several later editions), J.G. Sulzer promoted the study and collecting of prints as a critical factor in the formation of good taste, in itself a matter, he claimed, of national significance.[9] As we have seen, Sulzer (in a supplement published in the 1790s) was particularly concerned with the collecting habits of composers, describing C.P.E. Bach's considerable set of portrait prints, which might well have acted as a stimulus to Haydn. Print-collecting was also recommended in verses entitled 'The Hobbyhorse Riders' published in the *Lauerberger Genalogischer-Calender* for 1781, written by Anna Louise Karshin, and illustrated by her friend, the engraver Chodowiecki. In these verses a number of pastimes are discussed – book-collecting, natural history, antiquities, animals, food and heraldry – though all have certain drawbacks. Only print-collecting may be practised with total approbation.[10] Voltaire also recommended collecting prints, especially those 'after great Masters, an enterprise useful to humanity, which multiplies at little cost the merits of the best painters ... and which can introduce all schools [of painting] to a man who has never seen a picture'.[11]

Among Haydn's earliest acquisitions was perhaps a set of eight engravings by Chodowiecki illustrating an edition of works by G.A. Bürger, several of whose poems were set by Haydn.[12] By the end of the 1780s the collection was evidently well established. In common with collectors of contemporary prints throughout Europe, Haydn's preference was for English prints, the most popular of which were reviewed in German journals.[13] Writing to C.G. Breitkopf, his publisher in Leipzig, in April 1789, Haydn betrayed his enthusiasm: 'I would beg you at your convenience to send me a few *English* engravings, but beautiful ones – I will gratefully give you something of my work in return for any to send – for *I am a great amateur of them.*'[14] The English publisher John Boydell placed advertisements in a leading Leipzig journal, which between 1757 and 1811 gave notice of no fewer than 2,200 recent English prints. Haydn was therefore making use of contacts in Leipzig, where the desired commodity was easily available.[15] Later in 1789, in a letter to the Vienna agent of one of his patrons, Haydn was again requesting works to augment his collection.[16] However, only during his visits to London was Haydn fully able to indulge his interest and spend time viewing the print shops. In his first London Notebook (1791–92), for example, appears an entry describing the iconographic oddities of an engraving of Saint Peter he had seen in Oxford Street, where several print shops were located.[17]

By the time of his second visit, his penchant seems to have been sufficiently well known for acquaintances to present him with prints they thought would interest him. It was probably in October 1794 that he wrote thanking his friend the engraver and antiquarian Thomas Park for what the composer described as 'the two so charming Prints'.[18] The prints in question may be identified from Haydn's inventory as *Rosalie et Lubin* by William Beechey, showing the couple with a lamb beside a river, and *Lubin et Rosalie* by Richard Morton Paye, depicting Lubin retrieving the lamb from the river, leaving Rosalie grieving on the bank. Both were engraved by Park and published in 1790.[19] The subject matter of these works, derived from one of Marmontel's *Contes moraux*, was enormously popular in the later eighteenth century, both in England and in France, on stage as well as in print.[20] The story concerns two cousins, young shepherds, in love with each other. When the girl finds herself pregnant by Lubin – though neither understands how this could have happened – the bailiff informs them that they committed a mortal sin. A priest suggests that had they been rich, it would have been much easier to extricate themselves from their situation. Eventually, a kind-hearted lord rescues them by obtaining a dispensation for them to marry. The story struck a chord with a broad public, not only because it excited heartfelt sympathy for the plight of the couple, but also because it raised serious moral issues, challenging deep-rooted social and religious prejudices. Haydn was certainly mindful of these issues. One of his first set of English Canzonettas, to words by Anne Hunter probably written in the same year, had extended the story by imaging the girl's expressions of loss 'while Lubin is away'.[21] Subsequently, when Haydn was working on *The Seasons*, the story chosen for Hanne to relate in *Winter* was based on the same source.[22]

Haydn expressed his gratitude to Park for the prints by presenting his wife, presumably an amateur pianist, with what he described as 'a little Sonat', probably the D major sonata (Hob. XVI: 51), the only one of the three solo sonatas he composed in England distinguished by its ease and brevity.[23] When it was published, Haydn described it as 'composed in England for a Lady, who kept the original manuscript'.[24] The first-movement Andante is unique among Haydn's sonata-form compositions in being through-composed, the exposition having no repeat. This continuity lends the movement a narrative character, unusual in Haydn's writing for keyboard. It is tempting to suggest that this aspect of the piece was determined by the spirit of Park's pair of prints, for which the 'little' sonata was designed as a gesture of thanks. The main *cantabile* theme, with its *larmoyant* quality, and gentle triplet accompaniment, might well evoke the lovers at the waterside, whilst the more troubled development section suggests the rebukes of their elders, before the calm of domestic bliss, beside the river, is restored at the movement's close. The more tempestuous *Presto* Finale, with its rising and falling sequences of phrases, its surging rhythmic patterns, and its off-beat accents, might also have been understood to evoke the threat that the river presents in sweeping away the lamb and Lubin's attempt to rescue it, as illustrated in the second print.[25]

Haydn's facility in handling prints, even before he arrived in England, is evident in a letter he wrote to one of the London publishers interested in issuing his works, John Bland, who had apparently requested of the composer some portrait prints.[26] Haydn's willingness to procure such works for associates is further attested in correspondence by his friend, Burney, alluding to the composer having brought him '2 or 3 of the best prints of Metastasio that have been engraved in Vienna'. Burney intended having one of these re-engraved to illustrate his study of Metastasio.[27] Indeed Burney, one of the composer's earliest and closest acquaintances in England, almost certainly played an important part in impressing on Haydn the need for a musician, if he were to be taken seriously by educated society in Britain, to possess some understanding of the visual arts.

In his youth Burney had devoted much time to teaching himself about painting by studying the famous collection assembled by Sir Robert Walpole at Houghton (Norfolk), and by reading Vasari's *Lives of the Artists*.[28] Burney convinced himself that what had been done for the visual arts, by writers like Vasari, could work just as well for music. In many of his musical publications from the 1770s and later, Burney consciously introduced visual parallels. This was not simply a matter of suggesting the character of music, but a means of displaying his credentials as an educated gentleman, and thus of ensuring that his literary efforts to promote the respectability of music in society were well received. In his tours around continental Europe collecting information for the grand, multi-volumed *History of Music*, Burney always made a point of visiting the major collections and galleries, and then giving often extensive accounts of them which pepper the musical story he was telling. Important pictures by Italian and Netherlandish artists were seen, scrutinized and carefully recorded. At times, Burney's journals became more an exploration of painting than of music, a circumstance which he seems to have carefully engineered:

> During my residence at Venice, I was seized with such a rage for painting, that in perusing my miscellaneous journal [intended for publication] it seems more like a *Picturesque* tour than a musical one. And my remarks on pictures and styles of painting, will, I fear, be thought an affectation of *connoisseurship* by a professor of another Art, and naturally supposed to be ignorant of Painting.[29]

Burney was certainly not averse to flaunting his knowledge of the visual arts, nor of venturing his own critical views. At Turin, for example, he saw the collection of Signor Baretti, brother of one of his London friends:

> ... in [Baretti's] collection [there are] several good pictures, among which a *Susannah* [*and the Elders*] by Rubens, treated like that ... at Houghton, which is spoilt and thrown aside; but this is perfect. There are two fine old men's heads in it, on the left side a fountain and dog; it wants nothing but elegance in the figures and a more delicate beauty in the female, to make it one of the finest pictures in the world, which, in point of colouring it is at present.[30]

Evidently Burney had a good visual memory and confidence in his own judgement, though modern scholarship would take issue with him.[31] Respect for his expertise was such that he received invitations to Royal Academy dinners and was pleased to comment on the most notable pictures at the annual exhibition.[32] In private correspondence, he often moved effortlessly between debates on music and painting. In a letter to his friend Thomas Twining of 6 September 1783, for example, a discussion of Haydn symphonies is followed by mention of James Barry's recent *Account of a Series of Pictures* (Barry's own explanation of his paintings for the Society for the Encouragement of Arts, Manufactures and Commerce, which includes a depiction of Burney).[33] The letter also mentions Reynolds's jealousy of Barry, and ends with an indication that Burney hoped to get Haydn to London as an opera composer. When abroad Burney made special efforts to visit celebrated or unusual artists, especially when there was the possibility that they might offer a new insight into his understanding of music. In Florence in 1770, for instance, he managed to find time to see Mengs (then working on his *Noli me tangere* for All Souls College, Oxford), whom he found 'a very sensible and agreeable man': '[I] forgot my hurry so much as to stay chatting with him a couple of hours.'[34] The same year in Geneva, Burney met 'the ingenious M. Serre, a famous miniature *painter* who has written 2 very clever *musical* pamphlets, and is thought very deep in *the science of sound*'. In Turin he saw the tenor Gaetano Ottani (d. 1808), 'a master of his profession', and was pleased to discover that the singer 'likewise *paints* well, in the manner of Claude Lorraine and Du Vernet, and is sometimes *employed as a painter* by his Sardinian majesty'.[35] In Rome he met M. Zink, 'the famous *miniature painter* from Vienna', with whom he had a long conversation 'about German *music and musicians*'.[36] Burney was particularly pleased that his own nephew, E.F. Burney, a good amateur musician, became an artist, receiving approbation from Reynolds and other notable painters.[37] His uncle employed him for some of the plates illustrating his *Account of the Commemoration of Handel* (1785).

Burney's knowledge of the appearance of major paintings in Italy before going there stemmed principally from prints after them by his friend the Scottish engraver Robert Strange (1725–92), recognized as one of the leading engravers of his day. Several of Strange's works figure in Burney's will. Burney took with him to the Continent a quantity of Strange's prints, taken from drawings made in Italy, as gifts to those he visited.[38] Although Strange's Jacobite sympathies damaged his reputation in Britain, his prints after Old Master paintings, such as *The Celebrated Madonna of Correggio* (1771), were widely appreciated abroad.[39] Strange's great rival in this field was the Venetian Francesco Bartolozzi (1727–1815), who by the time of Haydn's visits to England had become the most popular and influential engraver in Europe. Bartolozzi's career was launched in the early 1760s when he was employed by the royal librarian, Richard Dalton, to copy many of the same Italian paintings on which Strange was engaged. A set of engravings after a collection of drawings by Guercino in Rome led to Dalton employing Bartolozzi to etch more Guercino drawings Dalton had acquired for George III (1765).[40] Bartolozzi recognized that the commercial opportunities in England for a good reproductive artist were considerable at this time, and he chose to remain in London for the next 37 years, only leaving when the Napoleonic wars caused the bottom to fall out of the English print market. A founder member of the Royal Academy, Bartolozzi soon diversified his range of subjects and techniques. His success with the public brought him numerous pupils and imitators. Burney felt it prudent, despite Bartolozzi's considerable fees, to employ him for the frontispiece of the Handel *Commemoration* and for ornaments in his *General History of Music*.[41] Bartolozzi's engraving of Reynolds's portrait of Burney (1784) also acted as frontispiece to later volumes of the *General History*.[42]

Bartolozzi's tremendous status as an engraver of popular prints helps to account for Haydn's interest in his work. He was responsible for at least 26 individual prints in Haydn's collection, the highest number for any engraver active in England. It seems clear that Haydn was himself acquainted with Bartolozzi, perhaps through Burney, whose *General History* was presented to Haydn in February 1791. In the list of Haydn's effects drawn up after his death, the cataloguer made a special point of noting the Italian's contribution to Burney's volumes: 'mit schönen Kupfern meißt von Bartolozzi'.[43] Shortly after the composer received Burney's volumes, Bartolozzi engraved Ott's portrait of Haydn. In May, Bartolozzi's name was cited in newspaper advertisements to promote a performance featuring Haydn at the King's Theatre, 'a new kind of concert', with dancers introducing 'ANIMATED PICTURES'.[44] The name 'Bartolozzi' presumably helped to sell the tickets, which he had engraved, and was appropriate to a concert calculated to appeal to an art-loving public. In 1792 he also engraved the frontispiece to a volume of Haydn's Scottish folksong arrangements for Napier. It was designed by William Hamilton, an artist Haydn seems to have particularly admired since he acquired all twelve plates of Hamilton's series of *Months*, published in 1788, and largely engraved by Bartolozzi.[45]

Haydn was also on close terms with Bartolozzi's son, Gaetano, a picture dealer and amateur violinist, and with his daughter-in-law, the celebrated pianist Therese Jansen. Haydn was a witness at the couple's wedding in St James's, Piccadilly, in May 1795. Gaetano met Haydn in Vienna in 1787 on a mission to persuade the composer to come to London as an opera composer, perhaps inspired by Burney.[46] He was later in contact with Artaria in Vienna on matters both musical and artistic.[47] Therese was the original dedicatee of Haydn's most brilliant pieces for keyboard, including the three trios (Hob. XV: 27–29) and the two solo sonatas (Hob. XVI: 50, 52).[48] She was probably also the original performer of a piece for piano and violin which Haydn entitled on the autograph 'Jacob's Dream'.[49] Dies heard from Haydn that this name, alluding to the story of Jacob's ladder reaching up to heaven, with angels ascending and descending (Gen. 28: 10–22), was an attempt to remedy an amateur violinist's habit of playing too close to the bridge in the high register: 'Miss J[ansen] ... noticed how the dilettante now ponderously, erratically, floundering, now in disarray, jumping, climbing up and down *this ladder*. The thing seemed so hilarious to her that she could not conceal her laughter ...'.[50] Haydn's decision to entitle this piece after an episode in the Bible may have been inspired by some recollection of a well-known painting then on view in Devonshire House, the *Dream of Jacob*, by one of the most admired of Italian landscape painters in eighteenth-century England, Salvator Rosa.[51] The painting was discussed by Reynolds in his Discourse of 1788. Rosa was of special interest to those who were musical because of the (groundless) view, substantiated by Burney, that he had been a composer as well as a painter. This probably explains why Handel acquired a set of etchings of Rosa landscapes by his erstwhile friend Joseph Goupy, including *Jacob's Dream*.[52] The painting would certainly therefore have been of interest to Haydn at a time when he was in close contact with the Bartolozzi family.

Not long after 1797 Gaetano and Therese visited Vienna. It was perhaps during this sojourn that Haydn received a fine print taken from a profile portrait of Francesco Bartolozzi by Violet, engraved by Bouillard.[53] This was published on 1 July 1797, so could not have been acquired by Haydn when he was in England. The fact that this portrait was in his collection at the time of his death therefore provides clear evidence of his esteem for, and friendship with, the elder Bartolozzi. Haydn would particularly have appreciated the allegorical scenes below the portrait, including Time presented with a medallion bearing a 'B', and Painting reclining against two volumes labelled 'BAR/OP.', in front of a pyramidal monument, on which a putto carves 'F. Ba . .'. The personification of Painting, shown as a gagged woman with a palette, derives from Ripa's *Iconologia*.[54] The motto accompanying this image, *Nulla dies sine linea* ('no day without a line'), explained in Pliny's account of Apelles (the most famous painter of antiquity), was apparently applied to himself by Haydn in old age, indicating that he never let a day pass without achieving something.[55] Perhaps Haydn learned the expression from Bartolozzi.

Haydn owned two prints engraved by Bartolozzi after Old Master paintings. One was 'A Picture of the Holy Family' by Andrea del Sarto, probably the *Madonna del Sacco*, a fresco in SS. Annunziata in Florence, painted about 1514.[56] The print was specifically mentioned in the sale of Gaetano's effects on 2 May 1795, as reported in *The Times*.[57] Haydn may have acquired his own print at this time. The *Madonna del Sacco* had always been among del Sarto's most famous works. Raphael Morghen produced another engraving of it in 1795, suggesting a growing interest in del Sarto during this period. Goethe saw a *Madonna and Child with the Infant Saint John* by del Sarto in the Fries collection in Rome in 1787, which Bartolozzi also engraved.[58] Describing it as 'a lovely painting, ... one cannot have any idea of it without having seen it', Goethe saw it in the company of Casti (Paisiello's librettist for *Il re Teodoro*).[59] Reports of such enthusiasm may have led Haydn to acquire his own del Sarto reproduction.

The other Bartolozzi Old Master print owned by Haydn was after a very celebrated painting universally believed in the eighteenth century to be by Correggio, showing St Mary Magdalen reading.[60] This *Penitent Magdalen* was then in Dresden, where the Electors of Saxony had formed the best collection of paintings by Correggio outside of Italy. Bartolozzi's print, 'Diva Magdalena', was published in 1790, but there were other engravings of it which may have been known to Haydn: by Burney's friend Strange (1780), and by William Ward (1792). Burney saw the actual painting in 1772 and, along with the other Correggios, was captivated by it, spending even more time in the picture gallery on their account than was usual for him. On his first viewing of the *Magdalen* he considered the painting to be 'beautiful and delicate beyond description'.[61] A second viewing enabled him to be more explicit: 'The little *Magdalene* is all beauty, softness, expression, and grace. The frame is ornamented with precious stones; and the late duke of Modena [a previous owner] prized this piece so much, that he never quitted his capital without taking it with him, nor could sleep if it was not in his chamber.'[62]

Haydn might have heard something of this directly from Burney in the early 1790s, when Correggio mania reached its zenith in England. Even leading politicians did not hesitate to admit their attachment to Correggio. This is evident in correspondence written in 1794 from Fox (who knew a lot about Italian painting) to his nephew (then on the Grand Tour in Italy), whose lack of enthusiasm for a favourite painter prompted firm reproaches: 'you were near losing all credit ... for speaking so coldly about the Correggio at Parma'; and '... our tastes are certainly not very like in painting, for to doubt about Correggio seems to me just as if a man were to doubt Homer, or Shakspeare, or Ariosto'.[63] Haydn could hardly have avoided hearing similar views. Perhaps in order to see the *Magdalen* for himself, he considered visiting Dresden on his return from London to Vienna in 1792, though it was only on his second return in 1795 that his itinerary permitted this. Incentives to make the detour were not lacking. Diderot mentioned the *Magdalen* in his *Salons* for 1763 and 1767.[64] But it was Correggio's staunchest champion before Stendhal, Mengs (whose own *Penitent Magdalen* was partly inspired by Correggio's version), who conveyed what the work ostensibly represented to the visual sensibilities of his age, in his account of Correggio first published in 1780: 'This sole image contains all the beauty which can be imagined in painting, for the diligence with which it is executed, the impasting of the colours, the softness, grace, and knowledge in the clare obscure.'[65] The painting gained additional celebrity in 1788, when it was briefly stolen. By this date it had been so frequently copied that even had it not been recovered, its appearance could hardly have been lost. Batoni, for example, possessed a copy of it, which probably inspired his own reworking of Correggio's composition, borrowing the saint's reclining pose, but changing Correggio's motif of the head resting on her arm so that her hands are clasped in front of her. This in turn became a well-known painting, likewise acquired for Dresden.[66] Burney says how his eye 'was caught by *the magic* of Battoni's Magdalen'.[67] Many others were also captured by its spell. J.S. Bach the Younger, for example, executed a drawing after the same work, an engraving of which was issued in 1780.[68] A print of it was sent to C.P.E. Bach in 1781, to help console the father for the premature death of his son.[69] Seven years later, Chodowiecki, in a conversation piece entitled *The Five Senses Drawn in India Ink*, exhibited at the Berlin Academy, characterized 'Seeing' as two men looking at a version of Batoni's painting.[70]

Batoni's reworking of Correggio's *Magdalen* was also engraved by Johann Pichler, an artist active in Vienna, who spent a short period in Dresden in the 1790s. Pichler was one of only a small number of Viennese artists represented in Haydn's collection. Another was Vincenz Kininger, who was personally known to Haydn, having laboured to update Guttenbrunn's portrait of the composer for Breitkopf & Härtel. Kininger gained a reputation for his representation of the Commendatore taking Don Giovanni by the hand on the title-page of the same firm's edition of Mozart's *Don Giovanni*, and for the title-page of their original publication of the full score of Haydn's *The Seasons*.[71] Haydn owned Kininger's set of twenty-nine illustrations of the 'new' uniforms in the Imperial army (engraved by Mansfeld).[72] Both Pichler and Kininger had been trained by Johann Jacobe, who did much to raise standards of engraving in Vienna. Jacobe spent a period perfecting his technique in London, executing prints after portraits by Reynolds, including the well-known *Omai*.

Like another Vienna-based artist, Unterberger, Pichler was particularly drawn to Correggio. He perhaps was influenced by Bartolozzi's prints of two paintings by Correggio in the Imperial Collection, published by Artaria in Vienna in 1785, with dedications to Joseph II.[73] English prints are known to have been displayed at the Academy in Vienna to inspire students of engraving. Pichler himself produced prints after two paintings by Correggio, the so-called *School of Love*, and its pendant, *Venus and a Satyr with Cupid*.[74] Haydn acquired one of these engravings, probably the *School of Love*.[75] The original was in Spain throughout the eighteenth century, but had a profound effect on painters like Benjamin West, who probably knew it through copies.[76] Mengs studied it when he was court painter in Madrid:

> The Duke of Alba owns a picture by Correggio ... representing Mercury who teaches Cupid to read in the presence of Venus. ... Cupid expresses all the innocence of youth. ... His little wings are treated in the manner of those of young birds, showing both the skin and the roots of the feathers. And in this picture, as in every other picture in which Correggio painted wings, they are so well attached – unlike what is seen in the work of other painters – that it would hardly be possible to remove them. ... As the owner of the picture said with reason on one occasion: 'Cupid's wings seem so perfectly placed that if it were possible for a child to be born with wings this is how they would appear.'[77]

Alba, who made this comment, was one of Haydn's principal patrons in Spain. His particular interest in Haydn's songs is known from Goya's last portrait of him. One of those probably in his collection, *Cupido*, about the mischievous pranks of a little boy, with wings and a bow, shares its name with the title by which Correggio's painting was known to Haydn.[78] It seems likely that Haydn was informed of some Spanish connection made between the painting and his song, which encouraged him to acquire the print when the opportunity arose.

Haydn's collection featured two further prints after Italian Old Master paintings, both engraved by the Facius brothers (Gottfried and G.S., sons of a Russian diplomat), who settled in London and worked together in collaboration. One was after a painting by Guercino executed in 1647, the *Persian Sibyl*, depicting a pagan counterpart of the Old Testament prophets in the act of writing, while resting her head against her other arm.[79] This picture, then in Rome, started to attract attention in 1761, when Mengs reworked Guercino's composition to produce his own *Sibyl*.[80] This was soon afterwards copied by West, then studying in Rome, for transmission to a patron in Pennsylvania.[81] Interest in Guercino at this time stemmed chiefly from Britain, where his paintings started being seriously collected around 1750.[82] By the 1790s a perceptive viewer of pictures, C.J. Fox, could rate Guercino above almost every other painter.[83] Meng's *Sibyl* was for a British patron, and shortly afterwards George III acquired his own Guercino, the *Libyan Sibyl*. This was the period when Bartolozzi was tempted to England by Dalton's offer to reproduce the newly acquired Guercino drawings in the royal collection, which greatly furthered the artist's reputation. About 1772, West, now based in London, executed a portrait of Lady Griffen, its composition modelled directly on Guercino's *Persian Sibyl*, clear evidence of the artist's familiarity with the painting and probably also of his patrons' admiration for it.[84] In the same year, a copy of Guercino's 'Sybil' (the account does not say which Sibyl, though it was probably the one in question) was imported into England from Italy, and three years later another was on its way to Scotland.[85] By the time, *c*.1790–91, therefore that Vigée-Lebrun painted Emma Hamilton's portrait 'en sybille', partly inspired by the *Persian Sibyl*, Guercino's painting would have been familiar to London viewers.[86] Vigée-Lebrun's painting – she considered it one of her finest works – stayed with her until 1819, used to demonstrate her abilities as she travelled throughout Europe.[87] In 1793 it was put on public exhibition in the residence of Prince Kaunitz in Vienna, where Haydn may have seen it between his two visits to London. After a showing in Rome in 1792, a British viewer described it as 'one of the most striking pictures I ever saw ... the attitude extremely simple with a great deal of dignity'.[88] Haydn would also certainly have known Vigée-Lebrun's portrait of 1798 of Princess Marie Hermenegild Esterházy (the wife of his last princely patron), the pose of which is ultimately derived from the same Guercino painting.[89] Haydn's acquisition of a print after Guercino's *Persian Sibyl*, a painting which had been seminal in inspiring several leading artists and collectors of the later eighteenth century, may of course simply represent his own personal taste, possibly conditioned by some of the instances of Guercino's late eighteenth-century popularity just mentioned. But it seems equally plausible that Haydn's interest in this particular Guercino betrays a well-developed appreciation of what excited a broad picture-loving public at the time he acquired it.

The same applies to the other Facius Old Master print in Haydn's collection, Guido Reni's representation of an unaffected Salome, holding up the head of John the Baptist on a salver (painted c.1638–39), known in the eighteenth century by the title *Herodias*.[90] The Facius engraving is dated 1779, but copies and variants of the original painting were in Britain at a much earlier date. Reynolds used it in 1772 to illustrate his view of Reni as an artist who represented figures for the sake of beauty, even when their context demanded expression.[91] Lanzi, writing in 1789, thought it the best of its type in Reni's oeuvre. West again made a detailed copy of this painting when he was in Rome in 1763.[92] Indeed West seems to have been particularly attached to it since he recommended it by name in 1788 in advice to the young German artist Heinrich Ramberg on pictures worth copying when studying in Italy.[93] Ramberg had come to London in 1781 and studied with West before returning to his native Hanover in 1788. Between 1790 and 1793 he studied in Italy, before making his way back to northern Germany. What is noteworthy about the advice he received from West in the context of Haydn's collection is that his chief recommendations closely coincide with the choices Haydn actually made for his own collection. West's partiality for Guercino's *Persian Sibyl* and Correggio's *School of Love* has already been mentioned, so it is not surprising that both painters are emphasized.[94] He also particularly recommended study of Rubens and Van Dyck, painters also represented in Haydn's collection. Since two prints after Ramberg's designs formed part of Haydn's collection, and the artist is known to have been in Vienna in 1793, when Haydn returned to Austria, between his two visits to London, there is a possibility that Haydn learned something of West's selections from Ramberg, a fellow German-speaker.[95] However, a better explanation is that Haydn received guidance directly from West himself.

West was at the height of his career during the period of Haydn's London visits. His election as President of the Royal Academy, following the death in 1792 of the first President, Reynolds, and the extensive patronage he was enjoying from the King distinguished him as the most enviable painter in England. Haydn was certainly aware of West, and could identify his style. He mentions the painter by name, together with an example of his work, in an entry in his Notebook recording the return journey of an excursion he made from London to the Isle of Wight in 1794: 'From there to Winschester [*sic*], where there is a beautiful gothic Cathedral Church, the altarpiece by West.'[96] This was the cathedral's large high altarpiece, depicting *The Raising of Lazarus*.[97] The painting was completed in 1780 and first shown publicly at the Royal Academy exhibition in that year.[98] It seems to have had an early success with the general public since a second plate of it had to be engraved by Valentine Green in 1783, the original one having worn out (Fig. 15).[99]

Churchmen from various denominations, however, were less enchanted. The founder of Methodism, John Wesley, writing in 1781, records how he went 'with great expectation' to see the 'celebrated painting' at Winchester, but was 'disappointed': 'I observed, 1. There was such a huddle of figures, that had I not been told, I should not have guessed what they meant. 2. The colours in general were far too glaring, such as neither Christ nor His followers ever were. When will painters have common sense?'[100] There seems to be no early comment on West's altarpiece by the cathedral clergy, perhaps reflecting the dilemma in the Anglican Church at the time on the appropriateness of prominent paintings in churches.[101] However, a local Catholic priest, writing in the 1790s, though very much in favour of paintings in churches for 'informing and exciting the minds of people', found West's painting prosaic: 'The apostles here are mere ordinary men, or at most thoughtful philosophers, or elegant courtiers ... Christ himself ... appears more like a physician, prescribing a medicine for the recovery of his patient, than the great Messiah, who is working an astonishing miracle.'[102] What is interesting about these criticisms by churchmen is that they were *not* widely shared. Haydn probably recorded this painting for the very reason that it was popular with the public. It seems likely indeed that he made a point of including Winchester on his itinerary in order to see a work which he already knew was 'celebrated'. Perhaps he had seen the engraving and wished to satisfy himself of the painting itself.

During the same trip to the Isle of Wight, Haydn visited Carisbrooke Castle, where he probably reflected on another print after a well-known work by West.[103] A visitor to Carisbrooke a year later recorded that 'The father of the person who showed us the castle ... was the *identical person* who is represented in the prints as supporting General Wolfe when he died. We saw the Indian sash, arms and stick of General Wolfe, which the father had left in the possession of his son.'[104] Presumably Haydn saw the father, the print and the artefacts for himself during his own visit. The print referred to was either William Woollett's 1776 engraving of West's famous *Death of General Wolfe*, one of the best-selling prints of the later eighteenth century, or the re-engraving of it (necessitated because the original plate had also worn out) of 1791.[105] West's painting commanded enormous admiration when first exhibited at the Royal Academy (1771), for the artist's ability to realize in paint a shocking event with convincing contemporary details, and also for the power of its composition to stir the feelings of viewers.[106] Because of the print's success and the sense of national pride it aroused, the painting long commanded public attention. Gillray's parody of it in 1795 indicates that it remained a potent image during the period Haydn was in England.[107] Shortly before he died (1805), Nelson, expressing regret for not having developed 'some power of discrimination' in art, is reported to have told West that 'there is *one picture* whose power I do feel. I never pass a print-shop with your

"Death of Wolfe" in the window, without being stopped by it.'[108] By the time Haydn visited Carisbrooke, in July 1795, it is most unlikely that he had not experienced for himself something of the fervour that viewing this composition provoked in Englishmen at this period.

Apart from the painting at Winchester, Haydn knew at least one other altarpiece by West. This was *The Last Supper* (1786) above the high altar in St George's Chapel at Windsor Castle, which Haydn visited on 14 June 1792.[109] Ever interested in prices, Haydn noted the vast cost of this and the huge stained glass window above it. The glass depicted *The Resurrection*, flanked by *Sts Peter and John Running towards the Sepulchre* and *The Three Marys Going to the Sepulchre*, all designed by West *c*.1782 and probably installed by 1787.[110] A drawing exhibited at the Royal Academy in 1785 had made public the design of this entire ensemble.[111] Since Fanny Burney, Mrs Papendiek (both probable acquaintances of Haydn's) and Hugh Walpole all record seeing the scheme *in situ*, it seems likely that friends encouraged Haydn to see it.[112] Haydn goes on to say: 'This year, 1792, above the side altar to the right, a smaller one [stained glass window], showing Christ appearing to the Shepherds, was unveiled. This small one is valued more highly than the large one [*The Resurrection*].'[113] This window had only been put on public view a matter of days before Haydn's visit, as is evident from a press report dated 12 June 1792: members of the Royal family 'inspected the New Window just arrived from the design of Mr West ... Their majesties were graciously pleased to signify the highest approbation at the sight of this elegant production. The window is situated at the East end of the South aisle of the collegiate church, and the subject is, the Angels' [*sic*] announcing the Birth of our Saviour. ... The group of Angels ... is composed with taste, and designed with character and expression, and executed in a soft tone of colour which never before appeared on painted glass ...'.[114] That he was among the earliest visitors to see this window suggests a special interest on Haydn's part in West's latest productions. Since this particular window cost *less* than *The Resurrection*, his comment that it was 'valued more highly than the large one' suggests he was reflecting an aesthetic judgement, perhaps influenced by local opinion. Walpole, viewing West's ensemble above the high altar in 1791, criticized several figures, especially the scale of the Judas in *The Last Supper*.[115] This sort of opinion provoked a defence of West which appeared in the *Windsor Guide* (1792): 'critics pretend that the figure of Judas is too predominant, 'though real judges esteem the whole a masterly composition'.[116] In viewing West's latest production, Haydn may have listened to a range of views on it, though found himself naturally siding with the members of the royal family, one of whose guests he may have been at the time.[117]

At the time that Haydn described these works, West was involved in such a quantity of work at Windsor Castle (including paintings for the Audience Chamber, the Chapel Royal and the Queen's Lodge) that he was given a room within the castle to work. Although Haydn does not mention these other schemes, it seems very likely that he saw something of them, perhaps in 1792, and plausibly during the period that he was on friendly terms with the King and Queen during his second visit to England when, like West, he was offered accommodation in the castle.[118] In 1792, however, Haydn's final recollection of Windsor was of the 'view from the terrace', which he found 'divine [*göttlich*]'.[119] West's own depiction of a view from Windsor Castle was probably painted around the time of Haydn's visit, and it is tempting to consider that West may himself have encouraged the composer to admire the prospect.[120] The main terrace had long been famous. Daniel Defoe claimed that 'neither at Versailles, nor at any of the Royal Palaces in France, or at Rome, or Naples, have I seen anything like it'.[121] Between the 1760s and early 1790s this terrace was popularized though numerous watercolours of it and its view by Paul Sandby.[122] Many of these belonged to Sir Thomas Banks, one of Haydn's most distinguished admirers, who perhaps personally recommended it to the visiting Austrian composer.[123] What is revealing about Haydn's comment on the excellence of the view at Windsor is that it shows him coming to terms with the value set by the English on viewing topography.

The publication of English prints after landscape paintings by Claude and Rosa earlier in the eighteenth century had stimulated a taste for finding equally impressive scenery in Britain. A chief criterion for determining the merit of views was by deciding 'between those, which please the eye in their *natural state*; and those, which please from some quality, capable of being *illustrated in painting*'.[124] The first leading proponent of 'the Picturesque', as it came to be called, was William Gilpin, whose popular *Essay on Prints* (1768) defines it as 'a term expressive of that peculiar kind of beauty, which is agreeable in a picture'.[125] Gilpin emphasized what he called 'roughness' and 'ruggedness' as key elements in distinguishing the Picturesque in landscape from the merely beautiful, meaning craggy mountains or ruins, rather than neat parkland or country-houses.[126] Tours of the Highlands of Scotland, the valleys of Wales, and later the Swiss Alps, were recognized as essential destinations for those seeking the Picturesque.[127] Such interests soon had musical repercussions. Shield's opera *The Travellers in Switzerland* (1794), with its setting in the Alps, is an example which Haydn probably knew.[128] More importantly, Haydn was certainly aware of London society's rage for 'folk-songs' from Scotland and Wales by the 1790s, stimulated in part by publication of tours of the Highlands and the Wye Valley, by Gilpin and others, since he became a prominent arranger of them.[129]

The remoteness of these regions for London residents led to interest in more accessible scenery, though less dramatic. Hampshire, with its forests and coastline, was one new destination to inspire both Gilpin and landscape painters.[130] Haydn's trip to the Isle of Wight in July 1794, taking in the Hampshire countryside, may be interpreted as his own attempt to experience something of the English fad for scenic tours.[131] His acquisition of an illustrated *Tour of the Isle of Wight*, published in 1790, suggests his seriousness.[132] Already in November 1791, on a visit to the Duke of York's estate at Oatlands, he noted that the house 'lies on a hillside and commands the most magnificent view [*herlichesten Prospect*]'.[133] His royal hosts also impressed on him the lengths to which an Englishman would go to heighten the appeal of his landscape: 'Among [the house's] many beauties is a most remarkable grotto which cost 25,000 pounds Sterling, and which took 11 years to create. It is very big and features many sections ...'.[134] After discovering 'views' at Oatlands and Windsor, Haydn was certainly interested in further Picturesque delights, such as 'the magnificent view [*herlichste aussicht*] over the sea' from the house of the governor on the Isle of Wight.[135] And there was more of the same noted at Bath and Bristol.[136] By the 1790s, even the River Thames between London and Windsor came to be looked on by some as suitable for a Picturesque tour.[137] Haydn's frequent mention of the Thames and his trips to notable places along this stretch of the river suggest an awareness of this recent popularization of the Picturesque. One of the items in his print collection also points in this direction: '1. scene in perspective with 4. prints which may be used to modify the views.'[138] Although the identification of this work is problematic, the description suggests that Haydn acquired in England an example of a publication designed to indicate how prospects might be changed by landscape designers influenced by the Picturesque, by adding folding sheets over a view depicting the present state of a landscape to illustrate suggested 'improvements'. For example, Humphrey Repton's *Sketches and Hints on Landscape Gardening*, published by Boydell in 1794, featured such a device, illustrating 'A park before and after improvement'.

The extent of Haydn's understanding of contemporary aesthetic attitudes in England may further be seen in his appreciation of ruins, an element of the Picturesque stemming from Gilpin's notion of 'roughness'. Ruins became an English obsession. During a visit to Waverley Abbey in August 1794, Haydn saw 'the ruins of a monastery which has already been standing for 600 years', describing it as 'this *beautiful wilderness* [schöne Wildniß]'.[139] This visit has often been discussed in relation to the strength of Haydn's Catholicism, since he ended the entry in his journal with 'my heart was oppressed at the thought that all this once belonged to my religion'. But this comment equally illustrates Haydn's understanding, not only of the English Dissolution of the Monasteries, but also of how, by the 1790s, many viewed the remains of such buildings with a nostalgia for a pre-Reformation era, and a recognition of the importance of the Gothic style of architecture to the English character.[140] Publications like *The Antiquities of Great Britain*, featuring engraved views of (mostly dilapidated) medieval buildings, had enabled the Picturesque to foster a popular antiquarianism, shifting understanding of the Gothic from a style associated with barbarians to one equating it with an unprecedented flourishing of the arts, culminating in the reign of Edward III.[141]

Haydn would probably have come to England with negative perceptions of Gothic. In Austria, where medieval monasteries were systematically remodelled in elaborate Baroque style in the eighteenth century, evincing a partiality for Gothic architecture would have been nearly incomprehensible at the time Haydn left. Austrians shared the contempt for Gothic still widely felt across Europe until late in the century, as in Rousseau's description (1768) of counterpoint being like the façades of Gothic cathedrals, or the disparaging comments of one of Smollett's characters, discussing York Minster (1771): 'The external appearance of an old cathedral cannot be but displeasing to the eye of every man, who has any idea of propriety to proportion ...'.[142] Haydn would also have known opera libretti requiring 'Gothic' sets to emphasize sinister or supernatural plots, as in the graveyard scene of some versions of *Don Giovanni*.[143] The dark or menacing side to the Gothic was particularly developed in England. It may have been extended for Haydn by knowledge of 'Gothic' novels, such as Walpole's *The Castle of Otranto* (1764). Despite creating one of the most celebrated of post-medieval 'Gothic' buildings, his house at Strawberry Hill, Walpole considered Gothic 'amusing', hardly on a footing with classical architecture: a style of 'unrestrained licentiousness', which one requires 'passion' to sense, in contrast to 'the rational beauties of regular [Grecian] architecture', which requires 'taste' to appreciate.[144] When Haydn, however, noted that the churches at Bath and Bristol were 'all in the old *gothic* style', he clearly saw nothing disparaging in this: Bath he considered 'one of the most *beautiful* cities in Europe'.[145] The view of Gothic he acquired during his period in England therefore involved no contempt. Nor was it considered in opposition to classicizing architecture, for which he also developed an eye. He noted, for example, the columns and proportions of the Royal Crescent at Bath, and pretentiously tried using architectural terminology.[146]

Haydn's positive attitude to Gothic was very much of the moment. One popular magazine after 1790 devoted an illustration and description of a Gothic building to almost every issue.[147] For the erudite, there were the publications of one of the greatest Gothicists of the period, the architect/antiquarian John Carter, something of whose work Haydn probably knew.[148] One of the highlights of Haydn's tour through Hampshire in 1795 was the visit to Winchester Cathedral, a building which he described as both 'beautiful' and 'gothic'.[149] Only four years earlier, in 1791, Fanny Burney, visiting the same 'poor dear old building', described nothing 'beautiful', and little that she thought 'Gothic'; instead she stressed the 'neglected' survivals 'from the original Saxon building', and 'its Saxon chiefs [tombs], its queer little niches, quaint images, mouldering walls, and mildewed pillars'.[150] The difference between Haydn and Fanny Burney in what they chose to emphasize at Winchester may partly be explained by the presence at the Cathedral in 1792 of Carter, whose Chapel of St Peter, sometimes cited as an early instance of Gothic being used in an ecclesiastical context in the eighteenth century, Haydn presumably saw.[151]

The Picturesque and the Gothic are two features of English taste which Haydn readily assimilated. Another was a preoccupation with Rubens and Van Dyck, two Flemish Old Masters who had worked in England, both included among West's recommendations. Haydn owned a pair of prints said to be after paintings by these artists, both engraved by Valentine Green.[152] Green had engraved both West's *Raising of Lazarus* and the same painter's designs for the great east window at St George's Chapel, Windsor, which is perhaps how he came to Haydn's attention. In 1789 Green was given permission to engrave 80 paintings from the collection of Carl Theodor, the Elector Palatine, at Düsseldorf, where he had been appointed professor of mezzotint at the Academy and established commercial relations. Haydn's engravings came from this ambitious undertaking, which perhaps particularly appealed to him because of the Elector's well-known patronage of music.[153] The 'Van Dyck', now considered a pupil's copy after a lost composition by Van Dyck, depicts (according to the inscription on the print) 'Antiope, Sleeping, Surprized By Jupiter in The Form of A Satyr', and was published in January 1792.[154] Since Van Dyck was much better known in Britain for portraiture, Haydn's choice might be thought unusual for an amateur collector, with little training. However, Reynolds's collection, auctioned at Christie's in March 1795 (three years after his death), included a 'Van Dyck' *Jupiter and Antiope*, which may have lent topicality to artist and subject when Haydn was in London.[155] Haydn's acquisition of Green's print after 'Van Dyck' therefore again shows him not only abreast of popular taste in England, but anticipating what was soon to become fashionable in German-speaking countries.[156]

The Rubens in Haydn's collection was published by Green and his son in June 1791. This was the famous *Castor and Pollux*, 'Carrying Off the Daughters of Leucippus' as the inscription expressed it, the subject having been identified in the *Teutscher Merkur* in 1777 (cf. Fig. 2).[157] Knowledge of Vogler's celebrated improvisations on Rubens, one of which was in front of this very painting, or perhaps Vogler's opera related to it, dating from the mid-1780s, may have stimulated Haydn's interest in Rubens. Vogler had been praised when he was in London in the 1780s by Joseph Banks and the Royal Society, an endorsement which might have been communicated to Haydn. Indeed some kind of sustained contact between Haydn and Vogler seems likely since the latter intended his own Requiem of 1809 to be performed at Haydn's funeral, though this was not permitted. Haydn also certainly knew Bianchi's opera on the subject of Castor and Pollux. He owned a copy of the libretto, and an aria from the opera was performed immediately after the first performance of Symphony No. 102 in February 1795.[158] The composer may also have heard something about Rubens's painting from friends at the Royal Academy, since Reynolds apparently saw a version of it when he visited Rubens's house in 1781.[159] Haydn's choice of a print labelled 'Castor and Pollux' may, in this light, be considered a reflection of a wider preoccupation with this subject matter, which, in juxtaposing the immortality of one twin with the mortality of the other, served as a reminder of human limitations. In the early 1790s there may even have been a political dimension to this aspect of the story. In the very year in which Haydn's print was first published, the *Académie royale de Musique* in Paris proposed 'revising' Rameau's *Castor et Pollux* (the libretto of which had provided the inspiration for those set by Vogler and Bianchi) in order to lend the score a topical element appropriate to the times. A favourable performance of this opera in 1792 was reported by at least one German source which Haydn might have known.[160]

Although Haydn possessed no further prints after Old Masters, he did express pleasure at seeing the work of one other seventeenth-century foreign painter who had worked in Britain. During the course of his trip to Hampshire, he records visiting Hampton Court, which reminded him of Eszterháza: 'there are here and there splendid statues in bronze, and very beautiful marble vases; especially fine the painting over the main staircase and the ceiling by the painter Verrio'.[161] In England Verrio had worked chiefly for a sequence of Royal patrons, decorating no fewer than 20 rooms at Windsor Castle, where Haydn probably first heard Verrio's name and admired his work. The painter's grand, late Baroque style probably put him in mind of similar work by Italian decorators in Austria, like Carlone.[162] What is interesting about Haydn's enthusiasm for Verrio is that the painter had completely fallen out of fashion by the time the composer was in England. Walpole, describing the very set of paintings by Verrio at Hampton Court commented on by Haydn, thought it 'as ill as if he had spoilt it out of principle'.[163] When Hazlitt described the paintings in the Royal Residences in 1823, the only comment he could manage on the artist's work were that 'there are *too many* of Verrio's paintings' at Windsor, and, 'We shall pass over ... the Verrios' at Hampton Court.[164] Within six years of this, Verrio's work at Windsor was so unpopular that George IV (Haydn's former benefactor) had much of it destroyed.[165] Had Haydn been shown the Verrios at Windsor, which seems likely, he almost certainly would have heard some disparaging remark about them. Despite both this and his concern with the popular, the example of Verrio shows Haydn's confidence in his own taste, defying the grain of current opinion. However, it is conspicuous that his reaction to the Verrio staircase, which he saw by himself, was really a personal matter, far removed from the commercial pressures which he faced in presenting newly composed music to London audiences. It was different when it came to prints, a populist medium, subject to commercial forces not dissimilar to those in the musical world in which he now operated. In this sphere he needed to feel the pulse of popular opinion, and so readily deferred to the judgement of others, such as West, whose experience in these matters was respected. This is not to suggest that Haydn was incapable of forming his own opinions, as the example of Verrio firmly contradicts; only that in developing his own preferences as a connoisseur, within the mould of popular taste of the time, the advice and views of those acknowledged for their expertise was helpful.

The key figure in this was undoubtedly Boydell, who had made a fortune through publishing prints and was elected Lord Mayor of London in 1790. Haydn was a guest at the Lord Mayor's banquet in the Guildhall on 5 November 1791, an occasion he described in detail. Four days later he attended a farewell dinner for Boydell at the Mansion-House.[166] The close relationship Haydn developed with Boydell, to whom he was perhaps introduced by Burney or Bartolozzi, is suggested by his comment that Boydell's wife 'is *Mylady* and remains so'.[167] Boydell's importance to British trade may be gauged from a tribute to him written shortly after his death, noting that English prints had 'produced an export of £300,000 per annum, chiefly from his own publications'.[168] As Haydn would have been well aware, the English print, as developed by Boydell, could be judged one of the most successful products of his time, known not only throughout Europe, but across the globe. In many respects this was the closest visual equivalent, in terms of popularity and distribution, to Haydn's own music. No wonder therefore that Haydn took a serious interest in Boydell productions, many prints in his collection having been published by this 'Commercial Maecenas', as he was termed by the Prince of Wales at the R.A. dinner of 1789.[169]

Boydell's early ventures included publishing Old Master paintings and landscapes. He was partly responsible for keeping Bartolozzi in England, issuing his set of etchings after Guercino's drawings. One of his greatest projects was reproducing the paintings in the collection at Houghton, which Burney had so admired, before it left for Russia.[170] The 162 prints in this publication involved teams of artists to prepare drawings of the paintings, and no fewer than 45 engravers, including Bartolozzi and Green. Boydell also encouraged British history painting on a grand scale, by promoting the exhibition of such paintings, and offering visitors the opportunity to subscribe to the publication of a print, a practice which was soon imitated. West's *Death of General Wolfe* was the most successful example of this strategy. The painting was originally exhibited at the Royal Academy, and the subscription launched a year later.

But Boydell's most ambitious enterprise was the Shakespeare Gallery, which opened in Pall Mall in 1789 with 34 paintings illustrating scenes from Shakespeare plays. The number of paintings gradually increased. The press was initially favourable, one newspaper calling the opening an occasion 'for public gratification, for it is a treasure of graphic excellence in the highest degree creditable to British genius'.[171] Visitors were encouraged to subscribe to the prints after the paintings, a catalogue of which was published in 1790. Almost certainly, Haydn was a visitor to the gallery. He knew its architect, Dance, as well as others concerned with the project. By the time he arrived in London, it was one of the most fashionable venues for being seen in the capital.[172] Indeed there is a possibility that Haydn himself subscribed to the early prints. The catalogue of his effects drawn up after his death includes an additional item, listed simply as '26 pieces, engraved theatre scenes', a collection which might describe the Shakespeare series, which started to appear in 1791.[173]

Haydn would also have visited Boydell's main shop, located close to one of the premises of his publishers, Longman & Broderip. A sense of what he as a foreigner would have found interesting there comes from an account by a German visitor in 1786:

> ... we visited Mr Boydell's shop, London's most famous print dealer. What an immense stock, containing heaps and heaps of articles! The shop is on ... one of the City's most populous thoroughfares, and has a view either side. ... I was struck by the excellent arrangement and system which the love of gain and the national taste have combined in producing, particularly in the elegant dressing of large shop-windows not merely in order to ornament the streets and lure purchasers, but to make known the thousands of inventions and ideas, and spread good taste about, for the excellent pavements made for pedestrians enable crowds of people to stop and inspect the new exhibits. Many a genius is assuredly awakened in this way. ... I stayed inside for some time so as to watch the expressions of those outside: to a number of them Voltaire's statement – that they stare without seeing anything – certainly applied; but I really saw a great many reflective faces, interestedly pointing out this or that object to the rest. ... And now we ... followed Mr Boydell, jnr, an excellent draughtsman, to an upper story, where he showed us the best pieces in the shop and a nice collection of fine paintings ...[174]

This visitor ended by describing those items which appealed to her, including 'a piece by Peters, a cleric'. The Rev. Matthew Peters was one of the most popular painters of the period.[175] An account of him published during Haydn's second London visit claimed that prints of Peters's *An Angel Carrying the Spirit of a Child to Paradise* (exhibited at the R.A. in 1782 and first engraved in 1784) 'were soon *dispersed through Europe*, and no print, we believe, *from any picture* of *whatever master*, had so rapid and universal a sale as what followed the publication from the plate we now mention'.[176] Perhaps this is the work seen by the German visitor to Boydell's shop, where Peters's compositions were still selling well in 1803.[177] The extent of its appeal may be gauged from an account in the *Morning Post* in 1786 indicating that an itinerant vendor was making a 'comfortable' living 'by shewing at a shilling a copy, from the print only, of the Angel and Child painted by [Peters]'. With its companions, *The Spirit of a Child arriv'd in the Presence of the Almighty* and *The Resurrection of a Pious Family*, purchasers seem to have been encouraged to take all three prints and form them into a triptych, with *The Resurrection* in the middle.[178] They were also successful in Germany, where all three appear in catalogues in the early 1790s.[179]

Haydn certainly acquired *The Resurrection*, the grandest of the set, engraved by Bartolozzi with a dedication to the Prince of Wales, and published 1 February 1790.[180] Seven figures, representing three generations of the 'Pious Family', are depicted rising from the midst of their shattered tombs 'at the Last Day' towards the eternal light. The accompanying inscription, quoting 1 Cor. 15: 55, clarifies the redeeming message: 'O Death! where is thy sting. O Grave! where is thy victory.' This vision and the religious sentiment it presents may have stayed with Haydn. Something not dissimilar reappears at the end of *The Seasons*, where (deviating from Thomson's poem, the oratorio's main textual source) truth and light are equated, and the family of soloists, having led blameless and uncorrupted lives, look forward to freedom beyond earthly existence, and to rising up to be at one with the Godhead. Haydn also owned a second print after Peters, possibly *The Spirit of a Child arriv'd in the Presence of the Almighty* (engraved by Bartolozzi in 1787), which presents a simpler variant of the same theme, though with the emphasis on innocence.[181] An image of a child accompanied by an angel might have particularly appealed to Haydn through some knowledge of the last of the 'Rosary' sonatas by the Salzburg composer Biber, which in the surviving manuscript is prefaced by a picture of a child with its guardian angel, as in Peters's print. Formally, Peters's religious pictures, like those which inspired Biber, owe much to Baroque painting in Italy, where Peters had studied. His mature style also reveals a clear debt to Correggio, from whom (like West) he made copies. Indeed Peters was the most consistently Correggesque painter working in Britain in the later eighteenth century, a quality that would have been a factor in Haydn's appreciation of his work.

2. A Popular Collection

Haydn's selection of prints after Old Masters shows him finely tuned into British collecting habits as they had developed by the 1790s. The particular choices he made also reveal another factor in English taste at the time, a preoccupation with images combining feminine sensuality with the power of virtue. The abduction scenes he owned by 'Van Dyck' and Rubens, featuring helpless women, their voluptuous bodies barely concealed from view, present this male predilection in its crudest guise: the women are manifestations of desire, though as innocent victims, they effectively repudiate for the viewer any lustful instincts.

In a more refined, though no less telling form, the seductive charms of women are also evident in the works he chose by Guercino and Reni. The yearning gaze of the Persian Sibyl looking directly at the viewer, her mind apparently distracted from her writing, might well convey more than a hint of carnality to a male onlooker, reinforced by the glimpse of her gently protruding breasts. But any lustful thoughts would of course have been sublimated by knowledge that the subject matter is quasi-religious: the woman in question is in the act of writing a prediction related to Christianity. Reni's 'Herodias' also stares wistfully and seemingly innocently – much too innocently – out at the viewer. Reynolds may have thought the painting typical of its artist in emphasizing the figure's beauty at the expense of expression, but this view catches only a part of what its eighteenth-century admirers are likely to have seen. The figure, as most viewers must have realized, actually represents Salome presenting the head of John the Baptist, her trophy for impressing on the King her fatal allure.[182] This puts the viewer into the role of Herod (Mark 6: 21–27), at first enchanted by his stepdaughter's comeliness, but subsequently appalled at his weakness in granting her whatever she wished. Salome's coy expression therefore suggests both the power of her sexuality, and also its dangers. The moral ramifications of this picture would certainly have been meaningful to Haydn at the time he acquired it, when he was discreetly conducting an affair with Mrs Schroeter.

Correggio's *Magdalene* presented an even more tantalizing dichotomy for the eighteenth-century viewer of taste, combining religious sentiment and sensual delight. Diderot used the figure as a kind of yardstick by which to measure sensuality in painting. Writing to Baron Grimm, he described Potiphar's wife in a painting by Deshays by noting, 'I have never seen so voluptuous a figure, not even in the figure of the Dresden Magdalene, whose print you keep with such care for the mortification of your senses.'[183] Correggio's reformed sinner, recumbent and resting her head against one arm, is reading a book supported with the other arm, a motif which underpins her conversion and acts as a reminder of Christian forgiveness (John 12: 4–6). But her fleshy, naked arms, delicate feet and partly exposed breasts, squeezed against the book, are distinct reminders of her past. The male viewer, entranced by her beauty, would find it difficult to escape from the role of voyeur.

The theme of the reformed penitent was undoubtedly an attractive one for Haydn. He owned the most popular visible expression of it in the late eighteenth century, George Morland's set of six prints engraved by J.R. Smith in 1789, illustrating the story of *Laetitia*.[184] The series was the period's answer to the *Harlot's Progress* (1732), Hogarth's illustration of the rise and fall of a London prostitute, though with an important distinction in its message. Whereas Hogarth's famous series acts like a cautionary tale, its ending sufficiently bleak to thwart any notion of following the same path, in the later series there is the prospect of hope and redemption, the 'Fair Penitent' being reconciled with her parents, having previously left the family home, seduced under a false promise of marriage. The first scene shows Laetitia with her family, occupied with sewing and reading. Above them hangs a caged bird, suggesting perhaps her secret feelings. In the second scene, Laetitia is shown leaving home, 'Lur'd by the gay Seducer's Art, To find a ceaseless train of woes, A ruin'd name a tortur'd heart', as the caption puts it.

The crux of the tale comes in the third scene, in which the fallen Laetitia, now a kept woman, returns home with gifts, but is rejected by her father. Morland underlines the Christian significance of the episode by showing the father raising his arms, a gesture indicating repulsion, but also echoing Christ's traditional pose, after rising from the dead, on seeing Mary Magdalene (*Noli me tangere*), a picture of which hangs on the wall immediately behind.[185] In view of his interest in the Magdalene, the religious dimension of the scene would certainly not have been missed by Haydn. Laetitia, still full of pride, and dressed in sumptuous fashions of the day, is as yet in no position to receive forgiveness. The next two scenes complete her fall from grace: they show her dressing for entertainments in front of her lover, an aristocratic rake, and then forced onto the streets, where she is obliged to solicit at the door to the inn to keep herself. The final episode is tellingly set in front of another door, this time to her parents' cottage, where she has collapsed in front of her father, who now receives her and pulls her to her feet: 'Repentance leads the mourner home, To find a friend and Father there.'

The redeemed child, accepted again by her father after being led astray by a seducer, was the subject of another of Haydn's prints: *Doctor Primrose finds his daughter Olivia in distress*, a pair with *Esq. Thornhill persuades Olivia to elope*, also in Haydn's collection. These are illustrations to Goldsmith's popular *Vicar of Wakefield*, engraved by Bartolozzi after drawings by Ramberg, and published in 1787.[186] Haydn would certainly have admired, and perhaps even identified with, the main character in the novel, Dr Primrose, who survives a sequence of adversities. The novel's mixture of sentiment and religiosity parallels his taste in print culture, and, in the episode of Olivia's elopement, anticipates Hanne's story of attempted seduction from *Winter* in *The Seasons*.

Haydn's interest in the relationship between beauty and virtue explains his acquisition of a print depicting Lady Elizabeth Lambert, the only portrait in his collection to represent neither a personal acquaintance, nor a major public figure of the time.[187] Lady Lambert was the subject of a series of scandalous speculations concerning her conduct, reported in the *Morning Post* shortly before Haydn's arrival in England.[188] Haydn was certainly partial to press gossip about reputedly beautiful women and their affairs, though in none of these cases does his interest seem to have extended to purchasing a portrait of them. What distinguished Lady Lambert was that the suggestive innuendo in the press had nothing to support it. At any rate, that was what Lady Craven, Lady Lambert's mother, determined to prove by suing the proprietor of the newspaper in question, Richard Tattershall, a key figure in the Turf, for £10,000. The jury agreed with her that Lady Lambert having lost one of (what Lady Craven claimed were the only) two ways of gaining a husband, her (good) character, the culprit responsible for this should recompense her daughter by supplying the second method, money. Damages were assessed at £4,050 and an apology. In the eye of the public, therefore, Lady Elizabeth's virtue remained intact. Her beauty had already been captured in 1788 by Downman in a drawing depicting her as Una (the representation of Religion) from Spencer's *Fairy Queen*. Guttenbrunn's portrait of Lady Elizabeth, which Haydn owned, was doubtless designed to cash in on her unsolicited celebrity.

The relationship of beauty to virtue is also explored in a pair of magnificent prints owned by Haydn, illustrating scenes from Milton's *Comus*.[189] Taken from paintings by Thomas Stothard, one of the most prolific illustrators of English literature of the period, and engraved by Stothard's friend Edmund Scott, the prints were published on 7 February 1793; Haydn would have acquired them during his second London visit.[190] *Comus* originated as a masque, but remained popular in the eighteenth century on stage, especially in the musical adaptation by Arne (1738), to which Handel added some numbers in 1745.[191] Burney found much to admire in it. Haydn would have had many opportunities to see it in London, where a revised version of 1772 continued to be performed until the end of the century. The importance of Milton to English culture would also have been impressed on him at Vauxhall Gardens, where he noted seeing Roubiliac's statue of Handel: matching this was the same sculptor's *Milton*, represented as the poet described himself in *Il Penseroso*, listening to 'sweet music'. A star attraction at the same venue was the elaborate 'Temple of Comus' which, taking its cue from the opening of Milton's masque, was 'embellished with rays', and above, a large sun or star, apparently illuminated at night.[192]

The episodes from *Comus* owned by Haydn were *The Brothers Driving off Comus and his Spirits* and *Sabrina Releasing the Lady from the Enchanted Maid*. The first scene had been illustrated by Hayman in 1752, a design which was republished in 1773.[193] But it was probably the success in 1785 of Joseph Wright of Derby's *The Lady in Milton's Comus*, illustrating the passage in which moonlight gives the Lady 'new enliven'd spirits', which first captured pictorially for public delectation the charm of Milton's verse.[194] The artist himself wrote that he had 'never painted a picture so universally liked'. Its purchase by Josiah Wedgwood, who understood the commercial possibilities of the visual arts, is a sure sign of the painting's wide appeal and of a reawakening of interest in the visual possibilities presented by *Comus*. When Thomas Macklin opened his Poets' Gallery in Fleet Street in 1788, therefore, he included a *Comus tempting the Lady* as one of two subjects from Milton; and at the Royal Academy, a German engraver, Conrad Metz (who may have known Haydn), exhibited a painting of *The Lady in Comus* in 1791, the same year that E.F. Burney designed a frontispiece to *Comus* for Bell's British Theatre series.[195] The standing of Wright's *The Lady* was further enhanced with the publication in 1789 of the mezzotint after it by J.R. Smith, who also published the prints after the Stothard designs owned by Haydn.[196]

As a publisher, Smith's greatest success was issuing prints after works by Morland, whose commercial potential he recognized at an early stage. His showrooms, known as the Morland Gallery, were based on a collection of Morlands purchased in 1792, for which he issued a catalogue inviting subscriptions for the engravings.[197] Apart from the *Laetitia* series, Haydn acquired a set of four animal scenes by Morland, also engraved by Smith and published by him in August 1794.[198] With no fewer than ten prints after Morland engraved by Smith in his collection, and a further four prints by the same engraver, there would seem to be a strong possibility that Haydn frequented Smith's premises in King Street, Covent Garden. If so, he might also have seen there the print after Wright's painting. Its magical representation of the moon breaking through clouds, providing comfort to the Lady in her perilous plight, may have remained with him when he composed the music for the rising moon in *The Creation*, a work partly derived from Milton's later epic, *Paradise Lost*. In this, much of the thematic material of *Comus*, especially the triumph of Virtue over Vice, and the temptation of a virtuous victim by means of deceptive reasoning, is developed further. It was, however, the pictorial aspects of Milton's poetry which were to make the greatest impact on Haydn.

His acquisition of prints after Stothard's *Comus*, in preference to the print after Wright's painting, may have been influenced by some personal connection with their engraver. Haydn acquired two further prints by Scott of entirely different character, which he had mounted and displayed at Gumpendorf. These were after a pair of small, sentimental drawings by 'Miss Metz', probably Conrad Metz's daughter, published by S.W. Fores on 8 March 1793.[199] *Jump Pussy* (c.1790), for example, shows a crouching child playing with a cat; the child smiles, looks down at the animal, and embraces it in her arms. The content here is a long way from the world of *Comus*. But both pairs may have had special significance for the composer, whose circle of acquaintances, including the Duke of York and Francesco Artaria, connected him with Scott.[200]

In *Comus*, 'the Lady' represents virtue and beauty. When she is captured by Comus, the personification of hedonism, her brothers search for her. The eldest maintains that the Lady's perfect virtue will protect her, though the 'Second Brother' fears for her since beauty requires protection. Comus tries to overcome the Lady by arguing that beauty is for enjoyment. Refuting this, the Lady maintained that Nature's gifts should be used abstemiously, excess of Luxury only breeding ingratitude. The dramatic first scene owned by Haydn illustrates the point at which the brothers enter Comus's palace, overwhelming his debauched followers, just when Comus is about to renew his offensive. The Lady, however, is only released from Comus's power when the river nymph, Sabrina, is summoned, the episode depicted in Stothard's second scene.

The connection between virtue and beauty presented in *Comus*, a pervasive bond in debates on aesthetics in eighteenth-century Britain, would certainly not have been lost on Haydn. It was explored further in another pair of prints he owned, both designed and engraved by J.R. Smith, and published on 1 September 1791. These are two representations of women, inspired by verses quoted beneath.[201] *Albina*, posed somewhat like Guercino's *Persian Sybil*, illustrates a poem by Edward Jerningham, one of the most admired of contemporary poets. It describes the retreat of a woman with a broken heart, 'Where Virtue loves with thee to dwell, / Remote – unseeing and unseen.' Its pair, *Eloisa*, shows a nun looking towards a crucifix. It illustrates Pope's poem based on the famous twelfth-century letters concerning the unfortunate love affair of Abelard and Eloise, among 'the most distinguish'd persons of their age in learning and *beauty*', which give 'so lively a picture of the struggles of grace and nature, *virtue* and passion'.[202] The relationship between the theme of this poem and that of *Comus* is clear from Pope's borrowing of a line from Milton's masque. Whether Haydn knew this cannot, of course, be established; but his admiration of Pope is evident from his possession of a print entitled *Lodona*, illustrating the beautiful nymph of this name, the daughter of Father Thames, whose story appears in *Windsor-Forest*.[203] Lodona, who 'scorn'd the Praise of Beauty', set Pan 'burning with Desire'. He pursued her, but her virtue was protected when she dissolved into a stream named after her, the Lodden, which flows into the Thames. The print was by Bartolozzi after a painting by Maria Cosway, exhibited in 1792 at Macklin's Poet's Gallery, where Haydn might have seen it.

Lodona, illustrating a tale of chastity threatened though preserved, is another example of a print in Haydn's collection in which a subject chosen for its sexual interest is sublimated by presenting it as illustrative of virtue. Many of the female subjects in prints of this period attained their popularity with male collectors because they addressed an interest in sex, either through the reputed beauty, reputation, or literary context of the person represented. But the sexual aspect is usually only implied, its essence deflected into an acceptable theme, often religious. Women with broken hearts depicted in seclusion, as in *Albina*, hint at the religious life, and in its companion, *Eloisa*, this is explicit: as Pope makes Eloisa say from within her convent's wall on recollecting Abelard, 'Not on the Cross my eyes were fix'd, but [on] you'. The late eighteenth century developed a particular fascination for images of nuns. A depiction of a veiled woman in Henry Morland's *The Fair Nun Unmask'd* (published in 1769), for example, illustrates more lines from Pope: 'On her white Breast a sparkling Cross she wore, / Which Jews might kiss and Infidels adore.'[204] Pictures of nuns often suggested to viewers of this period women with dubious histories, who, like Mary Magdalene, ended up exchanging indulgence for virtue. The extent of this fascination is clear from the case of Matthew Peters, sent by his aristocratic patron to Paris in 1782 to copy Le Brun's portrait of Louis XIV's notable mistress, Louise de la Vallière, painted after she had retired to a convent.[205] Peters's *La Vallière* was itself copied more than once, so the subject's wider appeal is undoubted. Apart from *Eloisa*, Haydn also shared in this fad by acquiring Westall's *The Nun*, engraved by Cheesman.[206]

Haydn owned three further prints after Westall, including *Cupid Sleeping*, Nutter's engraving of which was dedicated to the celebrated Whig socialite Georgiana, Duchess of Devonshire.[207] Below this oval image are verses by the poetess-actress Mrs Robinson, the Duchess's protégée, who achieved special notoriety as the Prince of Wales's first love and for her subsequent affair with Fox. The stanzas quoted could be interpreted as an exoneration of the Prince's behaviour to her. This was perhaps one factor in the popularity of the print, which many apparently took to be a portrait of the Duchess. Though widely admired for her beauty and as 'the people's Duchess', Georgiana was known for her own indiscretions: she gave birth to an illegitimate daughter during Haydn's first London visit.

Many of Westall's paintings were engraved by J.R. Smith and his pupils, which is perhaps how he came to Haydn's attention. Like other artists in this circle, he was drawn into illustrating Milton, including another version of *Sabrina Releasing the Lady*. Later, he collaborated on an edition of *Paradise Lost* with the artist most consistently drawn to subjects from Milton during and after the period of Haydn's London visits, Fuseli. Although Fuseli's 'Milton Gallery' did not open until five years after Haydn's final departure from London, the artist's enthusiasm for the poet was already the subject of satire during the composer's first visit. Gillray's *Sin, Death and the Devil*, published 9 June 1792, is a political parody of Fuseli's *Satan encount'ring Death, Sin interposing* (from *Paradise Lost*), completed only a fortnight before.[208] Gillray's inscription, recommending the scene to 'Messrs, Boydell, Fuseli and the rest of the Proprietors of the 385 editions of Milton, now publishing', is clear evidence of how Milton-mania was dominating ventures in London publishing houses.

Haydn owned no prints after Fuseli of Miltonic subjects, but his admiration for the artist is clear from the two prints he did acquire. One was the *Death of Oedipus*, engraved by Ward and published by J.R. Smith in 1785, after Fuseli's painting exhibited at the Royal Academy in 1784.[209] The scene, derived from Sophocles's *Oedipus at Colonus*, shows the aged and blind Oedipus, seated on the ground, staring out towards the viewer. His two daughters clasp him desperately, knowing from the thunder and fire around them that his end is approaching. Fuseli was certainly successful in conveying the terror of the event to contemporary audiences, even if they knew nothing of Sophocles' play. According to one report of its first exhibition, a viewer asked Fuseli what the old man was afraid of, to which the painter replied: 'Afraid Sir, why of going to hell!'[210] Haydn perhaps chose this scene because he knew its treatment in *Oedipe à Colone*, the opera by Sacchini, a composer much admired by Burney and performed by Haydn at Eszterháza.[211]

The second print was *The Weird Sisters*, illustrating the witches in *Macbeth* (I, 3). Fuseli's original painting had been exhibited at the Academy in 1783, and was often copied and engraved. Haydn owned the earliest print after it (Fig. 16), engraved and published in 1785 by J.R. Smith, who in the inscription called himself 'Mezzotint Engraver to his Royal Highness the Prince of Wales'.[212] This was the year the great tragic actress, Mrs Siddons, first performed the role of Lady Macbeth on the London stage, giving the play a new lease of life. Even had Haydn not seen it, he would certainly have heard about it.[213] He probably also knew something of Mrs Siddon's other well-known parts, especially the main characters in *Jane Shore* and *The Fair Penitent*, popular plays which kept the issue of fallen women at the forefront of public consciousness.[214]

The success of Fuseli's *Weird Sisters* and of Mrs Siddons in *Macbeth* were factors behind the creation of the Shakespeare Gallery. Both excelled in conveying the supernatural aspects of Shakespeare through the Gothic sublime, drawing out the horror of a scene using exaggerated gesture and grotesque expression, which, with limited or heightened lighting, left a devastating impression on the viewer's mind. The extent to which Fuseli's *Weird Sisters* grasped the public imagination is suggested through Gillray's use of it in his provocative visual commentary on the lasting political consequences of the King's temporary insanity of 1788–89: *Weird Sisters; Ministers of Darkness: Minions of the Moon* (1791). In this the witches become members of the government contemplating a crescent moon, the dark side formed by the dozing head of the King, the bright side showing the Queen, now shining out as a result of the crisis.[215] To sense all the ramifications of this brilliant caricature, an audience would have had to have known the original by Fuseli, to whom Gillray 'respectfully dedicated' his own print.

Gillray in fact provides a useful measure of the popularity of a number of prints in Haydn's collection. *The Accusing Spirit*, also published in 1791, 'Dedicated (without permission) to the Rev.d Mr Peters', is a disrespectful parody of Peters's *The Spirit of a Child*.[216] *Connoisseurs admiring a collection of George Morland's* (1807) may be understood as a grudging tribute to Morland the year after his early death, stressing his animal pictures; Haydn acquired prints after four such paintings.[217] But perhaps the most interesting of Gillray's derivations was *The Smoking Club*, showing members of the government and opposition blowing smoke in each other's faces. The

Fig. 1 Paolo Veronese, *Marriage Feast at Cana*. Paris, Louvre (The Bridgeman Art Library)

Fig. 2 Rubens, *Abduction of the Daughters of Leucippus*, or '*Castor and Pollux*'.
Munich, Alte Pinakothek

Fig. 3 Pietro Fabris, *Concert Party*, showing Wolfgang Amadeus Mozart, Leopold Mozart, Sir William Hamilton and Pietro Fabris and others. Edinburgh, Scottish National Portrait Gallery

Fig. 4 Angelica Kauffman, *Self-portrait with Painting and Music at the Crossroads*. Nostell Priory (National Trust Photographic Library/John Hammond)

Fig. 5 Antonio Canova, *Monument to Archduchess Christine*. Vienna, Augustinerkirche

Fig. 6 Title-page to the keyboard edition of Haydn's *The Seasons*, designed by Johann David Schubert, engraved by Friedrich Wilhelm Nettling, first published by Breitkopf & Härtel, Leipzig, 1802. London, British Library, E.409.w

Fig. 7 Karl Anton Hickel, *The House of Commons*, 1793. By courtesy of the National Portrait Gallery, London

Fig. 8 Franz Xaver Messerschmidt, *Ein absichtlicher Schalknarr* (A Deliberate Prankster). Vienna, Barockmuseum.

Fig. 9 Nicolas Poussin, *Eucharist*. Collection of the Duke of Sutherland, on permanent loan to the National Gallery of Scotland, Edinburgh

Fig. 10 Francisco Goya y Lucientes, *Si sabrà mas el discipulo?* (Might not the pupil know more?), *Los Caprichos*, No. 37. London, British Museum

Fig. 11 Giovanni Battista Tiepolo, *The Banquet of Cleopatra*. Melbourne, National Gallery of Victoria (The Bridgeman Art Library)

Fig. 12 'Magic Picture' scene from *Zémire et Azor*, engraved by Pierre-Charles Ingouf, after a gouache by François-Robert Ingouf. Paris, Bibliothèque Nationale de France

Fig. 13 *Joseph Haydn*, engraved by Johann Ernst Mansfeld, published by Artaria &
Co., Vienna, 1781

Fig. 14 John Hoppner, *Joseph Haydn*. Royal Collection, © Her Majesty Queen Elizabeth II

Fig. 15 Benjamin West, *The Raising of Lazarus*, engraved by Valentine Green, published by V. Green & Son, London, 1780. London, British Museum

Fig. 16 Henry Fuseli, *The Weird Sisters*, engraved by John Raphael Smith, London, 1783. London, British Museum

Fig. 17 Henry Bunbury, *Bethnal Green* ('Hie away Juno!'), published by W. Dickson, London, 1792. London, British Museum

Fig. 18 Philippe de Loutherbourg, *The Battle of Valenciennes . . . on the Twenty-Fifth of July 1793*, engraved by William Bromley, published by R. Cribb and C. de Mechel, London, 1801. London, British Museum

Fig. 19 Edward Francesco Burney, *Louiherbourg's Eidophusikon showing Pandemonium from Milton*. London, Victoria & Albert Museum (The Bridgeman Art Library)

Fig. 20 'Drawn by an Amateur' and engraved by James Gillray, *Farmer Giles & his Wife Shewing Off their Daughter Betty to their Neighbours, on her Return from School*, published by H. Humphrey, London, 1809. London, British Museum

composition of this was borrowed from a print of the same name by Henry Bunbury, one of the most admired caricaturists of the final decades of the century. As well as *A Smoking Club*, Haydn owned a further five prints after drawings by Bunbury.[218] The composer's special interest in the work of Bunbury, the best-known amateur artist of the period, is evident from his selection of *three* of these Bunbury prints for framing and display at Gumpendorf, more than any other artist in the collection.[219] Coming from a country where censorship had prevented the emergence of any comparable tradition of visual satire, it may have taken Haydn some time to understand the humour of the English caricature; but that he made the effort to appreciate this aspect of British public life, and was aware of the place it occupied in a country which prided itself on its freedoms, of speech and of the press, is again evident from his notebooks.

Haydn was particularly fascinated by the double entendres and other wordplays on which the caricaturists depended as the starting point for a joke. After studying what appears to have been one such caricature, he noted its caption in both German and the original English: 'Trip to JERSEY, or – divorce a la mode'. He then commented: 'Jersey is the name of the Prince of Wales' new mistress. THAT'S WHAT THEY SAY ...'.[220] Haydn clearly understood the fun this caricaturist, like others, had with the word 'Jersey'. He probably also grasped the reference to Hogarth's satirical cycle 'Marriage a la Mode' (1743), popularized in German-speaking countries through Lichtenberg's commentaries on Hogarth, published between 1784 and 1796.[221] Haydn may have seen the paintings themselves at the Shakespeare Gallery, where from 1792 they were exhibited to publicize new engravings of them published by Boydell.[222] Immediately after working out the meaning of the 'Jersey' caricature, Haydn himself attempted such wordplay (in German rhyming verse), choosing as his victims his own impresario and one of the great tenors of the day, both of whom happened to have the names of Old Testament kings: 'Salomon and David were great sinners / had beautiful wives, made many children. / When they couldn't do it any more and old-age caught up with them, / the one wrote songs and the other wrote psalms.'[223] Haydn may have been inspired into making this attempt at English-style satire from knowledge of one of the earliest caricatures addressing the Prince of Wales's affair with Lady Jersey, Isaac Cruikshank's *MY GRANDMOTHER, ALIAS THE JERSEY JIG, ALIAS THE RIVAL WIDOWS* (26 August 1794), in which the Prince, with beard and appropriate garb, appears in a portrait labelled 'Solomon', inscribed 'Solomon had 300 Wives and 700 Concubines'.[224] Lady Jersey appears as the grandmother. *My Grandmother* was also the title of an opera by Stephen Storace (1793), the plot of which centred on a portrait.[225] The cartoon clearly draws on the popularity of this musical entertainment. Since it was composed by one of Haydn's London friends, a familiarity with both opera and caricature seems likely. The latter could be seen at the showroom of the publisher, who, according to the inscription, had 'jus[t] fitted up his Exhibition in an entire Novel stile. Admittance one shillg [*sic*]'.

Although Haydn's attempt at the wordplay of English visual satire only amounts to a crude effort, it indicates his eagerness to understand English popular culture at its most agreeably vulgar. Haydn probably met in person the most visually astute of all political caricaturists, Gillray.[226] His preference, however, was for the gentler, though no less perceptive humour of Bunbury. Two of Haydn's Bunbury prints were literary in inspiration. *Marian* (engraved by P.W. Tomkins, a pupil of Bartolozzi, and published in 1792) illustrates an episode from *The Shepherd's Week* by John Gay, author of *The Beggar's Opera*.[227] It depicts a country girl, whose love is unrequited, turning to gypsies to read her palm. Though the prognostication is not good, it turns out to be false. The subject of gypsy fortune-tellers commanded special interest at this date, since it drew attention to the credulity of young women, in both its comic and moral aspects.[228] Its popularity probably affected the decision by Haydn's publishers to title the Finale of his most celebrated trio 'Rondo in the Gypsies' style', when it was first issued in October 1795.[229] Since he actually owned a print testifying to this fad, it seems that it was Haydn himself who recognized that a composition using thematic material associated with gypsies would succeed in London. Some of the tunes were adapted from those he had heard performed by gypsies at Eszterháza, a procedure already exploited in the 'Menuetto alla Zingarese' in the D major quartet from Opus 20.[230] Haydn may also have been attracted to Bunbury's print because it shared its title with a recent opera by Shield, a composer whose work for stage Haydn certainly followed.[231]

The pair to *Marian* which Haydn owned was *The Mouse's Petition*, engraved by Bartolozzi and published by Macklin on 20 November 1791. This illustrates Mrs Barbauld's popular 1773 poem of the same name, the opening stanzas of which are quoted beneath, beginning:

> Oh! Hear a pensive prisoner's prayer,
> For liberty that sighs;
> And never let thine heart be shut
> Against a wretch's cries.

The print shows a caged mouse, set on a table in a garden, looked on by a lad, two women and an old man. Ostensibly, this is an example of heightened sensibility, the mouse arguing its own case for freedom. At this level, the theme was evidently very successful, judging from later prints depicting trapped mice with similar titles.[232] However, Bunbury's design probably held further connotations for viewers like Haydn, seeing it in 1791. The poem's full title showed that it had originally been written after observing the use of animals in scientific experiments conducted by Dr Joseph Priestley, who responded to the 'petition' by releasing one intended victim.[233] Reviewers took this seriously, commending the author for providing 'this opportunity to testify our abhorrence of the cruelty practised by experimental philosophers'. By 1789, the date Mary Wollstonecraft republished the poem in the *Female Reader*, the tale of a captive seeking freedom, with its colourful images of oppression ('a tyrant's chain', 'with guiltless blood'), could be seen in light of the fall of the Bastille.[234] Two years later, when leading radicals like Priestley were celebrating the second anniversary of the Bastille's fall, the political tide in England was moving against them. Shortly afterwards, the reaction was such that Priestley's house and laboratory were destroyed by fire.[235] Bunbury's print, with its allusions to Priestley's humanity, was evidently conceived with these events in mind.[236] It seems very likely that Haydn would have grasped the political impact of such imagery at this time, though he also enjoyed its lighter side since he owned another print based on the theme of a trapped mouse, without the political dimension. *The Mouse Trap*, engraved by his friend Thomas Park in 1786, after a design by J.G. Huck (a pupil of Valentine Green), may allude to Shakespeare's *Hamlet* (a play Haydn saw in London), in which the Prince calls the performance devised to detect Claudius's guilt 'a mousetrap'.[237] Huck, whose father ran a print shop in Düsseldorf, would certainly have known the Shakespeare reference and perhaps intended viewers of his work to have it in mind. His design, however, is entirely innocuous, and depicts a woman, her children, two cats and the trap.

    Bethnal Green (Fig. 17), published in June 1792, also alludes to the theme of entrapment.[238] This is the kind of print on which Bunbury built his reputation, poking fun not at individuals, but at whole social groupings and their behaviour. It depicts a well-to-do, portly man and his dumpy wife outside the fence of their country residence, the entrance to which has a warning labelled 'Men Traps', to deter poachers. The residence itself is a Chinese pagoda, modelled on the one by Sir William Chambers at Kew dating from the early 1760s, a sure sign of the couple's pretentious and out-moded tastes.[239] The man is preparing for a shooting expedition by loading his gun, posing in the manner of a figure in a painting by Stubbs, though without the poise, the size of the gun emphasizing his short stature. Beside him is his dog, probably a foxhound bitch, carrying only a bone, hinting perhaps at the emptiness of the expedition. Bethnal Green was a pleasant London suburb at this time with a fast-rising population, though it seems doubtful that it would have been a good place to shoot. The main target of Bunbury's satire is reserved for the wife, who wears a riding habit. Her role in the outing is unclear. She is undoubtedly bored; and her indifference to standards of fashion and bearing are suggested by her posture and the carrying of her husband's wig and an umbrella, held upside down. The brim of her extravagant hat casts its shadow over her eyes, a motif borrowed from Bunbury's friend Reynolds, used here to suggest her lack of vision.[240] This is emphasized by the horse with blinkers shown immediately behind, and by contrast with the far-seeing man at the top of the pagoda, viewing the landscape with a telescope. The horse is pulling a trap, which was probably intended not only as a pun on the woman's own trappings, but also on her role in the couple's marriage. Bunbury draws clear attention to this theme because the sign warning of 'Men Traps' sticks up immediately behind her. A pretty woman was sometimes called during this period 'a man-trap', the title of one popular print showing a coy beauty.[241] Viewing the woman in Bunbury's print in these terms was clearly a huge joke for purchasers like Haydn. Its subtitle, *Hie away Juno*, serves to complete the ridicule: exertion seems to be the last thing on the woman's mind, and she evidently has little in common with the stately beauty of Jupiter's jealous wife.

Bunbury was renowned for his ability to make people laugh. Cowper considered that 'Bunbury sells Humour by the yard', and thought that if his caricatures were matched with verse and set to music, they would make 'the world die of laughing'.[242] There is no doubt that people found his work genuinely funny and those of good taste particularly appreciated that they contained 'no ribaldry, no profaneness, no ill-natured censure'.[243] The tone set in such caricatures made them safe viewing at court.[244] Indeed in 1788 Bunbury became equerry to the Duke of York, through whom the artist perhaps first came to Haydn's attention. *Bethnal Green* seems to have been aimed at amusing men, like Haydn, who longed to escape their wives' control.[245] This helps to account for Haydn's decision to display *Bethnal Green* at Gumpendorf, where his wife may have seen it, though without understanding its gist. Haydn's fondness for hunting would also have drawn him to it. The transparently exaggerated stories about his supposed shooting skills he later told the credulous Griesinger show him developing his own verbal wit along the lines seen in Bunbury's prints.[246]

Haydn was probably sufficiently well tuned into English popular culture to recognize that the print drew part of its humour by subverting a story previously associated with Bethnal Green, that of the blind beggar and his beautiful daughter, well known as the basis of an opera by Arne and a painting by Opie.[247] Bunbury illustrated it in 1790.[248] Its humour lies in the father's inability to see that his success in begging depends on his daughter's comeliness, of which he is ignorant. By the time *Bethnal Green* was published, drawing attention to an inability to see could hardly avoid a political dimension in the field of caricature. Caricaturists at this time, for example, frequently made use of Burke's spectacles to suggest foresight or lack of it.[249] Bunbury encourages a political reading of *Bethnal Green* with other strategically placed motifs. The wig, which the husband has discarded, clearly refers to the Whigs, and in particular to prominent members of the party falling out over their responses to the French Revolution. *A Barber's Shop* (1785), Bunbury's lampoon on the intense Westminster election campaign of 1784, provides clear evidence that prominent wigs refer to Whigs.[250] A wig set aside, as in *Bethnal Green*, probably had the sense of disillusionment with the party, suggesting a hardening of attitude along the lines set out by Burke.[251] The dog's bone may also have brought to mind contemporary contention among Whigs.[252] The woman's yawn, a favourite Bunbury motif, also had a political origin in English caricature. George Bickham's *Great Britain and Ireland's Yawn* (1743), depicting a yawning head, refers to the long administration of Sir Robert Walpole, as do the lines from Pope's satirical *Dunciad* quoted beneath: 'And Chief-less Armies doz'd out the Campaign; And Navies yawn'd for Orders on the Main.'[253] In *Bethnal Green*, the yawning woman holding her husband's wig doubtless comments on the tedium of Whig infighting at the time.

Bunbury had numerous family connections with Fox, the Whig leader, so it is hardly surprising that oblique comments on Whig fortunes are part of the fun of his caricatures during the early 1790s.[254] Another of Haydn's Bunbury prints, *A Smoking Club*, showing four male smokers, seated in silence and consumed with pleasure, presents a further example. On the wall hangs a *Vox populi* print of Fox, partly obscured by smoke rising from the peg-legged smoker seated in front, perhaps a visual metaphor for Fox's standing when the caricature was published in 1792. The smoker was probably intended to allude to the one-legged actor Moses Kean, who was celebrated for his impersonations of Fox, thus completing the ridicule.[255] The extent to which Haydn was aware of these allusions cannot now be determined with certainty. But given his close association with many of the figures concerned, it seems very likely he had more than an inkling of the full extent of this humour, especially taking into account his own reputation for wit.

Smoking was a pastime which had become unfashionable with the gentry and nobility across much of Europe during the third quarter of the eighteenth century, replaced by the more refined habit of snuff-taking. Smoking tobacco was often considered the cause of much domestic disharmony, hence the creation of clubs for men to indulge their addiction without fear of being pestered by their wives. Haydn, though apparently not a smoker himself, was certainly conscious of the association of smoking with discord in the home. In one of his first Esterházy symphonies, written shortly after his own marriage, he quotes at length a popular song by Gluck, the words of which focus on how tobacco foments strife between husband and wife.[256] In London, 30 years later, smoking was once again becoming acceptable, at least within certain circles with which Haydn seems to have been connected. Judging from prints like Bunbury's, and others of the period more overtly political in their message, pipe-smoking at the beginning of the 1790s (before the massacres in Paris in October 1792) was a sign of radicalism, and of support for the French Revolution in particular.[257] Even when smoking was completely out of fashion with the well-to-do it had remained popular with the poor and the working classes. When Pitt imposed a new tax on tobacco in 1789, some followers of Fox considered this an attack on the poor and promoted the habit very visibly themselves in order to show their solidarity with the less fortunate in society.[258] One of the best-known fictional characters of Revolutionary France, the plain-speaking Père Duchesne, who talked common sense in the language of the street, perhaps encouraged this attitude in England: his image, pipe in hand, smoke rising from its bowl, decorated the cover of every edition one of the most widely read publications of the early 1790s.[259] Haydn was almost certainly in tune with these developments through his connections with prominent Whigs. Apart from Bunbury's *A Smoking Club* he also owned one of the most famous smoking prints of the period – also published in 1792 – showing an old country labourer striding out on a winter morning, his spirits uplifted by the smoke inhaled from his pipe, an image used to decorate tobacconists' shops in London until the mid-nineteenth century.[260] More significantly, Haydn reveals himself in his notebooks to have purchased a tobacco box in December 1791, notwithstanding the fact that he was not himself a smoker.[261] He found himself soon afterwards obliged to give it to an admirer who wanted a memento of Haydn, and gave his own to the composer in exchange. The conventional gift at this time would have been of a snuffbox, which Haydn, like notable artists and composers, had received on several occasions from leading patrons. The exchange of tobacco boxes late in 1791, while ostensibly an act of homage, probably also signified a political stance, implying both men were sympathetic to Fox's position on the desirability of the initial aims of the French Revolution.

Haydn may have enjoyed the political aspects of Bunbury's *A Smoking Club*, but the print may well have caught his eye initially because the arrangement of the four seated figures and their gestures closely corresponds to the traditional grouping of the members of a string quartet when performing. Indeed Haydn, and others, may well have recognized the print as serving as a parody of such a musical performance.

3. Looking and Listening in London

The ceiling of the main concert hall at the Hanover Square Rooms, the venue where Salomon and his orchestra performed during Haydn's first London visit, was decorated with 'beautifully painted' scenes by Cipriani, Bartolozzi's friend and one of the leading decorative artists in Britain.[262] These paintings – like the venue itself, they are no longer extant – are an indication that the original organizers of the concerts thought listeners might be especially attentive to the music if they had something worthwhile to look at. Indeed, when the auditorium at Hanover Square was first opened (1775), this principle seems to have been uppermost in the minds of the promoters. The main concert hall included many other large paintings, by West and Gainsborough, as well as by Cipriani, leaving such an impression that it was considered 'the most elegant room in town'. Some of these were apparently painted on transparencies, with light shining through from behind, sufficient to illuminate the entire room with no further lighting. J.C. Bach and Abel, who conceived this effect, clearly thought that it would put listeners into the right frame of mind for listening to their music. However, there were those in the audience who objected to this feature (because the transparencies amusingly projected strong colours onto their powdered wigs), so the offending paintings were removed. When one lady subsequently voiced disappointment about their banishment, Bach told her that the paintings in question 'had not absolutely deserted us', for in the performance itself, he hoped 'your ladyship will *hear* them all'.[263] Although by the time Haydn performed at the Hanover Square Rooms the illuminated paintings had long since been removed, it seems likely that something of Bach's audio-visual intentions remained, through the remaining works by Cipriani. There is no doubt that the composer became interested in Cipriani. His print collection included a number of Cipriani's designs, though the cataloguer was sadly insufficiently detailed in his descriptions to enable all these to be identified.[264]

Cipriani was not only responsible for much of the decorative work at the most prestigious venue for concerts in London, but also at the equivalent venue for exhibitions of the visual arts, the Royal Academy in Somerset House, including four allegorical paintings for the ceiling of the library. At the centre of these was a work by the Academy's President, Reynolds, representing 'the *Theory of the Art* under the form of an elegant and majestick female, seated in the clouds, and looking upwards, as contemplating the Heavens. She holds in one hand the Compass, in the other a Label, on which this sentence is written: *THEORY is the Knowledge of what is truly NATURE.*'[265] Haydn probably owned the engraving of this painting published in 1785.[266] He perhaps approved the sentiment on Theory's label, and doubtless wished to have a reminder of work by the leading English painter of his time, in the allegorical style he particularly admired.[267] Haydn may also have acquired prints after four allegorical paintings by Angelica Kauffman, which (together with paintings by West) were executed *c.*1780 to decorate the ceiling of the Council Chamber of the Academy, where Reynolds delivered his Discourses.[268] Kauffman's paintings, engraved by Bartolozzi in 1787, represent *Invention, Composition, Design* and *Colour.* Like *Theory,* these works draw special interest in the practice and display of the visual arts in London. His choice also suggests a responsiveness on his part to the ways listening audiences in London at the time were in part conditioned in their reactions to music by viewing of the visual arts, especially in their most accessible form, at the galleries and showrooms linked to the commercial production of images, print-making.

By the time Haydn appeared in London, audiences were quite used to the notion that at certain venues entertainment for the ear might be accompanied by diversions for the eye. This was only to be expected in theatres performing opera or equivalent musical amusements; but in London the premise was extended to reach much larger sections of the public at popular places of recreation, like Vauxhall Gardens, where attentive looking and listening were demanded to maximize the benefits of a visit. Such conditioning suggested more refined forms of visual and aural interchange. The success of Bunbury's *Long Minuet* led, for example, to its being recreated on stage by dancers, and set to music.[269] Although *tableaux vivants* were becoming popular elsewhere in Europe, in London they seem to have had a special appeal. At the King's Theatre on 19 May 1791, for example, was given what was advertised as 'a new kind of concert'.[270] Although this may have been prompted by Gallini's problems in securing a licence to perform opera, the results none the less are intriguing. Haydn's Symphony No. 73 was performed, as well as a song of his own composition, which he accompanied. The evening ended with a ballet. But its most exceptional element was the 'New divertisement' with which it began, executed by dancers, introducing 'the animated pictures'. Perhaps these followed in the spirit of Samuel Arnold's *The Enraged Musician*, a through-composed afterpiece first performed in May 1789, bringing alive Hogarth's celebrated comic print of the same title (1741).[271] In this, the music and goings-on of the street are contrasted with the cultivated, foreign violinist, shown practising indoors, who evidently abhors the racket outside.[272] Hogarth drew part of his inspiration from the tradition of the Cries of London in its printed manifestation, and this was taken up musically in the Finale of Arnold's opera, featuring such street-cries as 'Knives to grind', 'Pots to mend', 'New mackerel' and others.[273] According to Mrs Papendieck's account of a Haydn symphony performed at what she claimed was the first concert of the 1791 season, 'One of the movements was to imitate the London cries, and "Live cod" was to be traced through every instrument that could produce the effect. The cry began the piece and ended it, and Salomon was wound up to a pitch of enthusiasm beyond himself. The public was satisfied, and Haydn was very properly taken up.'[274] Which movement Mrs Papendieck's account refers to is unclear. It may be that several symphonies composed after Haydn reached London incorporate what were then recognized as elements of street-cries. It has also been suggested that her memory was faulty, and that her account actually relates to Symphony No. 104, first performed 4 May 1795, the Finale of which certainly fits her description.[275] If the principal theme here was based on a street-cry, which seems likely, Haydn must have calculated its effect on the audience very carefully. A new series of fourteen small pictures of *The Cries of London* by Francis Wheatley were exhibited at the Royal Academy between 1792 and 1795.[276] These were engraved, starting in 1793, and proved to be enormously popular. Three were issued on 1 January 1795, about the time Haydn would have been composing this symphony, including 'New Mackrel, New Mackrel', which Mrs Papendiek might have understandably confused with 'Live cod'. The print was by Schiavonetti, who had previously engraved Guttenbrunn's London portrait of Haydn, a connection which may have encouraged Haydn to follow Schiavonetti's latest productions. Haydn would have known that many in the audience were subscribers to this series, so when they heard the cries referred to in the prints in the symphony, their experience of the music would have been enhanced by calling to mind the street scene as Wheatley depicted it. This was evidently a very special way of paying tribute to a London audience, leading one commentator to remark that 'for fifty years to come Musical Composers would be little better than imitators of Haydn; and would do little more than pour water on his leaves'.[277]

In such a procedure, Haydn was acknowledging the ways London's musical audiences were also experienced in looking at recent artistic productions, and accustomed themselves to finding connections between the world of the concert hall and the exhibition room. One clear example of this Haydn already knew was *A Representation of the Execution of Mary Queen of Scots*, by his friend, the Earl of Abingdon, the music for which was still in his library at Haydn's death.[278] Opie's picture of the same subject, painted for Bowyer's Historic Gallery in 1787, was the most famous of a series of representations of events associated with the Scottish Queen exhibited in London at this time.[279] Another Opie picture on a tragic scene from the life of Mary Queen of Scots was presented by Boydell to the Guildhall about 1794.[280] Opie's *Execution* was well known through prints, and was even one of the targets of criticism in Gillray's splendid satire on Boydell, *Shakespeare-Sacrificed* (1789).[281] Many listeners to Abingdon's piece would therefore have been conditioned in the way they perceived it through having viewed Opie's picture. The movement to portray Mary as tragic victim of events, rather than their perpetrator, gained strength from the execution of another Queen, Marie-Antoinette, in 1793. This event, and the background to it, were likewise enthusiastically taken up by composers and artists, anxious to enable the public to relive the Queen's ordeal. Dussek's *Le Tableau de Marie Antoinette*, a monodrama with set scenes, ends with 'la guillotine tomba', and a swift falling sound in the music. Storace's *Captivity* (1793) concentrates on the Queen's fate after the execution of her husband.[282] Its graphic images ('I see th'assassin's blood-stain'd sword, The Headless trunk, the bosom gor'd') seem to have been too much for listeners to stomach, and the piece was unsuccessful. He tried again soon afterwards with *A Lamentation of Marie-Antoinette, late Queen of France, on the Morning of Her Execution*. Like the painters and printmakers, Storace was here careful to avoid showing the blood, emphasizing instead the Queen's ordeal and her noble demeanor in the face of adversity.[283] Nevertheless, it is clear that looking at such works provided listeners to Dussek and Storace with appropriate preparation for experiencing the music.

Opie, whose work was represented in Haydn's collection, was a protégé of Dr John Wolcot. Under the name Peter Pindar, Wolcot wrote a series of satirical *Lyric Odes to the Royal Academicians*, published between 1782 and 1786. His artistic interests were matched by musical ones – he translated at least one opera libretto for Covent Garden – and in many ways he emerges as a key figure in establishing a visual way of experiencing music, especially in relation to Haydn. The text for Haydn's 'Madrigal' *The Storm*, first performed 24 February 1792, was by Wolcot, with whom the composer was presumably on good terms by this date. The words provided Haydn not only with an opportunity to demonstrate his ability to set an English text, but also to show that he understood how the English liked 'to see' through music. Lines like 'Hell's Genius roams the regions of the dark' and 'From cloud to cloud the moon affrighted flies, Now darken'd and now flashing through the skies' were vividly given musical expression. The endeavour was not lost on listeners. 'The Storm is a fine effort of musical *painting*; the vicissitude of the calm, and the tempest are remarkably striking', wrote one reviewer.[284] Another critic called it 'an exquisite specimen of *imitative* harmony ... the horrors of a tempest, contrasted with the gradual serenity of a calm, were finely represented, and highly admired'.[285] Some in the audience might well have brought to mind in listening to this example of 'representative harmony' (the term applied to it in the review in the *Morning Herald*) particular representations they had recently seen. For example, Morland exhibited a *Sea Storm and Shipwreck* at the Society of Artists in 1791, which Walpole noted as 'very fine'. Such storm imagery proved irresistible to the English, and Morland often repeated the subject.[286] Its other great exponent was Loutherbourg, whom Haydn knew. The moonlight effects in Wolcot's text would have also called to mind the memorable depictions of moons in paintings by Joseph Wright, especially *The Lady in Milton's Comus*. A London audience at the first performances of Haydn's *The Storm* might have had their attention particularly drawn to this because of recent publicity given to the Lunar Society of radical philosophers, with which Wright was associated, and whose members included Priestley, Darwin and Wedgwood.[287] The emergence of light out of darkness, seen in this and other pictures by Wright and described in Haydn's 'Madrigal', may have also had special significance for Freemasons, since it alluded to the important Masonic device *Lux e tenebris* ('Light out of darkness'). This would have been especially meaningful to Haydn, as well as several artists he knew or admired in London, including Bartolozzi, Loutherbourg, Peters and Wright, all of whom like him were Freemasons.

The Storm was first heard at a concert which included a performance of Symphony No. 93. When this was first given, a week earlier, one reviewer, desperate to find words to convey his excitement, wrote:

> Such a combination of excellence was contained in every movement, as inspired all the performers as well as the audience with enthusiastic ardour. Novelty of idea, agreeable caprice, and whim combined with Haydn's sublime and wanton grandeur, gave additional consequence to the *soul* and feelings of very individual present. The *Critic's eye brightened with additional lustre* – then was the moment that *the great Painter might have caught* – that which cannot be thrown on the human frame, but on rare and great occasions.[288]

Unfortunately, the writer did not say which 'great painter' (s)he had in mind; but the review clearly establishes that audiences experienced visual sensations when listening to purely instrumental music, as well as to vocal music, in which texts presented imagery, as in *The Storm*. The reviewer was also indicating Haydn's peerless position in the sphere of music, and that the full extent of his matchless achievement could only be suggested by evoking the thought of Old Masters painters, whose greatness need not be questioned. Of course, in writing this, it is assumed that the musical reader would have an understanding of the visual arts to make sense of such concepts. It further implies that Haydn himself intended communicating with his audience in visual terms. Haydn would have observed how other composers of this period in London managed this, and though without following them, learned from their example. Kelly, in discussing Stephen Storace's *The Pirates* (first performed November 1792), for example, says that the 'picturesque and beautiful' scenery for the opera was based on designs by the composer himself, 'taken on the spot ... at Naples'.[289] Storace is known to have been 'fond of Drawing' when he was in Italy, where he sought the company of British artists, including James Northcote.[290] Kelly's story is attested by the title-page of the opera's vocal score, decorated with a view across the Bay of Naples, which was probably taken from the set for the opening scene.[291] Storace therefore was one composer, with artistic ability, who used his combined talents to control the experience of his work both musically and visually simultaneously. Why he felt the need to do this for the first time late in 1792, when he had been composing operas since 1785, and had made the drawings in Naples in the mid-1770s, is unclear. Possibly he was responding to recent developments in the concert hall.

Haydn was not in London at the time of the première of *The Pirates*, but he was certainly aware of other developments concerning the relationship of music to painting, also in the field of opera. On 10 December 1791 he saw Shield's opera *The Woodman*, 'performed with universal applause' at Covent Garden.[292] One of Haydn's own publishers, Longman & Broderip, paid Shield the considerable sum of 1,000 guineas for the rights to print the music. Part of the plot is set in a hop field and includes a big chorus of hop pickers. In 1765 Walpole, travelling through Kent on his way to Paris, saw hop fields and hop pickers and considered they 'would make a lively picture ... what I never saw painted'.[293] The success of Shield's opera therefore enabled one artist, Westall, to identify an under-exploited subject and produce his own version of it, *Hop-pickers*, the engraving of which by William Ward was published in 1792.

However, whilst Shield's music had consequences for printmaking, the opera itself, in its turn, owed part of its initial appeal to the same field. In 1787, Gainsborough painted *The Woodman*, one of his last works and the one in which he expressed greatest satisfaction. It was taken to Buckingham House for the King to see early in 1788, and this, together with the fact that Gainsborough specifically mentions the painting in his final reconciliatory letter to Reynolds, from whom he had been estranged for several years, leant the painting a certain notoriety.[294] After Gainsborough's death in 1788 it was placed on exhibition at the painter's residence in Pall Mall, where it caught the public's imagination. An engraving of it by Peter Simon was issued in 1791. There can be no doubt that Gainsborough's painting was an important source of inspiration for Shield because the opera's librettist, Henry Bate-Dudley, had been a close friend of Gainsborough and the painter's leading champion. Bate-Dudley wrote Gainsborough's obituary, one of the best sources of the artist's objectives. It was published in the *Morning Herald*, the newspaper Bate-Dudley had founded in 1780, in which many of the most important early reviews of Haydn's London compositions subsequently first appeared.[295]

Gainsborough's *Woodman* became so well known that, beginning in 1789, it formed the basis of a series of imitations by a young artist called Thomas Barker. When Barker came to the attention of Bate-Dudley, the latter wrote a damning piece in his newpaper, attacking 'the execrable impostor at the brush who resides at Bath, who has been labouring for months past to impose on the taste of the public by pictures and drawings in Gainsborough's stile'.[296] Despite this, one of Barker's variations, showing an old woodman setting out for work with his dog on a winter morning, proved irresistible in the eyes of the public. It was borrowed, and subsequently purchased, by Macklin for display in his Poets' Gallery, where it illustrated a passage in Cowper's poem, *The Task*.[297] Bartolozzi's engraving of it in 1792 helped to extend its reputation well into the nineteenth century.[298] The print was acquired by Haydn, who had probably seen the painting when displayed in the Poet's Gallery.[299] Macklin doubtless wanted such an image at this time because it cashed in on the publicity then stemming from Shield's opera. Haydn was a willing sucker for this ruse, the print acting partly as a reminder of the performance, and, in his case, partly as a memento of his friendship with Shield.[300] When Haydn composed *The Seasons* much later, Barker's *Woodman* conceivably played a part in the characterization of Simon, the labourer.

Given the nature of the relationship in the public sphere between the visual arts and musical entertainments during the early 1790s, it is to be expected that Haydn himself would draw on this in order to endear his music to a London audience. The most popular composition of his first visit, Symphony No. 94

(1791), is well known to have caught the attention of his audience, chiefly because of the sudden *fortissimo* chord in the slow movement, which soon gave it the nickname 'The Surprise'.[301] Griesinger's reporting of Haydn's own explanation of the effect seems the most reliable of several early accounts of the composer's intentions: 'It was my aim to *surprise* the public with something new, and making my debut [to the new season of concerts] in a brilliant manner ...'.[302] Those later anecdotes suggesting that Haydn was hoping to startle particular elements in the audience, such as ladies of a delicate disposition, or sleepy old gentlemen, were therefore almost certainly devised as a way of explaining, misleadingly, how Haydn conceived his 'idea'. What it is here suggested may have been Haydn's starting point for his desire to surprise on this particular occasion, as many in the audience may have recognized, was a painting exhibited at the Royal Academy in 1791 entitled simply *Surprise*. This was one of a long series of self-portraits by the prominent French painter Ducreux illustrating various expressions, developed from Le Brun's treatise. Ducreux's representations of the expressions are a painterly equivalent of Messerschmidt's heads, discussed in Chapter 3, though without the menace. He arrived in England only a few days after Haydn in January 1791 as an *emigré*, but stayed only until August. This gave him time to exhibit not only *Surprise*, but also *Surprise Mixed with Terror*, both of which, with other works, were etched and published by Ducreux, in London, on 21 February 1791.[303] In the accompanying inscriptions, he called himself 'Painter to the King of France, to his Imperial Majesty, & Principal Painter to the Queen of France', titles intended to impress the public, and which would certainly have attracted Haydn's attention. The potential in Haydn's adaptation of this expression, giving it musical form, to stimulate the imagination visually is evident from an early review, which conveys the notion by conflating two types of popular print, the pastoral scene and the shooting piece: '[Haydn's] surprise might not be unaptly likened to the situation of a beautiful Shepherdess who, lulled to slumber by the murmer of a distant Waterfall, starts alarmed by the unexpected firing of a fowling-piece.'[304]

The greatest success of Haydn's second London visit was Symphony No. 100, soon known by the title 'The Military', and with even greater powers to stir the visual imagination of listeners. One early reviewer wrote:

> the middle movement was again received with absolute shouts of applause. ... It is the advancing to battle; the march of men, the sounding of the charge, the thundering of the onset, the clash of arms, the groans of the wounded, and what may well be called the hellish roar of war increased to a climax of horrid sublimity! Which, if others can conceive, he alone can execute; at least he alone has effected these wonders.[305]

Another reviewer sensed very similar images. Commenting in particular on the use of percussion instruments in the symphony, (s)he noted:

> The reason for the great effect they produce in the military [i.e. the
> second] movement is that they mark and tell the story: they inform us that
> the army is marching to battle, and, calling up all the ideas of the terror of
> such a scene, give it reality. Discordant sounds are then sublime; for what
> can be more horribly discordant to the heart than thousands of men
> meeting to murder each other.[306]

Almost certainly this was the kind of response Haydn had calculated. On 1
February 1793, when he was in Vienna restoring his energies between his two
London visits, France declared war on England. A British force, commanded
by the Duke of York, was sent to support the Austrian Netherlands against the
French attack. The War, in which Austria and Britain were allies, naturally
brought military themes and fierce patriotism to the fore.

During his first London visit, Haydn had probably observed how the British
relished their military successes, especially those gained in the face of
particular adversity. Haydn would have known about General Wolfe's victory
in Quebec, for example, from Mrs Schroeder, who grew up in the house where
Wolfe had previously lived; and, as already indicated, there is evidence
suggesting he knew the print of West's famous picture of Wolfe's dying
moments. The composer would also not have been able to avoid English pride
concerning the siege of Gibraltar, which lasted from 1779 to 1783, during
which the British successfully withstood a combined force of Spaniards and
French. Haydn was already well acquainted with the event because *L'assedio
di Gibilterra*, an Italian opera by an unidentified composer, was performed
with lavish sets at Eszterháza in 1783. Perhaps this was somehow related to
Shield's *Siege of Gibraltar*, performed at Covent Garden in 1780. The subject
was quickly taken up in the visual arts. Wright's *A View of Gibraltar during
the Destruction of the Spanish Floating Batterie*, depicting an event of 1782,
for example, was the centrepiece of his one-man exhibition in London in 1785,
which also featured *The Lady from Comus*.[307] In 1788 Boydell had hung
Reynolds's portrait of the victorious English general of the siege in his
Shakespeare Gallery, surrounded by four paintings of the siege by Paton. But
the most celebrated painting of the event was by the American artist John
Singleton Copley. His dramatic *Siege of Gibraltar* was commissioned by the
City of London and first exhibited (according to the invitation to subscribe to
a print), 'in a Pavilion, erected by gracious Permission of the King, for that
purpose, in the Green Park', in 1791.[308] Haydn, on his visits to Mrs Schroeder,
who lived nearby, could hardly have missed the structure and, like 60,000
others, probably paid his shilling to see it. The admission ticket, engraved by
Bartolozzi, shows the interior of the pavilion with visitors admiring the
painting, a clever piece of publicity, since it acted both as an incentive to
subscribe to the print, and as a memento of the visit. Such elaborate tickets
seem to have been a London speciality during this period. The possibility that
the '4. Visitbillets' catalogued in Haydn's print collection may have been of

this type, including the one permitting admission to see Copley's *Siege*, therefore seems highly likely.[309] If so, then he must have visited other exhibitions of this type.

One likely contender, exhibited during Haydn's second visit, may be closely connected with the emotions which the Military Symphony stirred up in its first listeners. This is Loutherbourg's large painting, *The Grand Attack on Valenciennes* (Fig. 18), representing an early triumph against the French of the joint British and Austrian forces, under the command of the Duke of York, in July 1793.[310] When news of victory reached London, Valentine Green and his son Rupert, in partnership with Mêchel, the Basel print-seller (who was briefly Dies's teacher), commissioned Loutherbourg to paint the picture with a view to exhibiting it for profit and inviting subscriptions for a print. By contrast with Copley's *Siege*, Loutherbourg's picture had a distinguishing incentive for the public paying to see it, a quality of authenticity. The painter re-created the scene by visiting the battlefield to draw the setting from life. Gillray was employed as his assistant, to sketch the leading personalities and details such as uniforms. After making these arrangements public, one newspaper mockingly inquired whether the attack would be re-enacted for the painter's 'amusement and instruction'.[311] After spending a month in the vicinity, 'Everyone [in London] was eager to see what they had seen.'[312] The artists were even summoned to show the King their drawings. Loutherbourg completed the picture in the spring of 1794, and it went on public view at the Historic Gallery, Pall Mall, for a shilling per head.[313]

For many listeners to early performances of the Military Symphony, knowledge of this painting and the achievement it commemorated are likely to have coloured the way the music was perceived. The account by the critic quoted above might almost be a description of the painting. The theme of the second movement, which was particularly distinguished as 'Militaire', had already been heard in London, in a version of the third concerto for lire organizzate. By reusing this music, Haydn could count on a certain sense of familiarity on the part of the audience. But this essentially served to draw attention to the additions he made, in the orchestration and in the extended coda. The battery of 'Turkish' instruments and the prominence given to an augmented woodwind section would have done much to hint at marching infantry. But it was the trumpet call (possibly a fanfare used by the allied troops) and the crescendo roll on the solo timpani, leading to a *fortissimo* crash of the full orchestra, gradually subsiding, which suggested a call to arms and the subsequent terror of engagement.

Military aspects to the music, however, may be detected throughout the symphony. Both principal subjects in the first movement may be shown to carry implications of armed forces, and the two tremendous climaxes in the development section have the potential to call to mind the surging of troops. Even the *Menuet*, composed first in Vienna (though after the outbreak of war), has a whiff of military precision about it, perhaps written by Haydn after observing officers at the Viennese balls for which he composed the dance music. Marked *Moderato*, this is certainly much slower than other minuets in the second group of London symphonies, most of which probably struck members of the audience for the impossibility of attempting any dance to them. The vigorous *allegro* and *allegretto* markings of these third movements are certainly far from the stately character of, for example, Bunbury's *Long Minuet*. It probably occurred to some listeners that Haydn, in these fast 'minuets', may have been sending up this tradition, in the manner of Gillray's parodies of famous paintings, whether or not this was his intention. The Finale of Symphony No. 100, the main theme of which came to be associated with one distinguished military figure, features many further devices to encourage listeners to imagine the scene on the battlefield. Though none of these was new in itself, when heard in combination with each other, and in the context of what has gone before, they would surely have been very suggestive to the visual imaginations of early listeners. In the development section, for example, the frequent tutti rests and general pauses which fragment the music's flow, and the constantly evolving tonality (the modulations never returning to the same key), not only create a mood of uncertainty, but might imply a range of tentative actions, such as the manoeuvres of troops in preparation for battle, and the fearful anticipation accompanying them. The sudden *fortissimo* of the timpani solo at bar 122 could suggest the first sound of cannon or gunfire. Cavalry might be called to mind through the 6/8 time signature and other *chasse* elements. And the reintroduction of percussion instruments at bar 286 ends the movement on a decidedly triumphant note.

When Haydn was in Portsmouth a few months after the first performance of the Military Symphony he recorded meeting Loutherbourg in his Notebook. The painter was then collecting material for a pendant to *The Great Attack*, again with Gillray as assistant, on the subject of Lord Howe's naval victory over the French, which had taken place on 1 June. Haydn may have attended Sheridan's spectacular tribute to the victory, *The Glorious First of June*, hastily put together with music by Storace a few days before he left London.[314] The captured ships and their men were then in port at Portsmouth, and Loutherbourg was studying them in the interests of documentary accuracy. Haydn was fascinated by English reactions to this victory. He noted the violent celebrations in London following the capture of French warships, and at Portsmouth he wrote down the number of sailors in hospital as a result of the battle, and commented on the prisoners, the barracks, the defences, the cannon and the enemy's ships.[315] He described the various kinds of warship, their masts and sails, even making a superficial sketch. He also wanted to enter the dockyard, though as a foreigner, this was refused.[316] Since the entry in his Notebook on Loutherbourg – he refers to him as 'the famous painter' – comes in the midst of this description, it seems conceivable that Loutherbourg may himself have shown Haydn around Portsmouth. For Haydn to recognize him suggests that they were already on good terms, which implies some kind of previous contact. If the impression given in the notebook that Haydn developed a fascination with Loutherbourg and his current work is not misleading, then perhaps one reason why Haydn was so keen to go to Portsmouth was to familiarize himself with the painter and his working methods. He may even have sensed that works in the spirit of *The Great Attack* might have a relevance to his own future compositions, at least in the sense of gauging audience reactions and enthusiasms for certain kinds of aesthetic effects. Haydn certainly had many London contacts who might have introduced him to Loutherbourg. John Hunter, the surgeon who attempted to operate on Haydn's nasal polyp, knew him, as did Wolcot and the Prince of Wales.[317]

One obvious outcome of contemplating the visual evidence of Lord Howe's naval battle, perhaps as guided by Loutherbourg, was Haydn's *Sailor's Song*, setting words by Anne Hunter, the surgeon's wife:

> High on the giddy bending mast, the seaman furls the rending sail, and, fearless of the rushing blast, he careless whistles to the gale. ... The hostile foe his vessel seeks, high bounding o'er the raging main, the roaring cannon loudly speaks, 'tis Britain's glory we maintain.[318]

But it seems possible that large-scale instrumental compositions may also have taken shape as a result of experiencing Loutherbourg preparing for *Lord Howe's Victory*, or viewing the painting and its pair.[319] Seeing the results of violent conflict at first hand, the full horror of its destruction and maiming, could not have failed to make an impact on any viewer. Surveying the scene with the aid of the eyes of a painter committed to recording the event itself could have only intensified the experience. It seems not unlikely that for a serious composer like Haydn, the experience itself might have suggested creative possibilities. The intensification of aspects of Haydn's composition at this time may perhaps have been one outcome of taking the trouble to study the visible remains of an event which totally captured the public imagination and dominated the media. The impetus to make use of the occasion itself and the public mood it inspired would have been difficult to resist for a composer like Haydn, who by this stage in his career was seeking new ways of projecting his work in the public sphere. Haydn was interested in satisfying the public, and in 1794 and 1795, this was what was preoccupying the public.

In the slow introductions to the symphonies of Haydn's last London season, for example, the music has a more searching and intense quality compared with the previous symphonies, shared by those sections of the slow movements in minor keys. Their unsettling harmonic shifts, with the principle interest often in the lower parts, resulting in darker, more mysterious textures, set the compositions as entities in the context of an uncertain world.

A similar musical idiom is found in two of Haydn's songs of this period, the words of which, again by Mrs Hunter, suggest the associations contemporary audiences may have made listening to these introductions. *The Wanderer* is marked *Poco Adagio*: 'To wander alone when the moon faintly beaming with glimering lustre darts thro' the dark shade, where owls seek for covert, and night birds complaining add sound to the horror that darkens the glade.' Here and there isolated interjections on various wind instruments suggest the sinister cries of such birds in these symphonies.[320] In *The Spirit's Song* (*Adagio*), portraying a spectre at the tomb, the line 'my spirit wanders free and waits till thine shall come' is expressed in the music with deep poise and solemnity. The aesthetic mode of such compositions may have suggested to some the contemporary Gothic novels of Mrs Radcliffe.[321] But the visual arts provide more likely inspiration for Haydn, and appropriate images in the minds of listeners. For example, Loutherbourg's *Philosopher in a Moonlit Churchyard* (1790), showing a figure before a tomb, combines several elements in which Haydn is known to have taken an interest: moonlight, Gothic ruins, and the forsaken, frightened individual.[322] Haydn's prints after two works by Fuseli, designed to elicit terror and vulnerability, were evidently studied by the composer at this time, and show him engaging with a distinctly English aesthetic.

The only symphonic introduction specifically mentioned in the earliest reviews of Haydn's London compositions is that of Symphony No. 103, which is said to have 'excited the deepest attention'.[323] The power of such music to capture the visual imagination of listeners was given full expression in at least two detailed programmes for this symphony's first movement, one by Lacépède (which cannot now be traced) and the other by the French theorist Jérôme-Joseph de Momigny, writing in 1806.[324] According to Momigny, the introduction is set in a church, where the inhabitants of a village have gone to pray for deliverance from a storm. The drum-roll represents thunder. Almost every major development in Haydn's score is given some programmatic interpretation, usually visual, which builds into a complete narrative. The second subject (beginning at bar 79), for example, depicts a country dance performed by shepherds and shepherdesses. Throughout his analysis, Momigny discusses the work as though it were a painting. Thus in the development section, he uses expressions like: 'Madness is *painted* on each face'; 'In the *painting* that Haydn makes of this scene'; 'Haydn's *picture* is finished'; and 'the different instruments ... *colour the drawing*'.[325] Although the precision of Momigny's programme is unique, the general principle that it was possible to 'see' Haydn's music seems to have been widely experienced. An account in the *Jahrbuch der Tonkunst von Wien und Prag* for 1796, for example, concerning the music-making activities of Count Apponyi and the quartets Haydn dedicated to him (Op. 71 and 74, first performed in London in 1794), describes how: 'An enchanting harmony prevails in [Haydn's] quartets, though their progress also includes the extraordinary, in the way they attract attention right at the beginning, hold it, and then as in a labyrinth, draw one now to a flowery meadow, now to a whispering brook, now once again through a roaring flood.'[326] This pictorial quality detected in Haydn's compositional style, dating from the period immediately after his first visit to England, is uncanny in the sense that it was only shortly before this that he himself was engaging with the English predilection for the Picturesque. That he was able to convey something of this to listeners elsewhere is further indicated by the nickname 'The Rider' given to the last quartet in this series, generally considered to derive from the leaping motif in the first movement.

In the context of the history of Western visual culture what is interesting about the reception of Haydn's music of the period in question is that many listeners believed they could experience images in the music, and this was prevalent. When Carpani says that he thought Haydn was a master of landscape, and that his instrumental compositions conveyed the sensations of surveying a fine prospect or looking at a painting by Claude, he was probably drawing on prevalent opinion.[327] In England this kind of thinking is first evident in connection with Haydn's arrangements of traditional Scottish songs. In the following newspaper report, announcing Haydn's settings, the melodies themselves are described in terms close to those previously used to suggest the Picturesque character of Highland scenery: 'Nothing, perhaps, can be a stronger instance of the superior genius of this great master [Haydn] than the facility with which he seized the *wild*, but *natural* and *affecting beauties* of the Scots airs now in great forwardness for publication, the taste with which he has entered into *their genuine spirit*, and the felicity of adaptation ...'.[328] Haydn is here complemented for his ability to convey these characteristics, the appreciation of which was particular to British taste in the pictorial arts at the time, through his music.

This quality may be extended to the comic elements in music Haydn composed for England. There was, of course, nothing new about Haydn bringing a smile to the lips of listeners through his compositions when he first arrived in London, as this book has already indicated. By the 1780s parody became practically instinctive to Haydn's compositional practice.[329] What often distinguishes the jokes of this period, however, is that they seem to have been crafted observing the conventions of English caricature and other kinds of visual humour. Examples of comic impropriety (vulgarity), poking fun at authority, mimicking conventions and even double entendre may all be detected in compositions of the period. The slow movement of Symphony No. 93 (first performed 17 February 1792) provides an example of a joke bordering on the obscene in the English tradition of popular visual culture. Most of the movement is characterized by music of great charm and delicacy (e.g. bars 1–16), as well as an episode of Handelian splendour (bars 17–22), of a kind which many in the audience might have associated with the most venerable traditions of English music-making. At bars 72 to 79 the last phrase of the movement's main theme is teasingly broken up through several repetitions, ending with two *pianissimo* retorts between violins and flutes in the high register. This calm is broken by an unexpected low note, played *fortissimo* on the bassoons, after which the full orchestra concludes the movement with a coda. This is surely the musical equivalent of those caricatures featuring a blast emanating from the backside of some public figure, which seem never to have been discussed in English commentaries, but which are known to have delighted foreign observers and provoked their comment.[330]

The first movement of Symphony No. 98 (1792) suggests an example of a different brand of humour inspired by English experience. The *Adagio* introduction is based on the light, opening theme of the *Allegro*, only performed slowly, very deliberately, in the minor, and with (in part) great Handelian pomp. The theme acts like a foundation stone of English respectability and taste, dominating the entire movement. But on its last appearance (bars 300–304) any vestige of seriousness remaining in it is ridiculed by a loud and rather pompous off-beat accompaniment. This, it may be suggested, is more than just a parody of material previously heard. It hints at a sending up of a whole tradition of venerable music-making and concert attending, much as Gillray's 'imitations' of celebrated works by Fuseli, Peters and others not only parody individual paintings, but undermine the whole convention of public picture-viewing on which such works depended.

Another aspect of Haydn's 'English' humour is his ability to mock himself by subverting his own much admired compositional devices and his audience's expectations. Haydn had always had a lot of fun teasing audiences with the return of principal themes (especially in Finales), endlessly repeating and varying opening motifs so that the listener is uncertain when the return proper will begin. But in the Finale of Symphony No. 102 (1795) he takes this toying with his listeners a stage further by implying a kind of ineptitude on the part of the performers to understand where the composition is going. Having brought the music to a close in the tonic at bar 230, Haydn hints that he intends to reintroduce the main theme (bars 232–39), only the orchestra cannot seem to manage it. After several false starts and an attack of bad temper (an important motif suddenly played tutti and *forte*, and in the wrong key, at bars 283–84), the orchestra gives up, and after a passage introducing a further note of uncertainty (bars 287–98), the movement concludes with the coda. This clearly pokes fun, both at the audience, for trying to second-guess where the music is going, and also at the orchestra, for seemingly being unable to get it 'right'. Haydn here seems to take up one strand of English caricature of the period making an audience the object of the satire, and by implication the viewer (or listener) himself or herself.[331] The unexpected pauses, shifts into the 'wrong' key, and 'false starts' of the last movement of the piano sonata in C major (Hob. XVI: 50), and to a lesser extent the equivalent movement of the

E flat major sonata (Hob. XVI: 52), take up this farcical element. These were compositions dedicated to a performer who is known to have had the capacity to laugh aloud at other music by Haydn, and perhaps this is what he was trying to provoke again in performer and listener alike. However, from the point of view of many listeners in England in the early 1790s, such obvious subverting of the primary material, as in the English tradition of caricature, might also be construed as accommodating a political dimension. Although the issues raised by such devices are usually comfortably resolved in Haydn's music during this period, these elements have an anarchistic aspect to them which, given the political background to the times in which they were first heard, must have been recognized and appreciated by a section of his audience. Haydn, it may be suggested, played a role in commenting on the affairs of this period, and persuading his listeners to address them, in the same humorous spirit as the Bunbury caricatures he so much enjoyed.

Passages in Haydn's instrumental music of the London period, such as those just mentioned, must frequently have resulted in barely stifled laughter at early performances, as in the documented case of Theresa Jansen performing 'Jacob's Dream'. In correspondence Haydn indicated how he had to 'change many things for the English'.[332] What appealed to an English sense of humour was doubtless one of the 'things' which he felt required changing. Obviously one of the factors which initially appealed to English audiences in Haydn's music was his capacity for wit and humour. But a component of his overwhelming success when actually writing with English audiences uppermost in his mind was turning this quality into one – to borrow a term derived from Leopold Mozart's advice to his son – with the right 'accent'. Haydn's evident appreciation of English visual culture provided him with indications just how this might be managed.

CHAPTER SEVEN

'Picture after picture':
The Creation and *The Seasons*

1. Creating Waves

When Haydn returned to Vienna in 1795, symphonic composition had ceased to be a priority for him. On the title-page of his last symphony (No. 104), he wrote, with a decisive note of finality, 'The 12th which I have composed in England', as though to draw a line under this aspect of his achievement. Henceforth Haydn had in mind grander projects to safeguard his reputation.

Music for voices, rather like the exhibitions of modern history paintings (by Copley, Loutherbourg and others) Haydn had attended in London, was a means of reaching still larger audiences. Voices allow greater scope for rhetoric, thereby permitting artists to stir intellects and sensibilities in favour of the common good, as Shaftesbury (an author read by Haydn) had advocated at the beginning of the century. A further incentive in this direction came from notions of the role of music in the service of the state, stemming from France. Haydn owned a German edition of one of the most influential writings advocating such changes, the *Voyages du jeune Anacharsis*, a dialogue set in Plato's time, by the Abbé J.J. Barthélemy, a former keeper of the king's Cabinet de Médailles.[1] Here, the case for music promoting public virtue is argued, but only in relation to vocal compositions. Barthélemy's argument has been seen as a factor in J.-L. David's conspicuous use of music in Republican ceremonial of the 1790s and possibly even in the early development of national ritual in the United States.[2] However, Barthélemy disapproved of devices like flutes imitating the song of nightingales, finding them a distraction from society's real needs.[3] Since *The Creation* features exactly this imitation, it seems possible that Haydn, whilst taking on Barthélemy's case for the social utility of music, sought to disprove this view by delighting in the very popularity of such imitations, and by using them as an expression of the diversity of God's creation.

Before settling back into Viennese life, Haydn had been principally celebrated as a composer of instrumental music. However, he himself had always recognized that it was vocal music which commanded greater universal respect.[4] The experience of hearing Handel's oratorios performed by enormous forces in London, much larger than the composer himself had anticipated, allowed him to foresee what it would be like to work on a monumental scale. His contact in 1793 with van Swieten, who organized performances of many choral works in Vienna, encouraged him to start looking for a suitable vehicle for his talents.[5] Salomon also urged him in this direction in 1794–95, conscious that the development of choral societies in Britain would soon require works other than those presented by Handel to maintain interest on the part of both performers and audiences. The project to set Selden's *Mare Clausum* seems to have been an early move in this direction, but had to be abandoned.[6] But when Salomon proposed setting an old libretto on the subject of the Creation, Haydn's imagination seems to have been fired. Apparently written for Handel, though rejected by him, the libretto was probably rediscovered by Thomas Linley, perhaps in the archive of the Drury Lane Theatre.[7]

Ostensibly Haydn's principal duty on returning to Austria in 1795 was the composition of an annual mass to celebrate the name-day of Princess Marie Hermenegild, the wife of his new patron, Prince Miklós II. The six masses Haydn wrote between 1796 and 1802, however, can hardly have been the kind of vocal composition he had been considering in response to the entreaties of van Swieten and Salomon. These were works which satisfied religious conviction and obligations to his patron; they were not conceived at the time of composition as the kind of music to secure his reputation beyond his lifetime. As settings of the Catholic liturgy they were precluded from ready acceptance in Protestant countries. At least three of them were also conceived as responses to topical and local, rather than universal, concerns: the *Missa Sancti Bernardi de Offida* (probably written in 1796) for the beatification in May 1795 of St Bernard, a Capuchin monk with a reputation in Austria for sanctity and devotion to the sick and poor (his name-day almost coincided with that of the Princess); the *Missa in tempore belli* ('Mass in the Time of War', written in 1796) for the war with France (a call for general mobilization, forbidding talk of peace until the enemy had been expelled from Austrian territory, having been made by the government in August 1796); and the *Missa in angustiis* (literally 'Mass in Time of Anguish', of 1798) for the unstable strategic situation caused by the rise of Napoleon, in particular his attempts to establish a colony in Egypt. Haydn's interest in this last development is evident from his acquisition of an English plan of the battle of Aboukir, at which Nelson successfully routed the French fleet near Alexandria in 1798.[8] However, the very fact that these settings had an element of topicality about them probably served to provide them at their first performances with congregations particularly well predisposed to listen fervently. Haydn, anticipating this, may have sensed opportunities to satisfy this fervour with powerful emotional and dramatic effects, and to experiment in his native country with the kind of pictorialism with which he had captured audiences in London.

Although all six masses were widely successful, their musical formation may be seen as an extension of Haydn's symphonic development during the London period, not merely in formal terms, but also in their extensive use of out-of-the-ordinary musical devices, sufficiently captivating to exert a powerful hold on the imaginations of listeners, with the potential for suggesting a visual dimension. The formula of a slow introduction (used in four of the masses) is one obvious aspect of Haydn's late mass style owing something to the conception of the symphony developed for London audiences by 1795. Haydn had already used slow introductions in earlier masses, but in the works of the post-London period these musical prologues, with their more adventurous harmonic changes and darker textures, generate suspense and mystery as gripping as any in the equivalent sections of the late symphonies. In the last mass, the *Harmoniemesse* of 1802, the whole of the opening Kyrie was set as an immense and mysterious slow movement, extending the moment of suspense for the work's earliest audiences beyond what might reasonably have been anticipated. In all these introductory slow sections, sensations of apprehension and even vulnerability, such as Haydn himself may have experienced in viewing works in England, for example the prints he acquired after paintings by Fuseli, were given musical expression, only now heightened with the additional fervour of devotional conviction, which had largely been irrelevant to the works he had composed for concert performance in London. The *Missa in tempore belli*, in particular, reveals Haydn charging the music with features inspired by aesthetic trends studied in London, though given renewed vigour in a religious context. As in compositions of the later London years, the background of the war, its devastation and uncertainty, is crucial here. The evocative imitation of gunfire in the Agnus Dei of this mass, conveyed through a rapid motif repeated several times on solo timpani, gradually increasing in volume, provides one clear example of how the armed conflict with France intruded on the compositional process. Haydn told Griesinger that this should sound 'as if one heard the enemy approaching in the distance'. Like a number of the military associations in some of the late symphonies, conceivably intended to project images of battlefields or of victorious forces into the minds of early listeners, this example of musical painting was perhaps initially suggested by the analysis of the sublime by Burke, who specifically gave the example of the noise of artillery arousing 'a great and aweful [*sic*] sensation in the mind' in his discussion of 'Sound and Loudness' in his treatise on *The Sublime and Beautiful*, which Haydn owned.[9] The same source may have suggested the notion of writing a composition based on the theme of fear, the starting point of the *Missa in angustiis*. In the somber, restless and at times overpowering settings of the Kyrie and the Benedictus of this mass, Haydn seems to have set out to overwhelm listeners with sensations of anguish so forceful that they are not simply heard, but are almost felt physically.[10] In the *Missa in tempore belli*, a loud military-style fanfare heralds the first setting of the words 'Dona nobis pacem' (Grant us peace), followed by a contrasting second setting performed *pianissimo* (immediately before the closing section of the mass, marked *più presto*), a juxtaposition which in the context of the tense political situation of the time may be understood to allude to the government's ban on peace talks, tempered by every listener's inner longing for an end to the crisis.[11] The setting of the *Et incarnatus est* in the same mass also treats the words of this section in a highly distinctive idiom. Usually settings of this section imply reverence for the relevant article of Christian faith by giving the words a beautiful melodic line. In the *Missa in tempore belli*, however, the setting conveys not just awe and mystery, appropriate to the words, but also a palpable sense of fear and apprehension, which would certainly have stuck some early listeners as unconventional. Melodically, harmonically and rhythmically the music has much in common with one of Haydn's final compositions of the English years, the eerie setting of *The Spirit's Song*, to words by Anne Hunter. Both compositions are marked *Adagio*, are in triple time in a minor key, and open with a mysterious ascending motif in unison.[12] In the song, with its unsettling harmonic shifts and dark textures, Haydn convincingly captures the sense of mystery and unease of the spirit waiting at the tomb. In using a similar musical language in the mass, he put the emphasis on conveying sensations of fear of the supernatural, a novel aesthetic objective in the context of late eighteenth-century settings of the mass, but one frequently pursued by artists interested in the sublime in the London he had left little more that a year earlier.

In 1796 Haydn had a further opportunity to act on his knowledge of English aesthetic currents, when a group of travelling performers brought a programme of plays and singspiels to Eisenstadt, including a tragedy on the life of Alfred the Great.[13] This was a German translation of a play by Alexander Bicknell, published in 1788, called *The Patriot King, or Alfred and Elvida*. Bicknell had previously written a *Life of Alfred* (1777), which provided the inspiration for a famous painting by Benjamin West, *Alfred Dividing the Loaf* (1779).[14] Boydell commissioned it for Stationers' Hall, his first donation to a public building. Given Haydn's interest in West, the composer would almost certainly have known about Alfred either from the painting itself, or from the print Boydell published after it in 1782.[15] Haydn probably also knew something of Arne's *Alfred* (1740), even if the only music he actually heard from this masque was the ever-popular 'Rule Britannia!'.[16] The words for *Alfred* were in part by James Thomson, whose celebrated poem, *The Seasons*, was later used as the basis of the libretto for Haydn's oratorio of the same title. Arne's *Alfred* was revived in 1773 with celebrated sets by Loutherbourg. Haydn could not, of course, have seen this; but he knew enough about this artist to have heard something about them, and this may have played a part in his conception of the music he composed to accompany Bicknell's play in 1796. Haydn provided three items: a bellicose chorus of Danes; an aria for the Guardian Spirit, providing comfort for Elvida, and a duet for Alfred and Odun. Of these, it is the magical aria, in which Elvida responds to the Spirit with spoken text, that shows the composer thinking back to ways in which music in England was often used to reinforce a sense of image. It is scored for a sextet of wind instruments, the same combination Grétry had used in the magic picture scene in *Zémire et Azor*, a work that Haydn had performed in the 1780s.[17] In both compositions, the unusual combination of instruments and other common features serve to heighten the ethereal relationship between the supernatural and earthly worlds. Haydn perhaps recalled the famous scene from Grétry's opera at about the time he left England because preparations were being made to perform it the following season at the King's Theatre. It had previously been successful in London, and its libretto had been reworked for *Selima and Azor*, an opera by Thomas Linley, for which Loutherbourg again provided the sets.

Haydn used another unusual combination of wind instruments to express the connection between the supernatural and the earthly on one further occasion not long after returning from England. This is the instrumental *Introduzione*, composed as an insertion between Nos 4 and 5 of the vocal version of the *Seven Last Words*, a piece of grief-stricken intensity and chilling reflection, evidently conceived to enable listeners to contemplate Christ's suffering, and also to call to mind the image of his body expiring on the cross. It was Haydn's experience of hearing a performance, in Passau in 1794, of the orchestral version of his *Seven Last Words*, arranged as a cantata, which provided a further indication that it was time to reconsider the genre of oratorio and exploit its possibilities. This arrangement impressed him, at least in the sense that it persuaded him that his own music, originally written for orchestra, was well suited to being sung. The addition of a text for the listening public might be deemed to lend further expression to Haydn's original series of meditations on Christ's death on the cross, and certainly helped audiences to visualize the scene. Haydn, however, knew he could do it better than the version he heard in Passau. A vocal version of his own devising would ensure that he himself gained from it commercially, rather than another party. Haydn took a copy of the cantata to van Swieten, who was only too willing to rearrange the words, recognizing that at last there was an opportunity to broaden the appeal of a genre of composition for which he had special enthusiasm, oratorio, by persuading the most renowned composer of the time to devote his energies to it. The collaboration proved a most fertile one, at least initially.

Although Haydn felt he needed van Swieten's literary expertise to furnish him with appropriate texts for setting to music, it does not follow from this that van Swieten contributed much more to the project than this, though the two men doubtless discussed their aesthetic objectives in working with each other. Van Swieten certainly provided Haydn with suggestions for setting the words in both *The Creation* and *The Seasons*, but Haydn ignored them more often than following them. It may be surmised from this that Haydn already had a good idea what he wanted to achieve before discussing these projects with the

Baron (even though he may as yet have been unsure exactly how to effect his aims), and that his initial inspiration came in part from his observations of London audiences, what they liked and the associations they made while listening to music. What is clear about the libretto Salomon gave Haydn, derived from Milton's *Paradise Lost*, was that Haydn evidently liked it. Had Haydn simply been concerned with composing an oratorio on the theme of the Creation story, as related in Genesis, he might well have asked van Swieten to prepare a text directly from the Bible. The libretto originally prepared for Handel, however, conveyed with it a considerable range of desirable features, not the least of which was its connection with Milton's poem, one of the best-known works of English literature, especially admired for the scope and distinction of its imagery. According to his own account, van Swieten's task was essentially to 'dress the English poem in German fashion', and to cut its length from almost four hours to one which even the most easily bored members of a late eighteenth-century audience might be expected to endure.[18] Haydn's experience of England showed him what a vital cultural heritage Milton had bequeathed. The same was true of Thomson, whose *Seasons* was not only read across most of Europe, but was reckoned the second most pictorial poem in English. Haydn would have recognized that both poems owed part of their popular success to their pictorialism. It was this feature he could extend further.

Throughout the eighteenth century, artists active in England found themselves drawn to Milton's writings. The portrait-painter and theorist Jonathan Richardson and his son wrote a commentary on *Paradise Lost* (1734), in which they argued that Milton in writing the poem set out to impress on the mind images in much the same way as a painter.[19] Richardson's main approach to Milton had already been set out in a treatise on *The Science of a Connoisseur* (1719), where he suggested everyone might be improved by amassing 'a fine Collection of Mental Pictures':

> what I mean is furnishing the Mind with Pleasing Images; whether of our own forming, or borrow'd from Others. This is a Collection which every one may have, and which will finely employ every vacant moment of ones time. I will give a Specimen or two of these in the Delicate, and in the Great kind, or to speak more like a Connoisseur, in the *Parmeggiano*, and in the *Rafaelle* Taste; and both out of Milton who alone is able to supply us abundantly.[20]

Richardson then quotes descriptive passages by Milton which he considered to have an effect on the mind very similar to looking at a real picture. In the later commentary, the Richardsons treat Milton primarily as an interpreter of visual phenomena, the main scenes in *Paradise Lost* being referred to as 'pictures', a list of which is actually added to the volume. Milton himself 'in all he Writes ... is a *Painter*, he Directs his Discourse to the Eye, next to the Heart, he Sets the Picture of Things Before us with all the Strength and Beauty that Words can *Image*.[21] At different stages in the commentary, Milton is compared with major artists. For example, to emphasize the classical inspiration of Milton's 'Grace, Majesty and Simplicity', the authors suggest that the poet has these qualities 'to a Degree beyond what We have ever found in Any Modern Painter or Sculptor, not Excepting *Rafaelle* Himself.'[22] In discussing the Adam and Eve 'picture', the form of their bodies compares with the 'Best of the *Greek* sculptors, *Rafaelle, Guido, Coreggio, Parmeggiano* ...'.[23] According to the Richardsons, when Milton was in Italy, before he went blind, he took some note of the great visual creations of the Renaissance, which in subsequent writings proved a fertile source of stimulation.[24] The Richardsons also hint that the painterly aspects of *Paradise Lost* are matched by musical ones, a perception which had consequences for the future.[25]

Two of the most noted composers working in eighteenth-century England, Handel and Arne, set texts by Milton. Parts of Handel's *L'Allegro* and *Il Penseroso*, which Haydn may have known, were especially admired for their pictorial effects.[26] As suggested in the last chapter, Haydn probably knew Arne's *Comus*, and was certainly familiar with artistic interpretations of the masque since he owned prints illustrating two of the principal episodes. The commentary by the Richardsons helped prepare illustrators for taking up Milton's work. During the course of the century, the appearance of interpretations of Milton in the visual arts increased in frequency. Burke's quoting of passages from Milton in his treatise on *The Sublime and Beautiful*, cited to elucidate the concepts he describes, alerted artists still further to the visual possibilities of *Paradise Lost*.[27] The first painting on a Miltonic subject to be shown at the Royal Academy was by Barry, Burke's protégé. *The Temptation of Adam*, exhibited in a prominent position in 1771, was favourably received.[28] In the catalogue to the exhibition Barry was at pains to emphasize that his source was Milton, rather than the Bible. The work perhaps inspired Reynolds, in his Discourse of 1778, to use Milton's description of Eve in *Paradise Lost* as an example of how, as in artistic sketches, much of the pleasure of experiencing such a work rests in what it leaves to the visual imagination, though a painter, 'when he represents Eve on canvas, is obliged to give a determined form, and his own idea of beauty distinctly expressed'.

When Haydn was in England, Barry returned to *Paradise Lost*, planning an extensive series of paintings, for which many sketches survive. Work on Fuseli's Milton Gallery was also begun at about the same time. These two projects were the most ambitious of several sets of illustrations to Milton, published or planned when Haydn was in London.[29] Three of these were by artists he is known to have admired, examples of their work having been acquired for his own collection: Stothard, Westall and Singleton.[30] Another artist represented in his collection, William Hamilton, executed some designs for *Paradise Lost* subsequently. And there were several others, including one by E.F. Burney.[31] The admiration of the artist's uncle, Dr Burney, for Milton is clear from several passages in his account of the Handel commemorations of 1784 and in the *General History*.[32]

Haydn therefore would have had every opportunity not only to appreciate the English preoccupation with Milton, but also how the poet had come to occupy a key position in visual culture of the period of his English visits. The tremendous appeal of Milton at this time was partly a result of the early favourable response to the French Revolution. Milton had himself been a republican, as was his biographer of this period, William Haley, who was friendly with several artists. By portraying the dignity and primacy of Man, *Paradise Lost* was perceived to lend support to republican ideals, which explains why an illustrated edition of the poem was published in Paris in 1792. In the later 1790s, interest in illustrating Milton temporarily waned as the war with France progressed, and the grander projects conceived earlier either failed, as in the case of Fuseli, or dried up, as with Barry. The main explosion of interest in illustrating Milton therefore coincided closely with Haydn's stay in England. Given Haydn's evident interest in English visual culture, it is reasonably clear why an old libretto based on *Paradise Lost* should have come to the fore at this time, and why Haydn should have taken a special interest in it.

Like Milton, Thomson was a poet whose works were closely associated with visual culture. As early as 1756, only eight years after Thomson's death, the historian of poetry, Joseph Warton, wrote that 'the Seasons of Thomson have been very influential in diffusing a taste for the beauties of nature and landscape', and even selected a number of episodes from the poem worthy of being turned in paintings.[33] Unlike many of his contemporaries, for whom it ranked far behind history painting, Warton esteemed landscape, arguing that 'Titian thought it no diminution of his genius, to spend much time in works of [this] species'.[34] Whilst promoting developments in popular taste in landscape, both in painting and gardening, it was recognized that Thomson's verse itself owed much to study of painting, especially landscape painting. In his last work, *The Castle of Indolence* (1748), he specifically invoked the names of the most celebrated landscape painters, Claude, Poussin, and Rosa, and also Titian, signalling an appreciation of colour.[35] Thomson himself had a modest collection of prints after Old Master paintings, as well as essential reference works on the visual arts, including a translation of Le Brun's essay on the Passions, Dubos's *Réflexions critiques*, and the major writings of de Piles.[36] From prints and his experience of Italy he knew the major sculptures of the Western tradition and inserted descriptions of some of them into his poetic landscapes. Thomson's greatest debt to the visual arts, however, was the scheme for his most celebrated work, *The Seasons*, the subject of which, with its division into four parts, had provided inspiration for numerous painters throughout Europe since the Renaissance, in many formats. No self-respecting painter in France by the first half of the eighteenth century could afford not to make his contribution to what almost amounted to a genre in its own right.[37]

Very often in this tradition the seasons are represented as personifications, who (following the Homeric *Hymn to Apollo*) are shown dancing to Apollo's music.[38] Haydn knew a variant of this theme at Eszterháza, where the ceiling of the *salon* is devoted to Apollo and in the corners of the room are representations of the Seasons. But in London he would have been bombarded with it. In the four designs by William Kent for *The Seasons*, which served to illustrate many editions of Thomson's poem between 1730 and 1782, episodes from the poem are set in landscapes with personifications shown in the sky; Apollo is featured in 'Summer'. Richard Wilson took up Thomson's challenge, 'who can paint the lover, as he stood, Pierced by severe amazement, hating life', with his *Celadon and Amelia* (1765), illustrating one of the set narratives of *Summer*, in which Celadon mourns the loss of his beloved Amelia, killed by lightening.[39] The composition became well known through Woollett's engraving, published in 1766. This seems to have been the earliest example of a picture derived from the poem, not intended to act as an illustration to an edition of the text. In the 1780s, this and the other set narratives from Thomson were taken up by, among others, Kauffman, strengthening the sense that the poem had a visual existence, independent of the text itself.[40] Her own version of *Celadon and Amelia* with its pair, *Damon and Musidora*, for example, were engraved by Bartolozzi and published in 1782. During his long career, Bartolozzi and his pupils were responsible for many prints illustrating *The Seasons*, not necessarily directly relating to Thomson's poem, but including various sets of personifications and fancy scenes, indicating how the theme gained increasingly popularity as the century progressed.[41] For example, one of Haydn's favourite artists, Westall, designed a *Spring* and *Summer*, engraved by Bartolozzi, published in 1791. Among Bartolozzi's other related engravings was one after Gainsborough's *Lavinia*, illustrating another of the poem's set narratives. This painting, published in 1790, was an early commission for Macklin's Poets Gallery. As Warton implied, once the poem itself became a kind of set book for those of discrimination, readers became accustomed to using it as a standard for judging the beauties of the natural world and sentiments associated with them, desiring to see the ideal realized.

In the early 1790s, many of the artists represented in Haydn's collection contributed to handsome editions of the poem. As with *Paradise Lost*, the most intense period of illustration of *The Seasons* coincided with the composer's English period. The year 1793, for example, saw a number of new editions featuring illustrations by Singleton, Stothard, Metz and William Hamilton.[42] Stothard contributed to an even grander edition in 1794. But perhaps the most seasoned illustrator of the poem was Hamilton, who provided fresh illustrations to editions in 1778, 1797 and 1802, as well as

1793. Haydn owned none of these, but his interest in illustration of this kind is evident from his purchase of Hamilton's set of months (1788), the compositions for which are close in spirit to his *Seasons* illustrations.[43] Indeed *The Seasons* was such a topical matter during this period that audiences found themselves automatically associating the richness of the pictorial world covered in Thomson's poem with the wealth of ideas featured in Haydn's symphonies of the period. After the first performance of Symphony No. 99 in February 1794, one reviewer apologized for the necessity of being brief, asserting that 'after all it may be best, when the *chef d'oeuvre* of the great HAYDN is the subject. "Come then, expressive SILENCE, muse his praise."'[44] In quoting the last line of the concluding *Hymn* from *The Seasons*, which it was assumed readers would know, the critic was suggesting not only that the experience of listening to the symphony was comparable to the totality of Thomson's huge poem – to its final line – but also that both works shared a pictorial quality, which recently published illustrations enabled everyone to appreciate, even those lacking imagination. Presumably one of Haydn's friends, perhaps the engraver Thomas Park (a later editor of *The Seasons*), identified the source of the quotation for him. Knowing that *The Seasons* was one of the most read poems in any language, and that it played a vital role in stimulating the visual sense in English musical audiences, would surely have been important factors in selecting a text for Haydn's second major musical collaboration with van Swieten. Since the composer himself knew that it was his music in particular which had effected comparison with Thomson's epic, it seems likely that the initial choice was his, and that his experience of English audiences was a crucial element in this. Van Swieten's knowledge of English taste was rather outdated by the time of their partnership. The struggle he had providing a parallel text in English for the oratorio (which following Haydn's practice in *The Creation* was a prerequisite for publication of the work) suggests that the poem may not have been his own choice, and that the idea came from Haydn. Indeed, it seems likely that Haydn may have been influenced in his choice of text by some knowledge of an earlier attempt to set Thomson's *Seasons*, a cantata in 20 movements by the Scottish composer Robert Barber, published in London in 1788.[45]

In setting parts of the two most iconic poems known to Western culture, both treating topics of immense scope and variety, Haydn was clearly making a bid to ensure the lasting survival of his own reputation.[46] His audacity in taking on such subjects, which most other composers had shunned, shows the extent of his ambition. But for the projects to work he needed to develop a form of musical expression which matched those features of the poems which attracted readers to them as he had particularly observed in England. This meant musical pictorialism, a realm which many critics already considered unworthy of composition, either because the notion was a distracting contradiction in itself, or because it pandered to the most vulgar kinds of taste.

Although some of Haydn's later acquaintances considered him a novice in the field of aesthetics, Haydn could hardly have been unaware of the kinds of objection this raised, but was intent on relying on his own judgement to determine how far he could go.[47] It may be argued that his principal concern, shared by van Swieten, was to sustain a universal popularity, to develop a mode of composition, which could be applauded on account of its scale and ambition, like history painting in the visual arts, but which simultaneously appealed to a very broad base, like the sentimental engravings produced in vast quantities in London. According to van Swieten's own account of the origin of the libretto for *The Creation*, it was Haydn's own instinct that the text he received from Salomon was suitable for him to set. The Baron simply agreed 'with the judgement *he* [Haydn] had made', and encouraged him to set the text since it provided *the* opportunity 'to demonstrate the whole range of his profound achievements and to express the full force of his inexhaustible genius'.[48] Although early sources indicate that it was van Swieten who was keen to build on the success of *The Creation* by embarking on a further oratorio, implying that Thomson's poem was his choice, this does not necessarily follow. The enthusiasm for another collaboration may have been the Baron's, but the choice of subject was probably Haydn's.

One witness of Haydn's activities during the composition of *The Creation*, the Swedish diplomat Silverstolpe, provides evidence of the composer relishing the pictorial aspects of his score, evidently convinced that it was possible to suggest images to listeners through music, even though he may have tried to make light of what he gauged some might think absurd. After playing the 'Representation of Chaos' to Silverstolpe (on the piano), Haydn remarked: 'You have certainly noticed how I avoid the resolutions that you would most readily expect. The reason is, that there is no form in anything [in the universe] yet.'[49] Later, Haydn showed Silverstolpe Raphael's first aria, saying: 'You *see* how the notes run up and down like the waves; *see* there too, the mountains that come from the depths of the sea?' Silverstolpe indicates that Haydn said this very much with his tongue in cheek. But the fact is that this is exactly what the music does and the passage in question is certainly serious in character. In testing excerpts from his score on discerning listeners, Haydn may have been trying to predict audience reactions to his pictorialism. He knew perfectly well that such devices were despised in some quarters, and therefore belittled his efforts in order to provoke a reaction. Whilst fully aware that some musical purists would dislike what he was doing, his real concern was to ensure that such a tidal wave of musical–visual effects would be comprehensible to and delight the general public.

A few years later Haydn recounted to Dies the experience of writing one of his earliest pieces for the stage, *Der krumme Teufel*. He claimed that in order to get the commission, his impresario, performing a comic role, made him improvise music at the keyboard to his actions:

'Suppose now that Bernadon has fallen into the water and is trying to save himself by swimming.' Then he shouts to his servant, throws himself on his stomach lying horizontally across the chair, makes the servant drag the chair backwards and forwards around the room, his arms and legs kicking like a swimmer, while Haydn expresses in six-eight time the play of the waves and the swimming. Abruptly Bernadon springs up, hugs Haydn, and virtually smothers him with kisses. 'Haydn, you're the man for me!'[50]

Haydn claimed to be 21 when this occurred. But the story, which the old Haydn remembered in such detail, shows that he was well equipped to devise music to express a visual dimension from the starting point of his career, and this was expected of him in order to succeed, or at any rate to succeed with music for *popular* theatre. Haydn told Dies that after two acclaimed performances the *singspiel* was banned.[51] However, the association of pictorial music with the popular, or even the vulgar, is implicit in the story, and explains why caution was necessary in employing this mode thereafter. The Haydn who returned to Vienna from England, flushed with success, could again afford to risk such musical improprieties, confident that his chosen idiom, and the taste with which it was employed, could persuade most listeners of his vision.

2. 'Pictures for the ear'

The first performances of *The Creation* proved enormously successful. Commentators were in no doubt that Haydn's achievement was in large measure a result of the power of the oratorio's music to convey vivid visual impressions of every aspect of Creation. In Wieland's poem praising the composition, which Griesinger reports gave the composer 'much joy', many of these images are listed. When it came to the creation of Adam and Eve, the poet did not mince words: 'We *see* the first-made couple *depicted* in thy sounds.'[52]

The earliest reviews not only acclaimed the composition, but readily pointed out its pictorial aspects, describing them in the language of the visual arts. One, following a packed performance of the oratorio in Berlin, attended by the King and Queen of Prussia, began by asserting that it was a work which can only be compared with itself, and 'Among all products of recent German Art', it is 'undoubtedly the most original and liberal':

> That there really is light, and that one who can create such a chaos can also create light when called on to do so, need hardly be mentioned. ... There is immeasurable worth in this tone-poem [*Tongemählde*], which can scarcely be compared with the slender brush strokes [*Pinseleyen*], lacking power and conviction, with which some incredible people ask the public to dine, to serve them with deaf old vegetables, warmed-up motifs

and old fugal steaks. No! This is no *Historia* of Susanna or Bathsheba that is being dished up, but the true imagination of a great minds which ought to, and does, inform the inner being of immense forces, gradually giving way to order. And in this spirit I see the whole work.[53]

The same reviewer went on to characterize the work as a kind of exhibition of paintings. The listener is encouraged to perceive the music just as the viewer might a series of exhibits:

Here one may see precisely how only a vivid imagination can create picture after picture [*Bild an Bild*], describing natural phenomena as easily and with as few strokes as they were painted [*mit wenigen Stricken zu mahlen*] originally. The most vital event has occurred; light is there, and at the same moment the artist delightfully conjures up wind and weather, snow and hail, and the text says each time: this was the storm, these were the strokes of lightning, this was the thunder, rain, snow. ... for the physical aspects of nature ... are brought together here as thoroughly as in an encyclopedia; and he who does not want to experience it directly himself, needs only look here, and if he knows how to look, he will find.[54]

The idea that *The Creation* might usefully be understood as a sequence of pictures was emphasized in a review of the score published in 1802. In this it is asserted that 'all Haydn's instrumental compositions are [of] an entirely new kind, created by him alone, of Romantic pictures for the ear [*romantischer Gemälde für das Ohr*], which cannot be conveyed in words or thoughts'. *The Creation* takes this notion a stage further: 'The poem is a collection of pictures [*eine Zusammenstellung von Bildern*], derived from the works of nature, and is like a sequence of paintings [*eine Folge von Gemälden*] before which we pass; by means of genuine music, these things are described and advanced.' Individual items show Haydn creating as a painter might. Discussing the opening aria in Part II, for example, the reviewer claims 'the composer could do nothing but *paint* the words of the poet [*als die Worte des Dichters ganz malerisch zu behandeln*]'.[55]

Initial reactions to *The Seasons* were not dissimilar. When Carpani called the oratorio 'a gallery full of paintings, all different in style, subject and colouring', he was restating a point of view already published in a review of the score which appeared in 1804: 'The overall impression of *The Seasons* is that of a gallery, an apartment of paintings, where the various pictures of natural objects are at the same time exposed to mindful reflection.'[56] After some criticism of composers who misuse 'musical tone-painting' (*musikalischer Malereyen*), the reviewer proceeds to discuss the entire oratorio, explaining why Haydn's particular kind of painting is acceptable. The painting starts at the outset, the Introduction, which van Sweiten's text says 'depicts the passage from winter to spring':[57]

We called the work under discussion ... a gallery of pictures, and we see this as the basis of the entire piece; we even see it as the basis for the cycle in which this artistic genre is and has to be framed ... The Overture ...

describes winter. Much may be said against any proposal to *paint* winter by musical means [*den Winter durch musikalische Mittel zu mahlen*], and if a composer were asked to undertake such a responsibility he would certainly complain, and the entire world would agree with him. ... 'How can one *paint* winter? How can one *depict* frost and cold, snow and ice, discomfort and the unpleasantness of hostile nature, which man, precisely through his enlightenment, succeeds in overcoming by artificially clothing his body, by heating his environment so that his love, his hate and all necessities may survive the winter?'

According to the reviewer, Haydn answers all such questions with conviction:

> The character of the ensuing *Vivace* [in the Overture] is raw, bleak seriousness; cold and severe, it displays icy tentacles which grip whatever cannot escape it. A shattering and a raging assault our ears, but only our ears, for all sensible folk have found safety; and this tone-painting turns into an exceptional piece of Romanticism of its kind [*diese Mahlerey zu etwas so ausgezeichnet Romantischen in seiner Art*], which we experience, not without the greatest, most opulent and most delectable sense of pleasure, and ever more joyously as we intellectually grapple with the fountainhead from which so much unfamiliar and exciting has whirled towards us.[58]

Indeed Haydn's unique success in this permits him to stand comparison with Michelangelo. Each individual 'picture' is subsequently described in the review. For example, the reader is told that, 'The ploughman appears, like a picture [*fast bildlich*], as he rushes to his field, striding behind his plough and along the lengthy furrows, whistling and sowing the seed in steady rhythm.'[59] Or again, in *Winter*, the scene of Hanne's story-telling is perceived as 'a work of antique art [*ein Werk antiker Kunst*], though the setting is from modern country-living'.[60] The process of breaking *The Seasons* down into a series of 'pictures' explains the detailed description Carpani was able to give his 'gallery': 'Four dominant pictures are shown among the smaller ones. The subjects of these larger pictures are: firstly, the snow, the ice and the North Wind; secondly, a summer storm; thirdly, a hunt; and fourthly, an evening gathering of country-people.'[61]

The visuality of Haydn's two last oratorios was evidently a source of delight for large numbers of listeners experiencing them at the time of the first performances. But there was also an increasing feeling that such reliance on musical painting was both detrimental to the art of composition and, because of its popular appeal, should be rejected as too vulgar. Following the earliest performance of *The Creation* in England, a press report dismissed it by suggesting that 'If it be again performed in this country, we recommend at least that the misnomer of CREATION be erased, and that of CHAOS *come again*, be substituted in its stead.'[62] The following year, a report of a performance of *The Creation* in Copenhagen pinpointed 'the paintings [*Mahlerein*] of the snowflakes (something visible!), of the roaring lions, the chirping larks, the cooing doves, the grieving nightingale (though the poet says that at that time nightingales did not yet grieve) and the *incessant painting* take us back to the days of Telemann, the creator of rainbows'.[63] The same journal, reporting earlier in the year on the first public performance of *The Seasons*, whilst admitting it to be moving and sublime, nevertheless again singled out examples of 'painting' for criticism: 'the imitation of the crowing cock at dawn [and] the exploding gun in the hunt represent for me a false notion of tone-painting in music, possibly even disgracing this heavenly art'.[64] In another leading journal a similar tone was set: 'it need not be questioned that this subject [the seasons] is best suited to the painter, then to the poet, and least of all to the composer'. The writer concedes that Haydn's painting successfully conveys images to listeners, even had the work included no words, and that this is undeniably delightful; but 'the predominant objects in nature are ... viewed by the poet [van Swieten] not in how they affect emotions, but merely as physical appearances in the natural world'.[65]

Criticism came to focus on the text of *The Seasons*, which was felt to be unworthy of the composer, and on the 'insignificant tone-paintings, for the existence of which the composer is least at fault'.[66] It is clear that a distinction was drawn in the minds of such reviewers between the tone-painting of the grander set pieces, like the Introduction to *Summer*, 'depicting the sunrise', which were recognized as conveying the emotional impact of such sights, and for which Haydn was generally praised, and the slighter musical imitations of individual creatures or plants, like the infamous frogs, which were considered degrading to music, and for which van Swieten received the blame. As one reviewer expressed it, 'the music in *The Seasons* has propelled to the ultimate degree what actually pertains to the realm of the pictorial through the association of ideas'.[67]

The theoretical underpinning of the notions expressed in these criticisms stemmed from the influential writings of Sulzer, Engel and others, whose names were occasionally invoked. Sulzer's *Allgemeine Theorie der schönen Künste* included sections on 'Tone-painting' (*Gemähld [in Musik]*) and 'Painting in Music' (*Mahlerey [Musik]*) in which, whilst it is admitted that some composers indulged in attempting to suggest images to the mind through music alone, this is really the sphere of poetry not music:

> Using only notes and rhythms, it is possible to imitate wind, thunder, the roar of the ocean, or the gurgle of a brook, a flash of lightening, and other such things. *Even* the most learned and skilled composers can be found doing this. But such painting *violates* the true spirit of music, which is to express the sentiments of feeling, not to convey *images of inanimate objects*. ...
>
> It is inconceivable to me how a man of Handel's talent could sink so low in his art by trying in an oratorio about the plague in Egypt to *paint* the jumping of locusts and other such tasteless things. A more nonsensical perversion of art can scarcely be imagined.[68]

Engel's *Über die musikalische Malerey* (1780) takes a much more positive view of the role of painting in music, but still emphasizes that 'the composer should always paint *feelings* rather than *objects* of feelings'.[69] According to Engel, however, it is possible for composers to 'suggest these objects to us by means of tones just as the painter tries to suggest his through colours'.[70] What he calls 'complete' painting 'brings the entire phenomenon before our perception ... Even colour is paintable. For the impression of a delicate colour bears some resemblance to the impression of a gentle tone on the soul.'[71] He illustrates his theory by citing a passage from Georg Benda's melodrama *Ariadne auf Naxos* (1774): 'The word "lion" merely stimulates a representation in my understanding; the picture of a lion actually places the phenomenon before my eyes. The word "roar" already has a sort of pictorial content; Benda's expression of it in *Ariadne* is an even more *complete painting* of a roar.'[72] This example was very relevant to *The Creation*, which also features a roaring lion.[73]

When van Swieten was preparing the libretti for Haydn's last two oratorios the notions of Sulzer and Engels were of course well known. They were closely repeated in one of the most authoritative musical compendia of the early nineteenth century, the *Musikalisches Lexikon* by H.C. Koch. In the article on 'Malerey', Koch emphasized that while music is capable of describing inanimate nature, this is largely undesirable because it is divorced from the true function of music, which is to stir the feelings. Only 'occasionally' can musical painting be justified, on the grounds that such cases relate directly to the expression of the inner soul.[74] Van Swieten could therefore rely on authorities like Sulzer and Engel to exonerate the possibility of musical painting, though he ignored their arguments concerning the wisdom of relying on it, perhaps because he assumed that the power of Haydn's music, even in musical painting, stirred the feelings in a manner (he believed) they sanctioned. As a provider of words, van Swieten may perhaps have been encouraged by references to Haydn in Grétry's *Mémoires*, published in 1789. The French composer argued that Haydn's instrumental works were like a huge dictionary, communicating such clear ideas that they yearned to be accompanied by words: 'Symphonic composers are like botanists who, having discovered a plant, wait for the physician to discover its properties.'[75] Possibly van Swieten, whose father had been the Empress Marie Theresa's doctor, saw himself as physician to Haydn's botanist. However, when the *Mémoires* appeared in German in 1800, their translator derided the notion that symphonies might be set to words. By the end of the century, though the analogy of music and the spoken word had been presented as incontrovertible in Kant's *Kritik der Urteilskraft* (1790), most critics, like Rochlitz, argued that music corresponded closely to emotions, with all their shades of expression. Language was denied this precise possibility because too many parts of speech may be considered simply essential mechanisms for conveying meaning, and had little to do with expressing emotionality in themselves.

But in evoking the visual in their collaboration, van Swieten and Haydn may be understood to have been trying to forge a new kind of aesthetic experience, which avoided the difficulties of the Grétry approach to Haydn, since the poetry inspired the music, not the other way round, but which nevertheless extended the impressions that listeners to Haydn's instrumental music had claimed to perceive. Both the aural and pictorial qualities extending from their approach were also consistent with the view that emotions were the main objective of music. In essays published at the time of the Haydn/van Swieten collaboration, Herder had taken Kant to task for ignoring music's appeal to man's inner feelings. The emotion stemming from this may be understood as the internal response to sensing natural phenomena, a process which leads to human awareness of notions such as truth, benevolence and beauty. The phenomena represented in *The Creation* and, even more so, in *The Seasons* certainly share this premise, as becomes clear by the end of both works. Although Herder put the emphasis on the power of music to draw out such emotions, referring to 'the clavichord within us which is our own inmost being', he had to raise the possibility of the pictorial playing a part in this, if only to dismiss it:

> A. Might it not be Castel's colour-keyboard, or a keyboard of visual shapes that is played within us?
> B. Visual shapes indeed! What have these to do with our inner responsiveness to emotional currents, vibrations and passions? You are implying that sounds *illustrate* things.[76]

Others, however, took this notion more seriously. The painter P.O. Runge developed a theory advancing the notion of a precise analogy between the musical octave and the colour spectrum.[77] After hearing a performance of *The Seasons* in 1803, Runge wrote: 'For the maintenance of one's pure nature and simultaneously for the innocence of one's mind', one must recognize that

> the symbolism of the proper poetry, i.e., the inner music of the three arts, in word, line and colour. ... Music, after all, is that which we call harmony in all the arts. Thus there must be music through words in a beautiful poem, just as there must be music in a beautiful picture and in a beautiful building or any kind of idea which is expressed through lines.[78]

The inspiration Runge drew from *The Seasons* is one measure of the impact that the oratorio was intended to make. The choice of subject and its musical treatment in this, as in *The Creation*, may have been Haydn's, but the conception of how both oratorios would work in the public sphere, and their aesthetic objectives, may in large part be attributed to his partner in the enterprise, van Swieten. Most of the adverse criticism which *The Seasons* received was directed primarily at van Swieten. He was one of the key figures in the cultural development of Austria in the last decades of the eighteenth century, best known today for his promotion of musical events in Vienna, including the championship of older, outmoded music (particularly works by J.S. Bach and Handel), and his enthusiasm for contemporary composers, like Mozart and Beethoven. As a man of the Enlightenment, for a time in charge of Austria's policy on education, van Swieten held a conviction that music was a key to ensuring that society remained cohesive, and did not fragment, as he believed had occurred in France.

Like most aristocratic patrons in his position, van Swieten's interests included the visual arts. As in music, however, his artistic tastes betray an unconventional concern with giving the forgotten a new lease of life. He was one of the first collectors, for example, who may be associated with the seventeenth-century Dutch painter Vermeer, whose *Allegory of Painting* was in his possession.[79] At this date Vermeer, whose name had then only recently been put into general circulation through the efforts of the Parisian dealer Lebrun, was an unusual painter to arouse interest.[80] Van Swieten's acquisition of this particular painting – a painting about painting, in the same way that Mozart's *The Impresario* was an opera about opera – suggests that he was probably extremely visually alert for his time. The picture depicts a painter at his easel, viewed from behind, painting a female model, who probably represents Clio, the Muse of History. She holds a trumpet, which may be interpreted as a symbol of fame. The painting is therefore concerned with the past and with issues of reputation. One element that van Swieten would have scrutinized is the map Vermeer painted on the back wall of the painter's studio. This is a real map, not dating from Vermeer's own time, but representing the Netherlands as it was in the sixteenth century (conceivably also the period intended for the costume of the painter depicted in the picture), ignoring the division between the Protestant north (which became an independent Republic) and the Catholic south (a territory which continued to be ruled as a province of the Habsburg Empire in van Swieten's time) of 1588.[81] An indication that the map was intended by Vermeer to be understood in terms of Habsburg politics comes from the chandelier, seen in front of it, which is decorated with a two-headed eagle, the imperial emblem of the Habsburg dynasty. It is usually considered today that Vermeer, a Dutch Catholic, was here making a point in relation to his art, perhaps nostalgically, about his own political sympathies and aspirations. Van Swieten, another Dutch Catholic, also owed his allegiance to the house of Habsburg. He assuredly recognized the political aspect of Vermeer's painting and probably identified with it. At the time he owned it, the Habsburg regents in the southern Netherlands (Archduchess Christine and Albert of Sachsen-Teschen) had recently been thrown out by the French, an event which would have lent the picture a particular kind of topicality for its owner.

Van Swieten's interest in Vermeer's picture may be seen as evidence of his visual alertness. As Prefect of the Imperial Library, he had access to the imperial collections of visual art, and certainly made use of them. A description of his apartment in the Hofburg in the diary of Count Zinzendorf indicates how this had direct access to the famous gallery of the Library, which Zinzendorf considered magnificent.[82] The Count was also struck with the Baron's tasteful interior decorations – he noted all the colour schemes – and recorded how the ladies in his party were entertained with prints from the imperial collection. In the 1780s, van Swieten's concerts actually took place in the splendid hall of the Imperial Library. Constructed in the 1720s after a design by J.B. Fischer von Erlach, the hall was decorated with a series of statues of the Emperor and his ancestors, and with frescoes by Daniel Gran forming an allegory of the imperial role in the promoting the arts.[83] Van Swieten presumably expected these paintings, which had been admired by Winckelmann, to remain a focus of attention during his musical performances. With the passing of the years, van Swieten became more intrigued by the possibilities of pictorialism in music, performing a number of Handel's compositions which had been criticized for this very element, including *Acis and Galatea* (1788), and *Alexander's Feast* (1790).[84]

When it came to libretti for Haydn's oratorios, van Swieten went so far as to provide the composer with notes elucidating his concepts for individual numbers, many encouraging Haydn to 'paint' the scenes. For example, in the opening number of *The Creation*, van Swieten, commenting on the words 'In the beginning God created', suggested to Haydn that 'The descriptive [*mahlerischen*] passages of the Overture could serve as the accompaniment to this Recitative.'[85] At the words 'And the spirit of God' which follow, van Swieten proposed that 'In the Chorus, the darkness could gradually disappear; but enough of the darkness should remain to make the momentary transition to light very effective.'[86] For the trio (no. 18), van Swieten advised that 'a simple and syllabic melody would probably be the best thing to have, so that the words can be understood clearly; but the accompaniment could paint [*mahlen*] the course of the brook, the flight of the bird and the quick movement of the fishes'.[87]

For *The Seasons* van Swieten's written suggestions to Haydn were even more plentiful and specific, though Haydn chose to ignore many of them. In one of Hanne's recitatives (no. 14), for instance, he states that 'I would like to hear also the murmuring of the brook, the humming of the insects, so that the *picture* given in Recitative may be fully realized.'[88] For the chorus at the end of 'Autumn', depicting the merry-making of the peasants, with drinking and dancing, van Swieten envisaged quite a complicated picture, with several activities taking place concurrently. For the passage he wrote mentioning various kinds of music-making – 'the tune of the fife', the roll of the drums, 'the squeak of the fiddle', 'the rattle of the hurdy-gurdy' and 'the bagpipes' long drone' – van Swieten advised Haydn that:

These instruments, when they are mentioned, must also be heard, and heard until the last entrance of the chorus. But since they are not grouped in one place but are spread throughout in various groups, they must have differing melodies and differing rhythms and come forth with the one or the other melody. Thus the fiddles could have the German *waltz*, the drums and pipes the 'Juch-he' and the lyre and bagpipes could sometimes be heard in the *waltzes*. The *Contratempi* should be useful in suggesting the varied places of the instruments.[89]

Van Swieten evidently wanted to suggest an expansive scene, with many groups of figures, viewed together, though in separately defined areas. To achieve this he urged Haydn to explore the possibility of a variety of distinct sonic effects overlapping each other, a suggestion which the composer only partly adopted. Van Swieten may have been inspired by paintings by Bruegel in the Imperial collection. Works like the *Battle between Carnival and Lent*, and more especially the *Peasant Dance*, both on view in Vienna since at least 1765, portray the kind of dense mixture of frenzied activity – including dancing, drinking and music-making, all taking place at the same time – which van Swieten wanted to convey in the oratorio. Van Swieten's attention would have been drawn to Bruegel's paintings when Chrétien de Mêchel was preparing the catalogue of the Imperial collection in the early 1780s, a rare example of systematic writing on Bruegel in the eighteenth century. Since Mechêl was working in close proximity to van Swieten, it seems very likely that the latter would have been stimulated to consider the compositional possibilities of such paintings at this time. He was probably not alone.[90]

3. Motion and the Dynamics of Light

The connection between van Swieten's work on *The Seasons* and Canova's design for the monument to Archduchess Christine (Fig. 5) has already been discussed in this book. The memorial's expression of the idea of life's progress, an innovation in eighteenth-century commemorations, and its reference to the ages of man perhaps owe their inspiration to plans for the oratorio. But there are other distinct aspects of the monument, as it was finally realized, which probably owed something to creative notions van Swieten and Haydn were exploring at the time Canova received the commission from Duke Albert: in particular the sense of movement Canova gave his figures, and his exploration of the contrast of light and darkness. But to analyse how these came into being and their significance, the context of this major commission must be taken into account.

In the treaty arranged in 1797 to prevent Austria falling to Napoleon, Austria conceded Habsburg possessions in Italy in return for the Veneto. As a consequence of this, Canova, a 'Venetian', travelled to Vienna in August 1798 to persuade Francis II to continue the pension he had previously received from the Venetian Republic. The Imperial court was more than prepared to grant the sculptor his pension and tried unsuccessfully to convince Canova to stay in Vienna permanently. Canova received several offers of commissions; but the only promising one was Albert of Sachsen-Teschen's proposal for a memorial to his wife, which offered him an opportunity to resuscitate his designs for the monument to Titian, abandoned in 1795.[91]

Christine had been the favourite daughter of Maria Theresa. The monument – a cenotaph rather than a tomb – was intended for the Augustinerkirche in Vienna, at the heart of the Hofburg, the collection of buildings which formed the powerhouse of the Austrian court. At the time of Canova's visit, the church had recently been stripped of its Baroque furnishings, leaving a rather spartan early fourteenth-century Gothic interior. This must have seemed a rather good prospect for the kind of monument Canova had planned for Titian – a major setting, with the best possible connections, and freshly prepared for new decorations. The site selected was against the outer wall of a bay in the middle of the south aisle of the nave; in other words, in a position where it might easily be seen by anyone visiting the church or attending services.

Austrians were desperate in 1798 for new public projects to bolster the standing of the Imperial family, which had recently received several setbacks.[92] The arrival of a major international figure in Vienna offered hope of something compelling. Canova, for his part, saw that creating a monument to Christine enabled him not only to complete earlier plans, but also to attempt something new. What was required was not a monument of the kind for which he had already made his name, like the tombs of Clement XIII and XIV, but a commemoration of love and devotion. Unlike the dynastic marriages of her sisters, Christine had been allowed to marry the husband of *her* choice, and the result seems to have been unusually close and heartfelt by the standards of most royal marriages in the eighteenth century. Although Canova originally envisaged quite a long identifying inscription for the Christine monument, the final, much simpler, inscription boldly displayed above the entrance-way says it all: 'Uxori optimae Albertus'.[93]

Before leaving Vienna, Canova probably discussed with Albert his objectives for the monument. Although the sculptor seems to have kept from his new patron the fact that he recycled an earlier design, Canova would have recognized that a straightforward adaptation of the Titian designs would not work. The drawing he sent to Vienna later in 1798 shows a clear relationship to the final plans for the Titian monument, but with several notable differences. The portrait medallion now shows Christine, and is supported by a female figure balanced by a putto bearing an olive branch. In the monument as it was finally erected the medallion gives the Archduchess's name and is framed with a snake biting its tail, an ancient allusion to immortality, sometimes used in Austrian monumental sculpture.[94] In the 1798 design, the seated Genius on the right now leans against a coat of arms. In the middle, the putti who had previously flanked the leading female figure have now become young girls. And on the left, the second mature female figure is no longer linked to a third female personification, but instead helps an elderly male figure, holding a lance and bent over with age, to climb the steps.

In a letter to Canova written in May 1799, Albert particularly commented on this male figure, suggesting the lance gave the mistaken impression that the figure represented a soldier. In a revised drawing sent to Albert in July 1799, Canova removed the lance and substituted a staff.[95] A sketch by Canova of this grouping shows the old man with a lance and therefore must have been executed by this date.[96] This is of great interest because it shows him toying with the idea of framing the group of the man and the supporting woman with two small children. Canova does not seem to have made anything more of these two children, though he opted to include a single male child tucked between the old man and the woman guiding him. This change strongly suggests that he was not trying to illustrate any fixed iconographic programme. Albert also wanted the composition to feature a lion behind the seated Genius. A suitably morose-looking lion was accordingly included in the revised drawing Canova sent to Albert, the form of the lion based on one he sculpted for the tomb of Clement XIII.

All of these features were included in the final monument, somewhat rearranged. As Canova told Albert in correspondence concerning the revised drawing he sent, his next task after agreeing the design was to make full-scale models of the figures and their setting so that they could be be examined in the round, with a view to ensuring that the arrangement was satisfactory.[97] Like other full-scale models, those for the Christine monument survive (incomplete) in Canova's home town of Possagno.[98] They were ready by July 1799 and exhibited in Rome later that year. In the monument in its final form, carved in marble and completed in early 1805, Canova included the floral swags hinted at in some of the earlier preliminary drawings; and also one further significant addition: a kind of carpet flowing from the entrance to the pyramid acts as a pathway leading the figures, seemingly inevitably, through the doorway of the tomb and to the darkness beyond.

Progress towards the completion of the Christine monument and its predecessor, the Titian monument, has been discussed in detail in order to emphasize important changes which took place in Canova's attitude towards the iconography of the two projects. In the Titian monument, the figures, mostly personifications, together formed an iconographic programme which viewers might ascertain and understand. This is what perceptive observers would expect to find in any grand tomb project, and what Canova assumed for his own early monuments. In the Christine monument, he was principally concerned with aesthetic considerations, ensuring that the figures were balanced, eye-catching and varied; any significance which may be attached to them is secondary. Canova's intentions concerning the monument's meaning were fluid. He himself implied that there was no allegorical significance in the figures: 'I hoped to group everything in a way that I could suggest *an immediate sense of movement*, rather than any allegory. Every artist has to be true to his own genius. ... For my part it seemed to be sufficient to represent *a sort of funeral procession* ... and if this purpose of mine can be clearly read, I am happy.'[99] Canova was here responding to Duke Albert's understandable attempt to make iconographic sense of the first design he was sent. Like other educated viewers of his time Albert tried to look for attributes which would identify what he believed must be personifications conveying a Christian message. For example, he thought at first that the old man being led by a woman might represent Charity, but recognizing that the motifs did not fit, he himself devised a meaning for them, calling the group 'Benevolence'. What is interesting about Canova's new approach – that is, beginning with the composition and the impression it creates, and worrying about its significance afterwards – is that he played on the expectations of the public to find concrete meanings by introducing motifs which were seemingly traditional. The lion, for example, might suggest to onlookers Fortitude. Had this been a medieval monument, the old man with staff might be taken for Sloth, a vice.[100]

In including this figure in the Christine monument, Canova may have hoped to tap quite a rich vein of popular associations in the mind of the public, without tying it down to any one. One of Aesop's fables, for instance, tells how an old man, weighed down by a load of wood, dropped the bundle and called on Death to release him from this burden; but when Death actually appears (usually represented in the form of a skeleton, seen frequently on eighteenth-century tombs), the man is so terrified that he pretends that all he wanted was help, the moral being 'Better to suffer than to die'.[101] Canova might also have sought to key into another story widely known in late eighteenth-century Europe, that of Belisarius, once a great general in the army of the Emperor Justinian, who through intrigue had been disgraced, blinded and reduced to penury. Canova's figure is also clearly blind. But despite these humiliations, so the story goes, Belisarius retained his dignity, which is what caught the imagination of the public in the Age of the Enlightenment, resulting in many painted versions of the story.[102] On the other hand, Canova's original intention to show the old man carrying a lance would have given audiences a reason for identifying the figure with Longinus, the centurion who stabbed the crucified Christ in the side. According to medieval legend, Longinus was cured of blindness when Christ's blood splattered his eyes.[103]

In eschewing any overt meaning in the figures on the Christine monument, Canova effectively took established religion out of the business of commemoration, even though the monument itself was erected in a church. In contrast to most eighteenth-century funerary monuments, there is nothing indisputably Christian about this one, and much which may be seen as pagan, such as the urn, the size of which points to the practice of cremation, not a

Christian custom at this date. The pyramid form itself may be seen in this light. Although the pyramid had long been understood as a Christian symbol of the life everlasting, by the time he modelled the Christine monument, a decade after conceiving the Titian monument, the form had been secularized under pressure from the French Revolution, gracing, for example, displays of the *Declaration of the Rights of Man*. This was anathema to the Church. Napoleon's attempt to acquire the real pyramids (coinciding with Canova's discussions with Duke Albert) and subvert their history for his own aims during his Egyptian campaign blighted any chance of the pyramid being reinfused with Christian principle. In view of these pagan associations, it is not surprising that one early commentator referred to the Christine monument as 'a scene from Sophocles carved at that time'. Perhaps Canova was responding in his avoidance of Christian symbols to one of the chief outcomes of the Enlightenment in Austria, the way Joseph II had succeeded in severely reducing the authority of the Catholic Church throughout his country; but it seems more likely that the de-Christianization of the monument was a result of trying to put into effect new creative aims.

Canova himself admitted that his overriding intention was to suggest a sense of *movement* through a procession of varied figures. This was evidently a notion that grew on him since it does not appear in the early bozzetti for the Titian monument; and the idea itself developed as Canova added more figures. Most funerary sculpture in the Western tradition shows static figures, which may communicate with one another but are rooted to the spot, illustrating allegorical programmes.[104]

The representation of motion itself in the procession – slow, but sure and dignified – is one of Canova's greatest achievements. Since the figures are principally seen from behind, he encourages observers, in viewing the monument, to identify with the procession, and join the figures on their journey towards the darkened abyss, a clear visual metaphor for life's progress towards death. Doorways on tombs, signifying the transition from this life to the next, may be traced back to ancient funerary monuments; Canova himself had featured one in the tomb of Clement XIII. In the Christine monument, however, the doorway takes on an entirely new significance since one can see through it to the space beyond. The space itself is unlit, appearing completely dark and void.[105] What is intriguing about this is that it hardly represents the traditional Christian imaging of the afterlife. The contrast in the monument between the light of this world and the darkness of the next is extremely potent. But by implying that the hereafter represented nothingness (being entirely devoid of light), Canova turned his back on the traditional Christian position. The point at which he fixed on this solution is hard to determine, because his intention is unclear in the bozzetti and drawings. It seems to have become concrete only during early stages of working on the monument in its Viennese manifestation. This also applies to the idea of a procession which represents life's progression, the figures covering all ages, from the most youthful to the old and infirm.

Canova's unprecedented depiction of forward motion in the Christine monument arguably owes its origins to the interest in motion in Haydn's late oratorios, especially *The Seasons*, on which the composer and van Swieten had probably just started work when Canova visited the Imperial court in 1798.[106] Motion was a key feature of Thomson's poem on which the oratorio was based and became a theme of overriding concern as the project unfolded. It would not have been difficult for Canova to grasp this in his dealings with the Imperial court: the very notion of representing movement, convincingly, and as a fitting expression of man's progress, became a key issue for composers and artists in Western culture from this point onwards.[107] Canova's spectacular use of light and darkness in the monument was also conceivably inspired by a major Viennese aesthetic preoccupation at the time he accepted the commission.

Of all the pictorial effects in Haydn's late oratorios, the one which made the most immediate and lasting impact on the public was the creation of light at the beginning of *The Creation*. The first performances were given for the benefit of Viennese society in April and May 1798. An eyewitness provides a vivid description of its reception:

> No one, not even ... Swieten, had seen the page in the score at which the origin of light is portrayed. This was the only part of the work which Haydn kept hidden. I think I can see his face even now, as this section was played by the orchestra. Haydn had the expression of someone who is considering biting his lips, either to cover his embarrassment or to keep a secret. And in the point where light shone for the first time, one might have said that rays shone from the composer's fiery eyes. The ecstasy of the electrified Viennese was so extensive that the orchestra could not proceed for several minutes.[108]

Almost all early accounts of the oratorio comment in particular on the power of Haydn's music to suggest to listeners the actual experience of sensing light being created. Griesinger reports that it was usual to break into applause at the moment of the creation of light at performances in Vienna.[109] Zelter wrote: 'That there *really* is light, and that one who can create such a chaos can also create light when called on to do so, need hardly be mentioned.'[110] To heighten the sense of exhilaration, some performances in the early nineteenth century are known to have kept the lighting in the venue down low for the Introduction to the oratorio, representing Chaos, turning up the gas-lamps to maximum brilliance at the appropriate moment.[111]

Haydn, whose previous career (as indicated earlier in this book) had thoroughly prepared him for this aspect of the undertaking, achieved this famous effect through what is seemingly the simplest of means: contrasting two sonic bases. The oratorio begins with a long unison C, sustained across the entire orchestra, suggesting the emptiness of the void which preceded the first act of Creation. The ensuing Prelude, which van Swieten called 'The Representation of Chaos', establishes a basic tonality of C minor, exploiting many harmonic and rhythmic ambiguities. This relies on numerous chromatic shifts and phrases, frequent and unusual dynamic variations, and a muted range of orchestral colours. Haydn evidently wished to create a dark and destabilizing impression in the minds of listeners. Playing it through to a friend in 1797, he explained his main compositional device: 'You will surely have noticed how I avoid the resolutions that you might well anticipate. The reason is that as yet there is no form in any thing.'[112] When form does arrive, coinciding with the last word of the phrase 'and there was *Light*', Haydn prepares by reducing the dynamic to *pianissimo* and the instrumentation to just strings, and then instantly changes the mood by introducing the full orchestra, playing a densely scored, *fortissimo* C major chord: the void is filled by dazzling white light and its impact is truly magnificent. The brilliance of the first act of Creation is conveyed through the brilliance of the sound picture. Something indisputably visual was presented unambiguously in music through a sudden harmonic and dynamic change, which thrilled early audiences. Considering its success, the device might well have been drawn to Canova's attention shortly after the first performances, encouraging him to adapt it for use in his monument to the music-loving Archduchess.

The striking audacity of Haydn's representation of the creation of light would have meant more to early audiences than an illustration to an Old Testament story. In a single chord, Haydn reconciled the most important basis of traditional Christian aesthetics with the eighteenth-century concept of Enlightenment (*Aufklärung*), whose proponents had generally found organized religion an impediment to humanity's progress. Haydn's musical gesture is a celebration of God in the same way that the stained glass of churches throughout Christendom acts as a commemoration of God by decorating light itself, which traditional Christianity had considered one of the clearest manifestations of Christ, that is God in his incarnation as Man. When Haydn stood in St George's Chapel, Windsor, admiring the gleaming window depicting the *Resurrection*, designed by West, he doubtless considered its function in this respect. He may even have seen a connection with his own numerous settings of the line 'Light from light' (*lumen de lumine*) from the Credo of the Mass.

In *The Creation*, however, Haydn found the means to express the connection between light and God more succinctly by resorting to Burke's ideas on the sublime, perhaps following a lead suggested by Sulzer.[113] Burke not only advocates 'A sudden beginning ... of sound' as having the power to rouse, but, in his section headed 'Light', specifically mentions 'a quick transition ... from darkness to light' as provoking the greatest of effects.[114] He continues by arguing that:

darkness is more productive of sublime ideas than light. Our greatest poet [Milton] was convinced of this; and indeed so full was he of this idea, so entirely possessed with the power of a well-managed darkness, that in describing the appearance of the Deity, ... he is far from forgetting the obscurity which surrounds the most incomprehensible of all beings ...

Burke illustrates his point by (mis)quoting two passages from *Paradise Lost* describing 'the divine presence'. He concludes from these that 'Extreme light, by overcoming the organs of sight, obliterates all objects, so as in its effect exactly to resemble darkness.'[115] An understanding of the relevance of Burke's notion of a close aesthetic relationship between light and darkness to Haydn's conception of the creation of light was probably a starting point for Canova's own conception of darkness and infinity in the Christine monument.

The Creation, however, does not need to be experienced in terms of Christian aesthetics. Its light is also the light of a new order, propounding freedom and justice. This is the light Paine used as a metaphor for truth in the *Rights of Man* (1792): 'such is the irresistible nature of truth, that all it asks ... is the liberty of appearing. The sun needs no inscription to distinguish him from darkness; and no sooner did the American governments display themselves to the world, than despotism felt a shock, and man began to contemplate redress.'[116] Haydn's is also the light Jefferson later promulgated in his design for the dome of the library of the University of Virginia (1812–26), natural sunlight symbolizing the spread of knowledge throughout the world.[117] Both Paine and Jefferson were, of course, drawing on a tradition of using light to express human aspiration, the 'illimitable freedom of the human mind' as Jefferson put it, to which Masonic thinking made an indispensable contribution. Novello, discussing Mozart's cantata *Dir, Seele des Weltalls, O Sonne* (1785) with Abbé Stadler in 1829, reports the latter to have found in 'the Masonic ode' 'the first germ of the idea of introducing a *piano* and *forte* to the expression of the word "Light", to give more effect by the sudden contrast – which idea Handel had before used in his *Samson* and Haydn afterwards used, with such extraordinary effect, in the oratorio of *The Creation*'.[118] In *Die Zauberflöte*, another Masonic composition, Mozart devised many other ways of expressing musically the contrast between light and darkness, representing goodness and evil, one of the opera's central themes, and certainly a stimulus for Haydn.

In the strand of Enlightenment thought with which Haydn and van Swieten were concerned, light is a means of banishing ignorance and promoting reason. In *The Creation*, darkness, once obliterated at the beginning of Creation, does not return. Van Swieten specifically requested Haydn to set the words 'and there was Light' only once, not merely for dramatic reasons, but to indicate that the contest between light and dark is finite, the act of creating light itself representing a moment of triumph. This interpretation of the manifestation of light was supported by scientific attitudes of the period. In the

Opticks, Newton had argued that what is perceived as darkness is merely the absence of light, there being no absolute state of blackness. For humanity, this implied that there was neither any intrinsic condition of being evil (equated with darkness), nor anyone for whom enlightenment was futile; hence *The Creation* has nothing to say about Original Sin. When a vocal score of the oratorio was published in Paris in 1801, therefore, the illustration devised for it emphasized light, not just for its spiritual potential, but specifically as a life-giving force, a view which reconciled traditional religion with Enlightenment thought.[119] The upper part of the image, depicting God dividing light from darkness, was based on the scene from Raphael's Loggie in Rome, a traditional representation of the opening of the Creation story.[120] The lower part, however, showing light streaming down from above to earth, where it promotes the growth of vegetation, was not essentially part of the story, and seemingly advocates a scientific reading of the oratorio itself.

That this was an interpretation of which Haydn and van Swieten would have approved is suggested by the treatment of light in *The Seasons*. In 'Summer', sunlight is extolled both as the source of life itself (*Lebens Quelle*), pervading the whole world of nature as well as empowering human existence, and as the 'most beautiful image of divinity' (*der Gottheit schönstes Bild*), which humanity owes to the Creator.[121] However, it is the sun which conspicuously receives praise, not God. This contrasts with the choruses in 'Spring', where God is unambiguously the subject of devotion. In 'Winter', although the oratorio ends with a vision of eternal morning, the gleam of light which eventually rescues the wanderer lost in the snow at night is very much a symbol of faith in humanity, not of religious faith.[122] This ambiguity partly stems from van Swieten's difficulties in adapting Thomson's deistic approach to his subject matter; but it also represents a deliberate dichotomy. Nature, and the light which supports it, provoke admiration in their own right, as well as for being expressions of an omnipotent Creator. Neither van Swieten nor Haydn wished entirely to lose sight of the religious dimension of their material. They did, however, want to show that nature's realm had replaced revelation as the basis of faith. The creative impulse behind Canova's Christine monument seems to represent an analogous attitude. Like *The Seasons*, the memorial is unconcerned with traditional Christian imagery. Its context, however, obliges it to be identified as a conventional com-memoration, just as *The Seasons*, as an oratorio, could not avoid religious expectations.

4. Observing Nature

For listeners, the idea that light might be perceived aurally was hardly a novelty at the time of the first performances of Haydn's late oratorios.

Newton's correspondence between the colours of the spectrum and the tones of the octave had already had a bearing on Haydn's compositions of the 1770s. What distinguished these late works was that they were written after their composer had benefited from opportunities to absorb other aspects of Newtonian science. When he first came to England in 1791, at least two poems written to celebrate his arrival saw fit to compare Haydn with Newton.[123] The one by Burney drew attention to Newton's theory of gravity, arguing that Haydn demonstrated this through 'the influence of A*ttraction*'. Burney pursued the scientific analogy by suggesting that Haydn's 'works alone supply an ample chart / Of all the mountains seas and fertile plains, / Within the compass of its wide domains.' Here, the great landscapes of *The Creation* and *The Seasons* seem already to have been anticipated.

Burney continued his eulogy by reaching out beyond terrestrial limitations, and drawing a parallel between harmony and astronomy. The music historian had a lifelong interest in astronomy. He lived in the house Newton himself had built to house his observatory, which Haydn would have been shown.[124] Burney's friendship with another musician who became a serious astronomer, Herschel, was probably behind Haydn's visit to see Herschel at Slough. Here he had the opportunity to see the astronomer's giant telescopes and learn something of his observations.[125] A telescope had featured in Haydn's opera *Il mondo della luna*; in this the instrument is the starting point of a farce in which false observations trick a credulous astronomer into making matches for his daughters which he would otherwise not approve.[126] This satire on seeing and believing is a far cry from the world of genuine observation with which Herschel was concerned. Assuming that, as seems certain, Haydn was shown the power of Herschel's telescope, it need not be doubted that the experience opened up new musical horizons for him. Indeed the relevance of observing the cosmos as a preparation for listening to music seems to have already been established before Haydn left England in 1795. One of the last concerts of this season featuring his music began with 'A LECTURE on ASTRONOMY, illustrated by a large Transparent Diagram'.[127] By 1796 discerning musical enthusiasts in Vienna also felt it necessary to keep abreast of developments in the understanding of the solar system, as did the composer himself in later years.[128]

When Haydn saw Herschel's telescopes, the astronomer's latest discoveries were the sixth and seventh satellites of Saturn (1789). By this date, telescopes designed for the domestic use of well-to-do Britons had been manufactured for several decades.[129] These may often be seen in the backgrounds of conversation pieces, suggesting the rise of a kind of culture of observation. Bunbury's *Bethnal Green*, which Haydn owned, provides a satirical comment on this practice.[130] The aesthetic and inspirational value of observing natural phenomena also applied to exploring the microcosm. A popular introduction to microscopy published in 1742, for example, emphasized how:

> The Works of Nature are the only Source of true Knowledge, and the
> Study of them the most noble Employment of the Mind of Man. Every
> Part of the Creation demands his Attention, and proclaims the Power and
> Wisdom of its Almighty Author. The smallest Seed, the minutest Insect
> shews the Skill of Providence in the Aptness of its Contrivance for the
> Purposes it is to serve, and displays an Elegance of Beauty beyond the
> utmost Stretch of Art.[131]

The disadvantage of such instruments, as Haydn noted in connection with
Herschel, was that serious use required long periods of solitude. Modified
microscopes (adapting the camera obscura principle), however, enabled
images of the tiny to be projected onto a screen for 'the convenience of
viewing any object by many persons at one and the same time'.[132] Detailed
viewing therefore became more socially acceptable.

This culture of observing nature reached a peak of popularity at the time of
Haydn's English visits following the publication of works like Gilbert White's
The Natural History of Selborne (1789), detailing observations of the
countryside and its flora and fauna over several years, and Erasmus Darwin's
long poem, *The Botanic Garden* (published in two parts in 1789 and 1791).
This epic work, describing the entire range of nature's realm, became one of
the most read poems of the time. The section beginning

> 'Let there be light!' proclaim'd the Almighty Lord,
> And trembling Chaos heard the potent word.

was particularly admired and probably played a part in bringing back to light
the libretto on which Haydn's *Creation* was based. One commentator called it
'a sublime description of the creation of the universe; not of our comparatively
small system, but of the infinity of systems beyond the reach of Herschel's
telescopes'.[133] The sense of enormity conveyed by the poem even impressed
Horace Walpole, not a man easily pleased: 'Darwin has destroyed my
admiration for any poetry but his own. ... The twelve verses that by miracle
describe and comprehend the creation of the universe out of chaos, are in my
opinion the most sublime passage in any author, or in any of the few languages
with which I am acquainted.'[134] Among other relevant topics treated in
Darwin's poem was an explanation of Castel's colour-organ, which he
connected with Newton's analogy between sound and colour, and a
demonstration of the parity between painting and music: 'they claim a right to
borrow metaphors from each other, musicians to speak of the *brilliancy* of
sounds and the *light* and *shade* of a concerto, and painters of the *harmony* of
colours and the *tone* of a picture'.[135]

In the preface to the poem, Darwin indicated that his purpose was 'to inlist
[*sic*] imagination under the banner of science', and to commend to readers 'the
immortal works of the celebrated Swedish Naturalist Linneus'. The
comprehensive system of plant classification developed by Linnaeus, giving
every plant a specific as well as a generic name, made a tremendous impact on

the way flora was viewed in the later eighteenth century, bringing order out of chaos and revealing clarity in God's work in the sphere of natural history. In 1788 the Linnaean Society was founded. The process of classification Linnaeus founded, however, required constant updating. One botanist who corresponded with Darwin about Linnaeus, for example, was Joseph Banks.[136] During his voyage to the south Pacific, Banks had collected huge numbers of plants unknown in Europe, some of which he was able to bring back to England, while others were captured in the drawings of Sydney Parkinson. All were eventually engraved for publication in Banks's *Florilegium*. Like Herschel, Banks occasionally attended meetings of Darwin's Lunar Society, whose members – they included Joseph Priestley and James Watt – were bound together by a belief in progress and perfectibility. As an acquaintance of Haydn's in London, Banks probably encouraged him to consider the realm of nature a fitting subject for musical expression, just as Darwin had addressed it in poetry, with popular acclaim.[137] One indication that Banks followed with interest Haydn's realization of this concept is Lady Banks's appearance on the list of subscribers to *The Creation*, suggesting that she, and presumably Banks himself, attended early performances of the oratorio in London.

Another figure who would have stimulated Haydn's interest in the compositional possibilities of the natural world was the distinguished surgeon and anatomical experimenter John Hunter, a friend and colleague of Banks's. Haydn was certainly friendly with Hunter's wife, Anne, who supplied the words to several of his English Canzonettas and later provided her own translation into English of van Swieten's word-book for *The Creation*, to which she and her son subscribed.[138] Haydn noted her husband's name, profession, reputation and address in his notebook for 1791–92.[139] He later told Dies that Hunter had offered to perform an operation to remove the polyp on his nose, and even attempted to force the reluctant composer into the surgeon's chair, though without success.[140] The story indicates how Haydn would have had the opportunity to familiarize himself with his extensive scientific collections, from which Hunter created a 'museum', designed to illustrate the entire phenomenon of life.[141] This featured all manner of exhibits concerning physiology, including stuffed specimens, drawings, paintings and casts, designed to excite wonder. Hunter also had a number of live animals kept in cages and was able to obtain the carcasses of ferocious beasts from the menagerie in the Tower of London for the purpose of dissection and experimentation. Like Lever's Holophusikon, another museum chiefly concerned with natural history, Hunter's museum presented animals, notably exotic species, which could not be seen by the public elsewhere in Britain.[142] The Holophusikon became so popular that it provided the setting for a scene in a contemporary opera, in which the stuffed animals are brought to life 'to the accompaniment of wildly rushing scales'.[143]

Haydn's musical depictions of every aspect of nature in his last two oratorios, especially of living creatures, may have led some critics, like Schiller, to consider them unworthy of him – 'Suitable only for the nursery, for use in Noah's Ark' – but to a public increasingly absorbed by nature's power to stimulate the eye, as Haydn was well aware, this aspect of his work proved immediately intelligible and irresistible.[144] The musical idiom Haydn employed in these pictures had a long ancestry. He probably knew Kircher's treatise on music in which the basis of a theory relating music to image – 'sound is the ape of light' – was propounded.[145] He perhaps also knew the 'representativa' sonatas by Biber, the Salzburg-based composer, who borrowed themes directly from Kircher's examples of the musical notation of birdsong (several of which were reinforced with pictures in the original treatise). Although such evocations were used extensively in the later Baroque period, especially in oratorios, it was the skill and frequency of Haydn's depictions in his own oratorios which impressed itself on their early audiences, suggesting the range of nature and providing a musical analogy to the collections of Banks and Hunter, and to Darwin's *Botanical Garden*.

Generally, Haydn presents each 'image' in music *before* the words elucidating their meaning are sung, thus giving the listener the opportunity to 'see' the pictures prior to the explanations offered by the text. In *The Seasons* this procedure is occasionally reversed to stress the sense of observation, the thrill of observing nature at first hand being firmly emphasized to the listener. In the *Freudenlied* in 'Spring', therefore, the soloists beseech listeners to 'see' in turn various effects of nature, which after being named are each given musical expression.[146] Although Haydn was challenged by some of the observations van Swieten selected, such as individual flowers ('the lily', 'the rose', etc.), his characterizations of other sights associated with spring (such as jumping lambkins, shoals of fish, swarming bees and flocks of birds) are wholly convincing. In this number, it was perhaps less essential to suggest comprehensive images musically since the identifications are sung first, and the main aesthetic objective was to convey the sense of joy on observing the whole of nature returning to life after winter. The notion that the experience of looking is treated in this oratorio as though it were a kind of recreation, a concept which was much more clearly defined by the late eighteenth century than in Thomson's time, is especially evident from the portrayal, in 'Summer', of the countryman resting on his staff, admiring the dawn.[147] This is wholly an invention of van Swieten's since it does not feature in his textual source.

Elsewhere in *The Seasons*, and throughout *The Creation*, the pictures are very clearly drawn. With the animals, the image often depends on their noises. For example, the cock crows, the dove coos, the nightingale sings and the lion roars.[148] But though it is sound which is imitated, for anyone familiar with these creatures the association cannot help but call to mind an image of each animal as it makes the noise. Not only has the composer witnessed these creatures, but the expectation from listeners is that they will have observed them also. This does not mean that either composer or listeners had actually observed all animals in the wild – which given the range of creatures concerned would not have been practical – but that familiarity with their appearance could be relied on because knowledge of them was likely from illustrations or paintings.

This applies to almost every living thing portrayed. Thus at the beginning of Gabriel's aria describing birds, Haydn seems to depict the eagle from at least three points of view: firstly, at close range, so that the viewer can see the magnificence of the bird and its strength in taking to flight; then, soaring in the sky; and finally, much more distantly, as it appears to fly towards the sun.[149] Haydn's imagination was perhaps stimulated by some of the numerous animal paintings by Philip Reinagle, exhibited in London during his stay there, or the stuffed birds displayed in attitudes of flight in the Holophusikon, which Reinagle used as models. His *The King Eagle Pursued to the Sun* provides a particularly good analogy, not only facilitating a view of the bird (and many other species) in flight, but illustrating the sentiment of van Swieten's words, suggesting the eagle as leader of the bird kingdom.[150]

In the period immediately prior to composition of Haydn's late oratorios, public awareness of the variety of animal life had greatly increased as a result of the greater availability of books on natural history, often with illustrations based directly on life. The year before Haydn arrived in London, Bewick published his *General History of Quadrupeds*, consisting of a deliberately populist, though informative text, illustrated by his own wood engravings.[151] This format proved commercially extremely successful, as it did again in his *History of British Birds*, the first volume of which appeared in 1797. Bewick made a point of emphasizing how his illustrations were taken from life to distinguish his productions from artists who worked from stuffed animals, who could not be relied on to convey accurately form or demeanour. The same point applies to the popular ornithological and entomological artist Sarah Stone. Haydn would have had the opportunity to see her work at Royal Academy exhibitions during his time in London. The publisher of John White's *Journal of a Voyage to New South Wales* (1789–90) vouched for 'the care and accuracy with which the Drawings had been copied from nature by Miss Stone', who supplied watercolours for most of the 65 plates in the book.

During his visits to England Haydn would have been aware that there was a tremendous burgeoning of books, especially illustrated books, on every aspect of natural history.[152] It was a sense of the rich diversity of the natural world which he wanted to convey in both oratorios. Although this could only effectively be managed by depicting token examples, he and van Swieten knew that audiences, conditioned by the contemporary predilection for observation and the development of popular natural history since the time of Captain Cook's voyages, would instinctively understand the works as universal in their frame of reference. There are some depictions, however, which are so distinct that they suggest Haydn himself may have been conditioned by particular experiences in London. When portraying the bounding tiger, for example, he would have recalled his visit, in the company of friends, to see the wild animals in the Tower of London. Perhaps this was arranged through some connection with Hunter.[153] According to Dies, the visit was memorable because the keeper unwittingly left open a trap door, which was only closed at the moment the tiger was about to escape.[154]

Haydn may have been able to study the tiger in more comfortable circumstances through representations of it by the most distinguished animal artist of the period, George Stubbs.[155] Both Banks and Hunter commissioned Stubbs to paint several examples of exotic animals.[156] Stubbs also worked for the Prince of Wales at the same time that the Prince was most closely connected with Haydn. A work like the *Red Deer Stag and Hind* which Stubbs completed for the Prince in 1792, with its noble depiction of the head and antlers of a stag, might well have impressed itself on Haydn's memory and played a part in his musical portrayal of the line 'The nimble stag bears up his branching head.'[157] Haydn would probably also have seen painted examples of Stubbs's favourite subject, horses. Hunter, for example, owned one of the various versions of Stubbs's *Horse Frightened by a Lion*, which may have contributed to the musical characterization of both the composer's lion and his horse.[158] Haydn perhaps saw the paintings exhibited at Stubbs's 'Turf Gallery', which opened in January 1794.[159]

Haydn, of course, knew what horses looked like, and probably lions also, without having to refer to pictures. However, striking images of animals – and there are few more striking in terms of their naturalism in the field of painting than those by Stubbs – help to fix the notion of the individuality of breeds in the mind. Since this was musically one of Haydn's aims, having a clear image on which to focus not only helped to reinforce the notion that animals were worthy of forming subject matter for all the arts, but also helped to demonstrate their significance in the scheme of God's creation, even if the picture the composer himself wished to suggest conveyed the idea of motion, when most portrayals were static. Clear evidence of Haydn's receptivity to using pictorial material in this way may be found in his thematic source for the hunting chorus in 'Autumn': the article on 'Airs de Chasse' in the *Encyclopédie*.[160] The plates in this not only provided the music for various horn calls, which Haydn borrowed, but also featured engravings of a series of hunting scenes after paintings by Elias Ridinger of Augsburg, which Haydn could hardly have ignored. Here, music and image were presented alongside each other. By the time of his late oratorios, Haydn attempted to 'paint' the scene within the composition itself.

5. Moving Pictures

Carpani's description of *The Seasons* being like a gallery, filled with pictures and dominated by four distinctive works, suggests that his conception of the oratorio (and perhaps that of van Swieten in planning it) may have been prompted by well-known paintings in the Imperial collection. The snow scene, the storm, and the hunt, for example, recall parts of a series of *Seasons* by Bruegel, which were described in Mechêl's *Catalogue de la galerie impériale et royale de Vienne*, on which van Swieten also seems to have drawn.[161] The get-together of country people on a winter's evening very much belongs to the world of another Flemish painter, Teniers, whom Carpani admired and who was popular in eighteenth-century Vienna.

Haydn may also have known these works; but his own musical characterization of the 'pictures' in both oratorios suggests that his conception for them was drawn from a quite different source, unknown to either van Swieten or Carpani. The pictorial qualities in a significant number of items in both oratorios may be shown to have been inspired by one of his London acquaintances, Loutherbourg. In particular, Haydn would have seen Loutherbourg's celebrated Eidophusikon, a small theatre showing what the artist himself called 'Various Imitations of Natural Phenomena, represented by Moving Pictures'. This cinema in embryo, opened in 1781, achieved its spectacular effects through an ingenious combination of coloured lights, image projection, reflectors, translucent screens, various painted devices, and a mastery of theatrical and mechanical presentation, which intrigued everyone who saw it. Reynolds and Gainsborough were among those known to have been transfixed by the entertainment.

Haydn, as previously indicated, certainly knew Loutherbourg ('the famous painter'), and probably admired those of Loutherbourg's paintings which had been commissioned by Mêchel during Haydn's London visits. The admiration seems to have been mutual. In 1801 Loutherbourg designed a sheet showing a series of cameos of celebrated musicians of recent times, displayed on a mountain, presumably representing Parnassus.[162] At the pinnacle of the arrangement are Haydn and Mozart, shown beneath Apollo's lyre, set against a blazing sun.[163] The design, published by Colnaghi with the title 'Apollini', is a musical equivalent of a similar arrangement devoted to English poets, published in 1793, apparently as the frontispiece to Bromley's *A Catalogue of Engraved British Portraits*.[164] An item in the catalogue of Haydn's print collection suggests that he may have acquired Loutherbourg's engraving, a small piece of evidence that the two men retained contact when Haydn was working on the late oratorios.[165]

As a young painter Loutherbourg had (as indicated in Ch. 4) achieved early success in Paris. Like Haydn, however, his subsequent career was motivated by a desire to extend the commercial possibilities of his art, and enable it to reach out and delight the largest audience possible. The opportunities available in London drew him to work as a stage designer at the Drury Lane theatre, where from 1771 he was employed by Garrick. In Paris, Loutherbourg had learned how to achieve the amazing stage effects – accomplished through movable coloured sources of light and resourceful mechanical contrivances – associated with Servandoni, whose magical productions at the Opéra-Comique Garrick wished to emulate in his own theatre. In London Loutherbourg brought about a complete transformation in the way audiences perceived theatrical performances, increasing emphasis being placed in newspaper reviews on the sense of spectacle, especially the convincing portrayal of nature, no longer static or artificial as in the formal perspective scenes stemming from the Baroque tradition, but seemingly ever-changing and credible. This fidelity to the natural world, managed chiefly through the development of new lighting techniques and transparencies, was often heightened by employing three-dimensional models to complete the illusion. In the 1773 version of *Alfred*, for example, he included a series of fully rigged model ships, which passed across the back of the stage, simulating a naval display. In the same year, in *A Christmas Tale*, his transformation of a forest setting, from spring to autumn, including all the colouristic changes in the foliage and the extremes of weather conditions (such as fog), and his representation of a palace burning down, led Walpole to describe the production as 'adorned with the most beautiful scenes'; they long remained in the memories of those who saw them.[166] In 1779, *The Wonders of Derbyshire*, with its picturesque settings noted for their topographical accuracy, inspired many expressions of praise.[167] One review called the scenes 'infinitely superior to every thing that has been seen since those of Servandoni, and with several advantages in the disposition and illumination'.[168] These included a setting sun, 'admirably imitated', 'a succession of beautiful, correct and masterly views', and 'a gloomy cave' transformed into 'a magnificent palace and gardens'; 'the piece ... deserves the highest praise, as it is on the whole generally superior to any we have ever seen'. Loutherbourg's next great success on stage was the production based on the life of Omai, subtitled *A Trip Round the World*, which one reviewer considered 'a spectacle the most magnificent that modern times had produced, and which must fully satisfy not only the *mind of the philosopher*, but the curiosity of every spectator'.[169]

It was, however, Loutherbourg's Eidophusikon which really captured the public imagination. 'By adding progressive motion to accurate resemblance', as the artist claimed in advertising the production, Loutherbourg intended that a series of spectacles exploring the diversity of nature would alone, without actors, hold the attention of an audience. As one journal, soon to carry an account of Haydn, expressed it:

> He resolved to add motion to resemblance. He knew that the most exquisite painting represented only one moment of time or action, and

> though we might justly admire the representation of the foaming surge, the rolling ship, the gliding water, or the running steed; yet however well the action was depicted, the heightened look soon perceived the object to be at rest, and the deception lasted no longer than the first glance. He therefore planned a series of moving pictures, which should unite the painter and the mechanic; by giving natural motion to accurate resemblance.[170]

The excitement caused by the entertainment was such that one newspaper complained of audiences not sitting still: 'the eagerness of curiosity is so great, that as the scenes follow each other in a quick succession, the spectators too frequently rise from their seats so suddenly, as to destroy the perspective effects of the pictures'.[171]

After a successful first season, Loutherbourg reopened his spectacle in 1782, and again in 1786, each time with new 'pictures'. By the time that Haydn was in London, Loutherbourg had sold his interest in it, and after being presented in Dublin, it reopened in London in 1793. Haydn probably had an opportunity to view it after his return to England in 1794, though he undoubtedly would have heard about it beforehand. The importance of the Eidophusikon for Haydn is that it represented pictorially close equivalencies of episodes in both of his late oratorios. What impressed observers about the scenes in the Eidophusikon is that they were 'moving pictures', as the announcement designated them, an expression which also applies to the conception Haydn adopted in both oratorios. A contemporary account of the very first scene Loutherbourg exhibited, entitled 'Aurora; or the Effects of the Dawn, with a View of London from Greenwick Park', for example, describes not only the panorama stretching across the city into the distance, but also how, beginning with just a faint glow, the light gradually increased, changing the tints on the clouds, then on the trees, and lastly on the buildings. As day broke, cattle and horsemen were seen moving across the fields. The scene imitated the full light of day at noon, then slowly faded through a series of gradations of colour, representing sunset. As darkness fell, the moon was shown rising. The 'picture' ended with a storm, the scene featuring imitations of wind, rain, and flashes of lightning.

Although individual elements of 'Aurora', such as the sunrise and the sunset, had been features of the Western tradition of landscape painting since the sixteenth century, what distinguished Loutherbourg's 'picture' was that viewers could perceive these elements changing, as they do in nature. It was this particular pictorial quality that appealed to Haydn's compositional instincts, and which it is here suggested the composer discovered by engaging with Loutherbourg's inventions. The notion of seeing the sun rise by small degrees, becoming ever more brilliant, is represented in both *The Creation*, where the concept is based essentially on a slowly ascending D major scale (played on the first violins and flutes), and in *The Seasons*, where the upward movement is suggested by measured chromatic shifts.[172] In both works growing light is conveyed by increasing the orchestral and dynamic range. In *The Seasons*, Haydn depicts several nuances in the first light of the day, from hazy twilight, to the first rays of the sun, the reddish tinges in the sky giving way to blue, and the glint of gold on mountain tops. Although van Swieten derived these from Thomson's poem, Haydn's settings, using contrasting motifs and instrumentation to underline each change, gives such a strong visual sense of early morning that it is hard to escape the conclusion that this had been impressed on him by Loutherbourg.

To show the rising of the moon, with its softer, more mysterious light, Haydn used another scale, based on G major, this time played on cellos and basses, *pianissimo* throughout, the orchestration restricted to strings, conveying a glistening quality.[173] A sense that the moon reaches its apex, and then begins to descend in the sky, as was probably the case in 'Aurora', is suggested by the music's subsequent downward movement. In 'Summer' in *The Seasons*, many of the other features in 'Aurora' were represented, including the herdsman leading out his cattle, the blistering character of the midday sun, and a storm with flashes of lightning (represented by a disjointed descending motif based on a diminished chord, played on the flute).[174] Though this takes place in gloomy daylight, not after nightfall, Haydn ended his music for this season with the twinkling of the stars appearing after sundown (suggested by various brief motifs on the high woodwind), a motif which Loutherbourg also seems to have included.

The setting sun ('after a Rainy Day') and the rising moon were also the subjects of two separate scenes represented in the Eidophusikon, which made much of changes in the colouring of the sky and contrasting various sources of light. In another scene, entitled 'The Cataract of Niagara', various visual effects of water were contrasted, including a torrent, a waterfall, and 'the spungy foam' where the falling water hit the slower moving stream below. Similar contrasts are the subject of Raphael's aria 'Rolling in foaming billows', in which the music begins by expressing the sublime violence of rapidly moving water, and ends with the picturesque flow of 'the limpid brook'; every conceivable musical device is used by Haydn to stress the distinction, whilst maintaining the sense that the aria portrays different aspects of the same element by employing the same tempo and basic tonality throughout.

The most famous scene exhibited in the Eidophusikon was taken from *Paradise Lost* and depicted 'Satan Arraying his Troops on the Bank of the Fiery Lake, with the Raising of Pandemonium; from Milton'. A vivid description of this by an eyewitness captures the awe it inspired:

> Here, in the foreground of a vista, stretching an immeasurable length between mountains, ignited from the bases to their lofty summits, with many-coloured flame, a chaotic mass arose in dark majesty, which gradually assumed form until it stood, the interior of a vast temple of

gorgeous architecture, bright as molten brass, seemingly composed of unquenchable fire. In this tremendous scene, the effect of coloured glasses before the lamps was fully displayed; which being hidden from the audience threw their whole influence on the scene, as it rapidly changed, now to a sulphorous blue, then to lurid red, and then again to a pale vivid light, and ultimately to a mysterious combination of the glasses, such as a bright furnace exhibits in fusing various metals. The sounds which accompanied the wondrous picture, struck the astonished ear of the spectator as no less preternatural; for to add a more awful character to peals of thunder and the accompaniments of all the hollow machinery that hurled balls and stones with indescribable rumbling and noise, an expert assistant swept his thumb over the surface of the tambourine which produced a variety of groans that struck the imagination as issuing from infernal spirits.[175]

Although no section of *The Creation* corresponds precisely to this, the connection between Loutherbourg's vision of Satan's domain and Haydn's setting of how disorder gives way to the new-created world is unmistakable. In Uriel's aria 'Now vanish before the holy beams', the depiction of the new order is interrupted by an episode, with chorus, painting the retreat of Satan's army into oblivion.[176] Having established order at the beginning of the aria, with a gentle theme in A major, Haydn quickens the tempo, suddenly modulating into the remote key of C minor, which immediately suggests a Satanic presence. A repeated descending chromatic scale on the violins reinforces the descending melodic line sung by Uriel as he describes the abyss, and vividly conveys a picture of the falling demons. The chorus, in the C minor interlude, with its disjointed subject (sung first by the basses, then imitated in the other voices), based on a falling three-note motif and an octave leap (using most of the notes of the chromatic scale), conjures up a splendid image of the fiendish spirits plunging down and attempting to leap back. Although Haydn allows them a brief return after they had seemingly been banished, this menacing moment of uncertainty serves to intensify the establishing of the new order. This is conveyed partly by reasserting the A major tonality, and partly by introducing a simple melody (devoid of chromaticisms and octave leaps) sung in harmony. The rapid contrasts of colour and texture in this number, and its vigourous sense of physical movement, show Haydn taking up the aesthetic issues raised by Loutherbourg and making them very much his own.

The only surviving visual evidence for the Eidophusikon's appearance is a watercolour by E.F. Burney, showing members of an audience viewing the Pandemonium scene (see Fig. 19).[177] Beelzebub and thousands of demons are clearly indicated, as is one of the flashes of forked lightening which Loutherbourg introduced wherever appropriate. What is interesting about this record, however, is that immediately in front of the little stage, partitioned from the audience, is a harpsichord. Accounts of the Eidophusikon's first season record that between the displays, musical interludes, especially written by Michael Arne and sung by Mrs Arne, 'with the truest taste', were part of the entertainment, performed in front of special transparencies.[178] In subsequent seasons the sonic effects were fully integrated with the main performance. According to one announcement, 'The Music for the Scenes [was] composed and performed, By Mr Burney', who had at his disposal a singer to add 'a vocal part'. In 1793, music was provided by 'Master Hummell', singing to his own piano accompaniment, presumably Haydn's later successor as Eszterháza Kapellmeister, the composer J.N. Hummel. Loutherbourg recognized that adding music to his effects served to increase public interest. He undoubtedly appreciated how sound effects heightened the power of the visual illusions to engage with their audiences, as the account quoted above describing the Pandemonium scene demonstrates. All Loutherbourg's early sets for the London stage were designed to be seen in conjunction with musical entertainments. Occasionally evidence survives to indicate that his visual contrivances were conceived with the music in mind. In the final tableau of *Queen Mab* (1775), for example, a staged regatta, with moving barges and rowers, kept time to the music. The importance attached to music in the Eidophusikon may be demonstrated from the use of musical instruments in the theatre's interior decoration. The combination of sound and image which Haydn probably experienced for himself at the Eidophusikon would certainly have been further elucidated for him by one of its exponents, his friend Burney. In this coming together of music and image in the form of a popular entertainment clearly lies a major source for Haydn's own conception of how his late oratorios should be perceived.

Many of Loutherbourg's other pictorial interests, known from his paintings, some of which were exhibited in the foyer to the Eidophusikon, may also be paralleled in Haydn's later compositions, especially *The Seasons*. The blasts of severe winter weather at the beginning of the oratorio, especially 'the snows / Dissolv'd in livid torrents' flowing down the mountainside, recall the painter's pictures of avalanches, showing human figures, dwarfed by alpine scenery, helpless in the face of cascading drifts.[179] The iced-over lake described in 'Winter' may be related to the most complicated set Loutherbourg designed, that showing a frozen ocean in *Omai*, made up of no fewer than forty-two separate pieces.[180] Haydn had many friends who might have described this to him. In 1791, he probably saw Loutherbourg's *Deluge* at the Royal Academy exhibition, which would have reinforced the effects of torrential rain experienced in the Eidophusikon. The depiction of a tremendous downpour in Haydn's 'Summer' is certainly related to Loutherbourg's achievement in terms of its aesthetic aims and its effect on audiences.[181] There seems to be every likelihood that Haydn experienced Loutherbourg's work in this field for himself when he was in London.

It may be argued, however, that Haydn was not only interested in the purely picturesque or sublime aspects of Loutherbourg's creativity. The artist had been among the first to take up in paint Gilpin's suggestions that the emerging industrialization of the British landscape offered painters new pictorial possibilities. Describing the 'great forges of the Carron works' in Scotland in 1784, for example, the writer drew attention to the place 'where coal is converted into coke by discharging it of sulphur, and fire spread of course over a large surface; the volumes of smoke, the spiry flames, and the suffocating heat of the glimmering air, are wonderfully affecting. ... At night its glare is inconceivably grand ... Among the horrid ideas of this place, it is not the least, that you see everywhere, black sooty figures wheeling about, in iron wheel-barrows molten metal, glowing hot.'[182] In Loutherbourg's career, the move towards such subject matter followed on naturally from the changing effects of molten metal employed in 'Pandemonium'. In 1786 he made his own sketches of several ironworks, notably those at Coalbrookdale, which were later used as the basis of his painting *Coalbrookdale by Night* (1801).[183] Although Haydn could not have known this particular painting, he was almost certainly aware of this aspect of Loutherbourg's activities. Probably the earliest of Loutherbourg's landscapes to draw attention to the impact of industry on the British countryside is his *Labourers near a Lead Mine*, exhibited in 1783; this is known to have particularly interested E.F. Burney. It was published in London and also in Vienna (by Artaria) in 1788.[184] That Haydn was intrigued by the process of industrialization in Britain is evident from his notes on the amount of coal used in London and how it was transported from Newcastle.[185]

In Thomson's *Seasons*, the praise awarded to industry in 'Autumn' is essentially about the rewards to be derived from nature at harvest-time, though this leads to a digression on commerce and the importance of the sea for the nation's progress.[186] In this tradition, industry is viewed as a virtue leading to happiness, opposed to idleness, which ends in misery. Haydn would have been aware of this in England through reproductions after works by Hogarth and Morland expounding the concept, and through popular writings of the mid-century advocating it as one of the bases of Britain's prosperity.[187] In adapting Thomson's text, van Swieten presented this view of industry largely intact: those who diligently work the land are recompensed by Nature with the benefits of housing, clothing and food. It became a matter of common knowledge, however, that Haydn found many sections of van Swieten's text so unpoetic that it affected his health in setting them, the chorus on 'industry' marking the lowest ebb.[188] According to Griesinger, Haydn considered he had been 'industrious' throughout his life, but 'setting industry to music' had never occurred to him.[189]

What the music actually conveys seems to have little to do with earlier conventions for presenting either rural activities or virtues in music, suggesting that Haydn's actual inspiration stemmed from a very different notion of industry. The strict rhythmic impulse of the accompaniment in the first part of this number, featuring groups of tightly repeated notes on the strings, and short, tense motifs on each of the wind instruments in turn, certainly conveys a sense of busy human activity. But its relentless drive might also suggest an impression of motion of a more mechanical kind, such as printing presses, weaving machines, or the new steam-driven mills. The Albion flour mill, constructed in London by James Watt in 1786, consisted of two engines powered by steam, setting in motion fifty pairs of millstones. The mill became a popular venue for the fashionable to visit.[190] Although it famously burnt down three months after Haydn first came to London, it inspired Erasmus Darwin's lines of the same year:

> There the vast mill-stone with inebriate whirl
> On trembling floors his forceful fingers twirl,
> Feat without blood! And nourish human-kind.

Darwin went on to predict further benefits to mankind of steam power. In the second part of Haydn's number celebrating industry, the subject of the fugue, with its broad leaps, emphasized by *forzando* accents, and its brisker pace, confirm that this representation of industry is far from the orderly country pursuits, reflecting the agricultural reforms of Joseph II, which van Swieten seems to have had in mind. Haydn, at this point, seems to engage less with the seasonal labours of the Austrian country-dweller, and more with the process of industrialization which he had witnessed in England. In other words, Haydn's setting makes use of none of the musical conventions associated with the pastoral or with country activities, or even with earlier settings of texts promoting virtue (which Haydn had had cause to explore at an earlier stage in his career). Instead he developed a musical idiom which, it is here suggested, fits a much more modern impression of industriousness, which he would have seen in London, and perhaps have been encouraged to think about in viewing works by Loutherbourg.

A further symptom of Haydn's willingness to engage with up-to-date notions of industry is the apparent disparity between van Swieten's sense of a labourer's cottage and Haydn's. In the text to his number on industry, van Swieten translated the word *Hütte* as 'hut', implying that he envisaged the kind of hovels where the rural poor traditionally lived, which offered a very low standard of comfort. Although such dwellings had previously been kept out of sight of the wealthy (or at least of their residences), the picturesque movement incorporated them into an idealized view of the countryside, suggesting contented cottagers. This sentiment is well expressed by William Paley, writing in 1792:

> If the face of happiness can anywhere be seen, it is in the summer evening of a country village, where, after the labours of the day, each man at his door, with his children, among his neighbours, feels his frame and his heart at rest, every thing about him pleased and pleasing, and a delight and a complacency in his sensations far beyond what either luxury or

diversion can afford. The rich want this; and they want what they must never have.[191]

Haydn knew this image from works by Morland. But he also knew something of the reality, his earliest years having been spent in such a dwelling. By his own admission he was 'the product of utmost poverty', though benefiting from the 'industry' of his parents.[192] Haydn reminded himself of his impoverished origins by keeping a print of the family home at Rohrau, a peasant cottage, in his collection.[193] But even such a straightforward image was open to idealistic interpretation, in part because of its connection with Haydn himself. When, towards the end of his life, Beethoven was presented with a picture of the very cottage where Haydn was born, he is reported to have said 'It gave me a childish pleasure [to see] the cradle of so great a man!'[194] From about the time when *The Seasons* was first performed, Beethoven often repeated a desire to rent a peasant's cottage in the country, seeing this as a means of connecting with nature, and of serving 'the Infinite'.[195] In Austria, therefore, notions of the rural poor and their desirable state of living, derived chiefly from pictures, long exercised a fascination for the enlightened city-dweller. But in England, the distinction between image and reality was brought to the public's attention long before Beethoven sought rural tranquillity. In *The Village* (1783), a poem which Haydn may have known, George Crabbe describes what he saw as the true circumstances of the rural poor:

> I paint the Cot,
> As Truth will paint it, and as Bards will not.

But by the time this was written, a change was starting to take place in Britain. Some landowners were beginning to address their social responsibilities and improve their workers' living arrangements. In *A Series of Plans for Cottages or Habitations of the Labourer* (1781), John Wood proposed schemes for 'dwellings intended to be built by landowners and occupied by their tenants'. He shamed the gentry by indicating how labourers' cottages 'were become for the most part offensive both to decency and humanity; ... the state of them and how far they might be rendered comfortable to the poor inhabitants, was a matter worthy the attention of every man of property not only in the country, but in large villages, in towns, and in cities'.[196] By the end of the century, the word 'cottage' in Britain had come to imply, not a labourer's hovel (as in its original sense), but a new class of vernacular building, which became the subject of architectural dissertations. For example, Sir John Soane's *Sketches in Architecture* (1793) includes designs for 'cottages for the laborious and industrious part of the community ... calculated for the real uses and comforts of life, and such as are within the reach of moderate fortunes'. Perhaps Haydn's architect friend George Dance pointed this out to him. When Haydn therefore used the word *Hütte* in 1802 to describe his comfortable house in Gumpendorf, which he had recently had extended (by adding a floor, a clear point of distinction with the traditional single-storey cottages found in both England and Austria), he seems to have been using it in this new sense, not as van Swieten had implied.[197] Perhaps this was what Haydn had in mind in composing *The Seasons*, not long before.

It may be argued from this that Haydn was pursuing both progressive and social agendas in composing *The Seasons*. He was probably not interested in presenting an idealistic view of country life, looking back nostalgically to a by-gone era, but in expressing through music a sense of what was taking place at the time of composition. The numbers in *The Seasons* devoted to depicting industriousness and agricultural enterprise almost certainly, from Haydn's viewpoint, and perhaps van Swieten's, reflect notions of progress he encountered during his visits to England. He is very likely to have known, for example, Benjamin West's designs for one of the ceilings in the Queen's Lodge at Windsor Castle, executed between 1788 and 1791, the programme for which represented the Arts and Sciences in service to the nation.[198] According to an early guide, it

> consists of several subjects. In the centre ... is genius reviving the arts; in the four corners, are agriculture, manufactory, commerce, and riches, depicted by emblematical figures in the different vocations, with the symbols of the several sciences. The intermediate compartments are ... representations of astronomy, navigation, electricity, geography, fortification, gunnery, chemistry, and botany.[199]

The ceiling itself was created by a German artist called Haas. Haydn probably saw some of West's designs for it at the Royal Academy exhibition in 1791, and would have been shown the whole ceiling during his visit to Windsor Castle in 1792.[200] The centrepiece included figures portraying Painting, Architecture, Sculpture and Music, as well as symbols suggestive of various sciences. Astronomy, for instance, is suggested by a large telescope, pointed at a spot in the sky showing the symbol for the planet Uranus, which Herschel discovered in 1781. After visiting Windsor in 1792, Haydn saw Herschel's telescopes, noting their size and the ingenuity of the machinery enabling the viewing position to be shifted single-handedly.[201] West's programme, therefore, showed progress at the cutting edge. Judging from Haydn's own observations and comments, all of this fascinated him.

Progress was also applied to the depiction of 'Agriculture', as the title given it by West implies: 'Husbandry aided by Arts and Commerce'. The representation of 'Manufactory Giving Support to Industry' was even more of the moment. In the surviving sketch, the foreground shows vase painting, and features one of Wedgwood's copies of the Portland vase, first produced in 1789.[202] In the background are groups of workers at a loom and at a spinning-wheel. In *The Seasons* Haydn and van Swieten introduced a song and chorus about spinning (an activity not mentioned by Thomson), ostensibly to suggest a female activity for a winter's evening. Van Swieten asked Haydn to imply the whirling of the wheels in the accompaniment in the recitative leading up to the song, the text for which was borrowed from one of Haydn's favourite poets, G.A. Bürger. The preceding recitative calls for an 'artless, jolly song'; but Haydn's setting suggests something much more serious. Van Swieten, at this point in the score, envisaged a simple evening gathering, with the daughters spinning. The words cleverly link the making of the cloth to a young woman's aspirations in love:

> Weaver, weave it soft and fair,
> at the 'Kermis' I shall wear
> soft and white the kerchief.

Haydn's setting, however, presents a picture of much more substantial industry, despite the vein of the words. His evocation of whirling wheels is loud and energetic, hardly suggestive of the jollity his collaborator imagined. Set in D minor, the number has a dark, industrial quality, possibly inspired by knowledge of cloth manufacturing in England, the subject of West's ceiling design at Windsor. West's iconographic programme, presenting the range of human achievement in a distinctly modern and original context, was certainly influential. It has been recognized, for example, as a source for Goya's modern allegories representing *Industry*, *Agriculture*, *Commerce* and *Science*, painted for the antechamber of the prime minister of Spain, Manuel Godoy, c.1801.[203] This commission, with its wealth of political, scientific and social references, might well have caused ripples elsewhere, even in Vienna, where in some circles in government (as discussed elsewhere in this book) Goya's career was followed with interest.

A further incentive for the special emphasis on industry and agriculture as representatives of human progress in *The Seasons* was the Revolutionary calendar temporarily enforced in France in the mid-1790s. Although this failed to replace the Gregorian calendar, its implications continued to be felt for several years. Robespierre decreed 'Industry' as one of 36 annual celebrations (replacing Christian worship on Sundays), and 'Agriculture' was implemented in a scheme of seven festivals in 1795.[204] Two others were 'Youth' and 'Old Age', celebrated at times of the year corresponding to the cycle of life. This notion perhaps encouraged van Swieten to view the seasons as an allegory of life in planning his last collaboration with Haydn. The names given to the months in the Revolutionary calendar, derived from kinds of weather conditions and types of produce of various seasons, may also have reinforced the need to represent unambiguously such effects of nature in *The Seasons*, and perhaps in *The Creation* also. Audiences in Austria were conceivably expected to understand these in relation to recent events, and recognize that the oratorios presented alternatives to the kind of progress advocated in France.

Haydn was undoubtedly at pains to ensure that *The Seasons* conveyed the idea of progress to listeners. Usually this is suggested by the musical illustration of the motion of various human activities. Loutherbourg's Eidophusikon was one practical incentive for this. Another was probably some knowledge that motion in music had been an issue of controversy in mid-eighteenth-century England. Avison discusses it, arguing that whilst 'a Flow of even Notes' may invoke 'the murmuring of a Stream', as in a passage in Handel's setting of Milton's *Il Penseroso*, 'Notes ascending or descending by large Intervals, are not ... like the Stalking of a Giant', despite Handel's attempt to make such devices 'imitative of the Walk of Polypheme' in *Acis and Galatea*.[205] Avison here draws a distinction between musical imitation of natural sounds, which is acceptable, and that of motion, the very notion of which is abhorrent, reprimanding Handel for venturing it. Haydn, who would have known Handel's examples, certainly had no doubts on the issue. The fact that critics had specifically condemned it only furnished him with motivation to prove them wrong. Thus the ploughman in 'Spring' may not only be *seen* whistling as he moves along, represented by a piccolo, but also 'striding in the furrows', suggested by the firm rhythm and the substantial parts given to the bassoons.[206] The farmer actually 'whistles' one of Haydn's most famous tunes, the theme from the slow movement of the 'Surprise' Symphony. Early audiences would, of course, have instantly recognized this, and understood its use here to indicate that even the lowest orders of society appreciated and benefited from the composer's music. But since he conspicuously *quickened* the theme's tempo in the oratorio, Haydn (by implication) raised the question of speed in listening to the number.[207] It did not require any great perception to recognize that the change was made to suggest the pace of the hardworking countryman in going about his business.

In *The Seasons* an equivalent sense of movement may be experienced in several numbers, representing the idea that everything in life and in the natural world around us is always changing. Haydn takes the representation of movement far beyond anything Handel had attempted. He invites his audience not simply to *view* movement, but to *experience* it as though his listeners were part of it. In the Western pictorial tradition before this time, when movement in figures or animals is represented, it is shown as though seen from a fixed point: a hunt, for example, might be viewed in its midst in order to make it exciting, but the viewer's feet are firmly planted on the ground; a marching army may create a tremendous sense of motion, but the viewpoint representing it is itself fixed. The same conceit applies to earlier music, and there are plenty of hunting or marching scenes in earlier operas to illustrate this. In *The Seasons*, however, the listener more often than not cannot escape from being part of the movement, following the figure's actions at close range.

In 'Autumn', for example, one number deals with a man out shooting pheasants with his spaniel. In sporting art this was a popular subject of the period. Morland's *Pheasant Shooting*, etched by Rowlandson in 1790, lays out the whole scene in a single episode: the gunmen in a rural setting, the shot, the pursuing dogs and the frightened bird.[208] Haydn's music (not van Swieten's words), however, obliges the listener to perceive things at first from the dog's perspective, all excited as it sniffs along, seeking the scent. The music then gradually speeds up to suggest the increasing excitement and the rush as the prey is sensed. Suddenly a startled bird flies up; the music insists that the listener moves (metaphorically) to look up at it. Next, the shot is heard, the bird falls down, and musically the listener discerns it falling. Lastly, the dog goes off to fetch it, and the pleasure it feels in retrieving the bird is conveyed in the music. Although the text tells the story, it is the music which directs how one *sees* the scene.

There are numerous instances of this kind of vision in *The Seasons*.[209] There can be little doubt that Haydn and van Swieten together discussed the kind of pictorial effect they wished to achieve. A possible early reflection of their deliberations is Canova's conception of movement in the Christine monument, a work planned for a building adjacent to van Swieten's office (where Haydn had meetings with the Baron), during the time that the oratorios were written. The concept of life's progress towards death compelled Canova to devise that wonderful sense of forward motion in his figures, inviting the observer to participate in their progress. Perceptually, Haydn's solution to the problem of movement, as represented in *The Seasons*, may be seen to have even more far-reaching ramifications, as the starting point for a key effect of modern cinematography. When a camera closely follows the movements of a protagonist in a drama to encourage viewers to identify with him; or when, in natural history programmes, the camera amazingly manages to stay with, for instance, some bird on its flight path, the convention drawn on may be traced back to the aesthetic issues raised by Haydn and his collaborator *c*.1800.

CHAPTER EIGHT

'Last Judgement'

1. Evolutional Ends

Even before completing *The Seasons*, Haydn seems to have envisaged writing one further oratorio. As difficulties started to mount in setting van Swieten's text, and criticism took root concerning the Baron's contribution to *The Creation*, Haydn let it be known that he would have rather set the Last Judgement than *The Seasons*.[1] During the last months of 1801 false reports appeared in the press indicating that the composer was actually engaged in composing an oratorio on the subject of the Last Judgement.[2] Haydn's seriousness regarding this subject is evident from Griesinger's correspondence with Breitkopf & Härtel. Although van Swieten seems to have begun work on such an oratorio, Haydn himself was determined to find another collaborator.[3] A letter of 21 April 1802 shows the Empress, among others, urging Haydn to compose a further large-scale work; Haydn hoped that the poet Wieland, who had written a poem praising *The Creation*, would write the text:

> [Haydn] believes that the Last Judgement would provide rich material: namely, in the first part Death, in the second Resurrection, [and] in the third Hell and Heaven. The thought seems Baroque, but in the head of a genius it could perhaps be satisfactorily realized. . . . Haydn would work at it *con amore*, especially since it is one of the Empress's pet ideas.[4]

Griesinger was right to call this concept 'Baroque'. Something similar had been attempted in Giuseppe Cavallo's oratorio *Il giudizio universale* (*c*.1681), which portrays many of the terrifying manifestations of the Apocalypse, such as tidal waves, as well as the cataclysmic end of the world and the torments of the damned. Haydn is unlikely to have known anything of this piece. What, however, probably appealed to him about such subject matter was the range of its visual spectacle and the emotional impact this suggested. It can hardly have been the opportunities the Last Judgement offered for pointing to moral guidance, which lies at the heart of Cavallo's didactic approach, since this is so conspicuously absent from *The Creation*.

The composer's interest in setting one final grand choral work led to a number of texts covering a variety of topics being passed on to him for consideration; but Haydn would not shift from his original position: the subject should be the Last Judgement, and the libretto should be by a distinguished author. Writing in November 1802, Griesinger emphasized that 'A text on the Last Judgement remains a very heart-felt matter for the old Papa. Haydn expects something on the subject to be raised with Wieland and Goethe . . . The text should be *rich in pictures*, but not so long, no more than

1¹/₂ hours in performance.'⁵ The proposal, of course, came to nothing. No suitable text was forthcoming before Haydn's deteriorating health excluded all possibility of serious composition.⁶

The episode, however, is revealing because it shows Haydn still committed to composing 'in pictures', despite widespread criticisms levelled at his collaborations with van Swieten for dabbling too much in the realm of painting.⁷ Haydn seems to have perceived the problem lying with the standard of the text, not with the pictorial aspect of the material. Critics and intellectuals may have increasingly disapproved his pictorialism, but Haydn's instincts told him that there remained a *popular* appetite for composing in pictures; and in securing his reputation this, it seems likely, was what Haydn really cared about.

In a sense he was right. Although the critical heritage of Haydn's compositions in the nineteenth century shows an escalating sense of disillusionment with works by Haydn which had been well known in his lifetime, particularly the late oratorios, this was hardly matched in the public sphere, where these works never lost their power to charm. In many regions of Europe and elsewhere, *The Creation* remained a regular feature of the musical calendar, a sure sign that ordinary music-lovers continued to relish it. As one influential writer on musical taste in the mid-nineteenth century put it: 'Haydn's 'Creation' ... has been extensively admired in this country [the United States], and it continues to be performed in many places, now after the lapse of some thirty years, almost with undiminished interest.'⁸ After pointing out some of its 'faults' – including 'questionable traits of description', and the composer's penchant for 'the imitative' – the same writer asks: 'But what work is perfect? Haydn's music is too enchanting to have anything to fear from criticism.' This comment coincides with a period of some of the most dismissive views on Haydn from musicians of the generation after Beethoven. For example, after many years of listening to *The Creation*, Berlioz found its pictorial character – such as 'its light in C which dazzles one like a Carcel lamp' – deeply irritating: 'they make me want to murder somebody'.⁹

The younger Berlioz, however, was more sympathetic to Haydn's aims, though not necessarily to the principles behind them. In an essay on imitation in music published in 1837, Berlioz acknowledged such a thing as depiction in music, 'whose existence we are aware of *only through our eyes*'; but solely at an emotional level.¹⁰ As his starting point Berlioz took issue with some remarks of Carpani's in *Le Haydine*. While Carpani, in discussing *The Creation*, saw a direct correspondence between imitation of things audible in music (such as animal noises) and imitation of things visible in painting (his example is a battle), Berlioz considered that music works on listeners in its own distinct manner, though with the power to 'act upon the imagination in such a way as to engender sensations *analogous* to those produced by graphic art'. But even in such cases, 'the truth of the image will only appear if the listener has taken the pains to inform himself ahead of time about the subject treated by the musician'.[11] Although Berlioz once admitted that he knew 'nothing of painting', confessing at the same time that Michelangelo's *Last Judgement* left him feeling acutely disappointed, there is no doubt he was intrigued by the visual arts. His choice of the immense task of casting a famous sixteenth-century bronze sculpture as the basis of his opera *Benvenuto Cellini* is very revealing in this regard. Berlioz also invoked John Martin's celebrated print depicting *Satan presiding at the Infernal Region* from *Paradise Lost* as a means of describing a ceremony he witnessed in St Paul's Cathedral in London, thus demonstrating that visual culture was of use to composers and their audiences.[12] What is interesting about Berlioz's understanding of Martin's work is that at least one well-known contemporary writer actually found his own imagination stimulated visually in listening to Berlioz's own music, a clear comparison with Martin's work springing to mind:

> In fact, if we look for analogous productions in the art of painting we find *a perfect resemblance*, an elective affinity between Berlioz and the eccentric Englishman [Martin]: here we see the same daring conception of all that is stupendous and excessive, and the same impression of infinity. With the one, there are stunning effects of light and shade; with the other, a burning sense of orchestral colour.[13]

Berlioz himself predictably denied this connection when he read it some years later. But the point is that some mid-nineteenth-century listeners were prepared to find such connections, and felt them so strongly that they believed in them absolutely. Since one of the perceived points of connection was the subject matter of a Miltonic character, it is arguably the case that repeated performances of Haydn's *Creation* underpinned this kind of experience in listening to music. Perhaps Haydn, in toying with the idea of setting the Last Judgement, already envisaged the sense of immensity and awe later realized in the minds of listeners in relation to Berlioz and Martin.

Berlioz perhaps refuted any direct artistic analogies for his music because influential authorities often viewed musical pictorialism with distain. Throughout the nineteenth century, many professional literary figures who considered themselves in the know about music – as opposed to 'ordinary' listeners – went out of their way (like Berlioz) to deride Haydn's pictorialism, even when they were enthralled by the most famous examples of it. An early example is the writer Anna Seward who, in a letter to Haydn's former friend Thomas Park written in 1802, considered everything in *The Creation – except* for Chaos and the creation of light – to be inferior to works by Handel. Commenting in particular on Gabriel's aria (No. 16), she wrote: 'We saw *an attempt* in Haydn's oratorio to represent the soaring of the majestic eagle; but the strains more resemble the darting evolutions of the swallow.'[14] In Seward's opinion, such music was no match for the bird music in Handel's *L'Allegro, il*

Penseroso ed il Moderato, a work which seems to have enjoyed lasting popularity with literary audiences in England, partly on account of its connection with Milton. When this letter was quoted in a memoir of Park, published in 1885, the author could not resist commenting on Miss Seward's verdict since it reinforced a prejudice still popular with those who considered themselves knowledgeable about music during the period he was writing: 'Doubtless Mrs Park, though a personal friend of Haydn, ... concurred with her correspondent in placing him immeasurably *below* his great predecessor [Handel].'[15]

However, although over-familiarity with some of Haydn's compositions at this time led to expressions of indifference, many composers who felt this way thought differently on occasions when they listened objectively, free from prejudice concerning Haydn's (supposed) character and (presumed) musical aims.[16] What may be a more balanced sense of the average music-lover's view of Haydn in the mid-nineteenth century comes from Berlioz's friend the painter Eugène Delacroix, who made several commendatory references to Haydn's works in his journal. An entry in 1847, for instance, records the painter having listened to a 'Quartet by Haydn, one of the last he wrote. Chopin said that the perfection we *so much admire* was the fruit of experience.'[17] Delacroix never lost his esteem for Haydn. On 5 March 1855, he wrote: 'The short fragment of the Haydn symphony which I heard yesterday delighted me as much as I was bored by all the rest of the concert. The time has come when I can no longer consent to lend my ears or my attention to anything that is not *truly excellent*.'[18]

What the anti-Haydn tendency in later nineteenth-century criticism confirms is that Haydn's works were still listened to by large sections of the musical public. For some composers of this period, the mere popularity of something evidently from a former age could prove irritating. Haydn himself was partly responsible for subsequent reactions to his music. His determination to be thought of as a father-figure – he even taught his parrot to call him 'Papa' – may have fostered esteem from the generation of composers who were directly connected with him, but understandably provoked scorn in composers of the next generation (born at the time of Haydn's death), who were left with the impression of a figure from a bygone era, whose very popularity was an obstacle to their own success. Here was a basis for considering Haydn and his music ridden with naïveté, delightful to some, but seriously unattractive to others.[19]

Haydn's determination to set the Last Judgement, though undoubtedly justifiable on the basis of the most worthy of musical objectives, was also certainly connected in his own mind with securing his own reputation. The choice of this subject naturally, had it been composed, would have invited comparison with the most famous of Last Judgements, Michelangelo's fresco in the Sistine Chapel. For many – especially in the nineteenth century, Berlioz notwithstanding – this was the supreme masterpiece of Western visual culture, a view first articulated by Vasari and often repeated in later accounts of the history of art:

> When *The Last Judgement* was revealed it was seen that Michelangelo had not only excelled the masters who had worked there previously but had also striven to excel even the vaulting that he had made so famous ... *The Last Judgement* must be recognised as *the great exemplar* of the grand manner of painting, *directly inspired by God* and enabling mankind to see the fateful results when an artist of *sublime intellect* infused with *divine grace and knowledge* appears on earth. Behind this work, bound in chains, follow all those who believe they have mastered the art of painting; the strokes with which Michelangelo outlined his figures make every intelligent and sensitive artist wonder and tremble, no matter how strong a draughtsman he may be. When other artists study the fruits of Michelangelo's labours, they are thrown into confusion by the mere thought of what manner of things all other pictures, past or future, would look like if placed side by side with this masterpiece.[20]

Having already set the *beginning* of the Bible, in *The Creation*, it is understandable why Haydn might have turned his attention to a subject from the *end* of the Bible.[21] This parallels Michelangelo, who had secured his own reputation initially by illustrating the principal episodes from the Creation, on the ceiling of the Sistine Chapel, and was subsequently commissioned to paint the Last Judgement (in the same Chapel). Perhaps Haydn had heard about Vogler's extemporizations on Rubens's *Last Judgement* and wished to emulated them. He may also have been motivated by the comparison between Mozart and Raphael which became popular *c*.1800, and proved tenacious throughout the nineteenth century. If Mozart could be understood as a modern equivalent of Raphael, then this had implications not only for how Haydn himself might be viewed, but also, if Vasari's persuasive theory of progress and decline in the arts were followed, for what might generally be deemed to constitute the summit of current musical creativity as understood from an early nineteenth-century perspective. In having it in mind to set the Last Judgement, Haydn was arguably advancing a case for his own career to be understood in this light. The comparison tentatively made on a handful of occasions between J.S. Bach and Michelangelo may also have spurred Haydn into making a bid to secure the Michelangelo role for himself.

Haydn may have learned the Vasarian view of Michelangelo – the summit of artistic creativity – from several sources, his English friends perhaps providing a particular impetus. Reynolds's final *Discourse*, delivered to the Royal Academy in 1790, famously extolled Michelangelo, extending Vasari's view that his work represented a high point in the visual arts by arguing that, since his time, 'Art has been in a gradual state of decline.'[22] Similar views had already been expressed in the eighteenth century by Richardson and Mengs. Burney, who knew his Vasari very well and had been friendly with Reynolds, might have presented these to Haydn. He might also have drawn Haydn's attention to the role Michelangelo's *Last Judgement* played in the work of contemporary artists active in London, like Fuseli, West and Metz.[23] The latter is especially relevant because, after leaving London, he made a detailed study of Michelangelo's *Last Judgement*, culminating in a series of prints of the fresco, the first version of which is dated 1803.[24] Metz's prints did much to extend an appreciation of Michelangelo's painting across Europe in the early nineteenth century.[25] There was certainly an appetite for Michelangelo, especially *The Last Judgement*, at this time. In 1802, for example, Runge found himself drawn to this painting; and in the same year a comic opera, *Michel-Ange*, was staged in Paris.[26]

Although Haydn's infirmity prevented him from composing *The Last Judgement*, the issue of comparison with Michelangelo remained a real one. Carpani discusses it, as does Stendhal, who plagiarized and extended Carpani's biography.[27] Stendhal, for example, discussing Haydn's transition from summer heat to summer storm in *The Seasons*, considered this 'a picture that might have been conceived by Michelangelo'.[28] But both Carpani and Stendhal concluded that in general the analogy was not sustainable. Carpani resolved the issue by pressing an alternative, though less potent, comparison with Tintoretto.[29] Stendhal thought that 'only on two or three occasions' was Haydn able to rise to heights worthy of the comparison: 'but then he was Michelangelo and Leonardo da Vinci rolled into one'.[30]

The general comparison between visual culture of the Italian Renaissance and musical culture of Haydn's own age had been first advanced by writers like Rochlitz and Forkel. Haydn, perhaps sensing that this was a matter of popular interest in the first decade of the nineteenth century, seems personally to have encouraged the public to view him in terms of Michelangelo, even after the project to set the Last Judgement had been abandoned. The Michelangelesque gestures he adopted at his last public appearance at a performance of *The Creation* in 1808 provides evidence for this.[31] Whether consciously or not, he was playing on an early nineteenth-century view that audiences for compositions setting parts of the Bible might be conditioned in their responses by recollections of works by famous Renaissance artists. Stendhal, for instance, suggests that 'Libretti based upon the Holy Scriptures' owe part of their attraction to 'memories of Raphael, Michelangelo and Correggio'.[32] Although this point arises in the context of discussion of Rossini's *Mosè in Egitto* (1818), Stendhal implies a pre-existing tradition for such expectations. He points out that at this opera's first performance, Moses appeared wearing a costume copied from Michelangelo's *Moses*, decorating the tomb of Julius II.[33] The authority of Michelangelo was thereby deliberately invoked to guide perceptions of the opera. Discussing Rossini's music for the same scene, Stendhal calls it 'reminiscent of Haydn at his most sublime – perhaps too directly reminiscent'.[34] The idea of linking Haydn with this music was probably suggested to Stendhal by recollection of some previous association between Michelangelo and Haydn, stemming from Haydn's lifetime. Rossini himself may have been affected by the same association when composing the scene.[35]

In the longer term, however, it was Beethoven, not Haydn, who many commentators considered worthy of comparison with Michelangelo. An early example of this association occurred within Haydn's lifetime. In a letter written in 1808, Reichardt describes a concert at which he heard quartets by Haydn, Mozart and Beethoven. To emphasize the differences between them he drew upon architectural analogies:

> [Mozart] set more store by artistically developed work and in this way he built upon the lovely and fantastic garden-house that was Haydn's. Beethoven had at an early age made himself at home in this palace and it only remained to him, if he were to express his own nature also in his own forms, to erect his daring, stubborn tower, on the top of which no one could easily build anything without breaking his neck. Several times there occurred to me Michelangelo's proud, impudent idea of putting the marvellous Pantheon as a cupola on his St Peter's Church.[36]

In 1811, an anonymous critic, reviewing the Eroica Symphony, heard in it 'the picture of a battle', which is described as 'our musical Michelangelo's worthy painting'.[37] A few years later, Beethoven himself copied into his *Tagebuch* a related sentiment, the source of which is unknown: 'Unfortunately, mediocre talents are condemned to imitate the faults of the great masters without appreciating their beauties: from thence comes the harm that Michelangelo does to painting ... and, in our day, Beethoven to music.'[38] Stendhal extended this comparison in relation to Rossini, whose music 'possesses neither the strength which is so characteristic of Haydn, nor any of that wild impulsiveness in the manner of Michelangelo, which is a feature of the music of Beethoven'.[39] By the middle years of the nineteenth century the analogy was commonplace. Liszt, for example, found that 'Raphael and Michelangelo increase my understanding of Mozart and Beethoven [respectively]'.[40]

With the general acceptance of the comparison between Beethoven and Michelangelo, Haydn's position in the general analogy between Renaissance visual culture and modern music became more difficult to define. If Mozart was the modern Raphael, and Beethoven was the modern Michelangelo, where did this leave Haydn? Carpani's comparison with Tintoretto was not repeated (except by Stendhal), perhaps because the Venetian was insufficiently known to have made much impact on listeners.[41] Leonardo, one of the best-known artists of the Renaissance, whose impact on both Raphael and Michelangelo was generally acknowledged, was the obvious alternative; but with no correspondences in their biographical details the comparison lacked substance. Compared with Mozart and Beethoven, Haydn, with no clear parallel in the accepted canon of Renaissance art, was disadvantaged in terms of their developing reputations in the nineteenth century. This is evident, for example, from Liszt's description of his friendship in Rome with the painter Ingres, whom Liszt called 'an excellent musician as well as an incomparable painter': 'Mozart, Haydn and Beethoven speak to him in the same language as do Phidias and Michelangelo.'[42] However, when it came to Liszt and Ingres performing together – the painter was a noted violinist – their repertoire was dominated by Mozart and Beethoven, just as Liszt's experience of Rome was dominated by seeing Raphael and Michelangelo in the Vatican.[43] Indeed Liszt subsequently composed piano pieces inspired by both artists. For his part, Ingres, in painting several versions of *Stratonice and Antiochus*, is known to have been inspired by the hugely popular *opéra-comique* on the same subject by Méhul, a composer described by Ingres's friend Cherubini as 'the Michelangelo rather than the Raphael of music'. The kind of intense musical/artistic parallels promoted in the circles of Liszt and Ingres evidently found no place for Haydn (despite evident admiration). This was certainly a factor in Haydn's weakening critical position as the century progressed.

There was, nevertheless, one way in which Haydn retained a role in the early nineteenth-century analogy between Renaissance art and modern music. Vasari's account of the development of the visual arts up until the time of Michelangelo distinguished three epochs, which progressively saw art improve to a position of 'perfection and true expression'. When this scheme was adapted in the nineteenth century for the history of music, Haydn and Mozart were seen as the key figures of the penultimate stage in this development, before perfection and true expression were reached in the compositions of Beethoven. Wagner, for example, expressed this view; but its most popular general exponent was R.G. Kiesewetter, in his *History of European-Western Music* (1834).[44] In his account of the 'Epoch of Haydn and Mozart', Kiesewetter claimed Haydn's 'most brilliant period' to be from 1780 to 1800, when he

> composed the greater number of his very excellent quartetts and symphonies, his glorious masses, and, finally, his grand, imperishable oratorios, *The Creation* and *The Seasons*. It was Joseph Haydn who invented that most interesting kind of chamber music, the scientific and intellectual quartett, who gave a form to the 'grand symphony', and who brought combined instrumental music *to a degree of perfection which had never been foreseen.*[45]

Haydn's oeuvre lent itself readily to an evolutionary interpretation of music history, like that advanced by Kiesewetter. The notion that during Haydn's time music progressed to its 'classic' phase, one step short of perfection, would have seemed compatible with features of his late oratorios as understood from later nineteenth-century perspectives. Progress, both in nature and in human achievement, is a feature of *The Seasons* derived ultimately from its textual source.[46] *The Creation*, though consistent in its layout with the traditional Christian view of the origin of the universe, was constructed in such a way that it permitted allegorical interpretation, rendering it compatible with notions of evolutionism which started to receive serious attention at the time of the oratorio's conception. If the days of creation are considered as stages in the evolutionary process, then the oratorio may be understood to cover the history of the earth, including in order: its geological structure (featuring the volcanic origin of types of rocks and the action of rivers in carving out valleys); its flora and fauna, embracing the concept of progress from simple organisms to complex creatures, and ending with man as the most recent and most developed outcome of the process. The context of this interpretation certainly remains the fulfilment of a divine strategy, but with the emphasis on God having designed the universe so that evolution is the mechanism through which His plan is achieved.

The shaping of *The Creation* to allow for such a reading may be seen as responding to works advocating evolution which Haydn may have heard about in England. James Hutton's *Theory of the Earth*, for example, first published in 1788, provoked several attacks in the London press when Haydn was in England, resulting in an extended version of his thesis, published in 1795. Hutton took as his starting point the principle that geological phenomena may be explained through everyday processes of nature. His identification of the volcanic origin of many rocks and his recognition of the action of erosion, from wind and water, on the landscape led to his conclusion that the earth had been formed by causes operating gradually over considerable periods of time. But his observations did not undermine his belief in a Creator: 'what a comfort ... to think that the Author of our existence has given such evident marks of his good-will towards man, in this progressive state of his understanding!'[47] Herschel's observations of the cosmos led to similar conclusions. Shortly before Haydn visited him, Herschel had started publishing astronomical evidence for understanding successive states of nebulosity as representing stages in the evolution of star systems.[48] Although these findings lent credibility to Hutton's suggestions, firmly contradicting, for instance, the traditional calculation for Creation having taken place in 4004 BC, Herschel's observations in no sense undermined belief in an omnipotent God.[49] A similar position, combining evolution and deism, was taken up and popularized in Erasmus Darwin's *Zoomania*, published during Haydn's second visit to London.[50]

Evidence that some nineteenth-century listeners to *The Creation* found it compatible with early views on evolutionism comes from Liszt, who described it being 'like a small musical Buffon', and from Stendhal, who made several generalized comparisons between Buffon and Haydn.[51] Buffon was one of the best known of eighteenth-century natural historians inclined towards evolutionism.[52] In his vast *Histoire naturelle*, he argued 'that man and ape have a common origin; that, in reality, all the families among plants, in addition to animals, originate from a common ancestry'.[53] According to Buffon, the geological record demonstrated that the earth was at least 70,000 years old. He recognized six 'hypothetical' epochs in earth's history, stretching from the first, when the globe was covered by fire, to the sixth, when the two hemispheres divided, and Man began to shape his world.[54]

Buffon's identification of six epochs was hardly fortuitous. The scheme was designed to coincide with Genesis's version of the days of Creation in an attempt to reconcile science and theology. Listeners in the early nineteenth century familiar with Buffon's scheme would probably have recognized in Haydn's *Creation* an analogous bid to harmonize recent views on the origins of the world with conventional beliefs. When Charles Darwin listened to parts of *The Creation* in the 1830s, therefore, at the time he first contemplated the theory of the origin of species, it seems quite likely that he would have appreciated Haydn's gesture in the direction of science, in the same way that Liszt was slightly later to perceive Haydn's connection with Buffon.[55] Like many of his learned contemporaries, however, Darwin's preference by the 1840s seems to have been for Beethoven rather than Haydn.[56] This shift in taste coincided with Kiesewetter's evolutionary view of musical history, then starting to make an impact throughout Europe. The idea that Beethoven might be understood as the summit of Western musical achievement, even eclipsing Haydn, would have been a potent concept by the 1840s, forming a significant parallel to Darwin's own theoretic views formulated during this period. Musical evolutionism, stemming from evolutionary interpretations of the development of the visual arts, may therefore be seen to play a role in the development of opinion on the natural sciences.

Of course, had Haydn actually set the Last Judgement, his credibility as a progressive composer might well have been severely undermined. Spohr's setting of this subject (1826) may have proved enormously successful, but it never displaced *The Creation* in public esteem, nor did it enjoy the kind of lasting popularity associated with Haydn's oratorio. So although Haydn's early biographers considered that he fell short of approaching the scale of Michelangelo's achievement, his contribution to public awareness of recent views on the understanding of natural phenomena ensured that throughout the nineteenth century his late oratorios continued to be heard by fully attentive audiences. The content remained topical.

2. Still Courting Popularity

A caricature published on 1 January 1809, *Farmer Giles & his Wife Shewing Off their Daughter Betty to their Neighbours, on her Return from School* (Fig.

20), provides valuable evidence concerning Haydn's popularity in the year of his death. This print, the work of an anonymous amateur etched by James Gillray, shows Betty performing a popular song, '[The] Bluebell[s] of Scotland', which she presumably learned whilst away at school.[57] Haydn himself arranged this song for Thomson in 1801. It formed the principal content of a letter from Haydn to Thomson dated 2 January 1802:

> I send you with this the popular song [*aria*], the blue Bell of Scotland [*sic*], and I would like to have this little song printed by itself and dedicated in my name to the celebrated Mtris Jordan, as a minute, minute indication of my admiration for her; for although I have not enjoyed the honour of having met her, I have the deepest respect *for her great virtue and reputation*. I have not wanted to compose a more striking accompaniment, for that might have overwhelmed the expressive and pretty voice of so charming an artist.[58]

Since the title on the song-sheet Betty uses in her performance is followed by the words 'sung by Mrs Jordan', it seems likely that young women of Miss Giles's background learned the song in the version arranged by Haydn, with which he was especially pleased.[59]

As the first of '6 Admired Scotch Airs', the song appeared again in 1805, this time in London, together with a set of three variations, also by Haydn,[60] a publication which could certainly have been known to Gillray. The object of the caricaturist's satire is the recent gentrification of the class to which Farmer Giles, his family and friends belonged, a result not simply of wealth created from improvements in agricultural practice, but more specifically of increases in food prices, a consequence of inflation caused by the war. For most classes the long struggle against Napoleon brought misery and impoverishment. One casualty was the London industry in designing and manufacturing popular prints, which all but collapsed after 1800, notwithstanding the expanding interests of *nouveaux riches* farmers like Giles, or their daughters, as a contemporary source noted:

> ... the [farmer's] daughter, boasts a decent room
> Adorned with carpet, formed in Wilton's loom;
> Fair prints along the paper'd walls are spread ...[61]

For many farmers, in contrast to the majority of Britons, the French wars brought increased prosperity and social elevation. Close scrutiny of Gillray's print indicates that 'Cheese Farm' has recently been renamed 'Cheese Hall', a change in nomenclature reflecting the comfortable refurbishment of the old homestead, whose owner enjoys being served imported beverages and can afford to educate his daughter at boarding-school. Money, however, buys neither talent nor taste, as may be gauged from Betty's performance, and the varying reactions to it.

Haydn's name does not appear in Gillray's *Farmer Giles*; but it seems likely that contemporaries would have recognized that they were supposed to *hear* him in the print. Betty evidently learned Haydn's song for Mrs Jordan at school, suggesting his music was considered appropriate for the training of genteel, young women. Haydn's was the kind of music to which such classes aspired, retaining popularity, at least in circles – like those in which the Giles family mixed – where Sheridan's invective against him (discussed in Ch. 2) went unheeded. Since Betty herself chose to perform the song in front of her parents' neighbours, the music also presumably represents the choice of youth and therefore looks to the future, not just the past.

Such continuing devotion to his music in Britain Haydn himself took some trouble to promote. He was certainly very concerned about his continuing reputation in Britain after he left London in 1795, as the efforts he went to in order to gain notable English subscribers for the publication of the score of *The Creation* in 1799 testify. But Haydn was not only concerned with furthering his reputation through his grandest scores: the most modest of his compositions, the Scottish arrangements, were also crucial to expanding the audience for his work. In a letter to Thomson written late in 1801 concerning another batch of his Scottish songs, Haydn added that he flattered himself that 'with this work I shall go on living in Scotland many years after my death'.[62] Thomson, or one of his clerks, was so impressed with this that his memorandum of the letter's contents noted, with emphasis, 'Haydn ... mentioning HIS HOPE THAT HIS NAME WILL BY MEANS OF THESE AIRS LIVE IN SCOTLAND LONG AFTER HIS DEATH.'[63] Haydn's dedication of 'The Bluebell' to Mrs Jordan, a very popular London-based actress at the height of her fame in 1802, also points to his desire to ensure that his name continued to find public favour by associating it with that of another popular figure still most certainly in the public eye.

But there is a sense in Haydn's management of his reputation at this time that his striving for popular acclaim was such that he was almost overstepping the boundaries of good taste. His dedication of a song to Mrs Jordan and his expression of concern for his reputation in Scotland coincide with Sheridan's attack on him, and may be understood as a personal response intended to combat in Britain the damage Sheridan had inflicted on his standing. Mrs Jordan had, after all, been part of Sheridan's company at Drury Lane since 1785, so from Haydn's point of view the association of his name with hers may have been an attempt to placate that part of the theatre-going public who listened to the playwright's accusations. But if this had been in Haydn's mind, it would have been a doubtful strategy since many songs performed by Mrs Jordan had been published bearing her name on their title-pages (thus ensuring their sale), so Haydn adding himself to their number might have been construed in London not merely as respectful, but as rather commonplace. One song printed with Mrs Jordan's name on it had been arranged for publication by Sir William Parsons, Master of the King's Band, whom Haydn knew in London as Dr Parsons.[64] In September 1799 Burney, responding to Haydn's request to find subscribers for *The Creation*, informed the composer that he could include *Sir* William Parsons on his list.[65] Learning that his former acquaintance, for whom Haydn's respect seems to have been limited, had been honoured with a knighthood may have given the Austrian – who had received an honorary doctorate whilst in England – the idea that following Parsons's example in associating his name with that of a popular singer could lead to a restoration of public recognition for him in 1802. But as Haydn would certainly have sensed, re-establishing his name with the followers of theatrical life in London, and preserving his reputation in Scotland, were not the same as maintaining the reputation he had enjoyed in the early 1790s. From a London perspective, the perspective Haydn understood, musical and theatrical entertainments based on Scottish culture might be in vogue,[66] but a name connected with Scotland was no guarantee of anything, as his friend Burney, who had begun life as Macburney, might have informed him.[67]

Mrs Jordan's name was also a particularly dubious asset, for though she was a greatly admired performer, her personal reputation had not always stood high. After 1791 it was doubtful that she could ever be considered respectable in the ranks of society in which Haydn had mixed during his time in London.[68] In October of this year she became the mistress of the Duke of Clarence, thereby exposing herself to merciless public attacks by satirists and caricaturists, including Gillray, who produced a series of humiliating images based on the relationship, so damaging to her public persona that she fell ill.[69] Gillray's use of Mrs Jordan's name in the 'Farmer Giles' cartoon of 1809 may therefore imply particularly unfortunate taste on the part of the Gileses, which, if this is a correct reading, would have tainted Haydn's name by association.

Haydn, however, was well aware that in invoking Mrs Jordan's name at the beginning of 1802 there was the possibility that he was not only associating himself with the popular and the beautiful – Mrs Jordan was considered one of the most handsome women of her age, who performed before the King – but also with the notorious and the sinful. With Mrs Jordan, as with many other performers of her day, her public image as actress could become confused with her private life. When Haydn wrote to Thomson that he had 'the deepest respect for her great virtue and reputation', he probably intended his correspondent to understand that he was referring to Mrs Jordan's stage persona; but there is also the possibility of irony, Haydn being well aware of the reputation she had for her private life. During his first visit to London, he noted English reactions to Mrs Jordan in one of his notebooks:

> English Fanaticism. Miß Dora Jordan, a mistress of the Duc de Clarens and the principal actress at Drury Lane, wrote to the impresario [Sheridan?] one evening an hour before the beginning of the comedy in

which she was to perform, that she had been taken ill suddenly and therefore was unable to act. When the curtain went up to tell the public about it, and to say that the management intended to put on another piece [*Spectacul*], the whole audience began to shout that the comedy which had [previously] been advertised should be given immediately, with another actress taking la Jordan's role and reciting with the part in her hand. To begin with, the management took exception to this notion, but the public insisted, and its wishes had to be satisfied: Miß Jordan made herself wretched in the public's eyes because she rode blatantly in Hey [Hyde] Park with the Duc. But she begged for forgiveness in all the newspapers, and everyone quite forgave her.[70]

In writing to the press Mrs Jordan took care to disentangle her public and private personas in so far as this was possible, saying that she had 'submitted in silence to the unprovoked and unmanly abuse which, for some time past, has been directed against me; because it has related to subjects about which the public could not be interested; but to an attack upon my conduct in my profession ... I think it my duty to reply.'[71] Haydn, who scanned the London newspapers for mentions of his own name, would certainly have read this and pondered its significance. Judging from Haydn's interest in English caricatures, he would probably have observed those lampooning her life. One other Austrian resident in London at this time certainly relished them, suggesting Haydn may have done likewise.[72]

Although Haydn claimed never to have met Mrs Jordan, his knowledge of her clearly indicates that he saw her perform – hence his admiration and recollection of her a decade later. His 'respect for her great virtue and reputation' may also have remained with him because when in London he had seen some of the numerous paintings of her, or the engravings after them that were published to profit from 'Jordan-mania', the sensation her acting created in the public eye, both before and after the scandal surrounding her relationship with Clarence.[73] All the leading painters of the day portrayed her in roles in which she achieved her greatest successes, though none more frequently than her friend Hoppner, who certainly knew Haydn, having painted his portrait.

The image of Mrs Jordan which the composer probably knew best is Hoppner's portrayal of her as Viola, her most celebrated role, from Shakespeare's *Twelfth Night*.[74] Haydn's only Shakespeare setting, from his second set of English Canzonettas, used the very lines which are known to have particularly distinguished the actress's performance in this play, 'She never told her love', spoken by Viola in disguise.[75] This is probably the moment in the play chosen for Hoppner's portrait. It seems likely that Haydn conceived this song, one of his most touching, in relation to Mrs Jordan's performance, or more particularly to Hoppner's depiction of it, which he may have first seen in the artist's house in 1791. The painting was probably shown at the Royal Academy in 1796, catalogued simply as 'Portrait of a Lady' in order to observe propriety, but recognizable to many. Haydn perhaps intended that his song, published the previous year, would not only benefit commercially from exhibition of a related picture, but would consequently be heard with special attention on account of recollection of the portrait, a kind of combined aesthetic experience.

Haydn's interest in Mrs Jordan provides a good example of his fascination with reputations. In the commercial climate of the late eighteenth century, the public image of a leading personality might be devastated by private revelations. When the public saw Mrs Jordan on stage or in portraits, its view of her was coloured by the scandal transmitted in newspapers and caricatures, even though at a professional level her career proceeded relatively unscathed. Haydn observed the same process at work in several other women in England. When the scandal of the leading soprano Mrs Billington and her affair with the Duke of Sussex broke, Haydn noted down the details, not of the affair, but of its effect on the way she was perceived in the public sphere.[76] We learn from Carpani – who must have heard it from Haydn himself – that Mrs Billington was obsessed about how she might be viewed from looking at a portrait, turning to the composer for reassurance.[77]

It was for Mrs Billington's celebrated colleague and rival, Brigida Banti, that Haydn wrote one of his final London compositions, the *Scena di Berenice* from Metastasio's *Antigono* (Hob. XXIVa: 10), first publicly performed at his benefit concert in May 1795. The text, about a women despairing of abandonment by her lover, was perhaps chosen at the time because it had a certain topicality, relating to the circumstances of several handsome women, often noted for their musicality, who had been, or were about to be, abandoned by their royal (or imperial) lovers. They included Mrs Billington, Mrs Jordan, Mrs Robinson and Nancy Storace. Lorenzo Da Ponte's recollections of Banti, one of the greatest dramatic sopranos of her day, show clearly how her behaviour behind the scenes fell far short of the image she wished to project in the public sphere.[78] On her arrival in London in 1794 she took, according to Da Ponte, a string of young lovers, beginning with the manager of the theatre in which she was initially engaged to perform. Like another illustrious female singer who worked with Haydn in London, Gertrude Mara, who left her husband for a young flautist, Banti was ever having to negotiate her private life with the exacting demands of her public, as Haydn noted.

Another woman renowned for her beauty and musicality (though feigned rather than substantial) was Emma Hart, whom Haydn probably observed in London in 1791, when she became the wife of the celebrated antiquarian Sir William Hamilton. Like Mrs Jordan and Mrs Robinson, Emma's good looks made her one of the most frequently portrayed women of her age.[79] Her long-running affair with Nelson was of course known (though politely ignored) throughout Europe. In a sense this offered her some protection from hostile opinion during the admiral's lifetime, though it left her vulnerable afterwards.

Her public persona was partly shaped by her famous 'attitudes' – dramatic mimes, many based on figures in famous works of art – which became very well known through engravings and caricatures.[80] Haydn certainly recalled them in 1800 in composing for her (at her request) the cantata *Lines from the Battle of the Nile* (Hob.XXVIb: 4), which provided much opportunity for the kind of highly charged gesticulation with which she was associated. A newspaper report of Emma's performance of Haydn's cantata *Arianna a Naxos* (Hob.XXVIb: 2) with the composer as accompanist, which took place at Eisenstadt in the same year, noted her 'very handsome face', her exceptional demeanour, and 'her clear, very strong voice with which ... she filled the audience with such enthusiasm that they almost became ecstatic. Many were reminded of the pictures of the Goddesses Dido and Calypso ...'.[81] Some, however, who witnessed her during the two days she, Nelson and Sir William spent visiting Eisenstadt, found her an embarrassment; one witness thought her behaviour 'coarse, ill-mannered, [and] disagreeable', hardly matching up to the image promised by the portraits which had bolstered her reputation.[82] Not surprisingly, as the novelty of her performances wore off, and her good looks turned to barely concealed obesity, her prospects declined and she died in poverty in 1815.[83]

According to Griesinger, it was Emma Hamilton's choice to spend her two days as a guest of the Esterházy family exclusively in the company of Haydn, which, if true, may be considered mutually flattering.[84] Haydn, whose choice of prints acquired in London (discussed in Ch. 6) emphasizes his interest in observing women, their beauty, and (mis)fortunes, was frank with his early biographers in his later years in admitting his eye 'for pretty women'.[85] Griesinger quotes him as saying that 'it's all part of my *metier*'.[86] Dies reports how in his younger days Haydn 'is said to have been most susceptible to love', though the composer confessed himself baffled how women were attracted to him, given that 'his good looks could hardly have led them to it'.[87] But in the circles in which he worked in his youth in Austria, it was not unacceptable for him to take a mistress (the singer, Luigia Polzelli), who long remained a burden to him after their romance had evaporated, or for his wife to take a lover (Guttenbrunn), whom she remembered for the rest of her life. After all, his Prince (Miklós I) was quite open about his relations with his own mistress. In the contained world of Eszterháza, there was no need to consider what a public might think of such relations. The consequences of such affairs for the business of music and its productions were limited. But in the London Haydn knew in the 1790s, this could hardly have been further from the truth. The public's appetite for portrait images, and its knowledge of the personalities behind them (from the press), led to a nascent cult of celebrity, which Haydn studied in both its pictorial and journalistic manifestations. He knew that lasting reputations are built on public acclamation, and also on the ability to maintain such prestige. Association with celebrity – as, for example, in his proximity to Lady Hamilton in 1800 – might be beneficial in this regard, though Haydn would certainly have recognized that this was a hazardous strategy, yet one worth the risk in 1800. But in general terms he would have recognized that anything conceivably considered disreputable in private life which entered the public sphere had the potential to tarnish an image and any hope of enduring repute.

It is entirely understandable therefore why Haydn went to great lengths to safeguard all discretion in conducting his own affair in London with Mrs Schroeter.[88] She was 35 when it began; he was almost 60. No one seems ever to have suspected the nature of their relationship at the time. Neither friends nor acquaintances even hint at it. Only her love letters to him, which Haydn (secretly) copied for himself before returning the (lost, or perhaps deliberately destroyed) originals to their writer, and his subsequent admission of the affair to Dies towards the end of his life, testify to the nature of their liaison during his visit to London. By this date (1806) Haydn was perhaps beyond caring about personal details or, more likely, saw this revelation as a means of reinvigorating his renown now that amorous affairs were in some quarters beginning to be considered a prerequisite of celebrity. The absence of such letters dating from Haydn's second visit has led some commentators to assume that the affair must have ended by the time Haydn returned to Vienna in 1792. But in fact much evidence survives to indicate that Haydn retained his full esteem and love for Mrs Schroeter long after he returned to Vienna for the *second* time.[89] It seems very likely therefore that the dearth of letters between them from the period of Haydn's second London visit may simply be accounted for by assuming that for much of this time the two were so frequently in each other's company that there was no need for correspondence between them. If this is so, as seems very likely, then both Haydn and Mrs Schroeter were more discreet in carrying on their affair than may be claimed at the time for almost any other public figure in Britain (or elsewhere) known to have shared their circumstances. Had there been any grounds for suspecting them, the newspapers and caricaturists would doubtless have had a field-day, given Haydn's prominence in London society. That this never happened is a tribute to his understanding of exactly how publicity and celebrity worked. It is also a tribute to Rebecca's own experience in these matters. She had married her husband, the 'suave' composer Johann Schroeter (d. 1788), following an elopement and against the express wishes of her family, who at various points in their relationship threatened to disgrace her publicly and ruin her financially. Like Haydn, her interest in the early 1790s was in pursuing their affair, though without running the least risk of unfavourable publicity. In this aim both were entirely successful. Having learned lessons from observing the examples of Mrs Jordan and others, they would certainly have made it a priority to avoid any suspicion of the tainted image, with all its vulgar connotations.

3. Beyond the Crossroads

The relationship between music and the visual arts, which this book has argued achieved a special kind of proximity during the course of the eighteenth century, played a particular role in the career of Haydn, the leading cultural figure of his time. Music and the visual arts came together because of the commercial opportunities which opened up in the public sphere. Men and women from most social backgrounds in the Western world developed appetites for looking and listening which might be satisfied together, as well as separately. Haydn sensed this, and prepared himself for understanding the phenomenon by immersing himself in visual culture at its most popular, especially when he was in England. For Haydn, image – whether a portrait of Mrs Jordan, a Boydell print, a picture at an exhibition, or the *Eidophusikon* – was a test of what gripped the public imagination. His late oratorios may be considered the most developed outcome of this process of coming together because, although the visual aspects of the work stemmed exclusively from the aural experience of the oratorios themselves, it was their pictorialism which was the clinching factor in their subsequent popularity.

In a sense it was the very success of these works in gripping the visual imagination, in becoming part of popular culture, which pointed towards a parting of the ways for music and the visual arts in the early nineteenth century. What was popular became suspect. Serious composers and artists deliberately shunned the notion that their activities could really have much to do with each other; nor was it thought appropriate that they should have much to do with commercialism, at least not directly. It was only in literature that the relationship between music and visual culture continued to be explored, as indicated, for example, by the influence of Carpani's *Le Haydine* on Stendhal, by the works of Wackenroder and his followers, and by the English Romantic poets. But it was also the reassertion of literature as the leading art, by Sheridan for example, which obliged composers and artists to seek fresh alignments.

But this is not to suggest that the crossroads resulted in no lasting consequences. Almost every serious composer since Haydn has – it need not be emphasized here – experimented with the possibilities of suggesting images through musical means; and often composers have been open about acknowledging inspiration from paintings or sculptures. Artists have often been preoccupied with music and its effects. What it may be suggested was most crucial about the continuing performance of Haydn's works after his death, and of *The Creation* in particular, was that it fostered in ordinary listeners the desire to see and to hear more, together. It was this desire which Wagner in particular sought to satisfy, and which in the twentieth century has resulted in the development of cinematic and televisual arts media, which reach the broadest audiences, in sound and vision. Haydn also played a crucial part in giving Western culture the *instinct* for combining moving image with music, not just as in dance, simply relating human action to musical sound, but by implying that all things in nature – in creation, which is never static – are capable of musical expression. Haydn as a name may have quickly lost prestige in the decades after his death; but his achievement continued to have ramifications at the grassroots of popular culture right up to, and beyond, the beginnings of modern movie theatre.

Haydn's Collection

The following document is an extract (in translation) of a copy of the inventory of Haydn's artistic effects drawn up after his death.[1] The inventory was compiled in preparation for the sale of the items at auction. Haydn's artistic collection was therefore dispersed. Only those sections relating to his artistic interests are included here. His collections of instruments, printed music, books on music, opera librettos, etc. have been omitted (items 79–608, 614), as has a further document of the same period listing the contents of his library.[2]

The original version of the document here translated was compiled for the city authorities in Vienna.[3] The copy was drawn up with a view to items being acquired by members of the court.[4] This copy was annotated by Kapellmeister Joseph von Eybler, who indicated which items he considered ought to be purchased for the Imperial collections. When Eybler did this, he was unaware that in 1807 Haydn had agreed to all his musical effects being purchased from his estate (after his death) by Prince Miklós II Esterházy. These items, once part of the Esterházy archives, are now in Budapest.[5] Eybler, understandably, indicated no interest in Haydn's artistic collections, which seem therefore to have fallen into private hands.

Many of the items listed below are fully identified and discussed in the main text of this book.

ENGRAVINGS IN THE PORTFOLIO

1. 4 visiting tickets [*Visitbillets*] and 4 views of Rohrau
2. 6 portraits of composers [*verschiedener Tonkünstler*]
3. 2 drawn heads [*gezeichnete Köpfe*]
4. 1 'Monument' and 1 Other.
5. 'Lady Elizabeth Lambert' by Guttenbrunn
6. 'Misstresse [*sic*] Gautherot' by Bartolozzi
7. 'Marie-Antoinette, Queen of France' [*Mar. Antoine Königin von Frankreich*] by Dies
8. 'Admiral Nelson' by Neidl and
9. ditto another
10. 'Peter Hænsel' by Pfeiffer
11. 'The persian Sybille [*sic*]' after Guercino and
12. The 'Herodias' after Guido Reni, both by Facius
13. 'The Nun' after Westall by Chesmann [*sic*]

14. 'a Smoking Club' [*sic*]
15. 'Cupido' after Corregio [*sic*] by Pichler
16. 'J.L. Dussek'
17. 'Pleyel' by Nutter
18. 'Cramer'
19. 'Salomon'
20. Another portrait from the inscription [*Ein enderes Portrait von der Schrift*]
21. 4 oval entertainment pieces [*Unterhaltungsstücke*]
22. 'Age and Infancy' after Opie by Smith
23. 29 Sheets[:] pictures of the new uniforms of the Imperial and royal army [*Abbildung der neuen Adjustierung der k.k. Armee*] after Kininger by Mannsfeld [*sic*] on vellum
24. 4 animal pieces [*Thierstücke*] after Morland by Smith
25. 'The Judgment of Britania [*sic*]' by Bartolozzi
26. 6 decorative prints [*Unterhaltungen*] after Morland by Smith
27. 2 Sheets: 'Albinia' and 'Eloisa' by ditto
28. 'Ladana [*sic*]' after Cosway by Bartolozzi
29. Plan of the Battle of Abbukir, English
30. 12 sheets: the 12 Months, oval decorative prints after Hamilton by Bartolozzi and others
31. 2 sheets: 'Doctor primrose [*sic*]' and 'Thornhill', oval after Ramberg by Bartolozzi
32. 'The Nymph of immortality [*sic*]' after Cipriani by ditto
33. 'Diva Magdalene' after Corregio [*sic*] by ditto
34. 'John Earl of Chatham' after de Koster by Keating
35. 2 sheets: 'Sabrina regleasing [*sic*] the Lady from the Enchanted Maaid' [*sic*], and 'the Brothers driving off Comus and his Spirits' after Stotthard by Scott
36. A group of the Holy Family taken [*Eine Loge die heilige Familie vorstellend*] after del Sarto by Bartolozzi
37. 'The Boxing Match' after Einsle by Grozer
38. 2 decorative prints after Westall by Hogg
39. 'The Woodmann' [*sic*] after Parker [*sic*] by Bartolozzi
40. 'The Mouse-trap' after Huck by Park
41. 'Cupid sleeping' after Westall by Nutter
42. 'The Weird Sisters' after Fuseli by Smith
43. 1 sheet with the most famous composers by various masters
44. 'The Resurrection of a pious Family' after Peters by Bartolozzi
45. A mourning family at a deathbed [*Eine bei einem Sterbbette trauernde Familie*] after Peters by ditto, according to the inscription
46. 2 sheets: 'Rosalie et Lubin', then 'Lubin et Rosalie' after Beechey and Paye by Park

47. 2 sheets: 'The Mouse's petition' and 'Marian' after Bunburg [*sic*] by Bartolozzi and Tomkins
48. 'The Death of Œdipus' after Fuseli by Ward
49. 2 Sheets: 'Education'; then 'Natura' after Singleton by Bond and Godby
50. 'Bartolozzi' after Violet by Bouillard
51. 'Apollo and the Muses' after Guttenbrunn by Facius
52. 'Antioppe' after Van Dyk [*sic*] and
53. 'Castor and Pollux' after Rubens, both by Green
54. 1 decorative print by Grozer
     Note. After these the addendum beginning with No. 610 should be remembered. [*Nota. Nach diesen wird der nachtrag bei No. 610 anfangend, ausgerufen.*]

ENGRAVINGS UNDER GLASS AND FRAMED, THEN OTHER THINGS

55. 3 pieces: 'Patience in a punt', then 'Bethnal Green' and one other after 'Drawing' by Bunburg [*sic*]
56. 2 pieces: 'Pretty Dick' and 'Jump Pussey' after Metz by Scott
57. 2 decorative prints after Ciprian [*sic*] by Bartolozzi
58. 2 pieces: Prince and Princess of Walles [*sic*] by Orme
59. 2 oval groups of children [*Kindergruppen*] by Bartolozzi
60. 2 pieces: 'Comic readings', then 'Tragic readings' after Boyne by Knight
61. 'Cherubini' drawn [*in Handzeichnung*]
62. 'Gyrowetz' ditto oval
63. Emperor Francis [II] and his wife M. Theresa in medallions [*Kaiser Franz und Gemahlin M. Teresia in Medallions*], then
64. 'Lignovsky' [*sic*] ditto, all 3 plaster casts [*Gypsabdrücke*]
65. 'Mozart' ditto in plaster and
66. 'Bach', then a woman virtuoso from Scotland in silhouette [*eine Virtuosin aus Scottland in Silhouette*]
67. 'Michael Haydn' modelled [*? poußirt*] and
68. A plaster cast of a mythological scene [*ein mythologischer Gypsabdruck*]
69. 'Joseph Haydn' in porcelain [*in Porzelainerde*]
70. ditto in wax modelled [?] by Irwach
71. ditto as a wax bust under a glass cover [*als Wachsbüste unter Glassturz*] by Thaler [*sic*]
72. 'Monument': 'Rohrau gave him life' [*Rohrau gab ihm das Leben*]
73. Painted lampshade [*Gestickter Lichtschirm*]
74. An 'Apollo' in alabaster by Sack under a glass cover

75. 1 scene in perspective with 4 prints which may be used to modify the views [*1. Perspektiv mit 4 Zügen, wobey jedoch das Objektivglas abgehet*]
76. Joseph Haydn's bust in porcelain [*Büste aus Porzelainerde*] by Grassy [*sic*], left by him to Count v. Harrach
77. ditto in lead on a pedestal [*aus Bley auf Postament*]
78. Pero breast-feeding her father Conon in prison [*Die Pero ernähret ihren Vater, Conon im Gefängniß durch ihre Brust*]. Several figures modelled in wax under a glass cover

ADDENDUM OF ENGRAVINGS

609. 26 pieces engraved Theatre scenes [26. *Stück gestochene Theaterszenen*]
610. Various maps
611. 50 various portraits
612. 2 engravings with 2 portraits, namely: Joannes and Sigismundus Theopholus Staden
613. 2 old prayerbooks with painted covers

Notes

Notes to Chapter 1

1. Aristotle, *De sensu*, III, 439^b–440^a. Aristotle's analogy between sight and sound was based on notions of light and dark within a single colour, rather than a range of colours.

2. Aristotle, *Metaphysics*, 980^{a}22 ff.; *De sensu*, III, 437^{a}4–12. Plato, *Timaeus*, 47A–C).

3. Aelian, *Varia historia*, 2.44. For commentary on this passage, see J.J. Pollitt, *The Ancient View of Greek Art: Criticism, History, and Terminology* (New Haven, 1974), 201, 205.

4. For St Gregory: J.-P. Migne, *Patrologia Latina*, lxxvii (1862), cols 1027–28. For comment: G.R. Owst, *Literature and Pulpit in Medieval England*, rev. edn. (London, 1961); C.M. Chazelle, 'Pictures, Books and the Illiterate: Pope Gregory I's Letters to Serenus of Marseilles', *Word and Image*, 6 (1990), 138–53.

5. For discussions of St Thomas Aquinas's views on music, see: Herbert M. Schueller, *The Idea of Music: An Introduction to Musical Aesthetics in Antiquity and the Middle Ages* (Kalamazoo, Mich., 1988), 382–88; Umberto Eco, *The Aesthetics of Thomas Aquinas*, trans. Hugh Bredin (London, 1988), 130–36.

6. Mosche Barasch, *Theories of Art from Plato to Winckelmann* (New York, 1985), 98.

7. In the later Middle Ages, looking at an altarpiece while listening to a sung mass would be an example of this. In the twelfth century, possibilities for sound and vision coming into proximity with each other is demonstrated through the interests of Hildegard of Bingen. Hildegard's famous visions were turned into manuscript illuminations; she also provided musical settings for her sacred dramas. In both of these examples, however, it is clear that the main point of contact between sight and sound is a text.

8. For example, in the *Bestiaires d'amours* by Richard de Fournival (d. 1260), memory is said to have two doors, sight and hearing. An early fourteenth-century illumination of this idea shows memory personified as a woman with, on one side, a doorway containing an eye (which is related to 'painting') and, on the other side, an equivalent doorway with an ear (related to speech). For a discussion of this and the tradition to which it belongs (extending back to Plato), see V.A. Kolve, *Chaucer and the Imagery of Narrative* (London, 1984), 24–26, 381–82.

9. For examples of this, see: Charles W. Warren, 'Brunelleschi's Dome and Dufay's Motet', *Musical Quarterly*, 59 (1973), 92–105; Hans Ryschawy and Rolf W. Stroll, 'Die Bedeutung der Zahl in Dufays Kompositionsart: "Nuper rosarum flores"', in Heinz-Klaus Metzger and Rainer Riehn (eds), *Guillaume Dufay* (Munich, 1988), 3–73; Bonnie J. Blackburn, 'The Virgin in the Sun: Music and Image for a Prayer Attributed to Sixtus IV', *Journal of the Royal Musical Association*, 124 (1999), 157–95. The Dufay motet discussed by Warren presents a controversial example of the possible proportional relationship between architecture and music in the fifteenth century. That contemporaries, however, recognized that there existed the possibility of a true relationship between musical and architectural proportions is suggested by

Tinctoris's treatise on musical proportions, in which he praises the proportions of the chapel of Ferdinand of Sicily, to whom the treatise is dedicated.

10. The composer Francesco Landini (d. 1397) was the son of the prominent Florentine painter, Jacopo del Casentino (d. 1349), a founder member of the painters' confraternity in his home city.

11. In Hugh of St-Victor's classification of the arts and sciences, for example, music (following tradition) counts as one of the arts of quadrivium, based on mathematics. The visual arts (architecture, sculpture, and drawing) come under a section on construction, one of the seven non-liberal arts, concerned with men's occupations. For an account of this, see Schueller, *The Idea of Music*, 439–40.

12. For an account of Leonardo's thinking about music, see Emanuel Winternitz, *Leonardo da Vinci as a Musician* (New Haven, 1982). Although in his writings Leonardo was anxious to demonstrate the superiority of painting over the other arts, his arguments for this often also applied to music. His line of argument was therefore often confused.

13. For an introduction to this subject, see Rudolf Wittkower, *Architectural Principles in the Age of Humanism*, 3rd edn (London, 1962).

14. P. Egan, '"Concert" Scenes in Musical Paintings of the Italian Renaissance', *Journal of the American Musicological Society*, 14 (1961), 184–95; A.P. de Mirimonde, 'La Musique dans les allégories de l'amour', *Gazette des Beaux-Arts*, 68 (1966–67), 265–90, 319–46.

15. For a full account of Augustine's ideas on music, see Schueller, *The Idea of Music*, 239–56.

16. The most significant work by Bosch featuring musical imagery is the inner right wing of the early sixteenth-century triptych known as the *Garden of Earthly Delights* (Madrid, Museo del Prado), which is plausibly considered to represent hell. Its imagery is undoubtedly associated with sin. The sexual connotations of music, as expressed in this panel, are clearly evident from the visual device of a pair of giant severed ears, a knife arranged between them in such a way as to suggest the erect male genitalia. For Bosch's use of musical iconography, see H.H. Lennenberg, 'Bosch's *Garden of Earthly Delights*: Some Musicological Considerations and Criticisms', *Gazette des Beaux-Arts*, 58 (1961), 135–44.

17. Both pairings are suggested in the third part of *Ragionamenti accademici* (Venice, 1567) by Cosimo Bartoli, who wrote extensively on both the visual arts and music: James Haar, 'Cosimo Bartoli on Music', in *The Science and Art of Renaissance Music*, ed. Paul Corneilson (Princeton, 1998), 38–75.

18. Kathi Meyer-Baer, 'Musical Iconography in Raphael's Parnassus', *Journal of Aesthetics and Art Criticism*, 8/2 (1949), 88–95; John Onions, 'On How to Listen to High Renaissance Art', *Art History*, 7 (1984), 411–37; Thomas Connolly, *Mourning into Joy: Music, Raphael and Saint Cecilia* (New Haven, 1994).

19. A. Underwood, 'Apollo and Terpsichore: Music and the Healing Art', *Bulletin of the History of Medicine*, 5 (1947), 639–73; A. Carapetyan, 'Music and Medicine in the Renaissance', in D. Schullian (ed.), *Music and Medicine* (New York, 1948), 121; Andrée Hayum, *The Isenheim Altarpiece: God's Medicine and the Painter's Vision* (Princeton, 1989). For a well-documented case of music being used during this period as medicinal therapy in relation to a practising painter, see Peter Murray Jones, 'Music Therapy in the Later Middle Ages: The Case of Hugo van der Goes', in Peregrine Horden (ed.), *Music as*

Medicine: The History of Music in Therapy since Antiquity (Aldershot, 2000), 120–46.

20. *The Treasury of Petrus Alamire: Music and Art in Flemish Court Manuscripts 1500–1530*, ed. Herbert Kellman (Ghent, 1999).

21. For the Paragone tradition, see: Leonardo da Vinci, *Paragone: A Comparison of the Arts*, intro and trans. Irma A. Richter (London, 1949); *Scritti d'arte del Cinquecento*, ed. Paola Barocchi, 3 vols (Milan, 1971–77), i, 221–462; Leatrice Mendelsohn, *Paragoni: Benedetto Varchi's Due Lezzioni and Cinquecento Art Theory* (Ann Arbor, 1982); David Summers, *The Judgment of Sense: Renaissance Naturalism and the Rise of Aesthetics* (Cambridge, 1987), 32–41.

22. For a widely read example of hearing being considered superior to vision in the early sixteenth century, see Thomas Frangenberg, '*Auditus visu prestantior*: Comparisons of Hearing and Vision in Charles de Bovelles's *Liber de sensibus*', in Burnett et al. (eds), *The Second Sense*, 71–94.

23. Gregorio Comanini, *Il Figino, overo del fine della pittura* (Mantua, 1591), in *Tratti d'arte del Cinquecento*, ed. P. Barocchi, 3 vols (Bari, 1960–62), iii, 368–70. For a discussion of Comanini's account of Arcimboldo's colour music, see Lionello Levi's essay in Benno Geiger, *Die skurrilen Gemälde des Giuseppe Arcimboldi* (Wiesbaden, 1960), 198. For a more recent account of Arcimboldo in the context of the culture of his time, see Kaufmann, *Mastery of Nature*.

24. For examples of iconographic analyses of musical subject matter (with emphasis on musical allegories), see: Fischer, *Music in Paintings of the Low Countries*; Mirimonde, *L'Iconographie musicale sous les rois Bourbon*; Leppert, *The Theme of Music*.

25. For a study of one painting in the context of the period, see Keith Christiansen, *A Caravaggio Rediscovered: The Lute Player*, exh. cat., Metropolitan Museum of Art (New York, 1990); Franc Trinchieri Camiz, 'Music and Painting in Cardinal del Monte's Household', *Metropolitan Museum Journal*, 26 (1991), 213–26. For evidence implying that Caravaggio himself was not responsible for the musical inscriptions in his paintings, see Slim, 'Musical Inscriptions in Paintings by Caravaggio and his Followers', 241–63.

26. For discussion of several such points of connection, mostly arcane and distinctly literary (and not populist), see: Cropper, *Ideal of Painting*, 137–45; Fumaroli, *L'École du silence, passim*.

27. A.-P. de Mirimonde, 'Les Sujets musicaux chez Vermeer de Delft', *Gazette des Beaux-Arts*, 58 (1961), 29–52.

28. Wilson, *Nicholas Lanier*.

29. *Ars magna lucis et umbrae* (Rome, 1646), II, i, ch. 6. For discussion of Kircher's interest in optics and the camera obscura, see Kemp, *Science of Art*, 191. Kircher was probably in part inspired by the rather vague comparisons between light and musical proportions advanced earlier in the seventeenth century by Robert Fludd: see the illustrations and commentaries in Joscelyn Godwin, *Robert Fludd: Hermetic Philosopher and Surveyor of Two Worlds* (London, 1979), esp. 44–53, 76–80.

30. The sound/light analogy comes in a treatise on acoustics entitled *Magia phonocamptica, sive de echo*, part of Kircher's great compendium *Musurgia universalis sive ars magna consoni et dissoni*, 2 vols (Rome, 1650). For a discussion of Kircher's musical interests, see Joscelyn Godwin, *Athanasius Kircher: A Renaissance Man and the Quests for Lost Knowledge* (London, 1979), 66–71.

31. *Phonurgia nova, sive Coniugium mechanico-physicum artis et naturae*, 2 vols (Kempten, 1673), I, i, ch. 1 (the opening section is headed 'Sonus lucis simia est'). The German translation was published in Nördlingen in 1684.

32. Biber closely quoted Kircher's examples of birdsong in his *Sonata Representiva* (1681): R.D'A. Jensen, 'Birdsong and the Imitation of Birdsong in the Music of the Middle Ages and the Renaissance', *Current Musicology*, 40 (1985), 50–60.

33. Haydn's interest in the relationship between visuality and music is a major theme of this book. For further speculations on his use of the *Phonurgia nova*, see Ch. 7.

34. *Musurgia universalis*, II, 366: Godwin, *Kircher*, 71. The visual context of Haydn's *Creation* is discussed in detail in Ch. 7.

35. For *Ut pictura poesis*, the fundamental study is Lee, *Ut pictura poesis*. The phrase derives from Horace's *Ars poetica* and in a saying of Simonides that painting is mute poetry, and poetry a speaking picture. It was taken up in the sixteenth century by several influential writers, notably Leonardo da Vinci. In the seventeenth and eighteenth centuries, French and English critics were inspired by this notion to write elaborate formal analogies between the two arts, mostly with the aim of convincing readers that painting (and the other visual arts) was worthy of distinction as a liberal art in the same manner as poetry. The fact that such detailed texts continued to be written suggests that resistance to the notion that painting merited the position occupied by the literary arts was entrenched.

36. For examples of music's alliance with poetry, see: Anthony Rooley, 'Ficino and the Supremacy of Poetry over Music', in *Le Concert des voix et des instruments à la Renaissance*, Actes du XXXIVᵉ Colloque International d'Études Humanistes, Tours, Centre d'Études Supérieures de la Renaissance, July 1991, ed. J.-M. Vaccaro (Paris, 1995), 51–56; Claude V. Palisca, '*Ut Oratoria Musica*: The Rhetorical Basis of Musical Mannerism', in F.W. Robinson and S.G. Nichols (eds), *The Meaning of Mannerism* (Hanover, NH, 1972), 47–49; Robert Toft, 'Musick a Sister to Poetrie: Rhetorical Artifice in the Passionate Airs of John Dowland', *Early Music*, 12 (1984), 191–98; Howard Mayer Brown, '*Ut musica poesis*: Music and Poetry in France in the Late Sixteenth Century', *Early Music History*, 13 (1994), 1–64.

37. One example is Charpentier's *Les Arts florissants*, which features personifications of painting, architecture, music, and poetry. But poetry is closely aligned with music, and always has the upper hand.

38. Engraving by N. Tardieu (1731). For the relationship between the two men, see E. Dacier and A. Vuaflart, *Jean de Jullienne et les graveurs de Watteau au XVIIIᵉ siècle*, 4 vols (Paris, 1922–29). For musical subjects in Watteau's painting, see A.-P. de Mirimonde, 'Les Sujets musicaux chez Antoine Watteau', *Gazette des Beaux-Arts*, 58 (1961), 249–88.

39. *Opticks*, III, i, query 13 and 14. Newton had in fact devised his theory of correspondence between light and sound in the 1670s, perhaps under the influence of Kircher. For the development of Newton's thinking on this point, see A. Shapiro, 'The Evolving Structure of Newton's Theory of White Light and Color', *Isis*, 71 (1980), 211–35.

40. For discussions of Newton's theories of light and colour (especially in relation to the history of Western visual culture), and his attempt to reconcile an understanding of light through knowledge of musical harmony, see: Kemp, *Science of Art*, 285–88; Gage, *Colour and Meaning*, 134–43.

41. Algarotti's writings are discussed in Ch. 4. His essay on Newton (1737) was

translated into English three times, first in 1739. Algarotti's essay on opera (1762) contains the statement, 'All music, that paints nothing, is only noise.' This remark was quoted in the *Encyclopédie*, giving it a kind of common currency, which played an important part in bringing musical/visual relationships to the attention of educated audiences. The essay was translated into English in 1768, and dedicated to William Pitt, the Prime Minister. For Voltaire, see *Élements de la philosophie de Newton*, ed. Robert L. Walters and W.H. Barber, in *The Complete Works of Voltaire*, general editors W.H. Barber and Ulla Kölving, xv (Oxford, 1992), 386–95, and 16–21 (for comment). Newton's *Opticks* was first translated into French in 1720 and soon provoked (mostly) favourable discussion among scientists in France.

42. L.B. Castel, *L'Optique des couleurs* (Paris, 1740): Schier, *Louis Bertrand Castel*; Chouillet-Roche, 'Le Clavecin oculaire'; Franssen, 'The Ocular Harpsichord'.

43. In a letter published in the *Mercure de France* (Oct.–Nov. 1725), 2552–53.

44. *Esprit, saillies et singularités du P. Castel* (Amsterdam, 1763), 309, 369.

45. iii, 35.

46. Castel claimed to have introduced Rameau to Kircher's ideas about birdsong as set out in *Musurgia universalis* (1650), which perhaps influenced the composer's own compositions based on birds. Although Rameau distanced himself from Castel, he none the less accepted the notion that musical proportions were exactly analogous to proportions found in the most satisfactory visual arts (he cites ancient Greek architecture): Girdlestone, *Jean-Philippe Rameau*, 488. Telemann's interest in Castel will be discussed in Ch. 3.

47. From de Cahusac's *La Danse ancienne et moderne, ou Traité historique de la danse*, quoted in Graham Sadler, 'Jean-Philippe Rameau', in *The New Grove French Baroque Masters* (London, 1986), 263.

48. Kristeller, 'The Modern System of the Arts', in *Renaissance Thought and the Arts*, 163–227, esp. 196–212.

49. Jean-Baptiste Dubos, *Réflexions critiques sur la poësie et sur la peinture* (Paris, 1719).

50. Charles Batteux, *Les Beaux-arts réduits à un même principe* (Paris, 1746).

51. Paris, Louvre: Marco Boschini, 'Invenzione', in *Le ricche minere della pittura veneziana* (Venice, 1674); modern edition in Boschini, *La carta del navegar pitoresco*, ed. A. Pallucchini (Venice, 1966), 754–55.

52. For an insight into how the picture was viewed, see Stendhal, *Lives of Haydn, Mozart and Metastasio*, trans. Coe, 13. Whether or not Boschini was transmitting an accurate tradition for identifying these figures remains debatable: for a recent view see Rowland-Jones, 'The Minuet: Painter-Musicians in Triple Time', esp. 416–18.

53. *The Tatler*, ed. Donald F. Bond, ii (Oxford, 1987), 358–61, no. 153 (for 1 Apr. 1710). Avison's 'Analogies between Music and Painting' forms part of *An Essay on Musical Expression* (London, 1753), 20–28.

54. The painting was in the 'Cabinet du Roy': Florent Le Comte, *Cabinet des singularitez d'architecture, peinture, sculpture et gravure*, 2nd edn (Brussels, 1702), ii, 165–68 (cited by Bond, *The Tatler*, 358). One of the key figures in Rome who in literary form tried to express an understanding of colour in terms of the mathematical proportions of musical harmony was the engraver Pietro Testa. For Testa and the context of his ideas, and a discussion of Domenichino's motivation for reconstructing musical instruments of the ancients, see Cropper, *Ideal of Painting*, 137–46.

55. For a discussion of this, see Allard, 'Mechanism, Music and Painting', esp. 269–73.

56. André Félibien, *Conférences de l'académie royale de peinture at de sculpture pendant l'année 1667* (Paris, 1669), esp. 32.

57. A. Coypel, *Sur l'esthétique du peintre* (Paris, 1721), translated in Puttfarken, *Roger de Piles' Theory of Art*, 30. Coypel's son, the painter C.-A. Coypel, realized this musicalization of pictorial matter by designing a series of tapestries on classical subjects, not derived from the classical sources, but from recent operatic practice. His *Hercules brings Alcestis back from the Underworld* was inspired, for example, by Philippe Quinault's opera *Alcestis*: Thierry Lefrançois, *Charles Coypel, peintre du roi* (Paris, 1990), 284–320.

58. Walker, 'Salvator Rosa and Music'; *Poesie e lettere inedite di Salvator Rosa*, transcribed and annotated by Uberto Limentani (Florence, 1950), 7–9. Burney undertook research into Rosa as a composer.

59. Roger de Piles, *L'Art de peinture* (Paris, 1668), 209. In de Piles's later writings, the musical analogy is taken still further, perhaps reflecting influence from Newtonian ideas: *Cours de peinture par principes* (Paris, 1708).

60. By John Lockman: from the *Old Whig*, 4 Jan. 1738.

61. Quel sublime dessein! Que de riches tableaux!
Tu me vois transporté de tes accens nouveaux;
Partout y brille le génie.
Le pinceau de Rubens guide ton harmonie. *Mercure de France*, May 1756, 242.

62. For Vogler and his visual interests, see Graves and Graves, *In Praise of Harmony*, esp. 184–85, 233–37; Schweiger, 'Abt Vogler'.

63. The account describing Vogler's improvisations is somewhat confused, since the subjects of the paintings do not match the names of the artists mentioned. However, it is reasonably clear that the following paintings in the Elector's collection at Düsseldorf were treated by Vogler: the 'great' *Last Judgement*; the *Fall of the Damned*; and '*Castor and Pollux*'. *Betrachtungen der Mannheimer Tonschule*, 3 vols with supplements (Mannheim, 1778–81), i, 293–96. Some of these paintings had been particularly described by de Piles: Bernard Teyssèdre, 'Une Collection française de Rubens au XVIIIe siècle', *Gazette des Beaux-Arts*, 62 (1962), esp. 284–89.

64. Munich, Alte Pinakothek. That the painting was known as 'Castor and Pollux' at the time Vogler saw it is clear from the engraving of the painting made by Valentine Green (1791), which is thus entitled.

65. For the (eighteenth-century) identification of the subject of Rubens's painting, see Gert Schiff (ed.), *German Essays on Art History* (New York, 1988), 25–28. The subject had been recognized in 1777 by J.J.W. Heinse and published in the *Teutscher Merkur* for 1776–77. For a discussion of the subject in the context of Rubens's intentions and its historical ramifications, see Elizabeth McGrath, *Rubens: Subjects from History*, Corpus Rubenianum Ludwig Burchard (London, 1987), 121–31.

66. Vogler's *Castore e Polluce* was performed in Munich in 1787 and possibly earlier.

67. *La Kermesse, ou La Foire flamande*, apparently first performed in Paris in 1783. Rubens's painting had been acquired for Louis XIV in 1685. For an account of the painting, see Svetlana Alpers, *The Making of Rubens* (New Haven, 1995), 5–64.

68. Handel made use of various effects of tone-painting throughout his career. Some examples are discussed in Ch. 7.

69. Rosand, 'Handel Paints the Resurrection', 7–52.

70. The painting was by Michelangelo Cerruti: Kirkendale, 'Ruspoli Documents', esp. 234, 260.

71. Lowell Lindgren, 'The Staging of Handel's Operas in London', in Stanley Sadie and Antony Hicks (eds), *Handel Tercentenary Collection* (London, 1987), 93–119.

72. White, 'Rehearsal of an Opera', 79–90; Annalia Delneri and Dario Succi, *Marco Ricci e il paesaggio veneto del Settecento* (Milan, 1993), 101–3.

73. For example, one of the paintings (New Haven, Yale Center for British Art) appears to show some kind of dispute, or operatic rivalry between the singers. The mood is reflected in the large seascape behind, which shows a tempest brewing up.

74. For a useful discussion of this theme, see Diane Waggoner, 'Hogarth's "Beggar's Opera" Paintings and Italian Opera', in Bindman and Wilcox (eds), *"Among the Whores and Thieves"*, 41–55. A subsequent use made in a musical context of one of Hogarth's musical satires is discussed in Ch. 6.

75. Handel was hardly the first composer to set texts of this kind. Indeed *Admeto* itself was based on a libretto first set *c*.1660 in Venice. In the seventeenth century, portraits and painters occasionally feature in operas. Another example is *Il favore degli dei*, performed in Parma in 1690. What is important about Handel's operas of this kind is that they seem to have been the ones which found most favour with the public. *Admeto* was not only a great success when first produced, it was revived a number of times in the composer's lifetime and received the last performances of any Handel opera before modern times, in 1754. Other successful Handel operas with plots involving portraits are *Ottone* (1723) and *Rodelinda* (1725). *Silla* (1713), which may have been commissioned and/or encouraged by the art-loving Lord Burlington and performed privately, is a further example.

76. [John Mainwaring], *Memoirs of the Life of the Late George Frederic Handel. To which is added a Catalogue of his Works and Observations upon them* (London, 1760), 194. For eighteenth-century appreciations of the Farnese *Hercules* and the *Venus de' Medici*, see Haskell and Penny, *Taste and the Antique*, 229–32, 325–28.

77. Hugh McLean, 'Bernard Granville, Handel and the Rembrandts', *Musical Times*, 126 (1985), 593–601; Richard G. King, 'Handel's Travels in the Netherlands in 1750', *Music & Letters*, 72 (1991), 372–83.

78. Hughes and Royalton-Kisch, 'Handel's Art Collection', lot nos 6, 8, and 9.

79. *The true Representation and Caracter etc.*: BMC 3273.

80. For a documented account of the *Musick for the Royal Fireworks*, see *Handel: A Celebration of his Life and Times 1685–1759*, ed. Jacob Simon, exh. cat., National Portrait Gallery (London, 1985), 212–19. For a discussion of the *Fireworks Musick* and the accompanying spectacle in its political and social context, see Brewer, *Pleasures of the Imagination*, 25–29.

81. Edelstein and Allen, *Vauxhall Gardens*; Allen, *Francis Hayman*, 107–12.

82. S. Toupee, 'An Evening at Vaux-Hall', *Scots Magazine*, summer of 1739.

83. Roubiliac's statue of Handel for Vauxhall is discussed in greater detail in Ch. 7I.

84. Frederick was one of the leading patrons of the visual arts of his age: Kimberly Rorschach, 'Frederick, Prince of Wales (1707–51) as Collector and Patron', *Walpole Society*, 55 (1989–90), 1–76. He was one of the first members of a royal family to be depicted playing a musical instrument (the cello): *Philip*

Mercier 1689–1760, exh. cat., Iveagh Bequest Kenwood (1969), 32–34, nos 24–26. The Prince was also the promoter of the 'Opera of the Nobility' (1733–37), 'got up against the dominion of Mr Handel'.

85. George Bickham's *Musical Entertainer* (London, 1737–39): F. Kidson, 'Some Illustrated Music-Books of the Seventeenth and Eighteenth Centuries: English', *Musical Antiquary*, 3 (1911–12), 195–208, esp. 200–3.

86. *A Discourse on the Dignity, Certainty, Pleasure and Advantage of the Science of a Connoisseur* (London, 1719), 203.

87. *An Essay on the Theory of Painting* (London, 1725), 5.

88. Victoria, National Gallery of Australia. The poet is Metastasio. The artist is the painter of the picture, Jacopo Amigoni. The identity of the singer is uncertain (Burney calls her Faustina Bordoni). Wilson, 'One God! One Farinelli'; Heartz, 'Farinelli and Metastasio'.

89. Burney, *Present State of Music in France and Italy*, 211; *Musical Tours*, ed. Scholes, i, 151–53.

90. Burney also mentions instruments named after Correggio, Titian and Guido Reni. There were several others Burney did not recall by name. Presumably the notion of relating musical sound to experience of well-known painters was a reflection of Castel's colour keyboard. Apart from paintings by Amigoni, Farinelli's collection included six 'Velazquezs' and oil sketches by Luca Giordano.

91. Coll. Duke of Buccleuch: Roettgen, *Anton Raphael Mengs*, 48–49, cat. 2.

92. Clark, *Pompeo Batoni*, 270–71, cat. 202, pl. 6.

93. Donald Posner, 'Mme. De Pompadour as a Patron of the Visual Arts', *Art Bulletin*, 72 (1990), 74–89.

94. For examples of her work, see Jacques Levron, *Secrète Madame de Pompadour* (Paris, 1961), plates (between pp. 154 and 155).

95. These are discussed by Goodman, *Portraits of Madame de Pompadour*.

96. Executed in 1774–75, the portrait survives in two versions (both today at Versailles): *Marie-Antoinette, Archiduchesse, Dauphine et Reine*, exh. cat. (Versailles, 1955), 34–35, nos 33, 34. In the Queen's choice of decoration at the Petit Trianon at Versailles, the reception room, now the music room, includes plaster work featuring musical instruments and also palette and brushes.

97. For Mrs Delany's life, see *Mrs Delany (Mary Granville), a Memoir 1700–1788*, compiled by George Paston (London, 1900). For Mrs Delany's artwork, see *Mrs Delany's Flower Collages from the British Museum*, exh. cat., Pierpont Morgan Library (New York, 1986). For her musical interests, see Leppert, *Music and Image*, 28, 149, 224 n. 36.

98. Pointon, *Hanging the Head*, 34, pl. 34.

99. For example, in *Pride and Prejudice*, *Emma*, and *Persuasion*, scenes concerned with music-making are balanced with those involving images, such as drawing, inspecting portrait galleries, or portrait miniatures.

100. *Catalog of Carl Philipp Emanuel Bach's Estate*, ed. Wade.

101. For a reproduction of this, see Ottenberg, *Carl Philipp Emanuel Bach*, fig. 9.

102. Stechow, 'Johann Sebastian Bach the Younger'.

103. For surveys of Gainsborough's musical interests and their relationship to his own painting, see: *Gainsborough and His Musical Friends: A Celebration of the 250th Anniversary of the Artist's Birth*, exh. cat., The Iveagh Bequest, Kenwood House (London, 1977); Asfour and Williamson, *Gainsborough's Vision*, esp. ch. 5, 'Ut musica pictura'.

104. Gainsborough's friend William Jackson left several records of the great

painter's musicality and love of music. For examples, see Whitley, *Thomas Gainsborough*, 360–62. Jackson, a well-respected composer, was himself a practising artist. Interestingly some of his landscapes have been shown to derive from the backgrounds in the engravings in Bickham's *Musical Entertainer*, a source also used by Gainsborough: Asfour and Williamson, *William Jackson*, 12. For Gainsborough's letters to Jackson, often referring to music, generally together with aspects of painting, see *The Letters of Thomas Gainsborough*, ed. Mary Woodall (London, 1963), 107–19, nos 52–59. Romney, Opie and Hoppner were also musical artists. Even Hogarth joined the Academy of Ancient Music soon after it was founded.

105.   Letter of 17 Oct. 1763: *Mozart Briefe*, ed. Bauer, Deutsch,and Eibl, i, 105. Bout's triptych of the *Last Supper* is still in the church of St Peter's in Leuven.

106.   Letter of 19 Sept. 1765: *Mozart Briefe*, ed. Bauer, Deutsch and Eibl, i, 202 (cf. 106, 110, 192–98). Rubens's celebrated altarpiece was well known from an early engraving by Vorsterman. For some views of the altarpiece close in date to Leopold's visit see John Rupert Martin, *Rubens: The Antwerp Altarpieces* (London, 1968), 62–70. Leopold also particularly praised Rubens's *Christ's Charge to St Peter*, then in the church of St Gudule in Brussels. He claimed to have the image of the painting before his eyes day and night. This was a much less well-known painting, though Reynolds saw it in 1781 and described it rather disparagingly; he again mentioned it in his Discourse delivered in 1788. The painting is now in the Wallace Collection, London: John Ingamells, *The Wallace Collection.Catalogues of Pictures*, iv: *Dutch and Flemish* (London, 1992), 317–20. Leopold also particularly mentions Rubens's painting showing *The Holy Trinity with Angels*, which he saw in the Carmelite church in Antwerp: Max Rooses, *Rubens*, trans. H. Child, 2 vols (London, 1904), i, 31–32.

107.   Both portraits are now in the collection of the Internationale Stiftung Mozarteum in Salzburg.

108.   One example is Mozart's letter of 10 May 1779 to his cousin Maria Anna. Mozart crudely sketched his cousin's head as an illustration to part of an ode he quotes by Klopstock, beginning, 'Thy picture sweet, O cousin, Is e'er before my eyes' (*Letters of Mozart*, ed. Anderson, 653). For a reproduction of the page in question (British Library, MS Zweig 67), see Banks and Turner, *Mozart: Prodigy of Nature*, fig. 24.

109.   Memoirs of Nannerl Mozart (1800): Deutsch, *Mozart: A Documentary Biography*, 494.

110.   Novello, *A Mozart Pilgrimage*, ed. Hughes, 80.

111.   Ibid., 89.

112.   Letter of 3 Nov. 1781: *Letters of Mozart*, ed. Anderson, 776. The composition was the serenade for two clarinets, two horns, and two bassoons in E flat (K. 375).

113.   Salzburg, Internationale Stiftung Mozarteum. The portrait dates from 1789–90 and is unfinished. Novello reported that this was Constanze's favourite portrait of her husband, and according to her the best likeness. She would not have the picture finished lest it spoil the likeness. Mozart's sister owned a copy of it: *A Mozart Pilgrimage*, ed. Hughes, 79.

114.   This painting is one of a pair; its pendant features a scene of fencing taking place at the other end of the same room, its walls also displaying an array of paintings, drawings and prints (also Edinburgh, National Portrait Gallery of Scotland): Powell-Jones, 'A Neo-Classical Interior', 104–7; Lambert, *The Image Multiplied*, 164, 180; Jenkins and Sloan, *Vases and Volcanoes*, 128–30, nos 16a,

16b. Some of the figures in the paintings, including Sir William Hamilton, may be identified through inscriptions subsequently added to their versos. The Mozarts are not mentioned in these inscriptions, but their correspondence confirms that they were part of Sir William's circle during their visit to Naples in 1770. They had already met in London in 1764. Leopold mentions visiting Sir William in Naples in a letter of 19 May 1770. He refers to Lady Hamilton (a skilled harpsichordist) performing nervously in front of Wolfgang. He also describes the instrument on which she played. It is clear that both Mozarts also performed in Sir William's residence and probably those of other members of his circle (*Mozart Briefe*, ed. Bauer, Deutsch and Eibl, i, 194, 347, 362). The evidence of the inscriptions indicates that the setting in Fabris's paintings is a room in the residence in Naples of Lord Fortrose, one of Hamilton's close friends. Charles Burney, the music historian, met Fortrose in Naples later in 1770, and described his 'great talents and taste': 'he both draws and paints very well ... and plays the harpsichord' (*Dr Burney's Musical Tours in Europe*, ed. Scholes, i, 267). Given these interests, it is understandable why Fortrose's residence is the setting for a painting conspicuously combining musical and artistic pursuits. The painting featuring fencing continues this theme since one of the figures may reasonably be identified as the celebrated composer Nicolò Jomelli, behind whom may be identified works by or after Gavin Hamilton and Francesco Albani, as well as by Fabris and Fortrose themselves: Jenkins and Sloan, *Vases and Volcanoes*, 129. The two paintings in Edinburgh are signed by Fabris, among Sir William's favourite living painters, and dated 1771. It is clear that these works represent a selection of activities associated with Hamilton and Fortrose, and not a particular event. Fabris presumably sketched Leopold and Wolfgang performing some time before the works in question were executed.

115. Letter of 1 May 1778: *Letters of Mozart*, ed. Anderson, 531–32.
116. The surviving pages of the autograph of the horn concerto in E flat (K. 495) provide one example of this (New York, Pierpont Morgan Library, Mary Flagler Cary Music Collection). Mozart entered it in his own catalogue in 1786. For a reproduction, see Banks and Turner, *Mozart: Prodigy of Nature*, pl. X.
117. For a discussion of this, see the introduction to W.A. Mozart, *Neue Ausgabe sämlicher Werke*, ser. V/14, vol. v.
118. G.G. de Rossi, *Vita di Angelica Kauffman* (Florence, 1810), 16–18.
119. Innsbruck, Tyroler Landesmuseum: Roworth (ed.), *Angelica Kauffman*, pl. 8.
120. The Iveagh Bequest, Kenwood House: ibid., pl. 35.
121. Nostell Priory: ibid., 22, pl. 36; Shaw-Taylor, *Genial Company*, cat. 15.
122. For Shaftesbury, see Barrell, *Political Theory of Painting*, 27–32. For the significance of the *Choice of Hercules* theme in British visual culture of the eighteenth century, see David Mannings, 'Reynolds, Garrick, and the Choice of Hercules', *Eighteenth-Century Studies*, 17 (1983–84), 259–83. The theme was also treated musically: Fiske, *English Theatre Music*, 119–200. The subject was set as an interlude by Handel. Haydn, the key figure in the argument of this book, owned a German translation of the libretto set by Handel. Kauffman perhaps knew these German versions of the Hercules at the crossroads theme. But she was perhaps most familiar with the theme from the *festa teatrale* written by Metastasio to celebrate the first marriage of the future Emperor Joseph II in 1760 (*Acide al bivio*). This was originally set by Hasse and was subsequently taken up by other leading composers, including Paisiello (1780). The version by Righini (1790) seems to have been performed in several countries in the decades on either side of 1800 and may also have been known to Kauffman.

123.   Kauffman's self-portrait with personifications of painting and music is, of course, by no means the only image of this period suggesting a parity between painting and music in the public sphere. Many other portraits of the period around 1790 illustrate this. Another example is Romney's double portrait of Vicountess Clifden and Lady Elizabeth Spencer, daughters of the fourth Duke of Marlborough, as *Painting and Music*, by Romney (Los Angeles, Huntington Art Gallery). One sister is drawing, while the other plays a harp. An early example of this kind is J.H. Tischbein the Elder's *Self-Portrait with the Artist's Wife* of 1769 (Berlin, Gemäldegalerie), showing the painter himself in front of a canvas he is working on and his wife playing a clavier.

124.   From the *Public Advertiser*, quoted in Whitley, *Artists and their Friends*, ii, 71.

125.   Rennert, *William Crotch*, 46.

Notes to Chapter 2

1.   Or, to put it another way, to attain a popularity which might be found across the world *within this figure's own lifetime*.

2.   '... den bekannten Ruhm ihrer berühmten, allenthalben geschätzten Werke ...' (Haydn, *Briefe*, 405, no. 310).

3.   '... dal Messico a Calcuta, come da Napoli a Londra, da Pera a Parigi': Carpani, 3.

4.   Cf. Griesinger, 105. Griesinger, one of Haydn's other early biographers, made the same point about Haydn's compositions being heard across broad geographical regions, though in slightly different terms from Carpani: 'Haydn's quartets and symphonies, his oratorios and church pieces, please equally on the Danube and on the Thames, on the Seine and on the Neva, and they are prized and admired overseas as in our own corner of the globe' (ibid., 3).

5.   David C. Nichols, 'A Mexican Tribute to Haydn', *Haydn Yearbook*, 13 (1982), 231–32. See also Robert Stevenson, *Music in Mexico: A Historical Survey* (New York, 1952), 2, 176, 180, 189, 226.

6.   Landon, *Haydn at Eszterháza*, 673.

7.   For the early reception of Haydn's music in America, see Herter Norton, 'Haydn in America', 309–37; Lowens, *Haydn in America*, ch. 1.

8.   *Jefferson's Memorandum Books: Accounts, with Legal Records and Miscellany 1767–1826*, ed. James A. Bear and Lucia C. Stanton, 2 vols (Princeton, 1997), i, 580, 592, 603–5, 609, 626, 630, 638, 685, 693, 729, 734, 771.

9.   *Houdon in America: A Collection of Documents in the Jefferson Papers in the Library of Congress*, ed. Gilbert Chinard (Baltimore, 1930).

10.   Letter of 10 Dec. 1784: ibid., 32.

11.   Symphony No. 17. The manuscript copy (Salem Collegium Musicum) is dated 12 Dec. 1766: Lowens, *Haydn in America*, 16.

12.   The Handel & Haydn Society of Boston, founded in 1815, is still extant. It gave the first complete performance of *The Creation* in 1817.

13.   Carpani, 11.

14.   Penderel Moon, *The British Conquest and Dominion of India* (London, 1989), 259.

15.   Ian Woodfield, 'Haydn Symphonies in Calcutta', *Music & Letters*, 75 (1994), 141–43.

16.   Tolley, 'Music in the Circle of Sir William Jones', 528, 549.

17.   *The Letters of Sir William Jones*, ed. Garland Cannon (Oxford, 1970), ii, 736.

18. *A Collection of Portraits Sketched from the Life*, ii (1814, n. p.).
19. 'Meine Sprache verstehet man durch die ganze Welt.' Reported by Dies, 78.
20. 'With the passing of time it [music] became a kind of speech – even a language – by means of which the different passions of the soul are expressed', from D'Alembert's *Discours préliminaire*: translation from le Huray and Day, *Music and Aesthetics*, 59.
21. *Essai sur l'origine des langues*, ch. 12, published in *Traités sur la musique* (Geneva, 1781).
22. Quoted in *Diary and Letters of Madame d'Arblay, Edited by her Niece*, vi: *1793–1812* (London, 1846), 37.
23. For the notion of the 'homogeneity' of music in the later eighteenth century, and for its development into a 'lingua franca' resting on 'the uncontested dominion of Italian opera', see Daniel Heartz, 'Classical', in *New Grove*, iv, 451.
24. Johann Karl Friederich Triest (1764–1810), writing in *AMZ*, 24 (1801), col. 407, translated in Sisman (ed.), *Haydn and his World*, 373.
25. For evidence of Mozart's success as an opera composer and performer in Vienna during the last five years of his life (when it has often been assumed there was a decline in his fortunes), see Dexter Edge, 'Mozart's Reception in Vienna, 1787–1791', in Stanley Sadie (ed.), *Wolfgang Amadè Mozart: Essays on his Life and his Music* (Oxford, 1996), 66–119. It should be stressed that this evidence (including box office receipts) shows Mozart to have been one of a number of popular composers in Vienna at this time. It might also be used to suggest how Mozart's reputation during these years (by comparison with Haydn's) was sustained chiefly on a local basis, rather than internationally.
26. For example, one of Haydn's acquaintances in London later wrote: 'I have heard Haydn, while he was in England, declare that Mozart was the most extraordinary, original and comprehensive musical genius that was ever known in this or any age' (Parke, *Musical Memoirs*, i, 170). Haydn himself wrote in 1792 that it dismayed him that he was unable to convince the English of the Mozart's greatness: *CCLN* 125.
27. The anecdote concerning Joseph II's view of *Die Entführung aus dem Serail* was first recounted in Franz Xaver Niemetschek's *Leben des k.k. Kapellmeisters Wolfgang Gottlieb Mozart* (Prague, 1798). Dittersdorf's report of a discussion he had with Joseph II on the subject of Mozart and Haydn and their relative merits provides good evidence of considered opinion in the early 1780s: *The Autobiography of Karl von Dittersdorf*, trans. Coleridge, 252–53. Both Dittersdorf and the Emperor agreed that in Mozart's compositions there was too much formally, melodically and texturally for the listener to grasp, at least on first hearing. By implication, this 'deficiency' did not apply to Haydn, whose (chamber) compositions they confirm were known to have created 'a world-wide sensation'. To appreciate the beauties of Mozart required the listener to work hard and often, whereas those of Haydn were believed to be evident 'at first glance'.
28. Cf. Sutcliffe, *Haydn: String Quartets, Op. 50*, 66.
29. Letters of 11–12 and 14 Feb. 1778: Mozart, *Letters of Mozart*, ed. Anderson, 475, 481.
30. Letter of 5 Apr. 1778: ibid., 521.
31. Letter of 6 May 1778: ibid., 536.
32. Letter of 20 Apr. 1778: ibid., 529. Leopold repeated this sentiment on 6 May 1778.
33. Letter of 31 July 1778: ibid., 587.

34. Letter of 9 July 1778: ibid., 564.
35. Holcroft, *The Life of Thomas Holcroft*, ii, 143.
36. For Haydn's relations with Holcroft, see Schroeder, *Haydn and the Enlightenment*, 118–19.
37. Holcroft, *The Life of Thomas Holcroft*, ii, 193.
38. From the *k.k. priviligierte Realzeitung* for 6 Apr. 1775: quoted by Landon, *Haydn at Eszterháza*, 215.
39. Griesinger letter to Breitkopf & Härtel of 21 Jan., 1801: Olleson, 'Georg August Griesinger's Correspondence with Breitkopf & Härtel', 16.
40. Haydn, *Briefe*, 443–44.
41. The society was called the Gesellschaft bildender Künstler: A. Steininger, *Hundertfünfzig Jahre Pensionsgesellschaft bildender Künstler in Wien. 1788–1938: Festschrift zur Jubelfeier am 12. Mai 1938* (Vienna, 1938).
42. Hob. IX, 11, 12: Günter Thomas, 'Studien zu Haydns Tanzmusik', *Haydn-Studien*, 3 (1973), 5–16.
43. The evidence for this comes from Haydn's list of German opera librettos, which includes the following item: 'Auf das erste ballfest der Bildenden Künstle / Der Apoteker v [*sic*] ... umlauf' : Landon, *The Late Years*, 325. The list is reproduced in facsimile in *Haydn Yearbook*, 1 (1962), 139. 'Der Apoteker' is presumably a version of Haydn's 1768 opera *Lo Speziale*. Carpani (p. 134) mentions a piece by Haydn called 'Die Apoteche', otherwise unidentified. See also Günter Thomas, 'Haydns deutsche Singspiele', *Haydn-Studien*, 6 (1986), 1–63.
44. Landon, *Haydn in England*, 205–7.
45. Landon has amassed evidence for considering that Haydn's Deutsche Tänze were among the earliest to be danced in the manner of a waltz: *Haydn in England*, 208–12. To this may be added Carpani's statement that Haydn wrote 'arie di Waltzer pei festini del ridotto [i.e. the Redoutensaal]': p. 81. Although he says that these 'walzes' were among Haydn's earliest works, this is clearly anachronistic. The works Haydn wrote for the Gesellschaft bildender Künstler in 1792 were his only works for the Redoutensaal, so it seems likely that, as so often with Carpani, what he wrote is muddled, though based on authentic reports. Van Swieten, in his suggestions to Haydn on how to set *The Seasons*, refers to walzes, perhaps because he knew that the popularity of this new dance had something to do with Haydn.
46. *Wiener Zeitung*, 14 and 18 Nov. 1795, No. 91, quoted in Landon, *Beethoven*, 50. Another announcement for the same ball referred to Beethoven acting 'out of love for the artistic community': Albrecht (trans. and ed.), *Letters to Beethoven*, i, no. 20, 39–40. Beethoven's relationship with the Gesellschaft bildender Künstler continued for several years.
47. Holcroft, *The Life of Thomas Holcroft*, i, xxi, 6, 109–10, 118.
48. Paintings by Richard Wilson seem to have been particularly favoured by Tory landowners: see David H. Solkin, *Richard Wilson: The Landscape of Reaction*, exh. cat., Tate Gallery (London, 1982).
49. Haydn's collection and his relations with artists in England are fully treated in Ch. 6.
50. For Dies, see: Andreas Andersen, *Die deutschen Maler-Radierer des neunzehnten Jahrhunderts*, iii (Leipzig, 1878), 165–82; H. Seeger, 'Zur musikhistorischen Bedeutung der Haydn-Biographie von Albert Christoph Dies (1810)', *Beiträge zur Musikwissenschaft*, 1/3 (1959), 24–34.
51. Goethe, *Italian Journey*, trans. Auden and Mayer, entry for 22 July 1788.

52. *Annalen der bildenden Künste für die österreichischen Staaten*, ii (1802), 165–82. The commentary is in the form of a reply to a piece of art criticism by this journal's founder, H.R. Füssli, who had used Lessing's *Laocoön* to support his view that artists should not select subjects which ordinary amateurs of art could not understand.

53. Dies explains this in the introduction to his book, pp. 11–15. Grassi had sculpted a number of portraits of Haydn, which are discussed in Ch. 5.

54. Dies, 11.

55. Ibid., 12.

56. Ibid.

57. Ibid., 13.

58. Dies perhaps chose Denner as an example of a painter renowned for excessive naturalism partly because although he came from Hamburg, he was known in Vienna (Charles VI having paid the extraordinary sum of 600 ducats for a head of a woman by him), and partly because he was associated with two famous composers, Handel (who bequeathed two of his paintings to his librettist Jennens) and J.S. Bach (whom he depicted): *Zwei Hamburger Maler: Balthasar Denner und Franz Werner Tamn*, exh. cat., Hamburg Kunsthalle (1969); Börsch-Supran, 'Georg Friedrich Händel und Balthasar Denner'.

59. Dies, 24.

60. The *European Magazine* for 8 Oct. 1784: Brown, 'The Earliest English Biography of Haydn'.

61. *Letters of Dr Charles Burney*, i, ed. Alvaro Ribeiro, 54.

62. Ibid.

63. Gilreath and Wilson, *Thomas Jefferson's Library*, 110–11.

64. Burney, *A General History*, ed. Mercer, ii, 958.

65. Ibid., 959.

66. Ibid., 437.

67. For the mythologizing of Mozart's life, see Maynard Solomon, 'The Rochlitz Anecdotes: Issues of Authenticity in Early Mozart Biography', in Clifford Eisen (ed.), *Mozart Studies* (Oxford, 1991), 1–59; W. Stafford, *Mozart's Death: A Corrective Survey of the Legends* (London, 1991).

68. For an account of these, see Gruber, *Mozart and Posterity*, ch. 1.

69. *Leben des k.k. Kapellmeisters Wolfgang Gottlieb Mozart*, published in Prague.

70. 'Parallele zwischen Raphael und Mozart', *AMZ*, 2 (11 June 1800), cols 641–51.

71. For example, in 1858 Georges Bizet could quite unaffectedly refer to Raphael as being 'the same man as Mozart'; and later still, Dvořák, on looking at one of Raphael's Madonnas, was heard to utter 'That is Mozart!' Bizet had a special fascination for Raphael which he often associated with Mozart: Mina Curtis, *Bizet and his World* (London, 1959), 72, 77, 99; Georges Bizet, *Lettres*, ed. Claude Glayman (Paris, 1989), 53, 62, 81. For Dvořák, see John Clapham, *Dvořák* (Newton Abbot, 1979), 169.

72. *Dr Burney's Musical Tours*, ed. Scholes, ii, 100, 120.

73. Edward Bellasis, *Cherubini: Memorials Illustrative of his Life* (London, 1874), 109. It is probably relevant that one of Veronese's most famous paintings, the *Marriage Feast at Cana*, had been brought to Paris at the instigation of Napoleon the previous year.

74. Licht, *Canova*, 15.

75. Vincent Duckles, 'Johann Nicolaus Forkel: The Beginning of Music Historiography', *Eighteenth-Century Studies*, 1 (1968), 277–90.

76. *The Seven Last Words* (1795–96), *The Creation* (1795–98) and *The Seasons* (1798–1801).
77. Landon, *Late Years*, 403, no. 604.
78. The *Brevi notizie istoriche della vita e delle opere di Giuseppe Haydn* (Bergamo, 1809).
79. E.g., Nicolas Framery, *Notice sur Joseph Haydn* (Paris, 1810). Among other notices published in France was one by Haydn's former pupil Sigismund Neukomm (translated by his friend Rossel), which appeared as *Notice biographique sur Joseph Haydn* in 1809: Marc Vignal, 'A Side-Aspect of Sigismund Neukomm's Journey to France in 1809', *Haydn Yearbook*, 2 (1963–64), 81–87. The following year saw a *Notice historique sur la vie et les ouvrages de Haydn*, an obituary by J. Le Breton. In 1812 there appeared an anonymous *Essai historique sur la vie de Joseph Haydn*, published in Strasbourg. For Framery, see Landon, *Haydn at Eszterháza*, 757–63.
80. *Mozarts Geist: Seine kurze Biographie und ästhetische Darstellung seiner Werke. Ein Bildungsbuch für junge Tonkünstler* (Erfurt, 1803). For Arnold, see Michael F. Robinson, 'An Early Biography of Paisiello', *Haydn Yearbook*, 16 (1985), 208–11.
81. *Gallerie der berühmtesten Tonkünstler des achtzehnten und neunzehnten Jahrhunderts: Ihre kurzen Biographien, karakterisirende Anekdoten und ästhetischen Darstellung ihrer Werke* (Erfurt, 1810).
82. *Gallerie der berühmtesten Tonkünstler des 18. und 19. Jahrhunderts ... W.A. Mozart und Joseph Haydn: Versuch einer Parallele* (Erfurt, 1810; 2nd edn, 1816).
83. It appeared in the Weimar *Journal des Luxus und der Moden* in July 1805, 449–52. The article, though based on notes supplied by Griesinger, was actually written anonymously by Carl Bertuch, another Haydn enthusiast. The same information was later used by Gerber in an enlarged edition of his musical dictionary published in 1812.
84. Griesinger, 1.
85. Ibid., 5–6.
86. Examples include Cimarosa compared with Cervantes, Mozart with Shakespeare, and Salieri with Schiller.
87. For Carpani's career, see G.P. Marchi, 'Carpani, Giuseppe' in *Dizionario biografico degli italiani*, xx, 581–5. For a bibliography of Carpani's writings, see Stendhal, *Lives of Haydn, Mozart and Metastasio*, trans. Coe, 283–91.
88. It was subtitled *Lettere sulla vita e le opere del celebre maestro Giuseppe Haydn*.
89. The letters are dated between 15 Apr. 1808 and 30 Mar. 1811.
90. Several popular English novels had adopted this format. One early example is Samuel Richardson's *Pamela* (1740), which was very well known on the Continent, and had inspired one of Goldoni's most successful librettos, *La buona figliuola* (1756), set by Piccinni (1760) and others.
91. Carpani, 101.
92. Ibid., 221, 253. Such comparisons were *individually* not entirely new: Burney had likened the capacity of Haydn's music to attract listeners to Newton's theory of gravity, and Griesinger had seen in Haydn the realization of some of Kant's precepts on genius and rule-making in the fine arts. Burney's comparison comes from his poem on the composer's arrival in England: Landon, *Haydn in England*, 35. For Griesinger's comparison with Kant, whom he quotes, see

Griesinger, 113. For comment on perceptions of Haydn in connection with Kant, see Harrison, *Haydn: The 'Paris' Symphonies*, 18–20. In making a comparison with Kant, Carpani may have merely had in mind a straightforward comparison between two near-contemporary figures, both most distinguished in their separate fields. Some of his readers might have been prepared for this parallel by Abbé Vogler, who is known to have improvised on the theme of 'Kant's philosophy'. But Carpani may have intended to suggest more, drawing attention to the philosopher's view (expressed in *The Critique of Judgement*), that unlike the other arts, which owed their appeal to the intellect, music was emotive, speaking 'merely through sensations without concepts, and so [music] does not, in contrast to poetry, allow room for reflection, though it moves the mind in more varied ways and with greater intensity, but only temporarily' (*Kritik der Urteilskraft*, Berlin, 1790, 218).

93. Pestelli, 'Giuseppi Carpani'.

94. *Descrizione delle pitture della cupola di S. Celso in Milano*; *Piano generale di tutte le pitture del palazzo Serbelloni*; *Lettera su di un quadro di madama Le Brun*. These and several other titles are only known from C. Baseggio, *Biografia degli italiani illustri nelle scienze, lettere ed arti del scolo XVIII* (Venice, 1845). A *Dissertazione intorno alla maniera e lo stile manierato* sounds as though it might be a very early attempt to analyse the style now known as 'Mannerism'. The word *manierato* ('stylized'), commonly used in relation to the style of much Italian art between the time of Raphael (d. 1520) and Annibale Carracci (d. 1609), was then generally applied pejoratively. Carpani was probably following the great historian of Italian painting, Luigi Lanzi, who devised the term *manierismo* as a positive stylistic label for this period: John Sherman, *Mannerism* (Harmondsworth, 1967), 19.

95. In 1819 Carpani entered into a protracted debate with the critic, painter and amateur musician Andrea Majer, who had published a book which, among other things, asserted that art should appeal primarily to the senses rather than the intellect, maintaining that colour was the most important aspect of a painter's work, and that the Venetian school of painting, and Titian in particular, set the best examples to follow: *Della imitazione pittorica, sulla eccellenza delle opere di Tiziano e della vita di Tiziano scritta da S. Ticozzi* (Venice, 1818). Majer also emphasized the need for the artist to imitate nature truthfully in all its forms, sharply opposing ideas of neoclassicists like Winckelmann and Mengs, who advocated the pursuit of 'ideal beauty' stemming from study of the selective examples of sculpture believed to have been created in classical Greek antiquity. Carpani responded to this in a series of letters published in a well-read Italian journal (subsequently collected together in book form), in which he reaffirmed the value of Winckelmann's assertions, especially the artistic quest for ideal beauty: *Le Majeriane, ovvero Del bello ideale e delle opere di Tiziano. Lettere* (Padua, 1820). Several editions of *Le Majeriane* appeared. Majer pursued the polemic with his *Apologia del libro della imitazione pittorica ... contra tre lettere di Giuseppe Carpani* (Ferrara, 1820), to which Carpani retaliated by republishing *Le Majeriane* in 1824.

96. *Spiegazione drammatica del monumento della Arciduchessa Cristina, opera del Cavaliere Antonio Canova*, published by J.V. Degen. If this survives, it has not been possible to locate a copy of it. It was published in French, German as well as Italian versions.

97. Canova hardly enjoyed the kind of popular reputation gained by Haydn, his patrons being almost exclusively drawn from the aristocracy or leading

churchmen, but he none the less received commissions from almost every country in Europe, and later from America.

98. Duke Albert was the greatest collector of Old Master drawings and prints of his age, and a known supporter of Haydn. These aspects of his patronage are discussed in greater detail in Ch. 3.

99. James Stevens Curl, *The Egyptian Revival: An Introductory Study of a Recurring Theme in the History of Taste* (London, 1982), 74, 98–99, 155.

100. For interpretive possibilities, see *The Age of Neo-Classicism*, exh. cat., Royal Academy, London (1972), 526, no. 313.

101. E.C.J. Van de Vivere, *Le Mausolée de S.A.R. Marie-Christine ...* (Rome, 1805); C.F. Ferow, *Über den Bildhauer Canova und dessen Werke* (Zürich, 1806), 149–88.

102. E. Bassi, *La Gipsoteca di Possagno* (Venice, 1957), 93–102; Hugh Honour, 'Canova's Studio Practice – II: 1792–1822', *Burlington Magazine*, 114 (1972), 214.

103. The composer told him that the aria 'refers to me'. This led Neukomm to write that: 'In this wonderful masterpiece, [Haydn] really spoke from the very innermost part of his soul, for he became seriously ill when composing it and one had to assume that this was the decisive point in which the Lord giveth, the Lord taketh away, closing Haydn's glorious career and allowing him to see "his life's progress and his open grave" [quoting the text of the aria].' (Quoted in Landon, *Late Years*, 124.)

104. For a reproduction, see Fraenkel, *Decorative Music Title Pages*, no. 181.

105. For example, in Thomas Stothard's illustration *The Four Seasons* of 1794, the four personifications (all young women) hold hands in a circle with a zodiac ring shown above them.

106. A 'rather agreeable old fool': Olleson, 'Griesinger's Correspondence', 32. It was the work of V.G. Kininger, who designed many important musical frontispieces. Examples of his work were in Haydn's own collection (see Ch. 6).

107. *Journal des Luxus und der Moden*, 16 (1801), 414: quoted and translated by Landon, *Late Years*, 45.

108. *Zeitung für die elegante Welt*, 1 (1801), 427: quoted and translated by Landon, *Late Years*, 45.

109. Carpani, 212.

110. It also probably had a bearing on his lyrics for *In questa Tomba oscura* (1806), perhaps the most famous words of the period intended for musical setting. Within two years the words had been set no fewer than 63 times, by a range of composers, including Beethoven. The song's subject matter concerns the darkened tomb of a lover, whose beloved now finds herself also drawn to the grave. The darkened tomb of the song relates, of course, to the dark entrance to Canova's tomb. Carpani completed his guide to the Christine monument earlier in the year he wrote the song. For mentions of Canova in *Le Haydine*, see Carpani, 251, 259.

111. The first edition, published in Florence in 1792, covered only the southern Italian schools and included in its title 'per agevolare a' dilettanti la cognizione de' professori e de' loro stili'. The first complete edition was published in Bassano in 1795–96 and revised by the author in 1809 when Carpani started to put together *Le Haydine*. The *Storia pittorica* went through many later editions and was soon available in translation.

112. It seems likely that Carpani knew Lanzi when the latter moved to the Veneto in 1794 to oversee the publication of the *Storia pittorica* in Bassano. Carpani was

then still active in Venice and Lanzi is known to have come into contact with several scholars.

113. Carpani, 214.

114. Vasari's comments come from the second edition of his *Vite* (1568): translation from Vasari, *The Lives*, trans. Hind, iv, 23. For Fuseli on Tintoretto, see [Fuseli], *Remarks on Rousseau* (London, 1767), 7. That Tintoretto's work was also no longer held in high esteem within the Habsburg empire by the time Haydn started his career is suggested by the fact that at least one major painting by him was sold from the imperial collections (1749). For the circumstances of this sale, see Slim, 'Tintoretto's "Music-Making Women"', 45.

115. Paris, Louvre: Mirimonde, 'Le Sabier, la musique et la danse', 131–36. The musical-pictorial association seems to have been sufficiently well known for one near-contemporary of Carpani's, the American painter Washington Allston, who was trained in London and Rome, to claim of Tintoretto and Veronese that 'They addressed themselves, not to the senses merely, ... but rather through them to that region ... of the imagination which is supposed to be under the exclusive domination of music' (E.P. Richardson, *Washington Allston*, 2nd edn, New York, 1967, 60). For an example of Tintoretto's supposed musicality as noted in the seventeenth century, mention may be made of Ridolfi's *Life of Tintoretto* (1642), which states that in his youth the painter enjoyed playing the lute and other strange instruments of his own invention. Early sources mentioning the musical interests and abilities of Tintoretto and members of his family are discussed by Weddingen, 'Jacopo Tintoretto und die Musik', 68–119.

116. Roger de Piles, *Cours de peinture par principes* (Paris, 1708), appendix. An indication of how the *Balance des peintres* soon captured the public's imagination is that in later editions and translations of the book it was listed as a subtitle on the title-page, as being of use to those who wished to be instructed in the value of painting.

117. Carpani, 126.

118. Ibid., 50.

119. Ibid., 59, 148, 177.

120. Ibid., 254, 256.

121. Ibid., 67.

122. For discussion of the series by Wenceslaus Hollar (executed between 1637 and 1642, and reissued in 1648 and 1666), by Jacob Sandrart (1652) and the Comte de Caylus (1730), see Turner, *Inventing Leonardo*, 81–82. The Hollar heads were republished in London in 1786 as *Characturas by Leonardo da Vinci from Drawings by Winceslaus Hollar out of the Portland Museum*.

123. J. Mariette, *Recueil de testes de caractère et de charges, dessinés par Léonard de Vinci florentin, et gravés par M. C[omte] de C[aylus]* (Paris, 1730); C. Le Brun, *Conference de Monsieur Le Brun premier peintre du Roy de France ... enrichie de figures gravés par B. Picard* (Paris, 1698). See Montagu, *The Expression of the Passions*.

124. Carpani, 73.

125. The key publications concerned works by Leonardo in the Royal Collection at Windsor Castle and in the Biblioteca Ambrosiana, Milan: C. Gerli, Disegni di Leonardo da Vinci incisi e pubblicati da Carlo Giuseppe Gerli milanese, con prefazione dell'Amoretti (Milan, 1784); J. Chamberlaine, *Imitations of Original Designs by Leonardo da Vinci* (London, 1796); G. Venturi, *Essai sur les ouvrages physico-mathématiques de Léonard de Vinci* (Milan, 1797);

C. Amoretti, *Memorie storiche su la vita, gli studi e le opere di Leonardo da Vinci* (Milan, 1804).

126. Carpani, 126.
127. *Galerie des peintres flamands, hollandais, et allemands* (Paris, 1792–96). Elisabeth Vigée-Lebrun describes the pre-Revolutionary music-making in the rue de Cléry in her memoirs. After she left her husband, he continued the concerts, probably on a grander scale: de Place, *La Vie musicale en France*, 241–42.
128. Carpani, 175, 177.
129. Ibid., 99, 174, 215.
130. Ibid., letters 10 and 12.
131. Ibid., 174, 205.
132. Ibid., 164.
133. Ibid., 166.
134. Ibid., 169. Such works were clearly well known to van Swieten who, Carpani implies, thought that at the point he started working with Haydn the time was ripe for such effects to receive more extensive application in music.
135. Ora F. Saloman, 'La Cépède's *La poétique de la musique* and Le Sueur', *Acta musicologica*, 67 (1975), 144–55.
136. Translations from le Huray and Day, *Music and Aesthetics*, 182–83.
137. Ibid., 181.
138. Griesinger, 72; Dies, 180. Dies implies that Haydn thought that Grétry had imitated the sounds of croaking frogs in music, but several composers may have illustrated the point. Rameau's *Platée* (mid-1740s) provides one example. Others may be found in compositions by Biber and Rousseau. Haydn may have been particularly sensitive on this point because his quartet Op. 50/6 earned the nickname 'The Frog' on account of the opening theme of its last movement, the *bariolage* of which apparently reminded some listeners of the croaking of frogs. I have been unable to discover when the nickname was first applied, but of course the association may have been made from a date earlier than the genesis of *The Seasons*, possibly offending the composer.
139. See Gotwals, *Haydn: Two Contemporary Portraits*, 259–60.
140. The fifth movement of the suite representing 'April' in Werner's *Musikalischer Instrumental-Kalender* is labelled *Das Froschgeschrei*. Werner's *Kalendar* is further discussed in the next chapter of this book.
141. Griesinger, 71–72.
142. *CCLN*, 18–21; Haydn, *Briefe*, 76–82.
143. Haydn, *Briefe*, 78.
144. *A General History*, ed. Mercer, ii, 959.
145. Haydn, *Briefe*, 115.
146. It appeared in *Das gelehrte Oesterreich*, 1/3 (1776), 309.
147. Griesinger, 80.
148. Borthwick, 'The Latin Quotations in Haydn's London Notebooks'.
149. *Thayer's Life of Beethoven*, ed. Forbes, 1046.
150. The Englishman Alcuin used it in a letter to Charlemagne in the early ninth century. The Archbishop of Canterbury took the words as his text in his sermon at the coronation of Edward III. For many further examples establishing the antiquity of the phrase in England, see Morris Palmer Tilley, *A Dictionary of the Proverbs in England in the Sixteenth and Seventeenth Centuries* (Ann Arbor, 1950), 700; F.P. Wilson, *The Oxford Dictionary of English Proverbs*, 3rd edn, rev. (Oxford, 1970), 862.

151. *Aphorisms*, trans. Hollingdale, 51, no. D2.
152. *The First Epistle of the Second Book of Horace Imitated* (1737), lines 89–90. Haydn's library included Pope's *Essay on Man*: Hörwarthner, no. 76.
153. For discussion of examples of such prints, see Donald, *The Age of Caricature*, 60–62, 126. One of these prints is actually satirized in an engraving owned by Haydn, Bunbury's *A Smoking Club*: see Appendix, item 14 (see Ch. 5 for further discussion of this).
154. BMC 6594.
155. Haydn, *Briefe*, 493. The second anecdote, which Haydn unfortunately did not complete, intriguingly concerned 'Mr Fox's trousers', a sedan-chair carrier, and the loss and retrieval of £4,000: ibid., 509.
156. Hörwarthner, 194, no. 85. Haydn may also have seen one of Holcroft's plays staged when he was in London, like the very successful *The Road to Ruin* (1791), in which fast-living and fashion-conscious sons of the well-to-do indulge in a hedonistic lifestyle with neither consideration nor purpose. The play was thought by some to be a political satire, the object of which is clarified in a print of the same title by William Dent (1792) showing a horse race with the Prince of Wales, his brothers, their mistresses and others as the riders heading for a finishing-post labelled 'Styx', the river of the Underworld across which the souls of the dead were ferried: Donald, *Age of Caricature*, 99–100, fig. 109.
157. In writing to Burney about subscribers to *The Creation*, Haydn expressed his regret concerning the Duke's death: *Briefe*, 336–37. The Duke had been on good terms with Burney also.
158. Haydn, *Briefe*, 481.
159. According to the list of items in Haydn's print collection drawn up after his death: Appendix, item 34. The cataloguer listed the print as 'John Earl of Chatham [Pitt's brother] nach de Koster von Keating', but this was in fact a misidentification derived from the long inscription below the portrait which mentions members of Pitt's family before giving his name. The Austrian cataloguer could not read English well enough to work out which name in the inscription identified the name of the sitter.
160. Parke, *Memoirs*, i, 144 (referring to 1791).
161. Griesinger, 62; Dies, 107, 113.
162. See Mozart's letter to his father of 3 Nov. 1781: *The Letters of Mozart*, ed. Anderson, 776.
163. London, National Portrait Gallery: Richard Walker, *National Portrait Gallery: Regency Portraits*, 2 vols (London, 1985), 598–604.
164. 'The Exhibition is now fully open from 10 till 6, at No 28 Haymarket, of a Picture 15 feet wide 11 feet high representing the House of Commons, painted by Mr A. Hickel, commenced in the year 1793, contains 96 Portraits as large as life, taken by favour from the Honourable Gentlemen themselves. Admittance one Shilling. Subscriptions are received at the Exhibition Room for a Print to be engraved from the above size 30 inches wide by 22 high. Proofs six guineas, half to be paid on subscribing and the remainder on delivery of the Prints.' *The Times*, 8 May 1795 (quoted in Walker, *Regency Portraits*, 599–600).
165. 9 June 1795. Although evidently planned, the print was never executed. The complexity and cost in terms of time for the engraver may account for this failure, as much as any lack of subscriptions.
166. John Andrew Bernstein, 'Shaftesbury's Identification of the Good with the Beautiful', *Eighteenth-Century Studies*, 10 (1977), 304–25.
167. 'The Art which we profess has *beauty* for its object; this is our business to

discover and to express; ... it is an idea residing in the breast of the artist, which he is always labouring to impart, ... but which he is yet so far able to communicate, as to *raise the thoughts*, and *extend the views of the spectator*; and which, by a succession of art, may be so far diffused, that its effects may extend themselves imperceptibly into *public benefits*, and be among the means of bestowing on *whole nations refinement of taste*: which, if it does not lead directly to purity of manners, obviates their greatest depravation, ... and conducting the thoughts through successive stages of excellence, till that contemplation of universal rectitude and harmony which began by Taste, may, as it is exalted and refined, *conclude in Virtue*' (my italics). From the Ninth Discourse (1780): Reynolds, *Discourses on Art*, ed. Wark, 151.

168. Hörnwarthner, no. 45. Haydn's relations with Royal Academy members will be discussed later in this book. For a discussion of Haydn and Shaftesbury's thinking, see Schroeder, *Haydn and the Enlightenment*, 9–20.

169. Carpani, 4–11.

170. For Jones's views on Handel, see Tolley, 'Music in the Circle of Sir William Jones', 529.

171. Griesinger, 57–58.

172. Parke, *Memoirs*, i, 197.

173. Haydn, *Briefe*, 552–53.

174. Griesinger, 58.

175. The words of Griesinger (p. 101).

176. Such as prohibitions against marriage to Catholics for a member of the royal family. This was a subject of topicality at the time he arrived in England, because of the Prince of Wales's morganatic marriage to Mrs Fitzherbert, a Catholic.

177. Ward and Roberts, *Romney*, 53.

178. See *CCLN*, 290. Haydn kept Tattersall's *Improved Psalmody* in his library until his death: Landon, *Late Years*, 398, no. 341.

179. Haydn, *Briefe*, 507.

180. Dies, 124.

181. Haydn, *Briefe*, 157–58.

182. From the 'Reminiscences' of Samuel Wesley (British Library, Add. MS 27593, f. 70), written at the end of his life.

183. Part of a letter to Vincent Novello, dated 22 Nov. 1828: quoted from Landon, *Haydn in England*, 58.

184. For the interest of Methodists in Handel's oratorios in the later eighteeth century, see Winton Dean, *Handel's Dramatic Oratorios and Masques* (London, 1959), 140–44; Smith, *Handel's Oratorios*, 354–59. For the status of Methodism, see David Hempton, *Methodism and Politics in British Society, 1750–1850* (London, 1984).

185. Samuel Wesley's 'Reminiscences' (British Library, Add. MS 27593, f. 70).

186. For the officer, see Haydn, *Briefe*, 121–22; Carpani, 230–1. The officer has been identified as Sir Henry Harpur, and the marches as those he presented to the volunteer cavalry troop raised by the gentry of Derbyshire in response to the threat from France (Hob. VIII: 1, 2). For the young woman, see Haydn, *Briefe*, 31–32 (Griesinger) and Dies, 120. The song Haydn wrote for her is *Der schlaue und dienstfertige Pudel* (Hob. XXVIa: 38).

187. Pierre, *Histoire du Concert spirituel*, 175–77.

188. Landon, *Haydn at Eszterháza*, 590–95.

189. For the information which follows, see Harrison, *'Paris' Symphonies*, ch. 1.

190. See ibid., 103, n. 20. It may be noted that a description of the last movement of the Farewell Symphony and how it came into being is given by a contemporary Parisian diarist: *Mémoires secrets pour servir à l'histoire de la république des lettres en France depuis MDCCLXII jusqu'à nos jours*, xxv (London, 1786), entry for 15 Apr. 1784.

191. Quoted from Landon, *Haydn at Eszterháza*, 595.

192. Part of a letter dated 28 Aug. 1789: Haydn, *Briefe*, 212.

193. For example, the hen protecting her eggs appears in a print showing a clergyman (opposed to the Civil Constitution of the Clergy) holding one snake and blowing another (*serpent* was the name of a curved wind instrument), putting the new, as yet fragile, order of fraternity in France (represented by the hen and her eggs) in jeopardy: Cuno, *French Caricature*, 172, no. 56. The cock, of course, became an even more powerful symbol of French nationhood, specifically referring to the necessity for vigilance to protect the new freedoms. However, in pre-Revolutionary France, both the cock and the hen were associated with the popular view of the poor peasant, trying to sustain a living on the land. Feeding 'La poule' was perhaps the best-known activity connected with this view. For an example, see Guérard's print *L'homme de village* (*c*.1710), illustrated in Adhémar, *La Gravure originale*, 27.

194. It appears in the catalogue of his collection drawn up in 1809–10: Appendix, item 7.

195. For a detailed account of Haydn's popularity in Paris during the last years of the eighteenth and first years of the nineteenth centuries, see Johnson, *Listening in Paris*, 198–204.

196. *Tablettes de Polymnie* for 5 Apr. 1811; *Gazette de France*, 26 June 1818, 693: quoted and translated in Johnson, *Listening in Paris*, 198, 202.

197. See e.g. Haydn's letter to Pleyel of 4 May 1801: *Briefe*, 363.

198. Landon, *Late Years*, 340.

199. For this point, see Temperley, *The Creation*, 14.

200. Although van Swieten borrowed this story, something of its narrative was probably already known to Haydn since he owned a pair of prints illustrating parts of Marmontel's original *conte*. This will be discussed in greater detail in Ch. 5.

201. *Ein sehr gewöhnliche Geschichte* (Hob. XXVIa: 4).

202. *Die Verlassene* (Hob. XXVIa: 5).

203. For an account of Haydn's arrangements of Scottish songs, see Fiske, *Scotland in Music*, 55–74.

204. Cecil Hopkinson and C.B. Oldman, 'Haydn's Settings of Scottish Songs in the Collections of Napier and Whyte', *Edinburgh Bibliographical Society Transactions*, 3, pt. 2 [for 1949–51] (Edinburgh, 1954).

205. *Dr Burney's Musical Tours* , ed. Scholes, i, 254.

206. For Allan, see: Skinner, *The Indefatigable Mr Allan*, esp. 14, 20; Macmillan, *Painting in Scotland: The Golden Age*, 64–73; Jenkins and Sloan, *Vases and Volcanoes*, 223–24, 242–46. A large number of watercolours by Allan record daily activities in Naples and Scotland, many of them of a musical character. Members of the Cathcart family, which was associated with Allan throughout his career, took a keen interest in developing the visual arts in Scotland, notably their sponsorship of the Foulis Academy in Glasgow, the earliest 'Academy of Fine Arts' in Britain. Lady Cathcart was the sister of Sir William Hamilton, the British envoy in Naples. This connection explains Allan's particular concern with depictions of both Neapolitan and Scottish rural customs. Mozart and his

father met Sir William during their visit to Naples in 1770 (see Fig. 3). Haydn's music written for the court in Naples would also almost certainly have been performed at Sir William's residence. He, his second wife, Emma, and Nelson all became friendly with Haydn in Austria in 1800 (see Ch. 8). The main theme of the Finale of Haydn's Symphony No. 100 is known in arrangements connecting it with the Cathcart family, such as the title 'Lord Cathcart's Welcome to Scotland', probably referring to Sir William's nephew: Arthur W.J.G. Ord-Hume, *Joseph Haydn and the Mechanical Organ* (Cardiff, 1982), 26. Further indications that the pictorial enthusiasms of an artist like Allan were understood by some to be relevant to perceptions of Haydn's music comes from the interests of George Thomson, the Edinburgh publisher, who commissioned arrangements of Scottish songs from Haydn and also many vignettes from Allan to decorate his publications. It has been noted that the music and dance scenes represented by Allan may be considered expressions of an ordered society: Macmillan, *Painting in Scotland: The Golden Age*, 73. The same point may apply to Haydn's contributions to Scottish culture. It is relevant that Allan was on close terms with James Tassie, the Scottish portraitist for whom Haydn sat in London (see Ch. 5).

207. Haydn, *Briefe*, 538.
208. Griesinger (pp. 108–9) gives an anecdote about Tenducci's favourite air which he read in Haydn's (lost) London notebook, so it seems possible that the composer was informed of the kind of music with which the singer had previously been associated in London.
209. *The Life of Rossini*, trans. and ed. Richard N. Coe, 2nd edn (London, 1985), 462–63.
210. For an account of early arrangements of Burns's lyrics and the tunes they were intended for, see Peter Davidson, 'Song Arrangements', in *The Songs of Robert Burns*, ed. Donald Low (London, 1993), 934–48. Although the conventional scholarly view is that Haydn received only the melodies of the songs he arranged, not the words, this is unlikely to have been true in every instance.
211. Hadden, *George Thomson*, 303–8; Cecil Hopkinson and C.B. Oldman, 'Thomson's Collections of National Song, with Special Reference to the Contributions of Haydn and Beethoven', *Edinburgh Bibliographical Society Transactions*, 2, pt. 1 [for 1938–9] (Edinburgh, 1940).
212. Letter to Thomson, dated 26 Apr. 1793: *The Letters of Robert Burns*, ed. J. De Lancey Ferguson, 2nd edn, ii (Oxford, 1985), no. 559, p. 211.
213. Hadden, *George Thomson*, 303. For Haydn's celebrity in Edinburgh in the 1780s see Johnson, *Music and Society in Lowland Scotland*, 33, 41.
214. The same enthusiasm was subsequently taken up by Beethoven, who provided Thomson with almost fifty arrangements between about 1815 and 1818.
215. Hörwarthner, no. 75. For examples of 'Scottish' publications in Haydn's music library, see Landon, *Late Years*, 396–98, nos 279, 313, 339.
216. Hörwarthner, no. 35.
217. For Haydn's claim that he changed 'many things' in his music to satisfy the English public, see his letter of 2 Mar. 1792: *CCLN*, 131.
218. Hörwarthner, no. 6.
219. *Lichtenberg's Visits to England as Described in his Letters and Diaries*, trans. and ed. Margaret L. Mare and W.H. Quarrel (Oxford, 1938), 54.
220. W.C. Smith, *The Life and Activities of Sir Ashton Lever of Alkrington 1729–1788* (Manchester, 1965).
221. See James Clifford, *Hester Lynch Piozzi* (New York, 1986), 194.

222. A.M. Lysaght, 'Banks' Artists and his Endeavour Collections', *British Museum Yearbook*, 3 (1979), 9–80.

223. Lincoln, Usher Gallery: Erffa and Staley, *Benjamin West*, 487, no. 586.

224. On 24 Feb. 1791 Banks apparently attended a concert held in the Pantheon including a 'Grand Symphony' by Haydn and a quartet from Opus 64: Landon, *Haydn in England*, 48. The handbills are in the British Museum. He attended the concerts with his sister Sophia.

225. Landon, *Haydn in England*, 75. Haydn was probably acquainted with Banks through Burney, who was in close contact with both men.

226. Jacobe was described in an obituary as 'famous as one of the outstanding artists in this profession [mezzotinter] throughout the whole of Europe': quoted, with full reference, in Griffiths and Carey, *German Printmaking*, 86.

227. For an account of Omai's stay in England, see O'Brien, *Joseph Banks*, 179–90. For Reynolds's portrait of him (now at Castle Howard) see Penny (ed.), *Reynolds*, 271–72, no. 100.

228. For Shield's contribution, see Fiske, *English Theatre Music*, 469–72. For Loutherbourg's scenery, see Joppien, 'Philippe Jacques de Loutherbourg's Pantomime "Omai, or, a Trip round the World"', 81–136.

229. Obeyeskere, *Apotheosis of Captain Cook*, 129–30.

230. Fiske, *English Theatre Music*, 476–80.

231. *African Hopitality* and *Slave Trade* were published by J.R. Smith, whose showrooms, judging from the prints in his collection, Haydn probably visited. For the origin of Morland's paintings and their impact, see Winter, *Morland*, 39–42, 48–51; Oldfield, *Popular Politics*, 68–72.

232. Griesinger, 101.

233. Papendiek, *Court and Private Life*, ed. Broughton, ii, 134–35.

234. Landon, *Haydn in England*, 65–67; J. Wright, 'George Polgreen Bridgetower: An African Prodigy in England 1789–1799', *Musical Quarterly*, 66 (1980), 65–82.

235. For Soliman, see Braunbehrens, *Mozart*, 84–87.

236. Carpani, 88–90.

237. *Letters of the Late Ignatius Sancho, an African, to which are Prefixed, Memoirs of his Life*, 2 vols (London, 1782); *The Interesting Narrative of the Life of Olaudah Equiano, or Gustavus Vassa, the African. Written by Himself* (London, 1789).

238. Reyahn King, Sukhdev Sandhu, James Walvin and Jane Girdham, *Ignatius Sancho: An African Man of Letters* (London, 1997).

239. For example, Sancho had been on excellent terms with the actress Catherine Horneck and her husband, the artist Henry Bunbury, who designed a vignette for the fifth edition of Sancho's *Letters*. Haydn had a notable collection of Bunbury prints, and as will become evident later in this book, certainly knew him well.

240. Paul Geoffrey Edwards, 'Unreconciled Strivings and Ironic Strategies: Three Afro-British Authors of the Georgian Era, Ignatius Sancho, Oloudah Equiano, Robert Wedderburn', *Occasional Papers* No. 34, University of Edinburgh, Centre for African Studies (Edinburgh, 1992).

241. Tolley, 'Music in the Circle of Sir William Jones', 525–27, 540–41. For Haydn's notebook entries on China, see *Briefe*, 544.

242. Macartney's interest in Haydn may be shown from the fact that both he and his wife later subscribed to copies of the original publication of *The Creation*: Landon (ed.), *The Creation*, 628.

243. J.L. Cranmer-Byng, *An Embassy to China: Being the Journal Kept by Lord Macartney during his Embassy to the Emperor Ch'ien-lung 1793–1794* (London, 1962), 104, 364, n. 22.

244. Ibid., 104–5.

245. 'Slow, solemn music, muffled drums, and deep-toned bells were heard at a distance. On a sudden the sound ceased and all was still; again it was renewed, and then intermitted with short pauses ... At length the great band both vocal and instrumental struck up with all their powers of harmony, and instantly the whole Court fell flat upon their faces before this invisible Nebuchadnezzar. ... The music was a sort of birthday ode or state anthem, the burden of which was "Bow down your heads, all ye dwellers upon earth, bow down your heads before the great Ch'ien-lung, the great Ch'ien-lung." And then all the dwellers upon China earth there present, except ourselves, bowed down their heads, and prostrated themselves upon the ground at every renewal of the chorus.' Ibid., 131.

246. For an account of the embassy and for the quotations of the edict used here, see J.L. Cranmer-Byng, 'China 1792–94', in Peter Roebuch (ed.), *Macartney of Lisanoure 1737–1806: Essays in Biography* (Belfast, 1983), 206–43.

247. The portraits were presumably copies of those by Reynolds painted in 1779 for the Royal Academy, or possibly prints after them: Penny (ed.), *Reynolds*, 285–87.

248. Kelly, *Reminiscences*, ed. Fiske, 263.

249. The quintets were for flute, two violins, viola, cello and keyboard: Christopher Hogwood, 'In Praise of Arrangements: The "Symphony Quintetto"', in Biba and Wyn Jones (eds), *Studies in Music History Presented to H.C. Robbins Landon*, 82–104.

250. For a discussion of these, see *Letters of Dr Charles Burney*, ed. Ribeiro, i, 376–78.

251. Wheelock, 'Marriage à la Mode'.

252. A fifth collection, drawing on the London Symphonies, appeared in 1797.

253. Gray's famous *Elegy Written in a Country Church-Yard* is one example of near-contemporary popular verse which fragments of Haydn's music were made to fit. 'Gray's Elegy set to music by Thomas Billington, Harpsichord and Singing Master. Opera VIII, London. To sections set using airs by Haydn': Hoboken, *Thematisch-bibliographisches Werkverzeichnis*, ii, 293.

254. For the arrangement, see Dawes, 'William: Or the Adventures of a Sonata'. For Jane Austen's ownership of the items in question, see Wallace, *Jane Austen and Mozart*, 254, 270.

255. Fiske, *English Theatre Music*, 562–63. This was the same work which Haydn described as a 'National opera': *CCLN*, 294. Arnold also made arrangements of other instrumental compositions by Haydn for voice and keyboard: Dawes, 'William: Or the Adventures of a Sonata', 761.

256. For examples, see Alexander, *Affecting Moments*, 18, no. 5; Clayton, *English Print*, 234, pl. 249.

257. For examples, see Hoboken, *Thematisch-bibliographisches Werkverzeichnis*, iii, 375.

258. Hob. XXXIa: 168.

259. This point will be explored in greater detail later in this book.

260. *AMZ, Intelligenz Blatt XV* (June, 1799), cols 73–74: for the translation, see Landon (ed.), *'The Creation'*, 471.

261. For an account of some of these, see Temperley, *The Creation*, 38–39.

262. *The Banks Letters: A Calendar of the Manuscript Correspondence*, ed. Warren R. Dawson (London, 1958), 763, 807.
263. Landon, *Haydn: Late Years*, 196–98.
264. Ibid., 199.
265. The remark is taken from a letter from Sheridan satirizing Haydn and his achievement: see *The Letters of Richard Brinsley Sheridan*, ed. Cecil Price, 2 vols (London, 1966), ii, 168.
266. This passage comes from Dies (p. 188), quoting an article in *AMZ* (9 June 1802) which discusses Haydn's election, citing examples of criticism in the English press.

Notes to Chapter 3

1. The business of running both choir and orchestra had proved too much for the elderly Werner, who had been in Esterházy service since 1728.
2. The extent to which the composer was responsible, or even aware of this in the 1760s, is unclear.
3. Haydn's loyalty to Miklós I is especially notable. He appears to have received several offers of employment elsewhere by the end of the 1780s, but declined them all.
4. *Die Fürsten Esterházy: Magneten, Diplomaten und Mäzene*, exh. cat. (Eisenstadt, 1995). The title 'Prince of the Holy Roman Empire', first conferred in 1687, was made hereditary in 1712. By the beginning of the eighteenth century the Esterházy estates comprised 25 castles and approximately 1,500,000 acres of land.
5. I. Schemper-Sparholz, 'Illustration und Bedeutung: Inhaltliche Überlegungen zu den Fresken Carpoforo Tencalas', *Wiener Jahrbuch für Kunstgeschichte*, 40 (1987), 303–19.
6. J. Fischer, *Catalogue de la galerie des tableaux de Son Altesse le Prince Nicolas Esterhazy de Galantha, dans son Hôtel de Laxenbourg [Catalog der Gemählde-Gallerie des durchlauchtigen Fürsten Esterházy von Galantha, zu Laxenburg bei Wien]* (Vienna, 1812).
7. Two years later, most of the collection was transferred to Vienna, to the palace in Mariahilf which Miklós II had then recently acquired from Prince Kaunitz, where in 1815 it was regularly opened to the public, becoming one of the best-known attractions in the city. In 1870 the collection was purchased by the Hungarian government, becoming the nucleus of what is now the Museum of Fine Arts in Budapest: Garas, *The Budapest Gallery*, 11–12; Zsuzsa Urbach et al., *Masterpieces in the Museum of Fine Arts* (Budapest, 1990), 5. For Fischer, see Griffiths and Carey, *German Printmaking in the Age of Goethe*, 93–95.
8. Budapest, Museum of Fine Arts.
9. Budapest, Museum of Fine Arts: William R. Crelly, *The Painting of Simon Vouet* (New Haven, 1962), 153, no. 17.
10. This was probably acquired between 1812 and 1820. Crivelli died in 1495. The *Madonna* was originally part of an altarpiece from San Domenico in Ascoli Piceno. The remaining panels from this altarpiece eventually entered the National Gallery in London as part of a composite altarpiece featuring other Crivelli paintings in 1868: John F. Omelia, 'Addenda to a Recent Reconstruction of the Demidoff Altarpiece', *Marsyas: Studies in the History of Art*, 11 (1962–4), 10–32, esp. 30.

11. The same conditions help to account for Esterházy interest in Spanish painting.
12. Stendhal, who probably discovered the artist through Napoleon's transference of some of Crivelli's works to Milan, wrote disparagingly of the painter at about the time that the Esterházy Crivelli was acquired, castigating any partiality for Crivelli's painting on account of its perceived disparity with the ideal forms of Raphael: *Histoire de la peinture en Italie*, ed. V. Del Litto, 402. In general terms, it was only in the 1850s that Italian painting before Raphael started to be widely appreciated.
13. The story is told by A. Hirt in four issues of *Morgenblatt für gebildete Stände*, nos. 143–46 (15–18 June 1808).
14. The Prince later acquired what is generally accepted as a genuine Correggio: the *Madonna del latte* (Budapest, Museum of Fine Arts), a painting which was very well known in the eighteenth century through copies and engravings: Garas, *Correggio: Szoptató Madonna*. Miklós II also acquired copies of sections of Correggio's well-known frescoes at Parma.
15. Symphonies Nos 6, 7, 8. *Matin* opens with a sunrise. *Soir* ends with a storm (headed *La Tempesta*), which features lightening. Suggestions have been made for programmatic elements in other movements. For a convincing instance, see Will, 'When God Met the Sinner', esp. 196–208. According to some sources the main titles were given to Haydn by his patron.
16. According to Dies (p. 43), Haydn (before working for Morzin) was asked to write stage music with clear visual characteristics.
17. Gregor Joseph Werner, *Musikalischer Instrumental-Kalender für zwei Violinen und Basso continuo*, ed. Fritz Stein, Das Erbe deutsches Musik, 31 (Kassel, 1956); Stein, 'Der musikalische Instrumentalkalender', 390.
18. Landon, *Early Years*, 555.
19. Telemann himself published an account of Castel's instrument (listed in Mizler's Bibliothek for 1740), entitled *Beschreibung der Augenorgel, oder des Augenclavicembals, so der gerühmte Mathematicus und Jesuit in Paris, Herr Pater Castel, erfunden und ins Werck gerichtet hat.*
20. Haydn would certainly have known a set of ballets on the same theme, given in Vienna in 1755. These were by Hilverdig, with music by Starzer: Brown, *Gluck and the French Theatre*, 162. As far as I am aware, the suggestion that Telemann's *Die Tageszeiten* may have acted as a stimulus to Haydn has not previously been made. Although it is unclear how well Telemann's music was known in Vienna at this date, the evidence of his name being cited in subsequent Viennese denunciations of 'pictorialism' in music suggests that compositions by him were widely performed in the circles in which Haydn worked over a prolonged period. Some of his compositions feature in the inventory of Haydn's collection of music drawn up after his death: Landon, *Late Years*, 397, no. 295.
21. See, for example, Shesgreen, *Hogarth and the Times-of-the-Day Tradition*. Among musicians sensitive to the tradition of representing the times of the day in the visual arts was Burney. When visiting Sans Souci, the royal palace near Berlin, he particularly noted the three large pictures in the ceiling of the 'marble gallery', 'the subjects of which, are morning, noon, and night': *Dr Burney's Musical Tours in Europe*, ed. Scholes, ii, 178.
22. Obvious examples include descending motifs for setting the word 'descendit', ascending ones for 'ascendit' in settings of the mass. For the background to such word-painting, see Gernot Gruber, 'Musikalische Rhetorik und barocke Bildlichkeit in Kompositionen des jungen Haydn', in Schwarz (ed.), *Der junge Haydn*, 168–91. For more developed examples of Haydn's word-painting in the

1760s, see Kumbier, 'Rhetoric and Expression', esp. 231. Both the *Stabat mater* (1767) and the *Applausus* Cantata (1768) contain extensive and developed use of word-painting.

23. Although the main building still survives at Eszterháza, despite considerable neglect over a prolonged period, many of the features of the project which so impressed Haydn's contemporaries (such as the opera house, the marionette theatre, the sculptures decorating the gardens, the pavilions, and artificial features of the landscape) have been destroyed.

24. The designation of Eszterháza as 'le petit Versailles de l'Hongrie' occurs in the *Excursion à Esterhaz en Hongrie*, a description of the palace published in Vienna in 1784: the text of this guide is reproduced in Landon, *Haydn at Eszterháza*, 104–16. Visitors from Western Europe, however, are likely to have found the style and layout of the palace distinctly old-fashioned by 1784.

25. At Versailles, although music-making was a fundamental aspect of court entertainment under Louis XIV, there is little to suggest that any particular space (other than the chapel) was created with music in mind. Such considerations were certainly not at the heart of the palace's design. The opera house at Versailles was only added much later in the eighteenth century.

26. Quoted from a guide written in German to the palace, the *Beschreibung des hochfürstlichen Schlosses Esterhaz im Königreiche Ungarn*, published in Pressburg (Bratislava): for the translation quoted, see Landon, *Haydn at Eszterháza*, 27.

27. Some modern works on the palace at Eszterháza designate this room, the largest within the main building, as the 'banqueting hall'. However, early accounts of festivities at the palace, such as those celebrating the visit of Maria Theresa in 1773, show that the room used for banquets was the *sala terrena*, immediately below the hall, on the ground floor. Although there seems to be no documentary evidence to indicate where orchestral concerts took place at Eszterháza, it is reasonably assumed that they were held in the main *salle*, the only suitable space for performing to an audience within the main building.

28. For Louis XIV as the 'sun king' and the influence of this concept in European culture, see: Burke, *Fabrication of Louis XIV*; H. Sedlmayr, 'Allegorie und Architectur', in M. Warnke (ed.), *Politische Architektur in Europa* (Cologne, 1984), 157–74; Chandra Mukerji, *Territorial Ambitions and the Gardens of Versailles* (Cambridge, 1997).

29. F.B. Polleross, 'Sonnenkönig und Österreichische Sonne', *Wiener Jahrbuch für Kunstgeschichte*, 60 (1987), 239–56.

30. G.B. Doni, *Lyra Barbarina amphicordos*, ed. G.B. Passeri and A.F. Gori, 2 vols (Florence, 1763), i. Doni's researches became well known to musicians with an interest in the antique after this publication. Burney, for example, mentions Doni and his work on Apollo in his notes on Rome (1770): *Music, Men and Manners*, ed. Poole, 152–53. Elsewhere Burney was very critical of Doni's researches: *General History*, ed. Mercer, i, 107–8; ii, 511.

31. For a discussion of Doni's work on Apollo and his lyre, see Fumaroli, *L'École du silence*, 159–66, fig. 33. Doni also wrote a treatise entitled *De praestantia musicae veteris libri tres* (1647), which was dedicated to Cardinal Mazarin.

32. Haydn's early biographers make it clear that Haydn was unfamiliar with the baryton and its technical demands before being required to write for the instrument. The Prince's particular enthusiasm for the baryton is clear from the instructions Haydn received in 1765 to provide more compositions suitable for him to play.

33. The operas were Haydn's *Der Götterrath* and *Philemon und Baucis*, the first acting as a prelude to the second. The final scene depicted the descent from the clouds of the Habsburg coat of arms, supported by allegorical figures representing Justice, Wisdom and Leniency, with Fame shown above holding a crown. Kneeling in front were figures in Hungarian costume symbolizing Obedience, Devotion and Loyalty, singing the sovereign's praises. Evidence for the festivities connected with the Empress's visit comes from a number of sources, especially a contemporary description in French: Horányi, *Magnificence of Eszterháza*, 88–91. For the subject matter of the operas, see H.C. Robbins Landon, '*Philemon und Baucis*, Facsimile of the Printed Libretto of the First Version 1773', *Haydn Yearbook*, 22 (1998), 44–75.

34. For example, in 1765 Metastasio wrote a piece set by Gluck, entitled *Il Parnaso confuso*, to celebrate the second marriage of Joseph II. The parts were played by members of the imperial family. A painting of the performance was made by J.F. Griepel: for a reproduction, see Zaslaw (ed.), *Man and Music: The Classical Era*, 116, fig. 30. For earlier musical associations with Parnassus, see H. Colin Slim, 'Musicians on Parnassus', *Studies in the Renaissance*, 12 (1965), 134–63.

35. Fumaroli, *L'École du silence*, 35–45. In 1724, for example, Couperin published a sonata entitled *Parnassus, or the Apotheosis of Corelli*, noting in the preface that 'French and Italian taste have long shared the Republic of Music'. The sonata illustrates a programme concerning Corelli's reception onto Parnassus. Couperin published an equivalent sonata concerning Lully the following year.

36. Fumaroli, *L'École du silence*, 37.

37. Griesinger (pp. 10–11) gives the clearest early account of Haydn's obsession with Fux's treatise. Alfred Mann, 'Haydn as Student and Critic of Fux', in H.C. Robbins Landon and Roger E. Chapman (eds), *Studies in Eighteenth-Century Music: A Tribute to Karl Geiringer on his Seventieth Birthday* (London, 1970), 323–34; Alfred Mann, 'Johann Joseph Fux's Theoretical Writings: Classical Legacy', in Harry White (ed.), *Johann Joseph Fux and the Music of the Austro-Italian Baroque* (London, 1992), 57–71. For Haydn's annotations to Fux's treatise, see Fux, *Gradus ad Parnassum*, ed. Mann, intro.

38. In a letter to Artaria, his publisher, of 20 July 1781: Haydn, *Briefe*, 101; cf. CCLN, 31. Haydn is discussing recent songs by Hofmann and indicating how his own settings of some of the same texts were managed much better.

39. Van Schuppen (d. 1751) executed the ceiling painting of one of the best-known concert venues in Vienna, the hall of the Lopkowitz Palace, the iconographic programme for which is an excellent example of allegories of the visual arts being matched with figures playing music.

40. The concert took place on 30 May 1781. The programme for the concert is unknown. The venue suggests that it would have been a chamber concert. Landon suggests that it may have featured quartets from Haydn's Op. 33 set: Landon, *Haydn at Eszterháza*, 447.

41. Throughout the 1770s Duke Albert was Governor of Hungary. His official residence was the Castle at Pressburg (modern Bratislava), which was said to be within viewing distance of Eszterháza on a clear day, facilitating regular visits. When Albert was appointed Governor of the Austrian Netherlands in 1781, the visits to Eszterháza necessarily ceased. The couple came to Prince Esterházy's palace so frequently that they were given their own set of apartments for use whenever they chose.

42. Christine and Albert attend one of Mozart's earliest concerts in Vienna in 1768 and also the première of his penultimate opera, *La clemenza di Tito*, in 1791. Mozart's short opera, *The Impresario*, was especially commissioned to honour the couple in 1785.

43. For example, a family scene by Christine, depicting the opening of gifts on St Nicholas's day (based on a work by C. Troots), shows her to have been a competent draughtswoman (Vienna, Kunsthistorisches Museum).

44. Budapest, Hungarian National Gallery, no. 415. The identity of the painter is unknown.

45. The Duke is best known today as the founding collector of one of Austria's national institutions, the Albertina, which counts among the most extensive collections of Western graphic art in the world, housed today, as it was in his own time, in the Taroucca Palace, part of the Hofburg, the complex of imperial buildings in central Vienna. From the outset, Albert's acquisitions were purchased with a view to his collection being representative, paying as much attention to northern European schools as on the more fashionable Italian schools. The enthusiasm of Albert and his wife for collecting is often reflected in portraits of the couple. For example, one group portrait depicting several members of the imperial family, executed shortly after the couple's return to Vienna in 1776 from an extensive collecting trip to Italy – taking in Florence where Christina's brother was the Grand Duke, and Naples where her sister was queen – shows Albert and Christine distributing for discussion some of their new acquisitions (painted by Heinrich Friedrich Füger; Österreichische Galerie, Vienna, Inv. 2.296): Koschatzky, *Giacomo Conte Durazzo*, cat. 86 (with illustration). On the right, Christina's mother, the Empress Maria Theresa, holds one of their purchases admired by her eldest son, the great reforming Emperor Joseph II, best known today as one of Mozart's patrons. Behind, three other members of the family inspect another image. A portrait of Christina by Zoffany (Kunsthistorisches Museum, Vienna), also painted in 1776 when the couple was in Florence, shows the Archduchess beside a statuette of Athena, an obvious allusion to her love of the arts: Webster, *Zoffany*, 64, no. 81. In the fashion of the time she wears a bracelet with a portrait-miniature of her husband. These portraits were painted during the Italian phase of the couple's interests. This was subsequently complemented by a northern phase developed during the period Albert spent as governor of the Austrian Netherlands, from 1781 until he was thrown out by the French in 1792.

46. Durazzo's dual interests in music and the visual arts is clear from the best-known portrait of him, an engraving by Giovanni Vitalba. The ledge above the identifying inscription in this print shows attributes of music (a lyre and sheets of music) along with attributes of the pictorial arts (a portfolio, a palette and several brushes). The portrait for this engraving was based on one taken by a protégé of Durazzo's, the painter Giovanni David. For the original design for this engraving (Venice, Museo Correr, Gabinetto dei Disegni e delle Stampe) and other aspects of Durazzo's artistic interests, see Sandra Pinto, 'La promozione delle arti negli stati italiani dell'età della riforma all'unità', in *Storia dell'arte italiana*, ed. Paolo Fossati, 6/ii (Turin, 1982), 869, fig. 843.

47. Haydn evidently knew Duke Albert well at Eszterháza. In later years, Albert is known to have attended a number of early performances of *The Creation* conducted by the composer: for example, in Vienna on 22 Dec. 1799, and at Eisenstadt in Dec. 1800. In 1783, Haydn told his publishers that he valued Durazzo's house above all others. When Haydn travelled to England, it was

Kaunitz who provided him with introductions to facilitate his reception into English society. Mozart revealed that he considered Kaunitz to have been the most courteous patron he knew.

48. For a full account of this and the complete text from which the quotation is taken, see Bonds, 'Haydn's "Cours complet de la composition"', esp. 161–62.

49. Ibid., 161.

50. *Natural History*, 35. 36. 81–84. For interpretations of this phrase, see: Hans van de Waal, 'The *linea summae tenuitatis* of Apelles: Pliny's Phrase and its Interpreters', *Zeitschrift für Aesthetik und allgemeine Kunstwissenschaft*, 12 (1967), 5–32; E.H. Gombrich, *The Heritage of Apelles* (London, 1976), 15–17.

51. There are a number of accounts of the origins of this symphony. Griesinger (pp. 28–29) went out of his way to indicate that Haydn told him that this was the true background to the composition of the symphony, dismissing other versions in public circulation at the time he was writing. The idea, expressed in early accounts, that Prince Miklós refused to allow the wives and children of musicians to be in residence at Eszterháza is confirmed in contemporary documentation.

52. This procedure seems to have been followed at subsequent performances of the symphony. The oboist Parke indicates the symphony was often performed in London in the later eighteenth century. He gives an erroneous version of the origin of the symphony and implies that he himself participated in departing from the orchestra: Parke, *Musical Memoirs*, ii, 28.

53. '*Matin*', '*Midi*' and '*Soir*' were probably performed at the appropriate times of the day. Haydn's quotation of the night watchman's song in a number of compositions, including Symphony No. 60 (1774), may imply the lateness of the hour at which they were performed, suggesting that darkened conditions were helpful to perceptions of the music: Geoffrey Chew, 'The Night Watchman's Song Quoted by Haydn and its Implications', *Haydn-Studien*, 3 (1974), 106–24. Another example of controlling the visual circumstances in which Haydn's symphonic music was heard occurred during Maria Theresa's visit, when the musicians performed in 'Chinese' costumes. Although this reflects the general fad for things Chinese at this time in Austria, it may be suggested that it had a more precise purpose. In 1769 Joseph II imitated a Chinese ritual in which the Emperor ceremonially ploughed a furrow to encourage diligence in his subjects. The ritual was apparently repeated in different territories of the Habsburg Empire and recorded in contemporary prints. The Chinese origin of this ritual was widely known in the West from prints, paintings and even a comment by Voltaire: see Christoph Müller-Hofstede in *Europa und die Kaiser von China: Eine Ausstellung der Berliner Festspiele*, exh. cat. (Frankfurt, 1985), 302–5, pls 128–29. Dressing up as Chinamen in front of members of the imperial family in 1773 would, therefore, probably have had particular connotations of industriousness and enlightenment for members of the audience. Further examples of Haydn taking an interest in controlling visual aspects of the performance of his music will be discussed later in this chapter.

54. There had been several monumental musical settings of these services by the time Haydn was writing, notably those by Gesualdo, Charpentier, Alessandro Scarlatti and François Couperin.

55. Haydn made use of melodic elements derived from the plainsong for the Lamentations of Jeremiah on several other occasions, notably Symphony No. 26, known accordingly as 'Lamentatione'.

56. For these qualities perceived in the key of F sharp minor, see the texts quoted by Steblin, *History of Key Characteristics*, 272.

57. Ibid., 126, 222–23.

58. G.F. Vogler, 'Ausdruck (musikalisch)', in *Deutsche Encyclopädie, oder Allgemeines Real-Wörterbuch aller Künste und Wissenschaft*, 23 vols, ed. H.M.G. Köster and J.F. Roos (Frankfurt am Main, 1778–1804), ii, 386: quoted and translated in Steblin, *History of Key Characteristics*, 126.

59. The clearest evidence for this is Haydn's setting of the creation of light in *The Creation*, which will be discussed in detail in Ch. 7.

60. This suggestion is very plausible: Webster, *Haydn's 'Farewell' Symphony*, 116–17. Haydn's correspondence and other testimony reveal how he himself felt very cut off being at Eszterháza. He described the palace as being in a 'desert'.

61. *Rodelinda* (1724), Act II, final duet; *Tolomeo* (1728), Act II, final duet. Handel used this key on other occasions when the mood of parting or absence (between lovers) was required. Examples include the aria in Act III, Scene 5 of *Alcina* (1735) and an aria in Act III, Scene 2 of *Sosarme* (1732).

62. The overture to *Orlando* (1733), which sets the scene for Zoroaster's contemplation of the stars seen in the night sky, and the obscurity of their meaning.

63. Scenes of farewell, derived from literary sources, were of course regularly to be seen in opera and the visual arts throughout the eighteenth century. Examples in opera have already been mentioned. The subject of *Hector's farewell to Andromache* (from Homer) was particularly popular in the visual arts. Antoine Coypel, for example, was commissioned to design a tapestry on this subject (part of a sequence illustrating the *Iliad*), commissioned in 1717. However, these examples of 'farewell' representations obviously provide no precedents for Haydn's concept, as realized in Symphony No. 45.

64. Berlin, Gemäldegalerie: Adehémar, *Gravure originale*, 146–48. Chodowiecki consciously adopted the manner of Greuse in *Les Adieux de Calas*. The painting was exhibited in Berlin, but the engraving was widely distributed. The Austrian ambassador in Berlin at this time was Gottfried van Swieten, Haydn's later collaborator, who reported on cultural events in Berlin for Vienna.

65. Chodowiecki even studied documentation of Calas's trial to lend the scene authenticity: *Daniel Chodowiecki, Bürgerliches Leben im 18. Jahrhundert*, exh. cat., ed. Peter Märker, Städelschens Kunstinstituts un Städtischen Galerie (Frankfurt, 1968), 34.

66. The prints in question were in Lavater's collection: Mraz and Schögl, *Das Kunstkabinett des Johann Caspar Lavater*, cat. 98. Lavater's work on physiognomy and its impact on Haydn are discussed in Ch. 5.

67. For a full analysis of the extraordinary slow movement, see Sisman, 'Haydn's Theater Symphonies', 326–29.

68. The opening words of the epigram are identical to the title given to Haydn's symphony in early sources: John Foster, 'The *Tempora mutantur* Symphony of Joseph Haydn', *Haydn Yearbook*, 9 (175), 328–29. Apparently Owen's epigrams were well known in German-speaking countries. The epigram's popularity is attested by its appearance on clocks and sundials. Owen died in 1622.

69. The date of composition of Symphony No. 64 is undocumented. Stylistically it arguably follows directly from the three great symphonies dated 1772, Nos 45, 46 and 47. Its quirkiness and unpredictable aspects suggest that it pre-dates the symphonies known to have been composed in 1774 (Nos 55, 56, 57 and 60) and

probably also pre-dates the dated symphony of 1773 (No. 50), which originated in the overture to Haydn's marionette opera created for Maria Theresa's visit to Eszterháza, *Der Götterath*. Tension had been mounting in Austria's relations with neighbouring nations throughout 1771. In this year Austria collected a large force in Hungary ready to thwart any attempt by Russia to cross the Danube. In February 1772 Russia organized the treaty of Poland's partition, which was proclaimed in Austria (which claimed Silesia) in September. These political developments would certainly have made an impact on life at Eszterháza at this time. Perhaps they influenced Prince Miklós's decision to refuse permission for the families of most of his musicians to join them in Hungary.

70. BMC 3886: Carretta, *George III and the Satirists*, 71, fig. 32.

71. The British envoy in Vienna from 1763 until late 1772 was Lord Stormont, a Haydn enthusiast. Burney reports hearing quartets by Haydn played at the ambassador's residence in Vienna in September 1772: *Present State of Music in Germany*, i, 290. Stormont introduced Burney to Metastasio and Gluck. He was described by Winckelmann (whom he met in Rome in 1768) as 'the most learned person of his rank whom I have yet known'. In 1772 Stormont was also visited in Vienna by his friend Sir William Hamilton, who had then recently been in correspondence concerning Bute's activities in Italy, where the former Prime Minister had been engaged in studies of architecture. Even Burney, when he had been in Vicenza in 1770, had heard that Bute had recently been in the city commissioning drawings of buildings by Palladio. When Haydn returned to Vienna in the years around 1772, he would therefore have had opportunities not only to see English prints like *Tempora mutantur*, but also to hear about the erstwhile politician they were designed to denigrate. For evidence of English prints being collected in German-speaking countries by 1767, see Clayton, *English Print*, 269, 279.

72. Apelles's painting was known from the description given by Lucian, which was well known in the Renaissance. It was generally viewed, like reconstructions and imitations from the Renaissance and later, as a warning to rulers to avoid false judgements. This is presumably why elements of it (allegorical references to Envy, Ignorance, Truth and Folly) were incorporated in the caricature *Tempora mutantur*. Diderot's description of the painting helped to make it well known in the mid-eighteenth century. The subject matter of Apelles's picture was certainly studied at the Vienna Akademie in the early 1770s. For these points, see David Cast, *The Calumny of Apelles: A Study in the Humanist Tradition* (New Haven, 1981), esp. 171 (for uses of the Calumny tradition in Vienna).

73. When Dies asked Haydn in 1806 whether he had tried to treat literary ('wörtliche') subjects in his instrumental music, the composer's response was 'seldom' (Dies, 131). Haydn meant that he did not follow programmes in composing symphonies, quartets, etc. He would therefore have given the same response had he been asked if he had followed visual subjects.

74. Heinrich Franz Biber, *Sechzehn Violinsonaten*, ed. Erwin Luntz (Denkmäler der Tonkunst in Österreich, 25/xii/2; Vienna, 1905), with reproductions of the engravings. For comment, see E. Schmitz, 'Bibers Rosenkranzsonaten', *Musica*, 5 (1951), 235–39.

75. Landon, *Late Years*, 402, no. 585.

76. The quotations from Mattheson are taken from P. Spitta, *Johann Sebastian Bach*, 2 vols, rev. edn (London, 1951), i, 236.

77. Griesinger, 117; Dies, 131; Carpani, 70. There is no agreement which symphony Haydn had in mind. For suggestions (slow movements in Nos 7, 22, 26), see Webster, *Haydn's 'Farewell' Symphony*, 235; cf. Will, 'When God Met the Sinner'. Griesinger indicates that it was among Haydn's earliest symphonies.

78. This *Cantique spirituel* is reproduced by Adhémar, *Gravure originale*, 151. It was published by Letourmy at Orléans.

79. Christ is actually depicted twice, once on the cross and once on the ground.

80. 'moralische Charaktere' (Griesinger, 117).

81. Carpani, 71.

82. Green, '"Il distratto" of Regnard and Haydn', 183–95.

83. 'Maestro di scuola innamorato': Carpani, 71.

84. In Gerber's *Neues historisch-biographisches Lexicon der Tonkunst* (Leipzig, 1812–14), ii, col. 573, this nickname is given to Symphony No. 43 (*c.*1771). This may have been an error for No. 55, which has a similar opening in the same key. The second movement of No. 55 has contrasting *staccato* and *dolce* sections, which may have suggested the bookish schoolmaster and his love interest.

85. 'Sic fugit amicus amicum'. Haydn usually ended a composition with the words 'Fine laus deo'. But in the Op. 20 quartets, he wrote a different motto – all express piety – in each case, reinforcing the notion that the quartets were consciously written as a set to show variety.

86. Carpani, 73. For Le Brun, see Kirchner, *L'Expression des passions*; Montagu, *Expression of the Passions*.

87. Le Brun's other headings were boldness, esteem, veneration, disdain, horror, dread, simple love, desire, fear, hate, sadness, physical pain, joy, crying, anger and extreme despair.

88. Grétry has a section on the analogy between colour and sound (his starting point is Castel): *Mémoires*, iii, 234–39. As a friend of several painters, Grétry frequently draws parallels between painting and music. For example, he discussed the 'musical colours' of the landscape painter, C.J. Vernet: *Mémoires*, ii, 46–47. His interest in painting the Passions perhaps originally stemmed from contact with painters like Greuze and Ducreux, who both produced series of works based on Le Brun's principles.

89. *Mémoires*, iii, 264.

90. Ibid., ii, 248.

91. Ibid., ii, 373.

92. Ibid., ii, 280.

93. Ibid., i, 342–43.

94. Bars 25–41.

95. Motifs played backwards, of course, often feature in Haydn's music, especially in development sections, throughout his mature career, though particularly in the early 1770s. But the *Menuet al Roverso* seems to represent an extreme, which it was unnecessary to repeat.

96. Haydn reused the music in a keyboard sonata (in A major Hob. XVI: 26/II; 1773), part of a set of sonatas which formed the earliest publication of works by Haydn issued with the composer's consent. In many respects the first movement of this sonata shows Haydn at his (consciously) most quirky and irregular. This is an example of an 'irregular' exposition type, especially favoured by Haydn during this period, featuring a lengthy 'expansion section', preceded by a short opening group in the tonic, and ending with an even shorter codetta in the dominant: Michelle Fillion, 'Sonata-Exposition Procedures in Haydn's

Keyboard Sonatas', in *Haydn Studies: Proceedings of the International Haydn Conference, Washington D.C., 1975*, ed. Jens Peter Larsen, Howard Serwer and James Webster (New York, 1982), 475–81. In this A major sonata, the passage beginning in the dominant minor at bar 11 opens the long central section within the exposition, which lacks a proper (perfect) cadence until the codetta, finally establishing the dominant major (bars 11–27). This central passage, with its sustained harmonic and rhythmic instability, conveys a state of anxiety and apprehension which, like much other music by Haydn of the early 1770s, is disconcerting. Another instance of this quality occurs in the development section, where two long sequences suggest a human capacity to get carried away (bars 46–50, 50–55). Such sequences, like other devices used by Haydn at this date (for example, fugal finales used in some of the quartets), may be considered a deliberate echo of Baroque compositional practice (cf. Suttcliffe, *Haydn: String Quartets, Op. 50*, 16); but in this particular case the sequences are so extended that they seem to represent a conscious extreme, which the audience was expected to understand. Perhaps Haydn was here mimicking a well-appreciated convention of earlier music in order to provoke a humorous reaction in his listeners. It would be hard to parallel such extreme cases in music by Haydn and others before and after the period of the early 1770s. These sonatas (as published) were dedicated to Haydn's patron, Prince Miklós, so it seems likely that their portrayal of extremes and the reactions these might provoke were to his taste.

97.   Kris, 'Characterköpfe des Franz Xaver Messerschmidt'; Rudolf and Margot Wittkower, *Born under Saturn: The Character and Conduct of Artists. A Documented History from Antiquity to the French Revolution* (New York, 1963), 124–32; Pötzl-Malikova, *Franz Xaver Messerschmidt*.

98.   Together with the testimony of Kaunitz concerning Messerschmidt's illness, Nicolai's account of the sculptor's unusual views and behaviour have led to an interpretation of his series of heads as symptoms of psychosis: Kris, 'Characterköpfe des Franz Xaver Messerschmidt'. For recent alternative views, see: Jörg Oberhaidacher, 'Kunstgeschichte oder Psychologie? Zu den Charakterköpfen des Franz Xaver Messerschmidt', *Österreichische Zeitschrift für Kunst und Denkmalpflege*, 38 (1984), 25–42; Maria Pötzl-Malikova, 'Zur Beziehung Franz Anton Mesmer: Franz Xaver Messerschmidt: Eine wiedergefundene Büste des berümten Magnetiseurs', *Wiener Jahrbuch für Kunstgeschichte*, 40 (1987), 257–67.

99.   It has been pointed out that the single pizzicato G played by four instruments at the end of the *Largo e cantabile* movement of Op. 33/5 is a clear contrast with the serious mood and 'archaic' references of what precedes it: 'Having poured out his heart, so to speak, the composer now pokes out his tongue' (Suttcliffe, *Haydn: String Quartets, Op. 50*, 23). Among Messerschmidt's heads with their tongues sticking out are those subsequently (after the artist's death) entitled *Der Speyer* and *Der Gähner* (both now Vienna, Österreichische Galerie). For a fuller study of Haydn's compositional aspirations in Op. 33, see Gretchen Wheelock, 'Engaging Strategies in Haydn's Opus 33', *Eighteenth-Century Studies*, 25 (1991), 2–13.

100. Haydn had himself suffered from a serious illness. According to several sources this took place *c.*1770. However, Vincent Novello, in the introduction to his edition of Haydn's *Stabat mater* (1828), says that he had heard from Latrobe (who had heard it directly from Haydn) that the composer had written the *Stabat mater* in fulfilment of a vow to compose such a work if he recovered from

illness. Since the *Stabat mater* was written by late 1767, it seems possible that the illness dates from this year (though there is evidence of subsequent critical illness also *c*.1771). The darker, more intense mode of much of the *Stabat mater*, appropriate of course to the text, may therefore be related to Haydn's illness, though not necessarily an outcome of it. If Haydn was aware of Messerschmidt's illness by *c*.1773, it seems feasible that by then he would have wished to avoid going in the same direction as the sculptor. Although Haydn's compositions of the later 1760s, like the *Stabat mater*, often show a distinct tendency towards the serious and the intense, it was only after 1770 that these traits developed into the troubled, uncertain and dark characteristics associated here with the world of Messerschmidt. For one claim that Haydn's compositions 'bordered upon madness', see Landon, *Haydn at Eszterháza*, 496–97.

101. 'I found his gestures very interesting. He was able to inspire a large number of performers with the spirit in which his composition had been written and should be performed. One could read in every one of his [facial] gesticulations, which could hardly have been more exaggerated if he had tried, very distinctly what his intentions were in each passage and how he must have felt in composing them' (*AMZ*, 15 Jan. 1800, col. 282). Haydn's interest in grimaces is evident also from an entry he made in his English journal, reported by Griesinger. Under a heading '*Smorfie d'un Virtuoso* [Grimaces of a Virtuoso]', Haydn recorded a story about the singer Tenducci being unexpectedly interrupted while singing an air, implying a variety of reactions and expressions: Griesinger, 108–9.

102. *Versuch eines Farbensystems* (Vienna, 1771): T. Lersch, 'Von der Entomologie zur Kunst-theorie', in *De arte et libris: Festschrift Erasmus* (1984), 301–16.

103. Accepting Castel's colour circle, with its twelve divisions, as a standard expression of the colour spectrum, Schiffermüller noted that colours one or two divisions from each other clash, and therefore cannot be used for garments or in pictures. Colours removed from each other by two divisions generally provide adequate contrast, but colours opposite each other, such as red and sea-green, are rarely likely to please when seen together and are called by trained painters 'poisonous'. Following Castel, Schiffermüller argued that in addition to twelve colours (which Castel had linked with the twelve notes of the chromatic scale) there should be a tonal scheme of twelve points for each colour. *Versuch eines Farbensystems*, 15.

104. For the significance of this in the history of colour theory, see John Gage, 'Runge, Goethe and the *Farben-Kugel*', in M. Holl (ed.), *Runge, Fragen und Antworten* (Munich, 1978), 61–65.

105. For a reproduction, see Somfai, *Joseph Haydn*, fig. 85. Haydn was in contact with Hummel, so it is possible that the design of the title-page was agreed in consultation with Haydn. Hummel subsequently reused the sun motif for the much later publication of the 'Military' Symphony: Otto Erich Deutsch, 'Curious Title-Pages of Works by Haydn', *Musical Times*, 73 (June 1932), 516–18. Other publishers also copied the motif. Longman, Clementi & Co., for example, used it in their publication of the Op. 76 quartets in 1799.

106. There are several documented cycles of paintings depicting the Tobit story in the eighteenth century, most of them French. The best-known artist who repeatedly returned to the theme was Rembrandt: Julius S. Held, 'Rembrandt and the Book of Tobit', *Rembrandt Studies* (Princeton, 1991), 118–30; Christian Tümpel and Peter Schatborn, *The Book of Tobit* (Zeist, 1987). Haydn may well have had access to Rembrandt's prints illustrating episodes in the story, drawing attention to the themes of light he also explored. For the background to Tobias

in the visual arts, see: Gertrude M. Acherbach, 'The Iconography of Tobias and the Angel in Florentine Painting in the Renaissance', *Marsyas*, 3 (1943–45), 71–84; E.H. Gombrich, 'Tobias and the Angel', in *Symbolic Images: Studies in the Art of the Renaissance* (London, 1974), 26–35.

107. For a consideration of Haydn's use of word-painting in this oratorio, see Landon, *Haydn at Eszterháza*, 259–61.

108. For an account of the importance of vision during the Enlightenment, see M. Jay, *Downcast Eyes: The Denigration of Vision in Twentieth-Century French Thought* (Berkeley, 1993), 83–113.

109. Translation from Larsen, *New Grove Haydn*, 42.

110. No. 9: 'Rendi a Tobit la luce'.

111. Light, darkness, the sun and blindness are all themes which might be given a Masonic interpretation. Although Prince Miklós was certainly a Mason – when he was initiated is unknown – and Haydn was initiated in 1785 (though no evidence has come to light to indicate that he attended a lodge thereafter), there are insufficient grounds to suggest that the use of light as a theme at Eszterháza and in Haydn's music of the early 1770s had any Masonic significance. The issue, however, is far from being clear-cut. Tobias von Gebler's play *Thamos, König in Aegypten*, which certainly uses Masonic symbolism, including a greeting to the rising sun as the benevolent governing force, was performed at Pressburg in 1773 with Haydn as conductor. Presumably the incidental music composed by Mozart in 1773 was performed on this occasion. In the Eszterházy archives are versions of Mozart's choruses for *Thamos* arranged as motets. The possibility exists, therefore, that Masonic elements may have contributed to the form of the embellishment of Eszterháza, both musically and visually: Landon, *Haydn at Eszterháza*, 185; Landon, *Haydn in England*, 505.

112. Carpani, 8, 11.

113. The original licence granted to Artaria covered only trade in copper engravings. Dealings in printed music (especially from Paris) only began in 1776. Artaria only started publishing its own music in 1778: *Vollständiges Verlagsverzeichnis Artaria & Comp.: Beiträge zur Geschichte des Alt-Wiener Musikverlages*, ed. Alexander Weinmann, rev. edn (Vienna, 1985).

114. For evidence of Artaria selling English prints by 1775, see Clayton, *English Print*, 269.

115. *Der Verlag Artaria: Veduten und Wiener Alltagsszenen*, exh. cat., ed. G. Düriegel, Museen Stadt (Vienna, 1981).

116. For examples, see Brusatti, *Zauberflöne*, pls II/15, II/16.

117. Torricella was advertising pirated versions of early Mozart quartets. He failed to say which quartets he was selling, emphasizing only that they were to be had 'at a very cheap price'. His objective was almost certainly to benefit from the attention given to Mozart's latest series of quartets, published by Artaria and dedicated to Haydn. Artaria and Mozart countered Torricella's advertisement by placing a long notice of their own, drawing attention to the fact that their publication was of 'brand new' quartets and that the publishers had 'spared no costs in supplying this work to the *connoisseurs*', especially concerning 'the beauty and clarity of the engraving'. Torricella responded to this by reminding the public that no further recommendation was needed for the quartets he was offering for sale than that they bear the name of Mozart, the main point of interest to connoisseurs. For a full account of this aspect of the rivalry between Torricella and Artaria, see Landon, *Mozart: The Golden Years*, 131–32.

118. The *Divertissements* are arrangements of the octets for baryton, horns and strings composed for Prince Miklós in 1775. The page in question is reproduced in *CCLN*, pl. IV.

119. For a discussion of ancient sources touching on the significance of the Graces, see Edgar Wind, *Pagan Mysteries of the Renaissance*, 2nd edn (London, 1967), 26–35.

120. Cesare Ripa, *Iconologia* (Rome, 1603), 17.

121. G. Venturi, 'La grazia e le Grazie', in *Antonio Canova*, exh. cat., Venice, Museo Correr and Passagno, Gipsoteca Canoviana, 22 Mar.–30 Sept. 1992 (Venice, 1992), 69–72.

122. Baron d'Hancarville (P.F. Hugues), *Antiquités étrusques, grecques et romaines. Tirées du Cabinet de M. William Hamilton, Envoyé extraordinaire et plénipotentiaire de S.M. Britannique en Cour de Naples*, 4 vols (1766–67, actually published 1767–76); G.B. Piranesi, *Vasi, candelabri, cippi, sarcofagi*, etc., 2 vols (Rome, 1778).

123. *La música, poema por D. Thomas de Yriarte, con superior permesso: en Madrid en la Imprenta Real de la Fazete* (Madrid, 1779). For a discussion of Tomás de Yriarte's place in the history of Spanish music, see José Subirá, *Historia de la música española e hispanoamericana* (Barcelona, 1953), 599–601.

124. 'Sólo á tu númen, Háyden prodigioso / Las Musas concedieron esta gracia / De ser tan nuevo siempre.'

125. From the translation by John Belfour published in London in 1807 (with some changes of spelling and punctuation).

126. 'Arte no menos grato y necesario / Al hombre en sociedad que al solitario.' The plate, by G. Ferro, is illustrated in Subirá, *Historia*, 599.

127. Landon, *Late Years*, 402, no. 575.

128. *Collección de obras en verso y prosa de D. Tomás de Iriarte*, vol. 2 (Madrid, 1805), 81–89.

129. Lee, *Ut pictura poesis*.

130. [Cavaliere D. Giuseppe Niccola d'Araza], *Opere di Antonio Raffaelo Mengs primo pittore del re cattolico Carlo III* (Parma, 1780), vol. 1, p. lxvi. For Azara's part in publishing Mengs's writings, see Angelo Ciavarella, *De Azara-Bodoni*, Museo Bodoni (Parma, 1979). The painting by Mengs considered stylistically comparable with Corelli was an *Annunciation* for Aranjuez.

131. 'Pintura sin colorido'.

132. The development of *tertulias*, evenings of intellectual discourse on cultural trends in the arts and sciences, which took place at residences of leading aristocrats, often with music-making, provided a forum where such notions might have been discussed.

133. Carlos III particularly disliked opera. He also actively discouraged the publication of music. He did, however, play a part in promoting much dance music, both traditional in character and for occasions like masked balls. Such events, often open free of charge to the middle classes as well as to the nobility, were sponsored by the King in line with other measures to show interest in the cultural welfare of his subjects, and may be seen as part of a movement in Spain, gathering strength in the later eighteenth century, to safeguard indigenous artistic traditions, with their appeal to simple values and national pride, against imports like Italian opera (notwithstanding the fact the King had ruled in Naples before reigning in Spain). According to the English writer and aesthete William Beckford, who was allowed to wander through the royal palace in Madrid unhindered in 1787 in order to inspect the paintings, the closest the King came

to establishing personal musical tastes were the exotic birds in gilded cages, 'some in full song', competing with the musical clocks, 'sounding like the tones of harmonic glasses', which Beckford found in every room: William Beckford, *Memoirs*, 2 vols (London, 1859), i, 28–30.

134. Sabbini was appointed by the king in 1761.

135. According to a letter to his friend Zapater, Carlos greeted Goya and asked after his son, then resumed his playing.

136. *Anhang zur Wiener Zeitung*, no. 80 (6 Oct. 1781): translation from Landon, *Haydn at Eszterháza*, 453.

137. The score was written by one of Haydn's known copyists: Fisher, 'Group of Haydn Copies for the Court of Spain'. See also David Wyn Jones, 'A Spanish Source for Haydn's *Non nobis, Domine*', *Haydn Yearbook*, 17 (1992), 167–69.

138. Letter from Goya to Martín Zapater, dated 11 Jan. 1783: translation from Symmons, *Goya: In Pursuit of Patronage*, 59.

139. There is no contemporary source for this story. It was first reported by the composer's great-grandson (his biographer), having apparently been passed down through the family: Germaine de Rothschild, *Luigi Boccherini, his Life and Work*, trans. Andreas Mayor (London, 1965), 39–40.

140. Countess de Yebes, *La Condesa-Duquesa de Benavente: una vida en unas cartas* (Madrid, 1955); Nicolás Alvarez Solar-Quintes and Yves Gérard, *La Bibliothèque musicale d'un amateur éclairé de Madrid: la Duchesse-Comtesse de Benavente, Duchesse d'Osuna (1752–1834)*, in *Recerches III* (Paris, 1963).

141. Two letters between Lelis and Yriarte concerning Haydn have been published, as well as the 1785 amendment to the contract: Nicolás A. Solar-Quintes, 'Las relaciones de Haydn con la Casa de Benavente', *Anuario musical*, 2 (Barcelona, 1947), 81–88; Feder, 'Manuscript Sources of Haydn's Works and their Distribution', 133–39.

142. There is a watercolour by Carmontelle showing a group of celebrated performers playing together on these instruments.

143. *Spanish Journals of Elizabeth, Lady Holland*, ed. Earl of Ilchester (London, 1910), 195.

144. Ibid., 143.

145. Solar-Quintes, 'Las relaciones', 81. These minuets and other dances cannot now be identified.

146. Fundación Bartolomé March Servera, Palma de Mallorca: N. Glendinning, 'Goya's Patrons', *Apollo*, no. 336 (Oct. 1981), 236–47.

147. Madrid, Prado.

148. Translation from Symmons, *Goya*, 140.

149. Juliet Wilson-Bareau, *Goya: Truth and Fantasy. The Small Paintings*, exh. cat. (London, 1994), 157–71, 351–52.

150. For the sketches as well as the completed paintings, still in Valencia Cathedral, see ibid., 146–51.

151. Ibid., 212–25, 358–59.

152. Russell, *The Don Juan Legend before Mozart*, 88–89, 199, 213, 457.

153. J. Subirá, *La música en la Casa de Alba* (Madrid, 1927).

154. Prado, Madrid: Guidol, *Goya 1746–1828*, vol. 1, no. 333.

155. See Hoboken, ii, 244. No Spanish sources are known for any of these songs.

156. Francesco Bonmati de Codecido, *La Duquesa Cayetana de Alba, maja y musa de Don Francisco de Goya* (Valladolid, 1940); Susann Waldemann, *Goya and the Duchess of Alba* (London, 1998).

157. On the night of 12/13 Sept. 1795 the Alba library, together with that of the Villafranca family (to which the Duke of Alba belonged), was destroyed in a fire in the Palacio de Buenavista: Bonmati de Codecido, *La Duquesa Cayetana de Alba*, 188–90. The Alba archives were destroyed during the Spanish Civil War: Subirá, *La música en la Casa de Alba*, p. xix.

158. Haydn, *Briefe*, 136.

159. See Fisher, 'Group of Haydn Copies', 73, n. 43.

160. Alexander Jardine, *Letters from Barbary, France, Spain, Portugal, etc. by an English Officer* (London, 1788).

161. New York, Metropolitan Museum of Art: Ives Colta and Susan Alyson Stein, *Goya in the Metropolitan Museum of Art* (New York, 1995), 37.

162. From the 'Prado' manuscript: translation from Harris, *Goya, Engravings and Lithographs*. Some scholars believe Moratín, acting under guidance from Goya, wrote these commentaries.

163. The collection certainly aroused the indignation of the Inquisition, which seems to have harassed Martínez on account of some of his images being deemed indecent, though the authorities in Madrid seem to have gone out of their way to protect him: José Manuel Cruz Valdovinos, 'Inquisidores e ilustrados: la pinturas y estampas "indecentes" de Sebastián Martínez', in *El arte en tiempo de Carlos IV* (Madrid, 1989), 311–19.

164. 1777; Wadsworth Atheneum, Hartford, Conn. For the Martínez inventory (not all items are fully identified), see Pemán Medina, 'Estampas y libros que vió Goya en casa de Sebastián Martínez', 312–20 (the item in question is no. 163). One print after a Benjamin West painting clearly identified is no. 169 in the inventory. For West's *Saul and the Witch of Endor* and engravings after it, see Erffa and Staley, *Paintings of Benjamin West*, 311–12, no. 275. Saul and the Witch of Endor was a popular subject in England, partly because of a much admired picture on the same text by Salvator Rosa (whose work was particularly appreciated in eighteenth-century Britain), and partly because it was treated musically in one of Handel's most celebrated oratorios, *Saul* (1739).

165. Pliny, *Natural History*, 35. 73. The passage was widely discussed in the eighteenth century, particularly in England. For one view of it, by a devotee of Haydn, see the essay on the imitative arts by Sir William Jones.

166. Wolf, *Goya and the Satirical Print*, esp. 15–26.

167. Leandro Fernández de Moratín, *Diario (Mayo 1780–Marzo 1808)*, ed. R. and M. Andioc (Madrid, 1968): translation from Xavier de Salas, 'Light on the Origin of Los Caprichos', *Burlington Magazine*, 121 (1979), 711–16. For Goya in Moratín's diaries, see J. Baticle, 'L'Activité de Goya entre 1796 et 1806 vue à travers le "diario" de Moratín', *Revue de l'art*, 13 (1971), 111–13.

168. For recent scholarly considerations of *Los Caprichos*, see J. Carrete, N. Glendinning, J.M. Serrera and J. Vega, *Caprichos de Francisoco Goya: una aproximación y tres estudios* (Madrid, 1996).

169. *Diario de Madrid* for 6 Feb. 1799: translation from Harris, *Goya, Engravings and Lithographs*, i, 95.

170. *Gazeta de Madrid* for 19 Feb. 1799: translation from Harris, *Goya, Engravings and Lithographs*, i, 99.

171. There are two paintings in the same series by other artists, one of which is dated 1795, clearly pointing to the period in which all five canvases were executed: F. Torralba Soriano, *Goya en la Santa Cueva* (Saragossa, 1983); J.L. Morales y Marín, *Goya pintor religioso* (Saragossa, 1990).

172. S. Sebastián Lopez, 'El programa iconográfico de la Santa Cueva de Cádiz', in *Goya. Nuevas Visiones: homenaje a Enrique Lafuente Ferrari* (Madrid, 1987), 374–85.

173. Between 1716 and 1798 Poussin's 1644–48 series of the Seven Sacraments was in the collection of the Dukes of Orléans. The paintings in the collection were engraved in 1774, and this publication was part of Martínez's library: Pemán Medina, 'Estampas y libros que vió Goya en casa de Sebastián Martínez', 316, no. 140.

174. The quotation comes from the Abbé Du Bos: Solkin, *Painting for Money*, 170.

175. Count Zinzendorf records in his diary attending a performance of the *Seven Last Words* in Vienna on 26 Mar. 1787, so the first performance in Cádiz must have been in the same year at the latest.

176. Foreword to the oratorio version of *The Seven Last Words* published by Breitkopf & Härtel (1801): translation from Haydn, *Die sieben letzten Worte unsere Erlösers am Kreuze: Oratorium*, ed. Fodor Ákos (Budapest, n.d.), p. viii.

177. For an account of the origins of *The Seven Last Words* given by Haydn to the *Morning Chronicle* in 1791, in which he referred to his correspondence with 'the Bishop' of Cádiz, see Landon, *Eszterháza*, 617. For the original commission coming from the Santa Cueva, not the Cathedral of Cádiz, see Dénes Bartha, 'A "Sieben Worte" változatainak kéletkezése az Esterházy-gyűjtemény kéziratainalk tükrében', *Magyar Zenetörténeti Tanulmányok*, 8 (Budapest, 1960), 107–86 (esp. 146); Hoboken, *Werkverzeichnis*, i, 845.

178. Cranmer's *Magazin de Musik*, 1787, p. 1385 (correspondence dated 8 Apr.): translation from Landon, *Haydn at Eszterháza*, 618.

179. Dies, 56.

180. Ibid., 54.

181. Ibid., 54–55.

182. Ibid., 55.

183. Pemán Medina, 'Estampas y libros que vió Goya en casa de Sebastián Martínez', 319, no. 19. The edition is probably one published in 1799.

184. For an account of Beattie's thinking on music and relevant selections from his text, see le Huray and Day, *Music and Aesthetics*, 150–56.

185. See, for example, the musical analysis by Landon, *Haydn at Eszterháza*, 618–21.

186. One wonders whether he may have been connected with the Martínez family in Vienna, which all Haydn's early biographers relate to the composer in his early career, and which had been under the protection of Metastasio. See Helene Wessely, 'Martínez, Marianne' in *The New Grove*, ix, 721–22; A. Peter Brown, 'Marianna Martines' Autobiography as a New Source for Haydn's Biography During the 1750's', *Haydn-Studien*, 6/1 (1986), 68–70. I have found no evidence to establish any clear connection between the Martínez families in Vienna and Cádiz.

187. Dies (in the early nineteenth century) clearly indicates that the *Seven Last Words* continued to be performed in Cádiz every Good Friday at the time he was writing (pp. 53–55).

188. J. Vega, 'Goya's Etchings after Velázquez', *Print Quarterly*, 12 (1995), 145–65.

189. Translation from Glendinning, *Goya and his Critics*, 35.

190. Alexander Novotny, *Staatkanzler Kaunitz als geistige Persönlichkeit: Ein Österreichische Kulturbild aus der Zeit der Aufklärung und des Josephinismus* (Vienna, 1947), 124.

191. *The Knife-grinder* and *The Water-carrier* (both Budapest, Museum of Fine Arts): M. Haraszti-Takács, 'Scènes de genre de Goya à la vente de la collection Kaunitz en 1820', *Bulletin du Musée Hongrois des Beaux-Arts*, 64 (1975), 113–20; Wilson-Bareau, *Goya: Truth and Fantasy*, 308–11, 370–71.

192. At the time of the purchase of these Goyas, the Esterházys were just beginning to show an interest in acquiring works by earlier Spanish painters. In 1819 and 1821 Prince Miklós's son, Pál, bought 46 paintings in London and Paris from the collection of Edmund Bourke, the former Danish ambassador to Madrid. Most of these acquisitions were works by Spanish Old Masters.

193. Examples include Paisiello's *Il barbiere di Siviglia* (performed in Vienna between 1783 and 1788), Mozart's *Le nozze di Figaro* (1786, 1789) and *Don Giovanni* (1788) and Martín y Soler's *Una cosa rara* (1786–87).

194. Da Ponte, *Memoirs*, trans. Abbott, 171.

195. For examples of such parody, see Suttcliffe's discussion of Op. 50/6: *Haydn: String Quartets, Op. 50*, 99–103.

196. Cf. *Los Caprichos*, nos 24, 37, 38, 39, 40, 41, 42, 63. In *Los Caprichos* it is interesting to note that one of the prints featuring asses (no. 38) has a musical theme, while another (no. 41) shows an ass sitting for his portrait (the painter is an ape). The use of the image or sound of a donkey to ridicule an idea or belief may be traced back to pre-Christian times. In an early Christian context it is mentioned, for example, by Tertullian. In English caricature of the eighteenth century, images of asses are plentiful. For what may be a satire on Hogarth, see *Ape Painting the Portrait of an Ass*, engraved by G. Bickham (*c*.1753), a probable source for no. 41: Pears, *Discovery of Painting*, 140 (cf. 99). Goupy's caricature of Handel, the 'Harmonious boar', discussed in Ch. 1, is another example. For a caricature featuring an ass of the period when Haydn was in London, see James Sayers's satire on the Society for Constitutional Information, published on 12 May 1791, based on the figure of an ass, braying 'Rights of Man': Dickinson, *Caricatures*, no. 44.

197. Cf. *Los Caprichos*, nos 61, 63, 66, 68, 70 among others.

198. For examples, see *Los Caprichos*, nos 48, 61, 62, 64, 65, 66, 67, 68, 70, 72, 74, 75.

199. The idea of gradually quickening the tempo of music perhaps derives from operatic finales, in which a series of tempo changes intensifies the drama and sense of confusion at the end of the first half of an opera (especially in the 1780s). However, usually these changes are staggered and each introduces new musical material, whereas Haydn's achievement involves using the same material but perceived in a new light.

200. For a discussion of this, see Wolf, *Goya and the Satirical Print*, 59. The world upside down topos was widely used in popular imagery and literature of the later Middle Ages and subsequently, especially in England. For accounts of this, see David Kunzle, 'Bruegel's Proverb Painting and the World Upside Down', *Art Bulletin*, 59 (1977), 55–66; Jean C.S.C. Klene, 'Chaucer's Contributions to a Popular Topos: The World Upside-Down', *Viator*, 11 (1980), 321–34; Christa Grössinger, *The World Upside-Down: English Misericords* (London, 1997).

201. See, for example, Howard R. Patch, *The Goddess Fortuna in Medieval Literature* (Cambridge, Mass., 1927).

202. Handel's libretto for *Giustino* was written and originally prepared in the early 1680s, based on medieval sources first studied in the early seventeenth century. In this case, therefore, tracing how the concept of Fortune's wheel entered eighteenth-century culture is reasonably clear.

203. For one early commentator on the *Caprichos*, who saw allusions to individuals, see the well-known letter from Joseph de Maistre to the Chevalier de Rossi: 'There are eighty plates in all. One ridicules the Queen in the most forceful manner possible, and the allegory is so transparent that even a child could see it.'

204. For differing accounts of Goya's motivation in withdrawing the prints from sale and subsequently giving them to the king, see: Harris, *Goya, Engraving and Lithographs*, i, 99–106; Eleanor A. Sayre et al., *The Changing Image: Prints by Francisco Goya*, exh. cat. (Boston, 1974), 56–57.

205. F. Eibner, 'Die authentische Klavierfassung von Haydns Variationen über "Gott erhalte"', *Haydn Yearbook*, 7 (1970), 281–88.

206. The repetition Haydn himself identified when reading through the proofs is in Hob. XVI: 36/ii and 39/i. For the letter to Artaria requesting that an explanation for the repetition be printed, see *CCLN*, 25

207. For de la Gardie, see Glendinning, *Goya and his Critics*, 53–54.

Notes to Chapter 4

1. Bartha and Somfai, *Haydn als Opernkapellmeister*; Landon, 'Haydn's Marionette Operas', 111–98; Landon, *Haydn at Eszterháza*, 44–117, *et passim*.

2. For documentation on opera performances at Eszterháza, see J. Harich, 'Das Repertoire des Opernkapellmeisters Joseph Haydn in Eszterháza (1780–1790)', *Haydn Yearbook*, 1 (1962), 9–109. Examples of the number of performances given in various years (established by Harich) include: 90 performances (1782), 105 (1783), 104 (1784), 89 (1785), 125 (1786), 98 (1787), 108 (1788): Landon, *Haydn at Eszterháza*, 457, 468, 479, 668, 675, 683, 704.

3. The account of Eszterháza published in Cranmer's *Magazin der Musik* (1784), clarifies Prince Miklós's preference for the comic, especially when the humour was blatant. The relevant passage is quoted in Landon, *Haydn at Eszterháza*, 100.

4. Music by Gluck was, however, heard at Eszterháza. Haydn used ballet music from Gluck's *Paride ed Elena* in 1773: Landon, 'Haydn's Marionette Operas', 149–50.

5. When, for example, Dr Burney visited opera houses during his Continental tours of the early 1770s, he had a reasonable notion what to expect at individual centres, though his experience of staged opera had hitherto been restricted to London.

6. The account of Eszterháza published in Cramer's *Magazin der Musik* (1784) describes the opera house and continues, '[the Prince] often engages a troupe of players for several months at a time, and apart from servants he is the whole audience' (Landon, *Haydn at Eszterháza*, 100). Much the same must have been the case with the opera. Arguably, some of Haydn's early singspiels and marionette operas, and others of their kind, were aimed at broad audiences, embracing all social classes. The use of Viennese dialect points to attempts being made to appeal to the ordinary man and woman in the street.

7. Haskell, *Patrons and Painters*, 278. Alessandro Scarlatti's opera was performed in a bilingual arrangement. For more about the circumstances of its performance, see Ch. 1.

8. Heartz, *Mozart's Operas*, 91.

9. 'I have explained to Stephanie [the librettist] the words I require for the aria – indeed I had *finished* composing most of the music for it *before* Stephanie knew anything whatever about it ... everyone abuses Stephanie. It may be that in my case he is only very friendly to my face. But after all he is *arranging* the libretto for me – and, what is more, *as I want it* – exactly – and by Heaven, I do not ask anything more of him [my italics].' Letter of 6 Oct. 1781: *Letters of Mozart and his Family*, ed. Anderson, 3rd edn, 768–70.

10. Lionel Salter, 'Footnotes to a Satire: Salieri's *Prima la musica, poi le parole*', *Musical Times*, 126 (1985), 21–24.

11. Landon, *Haydn at Eszterháza*, 178.

12. See *New Grove*, xiii, 442.

13. For a survey of Algarotti's career and interests, see Haskell, *Patrons and Painters*, 347–60.

14. For a modern edition of Algarotti's writings, see *Opere di Francesco Algarotti e di Saverio Bettinelli*, ed. Ettore Bonara (Milan, n.d.). *Newtonianismo per le dame* later became an appendix to his more extended *Dialoghi sopra l'ottica Neutoniana* (1752).

15. Sir Isaac Newton, *Opticks or a Treatise of the Reflections, Refractions, Inflections and Colours of Light, based on the 4th Edition, London 1730*, intro. Sir Edmund Whittaker, Dover edn (New York, 1952), 126–29.

16. Ibid., 154–58.

17. Castel's approach to popularizing audio-visual principles, for example, was certainly not for Algarotti, whose views were chiefly aimed at high-minded aristocratic audiences and serious practitioners.

18. Algarotti's obsession with Newton was even recognized on his monument at Pisa (paid for by Frederick the Great). The inscription on this tomb included the line 'NEWTONI DISCIPVLO': see Haskell, *Painters and Patrons*, pl. G.

19. Algarotti's text for the Timotheus painting may be found in M. Precerutti Garberi, 'Di alcuni dipinti perduti del Tiepolo', *Commentari*, 9 (1958), 110–23, at 111–12. See further Michael Levey, *Giambattista Tiepolo: His Life and Art* (New Haven, 1986), 127.

20. Algarotti could not have seen the first performance of this opera since he had temporarily fallen out with Frederick during the course of 1742; but he would certainly have known about, and possibly even contributed to, the preparations for this event, including the strenuous efforts made to complete the theatre in order to satisfy Frederick's impatience for a new opera house in Berlin, and also the lavish stage sets intended to make the production the most brilliant in Europe, for which no expense was spared.

21. Levey, *Giambattista Tiepolo*, 127.

22. *Alexander's Feast* was one of the greatest triumphs of Handel's career: Winton Dean, *Handel's Dramatic Oratorios and Masques* (Oxford, 1959), 270–73.

23. Haskell, *Patrons and Painters*, 349.

24. Newman Flower, *Handel: His Personality and his Times*, rev. edn (London, 1959), 232.

25. St Petersburg, Hermitage.

26. The quotations are taken from an anonymous English translation of Algarotti's *Saggio sopra l'opera* of 1768. For the text, see Strunk, *Source Readings* (1981), 83–84; (1998), 909.

27. Melbourne, National Gallery of Victoria. For an account of this painting and Algarotti's part in its creation, see Haskell, *Painters and Patrons*, 352–53.

28. Michael Levey, 'Tiepolo's Treatment of Classical Story at Villa Valmarana: A Study in Eighteenth-Century Iconography and Aesthetics', *Journal of the Warburg and Courtauld Institutes*, 20 (1957), 298–317. For more general discussions of Tiepolo's interest in opera, see: William L. Barcham, 'Costume in the Frescoes of Tiepolo and Eighteenth-Century Italian Opera', in M. Collins and E.K. Kirk (eds), *Opera and Vivaldi* (Austin, Tex., 1984), 149–69; Baxandall and Alpers, *Tiepolo and the Pictorial Intelligence*, esp. 23, 44–45.

29. F. Whiley Hillis, *The Literary Career of Sir Joshua Reynolds* (Cambridge, 1936), 221, quoted by Levey, 'Tiepolo's Treatment of Classical Story', 299.

30. For an overview of Ariosto in the eighteenth century, see C.P. Brand, *Ariosto* (Edinburgh, 1974), 191–92.

31. Erffa and Staley, *Paintings of Benjamin West*, 262–63, 282–84. For a general survey of Ariosto in the visual arts, see Rensselaer Lee, *Names on Trees: Ariosto into Art* (Princeton, 1977); for Tasso in the visual arts, see the same author's *Ut pictura poesis*, esp. ch. 7, 'Rinaldo and Armida'.

32. See the list of engraved subjects from Kauffman paintings compiled by David Alexander in Roworth (ed.), *Angelica Kauffman*, 179–89.

33. For Mortimer, see John Sunderland, 'John Hamilton Mortimer, his Life and Works', *Walpole Society*, 42 (1986), 1–236, esp. 132, cat. 74, figs 121–29. For Fragonard, see Elizabeth Mongan, Philip Hofer and Jean Seznec, *Fragonard: Drawings for Ariosto* (London, 1947).

34. Adhémar, *La Gravure originale*, 150. Chodowiecki's almanack illustrations included Ariosto and twelve subjects from the history of the crusades, which may be considered Tasso-like in subject matter.

35. None of Haydn's Eszterházy operas enjoyed wide circulation. During the composer's lifetime *Orlando paladino* was performed (usually in German) in Pressburg (1786), Prague (1791), Vienna (1791–92), Budapest (1792), Dresden (1792), Mannheim (1792), Frankfurt (1793), Cologne (1793), Berlin (1798), Leipzig (1800), and Munich (1800). Haydn himself introduced a couple of its numbers to London during his visits there.

36. For a discussion of Haydn's opera based on Ariosto in the context of an analysis of different treatments of Orlando as a character in eighteenth-century opera, see Ellen T. Harris, 'Eighteenth-Century Orlando: Hero, Satyr and Fool', in Collins and Kirk (eds), *Opera and Vivaldi*, 103–28, at 107–8.

37. Cervantes's anti-hero was the subject of an early opera by Paisiello (1769) and a series of drawings by Fragonard.

38. The subject was derived from several classical sources, chiefly the play by Euripides and Ovid's *Metamorphoses*, 12.25–28.

39. *Von der musikalischen Poesie* (Berlin, 1752), quoted in Heartz, *Mozart's Operas*, 3.

40. F.H. Dowley, 'Carle Van Loo's *Sacrifice of Iphigenia*', *Master Drawings*, 5 (1967), 42–47; id., 'French Baroque Representations of the "Sacrifice of Iphigenia"', in *Festschrift Ulrich Middeldorf*, vol. 1 (Berlin, 1968), 466–75, pls cci–ccii; Gerd Bartoschek, *Die Gemälde im neuen Palais* (Potsdam-Sanssouci, 1971), 23, no. 188.

41. For Vanloo and Mme de Pompadour, see, for example, Perrin Stein, 'Madame de Pompadour and the Harem Imagery at Bellevue', *Gazette des Beaux-Arts*, 123 (1994), 29–44.

42. Richmond, Virginia Museum of Fine Arts, and London, Wallace Collection: John Ingamells, *The Wallace Collection. Catalogue of Pictures*, iii: *French before 1815* (London, 1989), 254–56.

43. For a list of the texts, see *Vanloo: premier peintre du roi*, exh. cat. by Marie-Catherine Sahut, Nice, Clermont-Ferrand, Nancy (1977), 78, no. 158, cf. 14. As a result of the controversy, several painters were prompted to treat the subject, including Zoffany: Webster, *Johann Zoffany*, cat. 3.

44. Quintilian, *Institutio oratoria*, 2. 13. 12–13. For the translation quoted here, other relevant texts and the full context, see J.J. Pollitt, *The Art of Ancient Greece: Sources and Documents* (Cambridge, 1990), 156–57.

45. Algarotti may have pointed Tiepolo towards operatic versions of the subject like Jomelli's *Ifigenia in Aulide*. This is not known to have been performed in Venice (where Tiepolo was based) before 1757, but was still well known, having been staged in Rome, Mannheim, Naples and Barcelona.

46. Letter written to Marie-Antoinette's sister, Maria Christine Josepha, a week after the event: quoted in Einstein, *Gluck*, 138.

47. Quoted in Johnson, *Listening in Paris*, 81.

48. As one contemporary commentator put it, the 'principal subject of the operas was the music rather than the text ... [It is] in the orchestra alone that true expression comes.' *Querelle des gluckistes et piccinnistes*, i, 291, quoted in Johnson, *Listening in Paris*, 138.

49. Edinburgh, National Galleries of Scotland: Clark, *Pompeo Batoni*, 224–26, cat. 59.

50. The painting arrived in Britain in 1743, but was probably in Scotland when Gluck was working in London two years later. However, Gluck could have been shown either the retouched *bozzetto* for the composition, the whereabouts of which is unclear in the 1740s, but which had certainly been in London for a long time by 1770, or a lost version of the painting also recorded in London in the 1770s. For the *bozzetto*, see Clark, *Pompeo Batoni*, 224, cat. 58. The lost version is mentioned by Clark on p. 226.

51. 'When I took on the composition of *Alceste*, I determined to strip it entirely of all those abuses, brought into it either by the shallow vanity of singers or by composers over-zealous to please, which have for so long spoilt Italian opera and turned the most splendid and beautiful of spectacles into the most ridiculous and laborious.' For the original Italian text (addressed by Gluck to Archduke Leopold of Tuscany in 1769), see *New Grove*, vii, 466, fig. 5.

52. Preface to *Alceste* (Vienna, 1769), p. xi.

53. Prefatory letter, addressed to Duke Giovanni of Braganza, in *Paride ed Elena* (Vienna, 1770): Nohl, *Musiker-Briefe*, 8–11.

54. Letter to M. Le Bailli du Roullet, July–Aug. 1776: *Révolution*, 43.

55. Ibid., 110–11.

56. For a balanced account of the relationship between Calzabigi and Gluck, see Patricia Howard, *C.W. von Gluck: Orfeo* (Cambridge, 1981), 22–26. In a letter to the *Mercure de France* (Vienna, 1 Feb. 1773), Gluck gave Calzabigi the main credit for 'the new form of Italian opera', but there may have been diplomatic and other not disinterested reasons why he would have wished to do this in 1773.

57. Written in 1778: quoted in Einstein, *Gluck*, 113.

58. Mentioned in a letter by Gluck of 2 Mar. 1780: *CCP*, 174.

59. Extracts from Von Mannlich's Paris memoirs, with mentions of Gluck, are in Henriette Weiss von Trostpaugg (ed.), 'Mémoires sur la musique à Paris à la fin du règne de Louis XV', *La revue musicale*, 15 (1934), 111–19, 161–71, 252–62.

60. *CCP*, 186–88, 192–93.

61. Ibid., 192.

62. For Moreau, see Owen E. Holloway, *French Rococo Book Illustration* (London, 1969), 40–58.

63. See *Fragonard, Moreau le jeune and French Engravers: Etchers and Illustrators of the Late XVIII Century*, ed. Arthur M. Hind (London, 1913).

64. Bruce Alan Brown, 'Durazzo, Duni, and the Frontispiece to *Orfeo ed Euridice*', *Studies in Eighteenth-Century Culture*, 19 (1989), 71–97.

65. *CCP*, 202.

66. Ibid., 195.

67. See ibid., n. 2.

68. For an account of Algarotti's connections with Winckelmann, see Wolfgang Leppmann, *Winckelmann* (London, 1971), 109–11, 220.

69. *Gedanken über die Nachhahmung der griechischen Werke in der Malerey und Bildhauerkunst.* For an introduction to Winckelmann's writings and thought, see David Irwin, *Winckelmann: Writings on Art* (London, 1972).

70. *Gedanken über das Schönheit und über den Geschmack in der Malerey* (Zurich, 1752) and *Riflessioni sopra i tre gran pittori Raffaello, Correggio, Tiziano e sopra gli antichi*, published by Giuseppe Niccola d'Azara (Parma, 1780).

71. For Kaunitz's policy towards the visual arts and music, and his relations with Winckelmann, see Szabo, *Kaunitz*, 24–26, 97–99, 200–202. Without its tourist trade, Kaunitz maintained, Italy would be impoverished. Batoni and Mengs were among the contemporary artists for whom he expressed enthusiasm. The gift the Chancellor presented to Winckelmann to try to entice him to consider seriously moving to Vienna may have provided a motivation for Winckelmann's assassination.

72. *Geschichte der Kunst des Alterthums.*

73. For a comprehensive account of Winckelmann's aims in the *Geschichte*, see Alex Potts, *Flesh and the Ideal: Winckelmann and the Origins of Art History* (London, 1994).

74. '... Just as the feelings that painting arouses in us do not originate in the colours, so the influence that music has over our souls is not the work of sounds. Beautiful colours subtly shaded are pleasing to the eye, but this pleasure is purely one of sensation. It is the drawing, the imitation that gives these colours life and soul: the passions they express stir our own; the lines of touching painting are still touching in an engraving or print: remove these lines from the picture, and the colours will no longer have any effect. Melody does in music precisely what drawing does in painting; it marks the lines and the figures, of which the chords and the sounds are but the colours ... Just as painting is not the art of combining colours in a manner pleasing to the eye, neither is music the art of combining sounds in a manner pleasing to the ear. If it only came to that, both would be counted among the natural sciences and not the fine arts. Imitation alone is what raises them to the rank of arts. And what makes painting an imitative art? Drawing. What makes music another such art? Melody.' *Essai sur l'origine des langues*, ch. 13: translation from Fubini, *Music and Culture*, 94–95.

75. Letter to the *Mercure de France*, Feb. 1773: *Révolution*, 10.

76. *Révolution*, 10.

77. Ibid., 259–70.

78. 'Our men of letters, with hardly an exception, have little love of the arts, do not encourage them and do not live with artists. They go to hear opera as they go to see pictures at the Louvre, so that they can discuss them at dinner, rank the artists according to their judgement and show that, with a bit of sense, one can

talk well about anything. ... M. de Laharpe has felt himself compelled, in his position as a journalist, to consider your works as marking an epoch in the history of the arts. That's fine; but he should, it seems to me, speak either as an historian or put himself into a position to speak with an informed voice' (ibid. 285–89).

79. Ibid., 292–3.

80. Ibid., 293–4.

81. Ibid., 299.

82. Suard continued the analogy by pointing out that: 'There are also qualities which are excluded because of the imperfection of human nature; the greatest talent has its limitations and the greatest artists have always sacrificed certain parts of their art in favour of those which affect them more profoundly. But, although Raphael has neither the brilliance of Guido [Reni], nor the colour of Titian, he is nonetheless the best of painters' (ibid., 309–10).

83. *Essai sur les révolutions de la musique en France*: *Révolution*, 153–90.

84. *Révolution*, 167.

85. Vatican Museum, Rome. For a survey of views on the *Laocoön* following its redicovery in the sixteenth century, see Margarete Bieber, *Laocoon: The Influence of the Group since its Rediscovery*, rev. edn (Detroit, 1967) and Haskell and Penny, *Taste and the Antique*.

86. Quoted from the translation of *The Aeneid* by W.F. Jackson Knight, rev. edn (Harmondsworth, 1958), 57–58.

87. Lee, *Ut pictura poesis*, 20–23.

88. *Révolution*, 175–78.

89. *Mercure de France*, 15 Sept. 1778: *CCP*, 144.

90. *Mercure de France*, 5 Oct. 1778: *CCP*, 158.

91. *Briefe eines aufmerksamen Reisenden die Musik betreffend* (Frankfurt, 1774–76).

92. Translation quoted in Strunk, *Source Readings* (1981), 134–35. Reichard begins with another pictorial/musical analogy: 'Do you not also know that the composer of operas is in this not very different from the painter of scenery, who must paint everything with great sweeping strokes of his brush in order that, at the distance from which the beholder perceives it, it may for the first time seem to be that which it would represent?'

93. Ibid., 128. The paralleling of light and shade in painting with musical effects perhaps derives from Gluck's preface to *Alceste* (1769). Reichardt's selection of 'a merry banquet or a furious battle scene' was possibly taken from Gluck's *La Rencontre imprévue* (1764), which is fully discussed below in the text.

94. Indeed, in the ideas on taste and beauty expressed in this letter, Reichardt seems closer to Algarotti than Gluck. See, for example, his criticism of composers employing the 'fashionable' rapid alternations of *forte* and *piano*, in which he compares the effect with the portrait of a sick man making violent contortions, an effect far removed from the beauty which is really required (he gives the example of Watteau): Strunk, *Source Readings* (1981), 129. Reichardt's criticism of Graun for concentrating on invention in harmony at the expense of variety in melody perhaps springs from the same prejudices as some of Marmontel's criticisms of Gluck, though the language used by Reichardt to express these ideas betrays his familiarity with Gluck's defence of his own position. Here Reichardt uses the analogy of the landscape painter's use of architecture and secondary figures in shade to draw attention to principal figures: Strunk, *Source Readings* (1981), 133.

95. The bust was destroyed in a fire at the Paris Opéra. Its form is known through a large number of copies in different media: Arnason, *Houdon*, 108, n. 67.

96. Paris, Musée du Louvre: Arnason, *Houdon*, 35–36. Arnould also sang the part of Eurydice in Gluck's *Orfée* in the same year.

97. Alexandre Anantoff, *L'Œuvre dessiné de J.-H. Fragonard (1732–1806)*, vol. 1 (Paris, 1961), 183, cat. 455.

98. Coll. M. Arthur Veil-Picard, Paris. For a resumé of the arguments, see Pierre Rosenberg, *Fragonard*, exh. cat. (New York, 1988), 159–60.

99. *Catalogues de vents et livrets de Salons illustrés et annotés par Gabriel de Saint-Aubin*, ed. E. Dacier, 6 vols (1909–21); E. Dacier, *Gabriel de Saint-Aubin, peintre, dessinateur et graveur*, 2 vols (Paris, 1929–31).

100. Edgar Wind, 'The Sources of David's *Horaces*', *Journal of the Courtauld and Warburg Institutes*, 4 (1940–41), 124–38. For a more recent survey of sources of David's painting, see Antoine Schnapper et al., *Jacques-Louis David*, exh. cat. (Paris, 1989), 162–68, cat. 67.

101. Wind, 'The Sources of David's *Horaces*', 135–37. David's relationship with the musical stage in Paris continued in the 1790s. For example, his 1799 painting, *The Intervention of the Sabine Women*, was satirized at the Opéra Comique in a burlesque called *The Painting of the Sabines*.

102. Crow, *Painters and Public Life*, 94–96; Fort, 'Voice of the Public', 384–90.

103. [J.B. Pujoulx], *Figaro au Sallon de peinture. Pièce épisodi-critique en prose et en vaudevilles* (Paris, 1785). Paisiello's *Il barbiere di Siviglia* was first given in 1782 and Mozart's *Le nozze di Figaro* in 1786.

104. 'Aujourdui je suis Critique[.] pour égayer mes leçons j'y melerai des chansons.' For a reproduction of this engraving and discussion of the pamphlet, see Wrigley, *Origins of French Art Criticism*, 180–1.

105. For the overwhelming reaction to Haydn in Paris at this time, see Harrison, *'Paris' Symphonies*, 15–20.

106. The extent to which Haydn followed cultural events in Paris at the time of the commission for these symphonies is unclear, though it seems likely that the cultural interests of Prince Miklós (who visited Paris in 1782) would have encouraged him in this respect. He might well have read some of the earliest criticisms of David's painting after it was first exhibited in 1785, such as the account by J.H.W. Tischbein, published in *Der teutsche Merkur* in February 1786: see *From the Classicists to the Impressionists: Art and Architecture in the Nineteenth Century. A Documentary History of Art*, vol. 3, ed. Elizabeth Gilmore Holt (New York, 1966), 16–24. Qualities perceived in the *Horatii*, as reported in sources available to Haydn, are clearly evident in at least one Haydn symphony written for Paris, No. 86 (1786). The first movement, in particular, impresses on listeners the range of emotions experienced on looking at David's painting: its bold design and 'masterly' arrangement, inspiring sensations of 'courage', youthful vigour, 'strength', 'enthusiasm' and 'reverence' (see Holt, esp. 18–19). Although these connections may be coincidental, given the increasing reciprocity between music and painting in the 1780s in the public sphere, it seems very likely that listeners to Haydn's music would have been reminded of David's imagery.

107. Julian Rushton, *'Iphigénie en Tauride*: The Operas of Gluck and Piccinni', *Music & Letters*, 53 (1972), 411–30; Elisabeth Schmierer, 'Piccinni's *Iphigénie en Tauride*: "Chant périodique" and Dramatic Structure', *Cambridge Opera Journal*, 4 (1992), 91–118.

108. *Iphigénie en Tauride* is not the only one of Gluck's serious operas to require

statues or other kinds of image as props. *Alceste*, in particular, requires such images in several scenes. In *Les Danaïdes*, the libretto for which was prepared for Gluck (though it was actually set by Salieri), a statue of the goddess Nemesis is required to be prominently seen in the middle of the stage throughout Act II.

109. The play was by Guymond de la Touche: see Robert R. Heitner, 'The Iphigenia in Tauris Theme in Drama of the Eighteenth Century', *Comparative Literature*, 16 (1964), 289–309.

110. H. Bloch, 'Tommaso Traetta's Reform of Italian Opera', *Collectanea historiae musicae*, 3 (Florence, 1963), 5–15; Daniel Heartz, 'Traetta in Vienna: *Armida* (1761) and *Ifigenia in Tauride* (1763)', *Studies in Music from the University of Western Ontario*, 7 (1982), 65–88.

111. Daniel Heartz, 'Operatic Reform at Parma: *Ippolito ed Aricia*', in *Atti del convegno sul Settecento parmense nel 2⁰ centenario della morte di C.I. Frugoni* (Parma, 1969), 271–300.

112. Hob. XXIVb: 10.

113. London, Tate Gallery: Erffa and Staley, *Painting of Benjamin West*, 260–61, cat. 186. The painting, sent for exhibition in 1766, had already made a deep impression when seen in the artist's studio.

114. Following a chorus of female assistants at the temple with Iphigenia and her companion (Act I, Scene 3), Orestes is brought before Iphigenia by Toante, the barbarian king of Thrace, accompanied by a chorus of soldiers (Act I, Scene 4). The painting corresponds to this part of the opera, except that Pylades is not featured in this scene.

115. Erffa and Staley, 339–40, cat. 323.

116. Haydn's relationship to Lavater's ideas is discussed in Ch. 5.

117. For a survey of such dream scenes and Fuseli's development of the subject, see Nicolas Powell, *Fuseli: The Nightmare* (London, 1973), esp. 37–52.

118. For Fuseli's drawing (Staatliche Kunstsammlungen, Dresden), see Gert Schiff, *Johann Heinrich Füssli 1741–1825*, 2 vols (Zurich, 1973), 431, cat. 332. In Traetta's opera, stage directions show that although Orestes sings, he is supposed to be asleep (Act I, Scene 4). The Furies surround him, singing and dancing menacingly. The ghost of his mother also momentarily appears. In Gluck's opera (executed 16 years later), a chorus of Furies also surrounds Orestes (Act II, Scene 4), threatening him in dance and in the words and music of their singing; Clytemnestra appears momentarily as a ghost in the middle of their chorus.

119. For example, Hogarth's *Garrick in the Character of Richard III* (*c.*1746; Walker Art Gallery, Liverpool) shows only the fear which the vision causes the king, and not the ghosts of his victims which he supposedly witnesses. For connections between the reform operas of Gluck and the changes in theatrical practice associated with Garrick, see Daniel Heartz, 'From Garrick to Gluck: The Reform of Theatre and Opera in the mid-Eighteenth Century', *Proceedings of the Royal Musical Association*, 94 (1967–68), 111–27.

120. It seems possible that musical stimuli inspired some of Fuseli's other representations of scenes featuring ghosts. In 1777, for example, he depicted the subject of Saul consulting the witch of Endor, who calls up the ghost of the prophet Samuel on the eve of a battle between the Israelites and the Philistines (1 Sam. 28: 3–20). Samuel predicted defeat for the Israelites and the death of Saul and his sons. This biblical example of necromancy had been the subject of a well-known painting by Salvator Rosa, which was certainly an influence on Fuseli and also two other artists working in London, Benjamin West and John

Hamilton Mortimer, who both executed versions of this subject at about the same time. But the timing of their versions and the public interest in the subject was probably a result of the treatment of the episode by Purcell, and more particularly by Handel, in his oratorio *Saul*, which was first performed in 1739, though only published in a complete edition a few years before the depictions by Fuseli, West and Mortimer. Although *Saul* is not an opera, Handel's approach to the material may certainly be considered operatic, and in performance singers might well be expected to suggest to an audience the action and spirit of the drama. The ghost scene in *Saul* was not only largely unprecedented in such a work, but also certainly captured the public imagination, which might well have had repercussions for artists. For Fuseli, see Schiff, *Füssli* (1973), 372–3; for West, see Erffa and Staley, *Benjamin West*, 83–84, 311–12; for Mortimer, see John Sunderland, 'John Hamilton Mortimer and Salvator Rosa', *Burlington Magazine*, 112 (1970), 524–25. For Handel, see Winton Dean, *Handel's Dramatic Oratorios and Masques* (Oxford, 1959), 302.

121. The libretto was by L.H. Dancourt, based on the earlier work of Lesage and d'Orneval. The origins of the opera are fully discussed by Brown, 'Gluck's *Rencontre imprévue*'.

122. For a discussion on the origins of the Vertigo character, see Brown, *Gluck and the French Theatre*, 410.

123. Loche and Roethlisberger, *Liotard*; Anne de Heidt, *Dessins de Liotard*, exh. cat., Musée du Louvre (Paris, 1992). Liotard was not the only French painter to have worked in Turkish Constantinople. J.-B. Van Mour (d. 1737) had also worked there. But Liotard was by far the most famous artist with an oriental connection in the 1760s.

124. 'Un être surnaturel'. For an account of the concept of genius in the eighteenth century, see: Jonathan Bate, 'Shakespeare and the Original Genius', in Murray (ed.), *Genius: The History of an Idea*, 76–97; Shawe-Taylor, *Genial Company*, 6–9.

125. See Jean Seznec, 'Le Socrate imaginaire', in *Essai sur Diderot et l'Antiquité* (Oxford, 1957), ch. 1.

126. For Apelles' paintings of 'things that cannot be represented in pictures', including thunder, see *Naturalis historia*, 35. 36. 96. For Falconet on Pliny, see Jean Seznec, 'Diderot and "The Justice of Trajan"', *Journal of the Warburg and Courtauld Institutes*, 20 (1957), 106–111; Benot, *Diderot et Falconet*.

127. Paris, Musée du Louvre. For eighteenth-century copies of Veronese's *Marriage at Cana*, see Jean Hubert et al., *Les Noces de Cana de Veronèse: Une œuvre et sa restauration*, exh. cat., Musée du Louvre (Paris, 1992), ch. 5.

128. For examples, see Wakefield, *French Eighteenth-Century Painting*, 47–49.

129. Pictures by Berghem and Cuyp present obvious examples. For the taste for such works in eighteenth-century France (imitated in Austria), see, for example, Oliver T. Banks, *Watteau and the North: Studies in the Dutch and Flemish Baroque Influence on French Rococo Painting* (New York, 1977).

130. The popularity of these early works by Loutherbourg encouraged him to reproduce the compositions as etchings.

131. Diderot, *Salons*, ed. Seznec and Adhémar, i, 225. Diderot's criticisms for the Salon of 1763 were published in instalments between September and November 1763. They would have been highly topical at the time that the opera went into production.

132. Liverpool, Walker Art Gallery: Joppien, *Loutherbourg*, cat. 2; Diderot, *Salons*, ed. Seznec and Adhémar, i, 225–26.

133. Loutherbourg maintained a reputation for painting grazing bulls. One of the odes on members of the Royal Academy in London, by the satirist 'Peter Pindar', emphasizes this feature in relation to Loutherbourg (1782): *Works of Peter Pindar* (London, 1826), 123.

134. Diderot, *Salons*, ed. Seznec and Adhémar, i, 226.

135. Ibid. Diderot helped to bring Loutherbourg's name to the attention of the public, not only through discussion of his paintings, but also because he hinted at a scandal involving Casanova's wife.

136. London, Tate Gallery: Joppien, *Loutherbourg*, cat. 46. This painting is discussed further in Ch. 7.

137. Diderot, *Salons*, ed. Seznec and Adhémar, i, 205.

138. This became some of the most popular music in the opera. Various arrangements of it are known in printed and manuscript sources: Brown, *Gluck and the French Theatre*, 419.

139. For Reynolds, see Penny, *Reynolds*, cat. 90. *Hymen* was the title of a musical interlude by Michael Arne (1764): Fiske, *English Theatre Music*, 310, 317.

140. The other characters in the scene utter a series of popular artistic terms in attempts to take Vertigo's mind off of the notion of marriage.

141. Diderot, *Salons*, ed. Seznec and Adhémar, i, 245.

142. For accounts of the importance of the Pygmalion legend to the development of visual and musical culture in the eighteenth century, see J.L. Carr, 'Pygmalion and the *Philosophes*', *Journal of the Warburg and Courtauld Institutes*, 23 (1960), 239–55; Mechtild Schneider, 'Pygmalion, Mythus des schöpferischen Künstlers: Zur Aktualität eines Themas in der französischen Kunst von Falconet bis Rodin', *Pantheon*, 45 (1987), 111–23.

143. Montpellier, Musée Fabre.

144. For this drawing, see Winter, *Pre-Romantic Ballet*, 103.

145. This opera is discussed in Diderot's *Le Neveu de Rameau*, written in the early 1760s.

146. For a discussion of Watteau's representation of 'Gilles', see Donald Posner, *Antoine Watteau* (London, 1984), 266–77, 291–92.

147. *Le Festin de pierre*, performed at the Foire Saint-Germain in Paris in 1713–14: Julian Rushton, *Don Giovanni*, 34.

148. Russell, *The Don Juan Legend before Mozart*.

149. For the relationship of stone statues and other monuments to the Don Giovanni story in opera, see Malcolm Baker, 'Odzooks! A Man of Stone', in Jonathan Miller (ed.), *The Don Giovanni Book: Myths of Seduction and Betrayal* (London, 1990), 62–69.

150. For Shakespeare's use of the Pygmalion legend, see Leonard Barkan, 'Living Sculptures: Ovid, Michelangelo and *The Winter's Tale*', *Journal of English Literary History*, 48 (1981), 639–67.

151. Bryan N.S. Gooch and David Thatcher (eds), *A Shakespeare Music Catalogue*, 5 vols (Oxford, 1991), iii, nos 18675, 18699.

152. For examples, see: Wind, *Hume and the Heroic Portrait*, 47, figs 55–57; Dennis Bartholomeusz, *The Winter's Tale in Performance in England and America 1611–1976* (Cambridge, 1982), 28–41.

153. Charlton, *Grétry and the Growth of Opéra-Comique*, 49–55. The term 'speaking [or talking] picture' derives from Sidney's *Defence of Poetry*, and ultimately from Horace's *Ars poetica*. The phrase was popularized in the eighteenth century because it appears in Samuel Richardson's *Pamela*. This novel was the basis of a number of operas, notably Piccinni's *La cecchina, o sia La buona*

figliola, with a libretto by Goldoni (1760). There was also a version by Duni, produced in Parma in 1756.

154.   Although this talking picture may today strike us as most unlikely to have ever fooled anyone, we have to remember that we live in a much more sophisticated age today. It was not so very long ago that murder mystery films, especially in the 1930s, not infrequently made use of a similar device, the assailant spying on potential victims through holes of the canvas of a portrait.

155.   *Annales du théâtre italien depuis son origine jusqu'à ce jour*, 3 vols (Paris, 1788), ii, 62; cited in Charlton, *Grétry and the Growth of Opéra-Comique*, 335–36, n. 1.

156.   Ranc was a pupil of Rigauld, whose formal style of portraiture, in which even the least promising sitters were made to seem imposing through judicious arrangements of costume and hair, was the starting point of his own portraiture. Ranc became a court painter in Spain. See Juan J. Luna, 'Hyacinthe Rigaud et l'Espagne', *Gazette des Beaux-Arts*, 91 (1978), 185–95; id., 'El pintor Francés Jean Ranc y la corte de Felipe V en Andalucía', *Historia*, 16 (1987), 94–104.

157.   A manuscript indicating the complete choreography of this scene survives: Winter, *Pre-Romantic Ballet*, 164.

158.   Charlton, *Grétry and the Growth of Opéra-Comique*, 98–108.

159.   The picture seems to have been Grétry's invention, not Marmontel's: Karin Pendel, 'The Opéras Comiques of Grétry and Marmontel', *Musical Quarterly*, 62 (1976), 409–34, esp. 427.

160.   Among representations of the magic picture scene in *Zémire* are: an engraving by P.-C. Ingouf after a gouache by F.-R. Ingouf; a drawing by Moreau le Jeune (1771); an engraving by Voyé le Jeune (dedicated to Marie-Antoinette), from a drawing by J.-L. Touzé (Paris, Bibliothèque Nationale de France, Estampes Tb1–402); and a representation by Gramont (Paris, Bibliothèque Nationale de France, Opéra. MUS. 1648).

161.   *Dr Burney's Musical Tours in Europe*, ii: *An Eighteenth-Century Musical Tour in Central Europe*, 8–9. For Burney's observations on Liotard and Grétry, see Burney, *Music, Men and Manners*, ed. Poole, 22.

162.   Just as today we might temporarily be taken in by the setting of a recent film.

163.   For Mozart's interest in Grétry's *Zémire*, see Francis van de Velde, *Mozart à Paris*, exh. cat. (Paris, 1989), 124, no 229. This opera was regularly performed in Vienna from 1781 to 1791. For reworkings of the opera in London, see Kinne, *Revivals and Importations*, 144–45.

164.   Kinne, *Revivals and Importations*, 123–25.

165.   These operas were matched by at least one other work performed on the Parisian stage at the same time: Fabre d'Eglantine's comedy *L'Intrigue épistolaire* (1791) included a role for an artist who paints on stage.

166.   The author was Prince Hoare. The work was performed 101 times between 1793 and 1799: Kinne, *Revivals and Importations*, 229.

167.   Krumbhaar, *Isaac Cruikshank*, 108, no. 787.

168.   Portraits or miniature portraits are key elements of the plots in the unfinished opera later called *Zaide*, as well as *Così fan tutte* and *Die Zauberflöte*. In *Don Giovanni*, the Don orders Leporello to entertain Masetto and his friends with 'la galleria', which presumably denotes a collection of pictures. The statue of the Commendatore has already been mentioned. In *Die Entführung aus dem Serail*, a reworking of the plot of Gluck's *La Rencontre imprévue*, Belmonte pretends to be an architect.

169.   Ingamells, *Mrs Robinson*, 11–15.

170. *The Miniature Picture* was staged, against its creator's will, by Sheridan at Drury Lane. Lady Craven composed her own music for her plays. See *Memoirs of the Margravine of Anspach*, 2 vols (London, 1826), esp. ii, 181–82.

171. Kinne, *Revivals and Importations*, 162.

172. The kind of iconic elements identified in this chapter may be found in operas by Cherubini, Verdi, Offenbach, Gilbert and Sullivan, Richard Strauss, Puccini, Hindemith, Barber and many others. Indeed, the tradition remains strong, as is evident from John Adams's opera *Nixon in China*, in which an icon of Chairman Mao comes to life and dances with his wife.

173. Ali's aria 'Ecco un splendido banchetto'. *L'incontro improvviso* was not the first Haydn opera to make use of a strong iconic element. Surviving accounts of *Philemon und Baucis* (1773) show that it featured several images.

174. The unfinished opera later known as *Zaide* and *Die Zauberflöte*.

Notes to Chapter 5

1. Haydn, *Briefe*, 538.

2. Haydn's London notebooks reveal how several leading personalities, whose portraits were well known in the public sphere, were studied by him. His comments particularly draw attention to the discrepancy between their public image and their (often scandalous) private lives. The case of the actress and singer Dora Jordan is discussed in Ch. 8.

3. The announcement was made in the *Wiener Zeitung*. The best account of Haydn portraiture is the 'Iconography of Authentic Haydn Pictures', in Somfai's *Joseph Haydn: His Life in Contemporary Pictures*, 212–25, which includes a useful catalogue and resumé of relevant texts and sources. It has been used extensively in the writing of this chapter. Somfai's catalogue numbers are given in the notes below. In many respects, however, Somfai's work should be used with caution since the catalogue is certainly not complete and the sources he cites are far from exhaustive. Also useful is Joseph Muller's 'Haydn Portraits' (*Musical Quarterly*, 18 (1932), 282–98), which includes a catalogue listing engravings after painted and sculpted portraits, and Jens Peter Larsen's *Zur Frage der Porträtlichkeit der Haydn-Bildnisse* (Budapest, 1970).

4. Alexander Weinmann, *Vollständiges Verlagsverzeichnis Artaria & Comp.* (Vienna, 1952).

5. The composer looks out to the viewer through a circular frame, inscribed 'IOSEPHUS HAYDN'. The frame, suspended from above, is set against, on the left, a hanging drape, and on the right, a view of a statue of a woman labelled 'EVTERPE', the muse of music. Below the portrait, a collection of musical instruments (lyre, flute, trumpet and keyboard) and sheets of music rest on a slab which features the inscription *Blandus auritas fidebus canoris Ducere quercus* ('And blandish the listening oaks with singing strings': Horace, *Odes*, 1. 12). The same quotation was in or shortly after 1799 used for the larger of the two porcelain busts of Haydn made in Vienna by the sculptor Anton Grassi.

6. Haydn, *Briefe*, 97.

7. Somfai, *Joseph Haydn*, 213, no. 1. The portrait is presumed to have been destroyed in 1945.

8. Somfai, 213, no. 8a. The whereabouts of this portrait is now not known. Somfai argues for a date *c*.1791, when Guttenbrunn knew Haydn in London, but in line

with most commentators this dating is rejected here on the grounds that the sitter appears to be aged less than 40, which fits the earlier period. For the second version of the portrait (Somfai, no. 8b), indeed painted in London, see below in the text.

9. Dies, 206–7.
10. Carpani, 93.
11. Dies, 206.
12. Haydn, *Briefe*, 98.
13. Ibid., 101. The Mansfeld engraving must have proved very popular in Haydn's circle, since in his letter to Artaria of 18 Oct. 1781 he requested another batch of them for his own use: *Briefe*, 104.
14. Anne Schnoebelen, *Padre Martini's Collection of Letters in the Civico Museo Bibliografico Musicale in Bologna: An Annotated Index* (New York, 1979), 489, no. 4121.
15. *Catalog of Carl Philipp Emanuel Bach's Estate*, ed. Wade, 107.
16. *Musical Tours in Europe*, ed. Scholes, ii, 219.
17. Werner Neumann, *Bilddokumente zur Lebensgeschichte Johann Sebastian Bachs*, vol. 4 of *Bach-Documente* (Kassel, 1979).
18. Hence Haydn's quip to Artaria that his image had at least provided employment for frame-makers and gilders.
19. Haydn's collection of prints and other works of art is discussed in detail in Ch. 6.
20. Appendix, no. 2.
21. *Briefe*, 175–76.
22. Ibid., 220. A silhouette of Haydn himself had been published in an Austrian calendar in 1786, and another taken a few years later; so Haydn may have been particularly curious about this newly fashionable form of portraiture, though the interest did not last: Somfai, *Joseph Haydn*, 213, nos 4 and 6; Peggy Hickman, *Two Centuries of Silhouettes: Celebrities in Profile* (London, 1971). Haydn's interest may have waned because a silhouette of him was used to decorate the publication of a set of three keyboard trios (called Opus 40, published by Bossler), issued under his name, with his authority, two of which were in fact by Pleyel. During the time he was in London, this matter became the subject of legal proceedings against Haydn.
23. That is Salomon, Pleyel, Dussek, Cramer and 'Lady Elizabeth Lambert'.
24. The main part of Gerber's dictionary as originally published was an expanded version of J.G. Walther's *Musicalisches Lexicon*, issued in Leipzig in 1732, often cited as the first music dictionary.
25. Haydn's interest in new musical manuals intended for use by the public may be shown from the help he gave to John Wall Callcott in preparing his *Explanation of the notes, marks, words &c. used in music* published in London in January 1792: see Otto Biba, 'Joseph Haydn and John Wall Callcott: A Miscellany Concerning Haydn's London Acquaintances', *Haydn Yearbook*, 20 (1996), 57–58. The *Explanation*, however, contains no consideration of musical portraiture.
26. For Latrobe and Burney, see Landon, *Haydn in England*, 31.
27. British Library, MS Add. 11730, fol. 112, quoted by Landon, *Haydn in England*, 57. The account is dated 22 Nov. 1828, and is part of a letter to Vincent Novello.
28. Haydn's contacts with Latrobe (who dedicated three piano sonatas to Haydn and was mentioned by the composer in his *first* London notebook), and Haydn's very limited command of English at the time of the visit, point to a date of first

meeting between the two men within months of Haydn's first arrival in London. For Haydn's mention of Latrobe, see *Briefe*, 498; cf. *CCLN*, 263.

29. In *The European Magazine, and London Review*: Landon, *Haydn at Eszterháza*, 496–506.
30. Vienna, Sammlungen der Gesellschaft der Musikfreunde. Ott's portrait was only rediscovered in 1996, having long been considered lost: see 'Haydn News 1996', *Haydn Yearbook*, 20 (1996), 59.
31. Haydn certainly had contacts with émigrés interested in him; one example was Alexandre d'Arblay, who married Burney's famous daughter, the novelist Fanny Burney, on 28 July 1793. The French constitutional arrangements of 1789, which Haydn, in common with many British subjects and emigrés in circles with which he associated, seems to have supported, still left hope for the survival of the French monarchy, ensuring that adequate relations and trading links were maintained (for the time being) between France and other nations. Events taking place in France, however, at the very moment when Ott's portrait was executed and engraved soon dashed any sense that such hope was well-founded. The anti-clerical measures of the 1789 Civil Constitution finally led in the spring of 1791 to the Pope officially condemning both the Constitution (to which the new French Assembly decreed that all clergy were obliged to take an oath of allegiance) and the Revolution in general, a step indirectly leading to the royal family's abortive escape from France, which spelt the end to the experiment in constitutional monarchy. Within a few months the Assembly had decreed that all prominent émigrés who did not return by 1 Jan. 1792 would be considered guilty of treason.
32. For pictorial reflections of the change in English attitude to Philippe Egalité, see Bindman et al., *Shadow of the Guillotine*, 46, 90, 136; cf. nos 17, 109.
33. Whitley, *Artists and their Friends*, ii, 67.
34. *Diary of Joseph Farington*, entry for 14 Nov. 1793.
35. For the Orléans collection, see L.-F. Dubois de Saint-Gelais, *Description des tableaux du Palais Royal* (Paris, 1727). For the fate of the collection, see Haskell, *Rediscoveries in Art*, 39–44 and *passim*. Clear evidence of the Duke of Orléans's high standing with Englishmen of moderate opinion at the time of Ott's portrait of Haydn is the portrait medallion of him produced and marketed by Josiah Wedgwood: Bindman et al., *Shadow of the Guillotine*, 98, no. 37d.
36. Griesinger's letter to Breitkopf & Härtel, 12 June 1799: Olleson, 'Georg August Griesinger's Correspondence', 10.
37. Haydn's collection of prints, many of which were English stipples, seems to bear this out.
38. Haydn, *Briefe*, 352.
39. Ibid., 363.
40. Pleyel's arrangements with Breitkopf & Härtel were announced in the *AMZ* on 6 Oct. 1800 (col. 40).
41. Somfai, *Joseph Haydn*, 215, no. 14; 219, commentary on text I. In the view of the present writer, in relating the Guérin–Darcis engraving to the drawing commissioned by Breitkopf & Härtel, Somfai overlooked its relationship with the Ott–Bartolozzi engraving, which would probably already have been well known in Paris.
42. *Briefe*, 415.
43. The portrait is now in the Royal College of Music, London.
44. *Briefe*, 218, 223. Haydn's relations with Bland are explored in Woodfield, 'John Bland'.

45. The three trios: Hob. XV: 15–17. Haydn already knew that trios featuring one or more flutes were particularly appreciated in England, where the flute was a popular instrument for male amateur musicians. In 1784 he had sent on commission from the London publisher Forster compositions based in part (perhaps to save time) on material drawn from his 1777 opera *Il mondo della luna*; they were issued as 'Six Trios for Two Violins & a Violoncello or a German Flute, Violin & a Violoncello Op. XXXVIII' (Hob. IV: 6–11). Further trios for flute combinations were written during Haydn's second London visit (Hob. IV: 1–4).

46. Quoted by Landon in *CCLN*, 95.

47. For one example, see Somfai, 'Zur Authentizität des Haydn-Porträts von Loutherbourg'.

48. *Briefe*, 437.

49. Somfai, 213, no. 8b. The engraving was issued with no day or month specified. Some of Somfai's commentary is either misleading or out of date: see Landon, *Haydn in England*, 133.

50. For the Grand-Duke of Tuscany's collection of self-portraits, see: W. Prinz, *Die Sammlung der Selbstbildnisse in den Uffizien*, 2 vols (Berlin, 1971); *Painters by Painters*, exh. cat., by C. Caneva, A. Natali, National Academy of Design, New York, and the Museum of Fine Arts, Houston (Wisbech, 1988).

51. The sitter was Lady Elizabeth Lambert: Appendix, items 5, 51.

52. 'Mahler: Mr Ott und Guttenbrun': Haydn, *Briefe*, 503.

53. Ibid., 513.

54. Griesinger acted as a go-between in the Leipzig publishers' dealings with Haydn.

55. Olleson, 'Georg August Griesinger's Correspondence', 10.

56. Ibid., 11.

57. Ibid., 12.

58. Ibid., 13. When Kininger was subsequently obliged to make a second drawing of the Guttenbrunn portrait in the possession of Haydn's wife, he was hindered by the fact that she had gone to Baden, taking the portrait with her, a clear indication of her devotion ot it. Ibid., 13.

59. Quoted in Landon, *Haydn in London*, 133.

60. Royal Collection, Windsor Castle: Oliver Millar, *Later Pictures in the Collection of Her Majesty the Queen*, 2 vols (London, 1969), i, 52, no. 843.

61. From the *Quarterly Review*: quoted in H.P.K. Skipton, *John Hoppner* (London, 1905), 68–69.

62. Reynolds's portrait of Mrs Billington is now in the Beaverbrook Art Gallery, Fredericton, New Brunswick. It was first exhibited at the Royal Academy in 1790.

63. Carpani, 231–33.

64. 'Haydn, immediately on his arrival, told Salomon that he should stay the summer in England, and that as he heard there were to be twelve concerts and two benefits during the season there would be ample time for him to compose his first symphonies after he had had an opportunity of studying the taste of the English. He was determined that his first production should both amuse and please the musical public and rivet them in his favour.' Papendiek, *Court and Private Life*, ed. Broughton, ii, 290.

65. The letter is not actually addressed to Papendiek, but Landon makes an undisputable case for Papendiek as the letter's recipient: *CCLN*, 156–57; cf. Haydn, *Briefe*, 323–24.

66. Haydn, *Briefe*, 324.
67. In a letter of 20 Dec. 1791 (ibid., 268), Haydn mentions that 'The Prince of Wales is having me painted just now, and the portrait is *to hang in his cabinet-room.*'
68. For an interesting near-contemporary account of a painter (Romney) and a sitter (Mrs Jordan) trying to decide on a suitable pose for a portrait, see Ward and Roberts, *Romney*, i, 69; ii, 86.
69. The same may have been the case for the gesture of resting one hand on a desk or keyboard on which are shown folios from musical manuscripts.
70. Carpani, 251–52. The image on this title-page was actually based on Guttenbrunn's early portrait of Haydn.
71. University of Oxford, Faculty of Music: Somfai, 215, no. 13.
72. See the texts cited by Somfai, 222.
73. Ibid., 215.
74. Appendix: item 22. Opie painted two versions of *Age and Infancy*, one in 1783, and another in 1786 for his diploma picture for the Royal Academy. It is therefore likely to have been quite a well-known work. For a discussion of the original painting, see Ada Earland, *John Opie and his Circle* (London, 1911), 60. Haydn may also have had an opportunity to reflect on this matter through a lost painting by Hoppner on a similar theme called *Youth and Age*, exhibited in 1786, but perhaps still in Hoppner's studio at the time Haydn sat for his portrait there in 1791: Algernon Graves, *The Royal Academy of Arts: A Complete Dictionary of Contributors and their Work from its Foundation in 1769 to 1904*, vol. 4 (London, 1905), 153.
75. Ronald Paulson, 'Youth and Age: The Romantic Triangle', in *Rowlandson: A New Interpretation* (London, 1972), 71–79.
76. The letter was published by Dies, 105.
77. Landon, *The Late Years*, 335.
78. 'Hin ist alle meine Kraft! / Alt und schwach bin ich' (Hob. XXVc: 5). The poem is by J.W.L. Gleim (d. 1803). The card was also printed in place of a final movement to Haydn's last, incomplete quartet, composed in 1803, as published in 1806.
79. Visit of 15 Mar. 1806: Dies, 116.
80. Berlin, Staatsbibliothek zu Berlin — Preussische Kulturbesitz: Somfai, 215, no. 14. Neither this, nor the published version (used on the title-page of the first volume of Brietkopf & Härtel's so-called *Oeuvres Complettes de Joseph Haydn* of 1800) can be considered a success, since it neither looks like the more authoritative portraits of Haydn, nor does it retain the suavity which Haydn seems to have admired in Guttenbrunn's original. Haydn doubtless, however, appreciated the fact that although Kininger 'aged' the portrait, the composer still looked younger than he really was, at least in its engraved version.
81. Somfai, 176, pl. 329.
82. Letter dated 20 July 1801: *Briefe*, 371.
83. Griesinger, 86.
84. Visit of 9 Dec. 1805: Dies, 90.
85. In 1805 he rearranged the Missa Brevis in F (Hob. XXII: 1) written in the 1740s, commenting to Dies that 'What especially pleases me about this little work ... is the melody, and a certain *youthful fire* [ein gewisses jugendliches Feuer], and this excites me to write down several bars daily in order to give the voices an accompaniment for wind-band.' Visit of 21 Nov. 1805: Dies, 75.
86. Haydn related the story to Dies on 28 May 1805: Dies, 65.

87. Related to Dies on 23 Feb., 1807: Dies, 149.
88. An indication of how successful Haydn was in this respect comes from the evidence of the visit he made by himself to Hampshire and the Isle of Wight in 1794. Despite the fact that by this date prints of Haydn had wide circulation in Britain, and the composer visited several towns and places of interest to tourists as indicated in guidebooks of the period, as well as travelling in the company of several others, no record has come to light that Haydn made this trip other than from the pages of his own notebooks. No newspaper, journal, diary or letter refers to him having made this visit, which is doubtless exactly what he intended. In other words, Haydn, in the sixty-second year of his life, was able to travel incognito, fully confident that no one could possibly recognize him, the image of him presented to his public being next to useless as a tool for positive identification of the man himself: Matthews, 'Haydn's Visit to Hampshire', 120–21.
89. Dies, 182.
90. Published by J. Burchall in 1784: Appendix, item 32. Haydn perhaps also knew Bartolozzi's frontispiece to Thomson's *The Seasons*, featuring Fame crowning Thomson, and decorated with medallion portraits of Bartolozzi himself, William Hamilton and Petro Tomkins. All three engravers had works represented in Haydn's collection.
91. For this and other representations of the crowning of Voltaire, see *Inventaire Voltaire*, ed. Jean Goulemot et al. (Paris, 1995), 452–55.
92. It was this very public recognition of the parity between musical composition and literature, reflecting popular support for Haydn's election in the same year as a foreign member of the newly formed Institut National des Sciences et des Arts (soon to become known as the Institut National de France) in the class of 'Literature and Fine Arts', which so incensed Sheridan, who held to the older view of the superiority of words over music. The practice of paying tribute to busts of musicians by placing a wreath on their heads or around their necks survives today in the ceremony honouring Sir Henry Wood at the Last Night of the Proms.
93. Gerber, *Neues Lexikon*, article 'Haydn', col. 548, quoted by Gotwals, *Haydn: Two Contemporary Portraits*, 261.
94. Somfai, 217, no. 25.
95. An account of the medal was given in the *AMZ* of 16 Sept. 1801.
96. Haydn's letter to the French musicians of 19 Aug. 1801: *Briefe*, 376.
97. Tassie is mentioned by Haydn in his London Notebooks; ibid., 513 (Haydn called him Daßie). An impression of Tassie's *Haydn* is in the National Portrait Gallery in Edinburgh: H.C. Robbins Landon, 'A New Haydn Portrait', *Soundings*, 9 (1979–80), 2. For a discussion of Tassie's portraiture, see James Holloway, *James Tassie 1735–1799* (Edinburgh, 1986).
98. A token of his celebrity is the complete set of Tassie's stock of casts ordered by the Russian Empress, Catherine the Great, in 1781. In 1791, at about the time he portrayed Haydn, Tassie's collection of impressions (numbering more than 15,000) was catalogued by Rudolph Erich Raspe (author of *The Adventures of Baron Münchausen*): J.P. Smith, *James Tassie 1735–1799* (London, 1995). Since Tassie's art was appreciated in many of the cultural centres where Haydn was particularly favoured, such as Madrid, Naples and St Petersburg, the two men may have shared a natural affinity for each other's work. The composer's meeting with Tassie doubtless led him to an appreciation of how visual allusions to classical antiquity could be as useful as the tags from Classical texts he was

fond of injecting into his own writings, particularly in his London notebooks, in order to lend emphasis to ideas or observations which he found especially interesting. Portrayals in profile, because of the history of such representations, may have the effect of attaching notions of authority and leadership to sitters.

99. Somfai, 214, no. 11. The Dance drawing exists in four versions, all apparently autograph. Their relationship to each other and original contexts have yet to be fully understood. For a discussion of the different versions, and for an account of Haydn and Dance, see Stroud, *George Dance*, 173.

100. Reported in Stroud, *George Dance*, 173.

101. For Farington's references to Haydn and Dance, see *Diary*, for 16 Dec. 1794, 15 June 1795, 30 Sept. 1798.

102. The composer gives a long description of the Lord Mayor's banquet which he attended in November 1791 in his first London notebook; Dance, with his connections at the Guildhall, may have been instrumental in obtaining the composer the invitation. This suggestion is made by Stroud, *George Dance*, 173.

103. *A Collection of Portraits of Eminent Characters Sketched from the Life since the Year 1793*, 2 vols (London, 1808, 1814), ii, n.p.

104. 12 June 1799. Olleson, 'Georg August Griesinger's Correspondence', 10.

105. Appendix, items 69, 70, 71, 76, 77.

106. Item 49 from Haydn's second will dated 7 Feb. 1809: Vernon Gotwals, 'Joseph Haydn's Last Will and Testament', 341.

107. Somfai, 215, no. 15. For Grassi's relations with Haydn, see Landon, *The Late Years*, 90.

108. George Savage, *Porcelain through the Ages* (Harmondsworth, 1954), 154; W. Mrazek and W. Neuwirth, *Wiener Porzellan 1718–1864* (Vienna, 1970), 37–40.

109. *Briefe*, 433. The mixing of Classical allusion with Haydn's music at the level of popular delectation reached its zenith in the year of Haydn's death, when the Vienna porcelain factory, where Grassi had formerly worked, produced a cup and saucer, the cup painted with a cameo-like portrait of Francis II in the style of a Roman emperor, inscribed 'Gott! Erhalte den Kaiser', and the saucer decorated with Haydn's music: Mrazek and Neuwirth, 177, no. 687, pl. 99.

110. Somfai, 215, no. 16.

111. Dies, 140–41.

112. Ibid., 140.

113. For a discussion of the popularity of English landscape gardening in continental Europe at this time, see the account of William Gould, a protégé of Capability Brown, in Simon Sebag Montefiore, *Prince of Princes: The Life of Potemkin* (London, 2000).

114. *Briefe*, 496. For Vauxhall Gardens, see T.J. Edelstein and B. Allen, *Vauxhall Gardens* (New Haven, 1983).

115. John Kerslake, 'The Likeness of Handel', in *Handel and the Fitzwilliam*, exh. cat. (Cambridge, 1974), 27.

116. For an account of Roubiliac's work on Handel's tomb, see Bindman and Baker, *Roubiliac*, 332–36, no. 15.

117. Georg Christoph Lichtenberg, *Aphorisms*, trans. R.J. Hollingdale (Harmondsworth, 1990), 131.

118. Ibid., 180.

119. 'Monumente deutsche Tonkünstler', *AMZ*, 2 (1800), cols 417–23.

120. Appendix, item 72.

121. Landon, *Haydn in England*, 201.

122. Landon, *Haydn at Eszterháza*, 596–97.
123. An engraving of the monument by Delattre was published in Dr Burney's *Account of the Musical Performances in Westminster Abbey* (1785).
124. Novello, 191.
125. Pohl, *Joseph Haydn*, iii, 99.
126. Quoted in Landon, *Haydn in England*, 49–50.
127. Roscoe, 'Haydn and London', 205.
128. Ibid., 206.
129. Dies's visit of 21 Dec. 1805: Dies, 95–96.
130. Cf. Landon, *Symphonies of Joseph Haydn*, 534–35.
131. Dies's visit of 19 Feb. 1806: Dies, 114.
132. Reported by Griesinger (pp. 105–6).
133. Ibid., 98.
134. Pohl, *Joseph Haydn*, i, 182–83. For the miniature in Vienna (Vienna, Gesellschaft der Musikfreunde), see Somfai, 213, no. 5. For the second portrait-miniature, see *Haydn Yearbook*, 18 (1993), vi, pl. 1.
135. Edmund Leach, 'Magical Hair', *Journal of the Royal Anthropological Institute*, 88 (1958), 147–63; Ann Charles and Roer de Anfrasio, *The History of Hair* (New York, 1970); *Hair Raising*, exh. cat. Whitworth Art Gallery (Manchester, 1987); Robert Bartlett, 'Symbolic Meanings of Hair in the Middle Ages', *Transactions of the Royal Historical Society*, 6th ser., 4 (1994), 43–60.
136. Blunden, *Leigh Hunt: A Biography*, 368–73.
137. Novello, 83, 93.
138. Ibid., 194.
139. Quoted ibid., 83.
140. *CCLN*, 144–45.
141. Ibid., 144.
143. *Briefe*, 438.
143. Arthur Searle, *Haydn and England*, 29.
144. Collin's poem was included in Griesinger's biography (p. 90).
145. Ibid., 88–89.
146. No. 24 in *The Creation* describes the creation of Adam, the first man, 'and in his eyes with brightness shines the soul, the breath and image of his God' (text of the original edition).
147. For an account of this well-known scene by Balthasar Wigand (destroyed during the Second World War), see Somfai, 216, no. 22. The moment depicted in the painting is apparently Haydn's reception by the audience before the performance, which was perhaps considered a more fitting tribute for presentation to the elderly composer himself.
148. Among those who are recorded as addressing Haydn as 'father' or 'papa' are Mozart, Cherubini, Hummel, Neukomm and Pleyel.
149. For example, the obituary notice of Haydn which appeared in the *Gentleman's Magazine* in July 1809 called him 'the Father of Musick in our time'.
150. Reported to Beethoven's biographer Thayer by Hüttenbrenner, who witnessed the composer's death: *Thayer's Life of Beethoven*, ed. Forbes, 1051, n. 59.
151. Ibid., 1050.
152. See Rudolf and Margot Wittkower, *The Divine Michelangelo* (London, 1964), *passim*.
153. See, for example, Wilfred Mellers, 'What is Musical Genius?', in Murray (ed.), *Genius: The History of an Idea*, 166–80, esp. 170–71.

154. In the later Middle Ages, the cult of the Name of Jesus had been especially developed in England. Its celebration for the entire Church on the second Sunday after Epiphany was prescribed by Pope Innocent XIII.
155. *Briefe*, 127.
156. Ibid., 512. For a suggestion concerning the identity of the 'Shaw' family, and further evidence of Haydn's relationship with them, see Tolley, 'Music in the Circle of Sir William Jones'.
157. Visit of 17 Aug. 1806: Dies, 140.
158. Quoted by Dies (p. 103).
159. Published in the *AMZ*, 3 (21 Jan. 1801), 296: Landon, *Years of the Creation*, 589.
160. Visit in connection with the visit of 8 Aug. 1808 (Dies, 170).
161. 'The Diaries of Joseph Carl Rosenbaum 1770–1829', ed. Else Radant, *Haydn Yearbook*, 5 (1968), 152.
162. Griesinger, 93. For Beethoven's funeral, see *Thayer's Life of Beethoven*, 1052–56.
163. Griesinger, 93.
164. Vienna, Haydn-Museum: Somfai, 217, no. 23; *Zauberföne: Mozart in Wien 1781–1791*, exh. cat. (Vienna, 1990), 583, no. IX/59.
165. Bindman and Baker, *Roubiliac*, 332.
166. Lessing, who died in 1781, is a good example of a German writer whose death mask was made the day after he died: *Gotthold Ephraim Lessing 1729 bis 1781*, exh. cat., Herzog-August Bibliothek (Wolfenbüttel, 1981), 88, no. 106. In France a death mask was taken of Voltaire in 1778 by Houdon: Honour et al., *Age of Neo-Classicism*, 252, no. 390. Although interest in taking death masks seems to have become widespread in the eighteenth century, the practice of taking them itself can apparently be traced back to the Middle Ages. There is evidence that a death mask of Dante was taken.
167. Franz Glück, 'Prolegomena zu einer neuen Beethoven-Ikonographie', in *Festschrift Otto Erich Deutsch zum 80. Geburtstag*, ed. Walter Gerstenberg et al. (Kassel, 1963), 200–209. The practice of taking life masks of celebrities may be particularly associated with Vienna at this time. For example, one seems to have been taken of Nelson when he was in Vienna in 1800.
168. Told by Dies in connection with his visit of 10 June 1805 (p. 69). Dies does not name the servant, but the context of the account makes it reasonably clear that it is Elssler to whom he is referring.
169. For an account of the fate of Haydn's head, see Neumayr, *Music and Medicine*, 86–92.
170. Translation from 'Diaries of Joseph Carl Rosenbaum', ed. Radant, 150–59 (entry for 4 June 1809).
171. [H.C. Robbins Landon, ed.,] 'Documentary Report on the Opening of Haydn's Tomb at Eisenstadt, 1909', *Haydn Yearbook*, 17 (1992), 175–80.
172. Pohl, *Joseph Haydn*, iii, 286: translated in Gotwals, *Haydn: Two Contemporary Portraits*, 263.
173. Julius Tandler, 'Über den Schädel Haydns', *Mitteilungen der Anthropologischen Gesellschaft* (Vienna, 1909), 260.
174. Novello, 147.
175. Ibid., 190.
176. Letter dated 4 Apr. 1827 from Anton Schindler in Vienna to Ignaz Moscheles in London: *Letters to Beethoven*, ed. Albrecht, iii, no. 477, 215.
177. The full title is: *Physiognomische Fragmente, zur Beförderung der*

Menschenkenntniss und Menschenliebe (*Physiognomical Fragments for the Promotion of the Knowledge and Love of Mankind*).

178. *Briefe*, 106.
179. Gerda Mraz, 'Musikerportraits in der Sammlung Lavater', in Otto Biba and David Wyn Jones (eds), *Studies in Music History Presented to H.C. Robbins Landon on his Seventieth Birthday* (London, 1996), 165–76.
180. Lavater's collection included prints obtained for him by Goethe by Schongauer, Dürer and Lucas van Leyden. Although it has been suggested that he made his silhouette of Haydn himself, it is more likely to have been one of the known silhouettes, or a version of one of them: see Somfai, 213, 220.
181. Quoted by Griesinger (p. 96).
182. Somfai, 213, no. 4.
183. '... um wenigstens im Bild mit Naumanns Bekanntschaft zu machen' (Griesinger, 159).
184. An account of the performance (of the oratorio *Die Auferstehung und Himmelfahrt Christi*) is given by J.N. Forkel in *Musikalischer Almanach für Deutschland auf das Jahr 1789*: Deutsch, *Mozart: A Documentary Biography*, 310. The performance took place in Vienna on 26 Feb. 1788.
185. The print was engraved by Houbraken: W.C. Smith, *Concerning Handel* (London, 1948), 125–28. *Alexander's Feast* was certainly known to van Swieten since he commissioned a reorchestration of it from Mozart in 1790.
186. In the 1870s, for example, Tchaikovsky's patroness Nadezhda von Meck wrote to the composer (whom she never met in person), requesting a photograph of him: 'I want to search out in your *features* those inspirations, those feelings which influenced you to compose music which transports a person into a world of sensations ... that life cannot fulfil.' *To my best friend: Correspondence between Tchaikovsky and Nadezhda von Meck 1876–1878* (Oxford, 1993), 4–9.
187. For Thaller, see E.J. Pyke, *A Biographical Dictionary of Wax Modellers* (Oxford, 1973).
188. Novello, 146.
189. L.E. Tanner and J.L. Nevinson, 'On Some Later Funeral Effigies in Westminster Abbey', *Archaeologica*, 85 (1932), 169–202.
190. *The Times*, 22 Mar. 1806, as quoted ibid., 198.
191. Soliman's remains were destroyed in 1848: Braunbehrens, *Mozart in Vienna*, 85–87.
192. C.F.A. Marmoy, 'The "Auto-Icon" of Jeremy Bentham at University College, London', *Medical History*, 2 (1958), 77–86. Bentham was born in 1748 and died in 1832.
193. *Essays on Physiognomy*, trans. T. Holcroft (1789), as quoted in Willard L. Valentine and D.D. Wickens, *Experimental Foundations of General Psychology*, 3rd edn (New York, 1949), 6.
194. Quoted in Louis Chevalier, *Labouring Classes and Dangerous Classes in Paris during the First Half of the Nineteenth Century* (London, 1973), 411.
195. Religion and morality were threatened.
196. By February 1802 Rosenbaum was absorbed by Gall's theory of phrenology: 'Diaries of Joseph Carl Rosenbaum', ed. Radant, 99–100.
297. Quoted in Neumayr, *Music and Medicine*, 88.
298. E.g., George Combe, *Elements of Phrenology*, 9th edn (Edinburgh, 1862), 128.
299. Mary Shelley, *Frankenstein*, ed. Maurice Hindle (Harmondsworth, 1992), 51.
200. For these references, see John D. Davies, *Phrenology, Fad and Science: A 19th-Century American Crusade* (New Haven, 1955), 9–10. The fascination with

such studies in Edinburgh eventually led to the famous case of Burke and Hare, who provided bodies for the anatomists' table by murdering victims. The hanged body of the criminal Burke in turn became the subject of phrenological study.

201. For an account of the significance of the Prometheus myth for the development of Western culture, see Carl Kerenyi, *Prometheus: Archetypal Image of Human Existence* (Princeton, 1963).

202. Letter dated 20 July 1801: *Briefe*, 371.

203. *Die Geschöpfe des Prometheus*. For the importance of the Prometheus myth for Beethoven, particularly in his third symphony, see Peter Schleuning, 'Beethoven in alter Deutung: Der "neue Weg" mit der "Sinfonia Eroica"', *Archiv für Musikwissenschaft*, 64 (1987), 165–94.

204. Quoted in *Thayer's Life of Beethoven*, 273.

205. *Lives of Haydn, Mozart and Metastasio*, ed. Coe, 117.

206. Stuart Curran, 'The Political Prometheus', in *Spirits of Fire: English Romantic Writers and Contemporary Historical Methods* (London, 1990), 260–84, esp. 274–79 and fig. 3.

207. In a review of *The Seasons* in *AMZ* (2 May 1801).

208. [Haydn] resembling Prometheus, through the immeasurable ether
    That from earthly earth separates high Olympus,
    Dared ... to light
    The torch. He himself becomes a creator.
    The chords ascend on high in thundering symphonies,
    Shattering now, and so they threaten the worlds with collapse.
    ... is Haydn not the creator of magical tones
    That bewitch us gods? ...
    For, as a mortal he knew how to win for himself
    Immortality's crown, to become like the gods!
    Dies, 211–12; translation from Gotwals, *Haydn: Two Contemporary Portraits*, 205. Gotwals (p. 265, n. 141) surmises that the verses were written by Dies himself.

209. Mary Shelley's enthusiasm for Haydn's *Creation* is well expressed in her letter to Leigh Hunt of 11 Dec. 1823; *The Letters of Mary Wollstonecraft Shelley*, vol. 1, ed. Betty T. Bennet (Baltimore, 1980), 389.

210. See Somfai, 215–16, nos 15, 18, 21.

211. 'Mit Würd' und Hoheit angethan, / mit Schönheit, Stärk', und Mut begabt, / gen Himmel aufgerichtet, steht der Mensch, / Ein Mann und König der Natur. / Die briet gewölbt erhab'ne Stirn / verkünd't der Weisheit tiefen Sinn, / und aus dem hellen Blicke strahlt der Geist, / des Schöpfers hauch und Ebenbild' (Uriel's aria, no. 24 from *The Creation*).

212. See the text of the aria quoted in the previous note.

213. One example is the poem quoted by Dies at the end of his biography, cited above. For another example, see the poem by Gabriele Batsányi (1799) also quoted by Dies (p. 174).

214. Ibid., 101.

215. For a discussion of this, see Białostocki, *Dürer and his Critics*, ch. 4; Keith Andrews, 'Dürer's Posthumous Fame', in C.R. Dodwell (ed.), *Essays on Dürer* (Manchester, 1973), 87.

216. Schlegel, *Ansichten und Ideen von der christlichen Kunst*, ed. H. Eichner (Munich, 1959), 60.

217. Quoted in Gruber, *Mozart and Posterity*, 83.

218. Dürer was considered as the founder of a German school by Christian Friedrich David Schubart in his *Vorlesungen über Mahlerey, Kupferstecherkunst, Bildhauerkunst, Steinschneidekunst und Tanzkunst* (Münster, 1777), 125. For this and other related late eighteenth-century views of Dürer, see Białostocki, *Dürer and his Critics*, 73–90.

219. *Johann Sebastian Bach: His Life, Art and Work, Translated from the German of Johann Nikolaus Forkel*, ed. Charles Sanford Terry (London, 1920), p. xxv. For an account of J.S. Bach's reputation at this period, see Ludwig Finscher, 'Bach in the Eighteenth Century', in Don O. Franklin (ed.), *Bach Studies* (Cambridge, 1989), 281–96.

220. *AMZ*, 3 (1800–1801), col. 117.

221. Ibid., col. 302.

222. *A General History of Music*, ed. Mercer, ii, 958 (note c).

223. Dies, 113.

224. Ruth M. Smith, 'Intellectual Contexts of Handel's Oratorios', in C. Hogwood and R. Luckett (eds), *Music in Eighteenth-Century England: Essays in Memory of Charles Cudworth* (Cambridge, 1983); Weber, *The Rise of Musical Classics*, ch. 8.

225. Schloss Esterházy, Eisenstadt: Somfai, 216, no. 20.

226. Appendix, item 74.

227. Rembrandt's *Aristotle contemplating a bust of Homer* (1653; New York, Metropolitan Museum of Art) and Rubens's *Four Philosophers* (with self-portrait and a bust of Seneca; *c*.1612; Florence, Pitti Palace) were influential in the eighteenth century in establishing such portraits with busts: Wind, *Hume and the Heroic Portrait*, 51.

228. The portrait of Garrick by Gainsborough was formerly in the Town Hall at Stratford-upon-Avon, and was destroyed by fire in 1946. The depiction of Mrs Yates 'in the character of the Tragic Muse' was engraved by J. Heath and published in 1783.

229. Penny, *Reynolds*, 287–88, nos 116–17. Angelica Kauffman's portrait of Reynolds also features a bust of Michelangelo. Other examples of painters portraying themselves with busts of earlier painters include: Richard Cosway's self-portrait with busts of Michelangelo and Rubens in the Fondazione Cosway at Lodi of *c*.1789 (there is a pendant depicting Maria Cosway with a bust of Leonardo da Vinci, and a painting by Constance Mayer (1775–1821), in which she portrayed herself in the act of painting, including in the same picture a portrait of her father pointing to a bust of Raphael (Wadsworth Atheneum, Hartford, Conn.).

230. *Lichtenberg's Visits to England as Described in his Letters and Diaries*, trans. and ed. Margaret L. Mare and W.H. Quarrell (Oxford, 1938), 35.

231. H. Besseler, *Fünf echte Bildnisse Johann Sebastian Bachs* (Kassel, 1956); H.O.R. van Tuyll van Serooskerken, *Probleme des Bachporträts* (Bildhoven, 1956), Werner Neumann, *Bilddokumente zur Lebensgeschichte Johann Sebastian Bachs* (Kassel, 1979).

232. Novello, 146.

233. The frontispiece of the third volume of J.-B.-P. Lebrun's *Galerie des peintres flamands, hollandais et allemands* (1796) may serve as an example of how busts of celebrated artists were already accepted within the Pantheon of the famous. The scheme here was based on a drawing by Peyron, exhibited at the Salon of 1791, entitled *Minerva Debating with Father Time Concerning the Placement of Portraits of Famous Artists in her Temple*, including busts of Raphael and

several other Italian artists: Rosenberg and Van de Sandt, *Pierre Peyron*, 217. In Lebrun's adaptation of this, the artists in the Temple of Fame are Dutch.

234. For a survey of images of Napoleon associated with the heroic, see Telesko, *Napoleon Bonaparte: Der 'moderne Held' und die bildende Kunst*.

Notes to Chapter 6

1. For example, Haydn's will mentions his portrait of Franck, his first music teacher, which he bequeathed to Franck's daughter. In 1809 the portrait was kept on the first floor of his house at Gumpendorf: Dies, 195.
2. For the significance of stipple in relation to line engraving to the print industry of the period, from the perspective of one of the leading publishers, see Josiah Boydell, *Suggestions towards Forming a Plan for the Encouragement, Improvement, and Benefit of the Arts and Manufactures in this Country on a Commercial Basis* (1805), p. iii.
3. Griesinger, 97.
4. Landon, *Late Years*, 401, item 518. The number of canons mentioned is 40, but this is probably inaccurate.
5. For a reproduction of this, see Landon and Wyn Jones, *Haydn*, pl. 200.
6. A well-known medieval canon in this form is Baude Cordier's *Tout par compas suy composés*. For Cordier, see Craig Wright, *Music at the Court of Burgundy: A Documentary History* (Henryville, 1979), 124–32. For a list of circular canons, see Slim, 'Dosso Dossi's Allegory', 53, n. 51.
7. Dies, 131–32.
8. For the significance of such collections, see Griffiths and Carey, *German Printmaking*, 18.
9. See the articles on 'Geschmack', 'Kupferstecher', and 'Kupferstecherkunst'.
10. This hobby is a very modest one
   It performs without stealing from Nature's colours
   Yet leads us easily and as far
   As any form of Art in the path of Beauty.
   Quoted in Griffiths and Carey, *German Printmaking*, 62.
11. From *Le Temple du goût*, quoted in Adhémar, *Gravure originale*, 121.
12. The edition owned by Haydn was apparently published in 1779: Hörwarthner, no. 26.
13. Timothy Clayton, 'Reviews of English Prints in German Journals 1750–1800', *Print Quarterly*, 10 (1993), 123–37.
14. Haydn, *Briefe*, 203.
15. The journal in question was the *Bibliothek der schönen Wissenschaften und der freyen Künste*: Clayton, 'Reviews of English Prints'.
16. 'I would like to have a portrait of His Highness [Prince Kraft Ernst Oettingen-Wallerstein], but only a silhouette, since *I am an amateur collector* of the leading figures.' Letter of 29 Nov. 1789: *Briefe*, 203.
17. Ibid., 491. I have not succeeded in identifying the print Haydn describes.
18. Ibid., 302; cf. *CCLN*, 144. This letter was considered by Landon to have been written by Haydn to John Parke, the distinguished oboist, an identification in which he has been followed by several other authorities, including Bartha and Fiske (in his article on the Parke family in the *New Grove*). In his letter, Haydn does not give a first name, but simply wrote the name 'Mr Park' and the address 'Piccadilly Nr 32'. John Parke and his daughter, Maria, a singer and

pianist, certainly knew Haydn and often performed with him. However, evidence that he was not especially close to this family, though he was noted in the *Memoirs* of John Parke's oboist brother, William Thomas, comes from Haydn's list of worthy musicians active in London, where neither Parke is mentioned under the heading 'Oboists', nor did Maria Parke appear under the 'Pianists': *CCLN*, 265. But to Landon, it (understandably) made sense that the 'Mistris Parck' mentioned in Haydn's letter, to whom he sent 'a little Sonat', should be Maria, who was something of a celebrity and wrote her own keyboard compositions.

On the other hand, Haydn's spelling of the surname ('Park', not 'Parke'), though hardly conclusive in itself (the two names frequently being confused), is none the less significant. More importantly, the address given by Haydn, at Piccadilly, is where Thomas Park certainly resided at this time. If Thomas Park were indeed Haydn's correspondent, then 'Mistris Parck' would refer either to one of Thomas Park's four daughters, or, much more likely, to his wife, who was also (confusingly) called Maria. The title 'Mistris' (sometimes abbreviated to 'Mrs') seems to have been used exclusively by Haydn (and others of the time) to designate a married woman (cf. Haydn's account of Mr Shaw and his family in his notebook for 14 Dec. 1791: *Briefe*, 512), and therefore is unlikely to refer to Maria Parke, who only married in 1815.

There is no doubt that Haydn was friendly with Thomas Park since there is independent evidence to verify it: Jenkin, *Last Gleanings of a Christian Life*, 7, 11.

19. Item 46: Le Blanc, *Manuel de l'amateur*, iii, 141, nos 7, 8. Pohl already connected the item on the Haydn inventory and his 1794 letter, though did not investigate the implications of this: *Mozart und Haydn in London*, ii, 40–41.

20. Marmontel's *conte* was called *Annette et Lubin*, and the story set on the banks of the Seine. It was first published in 1762. Fragonard soon produced several paintings inspired by it, some of which were engraved (1772). For further French prints on the theme, see Gustave Bourcard, *Les estampes du XVIIIe Siècle: école française* (Paris, 1885), 237–38. Mme Favart put it on stage: Brown, *Gluck*, 427. In England, the story was made into a short opera by Dibdin (1778): Fiske, *English Theatre Music*, 423–24. This may have stimulated a demand for prints relating to the story. For examples, see Clayton, *English Print*, 250, 307 (n. 83), pl. 300. Beechey's *Lubin et Rosalie* was also engraved by Marcuard: Frankau, *Eighteenth-Century Colour Prints*, 210.

21. 'A Pastoral Song', opening with the words 'My mother bids me bind my hair': Hob. XXVIa: 27.

22. See Ch. 2. Interestingly, Park subsequently published editions of both Thomson's *Seasons* and Milton's *Paradise Lost*, major literary sources for Haydn's last two oratorios, raising the possibility that the engraver may have been instrumental in drawing the texts to Haydn's attention.

23. A hint that Maria (wife of Thomas Park) was musical, and thus would have appreciated a gift of a sonata from Haydn, comes from the evidence that she corresponded with Dr Burney: Joyce Hemlow, with Jeanne M. Burgess and Althea Douglas, *A Catalogue of the Burney Family Correspondence 1749–1878* (New York, 1971), 29 (letter of 8 May 1791), 60 (letter of 6 Apr. 1813). It remains unclear whether the D major sonata that Haydn wrote in England is the sonata mentioned in the letter, as some scholars have suggested; but this seems very likely. Since it is much the easiest and shortest of the three keyboard sonatas he is known to have composed during the period of his London visits

(the other two were certainly originally dedicated to Therese Jansen-Bartolozzi, a professional performer), it might well have been calculated for the abilities of an amateur pianist, rather than the more secure technique of a Maria Parke or a Therese Jansen-Bartolozzi. When the D major sonata was reviewed following its publication in 1804 (*AMZ*, 31 July 1805, cols 711–12), its easy character was the main point noted: '[It] perhaps was written as an occasional piece for someone who was still not too experienced as a *Klavier* player yet wanted to play something by Haydn. ... If then, the little piece is to be recommended mainly to less experienced players, it still has something attractive for more serious friends of art.' (Translation quoted from Brown, *Joseph Haydn's Keyboard Music*, 55.) It seems unlikely that the 'little sonat' can be identified with the famous F minor Variations (Hob. XVII: 6), sometimes referred to as 'Un piccolo divertimento', since its character hardly seems appropriate as a gift to an amateur pianist, and the date on the autograph (1793, when Haydn was in Vienna) does not fit the date of the documentation with Park.

24. Hase, *Joseph Haydn und Breitkopf & Härtel*, 51.
25. Perhaps the dramatic climax and pause reached in bar 33 of this movement may be seen to represent the perception of crisis, when the lamb is swept away when it is first heard, and when Lubin himself is drowned when it is heard during the repeat.
26. Haydn wrote, 'Concerning the portraits you ask for, you must be patient until I arrive in Vienna.' Nothing more is (as yet) known about this matter. For Haydn's letter and the translation given here, see H.C. Robbins Landon, 'Four New Haydn Letters', *Haydn Yearbook*, 13 (1982), 216.
27. Letter to J.C. Walker: quoted in Landon, *Haydn in England*, 230.
28. For Burney's visits to Houghton, see Lonsdale, *Dr Charles Burney*, 41. For the background to collecting and viewing Old Master paintings in eighteenth-century England, see Pears, *Discovery of Painting*, esp. chs 3, 6.
29. *Musical Tours*, ed. Scholes, i, 148.
30. Ibid., 59.
31. Neither of the two versions of *Susannah and the Elders* known to Burney is today considered autograph by Rubens. The version formerly at Houghton (sold in 1779 to Catherine II of Russia, and now in the Hermitage, St Petersburg) is believed to be the closest copy of a lost original by Rubens. The Baretti version is not mentioned in the Rubens literature, but may perhaps be identified with that now in the Galleria Sabauda, Turin: M. Carter Leach, '"Rubens'" "Susannah and the Elders" in Munich and Some Early Copies', *Print Quarterly*, 5 (1976), 120–27; R.-A. d'Hulst and M. Vandenven, *The Old Testament*, Corpus Rubenianum Ludwig Burchard (London, 1989), 215–18, no. 64.
32. See, for example, Burney's letter of 26 Apr. 1784: *Letters*, ed. Ribeiro, i, 411–16.
33. Ibid., 373–82.
34. Burney, *Music, Men and Manners*, ed. Pool, 119; cf. 202, 205.
35. *Musical Tours*, ed. Scholes, i, 56.
36. Ibid.,, 225.
37. *Letters*, ed. Ribeiro, i, 436.
38. Cf. *Musical Tours*, ed. Scholes, i, 83, 147.
39. Strange was elected a member of the academies of Paris, Rome, Florence, Parma and Bologna. For an account of his career, see Clayton, *The English Print*, 174–75, 266–67.

40. Denis Mahon and Nicholas Turner, *The Drawings of Guercino in the Collection of H.M. the Queen at Windsor Castle* (Cambridge, 1989); Nicholas Turner and C. Piazzotta, *Drawings by Guercino from British Collections*, exh. cat., British Museum (London, 1991), 21–26.

41. *Letters*, ed. Ribeiro, i, 177, 449.

42. Penny, *Reynolds*, 296–97.

43. Landon, *Late Years*, 402, no. 573.

44. *Morning Chronicle* for 18 May 1791: quoted in Landon, *Haydn in England*, 77–78.

45. Item 30. *January* and *November* were designed by N. Gardiner, though the set was known as Hamilton's.

46. Haydn mentions the younger Bartolozzi in a letter to Artaria of 22 Nov. 1787: *Briefe*, 181; Landon, *Haydn at Eszterháza*, 599. Much useful information on Gaetano and his wife is contained in Oliver Strunk, 'Notes on a Haydn Autograph', *Musical Quarterly*, 20 (1934), 192–205.

47. See the letters published in Landon, *Haydn in England*, 457–58.

48. At the top of the autograph of E flat major sonata is the written 'Sonata composta per la celebre Signora Terese de Jansen'. The title-page of first English edition of the C major sonata reads: 'Grand Sonata for the Piano Forte. Composed expressly for and dedicated to Mrs Bartolozzi'.

49. Dated 1794. In 1795 Haydn adapted the piece as the second movement of a trio (Hob. XV: 31), first published in Vienna in 1803 and dedicated to Magdalena von Kurzböck.

50. Visit of 4 June 1807: Dies, 154–55.

51. The painting was in the collection of the Dukes of Devonshire and is now at Chatsworth House. For a discussion of it, see Michael Kitson, *Salvator Rosa*, exh. cat. (London, 1972), 35, no. 42, pl. 36.

52. Hughes and Royalton-Kisch, 'Handel's Art Collection', 21, 23.

53. Appendix: item 50.

54. Ripa, *Pictorial Imagery*, ed. Maser, pl. 197.

55. This observation was made by the composer Anton Reicha, who knew Haydn during the last years of his life: quoted in Bonds, 'Haydn's "Cours complet de la composition"', 161.

56. Item 36. See Shearman, *Andrea del Sarto*, 264–65, no. 74, pl. 134. The composition of the *Madonna del Sacco* includes St Joseph, and therefore fits the description in the inventory of Haydn's collection: 'Eine Loge die heilige Familie vorstellend nach del Sarto'.

57. Mentioned in Strunk, 'Notes on a Haydn Autograph', 198.

58. Ascott, de Rothschild Coll., National Trust: Shearman, *Andrea del Sarto*, 247, no. 58, pl. 85a. It is possible that this was the print Haydn actually owned, though it seems unlikely that a Madonna with Child and St John the Baptist would have constituted a 'Holy Family' to the cataloguer of Haydn's collection in 1809.

59. Goethe, *Italian Journey*, trans. Auden and Mayer, 361.

60. This small painting on copper has been missing since the Second World War: Gould, *Paintings of Correggio*, 280–81. The painting, which was described as 'famosissimo' as early as 1682, has been generally considered a Correggio autograph (Gould favoured the attribution), but authoritative modern opinion is no longer possible.

61. *Musical Tours*, ed. Scholes, ii, 143–44.

62. Ibid., 147.

63. Letters of 18 Aug. and 5 Oct. 1794: *Memorials and Correspondence of Charles James Fox*, iii, 82, 86.

64. *Salons*, ed. Seznec and Adhémar, i, 215; iii, 314.

65. Mengs, *The Works of Anthony Raphael Mengs*, ii, 31. For Stendhal's enthusiasm for the same painting, see his *Letters Concerning Metastasio*: Stendhal, *Lives of Haydn, Mozart and Metastasio*, trans. Coe, 233. For Mengs's own *Penitent Magdalen*, see Roettgen, *Anton Raphael Mengs*, 105–6, no. 29.

66. Missing since the Second World War. Painted *c.*1742 and in Dresden by 1753: Clark, *Pompeo Batoni*, 226–27, no. 60, pl. 56.

67. *Musical Tours*, ed. Scholes, ii, 147.

68. Stechow, 'Johann Sebastian Bach the Younger', 431.

69. *Letters of C.P.E. Bach*, ed. Clark, 171–74.

70. Helmut Börsch-Supan, *Die Berliner Akademie-Ausstellungen 1786–1860* (Berlin, 1971), 1788, no. 9; Netzer, *Daniel N. Chodowiecki*, 122–23, no. 44 (with plate).

71. The Mozart was published in Leipzig in 1801: Brusatti, *Zauberföne*, 367, cat. V/12. Haydn's full score of *The Seasons* was published in 1802.

72. Item 23.

73. Vesme and Calabi, *Bartolozzi*, nos 393, 431.

74. Le Blanc, *Manuel de l'amateur*, iii, 200, nos 19, 20. Pichler's prints were probably taken from copies or earlier engravings, since there is no evidence that he had seen Correggio's original paintings.

75. Item 15, 'Cupido nach Correggio von Pichler'.

76. London, National Gallery: Gould, *Paintings of Correggio*, 213–16, pls 173–76; Cecil Gould, *The School of Love and Correggio's Mythologies* (London, n.d.). For its influence on West, especially in one early painting, an influence acknowledged by the painter in later life, see Erffa and Staley, *Paintings of Benjamin West*, 232, no. 128. Sir William Hamilton owned a *Venus Disarming Cupid*, said to be by Correggio in the eighteenth century, which was sometimes treated as the companion to the *School of Love*: Jenkins and Sloan, *Vases and Volcanoes*, 278–80, nos 176, 177. The painting (now attributed to Luca Cambiaso) apparently caused a stir when it was in London during Haydn's period in England, and might well have contributed to his interest in such 'Correggios' of this character.

77. Mengs, *The Works of Anthony Raphael Mengs*, ii.

78. To judge from its entry in the inventory of Haydn's collection: 'Cupido nach Corregio ...' The song is Hob. XXVIa: 2.

79. Item 11. In the eighteenth century the original painting was in the Pinacoteca Capitolina, where it remains. For an account of it, see *Giovanni Francesco Barbieri, detto Guercino, 1591–1666: dipinti e disegni*, exh. cat., Bologna, Museo Civico Archeologico, ed. Denis Mahon (1991), 298–99, no. 111.

80. Roettgen, *Mengs*, 94–95, no. 23.

81. Erffa and Staley, *Paintings of Benjamin West*, 445, no. 510.

82. Russell, 'Guercino and England', 4.

83. Cf. *Memorials and Correspondence of Charles James Fox*, iii, 73, 75, 82.

84. Erffa and Staley, *Paintings of Benjamin West*, 512, no. 629. An early nineteenth-century guidebook to Audley End (Essex), the Robert Adam house for which West painted this and two other portraits at the same time, suggests that the portrait was well understood to be based on a work by Guercino, indicating that it had always been expected that the derivation would be recognized by viewers

of the picture, and that this was part of the delight of the work. Its pendant was based on Domenichino's *Cumean Sibyl*.

85. Account book of Sir John Stanley, National Art Library, MS 86 B 96 (cited in Pointon, *Hanging the Head*, 49); Correspondence of Patrick Home, Scottish Records Office, Doc. GD 267 17/16. Cf. Skinner, *The Indefatigable Mr Allan*, 27.

86. *Elisabeth-Louise Vigée Le Brun*, exh. cat., Kimbell Art Museum (Fort Worth, Tex., 1982), no. 36.

87. Vigée-Lebrun, *Memoirs*, 102–5. According to Vigée-Lebrun herself the painting was often rapturously received wherever she went, though doubtless part of its attraction lay in the fact that it represented a woman who aroused the curiosity of much of Europe, the wife of a leading antiquarian and the mistress of a famous admiral.

88. Quoted in Jenkins and Sloan, *Vases and Volcanoes*, 272.

89. Collection of the Prince of Liechtenstein, Schloss Vaduz.

90. Item 12. For an account of the painting, see Pepper, *Guido Reni*, 281, no. 175, pl. 205. Reni painted several versions of this subject, but the one represented in Haydn's collection, and known in the eighteenth century as the *Herodias*, was the most famous.

91. In Discourse 5 (10 Dec. 1772). For comment on this, see Barrell, *Political Theory*, 110.

92. Erffa and Staley, *Paintings of Benjamin West*, 447, no. 516,

93. Forster-Hahn, '"The Sources of True Taste"', 382. Ramberg came to London, under royal patronage, in 1781. Although he studied under West, his main interests seem to have been in learning the techniques of English caricature, which he continued to develop in his later career.

94. For further comment on West's obsession with Correggio, see: Erffa and Staley, *Paintings of Benjamin West*, 232, 327, 442; Solkin, *Painting for Money*, 181, 186.

95. Haydn would have known Ramberg's recent paintings in St James Church, where he witnessed the marriage of Gaetano Bartolozzi to Therese Jansen. For evidence of Ramberg's visit to Vienna, see Franziska Forster-Hahn, 'J.H. Ramberg als Karikaturist und Satiriker', *Hannoversche Geschichtsblätter*, NF, 17 (1963), 80–86, 145, 187.

96. *Briefe*, 540.

97. When Haydn saw it, the painting was set into a screen, decorated with classical urns. There is a watercolour by James Cane depicting the altarpiece *in situ* (1801) belonging to the Dean and Chapter of the Cathedral: E. Sabben Clare, 'The Raising of Lazarus by Benjamin West', *Winchester Cathedral Record*, 60 (1991), 42–43.

98. Now in the Wadsworth Atheneum, Hartford, Conn.: Erffa and Staley, *Paintings of Benjamin West*, 350–51.

99. Green seems to have taken the opportunity of increasing his price when the second print was published: Clayton, *English Print*, 235, 306, n. 9.

100. Journal entry for 9 Oct. 1781: *The Journal of John Wesley*, ed. Elisabeth Jay (Oxford, 1987), 220.

101. The best-documented instance of the ecclesiastical authorities rejecting the display of paintings in churches is the Bishop of London's ban on the proposal to redecorate St Paul's Cathedral with pictures by Royal Academicians in 1773: see the preface to 'Life of Dr Newton, Bishop of Bristol, by himself', in Thomas Newton, *Works* (London, 1782). For the background to such views, see Pears,

Discovery of Painting, 43–47. For feelings on the part of artists about the Anglican Church's attitude to pictures at this time (its main objection seems to have been based on the notion that such works in church might lead some to fear a 'restoration of Popery'), see the comments by the engraver Valentine Green in his *Review of the Polite Arts*, 38.

102. Milner, *Antiquities of Winchester*, ii, 39–40.

103. Haydn noted 'The Castle at Newport has a well 300 feet deep which is driven by a mule', which confirms the identification with Carisbrooke: *Briefe*, 544.

104. *Journal of a Tour round the Southern Coasts of England* (1805), quoted in Matthews, 'Haydn's visit to Hampshire', 117.

105. There were several other painted versions of Wolfe's death, but West's was much the best known. There can be no doubt that this is the work referred to in the account. For an account of the print, and the initial difficulties in publishing it, see Clayton, *English Print*, 238–41. The man seen in the print, shown supporting Wolfe, may be identified from the key supplied by Woollett as Major Isaac Barré, who died in 1802. The account of a visit to Carisbrooke in 1796, quoted in the text above, published in 1805, has an addition in parentheses to indicate that the figure in question had 'died a little while ago'. This tends to confirm the identification.

106. National Gallery of Canada, Ottawa: Erffa and Staley, *Paintings of Benjamin West*, 211–13, no. 93.

107. *The Death of the Great Wolf* (17 Dec. 1795), in which Pitt is substituted for Wolfe: Hill, *Gillray the Caricaturist*, 59–60.

108. *Life, Letters and Journals of George Ticknor*, ed. George S. Hilliard, i (Boston, 1876), 63, quoted in Charles Mitchell, 'Benjamin West's Death of Nelson', 265.

109. Detroit, Museum of Arts: Erffa and Staley, *Paintings of Benjamin West*, 354–55, no. 346

110. Neither the glass, nor West's cartoons survive. The compositions are known primarily through preliminary designs: Meyer, 'Benjamin West's Window Designs', 53–65; Erffa and Staley, *Paintings of Benjamin West*, 363–71, nos 360, 367, 369. West was paid £2,200 for the cartoon (30 x 30 feet) of the *Resurrection* window alone. The figure mentioned by Haydn is 50,000 fl., which presumably included the cost of the glass.

111. The entire scheme studied by Haydn can today best be appreciated from a print, *The Choir of St George's Chapel* (1804), after Frederick Nash: Roberts, *Views of Windsor*, ill. 6.1.

112. Fanny Burney, *Diary and Letters ... Edited by her Niece*, iii [1786 and 1787], 197; Papendiek, *Journals*, i, 277–78, Walpole, *Correspondence*, xi, 363. Burney's account is particularly interesting since she saw the cartoons in the position for which the designs were intended, and was fortunate to have West himself to elucidate them: 'Mr West, whom I had once met at Sir Joshua Reynolds's, was exceeding civil, shewing the cartoon himself, and explaining his intentions in it. He spoke of the performance with just such frank praise and open satisfaction as he might have mentioned it with, if the work of any other artist, pointing out its excellences, and expressing his happiness in the execution – yet all with a simplicity that turned his self-commendation rather into candour than conceit.'

113. *Briefe*, 513. For the window to which Haydn refers (no longer extant, and for which no cartoon survives), see Erffa and Staley, *Paintings of Benjamin West*, 329, no. 306. Haydn failed to identify or recall the subject accurately.

114. Quoted in Erffa and Staley, *Paintings of Benjamin West*, 329.

115. Letter of 9 Oct. 1791: Walpole, *Correspondence*, 363.
116. Quoted in Erffa and Staley, *Paintings of Benjamin West*, 355.
117. Haydn's visit to Windsor preceded a day (or perhaps longer) spent at Ascot Races, which he described in some detail: *Briefe*, 487–89. Haydn mentions the Prince of Wales several times in this, suggesting that the Prince may have been his host at this time. If so, the Prince may have invited Haydn to Windsor also.
118. There is circumstantial evidence to suggest Haydn knew West's ceiling decorations in the Queen's Lodge, executed in 1789, and engraved by Bartolozzi and published on 1 Oct. of that year: Erffa and Staley, *Paintings of Benjamin West*, 409–13, nos 435–39. Mrs Papendiek, who describes these paintings, says that the violinist Bridgetower, Haydn's 'pupil', performed for the Queen in a Haydn quartet at the Lodge in the early 1790s: Papendiek, *Journals*, ed. Broughton, ii, 134–35, 235–36. The choice of composition may have been determined by Haydn's presence. The subject matter of these paintings is pertinent to the origins and form of *The Seasons*. Haydn's understanding of the Queen's Lodge paintings and his knowledge of aspects of other works by West at Windsor will be discussed in the following chapter.
119. *Briefe*, 513.
120. Tate Gallery, London: Erffa and Staley, *Paintings of Benjamin West*, 433–34, no. 477. The date on the painting is hard to read. Erffa and Staley give it as '? 1792', though others have read '1791'. West's view is from the East Terrace and, judging from the appearance of the countryside, might well have been painted in June.
121. *A Tour through the whole Island of Great Britain* (London, 1725), ii, 77, quoted in Roberts, *Views of Windsor*, 60.
122. Roberts, *Views of Windsor*, 60–69.
123. Banks owned at least 59 depictions relating to Windsor Castle by Sandby: ibid., 22–23, 136.
124. Gilpin, *Three Essays*, 2nd edn, i [p. 3].
125. Gilpin, *An Essay on Prints*, 1st edn, 2. A fourth edition was published in 1792.
126. *Three Essays*, 6–7. This was published in 1792, with a 2nd edition in 1794. It was therefore popular during the period that Haydn was in London.
127. Gilpin wrote tours of the Highlands and the Wye valley. For a discussion of Scotland in this context, see James Holloway and Lindsay Errington, *The Discovery of Scotland*, exh. cat., National Gallery of Scotland (Edinburgh, 1978). The tour of Johnson and Boswell to the Western Isles in 1773 (published by Johnson in 1775 and by Boswell in 1785) was sufficiently famous to be satirized in the later 1780s: Penny, *Reynolds*, 385–87, nos 198, 199. One of the dedicatees of Paul Sandby's set of twelve *Views in Aquatint from Drawings in South Wales* (1775) was Joseph Banks: Peter Hughes, 'Paul Sandby's Tour of Wales with Joseph Banks', *Burlington Magazine*, 117 (1975), 452–57.
128. First performed at Covent Garden, 22 Feb. 1794, and given 21 performances in its first season: Fiske, *English Theatre Music*, 551–54. One character has a patter song listing famous musicians considered beneath him, including Haydn!
129. Beginning with his work for Napier in 1792.
130. Gilpin, *Remarks on the Forest Scenery ... in Hampshire* was published in 1791, with a further edition 1794, so might have been known to Haydn. Gilpin also wrote two other works relating to the scenery of Hampshire and the Isle of Wight: *Observations on the Coasts of Hampshire, Sussex, and Kent*, written in 1774, though published in 1804; and *Observations on the Western Parts of England ... To Which are Added, A Few Remarks on the Picturesque Beauties*

of the Isle of Wight, published in 1798. In 1774 Wheatley exhibited at the Society of Artists a painting entitled *A study of the Coast of the Isle of Wight, the figures by Mr Mortimer.*

131. That Haydn was introduced to the principles of the Picturesque as defined by Gilpin seems very likely. It is just possible that he may have known something of three more sophisticated writings on the subject all dating from the last two years of his time in England: Richard Payne Knight's *The Landscape, a Didactic Poem* (1794); Uvedale Price's *Essay on the Picturesque* (1794); and Humphrey Repton's *Sketches and Hints on Landscape Gardening* (1794). These works were enormously influential on the development of the Picturesque movement in Britain.

132. This has been identified as a *Tour of the Isle of Wight* in two volumes, dedicated to the Duke of Clarence, with drawings engraved in aquatint by John Hassell: Hörwarthner, no. 82.

133. *Briefe,* 508. Haydn was invited to Oatlands by the Prince of Wales, the day after the London marriage ceremony of the Prince's brother, the Duke of York, to the Prussian Princess, Friederike Charlotte, who was to become one of Haydn's closest royal supporters in England. The view and grounds at Oatlands had become well known following publication of prints of them by Jean Pillement (*c.*1761).

134. *Briefe,* 508.

135. Ibid., 530.

136. Ibid., 541.

137. Gilpin wrote a Thames tour as early as 1764, though he did not publish it: Brownell, 'William Gilpin's "Unfinished Business"', 63–78. In 1794 Boydell published the first volume of *An History of the River Thames* (originally to have been entitled *Picturesque Views of the Thames* ...), a picture book with illustrations by Joseph Farington, who discusses their progress in his diaries.

138. Appendix, item 75.

139. *Briefe,* 551. Waverley, largely dating from the twelfth and thirteenth centuries, was the first Cistercian foundation in England.

140. For the religious context of the English enthusiasm for ruins, see Margaret Aston, 'English Ruins and English History: The Dissolution and the Sense of the Past', *Journal of the Warburg and Courtauld Institutes,* 36 (1973), 231–55.

141. *The Antiquities of Great Britain,* by Thomas Hearne and William Byrne, began publication in 1778 with four engraved views. Fifty-two engravings had been issued by 1786, when the set was published complete as Volume 1. Work on Volume 2 was only begun a decade later. See Morris, *Thomas Hearne,* 24–51.

142. Tobias Smollett, *Humphry Clinker,* ed. Angus Ross (Harmondsworth, 1967), 215.

143. For examples, see some of the librettos published by Russell in *Don Juan Legend before Mozart.* The contrast of classicizing and Gothic sets in music theatre may be traced back to Serlio's publications in the sixteenth century. Recommendations for 'Gothic' scenery were well known in early eighteenth-century opera. For an example, see 'Pier Jacopo Martello on Opera (1715): An Annotated Translation', *Musical Quarterly,* 66 (1980), 378–403.

144. Horace Walpole, *Anecdotes of Painting,* i (London, 1762), 107–8.

145. '... alle in alt gottischen geschmack'; 'Bath ist eine der schönsten Städte in Europa': *Briefe,* 541, 539. Haydn's use of the word 'alt' here might imply that he understood the difference between medieval (old) Gothic and contemporary

(Strawberry Hill) Gothic; but this may be reading too much into his choice of words.

146. He had failed to learn how to distinguish the Classical orders, and confused the Corinthian with the Ionic.

147. *The Gentleman's Magazine*: Clark, *Gothic Revival*, 72.

148. Haydn might have known something of *Views of Ancient Buildings in England* (1786–93) or *Ancient Architecture of England* (1795 and 1807). For Carter, see Clark, *Gothic Revival*, 72–79, 102–9.

149. *Briefe*, 540. Haydn was presumably most impressed by the late fourteenth-century Gothic nave, and did not have in mind the earliest parts of the Cathedral.

150. *Journals and Diaries of Fanny Burney*, ed. Hemlow, i, 19–20. In a long description, Burney did find the chapel and monument of Bishop Langton 'of valuable Gothic workmanship', and considered that Inigo Jones's 'screen of Grecian Architecture' was misplaced 'in a Cathedral of Gothic workmanship'.

151. Details of this chapel are known from the description by John Milner, the Roman Catholic priest and 'preservationist', who also commented on West's altarpiece for Winchester: *Antiquities of Winchester*, ii, 229–48. It was destroyed in the twentieth century.

152. Items 52, 53: Whitman, *Valentine Green*, nos 277, 278.

153. In describing Carl Theodor's 'famous' court to his son in 1777, Leopold Mozart stressed how its 'rays, like those of the sun, illuminate the whole of Germany, nay even the whole of Europe': *Letters of Mozart*, ed. Anderson, 367. Haydn would have held a similar view.

154. The painting is in the Alte Pinakothek, Munich, no. 864. Van Dyck certainly painted a *Antiope and Jupiter*, which survives with variants, though the composition is quite distinct.

155. [Editorial] 'Sir Joshua Reynolds' Collection of Pictures', *Burlington Magazine*, 87 (1945), 133–34, 211–12, 263–73 (no. 36). Van Dyck's *Antiope and Jupiter* had been influential in the earlier eighteenth century, when it acted as a model for Carle Vanloo's version of the subject commissioned by the future Marquis of Marigny in 1752: Sahut, *Carle Vanloo*, cat. 129. Haydn might also have known Sir William Hamilton's *Jupiter and Antiope* by Palma il Giovane (a source for Van Dyck), or the engraving of it published in 1773: Jenkins and Sloan, *Vases and Volcanoes*, 276, no. 173.

156. Green's print, or another source related to Van Dyck, influenced a *Jupiter and Antiope* by J.A. Nahl (a pupil of Tischbein), engraved in the late 1790s by Neidl, whose prints were represented in Haydn's collection: Griffiths and Carey, *German Printmaking*, 107, no. 60.

157. See Ch. 1.

158. Landon, *Late Years*, 322; Landon, *Haydn in England*, 286. Bianchi's opera was first performed in Florence in 1779; the libretto was closely related to the one set by Vogler.

159. Although Rubens was not admired by all London-based artists at this time, Reynolds's visit to the Low Countries marks an import shift in his own attitude towards the Flemish painter, which was enthusiastically taken up by other English painters in the 1780s, notably Richard Cosway. It was about the time of Reynolds's visit to Flanders that Lord Orford commissioned Cipriani, an artist whose work subsequently made an impact on Haydn, to paint a *Castor and Pollux* for Houghton, which along with the rest of this collection was soon after acquired by Catherine the Great; Christie's, 20 April 1990, lot 54. Cipriani's *Castor and Pollux* was one of a number of paintings commissioned by Orford.

For Cipriani in Haydn's collection, see items 32, 57. Haydn's choice of this subject matter may also have been governed by the recognition of the figure of Castor on a celebrated Classical vase owned by Sir William Hamilton, which was known through reproductions, and its inclusion in the monumental portrait of Hamilton by David Allan painted in 1775 for the British Museum: Jenkins and Sloane, *Vases and Volcanoes*, 106–9, nos 1, 2; cf. 176–77, 180–81, nos 51, 55. A celebrated Classical sculpture in Madrid of two male figures, usually identified as Castor and Pollux, also drew attention to the story of the two brothers and their loyalty to each other, and was widely known through casts, including one owned by Carl Theodor: Haskell and Penny, *Taste and the Antique*, 174.

160. Reichardt, *Vertrauter Briefe über Frankreich* (Berlin, 1792–93), no. xxvi, cited in Girdlestone, *Jean-Philippe Rameau*, 575.

161. *Briefe*, 537.

162. Such as Tencalla's work at Eisenstadt.

163. Horace Walpole, *Anecdotes of Painting in England* (1763), quoted by Wind, *Hume and the Heroic Portrait*, ed. Anderson, 53.

164. *The Collected Works of William Hazlitt*, ed. A.R. Walker and Arnold Glover, ix (London, 1903), 37, 42.

165. The scheme Haydn is most likely to have known at Windsor was in St George's Hall, which included a scene showing the captured French king, Jean le Bon, being led in a triumphal procession by the Black Prince. Pope mentioned these paintings in *Windsor-Forest* (line 307), a poem Haydn may have known since he owned a print illustrating part of it. Verrio's scheme may be partly reconstructed through descriptions and illustrations, especially those in W.H. Pyne's *The History of the Royal Residences*, ii (London, 1819). A portrait of Charles II by Verrio, part of this destroyed scheme, was rediscovered in 1996, and is now in the Royal Collection.

166. *Briefe*, 481–83, 503.

167. Ibid., 483.

168. Quoted in Clayton, *English Prints*, 262. At the end of his life Boydell himself summed up his achievement, writing: 'When I first began business [c.1745], the whole commerce of prints in this country consisted in importing foreign prints, principally from France, to supply the cabinets of the curious in this kingdom. Impressed with the idea that the genius of our own countrymen, if properly encouraged, was equal to that of foreigners, I set about establishing a School of Engraving in England; with what success the public are well acquainted. It is, perhaps, at present, sufficient to say that the whole course of that commerce is changed, very few prints being now imported into this country, while the foreign market is principally supplied with prints from England.' Letter from Boydell to Sir John Anderson, 4 Feb. 1804, quoted in A. Chalmers, *Biographical Dictionary* (London, 1812), under 'Boydell'.

169. Friedman, *Boydell's Shakespeare Gallery*, 74.

170. Gregory Rubenstein, 'The Genesis of John Boydell's *Houghton Gallery*', in *Houghton Hall, the Prime Minister, the Empress and the Heritage*, ed. Andrew Moore (London, 1996), 65–73.

171. The *Universal Chronicle* for May 1989, quoted in Vickers, *Shakespeare*, 508.

172. Friedman, *Boydell's Shakespeare Gallery*, 74.

173. Appendix, item 609. The cataloguer was too tired to give any further details. By this stage in the process, he was much briefer in his entries than at the outset.

After Haydn left England for the last time, the Shakespeare Gallery declined in public esteem. Both paintings and engravings were criticized. Eventually, too much capital having been tied up in the project, and the Napoleonic Wars having restricted European markets, the paintings were disposed of in a lottery, then auctioned off by the winner at comparatively low prices.

174.   *Diary of Sophie v. La Roche*, trans. and ed. Clare Williams, 37–39.

175.   Manners, *Peters*. For a recent account of Peters, see Pointon, *Strategies for Showing*, 242–72.

176.   *Freemason's Magazine* for Oct. 1794: quoted in Pointon, *Strategies for Showing*, 300, n. 104.

177.   Judging from their appearance in Boydell's catalogue, quoted by Manners, *Peters*, 63–65.

178.   They are discussed in this arrangement in the *Freemason's Magazine* for Oct. 1794: quoted in Pointon, *Strategies for Showing*, 300, n. 104.

179.   Clayton, *English Print*, 248, 307, n. 77.

180.   Appendix, item 44.

181.   Appendix, item 45. The identification of this print in the catalogue drawn up after Haydn's death presents problems. The cataloguer wrote 'Eine bei einem Sterbbette trauernde Familie nach Peters ...'. This sounds like a German translation of the print already catalogued, with its English title, under item 44. This is possible. However, it seems unlikely that Haydn would have acquired two versions of this particular print. In one other case where Haydn owned two copies of the same print (items 8 and 9), the cataloguer wrote for the second one 'detto andres', which he might also have been expected to write had item 45 simply repeated item 44. The cataloguer does say that item 45 was a print by Bartolozzi. If it were a print related to *The Resurrection*, though different, then *The Spirit of a Child*, which was also engraved by Bartolozzi, is a strong possibility, the iconography of the print conceivably being covered by the title which the cataloguer gave it. Why the cataloguer wrote the title in German is unclear, unless this was a special edition for distribution in German-speaking countries. Perhaps Haydn acquired it on the Continent, rather than in England, or perhaps the words were missing. Bartolozzi also engraved *The Angelic Child*, the third part of the triptych, though not until 1801. On balance, therefore, the evidence suggests that item 45 was not identical with item 44, and that in common with most other prints in the collection, it was acquired by Haydn in England. *The Spirit of a Child* seems the only satisfactory identification. The print is reproduced in colour in Clayton, *English Print*, pl. 270.

182.   For interpretations of the sexual aspects of Reni's painting, see Richard E. Spear, *The 'Divine' Guido: Religion, Sex, Money and Art in the World of Guido Reni* (New Haven, 1997).

183.   *Salons*, ed. Seznec and Adhémar, i, 215. See M. Ingenhoff-Danhauser, *Maria-Magdalena: Heilige und Sünderin in der italienischen Renaissance* (Tübingen, 1984), 95–96 for further relevant commentaries.

184.   Appendix, item 26. The cataloguer described the prints as '6. Unterhaltungen nach Morland von Smith'. This is clearly a series, and the only example of this is the *Laetitia* set.

185.   For further comment on these elements and the *Laetitia* series as a whole, see D'Oench, 'Prodigal Sons', 333–36.

186.   Appendix, item 31: illustrated in Alexander, *Affecting Moments*, 50–51, nos 42, 43.

187.   Appendix, item 5.

188. Vincent Orchard, *Tattersalls: Two Hundred Years of Sporting History* (London, 1953), 134–35.
189. Appendix, item 35.
190. Alexander, 'Edmund Scott', nos 60, 61 (with illustration of *The Brothers*); Cannon-Brooks, *Painted Word*, 98, no. 99 (with illustration of *Sabrina*). According to Cannon-Brookes, *Sabrina* was included in J.R. Smith's catalogue of before 1787, though it is not clear what this refers to. The oil painting by Stothard (or possibly a sketch for, or reduced version of it) was sold at Sotheby's, London, 22 Mar. 1972, lot 8, pl. VIII.
191. Fiske, *English Theatre Music*, 179–88; Anthony Hicks, 'Handel's Music of *Comus*', *Musical Times*, 117 (1976), 28.
192. Inside the Temple was a painting 'in the Chinese taste', depicting 'Vulcan catching Mars and Venus in the historical net'. For the connection between the poem and the decoration of the structure, see Pointon, *Milton*, 46–47.
193. Allen, *Francis Hayman*, 190, no. 291. For further discussion and illustration, see Pointon, *Milton*, 49. In 1776 Wheatley exhibited at the Society of Artists *Mr Webster in the Character of Comus*: Pointon, 167.
194. Walker Art Gallery, Liverpool. The painting was exhibited at Robin's Rooms, Covent Garden, where Wright had organized a one-man exhibition of his work.
195. Pointon, *Milton*, 73–74, 88.
196. Alexander and Godfrey, *Painters and Engravers*, 56, no. 114; Tim Clayton, 'The Engraving and Publication of Prints of Joseph Wright's Paintings', in Egerton, *Joseph Wright*, 25–30; cf. 250, no. 169.
197. *A Descriptive Catalogue of Thirty-Six Pictures Painted by George Morland ... to be Engraved by Subscription by and under the Direction of J.R. Smith* (London, [1792]). The 'Morland Gallery' seems to have previously been owned by Daniel Orme, who displayed it at his premises in Bond Street.
198. Appendix, item 24. The cataloguer mentions four animal pieces by Morland engraved by Smith which can only be identified with the set issued on 1 Aug. 1794. Their titles are: *Dog and Cat*; *Fighting Dogs*; *Rubbing-down the Post-horse*; and *Watering the Carthorse*.
199. Appendix, item 56.
200. From 1788 Scott called himself 'Engraver to ... the Duke of York': Alexander, 'Edmund Scott'. A drawing, today in Vienna, of Francesco Artaria is catalogued as the work of Edmund Scott, and datable *c*.1790: Brusatti, Otto, et al., *Zauberföne*, 579, cat. IX/52.
201. Appendix, item 27: Chaloner-Smith, *British Mezzotint Portraits*, 1318, nos 191, 192.
202. Quoted from Pope's own 'Argument' to his *Eloisa to Abelard* (1717).
203. Appendix, item 28, misread as 'Ladana': Lloyd, *Cosway*, 134, no. 233. Verse by Pope was also included in the collection of English poetry owned by Haydn.
204. *The Rape of the Lock*, Canto II, lines 7–8.
205. For an important account of the popularity of images of nuns in English visual culture in the later eighteenth century, and their sexual aspects, see Pointon, *Strategies for Showing*, 270–72, where the example of Matthew Peters is discussed at length.
206. Appendix, item 13.
207. Appendix, item 41: Frankau, *Eighteenth-Century Colour Prints*, 213. The two remaining prints after Westall cannot clearly be identified.
208. Hill, *Mr Gillray the Caricaturist*, 147–48.

209. Appendix, item 48: Weinglass, *Prints*, 80, no. 74. The original painting is now in the Walker Art Gallery, Liverpool.
210. Allan Cunningham, *Lives of the British Painters*, 2nd edn (1830–33), ii, 290, quoted in Weinglass, *Prints*, 80.
211. Sacchini spent many years in London, composing several operas for the King's Theatre. His portrait was painted in 1775 by Reynolds. Fanny Burney, who thought the portrait 'charming', wrote that, 'Sir Joshua himself said that Sacchini was the highest type of manly beauty': diary entry for 27 Feb. 1775. *Oedipe à Colone* was composed for Paris in 1786. An early performance was attended by Michael Kelly, who thought it 'delightful and enchanting': *Reminiscences*, ed. Fiske, 146.
212. Appendix, item 42: Weinglass, *Prints*, 77, no. 73. What seems to be the original painting is now in Zurich, Kunsthaus.
213. Haydn certainly saw one of Shakespeare's tragedies, *Hamlet*, in London: Landon, *Haydn in England*, 274. Since the evidence for this comes from a review of the play – reviews only rarely commenting on those present at a performance – it seems possible that Haydn attended the theatre to see productions of Shakespeare plays on other occasions.
214. Asleton (ed.), *Sarah Siddons*, 4–5. Both plays are by Nicholas Rowe.
215. For a discussion of this print, see Donald, *Age of Caricature*, 73. Although the print as published does not identify the figures, they evidently were so well drawn by Gillray that there was no difficulty in generally recognizing them: the copy which belonged to Walpole (now Lewis-Walpole Library, Farmington, Conn.) gives the identifications written in Walpole's own hand.
216. Clayton, *English Print*, 248, pls 270, 307. Gillray's *An Angel gliding on a Sunbeam into Paradise* (1791) was probably inspired by Peters's *An Angel Carrying the Spirit of a Child to Paradise*, the only part of Peters's triptych not in Haydn's collection.
217. Appendix, item 24. Interestingly, from the point of view of the content of Haydn's collection, Gillray's original drawing for this print includes an inscription connecting Morland with Correggio, both of whom died in 'wretched' circumstances: Lionel Lambourne, *An Introduction to Caricature* (London, 1983), 16–17, pl. 20.
218. Appendix, items 14 (one print), 47 (two prints), and 55 (three prints). The catalogue entry for item 14 provides only the title of the print, not the name of the artist or engraver. This leaves open the possibility of identification with Gillray's print of the same title as Bunbury's. However, this is most unlikely. Bunbury's *A Smoking Club* was published on the same day as two of the other prints in the collection (*Patience in a Punt* and *Patience in a Punt* [2]), and it is clear Haydn acquired them all at the same time.
219. Item 55, catalogued immediately after the heading 'Kupferstich unter Glas und Rahme'.
220. *Briefe*, 543. The caricature recorded by Haydn is not listed in Dorothy George's *Catalogue of Political and Personal Satires in the British Museum*, v: *1771–83* (London, 1935); vi: *1784–92* (London, 1938); vii: *1793–1800* (London, 1942), and it has not proved possible to trace it. The possibility that Haydn devised it himself, having studied titles of caricatures of the same type, cannot be discounted, though it seems unlikely. The Countess of Jersey probably became the mistress of the Prince of Wales in 1793. The affair was well known in the public domain.

221. For Lichtenberg and Hogarth, see Innes and Gustav Herdan, *The World of Hogarth: Lichtenberg's Commentaries on Hogarth's Engravings* (London, 1966); H.L. Gumbert (ed.), *Lichtenberg in England* (Wiesbaden, 1977); Arnd Beise, 'Lichtenbergs Erklärungen zu Hogarths moralischen Kupferstichen', in *Georg Christoph Lichtenberg 1742–1799: Wagnis der Aufklärung*, exh. cat. (Darmstadt and Göttingen, 1992), 239–59.

222. On 5 May 1792 the *Morning Chronicle* featured an advertisement for 'The six pictures of Hogarth's *Marriage A-la-Mode* now exhibiting in Pall Mall'. The new engravings, by Richard Earlom, were published between 1795 and 1800.

223. *Briefe*, 543. Although it is not entirely clear that Haydn was the author of the verses, Landon (*CCLN*, 299) points out that the poem 'is written down with many corrections and improvements, which suggests that Haydn was probably the author (or translator?)'.

224. BMC 8485; Krumbhaar, *Isaac Cruikshank*, 108, no. 787.

225. Fiske, *English Theatre Music*, 521–52.

226. Gillray accompanied the painter Loutherbourg to Portsmouth in the summer of 1794 on a commission to execute works connected with Lord Howe's vistory over the French. Haydn was in Portsmouth at the same time and noted meeting Loutherbourg in his notebook: *Briefe*, 535.

227. First published in 1714. The relevant part of the text is quoted beneath the print: Cannon-Brookes, *Painted Word*, 94, no. 96 (with illustration).

228. For example, *The Gypsie Fortune Teller*, published by Sayer in 1789, is inscribed with the verse: 'The Gypsies they a Fortune telling go: The Misses they their Fortunes want to know: Credulous to believe each flattering story told, That mark on your hand will bring you much gold'. For a reproduction, see Clayton, *English Print*, pl. 249. The interest in gypsies in the later 1780s was probably in part a result of the repeal in 1783 of a sixteenth-century Act of Parliament outlawing gypsies in England.

229. Hob. XV: 25, first published by Longman & Broderip.

230. For an account of the thematic origins of the movement in question, see Landon, *Haydn in England*, 433–34. Landon points out that Haydn 'makes no distinction between Hungarian and Gypsy music'. For a print apparently showing gypsies playing music in the courtyard at Eszterháza, see Somfai, *Joseph Haydn*, 60–61, pls 95, 98.

231. William Shield's *Marian* was first performed in 1788: Fiske, *English Theatre Music*, 467–68. Its popularity led to performances during Haydn's London visits. Haydn certainly attended Shield's *The Woodman*, given 10 Dec. 1791. In using the name of Shield's 1788 opera for their print, Bunbury and his publisher were probably cashing in on its success.

232. For example, James Ward's *The Mouse's Petition* was engraved by William Ward and published in 1805: C. Reginald Grundy, *James Ward R.A.: His Life and Work* (London, 1909), 72, no. 90 (with colour plate); cf. no. 91. The mouse is shown in a trap, looked on by three children. For another example, see William Hamilton's *Children with Mouse-Trap*, engraved by Marcuard: Frankau, *Eighteenth-Century Colour Prints*, 210.

233. The poem's full title is *The Mouse's Petition to Doctor Priestley Found in the trap where he had been confined all Night*. Priestley's experiments testing gases and electrical currents using animals is documented in his correspondence with Benjamin Franklin and in his *History of Electricity*. For a resumé of this, see *The Poems of Anna Letitia Barbauld*, ed. William McCarthy and Elizabeth Kraft (Athens, Ga., 1994), 244–45.

234. Mrs Barbauld's position in favour of the changes in France was public knowledge. A caricature ridiculing Burke's views published on 1 Dec. 1790 shows Mrs Barbauld being egged on to 'cut the Jesuitical Monster to pieces': Robinson, *Burke*, 144.

235. For items commemorating these events, see J. Tann, S. Price and D. McCullen, *Priestley in Birmingham*, exh. cat., Birmingham Museums and Art Gallery (Birmingham, 1980), nos 43, 44.

236. The theme of captivity in the years leading up to 1793 would also have put people in mind of the position of the royal family in France, especially Marie-Antoinette, who would doubtless have been on Haydn's mind.

237. Appendix, item 40. The relevant scene from *Hamlet* was drawn by Chodowiecki in 1778, with the title *Mausfalle*, and etched in 1780. Given Huck's background in the German print trade, he would surely have known this.

238. BMC 8208: George, *Hogarth to Cruikshank*, 78, fig. 62.

239. Views of Sir William Chambers's Chinese designs at Kew were published in 1763.

240. For the shadow cast over the eyes motif in Reynolds, see (for examples) Penny, *Reynolds*, nos 13, 120. The motif probably derives from Rembrandt.

241. Published 6 Jan. 1780 by Carington Bowles.

242. *The Letters and Prose Writings of William Cowper*, ed. James King and Charles Ryskamp, iii (Oxford, 1982), 87–88 (letters of 1787–88), quoted in Donald, *Age of Caricature*, 75. Cowper's term 'humour by the yard' refers to Bunbury's most popular print of his lifetime, *The Long Minuet as Danced at Bath* (BMC 7229), which is seven feet long.

243. From an obituary notice of 1811, reprinted in Joseph Grego, *Rowlandson the Caricaturist*, i (London, 1880), 79.

244. Fanny Burney reports how members of the royal family enjoyed Bunbury's work: *The Diary and Letters of Madame d'Arblay*, ed. C. Barret, iii (London, 1905), 304, 308, 316, 323–24, 331, 481.

245. Haydn's wife, of course, remained in Austria during the period of his London visits. But it was an open secret that their relations had been antagonistic for decades. Several artists with whom Haydn may have come into contact in London were well known to have left their spouses or been on bad terms with them, including Loutherbourg, Romney and Fuseli.

246. Gotwals, *Haydn*, 20; cf. 220–21.

247. For Arne's *Blind Beggar of Bethnal Green* (first performed 1741), based on a seventeenth-century play by John Day, see Fiske, *English Theatre Music*, 207. For Opie's painting (he apparently made more than one version, all dating from the early 1780s), see Earland, *Opie*, 339.

248. *The Blind Beggar and his Daughter of Bethnal Green*, published 20 Aug. 1790 by Thomas Macklin.

249. A good example is *Mr Burke's Pair of Spectacles for short sighted politicians*, published 12 May 1791 (BMC 7858). For discussion of this and other themes connected with seeing in caricature of the period, see Robinson, *Burke*, 152–53.

250. In the foreground two dogs, labelled with the names of the candidates, pull at either side of a wig. The original drawing for this print, exhibited at the Royal Academy in 1785, was in the collection of Reynolds, who reportedly called it 'one of the best drawings he had ever seen ... it would be admired in every age and country': Wolf, *Goya and the Satirical Print*, 46–49, fig. 19.

251. A print published in February 1790, for example, shows Sheridan snatching off Burke's wig, exposing the label 'Tory' on his head: BMC 7627. Another of

March 1793 portrays Burke and other Whigs discarding their wigs on a pile to the dismay of Fox and Sheridan: BMC 8315.

252. See, for example, *Bone of Contention [Different Sensations]*, published 26 Feb. 1790 (BMC 7631): Robinson, *Burke*, 137–39.

253. BMC 2607: [Lionel Lambourne], *English Caricature 1620 to the Present: Caricaturists and Satirists, their Art, their Purpose and Influence*, exh. cat., Victoria & Albert Museum (London, 1984), 50–51, no. 41, pl. 16.

254. For a résumé of these complicated family connections, see Ewart, 'Henry Bunbury', 157.

255. Moses Kean 'was a very extraordinary mimic, particularly in his imitations of Charles James Fox'. J.T. Smith, *Nollekens and his Times* (London, 1949), 202.

256. The composition in question is the first movement of Symphony No. 8, *Le Soir*, quoting a song by Gluck beginning 'Je n'aimais pas le tabac beaucoup': Heartz, 'Haydn und Gluck', 120–35. For discussion of this composition as 'a marital feud', see Will, 'When God Met the Sinner'.

257. Smoking as a sign of a radical cast of mind was given clear expression in designs for prints published in 1793 by Richard Newton, all depicting a number of well-known radical figures, portrayed as political prisoners (some were guilty of sedition) or prison visitors, many of whom are shown very conspicuously smoking. Newton's prints include *Soulagement en Prison; or, Comfort in Prison* (BMC 8339) and *Promenade in the State side of Newgate* (BMC 8342): Bindman, *Shadow of the Guillotine*, 191–92, nos. 193–94; Alexander, *Richard Newton and English Caricature*, 34–41, 120–21.

258. For Pitt's excise bill for tobacco, see Compton Mackenzie, *Sublime Tobacco* (London, 1957), 219. One of the most vociferous of Pitt's critics in this respect was John Courtenay MP, a keen Foxite: R.G. Thorne, *The History of Parliament: The House of Commons 1790–1820*, 4 vols (London, 1986), iii, 509–11. Courtenay's support for tobacco is evident from his portrayal as a smoker in a caricature by Gillray showing the MP engaged in raucous banter with a group of friends, including Fox: *'The feast of Reason, & the flow of Soul'*, published on 4 Feb. 1797: D. Hill, *The Satirical Etchings of James Gillray* (New York, 1976), p. 112, no. 48.

259. *Le Père Duchesne* was the creation of Jacques René Hébert. It was published between 1790 and 1794.

260. Thomas Barker's *The Woodman*, engraved by Bartolozzi: Appendix, item 39 (discussed below in the text at greater length).

261. *Briefe*, 514

262. The visual features of the Hanover Square Rooms mentioned here are described in a letter from Mrs Gertrude Harris to her son written shortly after the venue opened in February 1775: quoted in Terry, *John Christian Bach*, 141–42. For a general description of the venue, see Forsyth, *Buildings for Music*, 35–39.

263. Terry, *John Christian Bach*, 142.

264. Appendix, items 32, 57. Item 32, which is identifiable, has been discussed in Ch. 5.

265. From the official guide, written by Reynolds's friend, Joseph Baretti, quoted in Penny, *Reynolds*, 284.

266. Appendix, item 54: '1. Unterhaltungen von Grozer': Joseph Grozer's engraving of 'Theory' was published 29 Mar. 1785. The cataloguer of Haydn's collection did not give a title for the item in question. Grozer's other prints have their titles clearly below them.

267. Reynolds's *Theory* became for some a kind of emblem of English cultural achievement. It was subsequently engraved by William Blake (despite his detestation of Reynolds and his principles) for the frontispiece to Prince Hoare's *Inquiry into the Requisite Cultivation and Present State of the Arts of Design in England* (London, 1806): Katharine A. McDowall, '*Theory*, or *The Graphic Muse* Engraved by Blake after Reynolds', *Burlington Magazine*, 11 (1907), 113–15; Robert N. Essick, *William Blake's Commercial Book Illustrations: A Catalogue and Study of the Plates Engraved by Blake after Designs by Other Artists* (Oxford,1991), 94, pl. 214.

268. Appendix, item 21: '4. Ovale Unterhaltungsstücke'. Although this entry does not specifically mention Kauffman's paintings, or the prints after them, there are few sets of four oval prints which may be identified with the wording given in the catalogue of an appropriate date for Haydn to have purchased them when he was in England. Kauffman's designs, reproduced by Haydn's favourite engraver, therefore seem a very likely identification: Vesme and Calabi, *Bartolozzi*, 583, 588, 597, 640. The paintings are today in the entry-hall of Burlington House.

269. There are records of Bunbury's *Long Minuet* being staged in this manner for 8 June 1789 and 9 Nov. 1795. It seems very likely, however, that it was given many times in between, though because it was a short item, it did not appear on published programmes. On the first documented occasion, it was presented in a series of such 'pictures', the rest of which are not identified by the artists' names.

270. The details given here come from the programme announcement given in the *Morning Chronicle* for 18 May 1791, quoted in Landon, *Haydn in England*, 77–78.

271. Fiske, *English Theatre Music*, 558.

272. Paulson, *Hogarth's Graphic Works*, 152.

273. Hogarth drew on *The Cryes of the City of London Drawne after the Life*, first published in 1687: Sean Shesgreen, *The Criers and Hawkers of London: Engravings and Drawings of Marcellus Laroon* (London, 1990); id., 'The First London Cries', *Print Quarterly*, 10 (1993), 364–73. The information about Arnold cited here is taken from Fiske. Apart from Hogarth, Arnold (and his librettist, Colman) may have looked at Paul Sandby's set of etchings, the *Twelve London Cries done from the Life* (1760).

274. *Journals of Mrs Papendiek*, ed. Broughton, ii, 297.

275. Landon, *Haydn in England*, 614–15.

276. Webster, *Francis Wheatley*, 81–85.

277. *Morning Chronicle*, 6 May 1795, quoted in Landon, *Haydn in England*, 308.

278. Landon, *Late Years*, 398, no. 329.

279. Strong, *And when did you last see your father?*, 130, 162. Cf. Helen Smailes and Duncan Thomson, *The Queen's Image: A Celebration of Mary Queen of Scots*, exh. cat., Scottish National Portrait Gallery (Edinburgh, 1987), 94–96, no. 47.

280. *The Murder of David Rizzio in the Presence of Mary Queen of Scots* (*c.*1787): Bruntjen, *John Boydell*, 264.

281. See Clayton, *English Print*, 258.

282. Girdham, *English Opera*, 234

283. For a survey of images concerning the fate of Marie-Antoinette, see Bindman, *Shadow of the Guillotine*, 150–53.

284. *Morning Herald*, 17 Mar. 1792, quoted in Landon, *Haydn in England*, 147.

285. *Diary; or, Woodfall's Register*, 25 Feb. 1792, quoted in Landon, *Haydn in England*, 137.

286. T.S.R. Boase, 'Shipwrecks in English Romantic Painting', *Journal of the Warburg and Courtauld Institutes*, 22 (1959), 332–46; George Landow, 'Iconography and Point of View in Painting and Literature: The Example of the Shipwreck', *Studies in Iconography*, 3 (1977), 89–104.

287. See David Fraser, 'Joseph Wright of Derby and the Lunar Society', in Egerton, *Joseph Wright*, 15–24.

288. *The Times*, 20 Feb. 1992, quoted in Landon, *Haydn in England*, 134.

289. Kelly, *Reminiscences*, ed. Fiske, 195.

290. The Welsh landscape painter Thomas Jones mentions Storace's attempts at drawing in his *Memoirs*: Fiske, *English Theatre Music*, 492–93.

291. Fiske, *English Theatre Music*, 514, pl. XVI.

292. *Briefe*, 509–10. Haydn gives a long description of his view of the performance. The quotation comes from the title-page of the opera as published: Fiske, *English Theatre Music*, pl. XVI.

293. Walpole, *Correspondence*, ed. Lewis et al., *Madame du Deffant Correspondence*, v, 258. Walpole evidently did not know George Smith's *The Hop Pickers*, published by Vivares in 1760: Clayton, *English Print*, 189, fig. 203.

294. The painting was destroyed in 1810.

295. The Reverend Henry Bate assumed the name Bate-Dudley in 1784 and was created a Baronet in 1813. He also founded the *Morning Post* in 1772, a newspaper of which he was proprietor and editor for several years. Gainsborough painted portraits of both him and his wife.

296. *Morning Herald*, 11 June 1989, quoted in Bishop, *Barkers of Bath*, 13.

297. The painting is now owned by the Torfaen Museum Trust: Bishop, *Barkers of Bath*, 27, no. 10; John Hayes, *British Paintings of the Sixteenth Century through Nineteenth Centuries*, National Gallery of Art, Washington (Cambridge, 1992), 6–9.

298. Barker's image was used to decorate jugs, and other items of Staffordshire pottery and Worcester porcelain. The print was used as the basis of signs on tobacconists' shops until at least the mid-nineteenth century: see James Ayres, *Two Hundred Years of English Naïve Art 1700–1900* (Alexandria, Va., 1996), 131.

299. It appears in the catalogue of his collection as 'The Woodmann nach Parker von Bartolozzi': Appendix, item 39.

300. The popularity of the woodman theme in the early 1790s was not restricted to Britain. During Haydn's return to Vienna in 1793 he would have been interested to find that Schikaneder was putting on a singspiel called *Die Waldmänner* ('The Woodmen') with music by Mozart's former associate, J.B. Henneberg: Honolka, *Schikaneder*, 151, 158, 223. The plot seems to have no connection with Shield's opera.

301. For the origins of the name, see Michael Kassler, 'On the Name of Haydn's "Surprise" Symphony', *Music & Letters*, 52 (1971), 106.

302. Griesinger, 56.

303. Carlson and Ittmann, *French Printmaking*, 296. It may be suggested here that Ducreux's range of expressions may also have suggested to Haydn the unusual designation of the Nelson Mass as *Missa in angustiis* ('Mass in [the time of] fear'); the origin of this title will be discussed at greater length in the next chapter.

304. *Oracle*, 24 Mar. 1792, quoted in Landon, *Haydn in England*, 150.

305. *Morning Chronicle*, 9 Apr. 1794, quoted ibid., 247.

306. *Morning Chronicle*, 2 May 1794, quoted ibid., 250–51.

307. The painting is now destroyed.

308. Prown, *Copley*, ii, 312. The painting was subsequently displayed in the New Common Council Chamber of the Guildhall and may be seen in that position in an illustration by Thomas Rowlandson and Augustus Pugin in Rudolph Ackermann's *Microcosm of London* of 1808: Stroud, *George Dance*, pl. 36.

309. Appendix, item 1.

310. Joppien, *Loutherbourg* (1973), no. 64. Loutherbourg was already celebrated, as indicated in another chapter, for painting battle pieces.

311. *Morning Post*, 30 Aug. 1794, quoted in Hill, *Gillray the Caricaturist*, 49.

312. Henry Angelo, *Reminiscences of Henry Angelo*, i (London, 1828), 382.

313. Valentine Green rented the room from Bowyer for 200 guineas a year.

314. Fiske, *English Theatre Music*, 527–28.

315. *Briefe*, 534–35, 537.

316. Ibid., 532, 534.

317. Farington has an anecdote about Hunter and Loutherbourg: *Diary* entry for 13 Sept. 1796. Wolcot (Pindar) included Loutherbourg in his *Odes*, though he was not favourable to his work. For pictures by Loutherbourg commissioned by the Prince of Wales, see Oliver Millar, 'George IV when Prince of Wales: His Debts to Artists and Craftsmen', *Burlington Magazine*, 128 (1986), 586–92.

318. Hob. XXVIa: 31.

319. National Maritime Museum, Greenwich: Joppien, *Loutherbourg* (1973), no. 65. The painting was completed in 1795 and, together with its pair, was exhibited in the Historic Gallery, Pall Mall, for three years. It is suggested here that aspects of Symphony No. 102, which was probably first conceived around the time, or shortly after Haydn met Loutherbourg in Portsmouth (the autograph is dated 1794 on the first page of music, and the first performance was given on 2 Feb. 1795), may have been inspired, consciously or subconsciously, by viewing Loutherbourg at work and the painting in progress. In the first movement, the *Allegro Vivace* features a motif opening with the interval of a rising minor seventh, marked *sforzando* on the upper note, then falling back down the scale. It occurs in the exposition at bars 56 to 60 in the bass, and at bars 92 to 97 in the first violins, and similarly in the recapitulation. These might be construed as gunshots, a ricochet, even being suggested by the wind emphasizing the *sforzando* a beat after it is first heard. In the development section, this motif forms the basis of a violent passage, full of dissonance and imitation, which might be understood as full-scale assault and the confusion which this brings (bars 160–84). The main feature of the second subject, two *fortissimo* unisons held for an entire bar (played by the full orchestra), followed by a general rest for a further bar, then a passage marked *piano*, may be considered the musical equivalent of the sound of explosions caused by cannon fire. In his Notebook, Haydn specifically recorded the number of cannon he saw and the scale of damage and loss of life each cannon ball might cause.

320. The following passages may be suggested as examples: flute 1, oboes and bassoon 1 in Symphony No. 102, I, bars 8–9; flute and oboes at several places in the introduction to Symphony No. 103, and also in the first *minore* variation in II, bars 53–74; oboe 1 in Symphony No. 104, I, bar 16. Haydn had, of course, already used wind instruments to suggest birds in *L'anima del filosofo* (1791).

321. *The Mysteries of Udolpho* was published in 1794. Stendhal, writing in 1816, implied he sensed a connection between Haydn and Mrs Radcliff. See Stendhal, *Rome, Naples and Florence*, trans. Coe, 208.
322. Paul Mellon Collection, Yale Centre for British Art, New Haven.
323. *Morning Chronicle*, 3 Mar. 1795, quoted in Landon, *Haydn in England*, 295. Since Haydn reintroduced the music of the introduction, opening with the famous drum-roll, towards the end of the movement, it would certainly have been especially memorable.
324. The account occurs in Momigny's *Cours complet d'harmonie et de composition*. See Cole, 'Momigny's Analysis', 261.
325. 'La fureur est *peinte* sur chaque figure ...'; 'Dans *la peinture* qu'Haydn fait de cette scène ...'; '... *le tableau* d'Haydn est achevé'; 'les divers instruments ... *colorent le dessein*'.
326. Quoted from László Somfai, notes to the recordings of Haydn's 'Apponyi Quartets' by the Tátrai Quartet (Hungaroton, 1982).
327. Carpani, 126, 177.
328. *Morning Chronicle*, 31 Jan. 1792, quoted in Landon, *Haydn in England*, 128.
329. For discussions of Haydn's use of parody in the early 1780s, see: Clark, 'Intertextual Play and Haydn's *La fedeltà premiata*', esp. 68–69; Sutcliffe, *Haydn: String Quartets, Op. 50*, 102–3.
330. See, for example, the account published in Salas, 'Light on the Origin of Los Caprichos', 712–13. Haydn might have seen [William Dent's] *Public Credit or the State Idol*, published 3 June 1791: Robinson, *Burke*, 158, fig. 168.
331. For examples of such caricatures turning the tables on audiences, see Penny (ed.), *Reynolds*, 366 (no. 176), 370 (no. 181).
332. Letter of 2 Mar. 1792: *Briefe*, 279.

Notes to Chapter 7

1. Hörwarthner, no. 17. The edition owned by Haydn, in several volumes, was either published in 1792–93, or in 1792–96.
2. For David, see le Huray and Day, *Music and Aesthetics*, 166. Thomas Jefferson, the key figure in shaping early constitutional ceremonial in the United States, owned a copy of Barthélemy's *Anacharsis*: Gilreath and Wilson, *Thomas Jefferson's Library*, 18.
3. Barthélemy is on this point quoting from Aristophanes's *Birds*: le Huray and Day, *Music and Aesthetics*, 172.
4. In listing compositions for which he had 'received the most approbation' in his autobiographical sketch of 1776, he listed only vocal compositions in introducing himself in the public sphere: three of his operas, *The Return of Tobias*, and the *Stabat Mater*.
5. Van Swieten seems to have proposed at this time a setting of a text by J.B. von Alxinger on the Apotheosis of Hercules, which he hoped Haydn would set 'in the spirit of Handel'. Haydn understandably rejected it.
6. The dire text, which must have been extraordinarily difficult for a non-native English speaker to conceive musically, and the incarceration of its instigator, Lord Abingdon, evidently combined to render the plan unfeasible.
7. Linley had been in charge of music at this theatre, under Sheridan's management, since 1776, delegating responsibilities to Storace and Kelly in later years.

8. Appendix, item 29.
9. Burke, *Philosophical Enquiry*, ed. Boulton, 82. Haydn owned a copy of Burke's *Enquiry* (Hörwarthner, no. 46), which he made considerable use of in his unperformed opera for London, *L'anima del filosofo* (1791), and also in the late oratorios.
10. In a section labelled 'Feeling. Pain', Burke wrote 'the idea of bodily pain, in all the modes and degrees of labour, pain, anguish, torment, is productive of the sublime; and nothing else in this sense can produce it': *Philosophical Enquiry*, ed. Boulton, 86.
11. The first performance of the *Missa in tempore belli* was held in Vienna on 26 Dec. 1796 in a service marking the entry to the priesthood of Joseph Franz von Hofmann, whose father was the Imperial Paymaster for War.
12. Textually, there is also a connection between the song and the relevant section of the mass since both refer to spirits (a secular spirit in the song, and the Holy Spirit in the mass) and to tombs (the place where the spirit dwells in the song, and the place where the body of Christ was first placed after the Crucifixion in the mass).
13. Landon, *Years of 'The Creation'*, 106–9, 183–89.
14. Erffa and Staley, *West*, 187–88, no. 48.
15. For the print, see Clayton, *English Print*, 237. For a survey of paintings on subjects related to Alfred in British art of this period, see Strong, *And when did you last see your father?*, 114–18, 156.
16. Haydn may have had the opportunity to hear Arne's *Elfrida*, another drama set to music on an Anglo-Saxon subject related to *Alfred*. Paisiello also set texts on related subjects of English origin.
17. The two pieces are both scored for pairs of clarinets, bassoons and horns.
18. *AMZ*, 1 (16 Jan. 1799), col. 254. Griesinger (p. 37) states that the original English libretto lasted nearly four hours.
19. *Explanatory Notes and Remarks on Milton's Paradise Lost*: see Oras, *Milton's Editors*, ch. 5.
20. *Two Discourses. II. An Argument in behalf of the Science of a Connoisseur* (London, 1719), 191–92.
21. *Explanatory Notes*, VII, 321. The Richardsons' whole method in discussing the poem is thought of in terms of the visual arts: 'We found This Book, as a Picture of the greatest Master, Obscur'd for want of a Proper Light; We hold it Up to Them in Such a One; but we Abhor to do what is Too often done by the Best pictures, We dare not Scour, much Less Retouch it.' *Explanatory Notes*, p. clxxvii.
22. *Explanatory Notes*, p. cxlviii. Richardson compares the treatment of common themes in Raphael with Milton elsewhere, finding Raphael deficient by comparison. Comparisons are also made with Michelangelo and Dürer.
23. Ibid., IV, 321.
24. For Milton's actual relationship with the visual arts, see Frye, *Milton's Imagery and the Visual Arts*.
25. *Explanatory Notes*, p. clvi. For a survey of musical settings of Milton in the eighteenth century, see Shawcross, *Milton*, 9–12.
26. Avison comments on Handel's setting: *Essay on Musical Expression*, ch. 3. Handel's *L'Allegro* and *Il Penseroso* were performed at Covent Garden on 4 Mar. 1795.
27. For one example, see *Philosophical Enquiry*, ed. Boulton, 59.
28. A mezzotint by Richard Earlom, after Charles Brandoin's *The Exhibition of the*

Royal Academy in the Year 1771, shows Barry's picture in the most eye-catching position. What seems to be the painting is now in the National Gallery of Ireland, Dublin.

29. For a survey of Milton illustration at this time, see Pointon, *Milton*, esp. ch. 3.

30. Stothard's main Milton illustrations were published in 1792–93 by Jeffreys. The first volume of *Paradise Lost* with illustrations by Westall was published in 1794. Another edition of *Paradise Lost*, with illustrations by Singleton, was published by J. Parsons in 1796. Although he could not have known this, Haydn may have seen the subject from Milton Singleton exhibited at the Royal Academy in 1795.

31. There were also important sets of depictions of subjects derived from *Paradise Lost* by Romney, Flaxman, Metz (whom Haydn perhaps knew) and, later, Blake.

32. This enthusiasm was taken up by his son, also Charles, who in 1790 wrote an account of Milton's verse in Greek.

33. Quoted in Hagstrum, *Sister Arts*, 243.

34. Quoted ibid., 258, n. 26.

35. Canto I, verses xxxviii, xliv.

36. McKillop, *Background of Thomson's Seasons*, ch. 5.

37. Examples include series of paintings by: Boucher, Lancret, Pater, Watteau (known today only through engravings). The theme was also occasionally treated musically, one version being a ballet by Lully (1695).

38. One of the best-known examples of this was Claude's *Apollo Leading the Dance of the Seasons*, one version of which was etched by the artist himself. In later eighteenth-century England, this subject was widely known through versions by Richard Wilson dating from the early 1770s and prints after them: Constable, *Richard Wilson*, 167–68, pls 26a, 26b. Wilson's design, showing the Seasons holding hands in a ring, probably formed the basis of Stothard's frontispiece to *The Seasons*, published in 1794.

39. Solkin, *Wilson*, 220–21, no. 112; Clayton, *English Print*, 190–91. Verses quoting the poem, including Thomson's challenge, appear beneath Woollett's print after Wilson's painting.

40. Thomas Hearne is another example of an artist illustrating *The Seasons* at this time: Morris, *Thomas Hearne*, 64–66.

41. Allegorical designs by Cipriani (engraved by Bartolozzi), for example, even featured on Chinese porcelain for the English market by *c.*1782. Bartolozzi was still producing sets of seasons in Portugal after leaving England in 1802.

42. For discussions of these illustrations and works by other illustrators of *The Seasons*, see Cohen, *Art of Discrimination*, ch. 5.

43. For example, *January* (owned by Haydn), showing a scene of skating, was evidently the starting point for Hamilton's illustration to *Winter* in 1797.

44. *Oracle*, for 11 Feb. 1794, quoted in Landon, *Haydn in England*, 234. The source of the quotation was identified by Landon in *Late Years*, 93.

45. Barker's cantata was called *Hymn to the Seasons*: Johnson, *Music and Society in Lowland Scotland*, 56.

46. According to a later source, repeating an account stemming from Haydn's London years, Haydn asked his friend, the violinist and composer F.H. Barthelemon, 'I wish to write something which will make my name last in the world. What do you advise me?' Barthelemon apparently replied that he should start at the beginning of the Bible, and this was subsequently understood as 'the first suggestion for *The Creation*'. The anecdote was given to the father of

C.H. Purday (d. 1885), who gave it to Grove, who in turn passed it on to Pohl: translation quoted from Landon, *"The Creation" and "The Seasons"*, 7.

47. For near-contemporary evidence (probably misinformed) that Haydn was ignorant of works by major eighteenth-century writers on aesthetics, see Landon, *Late Years*, 25.

48. *AMZ*, 1 (16 Jan. 1799), col. 255.

49. Mörner, 'Haydniana', 24: translation quoted from Landon, *Years of 'The Creation'*, 251.

50. Dies, visit of 9 May 1805 (p. 43).

51. According to Haydn (reported by Dies) 'because of obscene comments in the text'.

52. 'Sehn wir das erste Paar geführt von deinen Tönen': Griesinger, 68.

53. *AMZ*, 3 (21 Jan. 1801), col. 292. According to Dies this review was written by Zelter.

54. Ibid., cols 293–94.

55. *AMZ*, 4 (10 Mar. 1802), col. 389. This review is by Zelter.

56. Carpani, 205. The review (by Zelter) appeared in *AMZ*, 6 (2 May 1804), cols 515–16.

57. 'Die Einleitung stellt den Übergang vom Winter zum Frühling vor.'

58. *AMZ*, 6 (2 May 1804), col. 519.

59. Ibid., col. 520.

60. Ibid., col. 525.

61. Carpani, 205.

62. *The Morning Herald*, 1 Apr. 1800.

63. *Zeitung für die elegante Welt* for 22 Dec. 1801: quoted from Landon, *Years of 'The Creation'*, 600.

64. *Zeitung für die elegante Welt* for 26 Apr. 1801.

65. *Journal des Luxus und der Moden*, 16 (1801), 414; Pohl, *Joseph Haydn*, iii, 371–72.

66. *Zeitung für die elegante Welt*, 1 (1801), 1051: quoted in Landon, *Late Years*, 185.

67. *Zeitung für die elegante Welt* for 31 Dec. 1801: Pohl, *Joseph Haydn*, iii, 365–67.

68. *Allgemeine Theorie der schönen Künsten*, 2nd edn (1792), ii, 357, translated in Baker and Christensen, *Aesthetics and the Art of Musical Composition*, 90–91. The oratorio mentioned is *Israel in Egypt* (1739).

69. Quotations from Johann Jakob Engel's 'On Painting in Music' are taken from the translation by Strunk, in *Source Readings*, ed. Treitler, 954–65; 956.

70. Ibid., 955

71. Ibid., 955–56.

72. Ibid., 955.

73. The same passage in Benda's *Ariadne* also features a musical representation of a sunrise, another 'painting' introduced into *The Creation*.

74. Heinrich Christoph Koch, *Musikalisches Lexikon* (Frankfurt am Main, 1802), 924.

75. *Mémoires*, iii, 244.

76. *Kalligone* (Weimar, 1800), translation from le Huray and Day, *Music and Aesthetics*, 254.

77. Runge, *Hinterlassene Schriften*, i (Hamburg, 1840), 168.

78. Letter of 6 Apr. 1803: *Hinterlassene Schriften*, i, 42, translated in Bisanz, *German Romanticism*, 74.

79. Vienna, Kunsthistorisches Museum: P.T.A. Swillens, *Johannes Vermeer:*

Painter of Delft, 1632–1675 (Utrecht, 1950), 99–102; Svetlana Alpers, 'In Detail: Vermeer and the *Art of Painting', Portfolio*, 4 (Mar./Apr. 1982), 88–92; D. Arasse, *Faith in Painting* (Princeton, 1994); Arthur K. Wheelock, *Vermeer and the Art of Painting* (New Haven, 1995), esp. 129–39. The provenance of this painting is discussed in A. Blankert's *Vermeer of Delft* (Oxford, 1978), 163–64: according to notes by Count Czernin, who acquired the painting in 1813, it was purchased from the estate of Gottfried van Swieten, via a saddlemaker.

80. For Lebrun's role in promoting Vermeer, see Haskell, *Rediscoveries in Art*, 32–38; cf. 145–50. For a full view of the history of Vermeer's reputation, see Ben Broos, ' "Un celebre Peijntre nommé Verme[e]r"', in *Johannes Vermeer*, exh. cat., National Gallery of Art, Washington, ed. Arthur K. Wheelock (New Haven, 1995), 47–66.

81. J.A. Welu, 'The Map in Vermeer's *Art of Painting', Imago Mundi*, 30 (1978), 9–30.

82. Diary entry for 14 June 1782, described in detail in Landon, *Mozart: The Golden Years*, 241, n. 9.

83. For a full account of this, see Buchowiecki, *Der Barockbau der ehemaligen Hofbibliothek in Wien*, 38–39.

84. Some pictorial effects in *Acis and Galatea* and *Alexander's Feast* were condemned by Avison, in *An Essay on Musical Expression* (1753).

85. Translation quoted from Landon, *"The Creation" and "The Seasons"*, 84.

86. Ibid.

87. Ibid., 85.

88. Ibid., 192.

89. Ibid., 193.

90. Mêchel's catalogue (the *Catalogue de la galerie impériale et royale de Vienne*) was published in 1784. Landon (*"The Creation" and "The Seasons"*, 193) suggests that van Swieten may have influenced the treatment of the ball scene in Mozart and Da Ponte's *Don Giovanni* (1787), in which three separate orchestras perform different dances simultaneously (involving many cross-rhythms and contrasting textures), corresponding with separate activities on stage. Both Mozart (who knew van Swieten well) and Da Ponte may, however, have also been influenced by the exposure of Bruegel's paintings given by de Mêchel. The confused picture of a Viennese ballroom scene, with its clumsy participants trying to perform different dances at the same time, described by Joseph Richer in 1795, may also owe much to the same pictorial source. For this, and its possible relation to the episode in *Don Giovanni* (as conceived by Mozart and Da Ponte), see 'An Iconography of the Dances in the Ballroom Scene of *Don Giovanni*', in Heartz, *Mozart's Operas*, 179–93.

91. For an account of the preliminary designs for the Titian monument and its relationship to the monument prepared for Vienna, see Licht, *Canova*, 65–72. For Canova's bozzetti, see E. Bassi, *Il Gipsoteca di Possagno* (Venice, 1957), 93–99, nos 69–74.

92. First, there were the early deaths of two emperors in quick succession, both brothers of Christine, in the early 1790s. Then, although Austria had temporarily made peace with France, nobody doubted that the threat from Napoleon would return. French forces eventually entered Vienna only a matter of days after the Christine monument was unveiled in 1805. The war with France was, of course, a consequence of the French Revolution. The French initiated the conflict in 1792 by occupying the Austrian Netherlands (modern-day Belgium), which had

a direct impact on Albert and Christine, who had been governors of the province and were forced to flee. The following year the French guillotined their King and Queen. Marie-Antoinette was Christine's sister. The murder of an Austrian princess naturally built increasing resentment against the French in Vienna, soon to be compounded by a French-inspired uprising in southern Italy, which temporarily forced into exile the King of Naples and his wife, another of Christine's sisters.

93. 'Albert to his excellent wife'. Canova's original intentions concerning the inscription are shown on a drawing of its projected appearance which he sent to Albert after returning to Rome in the autumn of 1798: Veronika Birke and Janine Kertész, *Die italienischen Zeichnungen der Albertina*, iv (Vienna, 1997), 2055–56.

94. In Donner's *Apotheosis of Emperor Charles VI* (Vienna, Barockmuseum) of 1734, for example, an angel is depicted holding a snake biting its own tail above the Emperor's head.

95. Krasa, 'Antonio Canovas Denkmal', 67–69, pl. 22.

96. Edinburgh, National Galleries of Scotland: *Antonio Canova: The Three Graces*, exh. cat., National Galleries of Scotland (Edinburgh, 1995), 92, no. 21.

97. Hugh Honour, 'Canova's Studio Practice, 1: The Early Years', *Burlington Magazine*, 114 (1972), 156.

98. Bassi, *Gipsoteca di Possagno*, 99–103, no. 75.

99. Translated from the original text quoted in Mario Praz and Giuseppe Pavanello, *L'opera completa del Canova* (Milan, 1976), 108.

100. For an example of this iconography representing Sloth, see 'The Bedford Hours' (British Library, Add. MS 18850; made in Paris, c.1420), in which a figure labelled 'Peresse' (Sloth) is shown as an elderly man, semi-clad, moving forward with a staff. This is part of a series of representations of the deadly sins.

101. For an eighteenth-century illustration of this story, see Joseph Wright of Derby's *The Old Man and Death* (1774; Hartford, Wadsworth Atheneum): Robert Rosenblum, 'Sources of Two Paintings by Joseph Wright of Derby', *Journal of the Warburg and Courtauld Institutes*, 25 (1962), 135–36.

102. The best-known painted example is the one by J.-L. David (1781). This story was widely illustrated in the sixteenth and seventeenth centuries. It returned to popularity after Marmontel published a new version of it: Albert Boime, 'Marmontel's *Bélisaire* and the Pre-Revolutionary Progressivism of David', *Art History*, 3 (1980), 82–98.

103. Canova certainly knew Bernini's statue of Longinus in St Peter's in Rome and the associated legend.

104. There are certainly earlier tombs which show interest in motion; but in these, the sense of movement is implied rather than explicit, and such examples are most unlikely to have been known to Canova. One example is the tomb of Philip the Bold, Duke of Burgundy (d. 1404) designed by Claus Sluter at Dijon, which was much imitated in the fifteenth century. The four sides of the tomb depict a complete funeral cortège. For a discussion of this, see Kathleen Morand, *Claus Sluter, Artist at the Court of Burgundy* (London, 1991), 350–69.

105. It is actually a fiction, being merely a blackened surface.

106. The date Haydn and van Swieten started work on *The Seasons* is undocumented. However, early sources indicate that the project took longer than *The Creation*, on which Haydn was working throughout most of 1796, all of 1797 and the first months of 1798. A report dated 24 Mar. 1799 (published in *AMZ*, Apr. 1799, col. 446) indicates that Haydn was then known to have been working on *The*

Seasons, and that 'Spring' had already been completed. Considering that the first performances of *The Seasons* took place in the spring of 1801, and taking into consideration that the work is longer than *The Creation*, it seems very likely that the collaborators were already engaged on the project by the summer of 1798, within months of the first hugely successful performances of *The Creation*.

107. It lies beyond the scope of this book to discuss this point in any detail. But works representing different kinds of motion, like Turner's depiction of a moving train, or Wagner's orchestral interludes in *The Ring*, conveying a sense of movement from one place to another, may be mentioned to indicate examples of how this captivated the imagination of European artists in the nineteenth century. It may be argued that one outcome of this obsession was the development of motion pictures by the end of the nineteenth century.

108. The account is by the Swedish diplomat F.S. Silverstolpe: Mörner, 'Haydiniana', 28. In London, Burney recorded a similar reaction: 'When dissonance was tuned, when order was established, and God said "Let there be light! – and there was light" ... the composer's meaning was felt by the whole audience, who instantly broke in upon the performers with rapturous applause before the musical period was closed.' Lonsdale, *Dr Charles Burney*, 453. At the performance of *The Creation* attended by Haydn in 1808, the audience still broke into applause at the moment depicting the creation of light, even though this was a decade after the first performances.

109. Griesinger, 89.

110. *AMZ*, 3 (21 Jan. 1801), col. 292.

111. The Kapellmeister at Frankfurt, C.W. Ferdinand (1787–1848) is known to have favoured this effect.

112. Silverstolpe: Mörner, 'Haydiniana', 24.

113. In the *Allgemeine Theorie der schönen Künste* (2nd edn, 1792), Sulzer quotes the line 'And God said: Let there be light; and there was light' in a section treating the Sublime. In setting these very words at the beginning of *The Creation*, Sulzer might well have prompted Haydn (and van Swieten) to consult Burke's treatise on the Sublime for ideas on how to inspire awe. Burke's book, of course, was already in Haydn's library.

114. *Philosophical Enquiry*, ed. Boulton, 83, 80. For a fuller discussion of these particular passages in relation to *The Creation*, see Horn, 'FIAT LUX', 70–71.

115. *Philosophical Enquiry*, ed. Boulton, 80.

116. Thomas Paine, *Rights of Man*, intro. Eric Foner (Harmondsworth, 1984), 159.

117. William B. O'Neal, *Jefferson's Buildings at the University of Virginia: The Rotunda* (Charlottesville, Va., 1960); Buford Pickens, 'Mr Jefferson as Revolutionary Architect', *Journal of the Society of Architectural Historians*, 24 (1975), 259–79.

118. 'To thee, O Sun, Soul of the Universe': Novello, 167. The cantata was never finished by Mozart, and was actually completed by Stadler himself.

119. The engraving is signed by Pierre-Philippe Choffard. It acknowledges the debt to Raphael below the picture on the left side. For a reproduction, see Somfai, *Joseph Haydn*, fig. 312.

120. The fresco is generally considered the work of Penni, or another of Raphael's assistants in Rome. For the popularity of works from Raphael's school in France in the late eighteenth century, see Rosenberg, *Raphael and France*, ch. 8.

121. *The Seasons*, no. 11.

122. *The Seasons*, no. 32.

123. *Verses on the Arrival of Haydn in England* [by Charles Burney], published as a pamphlet in 1791; *The Importation of Haydn; or The Commerce of the Arts*, published in the *European Magazine* in March 1791. Both poems are reprinted in Landon, *Haydn in England*, 32–35, 55–56.

124. Burney was certainly very proud to occupy the former residence of such a distinguished scientist. Shortly after moving into the house, in 1774, he wrote in correspondence that 'I can throw out no temptation so great to an astronomer perhaps as telling you that I now inhabit the House where Sr Is. Newton long lived, & where he remained till within a few Days of his Death. His Observatory on the Top of the House is a conspicuous Object in Leicester fields': *Letters of Dr Charles Burney*, ed. Ribeiro, 180.

125. *Briefe*, 486. For Burney's friendship with Herschel, see Lonsdale, *Dr Charles Burney*, 80–83, 331, 348, 381–406.

126. The opera was based on a libretto by Goldoni, also set by Paisiello, Galuppi, Gassmann and Piccinni.

127. Advertised in the *True Briton* for 18 June 1795; quoted in Landon, *Haydn in England*, 314. The programme included an 'Overture' and a 'Sinfonia' by Haydn, among several other items. There were also 'readings' in Italian, French and English.

128. For example, Count Zinzendorf, a great chronicler of musical activities in Vienna, noted in his diary (4 Apr. 1796) how he had read in a Berlin journal about the probability of a central solar system, commenting 'greatness of God, infinite smallness of Man'. Haydn subsequently acquired a manual on popular astronomy published in 1804: Hörwarthner, no. 90.

129. See Walters, 'Conversation Pieces', esp. 136–40.

130. Appendix, item 55, discussed in Ch. 6.

131. Henry Baker, *The Microscope Made Easy*, quoted in Walters, 'Conversation Pieces', 141.

132. From a description of a 'solar' microscope by the instrument-maker George Adams: quoted in Walters, 'Conversation Pieces', 141.

133. Letter from Richard French to Horace Walpole dated 14 Feb. 1790: Walpole, *Correspondence*, ed. Lewis, xlii, 267–68.

134. Letter of 14 May 1792: *Correspondence*, xiv, 41, 110; cf. xv, 328–29.

135. *The Botanic Garden*, Part 2 (*Loves of the Plants*), Canto III. Darwin was evidently very taken with the notion of a relationship between music and painting. The same arguments appear in a note entitled 'Melody of Colours', appended to his poem *The Temple of Nature* (London, 1803), 88–89.

136. Dawson (ed.), *The Banks Letters*, 251–52.

137. Haydn may have been informed how Handel had collected plants to satisfy the botanical interests of Telemann. He certainly would have pondered the significance of Grétry's suggestion that he was like a botanist, which, though intended as a comment on his music, had some actual bearing since Haydn owned at least two books on common plants, their properties and cultivation: Hörwarthner, nos 20 and 28.

138. There is a letter from Haydn's publisher in Edinburgh, George Thomson, to Anne Hunter, in which Thomson regrets that Haydn had not 'been directed by you [Anne Hunter] about the words for *The Creation*. It is lamentable to see such divine music joined with such miserable broken English.' Hadden, *George Thomson*, 288. A clear indication of Haydn's respect for Anne Hunter is his setting of the words she sent him at the time of his final departure from London: 'O Tuneful Voice'.

139. *Briefe*, 484.
140. Dies, 125–26.
141. For a description of the museum, written when Haydn was still in London, see Foot, *Life of John Hunter*, 241–42, 261–70. According to Foot, 'the lustre of [the museum] ... captivated the attention of every true philosopher, and dazzled the eyes, and excited wonder in the minds of the uninformed vulgar'.
142. Lever's Holophusikon was originally displayed in Leicester House, but by the time Haydn was in London it had been sold and moved to a site near Blackfriars. After Hunter's death in 1793, the future of his collections remained uncertain until 1799, when they were acquired for the nation for £15,000 and given to the Royal College of Physicians.
143. Fiske, *English Theatre Music*, 432. The opera was Michael Arne's *The Choice of Harlequin* (1781).
144. For Schiller, see *Schillers Briefwechsel mit Ch. G. Körner: Von 1784 bis zum Tode Schillers*, ed. Karl Goedeke, 3rd edn, 4 parts in 2 vols (Leipzig, 1878), ii, 363, 365.
145. The *Musurgia universalis*, first published in 1650. Haydn owned a German translation of Kircher's related work on acoustics, the *Phonurgia nova, sive Coniugium mechanico-physicum artis et naturae* (1673), first published in 1684, which elaborates this idea: Landon, *Later Years*, 403, no. 597.
146. *The Seasons*, no. 8.
147. *The Seasons*, no. 10.
148. The cock is in *The Seasons*, no. 9; the doves, the nightingale and the lion are in *The Creation*, nos 15 and 21. For a discussion of how Haydn composed the lion's roar, see Temperley, *The Creation*, 68,
149. *The Creation*, no. 15. Measures 1–13 and 27–40 suggest a view up close; measures 14–26 (including material later used for the nightingale) suggest the idea of soaring; and measures 41–47 convey the distant picture with the flight towards the sun.
150. Jackson, *Bird Painting*, 104–5.
151. Bewick claimed that *The History of Quadrupeds* was 'intended as A *complete* Display of that Part of Animated Nature ...'. Although it was published in Newcastle, it was distributed in London (as indicated on the title-page). Proposals for a subscription were advertised in 1788.
152. Examples include: Moses Harris's *The Natural History of Insects* (first published in 1766); Oliver Goldsmith's *History of the Earth and Animated Nature* (1774); John Latham's *The General Synopsis of Birds* (2 vols, 1789, 1795); William Lewin's *The Birds of Great Britain* (7 vols, 1789–95); James Hutton's *Theory of the Earth* (Edinburgh, 1785); and Hunter's *Observations on Certain Parts of Animal Oeconomy* (London, 1786; 2nd edn, 1792).
153. Hunter had a special arrangement with the Tower to have the animals after they had died. Haydn's visit is reported only by Dies, who implies that it took place during the composer's second visit, by which time Hunter was dead. But this may have been a misunderstanding.
154. Dies, 157.
155. Stubbs's researches into the tiger were more thorough than those of any other artist of the time. As well as producing engravings of tigers (one dated 1788), Stubbs also began in about 1795 a stunning series of anatomical studies of the tiger for his projected *A Comparative Anatomical Exposition of the Human Body with that of a Tiger and a Common Fowl*. The project was still incomplete at the time of his death in 1806.

156. Hunter commissioned Stubbs to paint a rhinoceros, a yak and a baboon, as well as owning other works by this artist. One is known from the sale of Hunter's extensive collection of paintings at Christie's on 29 Jan. 1794. Banks's commissions to Stubbs included a painting of a kangaroo and drawings of lemurs.

157. Windsor Castle, Royal Collection: Basil Taylor, *Stubbs*, 2nd edn (London, 1975), pl. 126.

158. For examples, see Egerton, *George Stubbs*, nos 60, 66, 67. For evidence of Hunter's ownership of such a painting (which Haydn may have seen), see Royal College of Surgeons of England, *Letters from the Past: From John Hunter to Edward Jenner* (London, 1976), 21.

159. This venture was intended to comprise a series of portraits of famous horses, which were to be engraved and sold by subscription, and illustrate a 'Review of the Turf' since 1750. The project was not successful. Haydn's interest in the turf is indicated from his long description of a race meeting at Ascot in June 1792: *Briefe*, 487–89.

160. *The Seasons*, no. 28: Heartz, 'The Hunting Chorus'. The article was by Charles Georges Le Roy (d. 1789).

161. There were six paintings, dating from *c*.1565. One from the series is lost. *Stormy Day*, *Return of the Herd* and *Hunters in the Snow* have been in Vienna since at least the mid-seventeenth century (now Kunsthistorisches Museum). The *Corn Harvest* (New York, Metropolitan Museum) remained in Vienna until taken away by French forces in 1809. In the nineteenth century, the *Hay Harvest* (Prague) found its way into the collection of Princess Leopoldine Grassalkowitsch, who was born into the family Haydn served from 1761 until the end of his life.

162. Brusatti et al., *Zauberföne*, 558, cat. IX/14; also reproduced in Landon, *Haydn: A Documentary Study*, fig. 80.

163. According to the engraving, the likenesses were taken 'from Miniature Cameos by H. de Janvray'. The likeness of Haydn in the cameo reproduced in Loutherbourg's design was probably derived from Hardy's portrait of the composer painted in 1791.

164. See Pointon, *Hanging the Head*, 78, fig. 95.

165. Appendix, item 43: '1. Blatt mit den berühmtesten Compositeurs von verschiedenen Meistern'. The identification of this item with Loutherbourg's print is far from certain.

166. Henry Angelo, in his *Reminiscences* (1828–30), gives an account of how these scenes 'astonished the audience' and how they were achieved.

167. See Allen, 'Wonders of Derbyshire', 54–66.

168. The *London Packet*, for 8–11 Jan. 1779.

169. The *Daily Universal Register*, quoted in Allen, 'De Loutherbourg and Captain Cook', 209.

170. *European Magazine*, 1 (1782), 182. The first account of Haydn to appear in Britain was published in the same journal two years later.

171. *Morning Herald*, 1 Mar. 1781.

172. *The Creation*, no. 12; *The Seasons*, no. 11.

173. *The Creation*, no. 12, bars 26–36.

174. *The Seasons*, nos 10, 12, 17, 18 (end).

175. W.H. Pine [Ephraim Hardcastle], *Wine and Walnuts*, 1 (1823), 302–3. Pine apparently saw the scene in 1786.

176.   Affrighted fled hell's spirits black in throngs;
        down they sink in the deep of abyss to endless night.
        Despairing cursing rage
        attends their rapid fall.
        A new created world
        springs up at God's command.
        (*The Creation*, no. 2, quoted in van Swieten's English version.)

177.   British Museum: Rosenfeld, 'The *Eidophusikon* Illustrated'. Judging from the costumes, the watercolour was probably made about 1786.

178.   Mrs Arne also sang two songs by J.C. Bach.

179.   Loutherbourg's best-known painting of an avalanche is the one dated 1803 in the Tate Gallery, London: Joppien, *Loutherbourg*, no. 46. However, there were certainly earlier examples.

180.   *The Seasons*, no. 32.

181.   *The Seasons*, no. 17. Loutherbourg's painting is lost.

182.   Gilpin, *Observations*, 77–78.

183.   Science Museum, London: Stephen Daniels, 'Loutherbourg's Chemical Theatre: *Coalbrookdale by Night*', in Barrell (ed.), *Painting and the Politics of Culture*, 195–230.

184.   Joppien, *Loutherbourg*, no. 49.

185.   *Briefe*, 489.

186.   For the concept of industry in Thomson's *Seasons*, see Hagstrum, *Sister Arts*, 246.

187.   For Hogarth, see Paulson, *Emblem and Expression*, Ch. 58. For Morland, see Winter, *George Morland*, 39–51, 170, 225. Industry also enjoyed a place in visual culture in eighteenth-century Britain as a personification: for one example, see Roworth (ed.), *Angelica Kauffman*, 182. Industry is particularly stressed in essays by David Hume. See, for examples: *A Treatise of Human Nature*, ed. L.A. Selby-Bigge and P.H. Niddrich (Oxford, 1978), 587 (written in 1739–40); and 'Of Refinement in the Arts', in *Essays Moral, Political and Literary*, ed. Eugene F. Miller (Indianapolis, 1987), 271 (first published in 1752).

188.   *The Seasons*, no. 20.

189.   Griesinger, 70. Both Griesinger and Dies emphasize Haydn's love of industry: Griesinger, 116; Dies, 207–8. Dies stresses industry as one of van Swieten's merits also (p. 160). Even during composition of his last completed work, the *Harmoniemesse*, Haydn was still concerned with how his industry was perceived: letter of 14 June 1802 (*Briefe*, 404).

190.   Watt wrote to his partner, Boulton: 'What have Dukes, Lords and Ladies to do with masquerading in a flour mill?' Quoted in George, *England in Transition*, 108.

191.   William Paley, *Reasons for Contentment Addressed to the Labouring Part of the British Public*, quoted in Barrell, *Dark Side of the Landscape*.

192.   As related to Dies on 15 Apr. 1805 (p. 16).

193.   Appendix, item 1.

194.   *Thayer's Life of Beethoven*, ed. Forbes, 1046.

195.   See Solomon, 'Some Romantic Images in Beethoven', 274–75.

196.   Quoted in Cohen (ed.), *Studies in Eighteenth-Century British Art and Aesthetics*, 6.

197.   Letter of 30 July 1802: *Briefe*, 406. In his choice of the word *Hütte*, Haydn was probably being self-deprecating about his home in Vienna (he is describing a

visit by his Prince). In no sense could his house be described as a 'hut' or 'hovel', though Haydn himself might have considered it comparable to a 'cottage' designed by Sir John Soane.

198. Erffa and Staley, *Benjamin West*, 409–13, nos 435–39. The Queen's Lodge was destroyed in 1823. Only four of West's preparatory designs and some drawings are known to survive.

199. *Windsor Guide* (Windsor, 1792), 98–99, quoted in Erffa and Staley, *Benjamin West*, 410.

200. Bartolozzi made engravings of some of the designs, which Haydn may also have known. Mrs Papendiek says that 'Haydn's pupil', the violinist Bridgetower, performed at the Queen's Lodge during the period of Haydn's first English visit. Considering the intimacy Haydn enjoyed with the Queen during his second visit, and her invitation for him to stay permanently at Windsor, there is every reason to assume Haydn himself had been to the Queen's Lodge and viewed for himself West's scheme.

201. *Briefe*, 486.

202. See H. Hawley, *Neo-Classicism: Style and Motif*, exh. cat., Cleveland Museum of Art (Cleveland, Ohio, 1964), no. 77.

203. Isidore Rose-de Viejo, 'Goya's Allegories and the Sphinxes: "Commerce", "Agriculture", "Industry" and "Science" *in situ*', *Burlington Magazine*, 126 (1984), 34–39.

204. Kennedy, *Cultural History of the French Revolution*, 349–50.

205. Charles Avison, *An Essay on Musical Expression* (1753), quoted in Fubini, *Music and Culture*, 313.

206. *The Seasons*, no. 4.

207. The marking *Allegretto* in the oratorio replaces the marking *Andante* in the Symphony.

208. Wilder, *English Sporting Prints*, pl. 64.

209. Examples include the farmer ploughing (no. 4), the gentry hunting (no. 26) and the wanderer lost in the snow (no. 32).

Notes to Chapter 8

1. In a report on a performance of *The Seasons* on 25 April 1801 in the *Zeitung für die elegante Welt*, i (1801), 428: quoted in Landon, *Late Years*, 45.

2. One such report appeared in the *Pressburger Zeitung* for 27 September 1801: Marianne Pandi and Fritz Schmidt, 'Music in Haydn's and Beethoven's Time Reported in the *Pressburger Zeitung*', *Haydn Yearbook*, viii (1971), 281. In the *Zeitung für die elegante Welt* for 22 December 1801, a review of performance of *The Creation* in Copenhagen, mentioned *The Last Judgement* as though it had already appeared, though the editor denied this in a footnote: Landon, *Creation*, 601.

3. Carpani indicates that Swieten conceived an oratorio for Haydn related to the subject of the Last Judgement: *Le Haydine*, 216. Griesinger, in correspondence, also implies that Swieten had such a work in mind: Olleson, 'Griesinger's Correspondence', 26. Swieten died in 1803, by which date his plans seem to have come to nothing.

4. Olleson, 'Griesinger's Correspondence', 37.

5. 'Reich an Bildern': Olleson, 'Griesinger's Correspondence', 39.

6. Haydn perhaps was influenced in this choice of subject-matter by Salieri's

setting of a text dealing with this theme (which seems to have received little attention). Schickaneder also had a (musical ?) play in his repertory called *Das letzte Gericht*. I have been unable to discover its actual content.

7. The general tone of criticism of making too much use of 'painting' is summed up by Dies: *BNvJH*, 160–61.

8. Thomas Hastings, *Dissertation on Musical Taste*, 2nd ed. (New York, 1853), 238; quoted in Temperley, *Creation*, 42.

9. From a letter of 8 February 1859: translation from Temperley, *Creation*, 43.

10. Berlioz, 'L'Imitation en musique', in *Gazette musicale de Paris* , translated by Jacques Barzun in *The Pleasures of Music* (London, 1952), 211.

11. Barzun , *Pleasures of Music*, 217.

12. In Berlioz's *Soirées de l'orchestre*, 2nd ed. (Paris, 1854), 265: Jean Seznec, *John Martin en France* (London, 1964), 33. Martin's mezzotint was published in 1824. Berlioz calls the work a painting. Presumably because he assumed that the print was taken from a large-scale painting. No such work is known to have been executed: Thomas Balston, *John Martin* (London, 1947), 207.

13. Heinrich Heine, letter to the *Gazette dÁugsburg* of 25 April 1844, republished in *Lutèce* (Paris, 1863), 387–88: Seznec, *John Martin en France*, 34. For further discussion of this, see Lockspeiser, *Music and Painting*, 20–29.

14. Letter of 27 September 1802: *Letters of Anna Seward: Written between the Years 1784 and 1807*, 6 vols, ed. Archibald Constable (Edinburgh, 1811), vi, 46–47.

15. Jenkins, *Last Gleanings*, p. 30.

16. Several celebrated composers of the generation born *c.* 1810 were capable of treating Haydn's compositions in a matter-of-fact kind of way in their formal writings, but expressed unexpected appreciation on hearing a Haydn composition which for a time had been passed over. Wagner is an example of a composer whose admiration for Haydn increased the more he heard, as reported in the diaries of Cosima Wagner: *Cosima Wagner's Diaries*, ed. Martin Gregor-Dellin and Dietrich Mach, trans. Geoffrey Skelton, 2 vols (London, 1978), *passim*.

17. *The Journal of Eugène Delacroix*, ed. Hubert Wellington, trans. Lucy Norton, 2nd ed. (Oxford, 1980), 66. Delacroix went on to report Chopin as saying that Mozart did not require experience.

18. *Journal of Eugène Delacroix*, ed. Wellington, 270.

19. For a full analysis of common perceptions of Haydn and his music in the nineteenth century, see Botstein, 'The Consequences of Presumed Innocence: The Nineteenth-Century Reception of Joseph Haydn', in *Haydn Studies*, ed. Sutcliffe, 1–34

20. Vasari, *La Vita di Michelangelo*, 2nd ed. (1568): translation from Vasari, *Lives of the Artists. A Selection*, trans. George Bull (London, 1993), iii, 169, 172. For the early reception of Michelangelo's painting, see Bernardine Barnes, *Michelangelo's Last Judgement: The Renaissance Response* (Berkelely, Cal., 1998).

21. According to one version of the origin of *The Creation*, Haydn was reported to have said to Barthelemon, one of his colleagues in London ' "I wish to write something which will make my name last in the world. What would you advise me to do?" Barthelemon took up a Bible which was lying near and said, "There is the book: begin at the beginning" – and this was the first suggestion of *The Creation*.' (Quoted in Landon, *Complete Authentic Sources*, 7.) By implication,

if the beginning of the Bible inspired Haydn's first attempt to emulate Handelian oratorio, the end of the Bible might have suggested itself at the same time, a notion which perhaps remained with Haydn long after he returned from England. Olleson ('Origin and Libretto', 152) points out that the anecdote (at least as conveyed in one form) has 'an authentic flavour'.

22. Reynolds, *Discourses on Art*, ed. Wark, 246. The eighteenth-century origins of Victorian interest in England in Michelangelo is explored in Lene Østermark-Johansen, *Sweetness and Strength. The Image of Michelangelo in Victorian Britain* (London, 1998).

23. For an overview of the importance of the Last Judgement theme in the work of artists active in London, see Paley, *Apocalyptic Sublime*, 93–100. For West's interest in Michelangelo's *Last Judgement*, see Farington, *Diaries*, ed. Garlick and Macintyre, vi, 2246. Although he later changed his mind, Fuseli, writing in 1801 (in his third lecture delivered to the Royal Academy as professor) found the *Last Judgement* not only Michelangelo's masterpiece, but the highpoint of Western art. One of the starting-points for Fuseli's conviction at this stage was Reynolds's final *Discourse*, which he reviewed when Haydn was in England (*Analytical Review*, May 1791, 5). For Metz's clear interest in Michelangelo's *Last Judgement* when he was in London, see Pointon, *Milton and English Art*, 74–75, fig. 64.

24. *La Sistina riprodotta. Gli Affreschi di Michelangelo dalle Stampe del Cinquecento alle Campagne fotograiche Anderson*, ed. Alinda Moltedo, exh cat. (Rome, 1991), 179–87, no. 38.

25. For the use of Metz's prints in furthering knowledge of Michelangelo in northern Europe, see Griffiths and Carey, *German Printmaking*, 31. Among artists drawn to Michelangelo's *Last Judgement* in the early nineteenth century were Blake and Runge. Stendhal gave the work serious consideration in his *Histoire de la Peinture en Italie*, first conceived in 1811.

26. For Runge's correspondence concerning Michelangelo's *Last Judgement*, see *A Documentary History of Art*, iii, *From the Classicists to the Impressionists: Art and Architecture in the Nineteenth Century*, ed. Elizabeth Gilmore Holt (New York, 1966), 79 (letter of 1 December, 1802). For *Michel-Ange* (with music by Nicolo Isouard), see Felix Clément and Pierre Larousse, *Dictionnaire des Opéras* (Paris, 1905), 2, 738. Other German artists influenced by Michelangelo's *Last Judgement* at this time include Joseph Anton Koch (his early illustration to Dante's Inferno of about 1802–03, Kunstmuseum, Düsseldorf). Special interest in the *Last Judgement* seems to have begun in the mid-1790s, in the work of Asmus Jakob Carstens (d. 1798): see *Goethe und die Kunst*, ed. Schulze, 346, no. 219. A late set of drawings by Carstens were engraved by Koch in Rome in 1799, so the source of Koch's practical interest in Michelangelo's painting seems clear.

27. *Le Haydine*, 126, 206.

28. Stendhal, *Lives of Haydn, Mozart & Metastasio*, trans. Coe, 136.

29. This has been fully discussed in Ch. II.

30. Stendhal, *Lives of Haydn, Mozart & Metastasio*, trans. Coe, 74. The passage in question, derived from Carpani, is taken from a discussion of the relationship of opera to history painting.

31. See the discussion in Ch. V.

32. 'Libretti based upon the Holy Scriptures may have their attraction for a Bible-reading nation such as the English, or even in Italy, where they are sanctified by a tradition of miraculous aesthetic beauty, and by memories of Raphael,

Michelangelo and Correggio': Stendhal, *The Life of Rossini*, rev. ed., trans. Richard N. Coe (London, 1985) 318–19.

33. In the church of San Pietro in Vincoli in Rome.

34. *Life of Rossini*, trans. Coe, 320.

35. Rossini was certainly familiar with Haydn's late oratorios. He conducted both *The Creation* and *The Seasons* in 1811: *Life of Rossini*, trans. Coe, 48.

36. Johann Friedrich Reichardt, *Vertraute Briefe* (Amsterdam, 1810), i, 232: translated in Landon, *Late Years*, 409.

37. In *Haude- und Spenerschen Zeitung* for 1811: translated in Thomas Sipe, *Beethoven: Eroica Symphony* (Cambridge, 1998), 78.

38. Quoted from 'Beethoven's *Tagebuch*', in Maynard Solomon, *Beethoven Essays* (Cambridge, 1988), 272, no. 79.

39. *Life of Rossini*, trans. Coe, 53.

40. From a letter to Berlioz, dated 2 October 1839, published in the *Gazette musicale* for 24 October 1839, 417: translation from Franz Liszt, *An Artist's Journey: Lettres d'un bachelier ès musique 1835–1841*, trans. Charles Sutton (Chicago, 1989), 186. For a further example of Beethoven being compared with Michelangelo (and Mozart with Raphael), see Hippolyte Bardebette, *Beethoven: Esquisse musicale*, 1st ed. (Paris, 1859). For a discussion of Bardebette and other references to Beethoven being compared to Michelangelo, see Leo Schade, *Beethoven in France. The Growth of an Idea* (New Haven, 1942), 35.

41. For evidence of ambivalent attitudes to Tintoretto in northern Europe in the nineteenth century, see Haskell, *Rediscoveries in Art* , cf. 11, 17, 178.

42. Liszt, *An Artist's Journey*, trans. Sutton, 187.

43. Liszt, *An Artist's Journey*, trans. Sutton, 187, n. 7.

44. Wagner's view is encapsulated in the following: 'as soon as Beethoven had written his 1st symphony, the whole musical fraternity could do any amount of darning and patching in an effort to produce an absolute man of music, and not a wiry and sturdy man of nature. Haydn and Mozart could and needs must be succeeded by a Beethoven; the tutelary spirit of music required him urgently, and in a flash he was here; but in the field of absolute music, who can aspire to follow Beethoven in the way that he followed Haydn and Mozart? The greatest would not be able to achieve any thing further in that area, simply because the spirit of absolute music no longer needs it ...' Richard Wagner, *Gesammelte Schriften un Dichtungen* (Leipzig, 1907), iii, 100; translation from Klaus Kropfinge, *Wagner and Beethoven. Richard Wagner's Reception of Beethoven*, trans. Peter Palmer (Cambridge, 1991).

45. Raphael Georg Kiesewetter, *History of European-Western Music*, first English edition (London, 1848), 241. For a discussion of Kiesewetter's importance to the history of evolutionary views of music history in the early nineteenth century, see Webster, *Haydn's 'Farewell' Symphony*, 347–51.

46. Thomson certainly espoused the rise and decline view of the Arts. For comment on his comparison of the decline of classical sculpture with the decline of the Roman Empire, see McKillop, 'Background to Thomson's *Liberty*', 62.

47. James Hutton, *Theory of the Earth, with Proofs and Illustrations* (Edinburgh, 1795), ii, 239.

48. William Herschel, 'On Nebulous Stars, Properly so Called', *The Scientific Papers of Sir William Herschel Including early Papers Hitherto Unpublished* (London, 1912), i, 421–22 (originally published in the *Philosophical Transactions* for 1791).

49. Herschel emphasised how his observations, and the very enormity of Creation, only confirmed his sense of the universe having been set in motion through a divine plan: Greene, *Death of Adam*, 33–34.

50. Erasmus Darwin's clearest expression of his own position is found in the following passage, first published in 1794: 'From thus meditating on the great similarity of the structure of the warm-blooded animals, and at the same time of the great changes they undergo both before and after their nativity; and by considering in how minute a proportion of time many of the changes of animals described have been produced; would it be too bold to imagine, that in the great length of time, since the earth began to exist, perhaps millions of ages before the commencement of the history of mankind ... that all warm-blooded animals have arisen from one living filament, which the GREAT FIRST CAUSE endued with animality, with the power of acquiring new parts, attended with new propensities, directed by imitations, sensations, volitions, and associations; and this possessing this faculty of continuing to improve by its own inherent activity, and of delivering down those improvements by generation to its posterity, world without end?' *Zoomania: Or the Laws of Organic Life*, 4th American ed., Philadelphia, 1818, i, 397.

51. Letter of 25 May 1855: Franz Liszt, *Selected Letters*, trans. and ed. Adrian Williams (Oxford, 1998), 370, no. 316. The context of Liszt's remark is criticism of the continuing popularity of the oratorio: 'I went to see Franz, who remarked to me very wittily about [Haydn's] *Creation*: "So they're still presenting this menagerie to an enthusiastic audience!" To understand this witticism, you need to know that in *The Creation* there are numerous portrayals of animals: a lion, a stag, birds, etc. It is like a small musical Buffon.' For Stendhal, see *Lives of Haydn, Mozart & Metastasio*, trans. Coe, 36, 51, 57, 151. It is interesting that, although Stendhal's book on Haydn was largely a plagiarization of Carpani's, his comparisons between Haydn and Buffon were his own insertions, suggesting that an appreciation of Haydn in relation to scientific understanding was an emerging feature of his reputation after the period when Carpani was writing.

52. See A.O. Lovejoy, 'Buffon and the Problem of Species', in Glass, Temkin, and Straus (eds), *Forerunners of Darwin*, 84–113.

53. Buffon, iv (1783), 382.

54. Buffon, *Les Époques de la nature* (Paris, 1780), i. This first appeared as vol. v of the *Suppléments* to the *Histoire naturelle* (1778).

55. In the 1830s one correspondent wrote to Darwin signaling his delight in *The Creation*. Darwin himself wrote to his sister expressing his particular pleasure in one of the choruses in the oratorio, which, he wrote, 'seemed to shake the very walls of the college' where he heard it: *The Correspondence of Charles Darwin*, ed. Frederick H. Burkhardt and Sydney Smith (Cambridge, 1985–): i, 223; ii, 86. The context of these references suggests that *The Creation* was familiar listening in the Darwin family. Charles Darwin was the grandson of Erasmus Darwin.

56. A letter of 1846 refers to Darwin looking forward to hearing 'lots of Beethoven': *Correspondence of Charles Darwin*, ed. Burkhardt and Smith, iii, 338. Darwin's wife (his cousin) was a competent pianist, who had lessons from Chopin. She, among others, seems to have encouraged her husband to take Beethoven seriously.

57. *JHGBA*, 390.

58. In the letter quoted above Haydn originally added the line, 'To tell you the truth,

I am particularly proud of this work', which he subsequently crossed out: *JHGBA*, 391; cf. *CCLN*, 198.

59.   The autograph (BL, Add. MS 35275, ff. 28, 29) is signed by Haydn and dated 6 February 1805, though the signature and date may have been added at the time of the later publication.

60.   *The Parish Register*, 1807, quoted in M.D. George, *England in Transition* (Harmondsworth, 1953), 92–93.

61.   *JHGBA*, 386.

62.   *JHGBA*, 386.

63.   For Haydn's accounts of meetings with Parsons, see *CCLN*, 291, 305. For Parsons' song, see *Mrs Jordan: The Duchess of Drury Lane*, exhib. cat., English Heritage (London, 1995), 80, no. 57 (d).

64.   This information comes from Haydn's reply to Burney's letter: *JHGBA*, 336–37.

65.   Haydn himself attended two pieces 'in Scottish costumes', with music by Samuel Arnold, at the Little Haymarket Theatre on 28 July 1794. He described in his notebook the Scottish costumes in detail, but called the performance 'abominable trash': *JHGBA*, 538.

66.   The Burney family dropped the Mac aware that a Scottish name was no asset in the circles in which they hoped to succeed.

67.   For the full story of Mrs Jordan, see Tomalin, *Mrs Jordan's Profession*.

68.   In one caricature the couple represent 'Debauchery'; another labels them 'A Burning shame and Adulterous disgrace'; yet another shows her on horse-back, leading the royal family to ruin, with Clarence behind, a chamber pot perched on his head. Gillray and other caricaturists made particular use of chamber pots in their cartoons featuring Mrs Jordan since 'Jordan' was a common word for just such a pot. The most shocking and memorable of the images based on this idea is Gillray's 'The Lubber's Hole, alias The Crack'd Jordan' published on 1 November 1791. Mrs Jordan appears as a giant chamber pot with a large open crack down the side, through which the duke scrambles, crying 'Yeo! Yee! Yeo!' in imitation of a sailor's pleasure in singing a sea shanty.

69.   *JHGBA*, 516.

70.   Count von Staremberg, the Habsburg ambassador to the court of St James – a passionate music-lover, who in London held private concerts in which he (a flautist) and his wife (a pianist) participated – owned at least one cartoon featuring Mrs Jordan and the Duke of Clarence: *Symptoms of Cruelty*, by William Dent, satirises Clarence's support for the slave trade by showing the Duke, having discarded his cloths, wearing several instruments of torture, with Mrs Jordan behind him, whip in hand and uttering 'Now do you like it?' On his return to Austria in 1802, Von Starhemberg visited Eisenstadt, where he heard the first performance (7 September) of Haydn's last major composition, the Harmoniemesse, which he noted in his diary as '[A] wonderful mass, excellent new music by the famous Haydn, and conducted by him. ... Nothing is more beautiful nor could be better executed.' The same evening Von Starhemberg proposed a toast to Haydn, on which occasion the composer might well have taken the opportunity to catch up on the latest news from London. It does not seem farfetched to suppose that Haydn asked the Count about Mrs Jordan, and in so doing may have learned about Sheridan's attack on him.

71.   For 'Jordan-mania', see Tomlin, *Mrs Jordan's Profession, passim.*

72.   The Iveagh Bequest, Kenwood House: *Mrs Jordan: The Duchess of Drury Lane*, 30–31, no. 8.

73. For a detailed account of the moving and memorable way Mrs Jordan delivered the lines, as probably seen by Haydn, see Charles Lamb, 'On Some of the Old Actors', published in the *London Magazine* in 1822 and revised the following year: *Lamb as Critic*, ed. Roy Park (London, 1980), 52.
74. *JHGBA*, 486–87.
75. 'This *virtuosa* had been portrayed by the famous Reynolds. . . . La Bilington was represented as St Cecilia, her eyes turned towards heaven, where a choir of angels were shown in the act of singing. Mrs Bilington showed her friend Haydn the portrait and asked him his opinion of it. Our *maestro*, after observing it closely, turned to the *signora*, saying, 'the portrait is a good likeness, but I find a serious flaw in it.' 'What?' (Reynolds was present.) 'The painter', replied Haydn, 'has . . . painted *you listening to the angels*, whereas he should have shown *the angels listening to you*.' La Bilington, delighted with this lush speech, threw her arms around the neck of the kind-hearted critic who had contrived such a gracious observation, and with several kisses, thus rewarded him for the excellence of his judgement.' *Le Haydine*, 230–31. For Reynolds's portrait of Mrs Billington (Beaverbrook Art Gallery, New Brunswick), see *Reynolds*, ed. Penny, 39, fig. 24, 332–3, cat. 157.

Notes to the Appendix

1. The complete document was published (as written in German) by Landon in *Late Years*, 392–403.
2. Haydn's library has been studied and reconstructed by Hörwarthner in 'Joseph Haydns Bibliothek'.
3. *Catalog der hinterbliebenen Joseph Haydnischen Kunstsachen* (Vienna, Wiener Stadt- und Landesarchiv): Schusser et al., *Joseph Haydn*, cat. 62.
4. Österreichische Nationalbibliothek, Musiksammlung, cat. S. M. 4843: Landon, *Late Years*, 390–91.
5. National Széchényi Library.

Bibliography

Abrams, Ann Uhry, *The Valiant Hero: Benjamin West and the Grand Style of History Painting* (Washington, DC, 1985).

Ackerknecht, Erwin H., and Vallois, Henri V., *Franz Joseph Gall, Inventor of Phrenology and his Collection*, Wisconsin Studies in Medical History, 1 (Madison, Wis., 1956).

Ackermann, Peter, 'Struktur, Ausdruck, Programm: Gedanken zu Joseph Haydns Instrumentalmusik über *Die Sieben letzten Worte unseres Erlösers am Kreuze*', in Anke Bingmann et al. (eds), *Studien zur Instrumentalmusik: Lothar Hoffmann-Erbrecht zum 60. Geburtstag*, Frankfurter Beiträge zur Musikwissenschaft, 20 (Tutzing, 1988), 253–60.

Adhémar, Jean, *La Gravure originale au 18ᵉ siècle* (Paris, 1963).

Agawu, V. Kofi, *Playing with Signs: A Semiotic Interpretation of Classic Music* (Princeton, 1991).

Agueda-Villar, Mercedes, *Antonio Rafael Mengs 1728–1779*, exh. cat., Ministerio de Cultura, no. 7 (Madrid, 1980).

Airlie, Mabel Countess of, *In Whig Society, 1775–1818* (London, 1921).

Alberts, Robert C., *Benjamin West: A Biography* (Boston, Mass., 1975).

Albrecht, Theodore, trans. and ed., *Letters to Beethoven and other Correspondence*, 3 vols (Lincoln, Nebr., 1996).

Alexander, David, *Affecting Moments: Prints of English Literature Made in the Age of English Sensibility 1775–1800*, University of York, King's Manor Gallery (1993).

———, *Amateurs and Printmaking in England 1750–1830*, exh. cat., Oxford, Wolfson College (1983).

———, 'Edmund Scott as an Engraver', in *The Scott Family at Home: An Evening in the Victorian Parlour*, exh. cat., Hove Museum and Art Gallery (1988).

———, 'Printmakers and Printsellers in England, 1770–1830', in Cannon-Brookes (ed.), *The Painted Word*, 23–29.

———, *Richard Newton and English Caricature in the 1790s* (Manchester, 1998).

——— and Godfrey, Richard T., *Painters and Engravers: The Reproductive Print from Hogarth to Wilkie* (New Haven, 1980).

Alkon, Paul, and Folkenflik, Robert, *Samuel Johnson: Pictures and Words*, William Andrews Clark Memorial Library, University of California (Los Angeles, 1984).

Allanbrook, Wye Jamison, *Rhythmic Gesture in Mozart: Le nozze di Figaro and Don Giovanni* (Chicago, 1983).

Allard, Joseph C., 'Mechanism, Music, and Painting in 17th Century France', *Journal of Aesthetics and Art Criticism*, 40 (1981–82), 269–79.

Allen, Brian, *Francis Hayman*, Yale Centre for British Art (New Haven, 1987).

———— (ed.), *Towards a Modern Art World* (New Haven, 1995).

Allen, D.E., *The Naturalist in Britain: A Social History* (London, 1975).

Allen, G. Ralph, 'The Wonders of Derbyshire: A Spectacular Eighteenth-Century Travelogue', *Theatre Survey*, 2 (1961), 54–66.

————, 'De Loutherbourg and Captain Cook', *Theatre Review*, 4/3 (1962), 195–211.

Allentuck, Marcia, 'Fuseli and Lavater: Physiognomical Theory and the Enlightenment', *Studies on Voltaire and the Eighteenth Century*, 55 (1967), 89–112.

Almond, Philip C., *Heaven and Hell in Enlightenment England* (Cambridge, 1994).

Alpers, Svetlana, *The Art of Describing: Dutch Art in the Seventeenth Century* (Chicago, 1983).

Altick, Richard D., *Paintings from Books: Art and Literature in Britain 1760–1900* (Columbus, Ohio, 1985).

————, *The Shows of London* (Cambridge, 1978).

Anderson, Patricia, *The Printed Image and the Transformation of Popular Culture 1790–1860* (Oxford, 1994).

Andrews, Malcolm, *The Picturesque: Literary Sources and Documents*, 3 vols (Mountfield, 1994).

————, *The Search for the Picturesque: Landscape Aesthetics and Tourism in Britain 1760–1800* (Aldershot, 1987).

Arblaster, Anthony, *Viva la libertà: Politics in Opera* (London, 1992).

Arnason, H.H., *The Sculptures of Houdon* (London, 1975).

Asfour, Amal, and Williamson, Paul, *Gainsborough's Vision* (Liverpool, 1999).

———— ————, *William Jackson of Exeter (1730–1803)*, exh. cat., Gainsborough's House (Sudbury, 1997).

Ashton, Geoffrey, 'The Boydell Shakespeare Gallery: Before and After', in Cannon-Brookes (ed.), *The Painted Word*, 37–44.

Asleton, Robyn (ed.), *Sarah Siddons and Her Portraitists*, exh. cat., J. Paul Getty Museum (Los Angeles, 1999).

Avison, Charles, *An Essay Concerning Musical Expression*, rev. edn (London, 1753).

Ayling, S., *A Portrait of Sheridan* (London, 1985).

Bach, Carl Philipp Emanuel, *The Letters of C.P.E. Bach*, trans. and ed. Stephen L. Clark (Oxford, 1997).

Bailey, Colin B., 'Conventions of the Eighteenth-Century *Cabinet de tableaux*: Blondel d'Agincourt's *La première idée de la curiosité*', *Art History*, 69 (1987), 431–46.

Baker, Keith M., *Inventing the French Revolution* (Cambridge, 1990).

Baker, Nancy Kovaleff, and Christensen, Thomas (trans. and eds), *Aesthetics and the Art of Musical Composition in the German Enlightenment: Selected Writings of Johann Georg Sulzer and Heinrich Christoph Koch* (Cambridge, 1995).

Banks, C.A., and Turner, J. Rigbie, *Mozart: Prodigy of Nature* (London, 1991).

Banks, Sir Joseph, *Florilegium 1768–1771*, British Museum and Alecto Historical Edition (London, 1987).

Barasch, Moshe, *Modern Theories of Art*, i: *From Winckelmann to Baudelaire* (New York, 1990).

Barbier, Carl Paul, *William Gilpin: His Drawing, Teaching, and Theory of the Picturesque* (Oxford, 1963).

Barker, H., and Chalus, E., *Gender in Eighteenth-Century England: Roles, Representations, and Responsibilities* (London, 1997).

Barker-Benfield, G.J., *The Culture of Sensibility: Sex and Society in Eighteenth-Century Britain* (Chicago, 1994).

Barrell, John, *The Dark Side of the Landscape: The Rural Poor in English Painting 1730–1840* (Cambridge, 1980).

———, *The Idea of Landscape and the Sense of Place* (Cambridge, 1972).

———, 'The Private Comedy of Thomas Rowlandson', *Art History*, 6 (1983), 431–33.

———, *The Political Theory of Painting from Reynolds to Hazlitt: 'The Body of the Public'* (New Haven, 1986).

——— (ed.), *Painting and the Politics of Culture: New Essays on British Art, 1700–1850* (Oxford, 1992).

Bartha, Dénes, and Somfai, László, *Haydn als Opernkapellmeister* (Mainz, 1960).

Barthes, Roland, *Image, Music, Text*, Essays selected and translated by Stephen Heath (London, 1977).

Bate, Jonathan, *Shakespearean Constitutions: Politics, Theatre, Criticism 1730–1830* (Oxford, 1989).

Baumgärtel, Bettina, *Angelika Kauffmann (1741–1807): Der Raffael unter den Künsterinnen* (Düsseldorf, 1998).

Baxandall, Michael, *Painting and Experience in Fifteenth-Century Italy: A Primer in the Social History of Pictorial Style* (London, 1972).

Baxandall, Michael, and Alpers, Svetlana, *Tiepolo and the Pictorial Intelligence* (New Haven, 1995).

Bayard, Jane, and D'Oench, Ellen, *'Darkness into Light': The Early Mezzotint*, exh. cat., Tale University Art Gallery (1976).

Beaussant, Philippe, with Bouchenot-Déchin, Patricia, *Les Plaisirs de Versailles: Théâtre et musique* (Paris, 1996).

Beckford, William, *The Journal of William Beckford in Portugal and Spain: 1787–1788*, ed. Boyd Alexander (London, 1954).

Becq, A., 'Rhétoriques et littérature d'art en France à la fin du XVIIᵉ siècle: Le concept de couleur', *Cahiers de l'Association Internationale des Études Françaises*, 24 (1972), 215–32.

Beise, Arnd, 'Lichtenbergs Erklärungen zu Hogarths Moralischen Kupferstichen', in *Georg Christoph Lichtenberg 1742–1799: Wagner der Aufklärung*, exh. cat. (Darmstadt and Göttingen, 1992), 239–59.

Benot, Yves (ed.), *Diderot et Falconet: Le Pour et le Contre* (Paris, 1958).

Berman, Laurence, *The Musical Image: A Theory of Content* (Westport, Conn., 1993).

Bermingham, Ann, *Landscape and Ideology: The English Rustic Tradition 1740–1860* (London, 1987).

Bernstein, S., 'Fear of Music? Nietzsche's Double Vision of the "Musical Feminine"', in P.J. Burgard (ed.), *Nietzsche and the Feminine* (Charlottesville, Va., 1994).

Białostocki, Jan, *Dürer and his Critics 1500–1971: A Chapter in the History of Ideas* (Baden-Baden, 1986).

———, 'Das Modusproblem in den bildenden Künsten', *Zeitschrift für Kunstgeschichte*, 24 (1961), 128–41.

Biba, Otto (ed.), *'Eben komme ich von Haydn . . .': Georg August Griesingers Korrespondenz mit Joseph Haydns Verleger Breitkopf & Härtel 1799–1819* (Zurich, 1987).

——— and Wyn Jones, David (eds), *Studies in Music History Presented to H.C. Robbins Landon on his Seventieth Birthday* (London, 1996).

Bindman, David (ed.), *John Flaxman*, exh. cat., Royal Academy of Arts (London, 1979).

——— with contributions by Aileen Dawson and Mark Jones, *The Shadow of the Guillotine: Britain and the French Revolution* (London, 1989).

——— and Baker, Malcolm, *Roubiliac and the Eighteenth-Century Monument: Sculpture as Theatre* (New Haven, 1995).

——— and Wilcox, Scott (eds), *"Among the Whores and Thieves": William Hogarth and The Beggars Opera*, Yale Centre for British Art (New Haven, 1997).

Bisanz, Rudolf M., *German Romanticism and Philipp Otto Runge: A Study of Nineteenth-Century Art Theory and Iconography* (De Kalb, 1970).

Bishop, Philippa, Burnell, Victoria, and Fleming-Williams, Ian, *The Barkers of Bath*, exh. cat., Victoria Art Gallery (Bath, 1986).

Black, Jeremy, *The British Abroad: The Grand Tour in the Eighteenth Century* (London, 1992).

Blum, Carol, *Rousseau and the Republic of Virtue: The Language of Politics in the French Revolution* (Ithaca, NY, 1986).

Blunden, Edmund, *Leigh Hunt* (London, 1930).

Boase, T.S.R., 'Illustrations of Shakespeare's Plays in the Seventeenth and Eighteenth Centuries', *Journal of the Warburg and Courtauld Institutes*, 10 (1947), 83–108.

——, 'Macklin and Bowyer', *Journal of the Warburg and Courtauld Institutes*, 26 (1963), 148–77.

Bonds, Mark Evan, 'Haydn, Lawrence Sterne, and the Origins of Musical Irony', *Journal of the American Musicological Society*, 64 (1991), 57–91.

——, 'Haydn's "Cours complet de la composition" and the *Sturm und Drang*', in Sutcliffe (ed.), *Haydn Studies*, 152–76.

——, *Wordless Rhetoric: Musical Form and the Metaphor of the Oration* (Cambridge, Mass., 1991).

Bor, Margot, and Clelland, Lamond, *Still the Lark: A Biography of Elizabeth Linley* (London, 1962).

Borthwick, E. Kerr, 'The Latin Quotations in Haydn's London Notebooks', *Music & Letters*, 71 (1990), 505–10.

——, 'Haydn's Latin Quotations: A Postscript', *Music & Letters*, 75 (1994), 576–79.

Bösch-Supan, Helmut, 'Georg Friedrich Händel und Balthasar Denner', *Göttinger Händel-Beiträge*, 2 (1986), 178–93.

——, 'Gruppenbild mit Musikern: Ein Gemälde von Balthasar Denner und das Problem der Bach-Ikonographie', in *Kunst und Antiquitäten*, 3 (1982), 22–28.

Botstein, Leon, 'The Consequences of Presumed Innocence: The Nineteenth-Century Reception of Joseph Haydn', in Sutcliffe (ed.), *Haydn Studies*, 1–34.

Bott, Gian Caspar, 'Ut pictura musica. Zu Evaristo Baschenis' "Ricercata Quinta"', in Harald Heckmann, Monika Holl, and Hans Joachim Marx (eds), *Musikalische Ikonographie* (Laaber, 1994), 15–29.

Bowler, Peter J., *Evolution: The History of an Idea* (Berkeley, Calif., 1984).

Brago, Michael, 'Haydn, Goldoni and *Il mondo della luna*', *Eighteenth-Century Studies*, 17 (1983–84), 308–22.

Braunbehrens, Volkmar, *Mozart in Vienna*, trans. Timothy Bell (Oxford, 1991).

Brechka, Frank T., *Gerard van Swieten and his World 1700–1772* (The Hague, 1970).

Bredvald, Louis, *The Natural History of Sensibility* (Detroit, 1962).

Brewer, John, *The Pleasures of the Imagination: English Culture in the Eighteenth Century* (London, 1997).

Briggs, Martin S., *Goths and Vandals: A Study of the Destruction, Neglect and Preservation of Historic Buildings in England* (London, 1952).

Brookner, Anita, *The Genius of the Future: Essays in French Art Criticism* (London, 1971).

————, *Greuze: The Rise and Fall of an Eighteenth-Century Phenomenon* (London, 1972).

Brown, A. Peter, '*The Creation* and *The Seasons*: Some Allusions, Quotations and Models from Handel to Mendelssohn', *Current Musicology*, 51 (1993), 28–58.

————, 'Critical Years for Haydn's Instrumental Music: 1787–1790', *Musical Quarterly*, 62 (1976), 374–94.

————, 'The Earliest English Biography of Haydn', *Musical Quarterly*, 59 (1973), 339–54.

————, 'Haydn's Chaos: Genesis and Genre', *Musical Quarterly*, 73 (1989), 18–59.

————, *Joseph Haydn's Keyboard Music: Sources and Style* (Bloomington, Ind., 1986).

————, *Performing Haydn's Creation* (Bloomington, Ind., 1986).

————, The Sublime, the Beautiful and the Ornamental. English Aesthetic Currents and Haydn's London Symphonies', in *Studies in Music History Presented to H.C. Robbins Landon*, ed. Otto Biba and David Wyn Jones (London, 1996), 44–70.

Brown, Bruce Alan, *Gluck and the French Theatre in Vienna* (Oxford, 1991).

————, 'Gluck's *Rencontre imprévue* and its Revisions', *Journal of the American Musicological Society*, 36 (1983), 498–518.

Brown, Frank, *William Herschel: Musician and Composer* (Bath, 1990).

Brown, John, *Letters upon the Poetry and Music of Italian Opera* (Edinburgh, 1789).

Brownell, Morris R., *Alexander Pope and the Arts of Georgian England* (Oxford, 1978).

————, 'William Gilpin's "Unfinished Business": The Thames Tour (1764)', *Walpole Society*, 57 (1993–94), 56–78.

Bruntjen, Sven H.A., *John Boydell (1719–1804): A Study of Art Patronage and Publishing in Georgian London* (New York, 1985).

Brusatti, Otto, et al., *Zauberföne: Mozart in Wien 1781–1791*, exh. cat., Historischen Museums der Stadt Wien (Vienna, 1990).

Bryson, Norman, *Vision and Painting: The Logic of the Gaze* (London, 1983).

————, *Word and Image: French Painting in the Ancien Régime* (Cambridge, 1981).

Buchowiecki, Walter, *Der Barockbau der ehemaligen Hofbibliothek in Wien, ein Werk J.B. Fischers von Erlach* (Vienna, 1957).

Budd, Malcolm, *Music and the Emotions: The Philosophical Theories* (London, 1985).

————, *Values of Art: Pictures, Poetry and Music* (London, 1995).

Bukdahl, Else Marie, *Diderot critique d'art*, 2 vols, trans. J.-P. Faucher (Copenhagen, 1980).

Bull, Duncan, Cabe, Linda, and Nisbet, Peter, *Classic Ground: British Artists and the Landscape of Italy*, Yale Centre for British Art (New Haven, 1981).

Burden, Michael, *Garrick, Arne and the Masque of Alfred: A Case Study in National Theatrical and Musical Politics* (Lewiston, 1994).

Burke, Edmund, *A Philosophical Enquiry into the Origin of our Ideas of the Sublime and the Beautiful, London, 1757*, ed. J.T. Boulton (London, 1958).

Burke, Joseph, *English Art, 1714–1800*, Oxford History of English Art, Vol. 9 (Oxford, 1976).

Burke, Peter, *The Fabrication of Louis XIV* (New Haven, 1992).

Burnett, Charles, Fend, Michael, and Gouk, Penelope (eds), *The Second Sense: Studies in Hearing and Musical Judgement from Antiquity to the Seventeenth Century* (London, 1991).

Burney, Charles, *Dr Burney's Musical Tours in Europe*, i: *An Eighteenth-Century Musical Tour in France and Italy being Dr Charles Burney's account of his musical experiences as it appears in his published volume with which are incorporated his travel experiences according to his original intention*; ii: *An Eighteenth-Century Musical Tour in Central Europe and the Netherlands, being Dr Charles Burney's account ...*, ed. Percy A. Scholes (London, 1959).

————, *A General History of Music from the Earliest Ages to the Present Period*, ed. Frank Mercer, 2 vols (London, 1935).

————, *The Letters of Dr Charles Burney*, i [*1751–1784*], ed. Alvaro Ribeiro (Oxford, 1991).

————, *Music, Men and Manners in France and Italy, 1770; being a journal written by Charles Burney Mus D. during a tour through those countries undertaken to collect material for a General History of Music. . . . British Museum, Additional Manuscript 35122*, ed. H. Edmund Pool (London, 1974).

————, *The Present State of Music in France and Italy*, 2nd edn (London, 1773).

————, *The Present State of Music in Germany, the Netherlands, and United Provinces, or, The Journal of a Tour through those Countries, undertaken to collect Materials for a General History of Music*, 2 vols, 2nd edn (London, 1775).

Burney, Fanny, *Diary and Letters of Madame d'Arblay, Edited by her Niece*, 7 vols (London, 1842–47).

————, *Journals and Letters of Fanny Burney (Madame d'Arblay)*, ed. Joyce Hemlow *et al.*, 12 vols (Oxford, 1972–84).

Busch, Werner, 'From Time Immemorial to Time Unimaginable: Caspar David Friedrich and the Depiction of the Four Seasons', in *Philipp Otto Runge*, ed. Andreas Blühm (Zwolle, 1996), 17–31.

————, *Das sentimentalische Bilde: Die Krise der Kunst in 18. Jahrhundert und die Geburt der Moderne* (Munich, 1993).

Butlin, Martin, 'William Hamilton', in *Aspects of British Painting 1550–1800 from the Collection of the Sarah Campbell Blatter Foundation* (1988), 171–74.

Cannon-Brookes, Peter, 'From the "Death of General Wolfe" to the "Death of Lord Nelson": Benjamin West and the Epic Composition', in id. (ed.), *The Painted Word*, 6–22.

———— (ed.), *The Painted Word: British History Painting 1750–1830* (Woodbridge, 1991).

Carlson, Victor I., D'Oench, Ellen, and Field, Richard S., *Prints and Drawings by Gabriel de Saint Aubin* (Middletown, Conn., 1975).

———— and Ittmann, J., *Regency to Empire: French Printmaking, 1715–1814*, exh. cat. Baltimore Museum of Art, Minneapolis Institute of Arts (1984).

Carpani, Giuseppe, *Le Haydine: lettere sulla vita e le opere del celebre maestro Giuseppe Haydn* (Milan, 1812).

Carr, D.J. (ed.), *Sydney Parkinson, Artist of Cook's 'Endeavour' Voyage* (Canberra, 1983).

Carr, Gerald, L., 'David, Boydell and Socrates: A Mixture of Anglophilia, Self-promotion and the Press', *Apollo*, 136 (1993), 307–15.

Carretta, Vincent, *George III and the Satirists from Hogarth to Byron* (Athens, Ga., 1990).

Carter, Harold B., *Sir Joseph Banks 1743–1820* (London, 1988).

Cassirer, Ernst, *The Philosophy of the Enlightenment*, trans. F.C.A. Koelln and J.P. Pettigrew (Princeton, 1951).

The Catalog of Carl Philipp Emanuel Bach's Estate: A Facsimile of the Edition by Schniebes, Hamburg, 1790, ed. Rachel W. Wade (New York, 1981).

Causa, Raffaelo, et al., *The Golden Age of Naples: Art and Civilization under the Bourbons, 1734–1805*, exh. cat., Institute of Arts (Detroit, 1981).

Ceram, C.W., *The Archaeology of the Cinema* (London, 1965).

Chaloner-Smith, John, *British Mezzotint Portraits*, 4 vols (London, 1883).

Chambers, F.B., *The History of Taste* (New York, 1932).

Chappel, Milkes L., *Rubens in Prints*, exh. cat. (Williamsburg, Va., 1977).

Charlton, D.G., *New Images of the Natural in France: A Study in European Cultural History, 1750–1800* (Cambridge, 1984).

Charlton, David, *Grétry and the Growth of Opéra-Comique* (Cambridge, 1986).

————, 'Instrumental Recitative: A Study in Morphology and Context, 1700–1808', *Comparative Criticism: A Yearbook*, 4 (1982), 149–68.

Chazal, Gilles., 'Les "Attitudes" de Lady Hamilton', *Gazette des Beaux-Arts*, 96 (1979), 219–26.

Chew, Geoffrey, 'The Night-Watchman's Song Quoted by Haydn and Its Implications', *Haydn-Studien*, 3 (1974), 106–24.

Choillet, Jacques, *L'Esthétique des lumières* (Paris, 1974).

Chouillet-Roche, Anne-Marie, 'Le Clavecin oculaire du père Castel', *Dix-huitième siècle*, 8 (1976), 141–66.

Christensen, Thomas, *Rameau and Musical Thought in the Enlightenment* (Cambridge, 1993)

Christophers, John, *Antonio Canova and the Politics of Patronage in Revolutionary and Napoleonic Europe* (Berkeley, Cal., 1998)

Ciliberti, Galliano, 'Le passioni degli dei: musica e pittura tra Gluck e David', in Bianca Brumana and Galliano Ciliberti (eds), *Musica e immagine: tra iconografia e mondo dell'opera: studi in onore di Massimo Bogianckino* (Florence, 1993), 177–95.

Clark, Anthony M., Pompeo Batoni: A Complete Catalogue of his Work with an Introductory Text, ed. Edgar Peters Bowron (Oxford, 1985).

Clark, Caryl, 'Intertextual Play and Haydn's *La fedeltà premiata*', *Current Musicology*, 51 (1993), 59–81.

Clark, Kenneth, *The Gothic Revival: An Essay in the History of Taste* (New York, 1962).

Clayton, Timothy, *The English Print 1688–1802* (London, 1997).

Cohen, Bernard, *The Newtonian Revolution, with Illustrations of the Transformation of Scientific Ideas* (Cambridge, 1980).

Cohen, Ralph, *The Art of Discrimination: Thomson's 'The Seasons' and the Language of Criticism* (London, 1964).

————, *The Unfolding of 'The Seasons': A Study of Thomson's Poem* (London, 1970).

———— (ed.), *Studies in Eighteenth-Century British Art and Aesthetics* (Berkeley, Calif., 1985).

Coke, David, *The Muse's Bower: Vauxhall Gardens 1728–1786*, Gainsborough's House (Sudbury, 1978).

————, 'Vauxhall Gardens', in *Rococo Art and Design in Hogarth's England*, Victoria & Albert Museum (London, 1984), 74–98.

Cole, Malcolm S., 'Momigny's Analysis of Haydn's Symphony no. 103', *Music Review*, 30 (1969), 261–84.

Colley, Linda, *Britons: Forging the Nation 1707–1837* (New Haven, 1992).

Cone, Edward T., *The Composer's Voice* (Berkeley, Calif., 1974).

Constable, W.G., *Richard Wilson* (London, 1953).

Cooper, Martin, *Gluck* (New York, 1935).

Copley, S., 'The Fine Arts in Eighteenth-Century Polite Culture', in J. Barrell (ed.), *Painting and the Politics of Culture: New Essays on British Art, 1700–1850* (Oxford, 1992)

Coward, Georgia (ed.), *French Musical Thought, 1600–1800* (Ann Arbor, 1989).

Coxhead, A.C., *Thomas Stothard R.A.* (London, 1906).

Craske, Matthew, *Art in Europe 1700–1830: A History of the Visual Arts in an Era of Unprecedented Urban Economic Growth* (Oxford, 1997).

Crawford, Donald W., *Kant's Aesthetic Theory* (Madison, Wis., 1974).

Cripe, Helen, *Thomas Jefferson and Music* (Charlottesville, Va., 1974).

Croft-Murray, E., 'Decorative Painting for Lord Burlington and the Royal Academy', *Apollo*, 89 (1969), 11–21.

————, *Decorative Painting in England, 1537–1837*, 2 vols (London, 1962–70).

Croll, G, 'Mitteilungen über die "Schöpfung" und die "Jahreszeiten" aus dem Schwarzenberg-Archiv', *Haydn-Studien*, 3 (1974), 85–90.

Crook, John (ed.), *Winchester Cathedral: Nine Hundred Years 1093–1993* (Chichester, 1993).

Cropper, Elizabeth, *The Ideal of Painting: Pietro Testa's Düsseldorf Notebook* (Princeton, 1984).

Cross, David A.: *A Striking Likeness: The Life of George Romney* (London, 1999).

Crow, Thomas, *Emulation: Making Artists for Revolutionary France* (New Haven, 1995).

————, *Painters and Public Life in Eighteenth-Century Paris*, 2nd edn (New Haven, 1987).

Crown, Patricia, 'Visual Music: E.F. Burney and a Hogarth Revival', *Bulletin of Research in the Humanities*, 83 (1980), 435–72.

Cuno, James, et al., *French Caricature and the French Revolution 1789–1799*, exh. cat., Wight Art Gallery, University of California (Los Angeles, 1988).

Dahlhaus, Carl, *The Idea of Absolute Music*, trans. Roger Lustig (Chicago, 1989).

Daniels, Stephen, *Joseph Wright* (London, 1999).

Da Ponte, Lorenzo, *Memoirs of Lorenzo da Ponte*, trans. Elizabeth Abbott, ed. Arthur Livingston (New York, 1967).

Darlington, C.D., *Darwin's Place in History* (Oxford, 1959).

Darnton, Robert, *Mesmerism and the End of the Enlightenment in France* (Cambridge, Mass., 1968).

Dawe, George, *George Morland* (London, 1807).

Dawes, Frank, 'William: Or the Adventures of a Sonata', *Musical Times*, 106 (1965), 761–64.

Dawson, Warren R. (ed.), *The Banks Letters: A Calendar of the Manuscript Correspondence* (London, 1958).

De Grazia, D., *Correggio and his Legacy*, exh. cat., National Gallery of Art (Washington, DC, 1984).

Delany, Mary Grandville, *The Autobiography and Correspondence of Mary Grandville, Mrs Delany*, ed. Lady Llanover (London, 1861).

Deleuze, Gilles, *Kant's Critical Philosophy: The Doctrine of the Faculties*, trans. Hugh Tomlinson and Barbara Habberjam (Minneapolis, 1984).

De Man, Paul, *Blindness and Insight* (New York, 1971).

Deutsch, Otto Erich, 'Haydn und Nelson', *Die Musik*, 24 (1931–32), 436–40.

———, *Mozart: A Documentary Biography*, trans. Eric Blom, Peter Branscombe, and Jeremy Noble (Stanford, Calif., 1965).

Dickinson, H.T., *Caricatures of the Constitution 1760–1832* (Cambridge, 1986).

———, *Liberty and Property: Political Ideology in Eighteenth-Century Britain* (London, 1977).

Diderot, *Salons*, ed. Jean Seznec and Jean Adhémar, 4 vols (Oxford, 1957–67).

Didier, Béatrice, *Écrire la révolution, 1789–1799* (Paris, 1989).

———, *La Musique des lumières: Diderot, "L'Encyclopédie", Rousseau* (Paris, 1985).

Dies, Albert Christoph, *Biographische Nachtrichten von Joseph Haydn nach mündlichen Erzählungen desselben entworfen und herausgegeben von Albert Christoph Dies, Landschaftsmaler* [Vienna, 1810], ed. Horst Seeger (Kassel, n.d. [1959]).

Dillenberger, John, *Benjamin West: The Context of His Life's Work with Particular Attention to Paintings with Religious Subject Matter* (San Antonio, Tex., 1977).

Diment, J.A., *et al.*, 'Catalogue of the Natural History Drawings Commissioned by Joseph Banks on the "Endeavour" Voyage 1768–71, Held in the British Museum (Natural History)', *Bulletin of the British Museum, Historical Series*, 11–13 (London, 1984–87).

Dittersdorf, Karl Ditters von, *The Autobiography of Karl von Dittersdorf Dictated to his Son*, trans. A. D. Coleridge (London, 1896).

Dixon Hunt, John, *Theatre in Focus: Vauxhall and London's Garden Theatres* (London, 1985).

Dodson, Jessie, *John Hunter* (Edinburgh, 1969).

D'Oench, Ellen G., *The Conversation Piece: Arthur Devis and his Contemporaries* (New Haven, 1980).

———, 'Prodigal Sons and Fair Penitents: Transformations in Eighteenth-Century Popular Prints', *Art History*, 13 (1990), 318–43.

Donakowski, Conrad, *A Muse for the Masses: Ritual and Music in an Age of Democratic Revolution, 1770–1870* (Chicago, 1977).

Donald, Diana, *The Age of Caricature: Satirical Prints in the Reign of George III* (New Haven, 1996).

Döring, Jürgen, *Eine Kunstgeschichte der frühen englischen Karikatur* (Hildesheim, 1991).

Dorment, Richard, *British Painting in the Philadelphia Museum of Art from the Seventeenth through the Nineteenth Century* (Philadelphia, 1986).

Dowd, David L., *Pageant Master of the Republic: Jacques Louis David* (Lincoln, Nebr., 1948).

Dubos, Jean-Baptiste, *Critical Reflections on Poetry, Painting and Music*, trans. Thomas Nugent, 3 vols (London, 1748).

Dülmuen, Richard van, *The Society of the Enlightenment: The Rise of the Middle Class and Enlightenment Culture in Germany*, trans. Anthony Williams (Cambridge, 1992).

Dunlop, Ian, *Marie-Antoinette* (London, 1993).

Earland, Ada, *John Opie and his Circle* (London, 1911).

Edelstein, T.J., and Allen, Brian, *Vauxhall Gardens*, Yale Centre for British Art (New Haven, 1983).

Egerton, Judy, *George Stubbs*, exh. cat., Tate Gallery (London, 1984).

————, *Joseph Wright of Derby*, exh. cat., Tate Gallery (London, 1990).

Einberg, Elizabeth, *Gainsborough's Giovanna Baccelli*, exh. cat., Tate Gallery (London, 1976).

Einstein, Alfred, *Gluck*, trans. Eric Bloom, rev. edn (London, 1964).

Erffa, Helmut von, 'West's "The Washing of Sheep": Genre or Poetic Portrait? Some Lost and Doubtful Subjects from Thomson's "Seasons"', *Art Quarterly*, 15 (1952), 160–65.

———— and Staley, Allen, *The Paintings of Benjamin West* (New Haven, 1986).

Erhardt-Siebold, Erika von, 'Harmony of the Senses in English, German and French Romantisicm', *Publications of the Modern Language Association of America*, 47 (1932), 577–92.

Errington, Lindsay, and Holloway, James, *The Discovery of Scotland: The Appreciation of Scottish Scenery through Two Centuries of Painting*, exh. cat., National Galleries of Scotland (Edinburgh, 1978).

Esterly, David, and Sayce, Lynda, '"He was likewise *Musical* ..."': An Unexplored Aspect of Grinling Gibbons', *Apollo*, 151 (July, 2000), 11–21.

Evans, Dorinda, *The Genius of Gilbert Stuart* (London, 1999).

Everett, Nigel, *The Tory View of Landscape* (London, 1994).

Everett, Paul, *Vivaldi: The Four Seasons (Concerti Op. 8)* (Cambridge, 1996).

Ewart, Herbert, 'Henry Bunbury, Caricaturist', *Connoisseur*, 6 (1903), 85–89, 156–57.

Fabian, Bernhard, *The English Book in Eighteenth-Century Germany* (London, 1992).

Farington, Joseph, *Diaries*, ed. Kenneth Garlick, A. Macintyre, and K. Cave. 14 vols (London, 1978–84).

Farrell, Gerry, *Indian Music and the West* (Oxford, 1997).

Fauvel, John, et al. (eds), *Let Newton Be! A New Perspective on his Life and Works* (Oxford, 1988).

Feder, Georg, 'Die Jahreszeiten', in *Die Vier Jahreszeiten in 18. Jahrhundert: Colloquium der Arbeitsstelle 18. Jahrhundert, Gesamthochschule Wuppertal, Universität Münster, Schloss Langenburg vom 3. bis 5. Oktober 1983* (Heidelberg, 1986), 96–107.

————, 'Manuscript Sources of Haydn's Works and their Distribution', *Haydn Yearbook*, 4 (1968), 102–39.

————, 'Opera seria, Opera buffa und Opera semiseria bei Haydn', in *Opernstudien: Anna Amelie Abert zum 65. Geburtstag* (Tutzing, 1975), 37–55.

Fenner, Theodore, *Opera in London: Views of the Press 1785–1830* (Carbondale, Ill., 1994).

Ferry, Luc, *Homo Aestheticus: The Invention of Taste in the Democratic Age* (Chicago, 1993).

Feuchtmüller, Rupert, et al., *Joseph Haydn und seine Zeit*, exh. cat., Schloß Petronell (Vienna, 1959).

Fischer, P., *Music in Paintings of the Low Countries in the 16th and 17th Centuries* (Amsterdam, 1975).

Fisher, Stephen C., 'A Group of Haydn Copies for the Court of Spain: Fresh Sources, Rediscovered Works, and New Riddles', *Haydn-Studien*, 4 (1978), 65–84.

Fiske, Roger, *English Theatre Music in the Eighteenth Century* (London, 1973).

————, *Scotland in Music: A European Enthusiasm* (Cambridge, 1983).

————, and Johnstone, H. Diack (eds), *Music in Britain: The Eighteenth Century* (Oxford, 1990).

Flaherty, Gloria, *Opera in the Development of German Critical Thought* (Princeton, 1978).

Fleury, Michel, *L'Impressionisme et la musique* (Paris, 1996).

Flinker, Noam, 'Miltonic Voices in Haydn's *Creation*', *Milton Studies*, 27 (1991), 139–64.

Foot, Jesse, *The Life of John Hunter* (London, 1794).

Ford, John, *Ackermann 1783–1983: The Business of Art* (London, 1983).

Foreman, Amanda, *Georgiana, Duchess of Devonshire* (London, 1998).

Forster-Hahn, Franziska, '"The Sources of True Taste": Benjamin West's Instructions to a Young Painter for His Studies in Italy', *Journal of the Warburg and Courtauld Institutes*, 30 (1967), 366–82.

Forsyth, Michael, *Buildings for Music: The Architects, the Musician, and the Listener from the Seventeenth Century to the Present Day* (Cambridge, 1985).

Fort, Bernadette, 'Voice of the Public: The Carnivalization of Salon Art in Prerevolutionary Pamphlets', *Eighteenth-Century Studies*, 22 (1989), 368–94.

Foster, Jonathan, 'The Tempora Mutantur Symphony of Joseph Haydn', *Haydn Yearbook*, 9 (1975), 328–29.

Fothergill, Brian, *Sir William Hamilton, Envoy Extraordinary* (New York, 1969).

————, *The Strawberry Hill Set: Horace Walpole and his Circle* (London, 1983).

Fox, Charles James, *Memorials and Correspondence of Charles James Fox*, ed. Lord John Russell, 4 vols (London, 1853).

Fraenkel, Gottfried, S., *Decorative Music Title Pages: 201 Examples from 1500 to 1800* (New York, 1968).

Frankau, Julia, *Eighteenth-Century Colour Prints: An Essay on Certain Stipple Engravers and Their Work*, 2nd edn (London, 1906).

————, *John Raphael Smith: His Life and Works* (London, 1902).

Fraser, Flora, *Beloved Emma* (London, 1986).

Franssen, M., 'The Ocular Harpsichord of Louis-Bertrand Castel: The Science and Aesthetics of an 18th-Century *Cause célèbre*', in *Tratrix, Yearbook for the History of Science, Medicine, Technology and Mathematics*, 3 (1991), 15–77.

Frew, John M., 'Gothic is English: John Carter and the Revival of Gothic as England's National Style', *Art Bulletin*, 64 (1982), 315–19.

Fried, Michael, *Absorption and Theatricality: Painting and Beholder in the Age of Diderot* (Berkeley, Calif., 1980).

Friedman, Winifred H., *Boydell's Shakespeare Gallery* (New York, 1976).

————, 'Some Commercial Aspects of the Boydell Shakespeare Gallery', *Journal of the Warburg and Courtauld Institutes*, 36 (1973), 396–401.

Frings, Gabriel, '*Ut musica pictura*: Laurent de La Hyre's Allegory of Music (1649) as a Mirror of Baroque Art and Music Theory', *Gazette des Beaux-Arts*, 123 (1994), 13–28.

Frye, Roland Mushat, *Milton's Imagery and the Visual Arts: Iconographic Tradition in the Epic Poems* (Princeton, 1978).

Fubini, Enrico, *Music and Culture in Eighteenth-Century Europe: A Source Book*, ed. Bonnie J. Blackburn (Chicago, 1994).

Fuller, David, 'Of Portraits, "Sapho" and Couperin: Titles and Characters in French Instrumental Music of the High Baroque', *Music & Letters*, 78 (1997), 149–74.

Fumaroli, Marc, *L'École du silence: le sentiment des images au XVIIe siècle* (Paris, 1994).

Fux, Johann Joseph, *Gradus ad Parnassum*, ed. Alfred Mann [J.J. Fux, *Sämtliche Werke*, VII/1] (Graz, 1967).

Fyfe, Gordon J., 'Art and Reproduction: Some Aspects of the Relations between Painters and Engravers in London 1760–1850', *Media. Culture and Society*, 7 (1985), 399–425.

Gage, John, *Colour and Culture: Practice and Meaning from Antiquity to Abstraction* (London, 1993).

————, *Colour and Meaning: Art, Science and Symbolism* (London, 1999).

————, 'De Loutherbourg: Mystagogue of the Sublime', *History Today*, 13 (May, 1963), 336.

Garas, Klára, *The Budapest Gallery: Paintings in the Museum of Fine Arts* (Budapest, 1977).

————, *Correggio: Szoptató Madonna* (Budapest, 1989).

Gascoigne, J., *Joseph Banks and the English Enlightenment: Useful Knowledge and Polite Culture* (Cambridge, 1994).

Gatty, Hugh, 'Notes by Horace Walpole, Fourth Earl of Orford on the Exhibitions of the Society of Artists and The Free Society of Artists, 1760–1791', *Walpole Society*, 27 (1938–39), 57–88.

Gaunt, William, 'George Dance's Royal Academy', *Connoisseur*, 153 (1963), 182–87.

Gause-Reinhold, Angelika, *Das Christinen-Denkmal von Antonio Canova und der Wandel in der Todesauffassung um 1800* (Frankfurt am Main, 1990).

Gay, Peter, *The Enlightenment: An Interpretation*, 2 vols, 2nd edn (New York, 1969).

Geiringer, Karl, *Haydn: A Creative Life in Music*, rev. edn (Berkeley, Calif., 1982).

————, 'Haydn and the Folksong of the British Isles', *Musical Quarterly*, 35 (1949), 179–208.

George, Mary Dorothy, *Catalogue of Prints and Drawings in the British Museum: Division I. Political and Personal Satires*, Vol. V [1771–83], Vol. VI [1784–92], Vol. VII [1793–1800] (repr. London, 1978).

————, *England in Transition: Life and Work in the Eighteenth Century*, rev. edn (Harmondsworth, 1953).

————, *English Political Caricature: A Study of Opinion and Propaganda*, 2 vols (Oxford, 1959).

————, *Hogarth to Cruikshank: Social Change in Graphic Satire* (New York, 1967).

————, *London Life in the Eighteenth Century* (Harmondsworth, 1965).

Gerlach, Sonja, 'Haydns 'chronologische' Sinfonieliste für Breitkopf & Härtel', *Haydn-Studien*, 6 (1988), 116–29.

Gibbs, F.W., *Joseph Priestley* ([London], 1965).

Gilpin, William, *An Essay upon Prints; Containing Remarks upon the Principles of Picturesque Beauty, the Different Kinds of Prints, and the Characteristics of the Most Noted Masters*, 1st edn (London, 1768).

————, *Observations Relative Chiefly to Picturesque Beauty* (London, 1784).

————, *Remarks on the Forest Scenery, and the Other Woodland Views, (Relative Chiefly to Picturesque Beauty) Illustrated by the Scenes of New-Forest in Hampshire, in Three Books*, 2 vols (London, 1791).

————, *Three Essays: On Picturesque Beauty; On Picturesque Travel; And On Sketching Landscape; To Which is Added a Poem, On Landscape Painting* (London, 1792).

Gilreath, James, and Wilson, Douglas L., *Thomas Jefferson's Library: A Catalog with the Entries in his Own Order* (Washington DC, 1989).

Girdham, Jane, *English Opera in Late Eighteenth-Century London: Stephen Storace at Drury Lane* (London, 1997).

Girdlestone, Cuthbert, *Jean-Philippe Rameau: His Life and Work*, rev. edn (New York, 1969).

Girouard, Mark, *Windsor: The Most Romantic Castle* (London, 1993).

Glass, Bentley, Temkin, Owsei, and Straus, William L. (eds), *Forerunners of Darwin 1745–1859* (Baltimore, Md., 1959).

Glendinning, Nigel, *Goya and his Critics* (London, 1977).

Gluck, Christoph Willibald, *The Collected Correspondence and Papers of Christoph Willibald Gluck*, ed. Hedwig and E.H. Mueller von Asow, trans. Stewart Thomson (London, 1962).

Goethe, Johann Wolfgang, *Italian Journey*, trans. W.H. Auden and Elizabeth Mayer (Harmondsworth, 1970).

Golahny, Amy (ed.), *The Eye of the Poet: Studies in the Reciprocity of the Visual and Literary Arts from the Renaissance to the Present* (London, 1996).

Göllner, Theodor, *"Die Sieben Worte am Kreuz" bei Schütz und Haydn*, Bayerische Akademie der Wissenschaft, Philosphische-historische Klasse: Abhandlungen, Neue Folge, 93 (Munich, 1986).

Goodman, Dena, 'Governing the Republic of Letters: The Politics of Culture in the French Enlightenment', *History of European Ideas*, 13 (1991), 183–99.

Goodman, Elise, *The Portraits of Madame de Pompadour: Celebrating the Femme Savante* (London, 2000).

Goodreau, David, *Nathaniel Dance, 1735–1811*, Kenwood, The Iveagh Bequest (London, 1977).

Gordon, Catherine M., *British Paintings of Subjects from the English Novel 1740–1870* (London, 1988).

Gotwals, Vernon, 'The Earliest Biographies of Haydn', *Musical Quarterly*, xlv (1959), 439–59

———, 'Joseph Haydn's Last Will and Testament', *Musical Quarterly*, 47 (1961), 331–53.

——— (trans. and ed.), *Haydn: Two Contemporary Portraits* (Madison, Wis., 1968).

Gouk, Penelope, 'The Harmonic Roots of Newtonian Science', in J. Fauvel et al. (eds), *Let Newton Be! A New Perspective on his Life and Works* (Oxford, 1988), 101–25.

Gould, Cecil, *The Paintings of Correggio* (London, 1976).

Grant, Kerry S., *Dr Burney as Critic and Historian of Music* (Ann Arbor, 1983).

———, 'Dr Burney, the Bear, and the Knight: E.F. Burney's *Amateurs of*

Tye-Wig Music', in Thomas Baumann and Maria Petzoldt McClymond (eds), *Opera and the Enlightenment* (Cambridge, 1995), 43–60.

Graves, Floyd Kersey, and Graves, Margaret G., *In Praise of Harmony: The Teachings of Abbé Georg Joseph Vogler* (Lincoln, Nebr., 1988).

Green, Robert A., '"Il Distratto" of Regnard and Haydn: A Re-examination', *Haydn Yearbook*, 11 (1980), 183–95.

Green, Valentine, *A Review of the Polite Arts in France, at the Time of their Establishment under Louis the XIVth, Compared with their Present State in England* (London, 1782).

Greene, John C., *The Death of Adam: Evolution and its Impact on Western Thought* (Ames, Ia., 1959).

Greenhouse, Wendy, 'Benjamin West and Edward III: A Neoclassical Painter and Medieval History', *Art History*, 8 (1985), 178–91.

Grétry, André-Modest, *Mémoires, ou essais sur la musique*, 3 vols (Paris, 1789); rev. edn (Paris, 1797).

Griesinger, Georg August, *Biographische Notizen über Joseph Haydn* [Leipzig, 1810], with notes by Peter Krause (Leipzig, 1983).

Griffiths, Antony, and Carey, Frances, *German Printmaking in the Age of Goethe*, exh. cat. British Museum (London, 1994).

Grim, William E., *Haydn's Sturm und Drang Symphonies: Form and Meaning*, Studies in the Interpretation of Music, 23 (Lewiston, NY, 1990).

Gruber, Gernot, *Mozart and Posterity*, trans. R.S. Furness (London, 1991).

Guidol, José, *Goya 1746–1828: Biography, Analytical Study, and Catalogue of his Paintings*, trans. Kenneth Lyons, 4 vols (New York, 1971).

Gumbert, H.L. (ed.), *Lichtenberg in England* (Wiesbaden, 1977).

Haar, James, 'Music as Visual Language', in Irving Lavin (ed.), *Meaning in the Visual Arts: Views from the Outside. A Centennial Commemoration of Erwin Panofsky* (Princeton, 1995), 265–84.

Haas, Robert, *Gluck und Durazzo in Burgtheater* (Vienna, 1925).

Hadden, J. Cuthbert, *George Thomson, the Friend of Burns: His Life and Correspondence* (London, 1898).

Haeringer, Etienne, *L'Esthétique de l'opéra en France au temps de Jean-Philippe Rameau*, Studies on Voltaire and the Eighteenth Century, 279 (Oxford, 1990).

Hagstrum, Jean H., *The Sister Arts: The Tradition of Literary Pictorialism and English Poetry from Dryden to Gray* (Chicago, 1958).

Haimo, Ethan, *Haydn's Symphonic Forms* (Oxford, 1995).

Hammerlmann, H., and Boase, T.S.R., *Book Illustrators of the Eighteenth Century* (New Haven, 1975).

Hammerstein, Reinhold, *Die Musik der Engel: Untersuchungen zur Musikauschauung des Mittelalters* (Berlin, 1962).

Hammond, J.L., and Barbara, *The Village Labourer 1760–1832: A Study of the Government of England before the Reform Bill* (London, 1911).

Hanning, Barbara, R., 'Conversation and Musical Style in the Late Eighteenth-Century Parisian Salon', *Eighteenth-Century Studies*, 22 (1989), 512–28.

Harich, János, 'Das Repertoire des Opernkapellmeisters Joseph Haydn in Eszterháza (1780–1790)', *Haydn Yearbook*, 1 (1962), 9–110.

Harris, James, *Three Treatises. The First Concerning Art. The Second Concerning Music, Painting and Poetry. The Third Concerning Happiness*, 3rd edn (London, 1772).

Harris, Tomás, *Goya: Engravings and Lithographs*, 2 vols (Oxford, 1964).

Harrison, Bernard, *Haydn: The 'Paris' Symphonies* (Cambridge, 1998).

Harvey, A.D., *Sex in Georgian England* (London, 1994).

Hase, H. von, *Joseph Haydn und Breitkopf & Härtel* (Leipzig, 1909).

Haskell, Francis, 'The Apotheosis of Newton in Art', in *Past and Present in Art and Taste* (New Haven, 1987), 1–15.

———, *History and Its Images: Art and the Interpretation of the Past* (London, 1993).

———, *Patrons and Painters: A Study in the Relations between Italian Art and Society in the Age of the Baroque* (New York, 1971).

———, *Rediscoveries in Art: Some Aspects of Taste, Fashion, and Collecting in England and France* (Oxford, 1980).

——— and Penny, Nicholas, *Taste and the Antique: The Lure of Classical Sculpture 1500–1900* (New Haven, 1981).

Hassell, J., *Memoirs of the Life of the Late George Morland; with Critical and Descriptive Observations on the Whole of his Works Hitherto before the Public* (London, 1806).

Haydn, Joseph, *The Collected Correspondence and London Notebooks of Joseph Haydn*, ed. and trans. H.C. Robbins Landon (London, 1959).

———, *Gesammelte Briefe und Aufzeichnungen*, ed. Dénes Bartha (Kassel, 1965).

Hayley, William, *The Life of George Romney, Esq.* (Chichester, 1809).

Head, Matthew, 'Birdsong and the Origins of Music', *Journal of the Royal Musical Association*, 122 (1997), 1–23.

Heartz, Daniel, 'Farinelli and Metastasio: Rival Twins of Public Favour', *Early Music*, 12 (1984), 358–65.

——— 'From Garrick to Gluck: The Reform of Theatre and Opera in the Mid Eighteenth Century', *Proceedings of the Royal Musical Association*, 94 (1967–68), 111–27.

———, 'The Hunting Chorus in Haydn's *Jahrzeiten* and the "Airs de Chasse" in the *Encyclopédie*', *Eighteenth-Century Studies*, 9 (1975–76), 523–39.

————, *Haydn, Mozart, and the Viennese School, 1740–1780* (London, 1995).

————, 'Haydn und Gluck im Burgtheater um 1760: Der neue krumme Teufel, Le Diable à quatre und die Sinfonie "Le Soir"', in *Bericht über den Internationalen Musikwissenschaftlichen Kongress Bayreuth 1981*, ed. Christoph-Hellmut Mahling and Sigrid Wiesmann (Kassel, 1984), 120–35.

————, *Mozart's Operas*, ed. with contributing essays by Thomas Bauman (Berkeley, Calif., 1990).

Heck, Thomas F., et al., *Picturing Performance: The Iconography of the Performing Arts in Concept and Practice* (Rochester, NY, 1999).

Helen, E.E., *Music at the Court of Frederick the Great* (Norman, Okla., 1960).

Helm, William H., *Vigée-Le Brun, her Life, Works and Friendships* (London, 1916).

Hempton, David, *Methodism and Politics in British Society, 1750–1850* (London, 1984).

Herbert, Robert L., *David, Voltaire, Brutus and the French Revolution: An Essay in Art and Politics* (London, 1972).

Herdan, Innes, and Herdan, Gustav, *The World of Hogarth: Lichtenberg's Commentaries on Hogarth's Engravings* (London, 1966).

Herrmann, Luke, *British Landscape Painting of the Eighteenth Century* (London, 1973).

Herter Norton, M. D., 'Haydn in America (before 1820)', *Musical Quarterly*, 18 (1932), 309–37.

Hibbert, Christopher, *George IV, Prince of Wales* (London, 1972).

Hill, Draper, *Mr Gillray the Caricaturist: A Bibliography* (London, 1965).

Hilmar, Rosemary, *Der Musikverlag Artaria & Comp.* (Tutzing, 1977).

Hipple, Walter John, *The Beautiful, the Sublime and the Picturesque in Eighteenth-Century British Aesthetic Theory* (Carbondale, Ill., 1957).

Hoboken, Anthony van, *Joseph Haydn, Thematisch-bibliographisches Werkverzeichnis*, 3 vols (Mainz, 1957–78).

Hobson, Marian, *The Object of Art: The Theory of Illusion in Eighteenth-Century France* (London, 1982).

Hogwood, Christopher, and Luckett, R. (eds), *Music in Eighteenth-Century England* (Cambridge, 1983).

Hohl, Hanna, 'Philipp Otto Runge: The Four Times of the Day', in Andreas Blühm (ed.), *Philipp Otto Runge* (Zwolle, 1996), 9–16.

Hokky-Sallay, Marianne, *The Esterházy Palace at Fertőd*, trans. Zsuzsa Béres (Budapest, 1979).

Holcroft, Thomas, *The Life of Thomas Holcroft. Written by Himself, and Continued to the Time of his Death from his Diary, Notes and Other Papers by William Hazlitt*, ed. Elbridge Colby, 2 vols (London, 1925).

Holmström, K.G., *Monodrama, Attitudes, Tableaux Vivants: Studies of Theatrical Fashion 1770–1815* (Stockholm, 1967).

Holt, Elizabeth Gilmore, *The Triumph of Art for the Public: The Emerging Role of Exhibitions and Critics* (New York, 1979).

Honeyman, K., *The Origins of Enterprise: Business Leadership and the Industrial Revolution* (Manchester, 1982).

Honolka, Kurt, *Papageno: Emanuel Schikaneder, Man of the Theater in Mozart's Time*, trans. Jane Mary Wilde (Portland, Ore., 1990).

Honour, Hugh, *Chinoiserie* (London, 1961).

————, *Romanticism* (Harmondsworth, 1981).

———— et al., *The Age of Neo-Classicism*, exh. cat., The Royal Academy and the Victoria & Albert Museum (London, 1972).

Hope, W.H. St John, *Windsor Castle: An Architectural History*, 2 vols (London, 1913).

Horányi, Mátyás, *The Magnificence of Eszterháza* (London, 1962).

Horn, Hans-Jürgen, 'FIAT LUX. Zum kunsttheoretischen Hintergrund der "Erschaffung" des Lichtes in Haydns Schöpfung', *Haydn-Studien*, 3 (1974), 65–84.

Hörwarthner, Maria, 'Joseph Haydns Bibliothek – Versuch einer literarischen Rekonstruktion', in Herbert Zeman (ed.), *Joseph Haydn und die Literatur seiner Zeit* (Eisenstadt, 1976), 157–207; translated as 'Joseph Haydn's Library: An Attempt at a Literary-Historical Reconstruction', trans. Katherine Talbot, in Elaine Sisman (ed.), *Haydn and his World* (Princeton, 1997), 395–461.

Hosler, Bellamy, *Changing Aesthetic Views of Instrumental Music in 18th-Century Germany*, Studies in Musicology, 42 (Ann Arbor, 1981).

Howard, Irving, 'Haydn and Laurence Sterne', *Current Musicology*, 40 (1985), 34–49.

Howard, Patricia, *Gluck: An Eighteenth-Century Portrait in Letters and Documents* (Oxford, 1995).

————, *Gluck and the Birth of Modern Opera* (London, 1963).

Hudson, Roger, *The Grand Tour 1592–1796* (London, 1993).

Hughes, Alison Meyric, and Royalton-Kisch, Martin, 'Handel's Art Collection', *Apollo*, 141 (Sept. 1997), 17–23.

Hughes, Rosemary, 'Dr Burney's Championship of Haydn', *Musical Quarterly*, 27 (1941), 90–96.

Hunt, Frederick Vinton, *Origins in Acoustics: The Science of Sound from Antiquity to the Age of Newton* (New Haven, 1978).

Hunter, Mary, *The Culture of Opera Buffa in Mozart's Vienna: A Poetics of Entertainment* (Princeton, 1999).

————, 'Landscapes, Gardens and Gothic Settings in the *Opere Buffe* of Mozart and his Contemporaries', *Current Musicology*, 51 (1993), 94–105.

———— and Webster, James, *Opera Buffa in Mozart's Vienna* (Cambridge, 1997).

Huss, Manfred, *Joseph Haydn: Klassiker zwischen Barock und Biedermeier* (Eisenstadt, 1984).

Hutchison, Sidney, C., *The History of the Royal Academy 1768–1968* (London, 1968).

Hyde, Ralph, *Panoramania! The Art and Entertainment of the 'All-Embracing View'*, exh. cat., Barbican Art Gallery (London, 1988).

Ingamells, John, *Mrs Robinson and her Portraits*, Wallace Collection Monographs, 1 (London, 1978).

Irving, Howard, 'Haydn and Laurence Sterne: Similarities in Eighteenth Century Literary and Musical Wit', *Current Musicology*, 40 (1985), 34–49.

Irwin, David, *English Neoclassical Art: Studies in Inspiration and Taste* (London, 1966).

————, 'Fuseli's Milton Gallery: Unpublished Letters', *Burlington Magazine*, 101 (1959), 436–40.

Isherwood, Robert, *Farce and Fantasy: Popular Entertainment in Eighteenth-Century Paris* (Oxford, 1986).

Jackson, Christine E., *Bird Painting: The Eighteenth Century* (Woodbridge, 1994).

Jacobson, Dawn, *Chinoiserie* (London, 1993).

Jaffé, Patricia, *Lady Hamilton in Relation to the Art of her Time*, exh. cat., Kenwood House, London (1972).

Jander, Owen, 'Genius in the Arena of Charlatanry: The First Movement of Beethoven's "Tempest" Sonata in Cultural Context', in Irene Alm, Alyson McLamore and Colleen Reardon (eds), *Musica Franca: Essays in Honor of Frank A. D'Accone* (Stuyvesant, NY, 1996), 585–630.

Jardine, Lisa, *Ingenious Pursuits: Building the Scientific Revolution* (London, 1999).

Jenkins, Ian, and Sloan, Kim, *Vases and Volcanoes: Sir William Hamilton and his Collection*, exh. cat., British Museum (London, 1996).

Jenkins, Robert C., *The Last Gleanings of a Christian Life: An Outline of the Life of Thomas Park, F.S.A., Late of Hampstead. The Friend of the Poets Cowper, Hayley, and Southey; of Sir Walter Scott, of Haydn, and of Miss Seward* (London, 1885).

Jobert, Barthélémy, '"Excellent peintre, terrible débauché!" La fortune critique de George Morland en France de la fin du XVIIIe siècle à nos jours', *Revue de la Bibliothèque Nationale*, 50 (Winter 1993), 19–28.

Johns, Christopher, *Antonio Canova and the Politics of Patronage in Revolutionary and Napoleonic France* (Berkeley, Calif., 1998).

Johnson, David, *Music and Society in Lowland Scotland in the Eighteenth Century* (London, 9172).

Johnson, Dorothy, *Jacques-Louis David: Art in Metamorphosis* (Princeton, 1993).

Johnson, James H., *Listening in Paris: A Cultural History* (Berkeley, Calif., 1995).

Jones, Vivien, *Women in the Eighteenth Century: Constructions of Femininity* (London, 1990).

Joppien, Rüdiger, *Philippe Jacques de Loutherbourg, R.A. 1740–1812*, exh. cat., Kenwood House, London (1973).

———, 'Philippe Jacques de Loutherbourg's Pantomime "Omai, or, a Trip round the World" and the Artists of Captain Cook's Voyages', *British Museum Yearbook*, 3 (1979), 81–136.

———, *Die Szenenbilder Philippe Jacques de Loutherbourgs: Eine Untersuchung zu ihrer Stellung zwischen Malerei und Theatre* (Cologne, 1972).

——— and Smith, B., *The Art of Captain Cook's Voyages*, 2 vols (Melbourne, 1985).

Jordanova, Ludmilla J., and Porter, Roy (eds), *Images of the Earth: Essays in the History of the Environmental Sciences* (Chalfont St Giles, 1979).

Julien, Jean-Rémy, and Klein, Jean-Claude (eds), *L'Orphée phrygien: les musiques de la Révolution* (Paris, 1989).

Junod, Philippe, *La Musique par les peintres* (Lausanne, 1988).

Kann, Robert A., *A Study in Austrian Intellectual History: From Late Baroque to Romanticism* (New York, 1960).

Kaufmann, Thomas DaCosta, *Court, Cloister, and City: The Art and Culture of Central Europe 1450–1800* (London, 1995).

——— *The Mastery of Nature: Aspects of Science, Art and Humanism in the Renaissance* (Princeton, 1993).

Kelly, Michael, *Reminiscences*, ed. Roger Fiske (London, 1975).

Kemp, Martin, *Dr William Hunter at the Royal Academy of Arts* (Glasgow, 1975).

———, 'Ingres, Delacroix and Paganini: Exposition and Improvisation in the Creative Process', *L'Arte*, 11 (1970), 49–65.

———, *The Science of Art: Optical Themes in Western Art from Brunelleschi to Seurat* (New Haven 1990).

Kennedy, Emmet, *A Cultural History of the French Revolution* (New Haven, 1989).

Kerman, Joseph, 'Theories of Late Eighteenth-Century Music', in Ralph Cohen (ed.), *Studies in Eighteenth-Century British Art and Aesthetics* (Berkeley, Calif., 1985), 217–44.

Kerslake, J.F., 'The Richardsons and the Cult of Milton', *Burlington Magazine*, 99 (1957), 23–24.

Kimball, Fiske, *Jefferson and the Arts*, Proceedings of the American Philosophical Society, 87 (Philadelphia, 1943).

Kimball, Marie, *Jefferson: The Scene of Europe 1784 to 1789* (New York, 1950).

King-Hele, Desmond (ed.), *The Essential Writings of Erasmus Darwin* (London, 1968).

Kinne, Willard Austin, *Revivals and Importations of French Comedies in England 1749–1800* (New York, 1939).

Kirchner, Thomas, *L'Expression des passions: Ausdruck als Darstellungsproblem in der französischen Kunst und Kunsttheorie des 17. und 18. Jahrhunderts* (Mainz, 1991).

Kirkendale, Ursula, 'The Ruspoli Documents on Handel', *Journal of the American Musicological Society*, 20 (1967), 222–73.

Kivy, Peter, *Osmin's Rage: Philosophical Reflections on Opera, Drama, and Text* (Princeton, 1988).

————, *Sound and Semblance: Reflections on Musical Representation* (Princeton, 1984).

Klein, L.E., *Shaftesbury and the Culture of Politeness: Moral Discourse and Cultural Politics in Early Eighteenth-Century England* (Cambridge, 1994).

Klingender, Francis D., *Art and the Industrial Revolution* (London, 1947).

Kobler, John, *John Hunter: The Reluctant Surgeon* (New York, 1960).

Knight, Charles (ed.), *Les Delices des chateaux royaux; or, A Pocket Companion to the Royal Palaces of Windsor, Kensington, Kew, and Hampton Court* (London, 1785).

Koschatzky, Walter, *Die Albertina und ihr Gründer Herzog Albert von Sachsen-Teschen. Die Albertina und das Dresdener Kupferstichkabinet* (Dresden, 1978).

————, *Giacomo Conte Durazzo 1717–1794*, exh. cat., Albertina (Vienna, 1976).

————, *Old Master Drawings from the Albertina*, exh. cat., National Gallery of Art (Washington, 1985).

————, and Krasa, Selma, *Herzog Albert von Sachsen-Teschen 1738–1822: Reichsfeldmarschall und Kunstmäzen* (Vienna, 1982).

Kramer, Lawrence, 'Haydn's Chaos, Schenker's Order; or Hermeneutics and Musical Analysis: Can They Mix?', *19th-Century Music*, 17 (1992), 3–17.

————, 'Music and Representation: The Instance of Haydn's *Creation*', in Steven Paul Scher (ed.), *Music and Text: Critical Inquiries* (Cambridge, 1992), 139–62.

Krasa, Selma, 'Antonio Canovas Denkmal der Erzherzogin Marie Christine', *Albertina Studien*, 5–6 (1967–68), 67–84, 135–55.

Kris, Ernst, 'Die Characterköpfe des Franz Xaver Messerschmidt', *Jahrbuch der kunsthistorischen Sammlungen in Wien*, 6 (1932), 169–228.

————, *Psychoanalytical Explorations in Art* (London, 1952).

————, and Kurz, Otto, *Legend, Myth and Magic in the Image of the Artist: An Historical Experiment* (New Haven, 1979).

Kristeller, Paul Oskar, 'The Modern System of the Arts', in *Renaissance Thought and the Arts: Collected Essays* (Princeton, 1965).

Krumbhaar, E.B., *Isaac Cruikshank: A Catalogue Raisonné with a Sketch of his Life and Work* (Philadelphia, 1966).

Kumbier, William A., 'A "New Quickening": Haydn's *Creation*, Wordsworth, and the Pictorialist Imagination', *Studies in Romanticism*, 30 (1991), 535–63.

————, 'Rhetoric and Expression in Haydn's *Applausus* Cantata', *Haydn Yearbook*, 18 (1993), 213–47.

Lacépède, Bernard Germain Étienne de la Ville sur Illon, Comte de, *La Poétique de la musique*, 2 vols (Paris, 1785).

Lambert, Susan, *The Image Multiplied: Five Centuries of Printed Reproductions of Paintings and Drawings (London, 1987).*

Landon, H.C. Robbins, *Beethoven* (London, 1970).

————, 'Haydn's Marionette Operas and the Repertoire of the Marionette Theatre at Esterház Castle', *Haydn Yearbook*, 1 (1962), 111–98.

————, *Haydn Chronicle and Works: Haydn at Eszterháza 1766–1790* (London, 1978).

————, *Haydn Chronicle and Works: Haydn in England 1791–1795* (London, 1976).

————, *Haydn Chronicle and Works: Haydn: The Early Years 1732–1765* (London, 1980).

————, *Haydn Chronicle and Works: Haydn: The Late Years 1801–1809* (London, 1977).

————, *Haydn Chronicle and Works: Haydn: The Years of 'The Creation' 1796–1800* (London, 1977).

————, *Haydn: A Documentary Study* (London, 1981).

————, 'The "Loutherbourg" Haydn Portrait', in *Essays on the Viennese Classical Style* (London, 1970), 37–43.

————, *Mozart: The Golden Years 1781–1791* (London, 1989).

————, *The Symphonies of Joseph Haydn* (London, 1955).

———— (ed.), *"The Creation" and "The Seasons": The Complete Authentic Sources for the Word-Books* (Cardiff, 1985).

———— and Wyn Jones, David, *Haydn* (London, 1988).

Langford, Paul, *Englishness Identified: Manners and Character 1650–1850* (Oxford, 2000).

————, *A Polite and Commercial People: England 1727–1783* (Oxford, 1992).

Lanzi, Luigi, *The History of Painting in Italy*, trans. Thomas Roscoe [from the rev. Italian edn of 1809], 3 vols (London, 1818).

La Roche, Sophie von, *Sophie in London 1786, Being the Diary of Sophie v. la Roche*, trans. and ed. Clare Williams, foreword by G.M. Trevelyan (London, 1933).

Larsen, Jens Peter, 'Zur Frage der Porträtähnlichkeit der Haydn Bildnisse', *Studia Musiologica*, 9 (1970), 153–66.

————, with Feder, Georg, *The New Grove Haydn* (London, 1982).

LaRue, Jan, 'A "Hail and Farewell" Quodlibet Symphony', *Music & Letters*, 37 (1956), 250–59.

————, 'Multistage Variance: Haydn's Legacy to Beethoven', *Journal of Musicology*, 1 (1982), 265–74.

Le Blanc, Charles, *Manuel de l'amateur d'estampes*, 4 vols (Paris, 1854–90).

[Le Blond, Gaspard Michel], *Mémoires pour servir à l'historie de la révolution operée dans la musique par M. le chevalier Gluck* (Naples, 1781; repr. Amsterdam, 1967).

Lee, Rensselaer, *Ut pictura poesis: The Humanistic Theory of Painting* (New York, 1967).

Leith, James A., *The Idea of Art as Propaganda in France 1750–1799: A Study in the History of Ideas* (Toronto, 1965).

le Huray, Peter, and Day, James, *Music and Aesthetics in the Eighteenth and Early Nineteenth Centuries* (Cambridge 1981).

Lennox-Boyd, Christopher, Dixon, Rob, and Clayton, Tim, *George Stubbs: The Complete Engraved Works* (London, 1990).

Leppert, Richard, *Music and Image: Domesticity, Ideology and Socio-Cultural Formation in Eighteenth-Century England* (Cambridge, 1988).

————, *The Sight of Sound: Music, Representation and the History of the Body* (Berkeley and Los Angeles, 1993).

————, *The Theme of Music in Flemish Paintings of the Seventeenth Century*, 2 vols (Munich, 1977).

Lessau, Alan P., '"Imitation and expression": Opposing French and British Views on Music in the Eighteenth Century', *Journal of the American Musicological Society*, 27 (1974), 325–30.

Lesure, François, *Haydn en France* (Budapest, 1961).

———— (ed.), *Querelle des gluckistes et des piccinnistes*, 2 vols (Geneva, 1984).

Levallet-Haug, Geneviève, 'Philippe-Jacques Loutherbourg 1740–1813', *Archives Alsaciennes*, 16 (1948), 77–134.

Licht, Fred, *Canova* (New York, 1983).

————, *Goya: The Origins of the Modern Temper in Art* (New York, 1979).

Lichtenberg, Georg Christoph, *Aphorisms*, trans. R.J. Hollingdale (Harmondsworth, 1990).

Lichtenstein, J., *The Eloquence of Colour: Rhetoric and Painting in the French Classical Age*, trans. E. McVarish (Berkeley and Los Angeles, 1993).

Link, Anne-Marie, 'The Social Practice of Taste in Late Eighteenth-Century Germany: A Case Study', *Oxford Art Journal*, 15/2 (1992), 3–14.

Lipking, Lawrence, *The Ordering of the Arts in Eighteenth-Century England* (Princeton, 1970).

Lippincott, Louise, *Selling Art in Georgian London: The Rise of Arthur Pond* (New Haven, 1983).

Lloyd, Stephen, *Richard and Maria Cosway: Regency Artists of Taste and Fashion*, exh. cat., National Galleries of Scotland (Edinburgh, 1995).

Loche, Renée, and Roethlisberger, Marcel, *L'opera completa di Liotard* (Milan, 1978).

Lockspeiser, Edward, *Music and Painting: A Study in Comparative Ideas from Turner to Schoenberg* (London, 1973).

Loef, Carl, 'Die Bedeutung der Musik Oktave im Optisch-visuellen Bereich der Farbe', in M. Hering-Mitgau, B. Siegel, J. Ganz, and A. Morel (eds), *Von Farbe und Farben: Albert Knoepfl zum 70. Geburtstag* (Zurich, 1980), 227–36.

Lonsdale, Roger, *Dr Charles Burney: A Literary Biography* (Oxford, 1965).

Lovejoy, A.O., 'Some Eighteenth-Century Evolutionists', *The Scientific Monthly*, 71 (1950), 162–78.

Lowens, Irving, *Haydn in America* (Missoula, Mont., 1979).

Lynch, Deidre, 'Overloaded Portraits: The Excesses of Character and Countenance', in V. Kelly and D. von Mücke (eds), *Body and Text in the Eighteenth Century* (Stanford, Calif., 1994), 115–24.

Macmillan, Duncan, 'Old and Plain, Music and Song in Scottish Art', in Edward J. Cowan (ed.), *The People's Past* (Edinburgh, 1980), 124–36.

——, *Painting in Scotland: The Golden Age* (Oxford, 1986).

Maidment, Brian, *Reading Popular Prints 1790–1870* (Manchester, 1996).

Manners, Lady Victoria, *Matthew William Peters R.A.* (London, 1913).

Manwaring, Elizabeth Wheeler, *Italian Landscape in Eighteenth-Century England* (New York, 1925).

Marnat, Marcel, *Joseph Haydn: la mesure de son siècle* (Paris, 1995).

Matthews, Betty, 'Haydn's Visit to Hampshire and the Isle of Wight, Described from Contemporary Sources', *Haydn Yearbook*, 3 (1965), 111–21.

McCarthy, Michael, *The Origins of the Gothic Revival* (London, 1987).

McClellan, Andrew, *Inventing the Louvre: Art, Politics, and the Origins of the Modern Museum in Eighteenth-Century Paris* (Cambridge, 1994).

——, 'The Politics and Aesthetics of Display: Museums in Paris 1750–1800', *Art History*, 7 (1984), 438–64.

McKendrick, N., Brewer, John, and Plumb, J.H., *The Birth of a Consumer Society: The Commercialization of Eighteenth-Century England* (London, 1982).

McKillop, Alan Dugald, 'The Background of Thomson's *Liberty*', *The Rice Institute Pamphlet*, 38/2 (July 1951), 1–119.

——, *The Background of Thomson's Seasons* (Minneapolis, Minn., 1942).

Mechel, Christian von, *Verzeichnis der Gemälde der Kaiserlich Königlichen*

Bilder Gallerie in Wien (Vienna, 1783) [Mêchel, Chrétien de, *Catalogue des tableaux de la Galerie Impériale et Royale de Vienne* (Basel, 1784)].

Mellor, Ann K., 'Physiognomy, Phrenology, and Blake's Visionary Heads', in Robert N. Essick and Donald Pearce (eds), *Blake in his Time* (Bloomington, Ind., 1978), 53–73.

Mengs, Anton Raphael, *The Works of Anthony Raphael Mengs, First Painter to His Catholic Majesty Charles III, Translated from the Italian, published by the Chev. Don. Joseph Nicholas D'Azara, Spanish Minister at Rome*, 2 books and supplementary works in 1 vol. [trans. anonymously by Richard Cumberland] (London, 1796).

Meyer, Jerry D., 'Benjamin West's Chapel of Revealed Religion; A Study in Eighteenth-Century Protestant Religious Art', *Art Bulletin*, 57 (1975), 247–65.

————, 'Benjamin West's Window Designs for St George's Chapel, Windsor', *American Art Journal*, 11 (1979), 53–65.

Meyer, Jürgen, 'Raumsakustik und Orchesterklangen in den Konzertsälen Joseph Haydns', *Acustica*, 61/3 (1978), 145–62.

Meyer, Leonard B., *Music, the Arts, and Ideas* (Chicago, 1967).

Milner, John, *The History, Civil and Ecclesiastical, and Survey of the Antiquities of Winchester*, 2 vols (London, 1798–99).

Mirimonde, A.P. de, 'Les Allégories de la musique', *Gazette des Beaux-Arts*, 72 (1968), 295–324.

————, *L'Iconographie musicale sous les rois Bourbon: la musique dans les arts plastiques*, 2 vols (Paris, 1975–77).

————, 'Le Sabier, la musique et la danse dans les *Noces de Cana* de Véronèse', *Gazette des Beaux-Arts*, 88 (1976), 131–36.

Mitchell, Charles, 'Benjamin West's *Death of General Wolfe* and the Popular History Piece', *Journal of the Warburg and Courtauld Institutes*, 7 (1944), 20–33.

————, 'Benjamin West's Death of Nelson', in Douglas Fraser, Howard Hibbard, and Milton J. Lewine (eds), *Essays in the History of Art Presented to Rudolf Wittkower*, 2nd edn (London, 1969), 265–73.

Mitchell, Timothy F., *Art and Science in German Landscape Painting, 1770–1840* (Oxford, 1994).

Moelwyn Merchant, W., *Shakespeare and the Artist* (London, 1959).

Moir, Esther, *The Discovery of Britain: The English Tourists 1540–1840* (London, 1964).

Monelle, Raymond, *Linguistics and Semiotics in Music* (Chur, 1992).

————, *The Sense of Music: Semiotic Essays* (Princeton, 2000).

Mongrédien, Jean, *French Music from the Enlightenment to Romanticism 1789–1830*, trans. Sylvain Krémaux (Portland, Ore., 1996).

Montagna, Dennis, 'Benjamin West's *The Death of Wolfe*: A Nationalist Narrative', *American Art Journal*, 12 (Spring 1981), 72–88.

Montagu, Jennifer, *The Expression of the Passions: The Origin and Influence of Charles Le Brun's "Conférence sur l'expression Générale et Particulière"* (New Haven, 1994).

————, 'The Theory of the Musical Modes in the *Academie Royale de Peinture at de Sculpture'*, *Journal of the Warburg and Courtauld Institutes*, 55 (1992), 233–48.

Mörner, C.G. Stellan, 'Haydniana aus Schweden um 1800', *Haydn-Studien*, 2 (1969–70), 1–33.

Morris, David, *Thomas Hearne and his Landscape* (London, 1989).

Morrison, Jeffrey, *Winckelmann and the Notion of Aesthetic Education* (Oxford, 1996).

Morrow, Mary Sue, *Concert Life in Haydn's Vienna: Aspects of a Developing Musical and Social Institution*, Sociology of Music, 7 (Stuyvesant, NY, 1989).

Mozart, Wolfgang Amadeus, *The Letters of Mozart and his Family*, ed. Emily Anderson, 3rd rev. edn by Stanley Sadie and Fiona Smart (London, 1985).

————, *Mozart Briefe und Aufzeichnungen Gesamtausgabe*, ed. Wilhelm A. Bauer, Otto Erich Deutsch, and Joseph Heinz Eibl, 7 vols (Kassel, 1962–75).

Mras, George P., *Eugène Delacroix's Theory of Art* (Princton, 1966).

————, '*Ut pictura musica*: A Study of Delacroix's *Paragone'*, *Art Bulletin*, 45 (1963), 266–71.

Mraz, Gerda, Mraz, Gottfried, and Schlag, Gerald, *Joseph Haydn in seiner Zeit* (Eisenstadt, 1982).

———— and Schögl, Uwe (eds), *Das Kunstkabinett des Johann Caspar Lavater* (Vienna, 1999).

Mullan, J. *Sentiment and Sociability: The Language of Feeling in the Eighteenth Century* (Oxford, 1988).

Muller, J., 'Haydn Portraits', *Musical Quarterly*, 18 (1932), 282–94.

Mulvey, L., *Visual and Other Pleasures* (London, 1989).

Münster, R., and Angermüller, R., *Wolfgang Amadeus Mozart: Idomeneo 1781–1981: Essays, Forschungsberichte, Katalog*, exh. cat. (Munich, 1981).

Murray, Penelope (ed.), *Genius: The History of an Idea* (Oxford, 1989).

Myers, Robert Manson, *Handel's 'Messiah', A Touchstone of Taste* (New York, 1948).

Myers, S.H., *The Blue Stocking Circle: Women, Friendship and the Life of the Mind in Eighteenth-Century England* (Oxford, 1990).

Nebehay, C., *Aquarelle und Zeichnungen von Vincenz Georg Kininger* (Vienna, 1981).

Neff, Emily Ballew, and Pressly, William L., *John Singleton Copley in England* (London, 1995).

Netzer, Susanne, *Daniel N. Chodiewiecki 1726–1801*, exh. cat., Goethe-Institut, London (1989).

Neubauer, J., *The Emancipation of Music from Language: Departures from Mimesis in Eighteenth-Century Aesthetics* (New Haven, 1986).

Neumann, A.R., 'Philipp Otto Runge and Music', *Germanic Review* , 27 (1952), 165–72.

Neumayr, Anton, *Music and Medicine*, trans. Bruce Cooper Clarke (Bloomington, Ill., 1994).

Newman, William S., 'Programmists vs. Absolutists: Further Thoughts about an Overworked "Dichotomy"', in Wye Jamison Allanbrook, Janet M. Levy, and William P. Mahrt (eds), *Convention in Eighteenth- and Nineteenth-Century Music: Essays in Honor of Leonard G. Ratner* (Stuyvesant, NY, 1992), 517–35.

Newton, Sir Isaac, *Opticks, or a Treatise of the Reflections, Refractions, Inflections and Colours of Light, Based on the 4th Edition, London 1730*, intro. Sir Edmund Whittaker, Dover edn (New York, 1952).

Nicolson, Benedict, *Joseph Wright of Derby: Painter of Light*, 2 vols (London, 1968).

Nicolson, Marjorie Hope, *Newton Demands the Muse: Newton's Opticks and the Eighteenth-Century Poets* (Princeton, 1946).

Nohl, Ludwig, *Musiker-Briefe: Eine Sammlung Briefe von C.W. Gluck, Ph. E. Bach, J. Haydn, C.M. von Weber, F. Mendelssohn-Bartholdy* (Leipzig, 1867).

Northcote, J., *The Life of Sir Joshua Reynolds* (London, 1819).

Novello, Vincent and Mary, *A Mozart Pilgrimage, Being the Travel Diaries of Vincent & Mary Novello in the Year 1829*, transcribed by Nerina Medici di Marignano, ed. Rosemary Hughes (London, 1955).

Obeyesekere, Gananath, *The Apotheosis of Captain Cook: European Myth-Making in the Pacific* (Princeton, 1992).

O'Brien, Patrick, *Joseph Banks: A Life* (London, 1987).

Oldfield, J.R., *Popular Politics and British Anti-Slavery: The Mobilisation of Public Opinion against the Slave Trade, 1787–1807* (Manchester, 1995).

Oliver, A.R., *The Encyclopedists as Critics of Music* (New York, 1947).

Olleson, Edward, 'Georg August Griesinger's Correspondence with Breitkopf & Härtel', *Haydn Yearbook*, 3 (1965), 5–53.

————, 'Gottfried van Swieten, Patron of Haydn and Mozart', *Proceedings of the Royal Musical Association*, 89 (1962–63), 63–74.

————, 'The Origin and Libretto of Haydn's *Creation*', *Haydn Yearbook*, 4 (1968), 148–66.

Oras, Antas, *Milton's Editors and Commentators from Patrick Hume to Henry John Todd (1695–1801): A Study in Critical Views and Methods* (London, 1931).

Orrey, Leslie, *Programme Music: A Brief Survey from the Sixteenth Century to the Present Day* (London, 1975).

Ottenberg, Hans-Günter, *Carl Philipp Emanuel Bach* (Oxford, 1987).

Ousby, I., *The Englishman's England: Taste, Travel and the Rise of Tourism* (Cambridge, 1990).

Page, Janet K., 'Music and the Royal Procession in Maria Theresia's Vienna', *Early Music*, 27 (1999), 96–118.

Paley, Morton D., *The Apocalyptic Sublime* (New Haven, 1986).

Papendiek, Charlotte, *Court and Private Life in the Time of Queen Charlotte: Being the Journals of Mrs Papendiek, Assistant Keeper of the Wardrobe and Reader to Her Majesty*, ed. Vernon Delves Broughton, 2 vols (London, 1887).

Parke, W.T., *Musical Memoirs, Comprising an Account of the General State of Music in England, 1784–1830*, 2 vols (London, 1830).

Parslow, Christopher Charles, *Rediscovering Antiquity: Karl Weber and the Excavation of Herculaneum, Pompeii and Stabiae* (Cambridge, 1995).

Pasquin, Anthony, *Memoirs of Royal Academicians* (London, 1796).

Paston, George, *Social Caricature in the Eighteenth Century* (London, 1905).

Patten, Robert L., 'Conventions of Georgian Caricature', *Art Journal*, 63 (1982), 331–38.

Paul, Charles G., 'Music and Ideology: Rameau, Rousseau and 1789', *Journal of the History of Ideas*, 32 (1971), 395–410.

Paulson, Ronald, *Emblem and Expression: Meaning in English Art of the Eighteenth Century* (London, 1975).

————, *Hogarth's Graphic Works*, 3rd rev. edn (London, 1989).

Payne, Christiana, *Toil and Plenty: Images of the Agricultural Landscape in England 1780–1890*, exh. cat., Nottingham and Yale (New Haven, 1993).

Pears, Iain, *The Discovery of Painting: The Growth of Interest in the Arts in England 1680–1768* (London, 1988).

Pemán, María, 'La colección artística de Don Sebastián Martínez, el amigo de Goya, en Cádiz', *Archivo español de arte*, 51 (1978), 53–62.

Pemán Medina, María, 'Estampas y libros que vió Goya en casa de Sebastián Martínez', *Archivo español de arte*, 67 (1992), 303–20.

Penny, Nicholas (ed.), *Reynolds*, exh. cat., Royal Academy, London (1986).

Pepper, Stephen, *Guido Reni* (New York, 1984).

Perry, Gill, and Rossington, Michael, *Femininity and Masculinity in Eighteenth-Century Art and Culture* (Manchester, 1994).

Pestelli, Giorgio, 'Giuseppe Carpani e il neoclassicismo musicale della vecchia Italia', *Quaderni della Rassegna Musicale*, 4 (1968), 105–21.

Peter, Mary, *John Opie, 1761–1807*, exh. cat., Arts Council (1963).

Pevsner, Nikolaus, *Academies of Art, Past and Present* (Cambridge, 1940).

Pierre, Constant, *Histoire du Concert spirituel 1725–1790* (Paris, 1975).

Pittock, Joan, *The Ascendancy of Taste* (London, 1973).

Place, Adélaïde de, *La Vie musicale en France au temps de la révolution* (Paris, 1989).

Pohl, Carl Ferdinand, *Joseph Haydn*, i, 2nd edn (Leipzig, 1878); ii (Leipzig, 1882); iii, completed by Hugo Botstiber (Leipzig, 1927); all repr. (Vienna, 1970–71).

———, *Mozart und Haydn in London*, ii: *Haydn in London* (Vienna, 1867), 2nd edn (Vienna, 1971).

Pointon, Marcia R., *Hanging the Head: Portraiture and Social Formation in Eighteenth-Century England* (New Haven, 1993).

———, *Milton and English Art: A Study in the Pictorial Artist's Use of a Literary Source* (Manchester, 1970).

———, *Strategies for Showing: Women, Possession, and Representation in English Visual Culture 1665–1800* (Oxford, 1997).

Porter, Roy, *English Society in the Eighteenth Century* (Harmondsworth, 1982).

——— and Roberts, Marie Mulvey (eds), *Pleasure in the Eighteenth Century* (London, 1996).

Postle, Martin, *Angels and Urchins: The Fancy Picture in 18th-Century British Art* (London, 1998).

Potts, Alex, *Flesh and the Ideal: Winckelmann and the Origins of Art History* (London, 1994).

Pötzl-Malikova, Maria, *Franz Xaver Messerschmidt* (Vienna, 1982).

Poundie Burstein, L., 'Surprising Returns: The VII$_\sharp$ in Beethoven's Op. 18 No. 3, and its Antecedents in Haydn', *Music Analysis*, 17 (1998), 295–312.

Powell-Jones, Flora, 'A Neo-Classical Interior in Naples', *National Art Collectors Fund Annual Review* (1985), 104–7.

Praz, Mario, *Studies in Seventeenth-Century Imagery*, 2nd edn (Rome, 1964).

Pressl, Nancy L., *Revealed Religion: Benjamin West's Commissions for Windsor Castle and Fonthill Abbey*, exh. cat., San Antonio Museum of Art (San Antonio, Tex., 1983).

Pressly, William, *Johan Zoffany's Paintings of the Massacre at Paris, August 10, 1792* (London, 1999).

Prod'homme, J.G., 'Napoleon, Music and Musicians', *Musical Quarterly*, 7 (1921), 579–605.

Propper, R., *Die Bühnenwerke Johann Friedrich Reichardts* (Bonn, 1965).

Prown, Jules David, *John Singleton Copley*, 2 vols (Cambridge, Mass., 1966).

Puttfarken, Thomas, *Roger de Piles' Theory of Art* (New Haven, 1985).

Ratner, Leonard G., *Classic Music: Expression, Form and Style* (New York, 1980).

Raupp, Hans-Joachim, 'Musik in Atelier: Darstellungen musizierender Künstler in der niederländischen Malerei des 17. Jarhunderts', *Oud Holland*, 92 (1978), 106–29.

Raven, J., *Judging New Wealth: Popular Publishing and Responses to Commerce in England, 1750–1800* (Oxford, 1992).

Redford, G., *Art Sales: A History of Sales of Pictures and other Works of Art*, 2 vols (London, 1888).

Rennert, Jonathan, *William Crotch 1775–1847: Composer, Artist, Teacher* (Lavenham, 1975).

Reynolds, Sir Joshua, *Discourses on Art*, ed. Robert R. Wark, 2nd edn (New Haven, 1975).

Ribero, Aileen, *Dress and Morality* (London, 1986).

———, *Dress in Eighteenth-Century Europe, 1715–1789* (London, 1984).

———, *A Visual History of Costume: The Eighteenth Century* (London, 1983).

Rice, John A., *Antonio Salieri and Viennese Opera* (Chicago, 1998).

———, 'Sarti's Giulio Sabatino, Haydn's Armida, and the Arrival of Opera Seria at Eszterháza', *Haydn Yearbook*, 15 (1984), 181–98.

Ridley, Mark (ed.), *Evolution* (Oxford, 1997).

Riedel-Martiny, Anke, 'Das Verhältnis von Text und Musik in Haydns Oratorien', *Haydn-Studien*, 1 (1967), 205–40.

Riely, John, *Henry William Bunbury: The Amateur as Caricaturist*, exh. cat. (Sudbury, 1983).

———, 'Horace Walpole and "the second Hogarth"', *Eighteenth-Century Studies*, 9 (1975), 28–44.

Ringer, Alexander L., 'The *Chasse* as a Musical Topic of the Eighteenth Century', *Journal of the American Musicological Society*, 6 (1953), 148–59.

Ripa, Cesare, *Baroque and Rococo Pictorial Imagery: The 1758–60 Hertel Edition of Ripa's Iconologia*, ed. Edward A. Maser (New York, 1971).

Rix, D.B., *French Printmaking of the Eighteenth Century* (Toronto, 1988).

Roberts, Jane, *Views of Windsor: Watercolours by Thomas and Paul Sandby from the Collection of Her Majesty Queen Elizabeth II* (London, 1995).

Roberts, W., *Sir William Beechey R.A.* (London, 1907).

Roberts, Warren, *Jacques-Louis David, Revolutionary Artist: Art, Politics and the French Revolution* (Chapel Hill, NC, 1989).

Robinson, Nicholas K., *Edmund Burke: A Life in Caricature* (New Haven, 1996).

Robinson, Sidney K., *Inquiry into the Picturesque* (Chicago, 1991).

Robson-Scott, W.D., *The Younger Goethe and the Visual Arts* (Cambridge, 1981).

Roettgen, Steffi, *Anton Raphael Mengs 1728–1779 and his British Patrons* (London, 1993).

Rosand, Ellen, 'Handel Paints the Resurrection', in Thomas J. Mathiesen and Benito V. Rivera (eds), *Festa Musicologica: Essays in Honor of George J. Buelow* (Stuyvesant, NY, 1995), 7–52.

Roscoe, Christopher, 'Haydn and London in the 1780s', *Music & Letters*, 49 (1968), 203–12.

Rosen, Charles, *The Classical Style: Haydn, Mozart, Beethoven* (New York, 1972).

Rosenberg, Martin, *Raphael and France: The Artist as Paradigm and Symbol* (University Park, Pa., 1995).

Rosenberg, Pierre, and Sandt, Udo van de, *Pierre Peyron (1744–1810)* (Paris, 1983).

Rosenblum, Robert, *Transformations in Late Eighteenth-Century Art* (Princeton, 1967).

Rosenfeld, Sibyl, 'The *Eidophusikon* Illustrated', *Theatre Notes*, 18 (1963–64), 52–54.

————, *Georgian Scene Painters and Scene Painting* (Cambridge, 1981).

Rosenthal, Michael, *The Art of Thomas Gainsborough: 'a little business for the eye'* (New Haven, 1999).

Roth, W., *The London Pleasure Gardens of the Eighteenth Century* (London, 1986).

Roworth, Wendy Wassyng (ed.), *Angelica Kauffman: A Continental Artist in Georgian England* (London, 1992).

Rowland-Jones, Anthony, 'The Minuet: Painter-Musicians in Triple Time', *Early Music*, 26 (1998), 415–31.

Rudé, G. *Hanoverian London 1714–1808* (London, 1971).

Rumbold, Valerie, 'Music Aspires in Letters: Charles Burney, Queeney Thrale and the Streatham Circle', *Music & Letters*, 74 (1993), 24–38.

Rushton, Julian, '"Royal Agamemnon": The Two Versions of Gluck's *Iphigénie en Aulide*', in Malcolm Boyd (ed.), *Music and the French Revolution* (Cambridge, 1992), 15–36.

————, *W.A. Mozart: Don Giovanni* (Cambridge, 1981).

Russell, Charles C., *The Don Juan Legend before Mozart* (Ann Arbor, 1993).

Russell, Francis, 'Guercino and England', in *Guercino in Britain: Paintings from British Collections*, exh. cat., introductory essays by Michael Helston and Francis Russell, cat. by Michael Helston and Tom Henry, based on the researches of Denis Mahon, National Gallery (London, 1991).

Sahut, *Carle Vanloo: premier peintre du roi*, exh. cat., Nice, Clermont-Ferrand, Nancy (1977).

Saisselin, Rémy Gilbert, *Taste in Eighteenth-Century France: Critical Reflection on the Origins of Aesthetics, or an Apology for Amateurs* (Syracuse, NY, 1965).

Salas, Xavier de, 'Light on the Origin of Los Caprichos', *Burlington Magazine*, 121 (1979), 711–16.

Sambricio, V. de, *Tapices de Goya* (Madrid, 1946).

Sambrook, James, *James Thomson (1700–1748): A Life* (Oxford, 1991).

Santaniello, A.E., *The Boydell Shakespeare Prints* (New York, 1979).

Saunders, G., *Picturing Plants: An Analytical History of Botanical Illustration*, exh. cat., Victoria & Albert Museum (London, 1995).

Schama, Simon, *Citizens: A Chronicle of the French Revolution* (New York, 1989).

Scharlau, U., *Athanasius Kircher (1601–1680) als Musikschriftsteller* (Marburg, 1969).

Schering, Arnold, 'Bemerkungen zu J. Haydns Programmsinfonien', *Jahrbuch der Musikbibliothek Peters*, 46 (1939), 9–27.

————, 'Künstler, Kenner und Liebhaber der Musik im Zeitalter Haydns und Goethes', *Jahrbuch der Musikbibliothek Peters*, 38 (1931), 9–23.

Schier, D.S., *Louis Bertrand Castel, Anti-Newtonian Scientist* (Cedar Rapids, Ia., 1941).

Schiff, Gert, *Johann Heinrich Füssli 1741–1825* (Zurich, 1973).

————, *Johann Heinrich Füsslis Milton Galerie* (Zurich, 1963).

Scholes, Percy A., 'Burney and Haydn', *Proceedings of the Royal Musical Association*, 67 (1940–41), 23–24.

————, *The Great Dr Burney*, 2 vols (London, 1948).

Schroeder, David P., 'Audience Reception and Haydn's London Symphonies', *International Review of the Asthetics and Sociology of Music*, 16 (1985), 57–72.

————, *Haydn and the Enlightenment: The Late Symphonies and their Audience* (Oxford, 1990).

————, 'Melodic Source Material and Haydn's Creative Process', *Musical Quarterly*, 66 (1982), 496–515.

Schueller, Herbert M., 'Correspondences between Music and the Sister Arts, according to Eighteenth-Century Aesthetic Theory', *Journal of Aesthetics and Art Criticism*, 11 (1953), 334–59.

————, '"Imitation" and "Expression" in British Musical Criticism in the Eighteenth Century', *Musical Quarterly*, 34 (1948), 544–66.

————, 'Literature and Music as Sister Arts: An Aspect of Aesthetic Theory in Eighteenth-Century Britain', *Philological Quarterly*, 26 (1947), 193–205.

————, 'The Pleasures of Music: Speculation in British Music Criticism 1750–1800', *Journal of Aesthetics and Art Criticism*, 8 (1950), 155–71.

————, 'The Use and Decorum of Music as Described in British Literature 1700–1780', *Journal of the History of Ideas*, 13 (1952), 73–93.

Schulze, Sabrine, and Apel, Friedmar (eds), *Goethe und die Kunst*, exh. cat. (Stuttgart, 1994).

Schusser, Adelbert, et al., *Joseph Haydn*, exh. cat., Historisches Museum der Stadt Wien (Vienna, n.d. [1994]).

Schwarz, Vera (ed.), *Der junge Haydn* (Graz, 1972).

Schweiger, Hertha, 'Abt Volger', *Musical Quarterly*, 25 (1939), 156–66.

Scott, H.M. (ed.), *Enlightened Absolutism: Reform and Reformers in Later Eighteenth-Century Europe* (London, 1990).

Scruton, Roger, *The Aesthetics of Music* (Oxford, 1997).

———, 'Representation in Music', *Philosophy*, 51 (1976), 273–87.

Searle, Arthur, *Haydn and England*, The British Library (London, 1989).

Serwer, Howard, 'The Coopersmith Copy of Handel's Brockes Passion: A Haydn Connection?', *Händel-Jahrbuch*, 38 (1992), 99–107.

Shawcross, John T., *Milton 1732–1801: The Critical Heritage* (London, 1972).

Shawe-Taylor, Desmond, *Genial Company: The Theme of Genius in Eighteenth-Century British Portraiture*, exh. cat., Nottingham University Art Gallery (Nottingham, 1987).

Shearman, John, *Andrea del Sarto*, 2 vols (Oxford, 1965).

Shesgreen, Sean, *Hogarth and the Times-of-the-Day Tradition* (Ithaca, NY, 1983).

Simon, Robin (ed.), *Buckingham Palace: A Complete Guide* (London, 1993).

Sinko, Grezegorz, *John Wolcot and his School: A Chapter in the History of English Satire* (Warsaw, 1962).

Sisman, Elaine R., *Haydn and the Classical Variation* (Cambridge, 1993).

———, 'Haydn's Theater Symphonies', *Journal of the American Musicological Society*, 43 (1990), 292–352.

——— (ed.), *Haydn and his World* (Princeton, 1997).

Skinner, Basil C., *The Indefatigable Mr Allan: The Perceptive and Varied Work of David Allan, 1744–1796, Scotland's First Genre Painter*, exh. cat. (Edinburgh, 1973).

Slim, H. Colin, 'Dosso Dossi's Allegory at Florence about Music', *Journal of the American Musicological Society*, 43 (1990), 43–98.

———, 'Musical Inscriptions in Paintings by Caravaggio and his Followers', in Anne Dhu Shapiro (ed.), *Music and Context: Essays for John M. Ward* (Cambridge, Mass., 1985), 241–63.

———, 'Tintoretto's Music-Making Women at Dresden', *Imago Musicae*, 4 (1987), 45–76.

Smith, Bernard, 'Captain Cook's Artists and the Portrayal of Pacific Peoples', *Art History*, 7 (1984), 295–312.

———, *Imaging the Pacific in the Wake of the Cook Voyages* (New Haven, 1992).

Smith, Ruth, *Handel's Oratorios and Eighteenth-Century Thought* (Cambridge, 1995).

Smither, Howard, *History of the Oratorio*, ii: *The Oratorio in the Baroque Era: Italy, Vienna, Paris* (Chapel Hill, NC, 1977); iii: *The Oratorio in the Classical Era* (Chapel Hill, NC, 1987).

Solkin, David, H., *Painting for Money: The Visual Arts and the Public Sphere in Eighteenth-Century England* (New Haven, 1993).

Solomon, Maynard, 'Some Romantic Images in Beethoven', in Sieghard Brandenburg (ed.), *Haydn, Mozart and Beethoven, Studies in the Music of the Classical Period: Essays in Honour of Alan Tyson* (Oxford, 1998), 253–82.

Somfai, László, 'Haydn's Eszterháza: The Influence of Architecture in Music', *New Hungarian Quarterly*, 23/87 (1982), 195–201.

——, *Joseph Haydn: His Life in Contemporary Pictures* (New York, 1969).

——, *The Keyboard Sonatas of Joseph Haydn: Instruments and Performance Practice*, trans. Charlotte Greenspan (Chicago, 1995).

——, 'The London Revision of Haydn's Instrumental Style', *Proceedings of the Royal Musical Association*, 100 (1973–74), 159–74.

——, 'Zur Authentizität des Haydn-Porträts von Loutherbourg', *Österreichische Musikzeitschrift*, 23/5 (1968), 276–77.

Souper, F.O., 'The Pictorial Element in Haydn', *Monthly Musical Record*, 58 (1928), 259–60.

Spaeth, Sigmund Gottfried, *Milton's Knowledge of Music*, 2nd edn (Ann Arbor, 1963).

Stafford, Barbara Maria, *Body Criticism: Imaging the Unseen in Enlightenment Art and Medicine* (Cambridge, Mass., 1994).

Staley, Allan, *Benjamin West: American Painter at the English Court*, exh. cat., Baltimore Museum of Art (1989).

Starobinski, Jean, *1789: The Emblems of Reason*, trans. B. Bray (Cambridge, Mass., 1988).

—— et al., *Revolution in Fashion: European Clothing 1715–1815* (New York, 1990).

Steblin, Rita, *A History of Key Characteristics in the Eighteenth and Early Nineteenth Centuries*, Studies in Musicology, 67 (Ann Arbor, 1983).

Stechow, Wolfgang, 'Johann Sebastian Bach the Younger', in Millard Meiss (ed.), *De Artibus Opuscula XL: Essays in Honor of Erwin Panofsky*, i (New York, 1961), 427–36.

Steegman, J., *The Rule of Taste: From George I to George IV* (London, 1968).

Stein, Fritz, 'Der musikalische Instrumentalkalendar – zu Leben und Wirken von Gregor Josephus Werner', *Musica*, 11 (1957), 390–95.

Stendhal, *Histoire de la peinture en Italie*, ed. V. Del Litto (Paris, 1996).

——, *Lives of Haydn, Mozart and Metastasio by Stendhal (1814)*, trans. Richard N. Coe (London, 1972).

——, *Rome, Naples and Florence*, trans. Richard N. Coe (London, 1959).

Stern, Martin, 'Haydns "Schöpfung": Geist und Herkunft des van Swietenschen Librettos. Ein Beitrag zum Thema "Säkularisation" in Zeitalter der Aufklärung', *Haydn-Studien* 1/3 (1966), 121–98.

Stevenson, Sara, *A Face for Any Occasion: Some Aspects of Portrait Engraving*, Scottish National Portrait Gallery (Edinburgh, 1976).

Strong, Roy, *And when did you last see your father? The Victorian Painter and British History* (London, 1978).

Stroud, Dorothy, *George Dance Architect 1741–1825* (London, 1971).

Strunk, Oliver, *Source Readings in Music History*, iv: *The Classic Era* (London, 1981); rev. edn, ed. Leo Treitler (New York, 1998).

Subirá, J., *La música en la Casa de Alba* (Madrid, 1927).

Sutcliffe, W. Dean, *Haydn: String Quartets, Op. 50* (Cambridge, 1992).

———, 'Haydn's Musical Personality', *Musical Times*, 130 (1989), 341–44.

——— (ed.), *Haydn Studies* (Cambridge, 1998).

Symmons, Sarah, *Goya: In Pursuit of Patronage* (London, 1988).

Szazbo, Franz A.J., *Kaunitz and Enlightenment Absolutism 1753–1780* (Cambridge, 1994).

Taylor, F.H., *The Taste of Angels: A History of Art Collecting from Rameses to Napoleon* (Boston, 1948).

Telesko, Werner, *Napoleon Bonaparte: Der 'moderne Held' und die bildende Kunst 1799–1815* (Vienna, 1998).

Temperley, Nicholas, *Haydn: The Creation* (Cambridge, 1991).

———, 'New Light on the Libretto of *The Creation*', in Christopher Hogwood and Richard Luckett (eds), *Music in Eighteenth-Century England: Essays in Memory of Charles Cudworth* (Cambridge, 1983), 189–212.

Terry, Charles Sanford, *John Christian Bach*, 2nd edn with corrigenda by H.C. Robbins Landon (London, 1967).

Teyssedre, Bernard, *Roger de Piles et les débats sur le coloris au siècle de Louis XIV* (Paris, 1957).

Thayer, Alexander Wheelock, *Thayer's Life of Beethoven*, rev. and ed. Elliot Forbes (Princeton, 1970).

Thomas, Günter, 'Griesingers Briefe über Haydn: Aus seiner Korrespondenz mit Breitkopf & Härtel', *Haydn-Studien*, 1 (1965–68), 49–114.

Todd, R. Larry, 'Joseph Haydn and the *Sturm und Drang*: A Revaluation', *Music Review*, 41 (1980), 172–96

Tolley, Thomas, 'Haydn, the Engraver Thomas Park, and Maria Hester Park's *little sonat*', *Music & Letters*, 82 (2001), 421–31.

———, 'Music in the Circle of Sir William Jones: A Contribution to the History of Haydn's Early Reputation', *Music & Letters*, 73 (1992), 525–50.

Tomalin, Claire, *Mrs Jordan's Profession: The Story of a Great Actress and a Future King* (London, 1994).

Tomlinson, Janis Angela, *Francisco Goya: The Tapestry Cartoons and Early Career at the Court of Madrid* (Cambridge, 1989).

———, *Francisco Goya y Lucientes 1746–1828* (London, 1994).

————, *Graphic Evolutions: The Print Series of Francisco Goya*, Columbia Studies on Art, 2 (New York, 1989).

Tuer, Andrew White, *Bartolozzi and his Works*, 2 vols, 2nd edn (London, 1885).

Turner, A. Richard, *Inventing Leonardo: The Anatomy of a Legend* (New York, 1993).

Tuve, Rosemond, *Images and Themes in Five Poems by Milton* (Cambridge, Mass., 1957).

Vales, Robert L., *Peter Pindar (John Wolcot)* (New York, 1973).

Vasari, Giorgio, *The Lives of the Painters, Sculptors and Architects*, trans. A.B. Hinds (London, 1963).

Verba, C., *Music and the French Enlightenment: Reconstruction of a Dialogue 1750–1764* (Oxford, 1993).

Vervieba, Birgit, 'Transparent Painting and the Romantic Spirit: Experimental Anticipations of Modern Visual Arts', in *The Romantic Spirit in German Art 1790–1990*, exh. cat. (Edinburgh, 1994), 171–80.

Vesme, A. de, and Calabi, Augusto, *Francesco Bartolozzi* (Milan, 1928).

Vickers, Brian (ed.), *Shakespeare: The Critical Heritage, Volume 6, 1774–1801* (London, 1981).

Vigée-Lebrun, Elisabeth, *Memoirs of Elisabeth Vigée Le Brun*, trans. S. Evans (London, 1989).

Vignal, Marc, *Joseph Haydn* (Paris, 1995) .

———— (ed.), Joseph Haydn: autobiographie, premières biographiques (Paris, 1997).

Voogd, Peter de, *Henry William Bunbury 1750–1811: 'De Raphaël der Carricatuurteekenaars'*, exh. cat., Rijksmuseum (Amsterdam, 1996).

Wackenroder, Wilhelm Heinrich, and Tieck, Ludwig, *Outpourings of an Art-Loving Friar*, trans. Edward Morain (New York, 1975).

Wagner, W., *Die Geschichte der Akademie der bildenden Künste in Wien* (Vienna, 1877).

Wakefield, David, *French Eighteenth-Century Painting* (London, 1984).

————, *Stendhal and the Arts* (London, 1975).

Waldorf, Jessica, 'Sentiment and Sensibility in *La vera costanza*', in Sutcliffe (ed.), *Haydn Studies*, 70–119.

Walker, F., 'Salvator Rosa and Music', *Monthly Musical Record*, 79 (1949), 199–205; 80 (1950), 13–16, 32–36.

Walker, Stella, *Sporting Art in England, 1700–1900* (London, 1972).

Walkley, Giles, *Artists' Houses in London* (London, 1994).

Wallace, Robert K., *Jane Austen and Mozart: Classical Equilibrium in Fiction and Music* (Athens, Ga., 1983).

Wallace, Robin, *Beethoven's Critics: Aesthetic Dilemmas and Resolutions during the Composer's Lifetime* (Cambridge, 1986).

Walpole, Horace, *The Yale Edition of Horace Walpole's Correspondence*, ed. W.S. Lewis et al., 48 vols (New Haven, 1937–83).

Walter, Horst, 'Gottfried van Sweitens handschriftliche Textbüche zu "Schöpfung" und "Jahreszeiten"', *Haydn-Studien*, 1 (1965–68), 241–77.

Walters, Alice N., 'Conversation Pieces: Science and Politeness in Eighteenth-Century England', *History of Science*, 25 (1997), 121–54.

Wangermann, Ernst, *Aufklärung und staatsbürgerliche Erziehung: Gottfried van Sweiten als Reformator der österreichischen Unterrichtswesens 1781–1791* (Munich, 1978).

Ward, Humphry, and Roberts, W., *Romney: A Biographical and Critical Essay with a Catalogue Raisonné of his Works*, 2 vols (London, 1904).

Wax, Carol, *The Mezzotint: History and Technique* (London, 1990).

Weatherill, L., *Consumer Behaviour and Material Culture in Britain 1660–1760* (London, 1988).

Weber, William, 'The Contemporaneity of Eighteenth-Century Musical Taste', *Musical Quarterly*, 70 (1984), 175–94.

————, 'Learned and General Musical Taste in Eighteenth-Century France', *Past and Present*, 89 (1980), 58–85.

————, *Music and the Middle Classes* (New York, 1975).

————, '"La Musique ancienne" in the Waning of the Ancien Régime', *Journal of Modern History*, 56 (1984), 58–88.

————, *The Rise of Musical Classics in Eighteenth-Century England: A Study in Canon, Ritual, and Ideology* (Oxford, 1992).

Webster, James, 'The Falling-out Between Haydn and Beethoven: The Evidence of the Sources', in Lewis Lockwood and Phyllis Benjamin (eds), *Beethoven Essays: Studies in Honor of Elliot Forbes* (Cambridge, Mass., 1984), 3–45.

————, *Haydn's 'Farewell' Symphony and the Idea of Classical Style: Through Composition and Cyclic Integration in his Instrumental Music* (Cambridge, 1991).

————, 'Haydn's Sacred Vocal Music and the Aesthetics of Salvation', in Sutcliffe (ed.), *Haydn Studies*, 35–69.

Webster, Mary, *Francis Wheatley* (London, 1970).

————, *Johann Zoffany*, exh. cat., National Portrait Gallery (London, 1976).

Weddigen, Erasmus, 'Jacopo Tintoretto und die Musik', *Artibus et Historiae*, 10 (1984), 67–119.

Wehrli, R., *Lichtenbergs ausführliche Erklärung der Hogarthischen Kupferstiche* (Bonn, 1980).

Weinglass, David H., *Prints and Engraved Illustrations by and after Henry Fuseli: A Catalogue Raisonné* (Aldershot, 1993).

Weinmann, Alexander, *Vollständiges Verlagsverzeichnis Artaria & Comp.* (Vienna, 1952).

Weinshenker, Anne Betty, *Falconet: His Writings and his Friend Diderot* (Geneva, 1966).

Weiss, Piero, and Taruskin, Richard, *Music in the Western World: A History in Documents* (New York, 1984).

Weller, Philip, 'Frames and Images: Locating Music in Cultural Histories', *Journal of the American Musicological Society*, 50 (1997), 7–54.

West, Shearer, *The Image of the Actor: Verbal and Visual Representation in the Age of Garrick and Kemble* (London, 1991).

Wheelock, Gretchen, *Haydn's Ingenious Jesting with Art: Contexts of Musical Wit and Humor* (New York, 1992).

————, 'Marriage à la Mode: Haydn's Instrumental Works "Englished" for Voice and Piano', *Journal of Musicology*, 8 (1990), 357–96.

White, Eric Walter, *A History of English Opera* (London, 1983).

————, 'The Rehearsal of an Opera', *Theatre Notebook*, 14/3 (Spring 1960), 79–90.

Whiteley, J.J.L., 'Exhibitions of Contemporary Paintings in London and Paris 1760–1860', in *Saloni, gallerie, musei e loro influenza sullo sviluppo dell'arte dei secoli XIX e XX*, ed. F. Haskell, Atti del XXIV Congresso Internazionale di Storia dell'Arte (Bologna, 1979), 69–88.

Whitley, William Thomas, *Art in England 1800–1820* (London, 1928).

————, *Artists and their Friends in England 1700–1799*, 2 vols (London, 1928).

————, *Thomas Gainsborough* (London, 1915).

Whitman, Alfred, *Valentine Green* (London, 1902).

Wilder, F.L., *English Sporting Prints* (London, 1974).

Will, Richard, 'When God Met the Sinner, and other Dramatic Confrontations in Eighteenth-Century Instrumental Music', *Music & Letters*, 78 (1997), 175–209.

Wilson, Gladys, 'One God! One Farinelli: Amigoni's Portraits of a Famous Singer', *Apollo*, 140 (Sept. 1994), 45–51.

Wilson, Michael I., 'Gainsborough, Bath and Music', *Apollo*, 105 (1977), 107–10.

————, *Nicholas Lanier, Master of the King's Musick* (London, 1998).

Wind, Edgar, *Hume and the Heroic Portrait: Studies in Eighteenth-Century Imagery*, ed. Jaynie Anderson (Oxford, 1986).

Winn, James Anderson, *Unsuspected Eloquence: A History of the Relations between Poetry and Music* (New Haven, 1981).

Winter, David, *George Morland (1763–1804)* (Stanford, Calif., 1977).

Winter, Marian Hannah, *The Pre-Romantic Ballet* (London, 1974).

Winternitz, Emanuel, *Leonardo da Vinci as a Musician* (New Haven, 1982).

————, *Musical Instruments and their Symbolism in Western Art* (London, 1967).

Wittkower, Rudolf and Margot, *Born under Saturn: The Character and Conduct of Artists. A Documented History from Antiquity to the French Revolution* (New York, 1963).

[Wolcot, John], *The Works of Peter Pindar Esq.*, 2 vols (Dublin, 1795).

Wolf, Adam, *Marie Christine, Erzherzogin von Österreich* (Vienna, 1863).

Wolf, Reva, *Goya and the Satirical Print in England and on the Continent 1730 to 1850* (Boston, Mass., 1991).

Wood, Marcus, *Radical Satire and Print Culture 1790–1822* (Oxford, 1994).

Woodfield, Ian, 'John Bland: London Retailer of the Music of Haydn and Mozart', *Music & Letters*, 81 (2000), 210–44.

Wörner-Berlin, Karl, 'Joseph Haydn und die Programm-Musik seiner Zeit', *Die Musik*, 24/6 (Mar., 1932), 416–18.

Wrigley, Richard, *The Origins of French Art Criticism: From the Ancien Régime to the Restoration* (Oxford, 1993).

Wüthrich, Lukas Heinrich, *Christian von Mechel: Leben und Werk eines Basler Kupferstechers und Kunsthändlers (1737–1817)* (Basle, 1956).

Wyn Jones, David, *Beethoven: Pastoral Symphony* (Cambridge, 1995).

———, 'Haydn's Music in London in the Period 1760–1790: Part One', *Haydn Yearbook*, 14 (1984), 144–72.

——— (ed.), *Music in Eighteenth-Century Austria* (Cambridge, 1996).

———, *Music in Eighteenth-Century Britain* (London, 2000).

Young, M.J., *Memoirs of Mrs Crouch* (London, 1806).

Zaslaw, Neal, 'Mozart, Haydn and the *Sinfonia da Chiesa*', *Journal of Musicology*, 1 (1982), 95–124.

———, *Mozart's Symphonies* (Oxford, 1989).

——— (ed.), *Man and Music: The Classical Era* (London, 1989).

Zeman, Herbert, 'Von der irdischen Glückseligkeit: Gottfried van Swietens *Jahreszeiten*-Libretto – eine Utopie vom natürlicher Leben des Menschen', in *Die Vier Jahreszeiten in 18. Jahrhundert: Colloquium der Arbeitsstelle 18. Jahrhundert, Gesamthochschule Wuppertal, Universität Münster, Schloss Langenburg vom 3. bis 5. Oktober 1983* (Heidelberg, 1986), 108–20.

——— (ed.), *Joseph Haydn und die Literatur seiner Zeit* (Eisenstadt, 1976).

Index

MAY 21 '02

Heterick Memorial Library
Ohio Northern University

	DUE	RETURNED		DUE	RETURNED
1.			13.		
2.			14.		
3.			15.		
4.			16.		
5.			17.		
6.			18.		
7.			19.		
8.			20.		
9.			21.		
10.			22.		
11.			23.		
12.			24.		

WITHDRAWN FROM OHIO NORTHERN UNIVERSITY LIBRARY

Ohio Northern University

3 5111 00514 5614

HETERICK MEMORIAL LIBRARY
OHIO NORTHERN UNIVERSITY
ADA, OHIO 45810